Dialects in Culture

To
A. T. O'Dell
Teacher, Counselor and Friend
Who directed me into the study of English,
and who demonstrated through the achievements of his
students that the teaching of composition is
the most important business of English departments.

DIALECTS IN CULTURE:
Essays in General Dialectology
by
Raven I. McDavid, Jr.

Edited by William A. Kretzschmar, Jr.
with the assistance of
James B. McMillan, Lee A. Pederson, Roger W. Shuy, and Gerald R. Udell

The University of Alabama Press
University, Alabama

Library of Congress Cataloging in Publication Data

McDavid, Raven Ioor, Jr.
    Dialects in culture.

    Bibliography: p.
    Includes index.
    1. English language--Dialects--Addresses, essays,
lectures. 2. English language in the United States--
Addresses, essays, lectures. 3. Dialectology--
Addresses, essays, lectures. I. Kretzschmar, William A.
II. Title.
PE1702.M3   417'.2   79-18397
ISBN 0-8173-0501-7

Contents

PART I.   THEORETICAL DIALECTOLOGY

Although dialects are studied for various purposes, students may agree on
certain principles: primacy of the spoken language, synchronic description
before diachronic comparison, training in rigorous analysis, and careful
phonetic notation. Regional surveys provide frameworks for more intensive
local studies, studies of non-English dialects, and investigations of the
vocabulary of various cultural activities.

The differences between linguistic structuralism and linguistic geography,
however each may be defined, are not so much matters of essential truth as
matters of emphasis -- as attention to fundamental system as opposed to
inescapable detail. So long as each practitioner is aware of the limitations of his own approach, these differences should yield not hostility but
cooperation to mutual advantage.

Although linguistics as a formal discipline has achieved striking popularity
and prosperity since World War II, there are still few well-written overviews to draw the layman from casual interest to serious study. Of such
overviews, Mencken's *The American Language*, in its various editions, remains
without competition.

The study of language must emphasize both system -- the major patterns
through which the language functions -- and variety, the details that differ
according to the experience of the user of the language and the situation in
which the language is used. For both types of study the importance of close
observation, as a lifetime habit, cannot be exaggerated.

Standards of usage are not a simple matter of good and bad, but of continuous variation along at least nine scales. Almost any of these scales may
involve various aspects of communication -- kinesics, haptics, paralanguage,
suprasegmentals, segmental phonemes, morphology, syntax, and lexicon. Detailed examination of a linguistic feature -- such as the zero third-person
singular present indicative (*he does*) -- reveals a complex interrelationship
of the scales of variation that should discourage simplistic judgments.

like Kurath's *Word Geography* -- more complexity in American regional dialects than has hitherto been recognized. A summary of the regional projects accompanied by an updated map is followed by an outline, with characteristic forms, of the speech areas of the Atlantic Seaboard.

The development of dialectology in America is a reflection of the wide learning, the immersion in American culture, the administrative skill, the generous humanity, and the personal inspiration of Kurath. The ideas and techniques which he first developed in New England have been adapted in many other situations, especially in the study of social dialects.

Traditionally, differences in grammar are social; differences in vocabulary and pronunciation are regional. However, the American regional surveys have shown that the picture is more complicated. Some pronunciations may be social markers, though not in every region where they occur; the interrelation of regional and social status must always be kept in mind.

For many years the National Council of Teachers of English was pilloried by Mencken and other observers as a stronghold of old-fashioned normative grammar. In recent years, however, the picture has changed, and the organization has been repeatedly charged with fostering the abandonment of all standards; charges of its professional irresponsibility have been particularly heated during the savage attacks on the Merriam *Third*. The charges against the NCTE are to be considered an honor rather than a shame, since they reflect the growing interests of the organization in the serious study of language, especially through the work of C. C. Fries.

Although American dialectology has recently emphasized social variation in response to the problems of urban education, many of its traditional emphases are still valid: working from data to theory, recognition of the distinctiveness of each community, acceptance of a multivalent language standard. In this period, regardless of the extent to which the curriculum may be modified toward the needs of cultural minorities, a major role of dialectology will be the education of teachers and of the dominant culture in the nature of language variety.

The affiliations of linguistics and the social sciences -- accepted for some time by anthropologically-oriented structural linguists -- can also be demonstrated through the evidence of the regional linguistic atlases. Recent field work has gathered data illustrating the variety of problems in American society that lend themselves to interpretation through the responses of Linguistic Atlas informants and through their attitudes toward these responses.

Traditional pictures of American regional dialects need to be revised in the light of new information about settlement history and social structure. The loss of postvocalic /-r/, a characteristic "Southern" feature, is far from universal in South Carolina; its predominance seems associated with the spread of the plantation system into areas once dominated by small farmers. Evidence also suggests that new social values may alter the social status of /-r/.

Since the general tendency in American society is toward the elimination of striking dialect differences, new lines of dialect cleavage in urban centers probably derive from new fault lines in society. Examples are: 1) affectation of Northern standards by educated Southern Negroes; 2) preservation of Southern phonology and lexicon among younger middle-class Negroes in Middle Western cities; 3) dialectal subdivision of the speech of Catholic adolescents in Buffalo under the tutelage of nuns for whom English is not a native language.

burlesque serenade by which a community recognizes weddings, chiefly but not always unpopular ones. These terms are highly local. Few of them survive in the Middle West, and those that do are always in competition with the dominant term *shivaree* (French *charivari*) which had early become identified with New Orleans.

Although there are strong emotional attitudes toward the pronunciation of /h-/, or lack of it, in such words as *whip*, *whoa*, and *humor*, objective studies have long indicated that the variants are regional rather than social. Detailed examination of the Atlantic Seaboard records for the linguistic atlases show that among these words there are several patterns, suggesting diverse cultural origins whose details are yet to be fully analyzed.

The zero plurals of nouns of measure -- *three year*, *two pound*, *nine foot*, and the like -- are popularly associated with nonstandard usage, but each of these items investigated for the regional linguistic atlases has its own regional pattern. Furthermore, all of these zero plurals have been recorded in the speech of cultivated informants, though they would probably never write such forms. The explanation for these differences is probably to be found in demographic, economic, and cultural history.

Much of the folk vocabulary of New York State is shared by all American regions, by the North and at least part of the Midlands, or by all of the North. Ease of communication, however, has brought in many scattered regionalisms from further South. Within New York State Kurath has identified three major areas: Metropolitan New York, the Hudson Valley, and Upstate. Less well-defined areas are Long Island, the Western Arm, and the North Country. There is need for intensive follow-up investigations.

Although Upstate New York lies within the Inland Northern speech area, Midland influence is found in two areas: 1) the Upper Susquehanna, Finger Lakes, and Genesee Valley; 2) the Niagara Frontier and Lake Erie shore. On the Canadian side the Niagara Peninsula reflects a heavy settlement by Pennsylvania Loyalists. However, the total number of Midland forms is not impressive, and only one item, *piece* 'lunch' is not at least partially a trade term in origin. Canadian loans cluster in the Buffalo-Niagara area and north of the crest of the Adirondacks.

Northwestern Ohio is a characteristic transition area, settled late, with mixed population and no dominant early cultural focus. Examination of data -- lexical, phonological, and grammatical -- shows divided regional usage in every community and informant. Further studies of such transition areas need to be undertaken. Meanwhile, on the basis of this evidence, one should be skeptical toward claims of single Old World origins for any American dialect.

Although fewer than along the Atlantic Seaboard, regional grammatical differences are found in the North-Central States on every level of usage. Regionally distinctive forms usually reflect the usage of the Northern (especially Inland Northern) and South Midland regions. Arteries of communication, notably the Mississippi and its tributaries, have facilitated the southward spread of Northern forms and the northward spread of forms from the South Midland. Spectacular relic forms are rare, generally confined to Eastern Kentucky. Social differences in usage are not accurately reflected in the judgments of textbook writers.

of English. Examination of some of the varieties of English spoken in Greenville and Charleston, South Carolina, reveals contrasts that cannot be accomodated by a strict application of the Trager-Smith analysis, which however remains useful for many purposes.

Much solid information has been gathered on Southern dialects, chiefly through the Linguistic Atlas project, but much remains to be done. Highest priority should go to completing and publishing the Atlas surveys and Cassidy's *Dictionary of American Regional English*. Follow-up studies should include intensive investigations both of cities and of rural relic areas, of mountain whites, of various groups of Negroes (Southern and transplanted), and of non-English-speaking groups. It would also be desirable to study variations in kinesics, paralanguage, and suprasegmentals, and reactions to dialect differences.

Southern speech is extremely varied; the lists of traditional markers of Southern speech (often prepared by outsiders) are often inadequate and inaccurate. Along the Atlantic Seaboard the 'political' South includes a North Midland fringe and a wide South Midland area -- both derivative from Pennsylvania -- as well as the plantation areas of the Southern coast. Distinctive areas within the South include Chesapeake Bay, the Virginia Piedmont, Eastern North Carolina, the Cape Fear-Pee Dee Corridor, the Southern Mountains, the South Carolina Low-Country, and the Savannah Valley. Change is taking place in the wake of emigration, industrialization, and the development of new economic and educational opportunities; nevertheless, Southern linguistic diversity persists, with locality more significant than race.

The war resulting from the attempted secession of the Southern states in 1861 is known by a variety of names, reflecting the attitude of the participants and the proximity of their homes to the scene of the fighting. Most of the terms used by Southerners have strong emotional connotations, though the most widespread Southern term, *Confederate War* (hitherto not recorded in dictionaries), is a relatively simple denotation. With the passage of time many of the older terms are disappearing.

PART III. CRITICAL DIALECTOLOGY

The author has a favorable situation for developing definitive statements about the speech of the Smokies. That his findings are less convincing than they might have been is due largely to unsystematic gathering and classification of data and to the failure to make use of the framework provided by the field records for the Linguistic Atlas project.

Although academic linguists have done little to provide sound popularization of their discipline, Mencken has in large measure supplied the need. *Supplement One* continues his tradition of accurate observation and delightful statement that has drawn many to serious work in American English.

Supplement Two continues Mencken's successful interpretation of American

English, and of American linguistic scholarship where the national tongue is concerned, for the laity. It shows wide familiarity with recent scholarship, generally accurate appraisal of the work of scholars, and a delightfully irreverent attitude toward American society that make him a successful practitioner of anthropological linguistics whose work academicians would do well to emulate.

economical but more useful than the large maps used by earlier surveys.

Atwood's *Survey* is "the first large-scale study of English grammatical forms derived from . . . systematic sampling of the spoken language of locally and socially identifiable informants over a wide area." After classifying items that may reveal differences, Atwood charts the responses and determines the regional and social differences of competing forms. Recognizing differences in field worker practices and cautious in accepting recorded forms (excluding suggested and reported responses), he finds regional patterns supporting those for vocabulary set forth in Kurath's *Word Geography*. He indicates that judgments in handbooks are often at variance with the facts of cultivated usage.

Although oddly defensive about academic scholarship (a little of which would have made the work more useful), *Down in the Holler* is an informative and entertaining discussion of Ozark folk speech, derived from Randolph's life-long total immersion in the local culture.

The six hundred place names of Franklin County described by Ramsay show many cultural influences. Like all of Ramsay's work, this monograph shows that place-name research provides not only valuable data for linguistic and cultural history but a great deal of pleasure for the investigator.

Using the methods of linguistic geography, Haugen documents the shift in the Norwegian-American community from Norwegian (often of diverse dialects) through bilingualism to assimilation. It is a pioneering work which should appeal to many audiences.

Pop's work provides indispensable background for the history of linguistic geography. It offers tremendous detail (often accompanied by critical bibliographies) on a variety of projects, summarizes lessons in method, and provides indices and other apparatus to make it an extremely useful work of reference.

Drawing on the resources of the Southern Historical Collection at Chapel Hill, Eliason has produced an excellent description of an earlier stage of North Carolina English -- vocabulary, grammar, and pronunciation -- taking full account of the cultural forces that operated in the state. Although he might have made better use of the Linguistic Atlas, he has produced a work which admirably complements the Atlas findings.

Atwood not only adds to our knowledge of regional varieties of American English (especially in the Southwest) but suggests new techniques of investigation -- notably the use of student field workers for gathering lexical evidence and the mechanical sorting of responses. His evidence suggests: 1) complications in drawing boundaries; 2) an additional focal area, the

Maps

Preface

Whatever merit this collection may have, I must share with many others, and not only those with whom I wrote various articles.

The idea originated with James B. McMillan, during his affiliation with the University of Alabama Press. That he is both a long-time personal friend and one of the most widely read scholars in the field made the invitation doubly pleasant.

Selecting the papers for inclusion was more than I felt like doing alone. Although a scholar should not write unless he ultimately enjoys what he has written, he is not necessarily the best judge of which of his writings are most important. At my suggestion, Lee Pederson, Roger Shuy, and Gerald Udell -- three of my doctoral candidates with whom I had worked very closely -- chose what appealed to them. I made a few changes, substituting recent papers for older ones -- but generally agreed with their good judgment.

A good deal of editorial work was necessary, since the papers chosen had appeared over a quarter-century in some thirty publications. Maps had to be added or redrawn; some statements had to be updated; styling had to be made uniform; a single bibliography had to be provided. The first two of these tasks had been largely accomplished by 1969, and all corrected manuscripts were in the hands of the Alabama Press.

There they rested for some years. Like all publishers, the Press had many commitments. Events also cut into my free time: a serious illness in 1969; concentration on editorial work for the *Linguistic Atlas of the Middle and South Atlantic States* till 1976 (Kurath et al. 1979-; now continued at the University of South Carolina, it still draws a good deal of my attention); assumption of responsibility for the *Atlas* of the North-Central States on the death of Albert Marckwardt in 1975 (Marck-

wardt *et al.* 1980-); the planning of major conferences, two on language variety (1970, 1977) and one on lexicography in English (1972).

The delay brought some compensations. The IBM Selectric-II permits the economical composition of technical copy; out of editorial work on the regional atlases came a special phonetic element and several competent compositors, notably William Kretzschmar, who has worked with me since 1977 to make the final editorial decisions and produce the camera-ready copy for the present volume.

The collection includes nothing written after 1969; it is a coherent body of work, winnowed by several conscientious editors, the research for which the NCTE gave me the 1969 David Russell award. More than what has been written later, it reflects the early excitement of discovery as I learned my craft under Hans Kurath, Bernard Bloch, Albert Marckwardt, Leonard Bloomfield and others, and was developing the relationships with colleagues and students that made my professional and personal life so pleasant. It derives from field work, from early editorial operations, and from immersion in Mencken. Changes in the original text are indicated in square brackets; such changes are few, normally reflecting recent history and new information not available at the time the original piece was written. Sometimes I have changed my opinion in the light of new data; I have never suppressed the data for the sake of new opinions. The primary responsibility of a lexicographer or a dialectologist is to accept carefully the role of a "dull cataloguer of data" (Lees 1957:380) and to present the catalog as clearly and precisely as possible. Theories can wait. If with my students and colleagues I can continue the work begun by Kurath and Marckwardt, that will be enough for a lifetime.

Acknowledgments

Education, we know, is a cooperative process in which the teacher receives as much as he gives. Besides the editors, I am heavily indebted to a number who have gained some distinction in the profession: for example, Charles Billiard, Elizabeth Bowman, Thomas Creswell, Sarah D'Eloia, Robin Herndobler, William Kirwin, Muriel Kolinsky, Rosemary Laughlin, Michael Miller, Sarah Myers, Raymond O'Cain, Robert Peters, Dagna Simpson, Andrew Sledd; and as post-doctoral students from abroad, Guy Forgue and Wolfgang Viereck. Colleagues of longer standing who have helped fashion these papers are too numerous to mention, but two have a special relationship: Alva Davis, whom I first met at the Linguistic Institute of 1937 and with whom I have worked in innumerable situations over four decades; and my wife, Virginia McDavid, who has left her mark for the better on everything I have done since 1948. Beyond these lie the evidence and those who contributed to it: some 550 informants in over two hundred communities, of all ages and walks of life; not only did they give generously of their time, but most of them enjoyed participating in the process of discovery. In finding these informants, I used all kinds of local contacts, from barbers to bankers. But I would not have known what kinds of people to consult had it not been for the network of contacts my father had developed where I did my first field work during forty years of dealing with the public in South Carolina. Furthermore, though my first informant, he was unparalleled in his knowledge of our folk culture, in his definitions of terms, and in his suggestions as to how to elicit natural responses. For these reasons, as well as for what he did to provide me with a sense of cultural identity, I hope that these papers show that I learned the lessons he tried to teach me.

I would also like to express my appreciation for the permissions given by the following journals and publishers:

1. "Some Principles for American Dialect Study," from *Studies in Linguistics* 1.12 (1942).1-11, edited by George L. Trager. Used by permission.
2. "Structural Linguistics and Linguistic Geography," from *Orbis* 10 (1961).35-46. Used by permission.
3. "Mencken Revisited," from *Harvard Educational Review*, 34:2 (Spring, 1964), 211-25. Copyright (c) 1964 by President and Fellows of Harvard College. Used by permission.
4. "System and Variety in American English," from *New Directions in American English*, edited by Alexander Frazier, copyright (c) 1967 by National Council of Teachers of English. Used by permission.
5. "Historical, Regional, and Social Variation," from *Journal of English Linguistics* 1 (1967).25-40, copyright (c) 1967 by Journal of English Linguistics: used by permission; from *Culture, Class, and Language Variety*, edited by A. L. Davis, copyright (c) 1972 by National Council of Teachers of English: used by permission.
6. "The Relationship of the Speech of American Negroes to the Speech of Whites," from *American Speech* 26 (1951).3-17, copyright (c) 1951 by Columbia University Press: used by permission; "Addendum," from *Black-White Speech Relationships*, edited by Walt Wolfram and Nona H. Clarke, copyright (c) 1971 by Center for Applied Linguistics: used by permission.
7. "The Dialectology of an Urban Society," from *Communications et rapports du premier congrès international de dialectologie générale* 1.68-80, edited by A. J. Van Windekens, copyright (c) 1964 by Centre International de Dialectologie Générale: used by permission; under the title,

Institute, The University of Michigan. Used by permission.

29. "The Folk Vocabulary of New York State," from *New York Folklore Quarterly* 7 (1951).173-92, copyright (c) 1951 by New York Folklore Society. Used by permission.

30. "Midland and Canadian Words in Upstate New York," from *American Speech* 26 (1951).248-56, copyright (c) 1951 by Columbia University Press. Used by permission.

31. "Northwestern Ohio: a Transition Area," from *Language* 26 (1950).264-73, copyright (c) 1950 by Linguistic Society of America. Used by permission.

32. "Grammatical Differences in the North-Central States," from *American Speech* 35 (1960).5-19, copyright (c) 1960 by Columbia University Press. Used by permission.

33. "Word Magic: or, Would You Want Your Daughter to Marry a Hoosier?" from *Indiana English Journal* 1 (1967).4.1-7, copyright (c) 1967 by Indiana Council of Teachers of English. Used by permission.

34. "Problems of Linguistic Geography in the Rocky Mountain Area," from *Western Humanities Review*, Volume V, Number 3 (Summer 1951), pp. 249-264, copyright (c) 1951 by *The Western Humanities Review*. Used by permission.

35. "The Unstressed Syllabic Phonemes of a Southern Dialect: a Problem of Analysis," from *Studies in Linguistics* 2 (1944).51-55, edited by George L. Trager. Used by permission.

36. "/r/ and /y/ in the South," from *Studies in Linguistics* 7 (1949).18-20, edited by George L. Trager. Used by permission.

37. "The Position of the Charleston Dialect," from *Publication of the American Dialect Society* 23 (1955).35-53, copyright (c) 1955 by American Dialect Society. Used by permission.

39. "Needed Research in Southern Dialects," from *Perspectives on the South: Agenda for Research*, edited by Edgar T. Thompson, copyright (c) 1967 by Duke University Press. Used by permission.

40. "Changing Patterns of Southern Dialects," from *Essays in Honor of C. M.*

Wise, edited by Arthur J. Bronstein, *et al.*, copyright (c) 1970 by the editors. Used by permission.

41. "The Late Unpleasantness: Folk Names for the Civil War," from *Southern Speech Communication Journal* 34 (1969).194-204, copyright (c) 1969 by Southern Speech Communication Association. Used by permission.

42. "Review of Hall 1942," from *Language* 19 (1943).184-97, copyright (c) 1943 by Linguistic Society of America. Used by permission.

43. "Review of Mencken 1945," from *Language* 23 (1947).68-73, copyright (c) 1947 by Linguistic Society of America. Used by permission.

44. "Review of Mencken 1948," from *Language* 25 (1949).69-77, copyright (c) 1949 by Linguistic Society of America. Used by permission.

45. "Review of Thomas 1947," from *Studies in Linguistics* 7 (1949).89-99, edited by George L. Trager. Used by permission.

46. "Review of Kurath 1949," from *New York History* 31 (1950).442-44, copyright (c) 1950 by New York State Historical Association. Used by permission.

47. "Review of Turner 1949," from *Language* 26 (1950).323-33, copyright (c) 1950 by Linguistic Society of America. Used by permission.

48. "Review of Baker 1945," from *Studies in Linguistics* 9 (1951).13-17, edited by George L. Trager. Used by permission.

49. "Review of Dieth and Orton 1952," from *Journal of English and Germanic Philology* 52 (1953).563-68. Used by permission.

50. "Review of McIntosh *et al.* 1951," from *Journal of English and Germanic Philology* 52 (1953).568-70. Used by permission.

51. "Review of McIntosh 1952," from *Language* 30 (1954).414-23, copyright (c) 1954 by Linguistic Society of America. Used by permission.

52. "Review of Atwood 1953a," from *International Journal of American Linguistics* 20 (1954).74-78. Used by permission (now published by the University of Chicago Press).

53. "Review of Randolph and Wilson 1953," reproduced from *Journal of American*

Raven I. McDavid, Jr.
University of Chicago

Editors' Preface

The sixty titles included in this collection span more than a quarter of a century and represent less than one-sixth of McDavid's published essays -- theoretical, applied, and critical statements over a wide range of topics in general linguistics. Our selections here focus on his primary interest, which is general dialectology, that branch of linguistics concerned with the areal and social distribution of linguistic forms. This priority necessarily excludes a number of important contributions to other areas of linguistics -- his work with lexicography, for example, and his pioneering research in Burmese, but such work as that, we trust, will be considered by editors of another volume.

At this time, a collection of McDavid's writings in dialectology is particularly appropriate for several reasons. Although the three longer works to which Professor Kurath refers are certainly of great importance to our discipline and have already gained recognition as standard texts, most of McDavid's scholarly energies have been directed to the particulars of dialectology, and these studies have been reported in a large body of essays from which we have made our selections for this volume. Most of those writings first appeared in the professional journals of linguistics, dialectology, and the modern languages, periodicals which are not readily accessible to every reader, and the information included in these essays provides much of the material with which the longer works were constructed. Furthermore, it is no coincidence that McDavid's career has paralleled the development of dialectology in the twentieth century, and, through his writings, we can trace the evolution of modern dialect study from the rural-oriented survey of regional differences to the urban-oriented analysis of sociolin-

guistic problems. His contributions have identified the fundamental problems which needed to be solved, investigated the structure of the spoken language, and set the conclusions in clear perspective in light of both the changing social structure of the American English speech communities and the implications of his own research, which has always been at the vanguard of American dialect investigation. Finally, the current social direction of dialect investigation as it merges with the practical problems of pedagogy recommends a wider audience for many of these writings. Educators and curriculum planners often find themselves without data to support their intuitions regarding the language of their students or directions to follow after those intuitions have been confirmed. This problem is most frequently considered to be the special province of those concerned with the education of underprivileged children, when in fact all language instruction might be improved with a better understanding of its subject matter. Many of the essays included here do speak directly to the problems of compensatory education, but many more provide basic information on the nature of American English.

These essays are arranged in three sections, proceeding from assumptions about language and linguistic investigation from the dialectologist's point of view, through a set of essays dealing with specific problems of phonology, morphology, syntax, and lexicon on national, regional, and local levels, to a representative sample of those critical reviews which reflect the understanding of the theorist and the practical experience of the field linguist. Taken together, these essays offer a coherent statement of the methods of inductive dialectology: assumptions are based on previous field experience, clarifying principles and pointing to further investigation on the basis of the systematic collection and analysis of data. The articulation and explication of those principles are developed through particular summaries of larger projects, reports of local surveys, and the interpretations of data, most often based on McDavid's own field work. In the reviews the central position of the field experience is also clearly apparent. Personal experience with the problems of research, from design to analysis, gives these essays an uncommon credibility, taking the reader to the situations in which the language is actually used and often providing first-hand information to support or question the validity of the work under consideration. We have made only a few changes in the original texts of the articles, most often silently to provide additional bibliography.

Part I outlines the principles, methods, and accomplishments of dialectology by delimiting its field, characterizing its procedures, and balancing its goals and realizations. Other essays in this section respond to questions concerning the operations of the dialectologist frequently raised by students of linguistics and other behavioral sciences with little experience in areal linguistics. McDavid assesses the notion of a structural dialectology, which has often been discussed but never tested, in "Structural Linguistics and Linguistic Geography" (Ch. 2) with a constructive and thoughtful consideration of the kinds of problems confronting the dialectologist which turn him away from simplistic or mechanical solutions. Similarly, in "The Dialectology of an Urban Society" (Ch. 7), he juxtaposes the contradictory criticisms of Atlas methodology before considering the work to be done against the work already completed. Here, as elsewhere, McDavid is much more concerned with projecting the aims and accomplishments of the discipline rather than developing a formal apology for techniques of linguistic investigation which have already been proven. Another important contribution to the literature of sociolinguistic theory is the classic statement, written with Virginia G. McDavid, "The Relationship of the Speech of American Negroes to the Speech of Whites" (Ch. 6). The facts and folklore of Negro American speech are clearly set forth in this essay, which remains instructive almost three decades after its first appearance. The more recent "Sense and Nonsense about American Dialects" (Ch. 9) reflects the interpretation of new evidence to strengthen the original observations through an evaluation of current research and a critical reappraisal of a number of rather widespread misconceptions concerning dialect study. Closely related to these writings are those essays concerned with clarifying a number of statements about English usage and the scales suggested by others for its interpretation. Again, the evidence of experience in systematic dialect investigation leads McDavid to a reevaluation of overly simplified solutions, as in "Historical, Regional, and Social Variation" (Ch. 5), where the full range of linguistic variation is placed under consideration to provide a much more sophisticated instrument for the interpretation of usage than has appeared in any previous writing on the subject.

Part II includes essays which range from wide overviews of dialectology in "The *Linguistic Atlas of New England*" (Ch. 10) and "Hans Kurath" (Ch. 12) to the close analysis of the vowels in unstressed syllables in the speech of Greenville, South Carolina (Ch. 35). Here also appear a definitive statement, written with A. L. Davis, on the complicated problem of dialect blending or overlapping in a transition area, "Northwestern Ohio: a Transition Area" (Ch. 31), the remarkable description of the area of Charleston influence, which includes evidence from 136 Atlas interviews and maps which did not appear in the original publication, "The Position of the Charleston Dialect" (Ch. 37), and that groundbreaking essay in sociolinguistics, "Postvocalic /-r/ in South Carolina: a Social Analysis" (Ch. 17), which relates the incidence of pronunciation variation to social characteristics as well as to regional distribution. Several other essays in this section consider the application of dialectology to problems in the related fields of toponymic research, ethnolinguistics, psychology, and education. In addition to these are the regional word studies of "The Folk Vocabulary of New York State" (Ch. 29), "Midland

and Canadian Words in Upstate New York" (Ch. 30), and descriptions of regional characteristics from the North-Central, Rocky Mountain, and Southern states. In addition to the discussion of the word *Negro* in "A Study in Ethnolinguistics" (Ch. 19), the detailed regional distribution of *shivaree* and its related forms, written with A. L. Davis (Ch. 26), and "Word Magic: or, Would You Want Your Daughter to Marry a Hoosier?" (Ch. 33) are other important lexical studies.

Part III reveals the crucial problems of operational efficiency, comprehensiveness, and accuracy in dialect study. These critical reviews point up the contributions of the work under consideration through a careful description of the contents, an evaluation of field and analytical procedures, and an appraisal of the accomplishments of the work on its own terms. This is true whether he is dealing with an investigation as unsystematic as *The Phonetics of Great Smoky Mountain Speech* (Ch. 42) or an extremely well-organized survey, such as *The Social Stratification of English in New York City* (Ch. 60). Our decision to include reviews in this collection follows the reasoning that when a scholar makes valuable contributions to his field through the examination of works of widely disparate quality, and thereby formulates important concepts in the process while establishing criteria for the evaluation of other works, such essays represent an important aspect of his professional writing. We know of no other critic of dialectology who has scrutinized so many books so well.

As former students of Raven I. McDavid, Jr., we welcome this opportunity to help make available for a wider audience some of those insights which have been so profitable to us. In this effort we are especially grateful to James B. McMillan for his generous assistance and encouragement in every phase of our editorial work.

Lee A. Pederson
Roger W. Shuy
Gerald R. Udell
William A. Kretzschmar, Jr.

Introduction

In recent years two branches of linguistic science, structural linguistics and area linguistics, have made substantial contributions to our understanding of the ways of American English.

Research in the phonological, morphological, and syntactic structure of a great variety of languages has made it perfectly clear that every language, and every regional or social dialect of a language, has its characteristic structure, its peculiar system of sounds and forms, by means of which the inhabitants of an area or the members of a social class communicate in the transaction of their common affairs.

Applied to the American scene, this scientific point of view implies that every regional and social variety of our English is systematic in its own way. Hence a cultured Virginian's usage cannot be called wrong when it differs from that of his social peer in New England or the Midwest. Nor can folk forms that diverge from cultivated usage in any section of our country be regarded as errors, since they conform to the social norm. Thus the teacher's task is not to eradicate pronunciations, grammatical forms and syntactic features of folk speech, but to familiarize his students with cultivated usage -- for their own good.

Since the 1930's, research in area linguistics, traditionally called linguistic geography, has been supplying the basic evidence for delimiting speech areas in the United States and for characterizing the social dialects in the several sections of our country. Selective sampling from place to place on three broad social levels, using a standard questionnaire, is furnishing us with the necessary data for establishing the dialectal structure along the geographic and the social dimensions.

After the dialectal structure has been determined, the linguist is in a position to investigate its sociocultural background. He finds, among other things, that speech areas may be correlated with settlement areas or trade areas; that they may be focused on old political and cultural centers (active focal areas), lie off the beaten path (relic areas), or be situated between two focal areas (transition areas). From the dissemination of variants by social classes or age groups he may infer trends in usage within the several dialect areas or nation-wide shifts.

In all of these operations he is treating language in its social, cultural, and historical setting. The complexities of the social forces that shape linguistic usage are such that some of his interpretations are tentative rather than definitive, and others may be questionable or erroneous. However that may be, his search for the underlying sociocultural 'drives' is scientifically sound: language must be treated as an aspect of the culture of a people.

For more than twenty-five years the author of the scholarly papers reprinted in this volume has played a leading role in developing the study of American English from the perspective outlined above.

Four or five years of full-time field work in his native South Carolina, in Georgia, in the Great Lakes area, and in the valley of the Ohio have given him insights into the linguistic behavior of persons in several distinct culture areas and in all walks of life. There is no substitute for this kind of experience and no better way of acquiring a feeling for the social and cultural background of linguistic usage.

Very early in his career he undertook to interpret linguistic phenomena in social terms, carefully documenting them with precise data available to him in the collections of the Linguistic Atlas project. A remarkable command of American social and cultural institutions and practices and their history is manifest in these publications, written with apparent ease and in a lucid style.

More recently his interest turned to social dialectology and its implications for the practical problems confronting the teachers of English, especially in large urban areas with their diverse ethnic and racial element.

As director of the Linguistic Atlas project of the American Council of Learned Societies since 1966, Raven Ioor McDavid, Jr., has resumed the editing of the field records from the Middle Atlantic and South Atlantic States and expects to start publication in 1979. May the importance of this enterprise be matched by the financial support required for carrying out his plans. Scholars and teachers concerned with our English badly need these fundamental data.

Recently McDavid has organized and supervised the publication of the data of the Atlas of the North-Central States in which he collaborated with Albert Marckwardt in the 1940's -- a remarkable performance of a vigorous scholar.

I am confident that the stimulating papers presented in this volume, some of which first appeared in journals that are not readily accessible, will find many readers and that they will enjoy the vision and the humane spirit of the author. I also hope that after reading these essays the reader will turn to his larger publications: his chapter on American English dialects in W. Nelson Francis, *The Structure of American English* (1958); his skillful abridgement and updating of H. L. Mencken, *The American Language* (1963); and *The Pronunciation of English in the Atlantic States* (1961), in which he collaborated with me.

Hans Kurath
University of Michigan

Part I
Theoretical Dialectology

The study of American dialect is now being directly fostered by several organizations: The American Dialect Society, newly reorganized; The Linguistic Society of America, especially through its emphasis on descriptive linguistics; The Modern Language Association of America, through its discussion groups for practical phonetics and for present-day American English. At least two regional organizations -- the South Atlantic MLA and the South-Central MLA -- have more or less active committees on dialect study; the first of these is collecting materials for what it may soon issue as a Southern Dialect Dictionary, while the latter, more modestly, is seeking to encourage the preparation of local occupational glossaries, which it hopes may some day fit into a scientifically organized American Dialect Dictionary. [Such a dictionary is nearing completion with Frederic G. Cassidy's *Dictionary of American Regional English* (1981-), handsomely supported since 1965.] In addition, there are projects and publications not immediately under the control of any one organization: the Linguistic Atlas of the United States and Canada is sponsored by the American Council of Learned Societies, but each regional survey is autonomous; *American Speech*, with its series of monographs, is published by Columbia University and its editors are members of the Columbia Faculty, but through an entente with the American Dialect Society and the Present-Day English Group of the MLA, it has an editorial board representing other colleges and other sections; Mr. Harold Wentworth -- working independently, though utilizing the materials collected by the American Dialect Society -- is preparing an American Dialect Dictionary (Wentworth 1944) for popular sale; and at the University of Chicago Professor Hulbert is bringing to completion the *Dictionary of American English on Historical Principles* (Craigie and Hulbert 1936-44). It is likely that other independent projects exist.

It is obvious that these organizations and projects have sharp disagreements over the importance of dialect, the techniques of investigation, and the rigorousness with which material is to be analysed. The *DAE*, for example, though concerned with the peculiar development of the English language in America, tries -- somewhat inconsistently, it would seem -- to exclude all dialect words. [Mathews 1951 includes documented regionalisms, such as those that have come to light in the work of Kurath and his colleagues; so does Avis *et al.* 1967.] Wentworth would include only words that are exclusively dialectal. Others are content to record the facts of usage and let the development of the picture determine whether or not a form is dialectal. The *DAE* uses written and printed material exclusively and stops at 1900; *American Speech* (particularly in its series of monographs) emphasizes phonographic recording, accepts the use of printed and written material, permits field inquiries but does not encourage the sampling technique of formal work-sheets; the Linguistic Atlas is based on forms obtained through interviews organized around formal work sheets. Wentworth would exclude words in the occupational vocabulary; the South Atlantic MLA would accept and encourage the collecting of such words, along with others; the South-Central MLA, acting on a suggestion from Kurath[1] would organize its work around the occupational glossary. The Linguistic Society stresses rigorous phonemic analysis; *American Speech* does not. The Linguistic Atlas employs one phonetic alphabet; *American Speech* another; some linguists use other alphabets. A great deal of confusion exists over the difference between phonetic and phonemic transcription: to some students, a phoneme is apparently a character used in a phonetic alphabet. Some students rigorously define the phonetic values of the characters they use; others compel the reader to guess these values.

Because of these disagreements, and the confusion which they induce in the person just beginning to study dialect, it seems advisable to suggest a few principles which might enable students to work more economically and effectively.

All students of dialect, whatever their interest, should bear in mind the nature of their work.

Every American speaks at least one dialect, sometimes more. By some European standards, of course, there are no dialects of American English; by others, however, all speakers of American are dialect speakers, since there is no Standard American comparable to British Received Standard, Parisian French, Tuscan Italian, or Bühnendeutsch.

Every dialect is worthy of serious study. No one knows to what extent a record of linguistic fact may be of use to later or contemporary scholars.

The spoken language is primary evidence; the literary record is derivative, secondary. Literary records may be studied at a later date, or even by later generations; a spoken dialect, possibly an entire language, may be lost within a decade. For example, only one native speaker of the Catawba Indian language is left. At the worst, a war will leave a large number of records unhurt; conscription, migration, industrial expansion may alter the population and culture of a region in a few years, and profoundly modify its speech in a generation. Literary records may be interpreted from a knowledge of the spoken language, rarely the other way around.

All linguistic work is important only insofar as it is scientifically organized. Casual details are interesting, to be sure, like unplanned collections of antique bric-a-brac; but the best museums have long stressed the *plan* and the *arrangement* of their collections. Any important linguistic work is characterized by rigorous *method*, in preliminary planning, in investigation, and in the analysis of the results. Dialect study is no exception.

Methods of recording vary in practicality.

For dialect work, *field recording* in phonetic notation, using *work sheets*, is the most economical method of obtaining analyzable data.

Phonographic recording is helpful in the collection of *texts* after the dialect is analyzed, but for most dialect work it is ineffective: 1) it is very expensive in time and in money; 2) accurate recording machinery is often bulky and difficult to transport to the informants; 3) even the most willing informant is likely to feel constrained by the presence of a microphone (the elaborate stratagems often resorted to, to conceal the machine from the informant, fail as often as they succeed, and even if successful, consume additional time); 4) the material collected on phonograph records must be transcribed impressionistically, in phonetic notation, and the transcriptions must be arranged and classified -- at additional labor and expense -- before this material is useful for analysis; 5) phonographic recording reduces the possibility of error only insofar as the student may hear the same utterances almost exactly repeated (conditions not met with in actual speech); the additional operations required offer additional possibilities of error, mechanical or human. 'Dialect test' recordings, like *Arthur the Rat*, are useful only with sophisticated informants. [Lightweight equipment now available eliminates some of the physical problems, but the others remain.]

Random listening and *casual notation of forms* may be helpful in the preliminary stages of dialect work -- as, for example, in selecting an informant. For the actual dialect study, it is a wasteful procedure. [Undirected questioning may provide statistically useful evidence in a few items, but limits their number.]

A field worker should be aware of his own dialect, so that he will not exaggerate the unfamiliar or overlook the familiar. Every word -- or sound -- in an informant's speech, not merely the strange, is a part of his dialect.

It is impossible to write a *descriptive* and a *comparative* study at the same time. Frequently, of course, it may be desirable in the same study to compare a dialect under observation with contemporary dialects, or with an earlier stage of the language, but the two tasks should not be mixed. *Description must precede comparison*. If the two types of comparison are undertaken, *synchronic* and *diachronic*, the former should be undertaken first.

Accurate phonetic annotation is a basic tool of all dialect study -- as of all linguistic work. For some types of study, such as linguistic geography, the ultimate record may well be printed in the *phonetic symbols* themselves. For other types of study -- morphological and syntactic, or a complete grammar of a dialect or language -- the *phonetic transcription* would naturally be replaced by a *phonemic* notation.

Only folk lore demands an unusually keen ear for accurate phonetic transcription. Hearing sufficient for normal social purposes is sufficient for distinguishing the phonetic and prosodic features of a language, provided the student has had *training*. Without training, acuteness of hearing means nothing.

Training is best acquired under an experienced linguist. Intelligent students may, however, sometimes acquire considerable skill from carefully following a well written exposition.[2] Non-linguistic phonetic instruction, such as that offered by elocutionists and other purveyors of 'correct speech,' usually hinders the development of true phonetic skill, because it substitutes for a scientific interest in recording sounds as spoken an emotional attachment or revulsion to certain sounds for pseudo-aesthetic or pseudo-social reasons.

A teacher of phonetics is not to be judged by his virtuosity in sound production but by the ability of his students to do accurate independent work. [Bloch was a superb teacher.]

Phonetic training involves: a) dissociation of sound and conventional spelling; b) familiarizing oneself with a phonetic alphabet; c) intensive drill, especially in situations where one student may compare his transcriptions with those of others -- and of the instructor; d) projects approximating as nearly as possible the conditions of field recording.

In field recording, some phonetic alphabet is necessary. The use of a phonetic alphabet will not, alone, yield magic results. The alphabet is a tool, not an end in itself.

For effective transcription in dialect geography and in the early stages of all field work, the student should employ as *detailed* or *narrow* a notation as his training permits.

Any speech sound can be transcribed. Statements that certain speech sounds 'cannot be written down' are nonsense. They really mean that 1) the student has not had sufficient training to recognize the sound; or 2) he is using an alphabet that does not recognize the full range of possible speech sounds.

The choice of a phonetic alphabet is often determined by the type-fonts available. The most complete phonetic analysis is that by Bloch and Trager (1940, 1942); the symbols in their phonetic tables have varied, and they suggest the possibility of using still different phonetic symbols.[3] The phonetic alphabet employed in the Linguistic Atlas of the United States is less scientifically organized, but -- with a few exceptions (for which modifications are feasible) -- covers the range of possible sounds in American dialects; it has the advantage of familiarity and of association with a well-known research project. A student may adopt other alphabets, combine features of several, or devise one of his own, such as Bell's 'visible speech.' The kind of alphabet does not matter so long as it can register the phonetic facts.

Whatever the alphabet used, the student should explain it to the reader, using tables and whatever additional apparatus is necessary. See, for example, Kurath *et al.* 1939, Chapter IV, The Phonetic Alphabet. The mere fact that a type of alphabet is used by a learned society does not guarantee that a reader will understand it; it must be explained. Phonetic symbols are useless unless the reader is informed of the *range of sound* they represent. Such explanations should be precise: to say that a sound represented by a symbol is 'essentially the same as in normal American speech' is meaningless because 1) a reader might never have heard Americans talk; 2) there is no such thing as 'normal American speech.' Even within the Central-Western or so-called 'General American' area -- the most homogeneous of the major speech-areas in the United States -- there are many local variants. [This was discovered very early by A. H. Marckwardt and his colleagues, in the investigations in the Great Lakes region.]

Phonetic records, however minute, are not linguistic apparatus in themselves, but must be interpreted in terms of the *significant* classes of sound-types -- in a *phonemic* transcription. For some purposes, as in the distributional maps in the Linguistic Atlas, it is preferable to leave the *phonetic* transcription rather than attempt a reduction to *phonemic* notation; in the discussion of these maps, however, it is necessary to make a, *phonemic* analysis of the dialect or dialects under discussion.

A *phonemic analysis* is simply a statement of the significant classes of sound-types in a language or dialect, describing the phonetic range of each class. If a *phoneme*, or class of sound-types, contains more than one sound-type, it is necessary to describe the phonetic range of each sound-type, or *allophone* of the phoneme, together with the phonetic surroundings in which each allophone occurs.

In a phonemic analysis, the three principles that must be followed are *complementary distribution, phonetic similarity,* and *pattern congruity.* See Trager 1942; Bloch and Trager 1942: 40-46; Trager and Bloch 1941.

A phoneme is not a sound, but a class of sound-types.

Phonemic transcription is not the same as phonetic transcription. Phonetic transcription emphasizes minute differences; phonemic transcription emphasizes major similarities. In phonetic transcription it is desirable to have as many symbols as the training of the student permits him to use in recognizing sound-types; in phonemic transcription it is desirable to have as few symbols as the structure of the language demands. One symbol should represent only one phoneme; one phoneme should be represented by only one symbol.

Linguistic analysis is not possible until the language or dialect is reduced to phonemic notation.

Before attempting field work, every student should prepare a phonemic analysis of his own speech, including as full a statement as possible of the allophones.

Morphological and syntactic analysis may be conducted for American dialects as for any foreign language. See Bloch and Trager 1942: 53-79.

Most American dialect students are primarily interested in *English* dialects spoken in the United States.

The most important work dealing with English dialects in the United States is the Linguistic Atlas of the United States and Canada.

The Linguistic Atlas attempts to set off dialect areas by sampling techniques. Informants are chosen according to population distribution and what is known of the history of the area. Work sheets are arranged so as to include the phonemes of American English with their various allophones in all possible positions, and morphological and lexical samplings adequate to set off dialect communities from each other. To facilitate comparison, the work sheets attempt to deal with materials common to the region being studied.

The Atlas is far from complete. For New England, field work and editing have been completed, and two-thirds of the Atlas of New England has been published. More than four-fifths of the field work has been done for the Atlas of the South Atlantic States, about as much for the Atlas of the Middle Atlantic States; much editing has been done for both of these sections. Completion of field work depends on the finding of qualified field workers, the procuring of additional funds, and a more favorable turn in the war that might allow the extensive automobile travel necessary for field work. The Atlas plans for other sections are indeterminate; from the University of Michigan is being conducted a broad survey of the North-Central States, using relatively fewer informants, shorter work sheets, and several field workers. In some other sections surveys (mostly unsatisfactory because field workers are not uniformly trained) have been made on the basis of Atlas work sheets; these surveys will help the Atlas field workers at some future date, but are not a substitute for the Atlas. [With his transfer to Ann Arbor, and the editorship of the *Middle English Dictionary*, Kurath became *primus inter pares*, and each regional survey became an autonomous project. The *Linguistic Atlas of the Upper Midwest*, edited by Harold B. Allen (1973-76), was published before the materials from the Middle and South Atlantic States.]

The Atlas should outline the problems of American dialect study, by providing a frame of reference within which future studies may be conducted. It suggests types of material most helpful in setting off dialect areas and in tracing the interpenetration of dialects; it broadly outlines the major dialect areas and their principal subdivisions, indicating dominant areas, relic areas, and transition areas. It cannot be ignored by any student seriously intending to study American dialects.

The Atlas is a guide, rather than a fully definitive work. It does not provide a phonemic analysis, but leaves that problem to the student using the Atlas. It cannot offer a complete morphology, syntax, or lexicon. Editorial exigencies may cause the ignoring of interesting local dialects. The Atlas is an outline to be filled in by other research.

In order that future American dialect research may be intelligently organized, it is imperative that the Atlas be completed as soon as possible. For comparative and historical study, it would be desirable to have an Atlas of the British Isles. [*The Survey of English Dialects* (Orton *et al.* 1962-71) has published its Basic Materials, analogous to the New England Atlas.]

Outside the scope of the Atlas there are many types of dialect survey which may be conducted in any part of the country.

Smaller dialect areas, counties and townships, can be surveyed to determine their relationship to the general picture of American dialects.

Relic areas, such as Marblehead, or the Banks Islands of North Carolina, should be intensively studied for the recording of relic forms and for the light which the study may throw on earlier stages of the language. A student should remember, however, that the lateness with which communications were established does not of itself make a community a relic area: inaccessibility characterized some areas of recent settlement and dialect mixture, like the Great Smoky Mountains. Relic areas should be studied by field methods as soon as possible, before the local speech forms are supplanted.

Transition areas, whether between major dialect areas or in the vicinity of cultural centers within an area, should be investigated for dialect mixture, the effects of cultural influences, and the tendencies of change.

For convenience in comparison and to save time both in the preliminary stages and in the field, the Atlas methodology and work sheets should be employed as far as they are applicable. The number and class of informants should always be indicated, and some apparatus should be available for distinguishing and evaluating the responses of each informant. The work sheets themselves might be altered or abridged as time limitations demand or the peculiar culture of a community may suggest. Nautical terms, for instance, would not normally be elicited in a Smoky Mountain community.

In local, intensive studies it is imperative to make a clear phonemic analysis of the dialect. If it is a mixed dialect area, the student should make a phonemic analysis of each dialect in the area, with tables of comparisons and alternations.

American Indian languages, and dialects of them, may be studied like any other new language or dialect. See Bloomfield 1942; Bloch and Trager 1942. American Indian languages may borrow words from English or lend words to English, just as other languages do. For the effective study of such borrowings, it is advisable to know something of both languages involved.

Dialect studies may and should be undertaken among the communities in which non-English immigrant languages are spoken. [Within the past two decades and a half, several excellent studies have appeared, notably Reed and Seifert 1954 and Haugen 1953.]

No one has yet compiled a definitive list of non-English immigrant language communities in the United States. Until such a list is prepared, we can only speculate, judge empirically, or accept local folklore about the extent of opportunities for research in such dialects. Many of these dialects and languages, spoken by small communities, may be lost, unnoticed, unless scholars are informed where they exist. The first task in a systematic study of non-English immigrant dialects is the preparation of a list of communities where such dialects are spoken.

The study of non-English immigrant dialects involves all the problems of the study of English dialects, with special problems of its own: the interrelationship between non-English dialects and English dialects in the same community; the interrelationship between two or more non-English dialects in the same community, whether or not they are of the same linguistic stock.

Lexical research is not so much linguistic research as research in the culture of a community. However, since the beginner in dialect study is likely to start with lexical material, lexical research must be included in any discussion of dialect problems.

Odd lexical details may be of interest, especially if indicating form distribution different from that indicated by such reference works as the *Oxford English Dictionary*, the *DAE*, or the *English Dialect Dictionary* (Wright 1898-1905). Like other dialect research, though, lexical research is more effective if organized around a definite pattern.

Since lexical research is cultural research, it may be organized to include the lexicon of an area or the lexicon of a culture-activity. Of the two, the lexicon of a culture-activity is easier to undertake, since the frame of reference is more definite and could serve for a comparative lexicon of a culture-activity over a wide area. For instance, the technique of cotton farming differs little from Texas to Virginia or from Mississippi to Illinois; after once preparing a glossary of cotton farming in a single community, a student could easily employ a frame of reference and questionnaires that would enable him to prepare a glossary representing occupational usage in the entire cotton-raising area.[4]

Very few occupations, or other culture-activities (such as recreations or foods) have been adequately studied. Perhaps the most thorough lexicons of occupations are those prepared by Professor D. W. Maurer of the occupational vocabularies in the underworld.

Until many glossaries of culture-activities are prepared, it will be impossible to issue any kind of accurate dialect dictionary of the United States.

Lexical research differs from other dialect research in permitting 1) the use of written or printed sources; 2) the elicitation of responses by written questionnaires.

All dialect students should investigate thoroughly, define accurately, and carefully verify their evidence. When this is done, they should publish promptly. Too many excellent studies have been lost because the authors did not take the trouble to have them published. However, when doubt exists, the student should publish: a poor article published will be forgotten sooner or later; a good article, unpublished, can never be regained.

NOTES

[1] In a talk 'Star-Gazing,' delivered at the Linguistic Institute, Chapel Hill, North Carolina, July 10, 1941.

[2] The best short exposition is Bloch and Trager 1942: Chapter II, Phonetics, 10-37; see their bibliography, 80-81, for other recommended treatments.

[3] [Excellently conceived as it was, the Trager-Bloch phonetic alphabet never caught on. In fact, with the development of lightweight high-fidelity recording equipment, and with the recent emphasis on theoretical closet linguistics, relatively few good young field workers have come into the study of dialectology, though many have been trained for the mission fields by Kenneth Pike and his colleagues.]

[4] Plans for studying the vocabulary of cotton farming were outlined by J. B. McMillan and Willis Russell, of the University of Alabama, and adopted tentatively as a regional project by the Chairman of the South-Central MLA Dialect Committee; completion of these plans is naturally deferred until after the war. [It is not yet achieved.]

Every growing academic discipline expands its scope and develops its subsidiary fields of special interest.[1] After the older 'natural philosophy' (so-called in the bulletin of the United States Military Academy as late as 1930) became physics, physics in turn developed many branches, some of which have become highly (and indeed alarmingly) publicized in the last two decades. Similarly, as linguistics has left philology and become a recognized discipline in its own right, it has developed its own specialized branches. As yet it is not as difficult to become conversant with all of linguistics as with all of physics or chemistry, but linguists are increasingly specializing as the field becomes more complex.

As specialization increases, the practitioners of each specialty develop intense loyalties. At times there seems to be a compulsive urge among particular groups to convert the entire discipline to their specialty, to restrict (by the proclamation of dogma, if not by legislative action) the science to this specialty, and to cast everyone else into outer darkness. Less than a century ago, medicine was rocked by a feud between allopaths and homeopaths; there is still controversy over the proper place of psychoanalysis.

As emphasized at the 1960 Congress of General Dialectology, one of the current problems in linguistics is the relationship between the structuralist and the linguistic geographer. In the United States this relationship has been most sharply debated by the adherents to the structural analysis presented in Trager and Smith 1951. Unfortunately, the debate has too often taken the form of propaganda rather than of the urbane controversy represented by C. S. Lewis and E. M. W. Tillyard in *The Personal Heresy* (1939). As a worker on the American Atlas and with the Tragerian framework (ultimately derived, Trager points out, from Henry Sweet through Prince N. S. Trubetzkoy), I hope this paper may lead to some understanding of what each group is after, and to a recognition that each can render its best service to our discipline, not by being converted or repressed but by working to the logical conclusion of its fundamental assumptions. And it may well be that both can serve as correctives to the generous assumptions of the new school of transformationalists, whose Bible is Chomsky's *Syntactic Structures* (1957).

Perhaps a part of the problem is that our science is so new that linguists are not completely sure of themselves. Where a linguist is attached to an established department -- whether English literature, modern languages, classics, psychology or anthropology -- his colleagues often look upon him as a freak, at best as a Cerberus that must be satisfied before departmental candidates can pass on to the Elysian Fields of the doctorate. Where linguists are established in an independent department, most older departments denigrate them as interlopers engaged in power politics. In fighting the heavy-handed normative grammarians and slide-rule-and-compass language teachers, and in defining their position in relation to other disciplines, linguists have often not stated their case as clearly or as urbanely as they might, and have drawn bitter if misguided retorts from traditionally-minded teachers of composition and literature. These circumstances, and the lively disagreements among ourselves, do not encourage objectivity about our differences. In fact, we sometimes do not even agree about the basis of our disagreement.

To invade territory untrodden by angelic feet: the structuralist is generally concerned with the distribution of a linguistic element in terms of other linguistic elements, the linguistic geographer with the distribution of a linguistic element in terms of the geographical area and social complex in which it is found. The two approaches are not mutually exclusive. Any time the structuralist speaks about variations in more than one locality, he is working with the materials of linguistic geography; conversely, when the linguistic geographer describes patterns of contrast and lack of contrast -- the occurrence of a discrete second-person plural in certain American dialects or the homophony of *cot* and *caught* -- he is speaking structurally. The same linguist may operate at different times in both roles. As a structural linguist I insist that my students learn at least one systematic description of English, involving patterns on levels of increasing complexity, from the sound type to the sentence. I insist that all applications of linguistics, from second-language teaching to stylistic criticism, have a basis of such systematic description. In presenting these descriptions, especially in their earlier stages, it is not only permissible but necessary to assume a fictitious uniformity of structure, just as the classical presentation of the laws of falling bodies disregards the effects of atmospheric friction. On the other hand, in at least one significant application of linguistics -- the teaching of the standard language to speakers of non-standard varieties -- it is necessary to become an applied dialectologist and present the desirable forms primarily in terms of their regional and social status.

Structural linguistics and linguistic geography have many things in common. Both study the phenomena of language as found and record them without reference to arbitrary outside norms or notions of propriety. This does not mean ignoring social differences or value judgments. It is a part of the process of recording the use of a linguistic form to indicate what speakers use it and what social contexts, and what attitudes these speakers have toward it. In Charleston, South Carolina, for instance, cultivated speakers from the oldest and best families frequently use *ain't* in familiar conversation with their social peers; it is also a part of the record that such speakers would never use *ain't* in formal discourse, let alone any kind of writing except deliberate humor. It is a part of the record of middle-class usage in the Carolina Piedmont that many speakers of this group -- including members of the local squirearchy and other public figures -- habitually use in everyday discourse such non-standard verb forms as *the wind blowed*, *we seen him*, and *the road is all tore up*; it is equally a part of the record that such forms are rarely offered in response to direct questioning, and that when suggested, they are rejected with the scornful observation that 'ignorant folks say that.' The social as well as the linguistic context of every form is relevant, though they are to be examined on different levels.

Neither the structural linguist nor the linguistic geographer is concerned with individual forms out of their socio-linguistic context. Neither is content to list quaint and curious lore; each wants to know something of the environment in which the form occurs -- whether linguistic, historical or socio-cultural. This is equally true of the pronunciation /jumə/ 'humor,' of /dʌv/ as the preterite of *dive*, and of *hamestrings* as the designation of large fishing worms.

Both structuralists and linguistic geographers are concerned with grammar. They do not attempt to downgrade its importance, but in fact urge a more thorough and systematic examination of grammatical patterns than has been done in the past.

The structural linguist and the linguistic geographer agree that every language has a structure which can be described, though different descriptions may vary in detail.

They agree that a difference in the scale of the description means a difference in the amount of detail, just as a map of a scale 1:1000 can offer more detail than one of a scale 1:1000000; but on its own scale the first may be as accurate as the second. They agree that this method may be applied to any language, whether it has 100 speakers or 100 million, whether it has an extensive written literature, a small one, or none at all. The process of description may be complicated by the number of speakers or by literary tradition. The larger the speech community, the more opportunities for varieties to develop. And a literary tradition may preserve, in a special status, limbo forms that are no longer a part of everyday discourse. The King James Version of the English Bible, the Book of Common Prayer, and church custom preserve in this status the second-person pronouns *thou*, *thy*, *thine*, *thee* and *ye*, the *-st* second-person singular (present and preterite) indicative of the verb, and the *-th* third-person singular present indicative as occasional but still functioning linguistic forms for many speakers of English. But in accepting this fact we insist on two corollaries: 1) limbo forms are not peculiar to English, or to languages with a written literature; many languages have forms peculiar to ceremonial, prayer, poetry, proverbs and the like -- forms which must be included in the full inventory of the language, but which do not function in ordinary conversation; 2) one can describe a language so as to take full account of such limbo forms, though their inclusion may complicate the statement.

In short, structuralists and linguistic geographers emphasize the actual facts of the language, are concerned with the grammatical system, approach through speech rather than through writing, and insist that any structure can be described.

Our differences also exist. As human beings we have personal tastes, such as a preference for Debussy over Mahler. We may be influenced by academic training and position: one who holds a position in a department of English Literature and teaches an occasional course in Milton is likely to think in terms of cooperation with his literary colleagues; he is probably less likely than a linguist in a separate department to look upon the study of literature as superfluous, inconsequential or decadent. Contrariwise, the linguist attached to a department of anthropology or to a language-teaching program may be more actively involved in structural problems than one associated with departments of literature. The former has a drive to master a systematic treatment of structure, for learning a new language or for teaching the languages he knows already;

the latter may feel (often wrongly) that he has an adequate working knowledge of the structure and can devote his time to geographical, historical or etymological studies. Finally, perhaps irrelevantly, the linguist with literary training may sometimes judge a linguistic statement by its literary quality.

We further differ about the best means of attaining the same goal: of getting a greater awareness of linguistics to a larger number at an earlier stage in their education. Some would do this through departments of English, through better linguistic training of the undergraduate majors who will go out to teach English in the public schools. Others, as sincerely, would work through schools and departments of education, and try to influence all prospective teachers. Still others work most effectively with psychiatrists and psychologists, with anthropologists, or with special programs in American studies. However, all these differences at best indicate why a linguist may prefer one type of linguistic study to another; they do not describe the different approaches, or contrast them.

In defining these approaches, I shall touch only briefly on that of the structuralist -- only insofar as it is necessary to point out differences between the approach of some structuralists and that of some linguistic geographers.

At the outset, we should remember that structural linguistics is not monolithic, but embraces several schools and methods of operation. It does not depend on using a given set of terms or on following a given set of operations in a given order. Trager and Smith, Pike, Harris, Bloch, Firth, Fries, Hjelmslev, Martinet, Chomsky and Jakobson -- to mention only a few -- all insist that their own methods are rigorously structural, but at times some of these have warmly denied that others were structuralists at all. Even on the phonological level, where there seems to be most agreement, some would include stress and pitch and juncture as a part of the system of phonemes, while others would relegate these to a separate prosodic system.

What all structural linguists have in common is an interest in finding patterns of distribution of linguistic elements, with reference to other linguistic elements. Typically, the structural linguists insist that the elements in a pattern be on the same level of analysis, that the distribution of a sound unit be stated in terms of other sound units, of a morpheme in terms of other morphemes, and so on. They normally insist -- some more than others -- that no level of analysis should be presented until after the preceding ones have been worked out: that one must work out the phonology before approaching the morphology, the morphology

before the syntax, and so on. Practically, they are often less meticulous; in fact, Fries's *The Structure of English* (1952) concerns itself almost altogether with syntax, ignoring phonology and introducing morphology only to help determine word classes. But the aim is always the same: to determine the patterns in which linguistic forms occur. For his purposes, the structural linguist is seldom greatly concerned with phonic details or with vocabulary. Phonetics he may consider as a part of pre-linguistics, vocabulary of metalinguistics (Trager 1949).

The linguistic geographer, or dialectologist, is concerned with the distribution of linguistic elements within certain geographical and social limits. Where the structuralist takes a linguistic form and determines the linguistic contexts in which it occurs, the dialectologist sets up a context and finds out what forms occur in that context. The element which the context is designed to elicit may be the phonetic quality of the final /-l/ in *pull*, the final consonant phoneme in *blouse*, the plural of *ox*, the negative of *ought to*, the designation of a long wiggly creature dug from the earth to put on one's fishhook, the kind of machine that bears the name *go-devil*, or the salutation used by small boys on December 25. A dialect investigation may include any or all of these types of items. Furthermore, in making his preparations and interpreting his data, the linguistic geographer will utilize data outside the field of linguistics: population history, transportation routes, educational practices, ecclesiastical organization, political boundaries, economic interests, social structure or physical geography.

In linguistic geography there are as many differences in approach as there are in structural linguistics -- reflecting differences in the personality and training and interests of the investigator, and differences in the purposes for which the investigations are undertaken. These purposes are so varied that not even Pop's *La Dialectologie* (1950) has presented them all; the following list merely suggests some of the things which dialectologists hope to determine from their studies:

1. A simple regional description, for its own sake or for some ulterior purpose. Such an ulterior purpose (not unjustifiable in itself) might be the realistic presentation of regional speech in a movie or television show, or the effective functioning of a quiz show, like Henry Lee Smith's "Where Are You From?" Such a show might in turn be designed to convince the public of the importance of linguistics.

2. The details necessary to complete one's structural analysis -- these details depending in turn on the kind of structural analysis and the purpose behind it.

3. The extent to which a standard dia-

lect has spread at the expense of regional and local types of speech.

4. The centers of trade and culture that have exerted an influence on the speech of surrounding communities and areas, and the ways and extent of that influence.

5. The accurate delineation of a generally recognized speech boundary.

6. The limits of conservative areas which might reflect an early stage of the language and resistance to the standard language; along with this, the discovery of what parts of the language show the greatest resistance.

7. Important early routes of migration and trade.

8. Earlier political or ecclesiastical boundaries; their influence on the development of dialects.

9. The relics of earlier dialects of the same language.

10. The development of particular features of an early stage of the language, such as Latin /ka-/ or Middle English /o:/.

11. The basis for more accurate statements about dialect distribution at an earlier period of the language -- as one might wish to have in preparing a historical dictionary.

12. A more accurate knowledge of the structure of earlier dialects, to help in the study of dialect texts.

13. The relationships between the dialects of a colonial language and those of the mother country -- say, American English and British English.

14. The influence of other languages on the principal language of an area, such as French on Louisiana English, German on Pennsylvania English, English on Quebec French.

15. The extent of acculturation of immigrants and other minority stocks.

16. The direction of change in a language, or in its dialects, from one generation to another.

17. The relationship between social or educational status and the preservation of regional or local speech forms.

18. The distribution in the general population of items peculiar to a social group.

19. The best network for the rapid and efficient gathering of material for a dialect dictionary, or for a dictionary of usage.

20. The basis for the official language of an emerging national state.

Manifestly, these purposes are not mutually exclusive; it is possible for a single investigation to have all or most of them in mind. But the interests of an investigator will influence the kinds of data he records, and the interest of a person using the data will determine the kinds of use he makes of it. A person interested chiefly in phonology will not be concerned with the extent of the lexical coverage, nor will the lexicographer be impressed by the amount of phonological data.

Perhaps underlying all such differences is the investigator's notion of what a dialect is. Is a dialect a form of speech sharply contrasting with the standard language? Is each local dialect assumed to be pure or uniform? Is the standard language itself considered as a dialect? Does the standard language itself have regional varieties? The answer depends in part on the cultural situation, but in part also on the investigator.

In view of these differences in the aims of the projects and the attitudes of the investigators, we should be prepared for differences in the execution: in the density of the network, in the number of informants per community, in the types of informants interviewed, in the circumstances of the interview, in the length and composition of the questionnaire,[2] in the method of eliciting the responses (free conversation, guiding questionnaires, citation words, or passages to be read), in the notation for recording the responses (whether phonic or phonemic),[3] in the use of mechanical equipment, in the numbers and training of the field workers, and in the relationship of the personality of the field worker to the goals of the project. All of these variables are familiar to the dialectologist with field experience, but not necessarily to the theoretical structuralist, especially to the structuralist trained to apply a predetermined pattern of analysis.

In summing up the relationship between structural linguistics and linguistic geography, one must concede that the public relations between linguistic geographers and other linguists have suffered from two things:

1. A widespread notion that anyone can do dialect investigation, and that all one has to do is to go out to some reasonably isolated place and listen to the quaint sayings of the natives. The linguist who suggests a little rigor in dialect study is often accused of taking the fun out of 'dialect collecting.' This very language suggests that too many of those concerned with dialect investigations are mere collectors, not students.

2. The frequent unwillingness of students trained in one set of techniques to accept any other as valid. This is particularly common among those trained in the traditions of Gilliéron and the French Atlas. No one should deny the originality of Gilliéron's methods, or the extent of the contributions to dialectology by the French Atlas and its derivative studies. But too often since the appearance of *L'atlas linguistique de France* (Gilliéron and Edmont 1902-10), dialectologists, particularly those dealing with Romance lan-

guages, have taken as immutable laws the operational principles that Gilliéron set down for his research: one Atlas, with one technique; one questionnaire through the area in which the language is spoken; one informant per community, a speaker of 'the dialect'; one field worker throughout the area investigated, to record impressionistically and make no systematization, to be as nearly as possible a human recording machine; one recording of each item, the 'spontaneous, naive response.'

Not infrequently, European critics of the American Atlas have insisted that these are immutable laws, not to be tampered with. It is not surprising that structuralists should feel that these principles are inadequate, and from the arguments of their defenders conclude that all linguistic geographers are a bit old-fashioned.

It is therefore time to offer the following modifications of Gilliéron's principles.

We need many investigations, with all sorts of techniques, both in relatively uninvestigated areas and in areas where major projects have already been executed. Every language area is so complex, and every culture is subject to so many forces tending to level old differences and create new ones, that we can never have too much information about any regional or social variety of any major language. For years many prominent British scholars refused to support a linguistic atlas of the British Isles, feeling that Ellis and Wright had recorded everything; fifteen minutes with the field records which Guy Lowman made in southern England in 1938 is enough time to disprove this assumption. No field worker can come out of a community with the feeling that he has recorded everything of importance; at most he can get thorough coverage of an inescapably limited questionnaire.

We need different types of questionnaires, each designed to get a particular kind of data (McIntosh 1952).

We can determine the number of informants per community by the nature of the investigation. One good local informant may supply all one needs in a study of local variations in the folk vocabulary of a rural society; on the other hand, where a problem (as in phonology) is complicated or the social structure of the community is complex, a large number of informants will be needed.

We need many field workers, with some allocation of field workers to projects in terms of their individual interests and abilities.

We should welcome multiple responses, especially where the item under investigation has several variants differing in social prestige. It complicates the data but clarifies the social picture if a given informant offers *saw*, *see*, *seed* and *seen* as preterites of *to see*.

We should welcome the use of mechanical apparatus, but not expect the apparatus to ask the questions or analyze the data. At the very least, a permanent recording would enable any dispassionate scholar to check the accuracy of the transcriptions. And only by mechanical recordings can we have adequate data for determining patterns of stress, pitch and juncture.

Thus one returns to the problem of the relative roles of the American Linguistic Atlas and Trager and Smith 1951:

1. The Atlas does not attempt to separate levels of analysis, but leaves analysis to the individual scholar utilizing the data the field workers have recorded. In the strict sense of the word, linguistic geography cannot be analysis; it either provides raw material for analysis or fills in the local variants for elements in an analysis which has been previously sketched.

2. The Atlas does not provide full material for statements about intonation, juncture or stress. It concedes their importance, but leaves them to other types of investigations, preferably those utilizing permanent recordings.

3. The Atlas provides detailed information on the regional and social variants of lexical and grammatical items, on a scale beyond the scope of any ouline sketch.

4. The Atlas alone provides certain types of systematic phonological information: the distribution of clear /l/ in intervocalic or post-vocalic position; the aspiration of intervocalic voiceless stops; the open beginnings of up-gliding diphthongs, and the occurrence of long pure vowels or in-gliding diphthongs, especially for the vowels of *date* and *boat*. Such phenomena set off dialect areas, and the boundaries so determined coincide with boundaries determined in other ways.

Probably the hardest doctrinal differences to reconcile between the two approaches are these:

1. Do compromise phonemes exist? Does a speaker always have clear-cut phonemic boundaries, or does he sometimes straddle, as when he feels that /kɛtʃ/ is vulgar but that /kætʃ/ is affected?

2. Can we by definition phonemicize for more than one dialect, or even one speaker at a time?

3. Can we expect phonological data to fall into a single over-all pattern?[4] Or will a large language area, subject to change and constant dialect mixture, always provide some residue that can with difficulty be fitted in? Is not the concept of an over-all pattern a denial of the most important kinds of dialectal difference, those in structure, adequately supported by the findings of Kurath and R. McDavid 1961 in the United States and Catford 1957a,b in Scotland? And if we ac-

cept an over-all pattern, how tight a fit must it have? Or is Hockett's notion of a common core rationally more valid?[5]

Today we are still far from agreement on these questions, and may not reach it for some time to come. In fact, it is doubtful whether full agreement would be a good thing, or whether one should work all the time within any single framework. The mere fact that there are differences in approach should lead to cross-fertilization, to the discovery of phenomena that might be overlooked if one stuck to one framework. Proportionately, the area of disagreement is not large; we can convert from one phonemicization to another about 95 percent of the time; and what is most impressive is the high degree of correlation between dialect boundaries established by the two approaches. With so much unfinished work, in American English as well as in other languages, we should not despise any type of investigation that promises to increase our knowledge, so long as it is done honestly and carefully according to a clearly stated method. No single investigation will please everybody in all details; we shall all be the richer by accepting the multiplicity of results rather than rejecting an entire investigation because it is not done our way. It may have been good etiquette, but it was poor administrative policy for the ancient Chinese to behead generals who had won battles by violating the long-established principles of military science.

NOTES

[1] This paper was originally presented at a special seminar on the structure of English, directed by James H. Sledd, at the University of Chicago in January 1953. In its original version it went into greater detail about the diversity of approaches in dialectology. The problem has been discussed elsewhere, notably (in Saussurean terminology) by Witold Doroszewski at the Eighth International Congress of Linguists, Oslo, 1958.

[2] A questionnaire will rarely please many scholars besides those who drew it up. To the questionnaire for the American Atlas, for example, Henry Lee Smith has objected because it contains too many vocabulary items and too little phonology; Frederic Cassidy has said that it contains too much phonology and too little vocabulary. John Kepke has remarked that the Atlas has too many items emphasizing rural life of pre-automobile days; the late Eugen Dieth objected because the American Atlas included too much modern material (in his opinion, items like *library*, *railroad station*, *baby carriage*, *kerosene* and *automobile* cannot be considered a part of 'dialect' -- even though they show clear regional and social patterns of distribution). Other scholars have deplored the slighting of such fields of the vocabulary as sugar-beet farming, hard-rock mining, Spanish American architecture, thieves' cant, moonshining, and homosexual relationships. An equally broad range of objections could be raised against any questionnaire that anybody could devise for the study of problems in dialect distribution.

[3] Systematic differences -- that is, a difference in the number and kinds of phonemic contrasts -- are the most significant dialect differences in phonology. To indicate such differences, as well as the incidence of the phonemes, the investigator must sooner or later make a phonemic analysis. But there is sharp disagreement as to whether a straight phonemic analysis of a dialect previously uninvestigated is really possible. The rigid application of a preconceived phonemic framework, as urged by the more enthusiastic Tragerites, will not only make it impossible to discover new contrasts but will obscure the lack of contrasts in the new dialect.

[4] The term *over-all pattern* may have originated with Trager and Smith; it is proclaimed most enthusiastically by their school. In addition to a universally distributed pattern of four degrees of stress, four levels of pitch, two types of internal transition and three terminals, it would analyze all English syllabic nuclei in terms of nine vowels /i, ɨ, u, e, ə, o, æ, a, ɔ/ and three semivowels /y, w, h/, so that every 'long vowel' or 'diphthong' is to be analyzed as vowel-plus-semivowel, *beet* and *boot* being transcribed respectively as /biyt/ and /buwt/.

This analysis, because it emphasizes the diphthongal quality of most English vowels, has been widely adopted for the teaching of English to non-native speakers. However, it is far from universally accepted. In particular, linguists familiar with the dialects of the Southeastern United States, particularly James H. Sledd and myself, have repeatedly pointed out its inadequacies, though our arguments have not been fully recognized by the proponents of the Tragerian analysis (e.g., Hill 1958). In his *Short Introduction to English Grammar* (1959), Sledd has abandoned the Tragerian framework entirely. My own arguments, from an application of Tragerian principles to the dialects with which I am most familiar, will be found in "Confederate Overalls," in this volume, pp. 282-87.

[5] The concept of the 'common core' (which is roughly equivalent to what Kurath calls 'the system of the language') is presented in Hockett 1958.

Forty-five years after the first edition of H. L. Mencken's *The American Language* (1919), the state of American linguistics is a prosperous one. School people at all levels are interested in what linguists promise to accomplish. If we can believe some of the more eloquent tub-thumpers, linguistics can solve any of the vexing problems of American education, from elementary reading to international understanding.

Beginning with World War II, linguists have been drawn into programs for teaching foreign languages -- not only the "exotic languages" like Chinese, Malay, Hindi and Russian, but such more conventional academic languages (if less widely spoken ones) as German, French and Italian. Even languages spoken by relatively few people are of national concern if their habitat lies in an impoverished friendly nation or along the frontier of a potential foe: Korean, Azerbaijani, Pashto and Cambodian begin to appear in American graduate programs, and the Foreign Service Institute of the State Department is prepared to offer training in almost any language to foreign service officers who may need it. In addition, it is now in the national interest to develop programs and textbooks for teaching English to speakers of a wide range of languages, from Arabic to Vietnamese. Almost every university of consequence has such a program, and linguists who are conversant with such languages and interested in overseas programs for training teachers of English can almost name their working conditions.

Linguistics has appeared, not only in the teaching of foreign languages but in other parts of the curriculum as well. In such orthodox situations as the teaching of English composition and literature, some linguists have been very active, both in asking the basic questions and in offering tentative answers. In the elementary school the cooperation of linguists is being sought for improving the teaching of reading, and experimental programs involving linguists are already underway. Moving beyond conventional academic programs, some linguists have been very active in developing the theory of machine translation, in the hope that computers can be trained to cope with the exponentially growing mass of information printed in other languages. They are encouraged both by the federal government and by private industry, for the supply of scienti-fically and technically competent bilinguals shows no signs of increasing as fast as the amount of technical knowledge.

Not only the practical demands for their services but the professional activities of linguists have greatly increased during the last few decades. The membership of the Linguistic Society of America is several times what it was in the early 1930's. In addition, there are several local organizations, like the Linguistic Circle of New York [now rechristened the International Linguistic Association] and the Georgetown Linguistic Round Table, that issue their own journals and monographs; and several linguistic publications attached to universities, such as *Studies in Linguistics* [based at different schools at different times, it is now discontinued], *General Linguistics* (Kentucky) and *Anthropological Linguistics* (Indiana). Linguistic articles and reviews are not uncommon in the various journals of the National Council of Teachers of English, and even in local publications like the *Chicago Schools Journal*.

Despite snide comments, there is no rigid party line in American linguistics. The American anthropological tradition in linguistic studies, so firmly established by Franz Boas, Edward Sapir and Leonard Bloomfield, has had to compete not only with the older and still developing theories of the comparative grammarians, but with the insights of such European groups as the Prague School of Trubetzkoy and Jakobson; the Copenhagen Circle of Hjelmslev; the London group around J. R. Firth; and most recently the linguists of the Soviet Union. Out of this interchange have come the new grammatical theories of Kenneth Pike; of George L. Trager and Henry Lee Smith, Jr.; of Zellig Harris and Noam Chomsky, to mention only a few. Where a few years ago the followers of Trager and Smith were excoriating Pike and Fries for mixing levels of analysis, the less temperate disciples of Chomsky are now consigning to the ashcan all linguistic theory developed before 1956, only themselves to come under the guns of the mathematical linguists at Illinois Tech and elsewhere. It is not a time for timid souls to dabble with the science of language, but one of exciting intellectual debate, out of which may come a new theory of the role of language in human affairs.[1]

But this excitement and the current popularity of linguists are not without their disadvantages. One can detect a strong current of anti-linguisticism among the public at large, among the writers in the public press and among the academicians in in other disciplines. The hue-and-cry over the Merriam Company's *Webster's Third New International Dictionary* (1961) is only a single if most spectacular example of this attitude. Editorials and reviews in such publications as *The New York Times*, *The New Yorker* and the *Saturday Review* have opened fire not only on the imaginary or real defects of the *Third* (and there are some real defects, which have largely escaped notice so far), but on the entire body of principles from which structural linguistics has grown in the last generation.[2] The National Council of Teachers of English, whose minions once afflicted the American schoolroom with prescriptive grammar and Better Speech Week, is now assailed by the Radical Right for seeking to destroy the purity of the national tongue. The long debate over principles of usage, which seemed settled with the publication of Fries's *American English Grammar* (1940), has been renewed, and the unlaid ghosts of Lindley Murray and Richard Grant White return to haunt the American teacher.

If the linguists have become straw-men for the neoconservatives to clobber, it is easy for the linguists in turn to stuff their own straw-men and blame them for this reaction. It is true that the liveliness of linguistics, and the insistence of linguists on precise quasi-mathematical formulations, are abhorrent to the genteel tradition of conventional humanism, whose characteristic spokesmen too often have sought the ivory tower as a respectable address in which they would be safe from the rigors of exact knowledge and the dust and soot of everyday life. It is true, also, that some of the most active anti-linguists are eloquent popular writers on language, who have deliberately perverted their academic knowledge for the blessings of a fast buck, and who gripe because serious linguists not only reject them but expose their pretensions. Yet neither prissiness nor spite is enough to explain the reaction. A large part of the fault lies at the doors of the linguists themselves.

Granted that there can be no rational justification for the anti-scientific attitude of the literary lamas, this attitude has not been helped by either the style or the content of much recent linguistic writing. From the chaotic algebra of Harris's *Methods in Structural Linguistics* (1951) through the latest tortured exegesis on the transformational revolution, too many linguists have used their claim to scientific precision as an excuse for being incomprehensible to all save the trebly-baptized of their private cliques.[3] Furthermore, too many of the younger lin-

guists -- perhaps pardonably biased by the specific directions of their work -- deny the flux, the competing forms and styles, the endless possibilities for innovation that a language must possess if it is to be alive. Codified formulas and computerized rules are all very well in their place, and necessary for constructing models of language; and models in turn provide stimulating insights into the act of communication. But, as the Russian linguist Andreyev (1962) reminds us, people speak in languages and not in their models.

This emphasis on rigorous models, this denial of variety within language, aggravates rather than reduces the conflict between the linguists and the literary mandarins. As any serious linguist discovers from being brigaded with literary historians and critics, the professional student of literature fights shy of the speechways of the common man and has little use for them save when they are embalmed in the dialogue of long-dead writers such as Shakespeare, and hence subject to the veneration due literary monuments. The typical teacher of English, at whatever level, has withdrawn from the dust and heat of active life, in search of a dignified occupation, and finds the slightest interest in everyday mores a threat to his hard-won respectability.

This position makes it easy for the literary scholar to misinterpret what linguists say. The casual statement of the linguist that any variety of a language is worthy of serious study is *ipso facto* a threat to the humanistic stance: if *it's me* is acceptable and the rules for *shall* and *will* are nonsense, what is to set off the poor English teacher from her cousins in the dime stores and on sharecropper farms? In the same way, the insistence of the linguist on strict scientific statement denies the rationale of the usual inspirational teacher of literature, who either is incapable of making exact scientific statements or has rejected the ardors of scientific discipline as destructive of the good and the beautiful.

For this reason, the linguist has difficulty enough talking with his literary colleagues even when he stays in the center of the culture and insists on deriving his statements from living speech and actual documents; but at least he can communicate with the historian, the anthropologist or the social psychologist. When he discards real speechways for formulas and rules, he denies culture and destroys the basis for communication with social scientists as well as humanists. Lacking such communication, he invites the assaults on his discipline that we have seen in the past two years.

The contest is acerbated by the ironical fact that (leaving aside the sympathy for exact knowledge) the same personality types seem to be drawn to conventional literary study and to quasi-mathematical linguistics. Both disciplines are filled with refugees from the complications of the real world -- on the one hand the advocates of clean hands and perfumed sensitivities; on the other, the shattered personalities who trust machines more than human beings -- in search of dignity and security. Both tend to foster line integration:[4] working out, in a single dimension, an extrapolation of a routine statement in terms of a rigid program. In one instance a work of literature is macerated according to the dogmas of a particular school of criticism (and whether that school is New, Aristottering or Freudulent seems to make little difference); in another, the grammatical evidence from a language is racked to fit the preconceptions of a linguistic theory. The usual products of either climate are likely to be zombies rather than critical scholars; both climates are hostile to the point integrator, who takes a problem and insists on working simultaneously in as many dimensions as necessary to achieve a solution and on drawing on whatever disciplines may provide fruitful insights. With more years in Academe than I care to remember, I find that the point integrator is the far more stimulating teacher, however ill he may fit into preconceived programs. From Allan Gilbert in my incarnation as a Miltonist,[5] from Edward Sapir at my first Linguistic Institute, from Hans Kurath in a quarter-century of association on the Linguistic Atlas, I have received dazzling epiphanies that have enriched all my later work.

Nothing short of highly developed point integration, braced by thorough professional discipline, can produce an adequate view of language. The dimensions of relationships in any linguistic system -- regardless of the size of the speech community in which it is used -- are many, and to deny any of these dimensions prevents a full understanding, however powerful a restricted view may be for restricted ends. This multi-dimensional language is implicit in the better-known definitions, such as that by Herskovits out of Sapir and Sturtevant:

> A language is a system of arbitrary vocal signals by which members of a social group cooperate and interact, and by means of which the learning process is effectuated and a given way of life achieves both continuity and change. (Herskovits 1948: 448)

An exegesis of this definition will show the ramifications of linguistics. The *systematic* nature of language relates its study to all science; the formulaic way in which the system can be stated relates linguistics particularly to mathematics, and through mathematics to philosophy.

The means by which language communication typically and primarily takes place -- the *vocal signals* -- ties linguistics to human biology and to acoustics. The function of language in the *social group* links it to all the social and behavioral sciences, and its use as the vehicle of *cultural transmission* (including the appreciation of literature and the other arts and the attempts to understand the unknown) relates it inexorably not only to the social and behavioral sciences but to the theological sciences and the humanities as well. Any theory of linguistics that excludes any of these relationships is narrow, emasculated and self-defeating -- whether it be the humanistic approach that gags at precise statement of involvement in the social sciences, or the mathematical one that brushes aside the details of human relationships.

Viewed in this way, Mencken's *The American Language* is still a most important work, without any competition in the English-speaking world. As a work concerned with all the interrelationships of the mode of communication in a speech community, it respects exact knowledge, recognizes the biological and physical aspects of language, understands how a variety of language is intimately associated with the cultural matrix in which it is used, and comments sagely on the tension between the habitual mode of speaking and the linguistic practices of approved authors. Further, the history of *The American Language* reveals the many ways in which Mencken prodded academic scholars into supplying the necessary basic works on the national way of speech. As he often said, one of his important roles was that of a bird dog: to point out the quarry steadfastly until the hunters got around to bagging it.

In 1919, linguistics as a science was hardly recognized at all. Where the serious study of language existed, it was simply attached to traditional academic departments: English, Germanic, Romance or Classical Languages and Literature, and occasionally to anthropology. It was heavily biased toward historical grammar, for obvious reasons. The antiquarian interests of the Renaissance and Reformation (including the examination of Old English records by common lawyers seeking in precedent a bridle for arrogant kings) had drawn scholars toward historical problems; the discovery of Sanskrit by Sir William Jones (1786) and the subsequent formulation of Indo-European comparisons by Rask and Bopp had introduced the exciting possibilities of historical reconstruction; the publication of Darwin's *Origin of Species* (1859) only confirmed the existing historical and evolutionary bias of linguistics and the human sciences in general, and further diverted them from the task of rigorous taxonomic description.[6]

Not till the end of the nineteenth century did modern descriptive linguistics get under way, principally directed toward the aboriginal tongues of Asia, Africa and the Americas -- partly as an aid to colonial administrators, partly as a tool to enable anthropologists to understand disappearing cultures. Not till the 1930's were these rigorous descriptive methods applied to the culture-bearing languages of Europe, and then often to draw the resentment of literary scholars trained in the older tradition.[7]

If serious interest in language study for its own sake was barely tolerated in the universities of 1919, it had almost no status in the public schools. Our educational system was heavily biased toward the genteel tradition and the cult of respectability. Languages were valued chiefly as cultural ornaments; in the orgy of super-patriotism that engulfed the United States during World War I, the study of German was eradicated from most of the public schools, and departments of German were even abolished in some prominent universities. Higher education was openly designed for the favored few; it was accepted as a fact of life that less than one percent of fourth-grade students would obtain a college degree. Yet no dropout problem existed; it was assumed that those who lacked academic interest would be held back, term after term, until they disappeared from the schools into the world of practical affairs -- perhaps to succeed financially, but certainly to repay the condescension of the more fortunate with bitter scorn toward book-learning.[8]

Even worse, in language, as in other fields, there was little communication between those who professed learning and those who practised public education. Liberal arts colleges, by and large, neglected teacher training, and despised the institutions devoted to it -- an attitude still too common among the humanists.[9] In turn, the English teacher, cut off from the main intellectual currents, forced her charges toward a parroted perversion of eighteenth-century normative grammar, and viewed departures from that norm (even the tolerated quaintness of backwoods dialects) as badges of intellectual, social and moral obloquy. Students of my era learned little about the organization of the language, but much about the stigma of using non-standard forms; and even in Baptist communities afflicted with a high degree of Victorian prudery, *ain't* was the most horrendous of four-letter words. Even those who acquired some taint of higher education rarely recovered from this repressive attitude; needless to say, both the illuminati and the lower ranks of pedagogues casually assumed that American English was inferior to the British variety.

Finally, in 1919 the few professional linguists had no organization in which persons affiliated with various disciplines could talk with each other. They were scattered among a half-dozen societies: the Modern Language Association, the Philological Association, the Anthropological Association, the Oriental Society, the National Council of Teachers of English, and the Dialect Society. This last, the sole American organization concerned essentially with American English or any other variety of language, was largely manned by amateurs, antiquarian-oriented, as the membership had been at its foundation a generation earlier. Its aim (still unfulfilled in 1964)[10] was to produce an American Dialect Dictionary, analogous to the *English Dialect Dictionary* (1898-1905) and the *English Dialect Grammar* (1905) of Joseph Wright. Conversation among the students of language was possible only informally, in local groups. Even with our historical perspective, and the aid of A. G. Kennedy's *Bibliography of Writings on the English Language* (1927), we find it difficult to know what was happening at that time. The scholars of 1919 must have often been frustrated, though such giants as C. H. Grandgent and G. O. Curme produced memorable work. Certainly, no professional scholar of the time would have dreamed of presenting a discussion of the totality of American English. It took a layman, energetic and fearless and delighted in the American scene, to rush in where the academic angels feared to tread.

To resume our mathematical metaphor, Mencken was the epitome of point integration. His lack of formal training in linguistics (he had no more than a high school diploma, though it might be suggested that the Baltimore Polytechnic of the 1890's provided more nourishing intellectual fare than many American colleges of the 1960's) was an advantage, for he didn't know how impossible was the task that he had set himself. Bilingual in English and German, he knew intuitively the differences between linguistic systems. He read voraciously, both for sheer pleasure and as a part of his duties as a newspaperman. On his beats he had observed the rich dialectal diversity of Baltimore -- a city astraddle one of the major dialect boundaries in the United States,[11] once dominated by branches of the Virginia aristocracy but now rapidly industrializing, culturally enriched by Germans of the 1848 migrations, a market town for Pennsylvania German settlements, a rendezvous for oystermen, fishermen, crab-catchers and tobacco farmers, a magnet for miscellaneous proletarian whites, and a way-station for Negroes on the move from the South to New York. He had read fascicles of *Dialect Notes* and what was currently available about the study of language, notably the works of A. H. Sayce and William Dwight Whitney. His daily practice as a reporter had not only taught him a vigorous, natural style but had encouraged his amusement at the antics of *homo boobensis Americanus* and his delight at stirring up the animals. Finally, his muzzling by Attorney General J. Mitchel Palmer's Dogberrys during the heresy hunts of World War I[12] provided him with leisure in which he could draw together his observations on American English, some of which had appeared in the *Baltimore Sun* as early as 1910.

The claims Mencken made in the first edition were modest enough:

> It is anything but an exhaustive treatise upon the subject; it is not even an exhaustive examination of the materials. All it pretends to do is to articulate some of those materials -- to get some approach to order and coherence to them, and so pave the way for a better work by some more competent man. That work calls for the equipment of a first-rate philologist, which I surely am not. All I have done here is to stake out the field, sometimes borrowing suggestions from other inquirers, and sometimes, as in the case of American grammar, attempting to run the lines myself (vi).

But Mencken's delight in stirring up the animals led him to a calculated statement that the growing divergence of English and American would lead to mutually unintelligible languages. When this was added to his insistence that the American Vulgate was worthy of serious scholarship and his indication of wide areas which American academicians had left uninvestigated, many of the self-appointed guardians of the language took the work as a personal and professional insult. Some of the reviewers, like Bright of the Johns Hopkins (*Modern Language Notes*) and Hulbert of Chicago (*Modern Philology*), sought to draw the teeth from Mencken's arguments by pointing out his lack of formal linguistic training (freely conceded), or to excuse their failure to make a systematic study of the national idiom on the grounds that historical dictionaries and linguistic atlases had not been made. This last excuse only reinforced Mencken's argument; in his preface he had indicated:

> I soon found that no such work [i.e., a study of the differences between British and American linguistic practices] existed, either in England or in America -- that the whole literature of the subject was astonishingly meagre and unsatisfactory . . . . On the large and important subject of American pronunciation . . . I could find nothing save a few casual essays. On American spelling, with its wide and considerable divergences from English usages, there was little more. On American grammar there was nothing whatever. Worse, an important part of the poor literature that I unearthed was devoted to ab-

surd efforts to prove that no such thing as an American variety of English existed . . . (v).

Temperate reviewers, like Brander Matthews of Columbia (*The New York Times*) and Curme (*Journal of English and Germanic Philology*),[13] acknowledged the corn and conceded that Mencken had a sounder understanding of the roots of American speechways than any academic philologist currently in practice. For four decades the debate over *The American Language* has continued along the lines established by its earliest version: its appreciation varies directly with the depth of the reviewer's understanding of language as a manifestation and a vehicle of culture.[14]

For once Alfred A. Knopf underestimated the appeal of a book by Mencken: only 1500 copies of the first edition were printed, and the type was distributed, so that a reprint was impossible. But the demand was such that Mencken brought out an expanded second edition in 1921 and a still fatter third in 1923. These expansions showed not only the public interest in the work, as evidenced by voluminous correspondence, but Mencken's generosity in acknowledging corrections and his willingness to consult sources he had neglected. With the third edition he laid the work aside, to become *diaboli advocatus* during the saturnalia of optimistic hokum that led from Harding to Coolidge to Hoover. The era, and Mencken's role as moral theologian, ended with the *sauve qui peut* which converted the overpublicized Hoover Prosperity into the Great Depression.

But Mencken had won his point as an observer of American English. Whether it was simply that the times were ripe, or that the entrance of the United States into world affairs had made its scholars (if not its politicians) aware of the importance of languages, a tremendous growth took place in American linguistics between the first edition of *The American Language* in 1919 and the fourth in 1936. In 1921 appeared Sapir's *Language*, still the best written and most provocative work of its kind; in 1924, the Linguistic Society of America was founded, and J. S. Kenyon issued the first edition of his *American Pronunciation*; in 1925, George Philip Krapp brought out *The English Language in America* (with particular emphasis on historical phonology), Sir William Craigie started editing the *Dictionary of American English* at Chicago, and a group of scholars, egged on by Mencken, launched the journal *American Speech* (see Mencken *et al.* 1945); in 1929, Sapir and Edgar Sturtevant made the first moves toward the Linguistic Atlas of the United States and Canada; in 1933, Leonard Bloomfield issued his *Language*, still the basic work for the systematic linguist, and began his work toward improving the teaching of reading.

In 1936, Fries, then working toward the *American English Grammar*, established the Linguistic Institute on a permanent basis by bringing it to Michigan for five consecutive summers as a regular feature of the summer school.[15] Since that time, there has always been at least one distinguished summer program in linguistics at some American university, providing not only a wider variety of courses than any single institution could normally offer, but a forum in which established scholars could test their theories against the arguments and evidence of their peers and at which beginners could observe the depth and complexity of their discipline. During the same period, Benjamin L. Whorf was advancing his stimulating hypothesis of the interrelationships of language and culture, and a few pioneering institutions, such as Michigan, were establishing courses in American English -- naturally centered around Mencken's work.

Most literate Americans are aware that Mencken's impact as a social satirist declined after 1930. This was not an unmixed bane, however, for he was now able to return to *The American Language* and incorporate new evidence, both from his own observations and from the scholarship of others in the preceding decade. With a new organization of his material -- an organization virtually unchanged since[16] -- and a somewhat less belligerent tone (in recognition of the fact that American academicians had at last begun to fulfil their responsibilities to the language), he introduced a new thesis: instead of diverging, the branches of the English-speaking community were drawing closer together, but the increasing American influence in world affairs was likely to make English, in the future, a sort of dialect of American. Fortunately Mencken did not discard all that he had written: many of his happier statements, such as his capsule history of English noun inflection, have been retained even to the present version. The two Supplements of 1945 and 1948, enjoyable reading as they are, essentially amplify previous statements or revise them in the light of new evidence. The 1963 abridgement is the first weaving together of all of Mencken's observations.

The most important change in the climate of opinion since 1936 has been the discovery during World War II that professional students of language, like atomic physicists, could be used to implement military and diplomatic policy. As older linguists found their enrollments increasing and younger ones found themselves readily employable,[17] new outlets for publication and new forums for discussion were established. Reflecting the new order in international politics, the Germans and Japanese, already interested in American English, have begun to study it more systematically,[18] and their American seminars have been emulated not only by our official allies but by our coexisting competitors. This increased interest, at home and elsewhere, has led to a bibliographical explosion comparable to that in the physical sciences, so that the teacher (always more important in linguistics than in most of the humanities) has acquired an added responsibility for providing breadth and depth, and for developing students who can form their own conclusions and not merely parrot someone else.

In this new situation, Mencken's work has still much to commend it to a generation of technically directed linguists. In fact, these new developments make his work more relevant than ever. He provides a historical orientation to the American way of speech that can be found nowhere else -- a profound appreciation of the intricately intermingling influences that have made American English. In addition, he has shown how historical developments -- the opening of the West in the early nineteenth century, the rise of cities after the Civil War -- have been reflected in the changing fashions in linguistic processes and in modes of expression, and in changing attitudes toward both the American variety of English as a whole and toward specific words, pronunciations and grammatical constructions. With the historical orientation he mingles a strong cultural orientation, a concern that extends far beyond the section of Chapter II so designated. Not satisfied with the technical definitions, from John Witherspoon to Mitford Mathews, he repeatedly asks what are the common characteristics of the linguistic features that we will generally recognize as Americanisms, and why such linguistic features have arisen in English-speaking North America. Unanswerable questions? Perhaps. But few fundamental questions are ever answered completely.

There are many specific virtues. It is a beautifully written book, where every page proclaims the author a professional writer who enjoys the work of writing. The range of information, eclectically garnered, is immense. The style ranges from the delicate to the grotesque, from serious scholarship to outrageous buffonery. It is a work whose bulk requires the reader to put it down, but whose vitality leads him to pick it up again. It can be dipped into for five minutes or studied seriously all afternoon. One finds delight in controversy, generous acknowledgment of the help others have given -- especially the beginners in the field. The effect of this generosity cannot be **exaggerated**: in my own specific case, Mencken's generous acknowledgment and Leonard Bloomfield's encouragement combined to make me a linguist, against formidable odds.

The chief weakness of the book, as many observers have indicated, is Mencken's failure to understand formulaic structural statements, of whatever school. Part of this, to be sure, comes from the fact that Mencken left mathematics at the Baltimore Polytechnic and never returned. But this is not the whole truth, since Mencken always appreciated exact scientific statements. The rest comes from his suspicion, not without foundation, that many of the younger linguists used their mathematical designs and their gnarled, infelicitous style to conceal their muddled thinking. We must recognize that the public writing of most linguists is pretty bad, far worse than that of physicists or social anthropologists and sometimes approaching the obscurantism of literary critics. Too many linguists deliberately write for their own coteries and never present the evidence on which their argument depends. As a professional linguist attempting to keep up with developments in my field, I cannot deplore too warmly this apparent contempt for the reader, nor resent Mencken's impatience with the brethren guilty of such faults.

Mencken's work thus provides the younger linguist with perspective that their academic training does not give. It also provides a unifying theme to the somewhat diffuse discipline of American studies, since it relates language to the total complex of social and cultural developments in the United States. On a larger scene, it should stimulate the students of language in culture, as a model for relating linguistic phenomena to the totality of human behavior. Whatever language one is interested in (and the resources of English are far from exhausted), it sug-gests how one may take the best linguistic evidence and interpret it against the ground of all the associated aspects of human activity, as studied in sociology, anthropology, psychology, folklore and literature. Here is challenge enough for an army of the intellectually adventurous.

I pointed out earlier the caution of Andreyev: that people speak in actual languages, and not in their models. To this may be added Mencken's observation that his principal purpose was to convince the academic brethren that the study of American English, in all its complexities, can be interesting -- and more than interesting, important. The linguist who shrinks not from designing his model, but remembers that it is only a model, and that new and unpredictable combinations of linguistic forms can be expected from a speech community of 250,000,000 people, "many of them amusing, and some of them wise," is on his way to establishing his discipline in its place as the unifying force among the humanities and social sciences.

CHRONOLOGY

1880	H. L. Mencken born.
1910	First articles on American English, *Baltimore Sun*.
1919	*American Language*, first edition.
1921	*American Language*, second edition.
1923	*American Language*, third edition.
1936	*American Language*, fourth edition.
1945	*American Language*, Supplement One (cf. McDavid 1947, in this volume pp. 325-28).
1948	*American Language*, Supplement Two (cf. McDavid 1949e, in this volume pp. 329-34). Mencken's writing career terminated by the first of a series of strokes.
1956	(February) Death of Mencken.
1963	Raven I. McDavid, Jr. edition.

NOTES

[1] The most promising theoretical approach is that of Pike 1967.

[2] *The American Heritage Dictionary* (1969) has so blatantly tried to capitalize on resentment against the *Third* -- and the structuralists -- that it has been humorously called the *Joe McCarthy Dictionary*. As a part of his own campaign against the structuralists, Noam Chomsky, *Reichsführer* of the transformationalists, has told English teachers that transformational grammar is just like the school grammar they are accustomed to teaching. This incredible statement is probably best interpreted in terms of Chomsky's recent proclamation that he is more interested in politics than in linguistics.

[3] For example, Harris 1951: v, "This book is, regrettably, not easy to read." Among the transformationalists there is an exasperating practice of publishing only revealed dogma, and referring the readers, for evidence, to inaccessible seminar papers.

[4] *Line integrator* and *point integrator*, as personality types, were first used by Edward T. Hall, Henry Lee Smith, Jr., and George L. Trager in the working seminars of the Foreign Service Institute, Department of State, c. 1950. The most detailed exposition is to be found in Trager and Hall 1953: 43-44:

It is well at this point to repeat what our analysis has indicated: A: there are two ways in which experience is integrated or learned, or two ways in which the organism is modified; also, as in the case of sex, these do not exist in their pure state, i.e., each has characteristics of the other in varying degrees and there are inter-grades. B: these two things exist in complementary relationship to each other and are both necessary; also, as in the case of the sexes, different cultures may enhance or value or emphasize one more than the other. C: within each there will be a hierarchy; just as some men are more masculine than others and some women more feminine, there is also a hierarchy within the two types of integration.

In order to avoid invidious distinctions, we have termed these two *point* and *line* integration. Both can be either high or low order in their own class, or they can fall between the extremes. They are characterized as follows:

The *line integrator* works within a given system or systems. His function is to make systems go, and his intellectual eyes are turned inward, as it were, towards improving and working within, or manipulating his own frame of reference. When he is a high order line integrator, he learns very rapidly and with great ease, as long as what is given him is integrated into some type of system. Memory work is not arduous to him. By and large he ignores contradictions between the internal logic of his own systems and events which are outside his systems. It must not be assumed that line integrators are not scientists; one can say that some of the best scientific work is done by persons of this type. This is because, given a system, they then go to work and build the solid foundation which gives the system substance . . . .

The *point integrator* has to make each system his very own, and consequently may learn more slowly than a line integrator. He is likely to question his teachers and professors about the 'principles' involved in a given scheme. He is deeply disturbed by contradictions, either within a given frame of reference or between that frame of reference and what is outside. There are times when he has difficulty with line integrators who do not get his points. His function in regard to society is to create new systems as conditions change; he is, however, restless in a static situation and tends to suffer if he isn't permitted to integrate his points. Having discovered the points, however, he is likely to lose interest and move on, leaving line integrators to fill in the picture, so that in the realm of science he is often accused of being 'unscientific' or lacking proof for his points. Professor Einstein would be an example of a point integrator of the highest order, Napier a line integrator. No one can deny the contribution of either.

[5] It was typical of Gilbert to make himself an expert horseman in his late forties, to verify the story of a similar feat by an Italian Renaissance figure. During the nearly three decades since I received my doctorate he has never expressed a regret that I deserted Milton for linguistics; rather, he points to what success I have achieved as evidence in support of his theory of education -- that an adequately trained scholar can find his own field, regardless of the discipline in which he was trained.

[6] This was pointed out repeatedly by A. L. Kroeber, in the University of Chicago seminar before the Darwin Centennial Celebration of 1959.

[7] It is a common argument, among the foes of scientific linguistics, that the descriptivists attempt to apply to the vehicles of great civilizations the same techniques used (as they would put it) to analyze the gibberish of a few dozen half-naked savages. The linguist would reply that the method is valid, whatever the language, though the statements may be more complicated where the speech community is larger and the records extend over longer periods of time. Working anthropologists have often discovered complicated stylistic variations in aboriginal languages, just as in those of the dominant Western cultures.

[8] From my personal experience: in 1919, when I entered the second grade, there was a student in my room a head taller than I was and wearing long pants -- at that time a badge of manhood never assumed before the age of 16. He disappeared before the end of the year, and I never saw him again.

[9] As an exception to the prevalent pattern of the time, I cite James L. Mann, local superintendent of schools (Greenville, S.C.) in my boyhood, a Ph.D. from the University of Berlin and a man of deep appreciation of serious learning. In one of our last conversations, just before I entered graduate school, he urged me to take Old English right away, and Gothic whenever I had a chance. He was the first person to direct me toward courses in linguistics.

[10] In 1965 Frederic G. Cassidy of the University of Wisconsin, a former dialect field worker in the North-Central States and one of the editors of the *Dictionary of Jamaican English* (1967) began assembling evidence toward the *Dictionary of American Regional English* (Cassidy *et al.* 1981-; commonly called *DARE*) with the help of a grant from the U.S. Office of Education. [It is now nearing completion.]

[11] For the position of Baltimore see Kurath 1949 and Kurath and McDavid 1961.

[12] The venom of these heresy hunts was more virulent than that of the age of McCarthy I. One of my noblest friends, John P. Grace, publisher of the Charleston (S.C.) *Mercury*, twice mayor of his city, and a fearless crusader for human rights (among other things, he broke the peonage system on the Sea Islands), was similarly forbidden to write in his own paper because, being of Irish descent, he could not swallow the notion that the English were emblems of unalloyed moral rectitude.

[13] Curme published two volumes of a projected *Grammar of the English Language* -- *Accidence* (1935) and *Syntax* (1931) -- the largest-scale work of its kind ever undertaken by an American.

[14] The latest version of *The American Language* -- the Fourth Edition and the Two Supplements, abridged with annotations and new material, by Raven I. McDavid, Jr., with the assistance of David W. Maurer -- appeared in November 1963. [It was reprinted in paperback in 1977.]

[15] Previous Linguistic Institutes had been

offered by Yale and by the City College of New York, but they carried no credit and there had been no continuing tradition. A history of Linguistic Institutes, by A. A. Hill, is included in the final announcements of the 1964 Institute, to be held at Bloomington, Indiana, under the auspices of Indiana University.

[16] For the few changes in the current version, see the Editor's Introduction, pp. xi-xiv.

[17] Ironically, since most universities follow the economic rule of buying talent as cheaply as possible, some of the best linguists have had greater difficulty getting properly placed than have raw Ph.D.'s. At least one brilliant theoretician, who made his mark in the profession before 1940, did not achieve academic tenure till 1962; and several others have gravitated to unglamorous if sound institutions.

[18] Noteworthy is Hans Galinsky, of the American Seminar at the Johannes Gutenberg Universität, Mainz. [The Deutschen Gesellschaft für Amerikastudien has been seriously interested in American English.]

It is a timeworn observation that the person who comes from the longer settled areas of the United States experiences a sense of bewilderment at the newness and the rapid growth of our Pacific cities. As we all know, Los Angeles was a sleepy sunbaked village barely two generations ago; now it is the third city in population in the United States; it is threatening the second position of Chicago, my present home town, all of four generations old. But even Chicago impresses me as raw and new; I was the sixth generation of my family to grow up in Greenville County in the northwestern corner of South Carolina. I share this status, incidentally, with our distinguished neighbor here in Santa Barbara,[1] Harry Ashmore, the courageous publisher of the *Arkansas Gazette* who spoke out in Little Rock for decency and intelligence in the first major test of the Supreme Court decisions on desegregation. Yet Harry and I, who grew up a block apart, used to feel a little diffident in the presence of old families in Charleston, another century older than our community.

Each of these cities, however young or old, however small or large, is a manifestation of the same American tradition -- urbanization as an outgrowth of industrialization -- of the application of well-advertised Yankee ingenuity in devising machines to exploit the environment. Each of our cities is, in its own peculiar ways, a monument to the complexity of the human spirit -- to the strange mixture of good and evil of which we are all composed. The gracious living of Charleston was built on the backs of slaves; the gracious affluence of San Marino and the glamour of Beverly Hills are complemented by smog, choked freeways, and the sullen fury of Watts. Yet the fluid if imperfect American urban setting has produced something else -- what Sir Charles Snow describes as the most generously conceived system of education the world has ever known, a system of education based on the Jeffersonian principle that everyone should have the opportunity to gain that degree of education which will enable him to fulfill his potentialities as a human being. Toward this end the most important subject in the curriculum is English -- the official language of our nation, the vehicle of most of our instruction, the carrier of our traditions, the medium through which we most often interact with our fellow citizens.

Knowing that the interests of literature and composition will be well served by my colleagues on this panel, I shall confine my remarks to the position of the language itself, as one not ashamed to call himself a structural linguist in the American tradition.

I identify myself as a structural linguist because, as English teachers are fully aware, there are several actively competing groups of linguists, with different theoretical bases and different practical interests. Such differences, as we should know already and shall emphasize in various ways today, appear naturally in periods of intellectual ferment. It is not too much to say that in the past generation the expansion in our knowledge of language and of other aspects of human communication has been as striking as the expansion in our knowledge of the components of matter. And like the new knowledge in physics, the new knowledge in language has awe-inspiring potentialities for the destruction or the liberation of mankind; in fact, we may even say that the way we learn to use our new knowledge of language will decide whether our new knowledge of matter is a force for evil or good. It is thus not surprising that at this time we linguists are continually reexamining all our previous conclusions.

The need for such continual reexamination is particularly apparent in the branch of linguistics to which I have devoted most of my attention -- the study of American dialects through the Linguistic Atlas of the United States and Canada and related projects. Even before the original study along the Atlantic Seaboard has been published, several of our colleagues have begun new investigations in communities studied in the original project, to see what changes a generation has brought. Students of dialects are well aware that changes in ways of living are inevitably reflected in changes in ways of talking; and in consequence they have a well-developed Al Smith syndrome that makes them go back and look at the record to see if a situation is still what it was reported to be.

It should come as no surprise that laymen do not always share the feeling that data on our language must be repeatedly reexamined. In the agonizing deappraisals of the *Webster's Third New International Dictionary*, most of the adverse critics were working in a theoretical vacuum, ignorant even of their own serious use of forms they deplored. And dialect investigators frequently find their local contacts surprised that investigations on the spot are even necessary. In December 1947, when I was completing the Georgia field investigations for the *Linguistic Atlas of the Middle and South Atlantic States* (Kurath *et al*. 1979-), the Milledgeville clerk of court expressed surprise at my mission. "Isn't all of that," she asked, "in *Gone with the Wind*?" With somewhat more tact than I have been known to display on other occasions, I finally explained that I was aware that Miss Mitchell had undoubtedly used, with accuracy, a great deal of old-fashioned Georgia vocabulary. Nevertheless, there were differences: I wanted to see what had happened since Reconstruction; I wanted to get more accurate information on local pronunciation; I wanted to get information on a number of items that would simply not be recorded in a historical novel. After this explanation I did get an introduction to an excellent informant, who not only gave me full information, but so enjoyed the interview that he campaigned enthusiastically the next year for the reelection of the clerk of court.

But even scholars may fail to see the need to reappraise the evidence. A systematic dialect survey of Britain was not started until nearly two decades after the beginnings of the Linguistic Atlas of the United States and Canada. Scholars refused to believe that there was any need to probe beyond the limits of A. J. Ellis's survey of dialect pronunciation -- in the fifth volume (1889) of his *Early English Pronunciation* -- or Joseph Wright's *English Dialect Grammar* (1905) and *English Dialect Dictionary* (1898-1905). Wright, in fact, was sure he had been definitive; in the preface to his *Dictionary*, he stated that he had recorded all of the dialect words in English. However, a person who has seen only the prospectus for the *Linguistic Atlas of New England* (Kurath *et al*. 1939-43) would salute Wright's statement with a few bars of the "Colonel Bogey March." The lowly earthworm -- charted in the prospectus -- has an extraordinary variety of regional designations along the Atlantic Seaboard. The ordinary variety is known under such aliases as *angleworm, angledog, mudworm, fishworm, fishing worm, eaceworm, eastworm, ground worm, eelworm, robinworm,* and *redworm*; the larger ones as *dew worms, night crawlers, night creepers, night walkers, town worms,* and *hamestrings*; the patterns of distribution for these variants are such that most of the terms must have been brought to America by settlers from the British Isles. Wright, however, gives us little evidence; of these terms, he records only *angledog* and *eaceworm*. Even the new survey of English dialects, directed by Harold Orton (Orton *et al*.

1962-71), fails to use the American experience to rectify Wright's omission. Although it would have been easy to ask for lexical variants, Orton's investigators sought only the simplex *worm* for pronunciation; except for incidental forms in Orton's study our sole evidence for the British distribution of *fishworm, redworm,* and other names for the earthworm is a set of short field records which Guy Lowman made in 1937-38 (Viereck 1975).

But if some of us ignore the variety in English, others cannot recognize the system for the details. This approach is painfully evident in the drearily repetitious reviews of the *Third New International*. As scholars competent to evaluate a dictionary have observed, few if any of the adverse journalistic reviews have asked substantive questions about the system of selecting the vocabulary, about the system of representing pronunciation, about the system of labeling usage. Their attention is focused on a few items: 1) whether *ain't* (and the less shocking sexual and excretory four-letter words) should be included, and under what label; 2) whether *bi-monthly* should be recognized as meaning "twice a month" (for which I have good evidence in cultivated speech from 1930) or only as "every two months"; 3) whether *disinterested* should be recognized in its oldest English meaning "apathetic" (as used by John Donne) or only in the later meaning "unbiased." These critics have failed miserably in their responsibility; they have never looked at the history of lexicography in English to discover what are the generally accepted obligations of lexicographers and the areas generally recognized as outside their competence; only on such principles can a reviewer fairly appraise the achievement of a particular dictionary.

But, however important an understanding of system may be for an evaluation of dictionaries, it is far more important in the practical situations where some of us, especially the elementary teachers, must try to teach the use of standard language to those groups for whom the standard language is not native. On one hand we face children whose home language is something other than English. In Chicago, for instance, we have fifty-five elementary schools with at least fifty students with a home language other than English (until two weeks ago there was only one teacher in the Chicago schools permanently assigned to this problem; now there are three).

I do not know how many California children face this problem, but relatively and absolutely I suspect the problem is far greater here. For each of these home languages we need special materials dealing with differences within the system: the system of pronunciation, the system of grammatical endings, the system of sentence patterns.

The other group of children without standard English is comprised of those who have grown up in communities or sections of communities where they normally do not have a chance to develop a productive command of the patterns of standard English. Specifically, but not exclusively, the Negroes in our urban slums live in areas where people do not alternate -- as I trust most of us do -- *I do* and *he does*, *she makes* and *they make*. Instead, they may alternate *he does* and *he do*, *they make* and *they makes*, in patterns which can no doubt be described in terms of a set of situations, but patterns which are not the patterns of standard English as it is known today. However much we sympathize with the aspirations of these people, we face the fact that their grammatical practices are an obstacle to employment in clerical or sales positions and to any success in higher education. Yet the conventional English or language arts program in the schools does little to teach such students the habitual use of the proper concord of such forms as *I do* and *he does*. By and large the program emphasizes the finding and marking of discrete errors, a method that assumes that students already have had some exposure to the traditional middle-class norms on which our educational system is built. We cannot say we are adequately facing the problems of these students until -- to take this one example of many -- we have a program that produces an inevitable coupling of a singular noun or a third-person pronoun and the {-Z} form of the verb, so that we have *he keeps*, *she adds*, *it misses*, *the man has*, *the girl does*, *the paper says*, but *we keep*, *you add*, *they miss*, *the men have*, *the girls do*, *the papers say*.

In other words, we have to recognize that some groups in our society, productively if not receptively, have a somewhat different grammatical system from that of the standard language; we must recognize variety within the system itself.

Now if some observers are so preoccupied with varieties in detail that they ignore the system of the language, others are so interested in establishing a rigorous system that they overlook varieties. This has been especially true of the more eloquent advocates of the phonemic school which one may call *trageremics* and the syntactic school which one may call *chomskemics*. On some of us with a different body of experience, their categorical statements have the same effect as the appearance of a plug hat in a shanty Irish neighborhood after a heavy snow. Even before the official publication of the Trager and Smith *Outline of English Structure* (1951), some of us were already on record as recognizing that the widely advertised overall pattern could not accomo-

date certain significant elements in our pronunciation systems, and time has done nothing to lessen our skepticism. More recently, I find that by the time I have read six illustrative sentences in Chomsky's *Syntactic Structures* (1957), I have two disagreements on grammaticality: at least one sentence that he characterizes as grammatical I would reject in my normal discourse; one of those he rejects as ungrammatical would seem acceptable to me in some contexts. To accomodate our differences would require a far more intricate set of formulae, or "rules," than has yet been offered. In sum, within the system the phenomena of language are infinitely more varied than the designs laid down by Trager and Chomsky would recognize; investigators who work in the field with hundreds of informants in dozens of communities should not be surprised to find, on all levels of the language, variations they had not anticipated before. The system must accomodate the variations, but variations make sense only in terms of the system. In our teaching design we must **accommodate both system and variation;** else we lobotomize our students.

Now this kind of tension between pressures for order and pressures for variety is not new; it is not confined to the study of American English, or even to linguistics. In Europe, a century ago, the Young Grammarians were passionately enunciating *Die Lautgesetzesausnahmlösigkeit*, the principle that sound laws admit of no exceptions. The French dialectologists, on the other hand, were asserting with equal passion *"Chaque mot a son histoire"* -- that each word has its own history. Even earlier we had the debates over etymology between the analogists, who believed in regularity, and the anomalists, who didn't; some of the suggestions of the latter group were so bizarre as to provoke from Voltaire the quip that etymology was a discipline in which the consonants meant nothing and the vowels less. Literature, too, has seen the same kind of debate. Walter Pater's essay "Romanticism" (1876) points out the basic disagreement between the classical temperament which emphasizes order and the romantic temperament which emphasizes strangeness; John Livingston Lowes comments on the same kind of disagreement in *Convention and Revolt in Poetry* (1919). Nor are such disagreements limited to the humanities. American historians still debate the significance of the frontier or the economic bias of our Founding Fathers. And even in physics there is debate as to whether light is waves or particles.

Happily, in most disciplines we have seen a growing process of accomodation as scholars become more self-assured and more aware of the complexity of phenomena; it is possible that no one viewpoint provides all the answers, but that each has its own contributions to make. So physicists now are willing to accept light as waves for some purposes, as particles for others. In most American universities, English departments allow a wide range of critical attitudes; Chaucer and Conrad, Melville and Mark Twain, Milton and Henry James may provoke distinguished teaching and research. In historical linguistics, too, the disputation is less bitter than it used to be. We recognize that we must accept the regularity of sound change as a starting point; otherwise we get chaos. Then, when we establish our regular patterns of sound change, we do not ignore our apparent exceptions but classify them in turn and seek rational explanations. So in French we note that *l'amour* preserves its medieval vowel instead of following *le douceur*, *le chaleur* and the other nouns of its family; a southern French pronunciation has prevailed, probably influenced by the Provençal emphasis on courtly love. In the German Rhineland, the consonant changes that distinguish *Plattdeutsch* from *Hochdeutsch* are more widely spaced than we would expect; the limits of various changes follow the boundaries of German principalities that existed before the French Revolution.

In our discussions of modern English, we have barely reached the point where we can accommodate both the passionate belief in system and the passionate belief in variety. Perhaps we are too close to the phenomena in time; perhaps we are too close to the issues in emotional commitment. A full appraisal of the question demands that we recognize both the parts of the system and the dimensions of variation for each part.

Human communication, we have learned in recent years, involves far more than the system of arbitrary vocal signals that we call languages. There are many modes, each of them rigorously structured and as culturally determined as the mode of language; each is so habitual, so "normal," that we are sometimes surprised when people in other cultures act in accordance with other norms. Edward T. Hall was the first to assess the role of *proxemics*, of spatial relationships in human communication. In many places, notably his book *The Silent Language* (1959), he has shown that two American males, in face to face communication, normally maintain a distance of about twenty-three inches. A male coming within a foot of another male is suspected of unpleasant aggression; the normal reaction is either retreat or a physical countermeasure. But a Latin American male cannot communicate comfortably with another male if they are more than a foot apart; the North American who insists on his customary distance of two feet is described as cold or unsympathetic. After years of mutual misunderstanding, our State Department took the step of explaining to our Foreign Officers that the shorter distance between speakers is a cultural feature which visitors to Latin America must learn to accept.

Another feature of human communication which we are just beginning to study is *haptics*, the phenomena of physical contact, first examined by William Austin (e.g. Austin 1965). Very slight differences may indicate drastic changes in relationships; a boy and a girl may sit close beside each other on a sofa, with thighs touching, innocently studying their lessons, but an almost imperceptible shift in the amount or kind of contact can constitute an invitation to another sort of activity. As with proxemics, haptics can vary between cultures; in Mainz one summer I noticed that a boy and a girl thought nothing of applying half-nelsons and hammerlocks to each other as they walked along the street holding hands -- an activity probably innocent enough, but sufficient to get students in this country called up before a Dean of Women, if not before the Un-American Activities Committee.

Another mode of communication is that of *kinesics*, gestures and other body movements, most fully explored by Ray Birdwhistell (e.g. Birdwhistell 1952, 1956, 1970). The extent to which these movements contribute to human communication can be seen if one watches movies of unrehearsed situations. In a group discussion there is a rhythmic pattern of head and eye movements of the listeners, as they follow the speaker of the moment (McQuown 1971). Even more striking is the pattern of physical movement during a psychiatric interview; the gestures build up as hidden tensions work toward the surface, until a patient actually kicks her shoe off in unconscious emphasis. Or an overly protective mother may move between her son and his psychiatrist, negating with gesture the case she has been making orally.

Another mode of communication, analyzed by Trager, Smith, Hockett, and others, involves an assortment of nonlinguistic modulations of the stream of speech, lumped together as *paralanguage*. Some of these, such as drawl, we associate with regional types of speech. Some, such as extra-high or extra-low pitch, or the flattening of intonation contours, we associate with emotional states.[2] Some others we associate with public roles. Hillbilly music, for instance, seems to require heavy nasality, heavier than even the well-attested nasality of normal Southern Mountain speech. An army top sergeant uses pharyngeal rasp and extra loudness to browbeat his charges, as in the well-known command, "Suck up that gut!" A primary teacher traditionally uses an open pharynx and wheedling intonation, to achieve the so-called "Miss Frances" voice: "Children, behave yourselves and eat your lunch." A topkick trying the Miss Frances wheedle on a detail of recruits would be laughed out of the army; a primary teacher using the topkick's rasp and overloudness, however much her charges deserved it, might be hauled before the PTA. Paralanguage offers a profitable and almost uninvestigated field for the student of human behavior.

Proxemics, haptics, kinesics, and paralanguage are all outside the formal structure of language. A part of language in communication, though linguists still argue about its specific place in language, is the area of *suprasegmentals* or *prosodics*, of stress and intonation and juncture, to take these phenomena as they appear in English. The accurate use of these suprasegmentals is an even better clue than the pronunciation of vowels or consonants, when we come to setting off the native speaker from the foreign.

Finally we come to the system of language itself. There is a system of sounds, of phones and phonemes or of distinctive features and morphophonemes. We likewise have a system of forms, of inflections to mark grammatical relationships, and of derivations to make word-bases into words or one word into another. We have a system of arrangements which we call syntax -- patterns of making phrases and clauses and sentences. And finally we have what we might call a system of content, a body of words or morphemes with their meanings. The arrangements of meaningful words built up by derivational and inflectional suffixes, all pronounced by human beings in social contexts, constitute a language; and communication through language in turn is enriched by paralanguage, kinesics, haptics, and proxemics.

So complex is this process of human communication that we often seek to strip it of variables that may lead to misunderstanding. The urge for a stripped down kind of communication is especially strong in the field which Norbert Wiener called *cybernetics*, the science of directing machines to perform repetitive acts, sometimes of extreme difficulty and complexity. But these machines, as the men who mind them recognize, are high-speed morons; they cannot sort out stylistic differences but must have their tasks broken down into smaller steps. This barebones computer language is but an extreme case of what is true of all scientific and technical language: that there is a special vocabulary shared by writers and readers, even to the semantic implications, and there is a set of syntactic conventions for developing sentences. The need for explicit vocabulary and syntax becomes even greater in scientific abstracting, greater still in machine translation, where the computer cannot be expected to sort out subtleties of meaning

except at prohibitive cost; the machines will present comprehensible English versions of the *Bulletins of the Magnitogorsk Electronic Laboratories* generations before they will render the nuances of Sholokov's novels. [The complexity of translation led the armed forces to withdraw their support for machine translation, though not before it had stimulated a great deal of theoretical work in linguistics.]

In a smaller degree, of course, we find consistent meanings of words and relative uniformity of syntax in more familiar kinds of speech and writing. The language of communication, especially of commercial aircraft with each other, or with the ground, is rigorously restricted, since there is seldom a next time for someone to profit from a mistake. For the same reason, the structure of military field orders is rigidly prescribed; the words *not*, *or*, and *if* are forbidden, since they might lead an officer to speculation instead of action. On a more familiar level, manuals of instruction in the use of equipment, whether automatic rifles, electric blenders or dictionaries, need to explain unequivocably what the user is dealing with. For the same reason, conventional business correspondence follows set patterns, and elegant variations usually end up in the circular file of letters we never finished reading.

But even leaving out the uniformity of specialized fields of communication, we find that we share a great deal with other speakers of the language. There is little variation in the structure of pronunciation, derivation, inflection, or syntax. Word order in English is now fairly well fixed, so that in statements we cannot put objects before verbs and subjects after them. We even share much of the vocabulary; and among the words which we do not share, in a lexical inventory of some half million items, we can usually reach fair agreement on whether or not an unfamiliar word is a technical or scientific term.

Conceding this extensive agreement, we must still recognize a number of dimensions of variety in usage; Martin Joos and Harold Allen have so far presented the most elaborate pictures, but it is possible that other dimensions will be revealed by more detailed investigation.

One of the first dimensions of usage is that of medium; we cannot write exactly as we speak. When we write we necessarily exclude the effects of proxemics, haptics, kinesics, and paralanguage; at most they may be suggested by description or by using synonyms of the verb *to say* -- *whined*, *minced*, *roared*, or the like. We ordinarily disregard most of the features of pronunciation and let the reader supply them. This creates a problem for the teacher who is trying to get his students to write as naturally as they talk. A student who tries to write just as he talks may be misunderstood, because there is no way in writing to represent directly the suprasegmentals of stress, intonation, and juncture which in speech may produce special emphasis; instead, the writer must use syntactic devices in such a way that any reader will perceive where the emphasis lies. Even the vocabulary of speech may differ from that of writing. Few of the sesquipedalian terms of organic chemistry are ever spoken; such a term as *fice*, for a small noisy nondescript dog, is written only in local color fiction.

Another dimension is that of history. Many words or meanings or grammatical forms or pronunciations that were once used are not a part of twentieth-century English. The term *obsolete* indicates that there has been no evidence of use in a very long time; *archaic* that there has been little evidence in a long time, but not quite so long. The cutoff date chosen is always an arbitrary one, and decisions are subject to correction in the light of new evidence. The *Oxford English Dictionary* labeled as possibly obsolete the use of *disinterested* meaning apathetic, because it had no evidence since 1797, but the label was removed in the 1930 supplement after the readers had discovered ample evidence in 1928 standard British usage. A more subtle kind of obsolescence is that of words which are widely used but by the older and less sophisticated. Words of this kind are often labeled *dial*, but with the dialect unspecified: *old-fashioned* would probably be a better designation. In the other direction, we know that there are linguistic innovations, that some features have come in recently. The pronunciation of an *l* in such words as *calm* and *palm* would fall into this category. For practical purposes, dictionaries do not label items of this class; new features are not likely to be included in a dictionary until they are well-established.

Besides general history, there is a dimension of personal history or maturity. The keynote to this scale is that one acts and talks his age. Otherwise incongruity results, as when a plump middle-aged housewife appears in a bikini. We recognize a similar incongruity where a middle-aged woman describes a cake as *yummy*, an adjective associated with children in the primary grades or in commercials addressed to them. We know that college students do not use the slang of teenagers, and that we aging citizens use either type of slang at our peril, unless we restrict our use to that of the scientific observer (my own teenage savages will accept my use of slang in that role, but not otherwise).

A fourth scale of usage is what Joos calls the scale of responsibility. There is a general range within which we are tolerated; excess sloppiness or excess preciosity will be rejected. The fine

uninhibited fury of the late beats has run its course, with even Jack Kerouac now typed as a regurgitator of his own mannerisms. On the other hand, a writer or speaker may find himself out of rapport with his audience because he is too careful. Though the mores of one age may favor a more or less formal norm of responsibility than those of another, the tolerable range of deviation from the normal seems fairly constant.

A fifth scale, that of style, is well-known to us from Joos's *The Five Clocks* (1962). In the center is the style of the small committee, whose members understand each other enough to speak informally but must still supply background information. On one side, we find the formal language of public address and the highly concentrated style of great literature; on the other are the casual style, where background information is taken for granted, and the intimate, where a few words may convey as much as paragraphs of formal statement.

A dialectologist like myself is especially concerned with the sixth dimension, that of geographical extent. Certain scientific and technical terms are truly international; their use knows no language boundaries. In contrast, the cowcall *chay!* seems to be restricted, in North America to a small area in eastern South Carolina. Between these extremes, we have dialect areas and larger dialect regions and some national limits. A *homer* in the United States is a *home run* in baseball; in Canadian baseball *homer* also has this meaning, but in hockey Canadians use it to label an official suspected of favoring the home team. Canadians and Britons use *fridge* for refrigerator and *perm* for permanent wave; but Canadians and Australians, like us, have not adopted the British *telly* for television, a beautifully snide term that deserves immortality.

We also have a social dimension in language. *Them boys* tells us much about the status of the speaker; so does *he do* as the third singular present. But we must not let ourselves be tricked into believing that imparting the proper use of a few grammatical forms will fulfill our obligations as English teachers to bring into the center of our culture those groups who have not had our educational and social advantages. The extent of the problem was seen by Fries in 1940, in the final chapter of his *American English Grammar*. He concluded that vulgar English is chiefly distinguished from standard English, not by differences in the grammatical system or even by differences in grammatical details, but by a general impoverishment in language which is symptomatic of cultural impoverishment. The speaker of vulgar English has a smaller vocabulary, less variety in his sentence structure, a less extensive inventory of prepositions and conjunctions, fewer subordinate clauses.

Fries's conclusions have found recent support in the work of the British social psychologist Basil Berstein, who distinguishes between an *elaborate code*, characteristic of the middle class, and a *simple code*, characteristic of the working and lower classes. According to Bernstein, the difficulty of getting working-class people to accept middle-class values pivots upon their differences in the use of the language. The contrast is shown when a mother wants her child to go to the back of the bus and the child refuses. The middle-class mother will verbalize the request and attempt to reason with the child; the working-class mother will utter a peremptory command and reinforce it with a slap. Here, it is said, is part of the difficulty in educating the culturally disadvantaged child. Reports from the homes of such children indicate that there is very little effort to create habits of verbal interaction or word play; child management is basically a set of simple commands, physically reinforced. With little encouragement to practice sentence patterns and explore the possibilities of variation, it is small wonder that these children have difficulty in mastering the art of reading; it is a marvel that any succeed. [Labov 1972 is in many ways an attack on Bernstein's position, but the examples he cites seem to confirm rather than refute it.]

Our final dimension is that of associations, of language patterns shared with people we are brought in contact with. *Slang* is a matter of vogue; the speaker wants to be with it. *Hot* as a general term of approbation gave way to *cool*; now the vogue adjectives seem to be *tough* and *boss*. *Technical language* and *argot*, however different their connotations, are practically the same, as in-group modes of speech; Chicago critics and narcotic addicts are both distinguished by linguistic practices unknown to the uninitiate.

When we have indicated these dimensions and the possibility that others exist, we can sympathize with the lexicographer. All of these dimensions interlock; an accurate statement of usage would involve indications of the places on each scale where a word or meaning or grammatical construction or pronunciation happens to fit. Since lexicographers cannot have all the information about all dimensions for all entries, or represent them if they had, one who takes his duty seriously is tempted to throw up his hands and abandon all labeling.

A few illustrations will illustrate the complexity of the problem. Something which is historically of the past may be preserved regionally, such as the past tense *holp*, "helped," pronounced often as a homonym of *hope*. Such forms are especially common in *relic areas* as the coast of Maine or the outer banks of North Carolina. They may also be preserved socially; older preterite and participial forms, such as *driv* and *writ*, still occur among the uneducated.

Or a regional feature may acquire social and even ethnic overtones. The uninflected third singular present, as *he do*, is widely found in Southern England. Brought to the colonies, it has survived strongest in the Southeastern United States because poor communications, a rural economy, and a poor educational system gave it a greater opportunity to take root. In the same way, the economic and educational handicaps of the Southern Negro mean that such non-standard forms are more common among Southern Negroes than among Southern whites. Since the uneducated Southerners migrating to Northern cities are more likely to be Negro than white, and the Negro is more visible in the society, *he do* in Chicago becomes identified as a Negro form.

If the difficulties of describing usage are formidable to the lexicographer, they must seem overwhelming to those who would plan a program for the schools. It might be easiest to evade the question. But society will not let us evade it; people want to know what is "right," that is, what won't cause difficulties for them, and we are supposed to tell them.

Actually, we can do much.

When we look at our resources, we discover that we have very good evidence on some dimensions. We are perhaps best off in the historical dimension. We have a wide range of texts, from all periods; we have the incomparable *Oxford English Dictionary*; we have such other historical dictionaries as the Michigan *Middle English Dictionary*, the *Dictionary of American English*, the *Dictionary of Americanisms*, the *Dictionary of Canadianisms*, and the *Dictionary of Jamaican English*. For territorial differences, we can draw on the various parts of the Linguistic Atlas project, and soon we will have Cassidy's *Dictionary of American Regional English* (1981-). For social differences, we have good evidence from the Linguistic Atlas, supplemented by a group of intensive local studies, with more to come.

On the other hand, perhaps because all of these scales show shifting values, we can't sort out clearly the differences between styles, the area of responsibility, the maturational scale, or the range of associations. To take an example of the last problem, what was yesterday the argot of the brothel, or the narcotic addict, may be today's argot of the jazz musician and tomorrow's teenage slang. This drift has already gone so far that those who know the original meanings of present-day jazz terms sometimes find their blood curdling when the terms are used by innocent teenagers: *boogie-woogie*, for instance, originally meant tertiary syphilis.

Yet even here we can offer a few suggestions:

1) We can make our children aware of the problems of variation in language.

2) We should introduce them to the best sources of evidence, both primary (like the Linguistic Atlas) and secondary, like Atwood's *Survey of Verb Forms* (1953a).

3) We should encourage our students to observe and read widely and to become sensitive to contextual variations.

4) We should also encourage them to develop flexibility and versatility in their use of language and not to confine themselves to any one style.

5) Finally, we should make them willing to change their usage as they see the patterns of the culture change, and to accept change and variety in the usage of others.

NOTES

[1] This paper was originally presented before the National Council of Teachers of English Midwinter Institute in Santa Barbara, California, February 1966.

[2] The correlation between psychic depression and the flattening of intonation curves has been noted informally and intuitively by many lay observers; e.g. Friedan 1963.

What Sledd has called the "agonizing deappraisals" of *Webster's Third New International Dictionary* since its appearance in 1961 has shown that many Americans, in keeping with the national trend to simplistic interpretations, would make a sharp dichotomy between "good language" and "bad language," or between what is "correct" and what is "incorrect." In this same dichotomizing the villains of the piece are often the linguists, who are accused of advocating say-as-you-go attitudes in language practice and of letting down the bars where standards are concerned. Though it is perhaps no help to a linguist or lexicographer who has been clawed by an angry journalist or literary critic, the fact is that no responsible linguist has denied the existence of standards or refused to recognize that in any speech community some people are acknowledged as using the language better -- that is, in a fashion more worthy of emulation -- than others.[1]

There is not in language (or in any other form of human behavior) a simple opposition between good and bad, but a complicated set of interrelated variations; it is necessary for linguists themselves to sort out the many dimensions in which usage may vary and show how these variations are related to each other. This has been done in the past by several scholars; but as a way of introducing this topic it is well to repeat their findings.[2]

Among the scales on which a given detail of usage may be measured, the following have been suggested; others may of course be devised or discovered.

1. The dimension of the medium -- essentially writing as opposed to speech. There is little chance to use *antidisestablishmentarianism* in conversation, let alone the sesquipedalian terms of organic chemistry. Only in homely fiction (and the authorship of such a distinguished writer as William Faulkner does not refute the homeliness) is there a place for such a term as *fice* -- "a small, noisy, generally worthless dog of uncertain ancestry."

2. The dimension of responsibility, as Martin Joos puts it -- an understanding of the normal social expectations of the audience in particular or of the community at large. A politician who talks over the heads of his audience may be admired for his cleverness or even brilliance but will usually be denied the votes he is seeking. Some people -- like myself -- cannot read Henry James: he is too consciously superior in his style, which begins to seem a set of mannerisms after half a dozen pages. And it has been attested in a variety of situations that a person who is too meticulous in his observation of grammatical shibboleths and in avoiding the speech of his locality may rouse the distrust of his fellows.[3] On the other hand, a complete disregard of these expectations may be equally disastrous. The novelty of the "Beat" writers, free association with a minimum of revision, soon ran its course, except for the most case-hardened cultists; the reading public became impatient.[4]

3. The dimension of maturity -- the notion that one should speak as well as act one's chronological age. The sight of a plump hausfrau in a bikini is no more distressing than the sound of a middle-aged parent trying to keep up with the latest adolescent slang. Even finer distinctions are apparent: college students scorn the kind of language that delighted them in high school.

4. The scale of vogue. On one hand this is found in the slang of the year; on another in certain kinds of jargon and counter words. Both varieties of vogue language are exceedingly difficult to pin down; most of the time the vogue has passed before the lexicographers have settled down to recording and classifying.

5. The scale of association -- the argot or technical language of a group with which one has become identified. Every association group has this, not just the teenage gangs and the more formally parasitic subcultures of the underworld. The language of a stamp collector or a model railroad fan on the one hand, of Anglo-Catholic clergy or Chicago critics on the other, may be just as unintelligible to outsiders not of the true bond as is the lingo of safe-crackers or narcotics addicts.

6. The scale of relationship between the speaker or writer and his audience -- the "five clocks" of Joos 1962. In the center, as Joos reckons it, is the *consultative* style of the small committee or social gathering -- not more than six people -- where free interchange is possible but where background information must be supplied. On the one side are the *formal* style, typified in public address, and the *frozen* style, that of great literature (encompassing principally but not exclusively the high style or the sublime of traditional criticism) where the public

insists on the text being repeated intact. On the other are the *casual* style, where familiarity of speaker and audience with each other eliminates the need for background information, and the *intimate*, where close association makes possible many syntactic shortcuts. It is noticeable that the frozen and the intimate styles, as opposite poles, share the feature of high allusiveness, created in one by the genius of the author at compressing much into a small space and in the other by the closeness of association.

7. The dimension of history, paralleling to some extent the scale of maturity in the individual. Dictionaries have long recognized this dimension: words or senses that have not been observed for some centuries are labeled *obsolete*; those that have appeared only rarely in some centuries, and not at all for a few generations, are marked *archaic*. A more troublesome class is made up of those words and meanings which are still encountered, but only in the usage of the older and less sophisticated -- those that I would call *old-fashioned*; so far, there is no traditional label in lexicography, though everybody recognizes the items. Even more troublesome are innovations, which are seldom if ever marked, since by the time they are noticed they have generally become well established. A notorious example is the verb *to finalize*, which did not arouse the ire of the belletristes (because of its vogue in advertising) until a generation after it had been recorded in dictionary files, and much longer after it had first appeared.

8. The regional scale. At one end we have pronunciations, words, or meanings that are limited to a small part of the English-speaking world; at the other, things that are truly international in that they are shared by several language communities. *Chay* -- a call to summon cattle -- is found in the United States only in a small section of eastern South Carolina; it may still be heard in Northern Ireland. Most of the new terms of science and technology, including such everyday words as *telephone*, are found not only in all places where English is spoken but in other languages as well. Within the English-speaking world, there are words, meanings, pronunciations, and even grammatical forms characteristic of England proper, Ireland, Scotland, the United States, Canada, Australia, New Zealand, South Africa, and the West Indies -- to say nothing of more local sudivisions in each of these. To take a few examples, a *station* in Australia is the same as a *ranch* in western North America; a *tickle* in Newfoundland is an inlet; and the *telly* in Britain is the television.

9. The social scale. This means, simply, that some varieties of the language are more esteemed than others. It may be an alien variety of the community language, like British English in parts of the Commonwealth; it may even be an alien language, like French in parts of Africa. In most European countries it is a variety of the language used by the richer and better born and better educated in a focus of national life -- economic, cultural, or political -- which often turns out to be the area around the capital: Roman-Florentine in Italy, Castilian in Spain, Parisian in France, Muscovite in Russia, London in England. (It should be noted that the lower-class speech of the same areas has no prestige; in fact, as we are well aware when we look at traditional London lower-class speech, Cockney, it may be the least favored of all lower-class regional varieties.) The favored dialect of one century, even one generation, may not be that of the next. In extreme cases, another city may replace the older center of prestige, as London replaced Winchester after the Norman Conquest; in all cases tha favored dialect will change as new classes rise in the scale and set new fashions of language behavior.

The American situation, however, is different, both in the United States and in Canada. Partly through geography, partly through the independence of each of the early settlements from each other, partly through a stubborn tradition of individualism and local loyalty, no city has unqualified preeminence of the kind that Paris, London, and Vienna have in their countries. Each of the older cultural centers -- Boston, New York, Philadelphia, Richmond, Charleston -- had its own elite and boasted its own kind of excellence; as the nation expanded westward, such new cities as Chicago, San Francisco, Atlanta, St. Louis, and Salt Lake City developed their own prestige in their own areas. There is a good deal of ridicule exchanged between cities, most of it good natured, as to which local pronunciation (for grammar and vocabulary are strikingly uniform among urban educated speakers) is the most outlandish or the most pleasant; but for practical purposes the educated speech of one area is as good as another. And all varieties of uneducated speech are at a disadvantage, especially when the speakers move out of their own areas.

For six of the nine scales of variation the speaker has some freedom of choice. But for the last three -- history, region, and society -- he is more or less caught up in forces beyond his control. No man can change the generation or place of his birth; his attempts to change the social variety of his speech will be determined by the kind of education he receives and the kind of persons he associates with, and opportunities to make a drastic change are not as common as we would like.

Along all of these scales, for practical purposes, we can expect variation in a number of aspects of human communication. Outside language we have 1) *proxemics*, the phenomena of spatial variation, including the distances at which communication is effective; 2) *haptics*, the phenomena of body contact; 3) *kinesics*, bodily movements in communication, of which gestures are only a small part; 4) *paralanguage*, the nonlinguistic but communicatively significant orchestration of the stream of speech, involving such phenomena as abnormally high or low pitch, abnormally fast or slow tempo, abnormal loudness or softness, drawl, clipping, rasp, openness, and the like. These are all in the earliest stages of discussion; linguists and anthropologists recognize their importance but have just begun to develop systems of notation and means of comparison.[5]

Within the domain of language proper, but having a special position, are the *suprasegmentals*, the phenomena that in English include stress, intonation, transitions, and terminals of clauses and utterances. It should be noted that suprasegmentals, like the aspects of communication outside the language system, have so far had no systematic comparative discussion regionally or socially. Also, all these phenomena are attested only in a limited way historically, and in writing they have no direct reflection.

Within language proper there is a system of *segmental phonemes*, of vowels and consonants capable of variation in the structure of the system, in the articulation of the individual phonemes, and in their incidence in particular environments.[6] The system of *morphology* likewise varies in its structure, in the shape of particular morphemes (especially of inflections) and in their incidence in particular environments. There is a system of *syntax*, involving the selection and arrangement of morphemes.[7] And finally there is a body of meaningful forms -- the *lexicon* -- with various words possible for the same meaning and various meanings possible for the same word.

If we look at the history of English, we can see that all kinds of changes have taken place as the result of various forces, borrowing (both from other languages and from one dialect of English into another), phonetic change, and analogy.[8]

In the pronunciation system, we have kept four of the short vowels of Old English: /ɪ, ɛ, æ, ʊ/; Old English /y/, however, has unrounded to /ɪ/, so that *fill* and *will* now rhyme. Many of the words which had /u/ in Old English now have /ʌ/, and for most American dialects the low-back rounded vowel /ɔ/, as in *God*, has unrounded to /a/. In contrast to these slight changes, all the long vowels and diphthongs of Old English have changed their phonetic shape, and some of them have fallen together; for example, Middle

English /sæ:/ "body of water" and /se:/ "to perceive with the eyes" have fallen together as /si/.

The morphological structure of the language has likewise altered. The noun retains only the general plural and the genitive; the adjective retains comparison (though for many adjectives it is a periphrastic comparison with *more* and *most* instead of the historical inflected comparison with *-er*, *-est*) but has lost all markers of number, gender, and case. The pronoun system has been drastically simplified: only the neuter *it* retains the old accusative, here undifferentiated from the nominative; in all other pronouns the old dative has assumed all object functions. In the second person the historical dative plural has not only usurped the functions of the accusative but those of the nominative as well and (with rare exceptions) has become the standard for the singular in object and subject positions. In the third person, *she*, *they*, *their*, and *them* -- borrowings from Northern English dialects -- have supplanted the older forms. Throughout the pronominal system there has been a differentiation between the attributive genitive, as in *my book*, and the absolute, as *a book of mine*. The article and demonstrative pronoun are now distinct from each other; the demonstrative has lost all gender and case distinctions, with the historical neuter nominative-accusatives *this* and *that* in the singular, and developing new plurals.

The most spectacular morphological changes have taken place in the verb. It is still a two-tense verb, like all Germanic verbs, but many of the older strong or irregular verbs have become weak or regular, and the survivors have tended to level their principal parts: only *was/were* remains of the historical distinction between preterite singular and preterite plural, and for many verbs preterite and past participle have fallen together. Distinctions of person and number have been lost except for the verb *to be* and for the third singular present indicative. The subjunctive mode has been lost except for the hypothetical *if I (he) were you*, the very formal *if this be treason*, a series of petrified formulas, such as *resolved, that this house stand adjourned*, and *that*-clauses following such verbs as *urge* and *insist*.

Syntactic changes are also numerous. Word order, once flexible and capable of variation, as in classical Latin or contemporary Ojibwa, has now been fixed. New patterns of interrogative and negative structures have been developed, with the verb *do* as an auxiliary. And there has been a proliferation of very complicated verb phrases, capable of rendering far more subtle nuances of meaning than could have been rendered in Latin; if some of them rarely occur, as *tomorrow our house will have been being redecorated for two months*, they are comprehensible and acceptable when they do.

Changes in the vocabulary and in meanings are so numerous and familiar that it is almost useless to mention them; a few examples will suffice. *Starve*, originally meaning "to perish" like its German cognate *sterben*, came to signify "to perish of hunger"; as a general verb it has been replaced by *die*. The overworked *nice* originally meant *foolish*. *Flesh* has lost its meaning of "edible muscular tissue" and has been replaced in this meaning by *meat*, which originally signified anything edible (*sweet-meats* preserves the old meaning); *food* has assumed the general meaning.

To this stage of the presentation we have assumed a more or less linear development, recognizing but disregarding differences within the speech community. Yet we know by experience that no speech community of any size -- and the size may be only a few hundred speakers -- is without regional and social distinctions. Different communities use the language differently; some speakers are recognized as using it better than others do. The larger the speech community, the more complicated are the relationships between regional and social varieties.

Regional differences may arise in a variety of ways. The classical explanation -- which has been used to explain the differences in Modern German, before the new *Völkerwanderung* after World War II -- derives these differences from the original settlement by a group speaking a particular dialect of the same language. The population mixture in all of the early American settlements makes this explanation less cogent here, but such groups have left their traces. We can think of the Ulster Scots in western Pennsylvania, and less significantly in the Southern uplands and the South Midland derivatives to the west; of the Irish fishermen on Beaver Island in Lake Michigan and in various coves along the Newfoundland coast; of the East Anglian influence, through the early Puritans, on the speech of New England, especially east of the Connecticut River; and, in the American Middle West, of the preservation of New England speechways in the Western Reserve around Cleveland and in the Marietta speech-island where the Muskingum flows into the Ohio.

Settlements of speakers of a foreign language also leave their impact on a local dialect. The Palatinate Germans who settled in eastern Pennsylvania about 1700 have influenced to some extent the English of their area, not only in vocabulary but also in pronunciation, in syntax, and in intonation. In similar fashion the Scandinavians in Minneapolis have markedly influenced English intonation; even complete monolinguals cannot escape acquiring the speech-tune of the Swedish-Americans they played with as children. So have the Cajuns of southwestern Louisiana influenced the intonation of Louisiana English, and -- on all but the most educated levels -- caused a reduction of final consonant clusters and a loss of most inflectional endings.

Regional dialects also reflect historical patterns of migration and communication. In Germany the Rhine has disseminated the South German speech forms northward, and Northern forms southward; in the United States the Mississippi has done likewise with English. In the Middle West, settlers from New England followed the shores of Lake Erie westward and did not cross the swamplands of the Maumee and Kankakee, while settlers from the upland South moved north along the tributaries of the Ohio, taking up holdings in the bottom lands; today, despite subsequent industrialization, the speech of Ohio, Indiana, and Illinois is split between Yankee and Southern Highland. Conversely, even what now seems a trivial geographical barrier could inhibit the spread of settlement and speech: Chesapeake Bay isolated the Delmarva Peninsula from the focal area of the Virginia Tidewater and Piedmont; the Virginia Blue Ridge limited the westward spread of plantation culture, so that the Shenandoah Valley was settled by migration from western Pennsylvania, and in Vermont the crest of the Green Mountains marks the division between eastern and western New England speechways.

If a cultural focus exists, its speech forms spread into the surrounding countryside or even leap rural areas to become established in what one could call satellite cities. The prestige of Boston has led to the establishment of its speech as the model for eastern New England and as a type to imitate in much of the northern United States; Philadelphia dominates eastern Pennsylvania and Pittsburgh the western half of the state; the cultivated speech of Richmond and other Virginia Piedmont cities has been emulated not merely in the Shenandoah Valley but in cities of eastern North Carolina and as far west as Charleston, West Virginia. New York seems to be an exception; its vocabulary has spread but not its pronunciation, possibly because the city has for so long boasted very large foreign-language concentrations. Where communities have been geographically or culturally isolated, the opposite is true: the speech of the Maine coast, the southern Appalachians, or northeastern North Carolina does not spread and in fact gives way to outside models as these remote areas become accessible. Dialect mixture has been so common in American English from the beginning that consistent leveling in the present is probably rare.

Political boundaries old and new are reflected in Europe as limits of pronunciations or words; they are so recent in the United States, and so ineffective on the movement of people and goods, that they seldom cause linguistic differences -- though with purely political terms such as the Ontario *reeve*, or "township officer," linguistic and political limits may coincide. But in an indirect way, as in the quality of a school system, state boundaries may be significant. Folk pronunciations and folk grammatical forms survived much more strongly in western Maryland and West Virginia than in Pennsylvania, though the early settlers were the same kinds of people and the easy routes of communication cross state boundaries; but Pennsylvania had an earlier and deeper commitment to public education than the states further south.

By now it is possible to summarize in some detail the kinds of regional differences that appear in American English. In addition to the usual features of grammar, pronunciation, and vocabulary, there are probably regional variations in proxemics, haptics, kinesics, paralanguage, and suprasegmentals, though no systematic statement is possible. The entomologist Henry K. Townes has noted that some hand gestures seem to occur only in the South Carolina Piedmont; Southern speech seems to have a wider range of stress and pitch than the speech of other regions, especially the dialects of the Middle West; the so-called Southern drawl does not reflect a slower tempo -- Southerners normally speak more rapidly than Middle Westerners -- but rather this heavier stress, combined with prolongation of the heavily stressed syllables and shortening of the weakly stressed ones.

Within the pronunciation of American English, there is only one major difference in the system of phonemes; most dialects contrast unrounded /a/ and rounded /ɔ/, as in *cot* and *caught*, but some do not. Where the contrast does not exist, some dialects -- in eastern New England, western Pennsylvania, the St. Louis area -- have a low-back rounded vowel, while others -- the Upper Peninsula of Michigan, northern Minnesota, western Canada -- have a low-central or low-back unrounded one. Until recently, some dialects in the area of New England settlement had a falling diphthong /iu/ in such words as *blue*, *suit*, *grew*, where most speakers of American English have /u/ and others have /ju/; however, the /iu/ is generally considered old-fashioned, and it is rapidly disappearing.

Although general structural differences in the pronunciation systems of American dialects are rare, conditioned structural differences are more common. As we have indicated, the consonant sequences /tʃ-, dʒ-, nʒ-, stʃ-/ -- in such words as *tube*, *due*, *new*, *student* -- simply do not occur in some regions, though all of these con-

sonants are found in all American dialects. Dialects that contrast /a/ and /ɔ/, as in *cot* and *caught* may not have the contrast before /-r/, as in *barn* and *born*; this is especially true in some communities in the southern Midwest, in parts of the Southwest, and in the Rocky Mountains. All varieties of American English contrast /ɔ/ and /o/, as in *law* and *low*, but before /-r/, as in *horse* and *hoarse*, the contrast is retained chiefly in parts of the South. Again, only in parts of the South and some Atlantic Seaboard Yankee areas -- and probably not so common there as it used to be -- does one find the contrast between *met*, *mat*, and *mate* maintained before intervocalic /-r-/, in *merry*, *marry*, and *Mary*; from Cleveland west these words are generally homonyms. And in the older speech of the Charleston area there seems to be only one front vowel before postvocalic /-r/ or its derivative /ə/, so that *fear* and *fair*, *ear* and *air* are homonyms.

The phonemes may differ in phonetic shape: /e/ in *date* is an up-gliding diphthong with a high beginning [eɪ] in the South Midland, an up-gliding diphthong with a low beginning [ɛɪ] in the Delaware Valley and the Pittsburgh area, a monophthong [e·] in the Pennsylvania German area and an in-gliding diphthong [e·ə] in the South Carolina Low-Country. The /ɔ/ of *law* and *dog* has a high beginning and an inglide in much of the Middle Atlantic Seaboard, including old-fashioned New York City speech; in much of the South and South Midland, it has a low beginning with an up-glide and increasing rounding.

More familiar are differences in incidence of phonemes. Upstate New York has /a/ in *fog*, *hog*, and *on*; Pennsylvania has /ɔ/. The fish *crappie* has /a/ in the stressed syllable in Michigan, /æ/ in South Carolina. The North and North Midland prevailingly have /-s-/ in *greasy* and /ɪ/ in *creek*; the South and South Midland have /-z-/ and /i/.

Differences in inflection are less frequent than in pronunciation. Systematic differences are very rare: a few British dialects retain the old second person singular *thou*, *thy*, *thine*, *thee*; some American dialects have developed a new second person plural, *you-all*, *you-uns*, *mongste-ye*, *oona*, though none of these has standing in formal writing and only *you-all* has achieved the dignity of standard informal status; possibly some dialects have lost the distinctiveness of the third singular present indicative -*s* and consistently have either -*s* or zero throughout the present.[9] In the shape of the morpheme there are more differences: standard *drank* as a preterite, versus *drunk* and *drinkt*; standard *climbed* versus *clim*, *clum*, *clome*, *cloom*, and the like; and on the standard level, such variations as between *kneeled* and *knelt* or between *dove* /dov/ and *dived*.

It is notorious that the description of

English syntax is less adequate than that of its pronunciation or inflections. But even at this point we can recognize some regional patterns. In the South and South Midland such compounded auxiliaries as *might could* and *used to could* are common in educated informal speech; the New England settlement area forms the negative of *ought* by the periphrastic *hadn't ought*; in eastern Kentucky *used to* has become a sentence-initial adverb, as in *used to everybody around here baked their own bread*.

Regional differences in vocabulary still abound, despite the homogenizing effect of twentieth-century urban civilization. Perhaps few of our students today would recognize the Northern *whippletree* or Midland *singletree* by any name, and urban living has probably prospered *dragonfly* and *earthworm* at the expense of such regional designations as Northern *darning needle*, South Midland-Southern *snake doctor* and Southern Coastal *mosquito hawk*, or Merrimac Valley *mudworm*, Pennsylvania German *rainworm*, Southern Mountain *redworm*. But a dry-cleaning establishment in Boston is a *cleanser*; the New Orleans *poorboy*, a sandwich on a small loaf of bread, is a *submarine* in Boston, a *grinder* in upstate New York, a *hero* in New York City, a *hoagy* in Philadelphia; the grass strip between sidewalk and street, still unnamed in some regions, is a *boulevard* in Minneapolis, a *tree belt* in Springfield, Massachusetts, a *tree lawn* in Cleveland, and a *devil strip* in Akron. And similar differences in meanings persist. It may be only academic that in the Carolina mountains a *corn dodger* is a *small loaf*, in the coastal plain a *dumpling*, in Savannah a *pancake* and in Brunswick, Georgia, a *hush puppy*; but one who customarily uses *brat* to describe a noisy child may run into difficulties in parts of Indiana where it denotes a bastard, and the Middle Westerner used to ice cream in a *milk shake* will be disappointed in Boston, where it contains only milk and syrup.

If the basis of regional dialects is the fact that communities or regions differ in their history, the basis of social dialects is that people of different social standing in a given community will use different forms, and that the status of the linguistic forms will be determined by the standing of their users in the community.

Although this general principle has been recognized for generations, the procedures for discussing the correlation between speech differences and differences in status have been systematically worked out only in recent years and are still being refined. For a long time the difference between what was good and what was bad was more a matter of the observer's prejudices than of his observations. However, with Fries's *American English Grammar* (1940)

and the American Linguistic Atlas project (1933-, with the first publication in 1939), it has become customary to identify the social status of informants first, by nonlinguistic means, and then to describe, simply, the forms they use. A further refinement has been recently introduced by Labov, in his *The Social Stratification of English in New York City* (1966), by limiting himself to a smaller number of variables, by obtaining examples in a variety of contexts -- ranging from the reading of potentially minimal pairs to the account of an incident in which the informant thought he was going to be killed -- and by informants' identifications of the social status of particular variants. Labov has revealed that in pronunciation New Yorkers have a considerable gap between their target and their actual usage; whether such a gap exists in other regions -- I suspect it is less important in the South than in the urban Northeast -- can be determined only by further investigation. But whatever the answer, Labov has already rendered the profession an invaluable service by providing a kind of instrument for answering questions that have long been felt.

Although the situation in any given community is far more complex, a working evaluation of social dialects starts with a threefold classification: 1) uneducated, or folk speech; 2) common speech -- in the more general sense of everyday usage of the average citizen, not in the Southern pejorative sense; and 3) educated, cultivated, or standard speech. It is from the last group that speech with national prestige has developed. In the European situation, as we have pointed out, there is often a single prestigious variety of the language -- in origin, normally the upper-class speech of the capital or the surrounding area or of some other important center. In the New World, on the other hand, there are a number of prestigious regional varieties, deriving from regional cultural traditions; one has only to think of the differences in the speech origins of the last eight college-educated presidents: Calvin Coolidge (Western New England), Herbert Hoover (Northern Middle Western, modified by travel), Franklin Roosevelt (Hudson Valley), John F. Kennedy (Boston), Lyndon Johnson (Southern Texas), Richard M. Nixon (California), Gerald Ford (Michigan), and Jimmy Carter (Southwest Georgia).

When we have discovered the principal dialect levels in our society and their regional variants, we must still observe a few cautions. First, the social distance between levels is not the same in all communities. In, for example, the older plantation communities, the distance between common and cultivated -- the distance between plain, everyday people and the elite -- was greater than that between folk and common. On the other hand, in such urban centers as Detroit, Cleveland, and

Chicago, the distance between uneducated speech and common speech is greater than that between common and cultivated. In New York City the spacing between various levels may be fairly wide; in a small Midwestern town without heavy industry it may be narrow.

Second, who is or is not cultivated depends on local standards and is more or less relative. It is only a slight exaggeration to cite the experience of a graduate student from Georgia who went with his Harvard classmates to a performance of *Tobacco Road*. In their discussion afterwards, one of the New Englanders asked if Jeeter Lester and his family were really typical of rural Georgia. "Hell, no!" exclaimed the Georgian. "Back home we'd call people like that the country club set." It is very likely that in terms of absolute education and cultural exposure a storekeeper in a college community like Ann Arbor or Chapel Hill would rank above the local doctor or superintendent of schools in a county seat in southern West Virginia.

Third, local mores differ strikingly in the tolerated differences between formal and informal educated speech. Where social differences are based on tradition and on family status, as among the "county" families of England and their analogues in the older parts of the American South, informal cultivated speech addressed to equals or other intimates may differ remarkably from the norms of formal expository prose. For Middle Western suburbs, one may agree with the melancholy observation of Sledd 1964:473 that "any red-blooded American would prefer incest to *ain't*"; but in a community like Charleston one may encounter *ain't* a hundred times a day in conversation among the proudest families. So the educated Midwesterner often considers the informal speech of the educated Southerner as very careless; the educated Southerner, in turn, missing the familiar conversational cues to informality, often considers the conversation of educated Middle Westerners as strained and anxious. In short, each suspects the other's cultural credentials. Perhaps it is inevitable in an ostensibly open society that covert class markers become more significant as the material ones disappear.

Regardless of the degree of difference in a locality, there seem to be to basic situations in which social dialects arise. The most familiar one is that in which different groups within the same community acquire different status, thanks to differences in education and wealth and power, so that the speech of one group is deemed worth emulating and that of the other groups is not. This is the situation that has developed over the years in the small towns of much of New England, upstate New York, and the Southern up-

lands; it is probably the same kind of situation out of which the manners and speech of the gentry acquired status in rural England.

The other situation, perhaps more common in our industrialized and urbanized society, is that in which groups of original settlers differ in their social status or a large group of new immigrants may acquire a peculiar status in the community. Most of the time this peculiar status is that of social inferiority, though we can all think of exceptions: the outsiders who bring social prestige with them -- the English civil servant in the colonies; the Swedish pastor in Minnesota; the proper Bostonian in Rochester, New York; the Richmond family in Charleston, West Virginia. But these are atypical. The social dialect problems created by immigration are of three basic kinds:

1. The speech of those whose native language is something different from that of the community, whether Yiddish, Cajun French, Puerto Rican Spanish, or Hungarian.

2. The speech of groups who use a nonstandard dialect from the same region; a classic example is the speech of the rural Southern Negroes or poor whites who come to cities like Savannah or Birmingham in search of better jobs.

3. The third situation involves the migration into one region of speakers of substandard dialects of another region. Here we have not only the problem of clearly recognizable social differences but that of regional ethnocentrism: of the tendency to look upon what is regionally different as *ipso facto* inferior. Detroiters often overtly try to eradicate West Virginia vowels (or what they think are West Virginia vowels); South Carolinians often remark -- not so publicly as Detroiters, because they have a tradition of greater politeness or at least of a wry diffidence in such matters -- that to their ears educated Middle Westerners sound like uneducated Southerners, since the strong postvocalic /-r/ in *barn* and *beard* is in the South traditionally associated with poor white speech. To this category belong the language problems of Appalachian whites and Southern Negroes in such Northern and Western cities as New York, Cleveland, Chicago, and Los Angeles.

It is in this last situation that historical and regional and social differences intersect. For example, in much of Southern England the uninflected third singular present indicative, as *he do*, is found in old-fashioned rural speech. This feature must have been brought to all of the American colonies. However, it is unevenly distributed today because of differences in the cultural situation. The Southern colonies were more rural than the rest, more dependent on agriculture for a longer time, and on money-crop agriculture

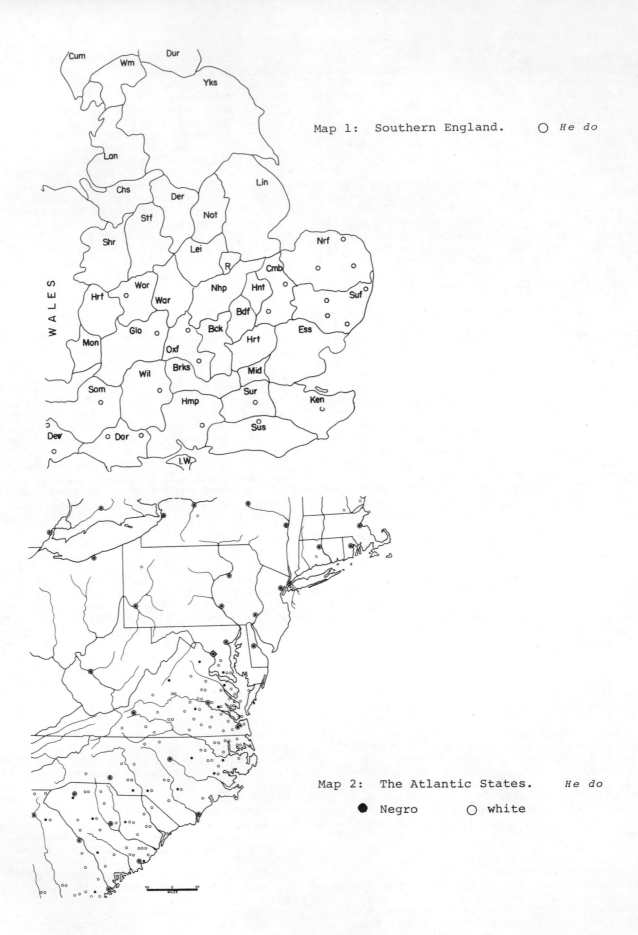

Map 1: Southern England.   ◯ *He do*

Map 2: The Atlantic States.   *He do*

● Negro   ◯ white

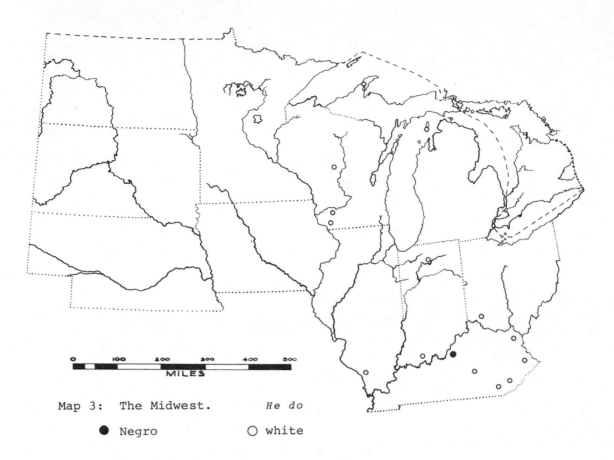

Map 3: The Midwest.   *He do*

● Negro   ○ white

that required a great deal of low-grade hand labor -- cotton and tobacco. The average income in the South is still lower than that in other regions; Southerners travel less; they have, on the average, fewer years of schooling and that is of an inferior quality to what is available in other regions. It is therefore not surprising that such forms as *he do* are today more widely distributed in the South and South Midland than in other dialect regions, simply because the conditions there were more favorable to their survival.

But this is not all. Within the South itself, a similar cultural differential operated to the disadvantage of the Negro -- long enslaved, and discriminated against even after emancipation. For a long time the Southern Negro population was more rural than the Southern white, more confined to agriculture and to the more menial kinds of agricultural work. The Southern Negro was less given to travel; his income was -- and is -- lower than that of his white neighbor; schooling is for fewer years and of poorer quality. For this reason, in the South, such forms as *he do* will be heard from a greater proportion of Negroes than whites. And since, in recent years, the migrants from the South to Northern and Western urban areas are more likely to be Negroes than whites and since Negroes are more likely to be identified as recent migrants, in such areas forms like *he do* are likely to be considered as simply Negro speech forms, though historically they are regional forms widely disseminated in Southern England, and regionally in the United States they are characteristically Southern. Though the origins of Negro dialects in the United States are undoubtedly more complicated than nineteenth-century observers suggested -- Turner's *Africanisms in the Gullah Dialect* (1949) has been particularly helpful in providing a new perspective -- for the most part, Negro usages that differ from middle-class white practice are largely the result of this kind of selective cultural differentiation.[10]

Our knowledge of none of these three dimensions -- historical, regional, and social -- is so complete that we can close our eyes to the need for adding further data. Yet even now we know enough to provide a richer understanding to all those who are concerned with dimensions of usage -- whether they are interested in dictionary labeling, school programs, or simply the phenomena of cultural history and social structure. If our statements are more complicated than some of our friends would wish, the fault is not in our science but in the tangled web of human relationships.

[41]

[1] Statements about regional dialects are drawn principally from the archives of the linguistic atlases of the United States and Canada, by permission of the American Council of Learned Societies. Many details have appeared in previous derivative studies, notably Kurath 1949, Atwood 1953a, and Kurath and R. McDavid 1961. This paper was originally presented to a meeting of Connecticut teachers of English at Middletown, in July 1966; an earlier version was published in the *Journal of English Linguistics* 1.25-40 (1967).

[2] Notably in Kenyon 1948; Joos 1962; Allen 1958, 2nd ed.:272-76.

[3] Examples have been cited by the late J. R. Firth, from British officers in India; by Kenneth L. Pike, from a variety of situations; and from my own experiences in the American South.

[4] The expectations extend to other behavior as well. The political backlash of 1966 among white middle-class and working-class voters was intensified by the way these expectations were disregarded by the irresponsible dress and behavior of certain well-advertised liberal groups such as the Berkeley Left and the Chicago Students against the Rank -- beards, stringy hair, sloppy clothing, noise, and general boorishness. The invasion of lower-middle-class Chicago suburbs by such groups did nothing to further desegregation of private housing; nor did similar invasions of the South in 1964 and 1965 further the civil liberties cause in that region. It will be noted that participants in the original sit-in movements in the South won a great deal of local respect for their essential cause by carefully observing local conventions in such nonessentials as dress and personal grooming, thus providing a striking contrast to the local poor whites who opposed them.

[5] E. Hall 1959, 1966; Birdwhistell 1956; Smith and Pittenger 1957; Trager 1958; Pittenger, Hockett, and Danehy 1960; Austin 1965. The last also appears in R. McDavid and Austin 1966.

[6] A phoneme is a minimal distinctive unit in the sound system; there are various competing analyses of the phonemes of English. In this paper the phonemic transcriptions, in slashes, follow the analysis of Kurath and R. McDavid 1961; phonetic transcriptions are in square brackets.

[7] A morpheme is a minimum meaningful form; it may be derivational, as for the making of abstract nouns from adjectives, or inflectional, as for the forming of the plural.

[8] For detailed discussions see, for example, Bloomfield 1933; Hockett 1958; Pyles 1964.

[9] See Paddock 1966:20-21 for aspectual differences formally signalled.

[10] The same forces would also help to preserve features of ancestral languages. As Turner points out, the relative isolation -- geographical and social -- of the Gullah Negroes of South Carolina and Georgia has preserved many relics of West African languages, and some of these could reinforce forms derived from nonstandard English dialects. The complex backgrounds of American Negro dialects require intense investigations.

Almost without exception, any scholar studying American Negro speech, whether as an end in itself or as part of a larger project, must dispose of two widely held superstitions: 1) he must indicate that there is no speech form identifiable as of Negro origin solely on the basis of Negro physical characteristics; 2) he must show that it is probable that some speech forms of Negroes -- and even of some whites -- may be derived from an African cultural background by the normal processes of cultural transmission. Such a necessity of refuting folk beliefs seldom arises when one is studying the English of other American minority groups. For these, it is generally assumed, though not necessarily in the terms anthropologists would use, that all linguistic patterns are culturally transmitted, that where a group with a foreign-language background -- such as the Pennsylvania Germans -- has been speaking a divergent variety of English for several generations in an overwhelmingly English-speaking area, there is nothing in their speech that cannot be explained on the basis of the culture contacts between the speakers of two languages. We are generous in recognizing Scandinavian linguistic survivals in Minnesota and the Dakotas, German in Wisconsin and Pennsylvania, and Dutch in the Hudson Valley. We do not explain this influence on the basis of Scandinavian hair color, German skull configuration, or Dutch mouth shape, but on the grounds that two languages were spoken side by side, so that bilingualism developed in the community (Haugen 1950a).

In forming judgments on the speech of the American Negro, however, the process has been reversed: the cultural transmission of speech forms of African origin has been traditionally denied, and the explanation of Negro dialects given in terms of a 'simple, childlike mind,'[1] or of physical inability to pronounce the sounds of socially approved English. So widely spread is this superstition that Gunnar Myrdal felt obliged to explain that Negro speech, like all other speech, is culturally transmitted;[2] as late as 1949 the author of a widely syndicated 'popular science' newspaper quiz explained that the Negro cannot pronounce a post vocalic /-r/ in such words as *car*, *beard*, or *bird* because his lips are too thick (Wiggam 1949).

There are reasons for this popular mis-interpretation. One of the most obvious is that the Negro, unlike other groups of foreign-language origin, is readily identifiable by skin pigmentation. Whatever differences the naive observer notices between his speech and that of the average Negro he encounters, he interprets as a function of the identifiable physical difference. The fact that the contacts between whites and educated Negroes are limited, the normal contact between the two races being in terms of the situation of white master and Negro servant, means that Negro speech is generally judged on the basis of nonstandard speakers, or at best on the basis of speakers from a different dialect area (Myrdal 1944:965).

Other reasons for such misconceptions can be seen in the history of Negro-white relationships. Most obvious is the historical fact that the Negroes constituted the only large group of the American population that came here against their will, and with their cultural heritage overtly overridden in the effort to fit them into the new pattern of the basic unskilled labor for the plantation system.[3] Rationalizing the institution of chattel slavery as a benefit to the Negroes required that the whites deny any consequential African cultural heritage. Then when slavery was abolished as an institution but replaced -- both in the South and elsewhere -- by a racially determined caste system, supported by discriminatory legislation or extralegal covenants, the need for rationalization continued.[4]

It is therefore difficult for the white scholar to approach dispassionately the problem of African survivals in American Negro culture in general and speech in particular. The scholar who accepts the theory of Negro inferiority tends to explain any apparent differences between Negro and white speech on the basis of the Negro's childlike mind or imperfectly developed speech organs. Or if he tries to be fair, he will probably deny that there are any essential differences. This was the position of the late George Philip Krapp:

. . . The Negro speaks English of the same kind and, class for class, of the same degree, as the English of the most authentic descendants of the first settlers at Jamestown and Plymouth.

The Negroes, indeed, in acquiring English have done their work so thoroughly that they have retained not a trace of any native African speech. Neither have they transferred anything of importance from their native tongues to the general language. A few words, such as *voodoo*, *hoodoo*, and *buckra*, may have come into English from some original African dialect, but most of the words commonly supposed to be of Negro origin, e.g. *tote*, *jazz*, and *mosey*, are really derived from ancient English or other European sources. The native African dialects have been completely lost. (Krapp 1924:190-95; cf. also Krapp 1925: 1.161-63; 2.226.)

But neither has the Negro scholar found the task an easy one. For a considerable period, he was as reluctant as the white scholar to admit a consequential African cultural heritage, reckoning Africa "a badge of shame . . . the reminder of a savage past not sufficiently remote, as is that of European savagery, to have become hallowed"(Herskovits 1941:32). The inevitable overemphasis of possible African survivals, which one sometimes discovers in the works of recent Negro scholars, is perhaps no nearer an objective presentation than the old attitude, but ultimately should be as salutary a corrective of perspective as it is inevitable.

At the beginning of the century, the opinions held concerning the relationships between Negro and white speech may be summed up in two ethnocentric statements, both frequently heard today:

1. The regionally ethnocentric statement by Northerners that the 'quaintness' and 'primitiveness' of what they considered Southern speech[5] was due to the influence of the Negro.

2. The racially ethnocentric statement that the Negro contributed nothing of himself from his African heritage except a few exotic words, but that the essential characteristics of Negro speech -- even of Gullah[6] -- were to be derived from British provincial speech or from lapses into quasi baby talk by a simple people physically and intellectually incapable of mastering the sounds and structure of English.

Both of these statements, we will find, contained elements of truth. But neither was the whole truth. The first statement has had comparatively little currency and done little damage.[7] But the second has been institutionalized as part of what Herskovits calls "the Myth of the Negro Past"(Herskovits 1941:1-2).

To cite a multiplicity of examples of these attitudes would add little to the argument. But from two examples one may see the myth in action.

In his single essay at linguistic analysis (1935), Cleanth Brooks sought in Wright's *English Dialect Grammar* (1905) and *Dictionary* (1898-1905) for the origins of what he called the "Alabama-Georgia dialect," recorded by his definition in Leonidas W. Payne's "A Word-List from East Alabama" (1908) and the Uncle Remus stories of Joel Chandler Harris. As a basic

premise, Brooks assumes that no Africanisms have survived (64), and that the speech of Negroes and whites may therefore be considered as the same.[8]

The first study of Gullah was that made by John Bennett (1908-09). His general conclusions were that Gullah was essentially derived from seventeenth-century British folk speech, as adopted or misinterpreted by a culturally inferior group physically incapable of making English speech sounds:

> To express other than the simplest ideas, plain actualities, is, however, difficult . . . (1908: 338).
> Intellectual indolence, or laziness, mental and physical, which shows itself in the shortening of words, the ellision of syllables, and modification of every difficult enunciation . . . (1909:40).
> It is the indolence, mental and physical, of the Gullah dialect that is its most characteristic feature . . . (1909:49).

Until the studies of Lorenzo Turner (1941, 1949), students of Gullah -- or those referring to Gullah speech in the course of other work -- largely took over Bennett's conclusions and words, with some slight rephrasing.[9] It would seem that the linguistic investigator had often formed his conclusions before he began his field work.

Even where the investigator is seriously interested in gathering new evidence for reinterpreting the old, he is likely to run into difficulties in the field. A Negro community that has been too often pointed out as a Negro community, and exploited as such by political and propaganda groups, is reluctant to accept the outside investigator, no matter how well-intentioned.[10] If the speech of the Negro group has a situational dialect variety employed to conceal information or attitudes from the white man, there is reluctance to give away the in-group secret to the investigator.[11] Where the Negro is accustomed to telling the white man what he thinks the white man wants to be told -- where, in fact, his survival often depends on his skill in guessing that -- the investigator may find informants too cooperative, too ready to offer evidence supporting a stereotype.[12] And in communities where the caste lines are most sharply drawn, even an experienced field worker may inadvertently lose rapport with his Negro informants by transgressing taboos of speech or manner (Turner 1949:11-12).

In spite of these difficulties, the last half century has seen much information gathered about both white and Negro speech, and the cultures in which they are used, so that we are now able to speak more intelligently, if somewhat more tentatively, than before. Perhaps the most important force in the revision of older attitudes has been the development of the culture concept by anthropologists (Kroeber 1950), with the realization that long-established ways of saying and doing things or thinking about them can persist in the face of almost inconceivable disadvantages, simply because they are what people are used to. More particularly, there has been a great deal of serious study of Negro communities in Africa and various parts of the New World, and a large-scale study of the American Negro under the direction of the Swedish sociologist Gunnar Myrdal and the auspices of the Carnegie Corporation.[13] There have been scientific studies, both descriptive and comparative, of African languages[14] and of pidgin and creolized languages, especially the studies of Melanesian pidgin (1943), Chinese pidgin (1944), Taki-Taki (1948), and Haitian Creole by Hall, of Haitian Creole by Comhaire-Sylvain (1936), of Louisiana Negro-French by Lane (1934-35), and of Papiamento (the creolized Negro-Dutch-Spanish of Curaçao) by Frederick Agard and C. Cleland Harris (1952). The South Atlantic records for the Linguistic Atlas of the United States and Canada provide material for comparing white and Negro speech in the same communities, and Turner has made a significant contribution by his seventeen years of research in Gullah.

The study of African languages has served two purposes, in addition to the obvious one of indicating actual or potential etyma for vocabulary items in American Negro speech. By providing a record of the structural features of African languages -- phonemics, morphology, and syntax -- it has enabled us to see that some features of American Negro speech may not be baby talk or the misinterpretations of ignorant savages, but rather the persistence of something from African speech. Moreover, the comparative work in African languages has revealed a high degree of structural similarity between the languages of the area from which most of the slaves were taken, so as to make for common trends in the speech of American Negroes, regardless of the mutual unintelligibility of their original languages (Herskovits 1941:79-81).

The study of pidgins and creolized languages has likewise facilitated the intelligent study of the relationship between white and Negro speech. It has repeatedly been shown that these languages are not linguistic freaks, with quaint and curious ways of saying things, but that each of them has its own definite structure, and that they are as worthy of serious study as the better-known languages of Western Europe. Consequently, the investigator of Negro speech in this country has precedent for making a scientific description, as one should make of any dialect. More immediately pertinent, the research into

Taki-Taki, Brazilian Negro Portugese, and Haitian Creole enables the student of American Negro speech to assay whether a particular structural feature is of African origin or not. If a certain feature of Gullah syntax, say, is also found in Brazilian Negro Portugese, in Haitian Creole, and in Papiamento, and resembles a structural feature of several West African languages, it is likely that it is not taken from British peasant speech (Hall 1950b:51-54).

The Linguistic Atlas project provides a tremendous mass of data for evaluating dialect relationships within English-speaking North America; and thanks to the cooperation promised by British scholars, it may soon enable us to state the interrelationships of all forms of present-day English. In their present state, the records for the Atlantic Seaboard area of original settlement, in which Hans Kurath -- the director of the project -- is particularly interested, show the comparable results of 1600 interviews in over 700 communities from southern New Brunswick to the Altamaha Valley and northeastern Florida. The regional surveys -- from the Midwest to the Pacific Coast -- include some 2500 more interviews of actual usage by living informants native to the communities investigated. These records include 40 Negro informants in the South Atlantic States, a few in New England and New Brunswick, and a large number in the Gulf States. These studies attempted to obtain data from Negro and white informants of the same economic and educational level in the same community; in such a way one can avoid the comparison so properly resented by Negro leaders and by serious scholars of all races, of juxtaposing the most cultured white and the least sophisticated Negro.[15] And with such data available, one finds -- as anthropologists have predicted -- that vocabulary and phonology are not matters of skin pigmentation but of the social contacts and economic opportunities of the informant.

Perhaps the greatest single contribution to an intellectual reappraisal of the relationships between white and Negro speech has been the investigation of the speech of Gullah Negroes by Lorenzo D. Turner. Though embodying only part of his findings, his book, *Africanisms in the Gullah Dialect* (1949), dispels effectively the notion that the American Negro lost all his language and his culture under the impact of chattel slavery and the plantation system. Turner's overt statement is impressive enough: that an investigation of Gullah speech discloses several thousand items presumably derived from the languages of the parts of Africa from which slaves were taken. But the implicit conclusions are yet more impressive: that many structural features of Gullah are also to be found in creolized languages of South America and the Caribbean, in the pidgin-like trade English of West Africa, and in many African languages -- this preservation of fundamental structural traits is a more cogent argument for the importance of the African element in the Gullah dialect (and, by inference, in the totality of Gullah culture) than any number of details of vocabulary.[16] Perhaps most significant of all, though hardly hinted at by Turner, is the evidence from phonological structure: like the languages of West Africa described by Westermann and Ward, Gullah has a far less complex system of vowel phonemes than any known variety of English; furthermore, Gullah has a remarkable uniformity, not only in phonemic structure but in the phonetic shape of vowel allophones, along a stretch of nearly four hundred miles of the South Atlantic coast, in the very region where there is a greater variety among the dialects of white speech than one can find elsewhere in English-speaking North America -- a uniformity difficult to explain by chance, or by any of the older explanations of Negro speech.[17] Turner's work has already made scholars aware of the importance of the African background in American Negro speech; though his descriptive grammar of Gullah was never completed, one can draw profitable inferences (Kurath 1972:118-21).

As by-products of the field work for the Linguistic Atlas and other dialect studies, several bits of evidence have been found that suggest how a comparative study of Negro and white speech may be useful in indicating areas of actual or potential interracial tension. It is not without significance that Chicago-born Negro students at the University of Illinois have preserved many characteristic Southern words that are unknown to white students of the same age and city, or that Michigan-born Negroes in the age group between twenty and thirty have the South Midland diphthongs in *dance* and *law*, although the dialect of older-generation Michigan-born Negroes is indistinguishable from that of their white contemporaries. Nor can one overlook the fact that educated Negroes in such Southern communities as Greenville and Atlanta tend to avoid the forms having prestige in local white speech in favor of their conception of New England speech. Even though this evidence is spotty and unsystematized, it already indicates that future community social analyses should include a study of dialect differences within the community -- and especially if the community contains a large Negro group (e.g., O'Cain 1972; Greibeslund 1970; Dorrill 1975).

In summary, we must evaluate the relationships between Negro and white speech in the same scientific spirit as any anthropologist studies acculturation. We must lay aside ethnocentric prejudices of all kinds -- no less the traditional Southern assumption of Negro inferiority than the equally glib statement of career Negroes (perhaps oftener in Africa than in the United States) that no study of Negro culture by whites can be valid because the white man doesn't understand the black man's mind. We must remember that conclusions are valid only insofar as they are based on valid data, and that the discovery of new data may call for new conclusions -- though we can hardly expect so drastic a modification of attitudes as that made possible in the last generation by the use of evidence from African languages and from creolized Negro speech elsewhere in the New World. What new conclusions we reach will probably come by revision of details within the following framework.

First, the overwhelming bulk of the material of American Negro speech -- in vocabulary as well as in grammar and phonology -- is, as one would expect, borrowed from the speech of white groups with which Negroes come in contact. Sometimes these contacts have been such that Negroes simply speak the local variety of standard English.[18] It is also likely that many relic forms from English dialects are better preserved in the speech of some American Negro groups than in American white speech -- not merely items of vocabulary but also items of grammar and even of pronunciation, so far as the occurrence of a given phoneme in a given group of words is concerned. After all, the preservation of relic forms is made possible by geographical or cultural isolation. If Africanisms survive, say, in Gullah because of the long inaccessibility of the Gullah-speaking communities and because of the Southern caste system which limited contacts between white and Negro speakers, so can relic forms from seventeenth-century English.

Nevertheless, the borrowing has not been all in one direction. The Linguistic Atlas indicates that many words noted by Turner as of African origin have been taken over by Southern whites and spread far beyond the areas in which the plantation system flourished.[19] The foci from which these words have apparently spread had large Negro populations early in their history (Petty 1943). *Pinto*, 'coffin,' has been recorded sporadically from the Pee Dee to Savannah -- chiefly from Negroes, but sometimes offered by white informants as a characteristic 'Negro word.'[20] *Buckra*, 'white man,' has spread into the South Carolina Piedmont, especially in the contemptuous designation of poor whites as *poor buckra*. *Joggling board* (cf. Gullah [ʤɒgɑl-bɔd, ʤɒgɒl-]), less often applied to a seesaw than to a long limber plank anchored at both ends and used, as a swing might be used, by nurses dandling infants, by children at play, and by courting couples. The artifact is known throughout the plantation country from Georgetown to the Altamaha River, and in inland communities frequented by plantation families in the malaria season. *Jinky board, janky board* (cf. Gullah [cìka-bod]) is a name for the seesaw in Berkeley County, South Carolina. *Pinder*, 'peanut,' has been recorded in all parts of South Carolina; *goober*, 'peanut,' is found from Chesapeake Bay and the Potomac River southwest through the Piedmont of South Carolina and Georgia, and along the coastal plain from Georgetown south. *Cooter*, 'turtle,' is found throughout the coastal plain and the lower Piedmont from the Cape Fear River to Florida. *Cush*, 'a kind of mush,' is frequently recorded in the coastal plain.[21] Of words not recorded in the Atlas, *hoodoo* (noun and verb) has spread far beyond the South; *okra* is a staple Southern vegetable; *gumbo*, 'a thick soup with an okra base,' (cf. Gullah [gʌmbo] 'okra') is nationally known; *benne*, 'sesame,' is a common ingredient of cookies and candy in the Charleston and Savannah areas; *da* is the usual Charleston name for a child's Negro nurse; *Geechee* is commonly used, with mildly insulting connotations, by Up-Country South Carolinians as a nickname for any Low-Countryman, especially one from the Charleston area; *jigger* (or *chigger*) is the common Southern name for a minute insect with a proclivity for burrowing in human flesh; *war mouth*, also known as *moremouth* (cf. Gullah [wʊmeʊt], Mende [wɔ] 'large'), is a common coastal plain name for a kind of catfish; *pojo*, 'heron,' is widely known in the Charleston area; *tabby*, 'a type of structural material made of cement and oyster shells, often with pieces of brick intermixed,' is frequently used for foundations or house walls in South Carolinian and Georgia coastal communities; *shout*, 'religious dance,' is a typical practice of the less formally organized Protestant groups in the South, white as well as Negro.[22]

So far as Gullah word formation is concerned, dialect geography supports Turner's suggestion that many Gullah compounds and onomatopoetic expressions may reflect African practice: *yard ax*, 'poorly trained irregular preacher,' and its synonym *table tapper* have been recorded chiefly in the Georgetown and Charleston areas and in the Santee Valley; *huhu owl*, 'hoot owl, large owl,' is found occasionally in the South Carolina coastal plain; *bloody-noun*, 'large bullfrog' (cf. Gullah [blʌdɪnɒn]), has been recorded in the Santee and Savannah valleys, and along the coast from Georgetown to the Florida line.[23] Not recorded in the Atlas but commonly considered to be of Negro origin are such metaphors as *sweet-mouth*, 'to flatter,' and *bad-mouth*, 'to curse.'[24]

From Negroes -- whether the form is in origin an Africanism or a relic of early English usage -- many white folk speakers along the South Carolina coast have taken *for* as the particle with the infinitive of purpose, as *he come for tell you* rather than the standard *to* or the widespread folk form *for to*. It may possibly be that the Negro playmates of well-to-do white children (especially boys) and the Negro servants to whom they have been accustomed are at least partially responsible for the more frequent occurrence and the higher degree of cultural tolerance for nonstandard forms in cultured speech in the South than elsewhere.[25] In phonology, many white folk informants in and near the Gullah country use the bilabial /f,v/ [Φ,β] or replace both /v,w/ by one bilabial voiced spirant [β], as in Gullah (Turner 1949:241-42). Perhaps the greater tendency in Southern speech to simplify final consonant clusters is encouraged by the fact that Gullah and African languages have relatively less complex final clusters than English dialects in other parts of the United States. Furthermore, the striking intonation patterns noticed in such communities as Charleston and Georgetown suggest the possibility that Negro influence in this feature might well be investigated.

With so much apparent, the next step is to plan future work. Herskovits (1941: 327-37) has already made suggestions as to places to be investigated and types of linguistic investigation to be conducted. To these one might make a few additions. Americo-Liberian English should be studied, to see both the extent of reacculturation to Africa and the survivals of traits of Southern American English.[26] One should investigate such old Negro communities outside the South as the Dowagiac-Cassopolis area in Michigan or Dresden in Ontario (both settled by refugee slaves brought out of the South along the Underground Railroad) or the relics of the New Brunswick settlements by the slaves of New York Loyalists and the Nova Scotia settlements by Jamaica Negroes (Herskovits 1941:94). For controls -- communities where relic forms might be expected to occur, but where Negro influence is improbable -- we should have an early survey of Newfoundland, and intensive study of selected communities in the Maritime Provinces and of the Banks Islands on the North Carolina coast between Manteo and Wilmington. Furthermore, in community studies where Negroes are interviewed, the field worker should not only interview representatives of several age groups and educational groups, but should also make a selection in terms of the number of generations the families of informants have been resident in the community.

In this way it should be possible to establish a procedure for determining whether a form found among Negroes in the South is likely to be African or folk English in origin. The investigator should check its occurrence in Newfoundland, the Banks Islands, New Hampshire and Maine, Cape Ann, Cape Cod and the offshore islands -- all known to be relic areas without probable Negro influence. If the form is found in the latter communities, whether or not it is found in the British Isles, it is reasonable to suspect that its etymon is not African, though one may concede a reinforcement by African influence.[27] Conversely, forms not found in such communities but found, say, in Gullah and Papiamento probably have African origins.

As with many other aspects of dialect investigation, the half century of investigations of Negro speech and its affiliations with white speech has left many questions unanswered. But it has provided a framework within which these questions can be both asked and answered more intelligently than heretofore.[28] The linguistic scientist has learned not to look down upon other forms of speech that happen to differ from his own; he can hope that the public will cease to look down upon the speech of those whose skin pigmentation or hair form may be different, or to fancy any necessary correlation between the pigmentation of a speaker's skin and the phonemic system of his dialect.

ADDENDUM[29]

The suggestion that a wide range of evidence be drawn on before sweeping conclusions are reached is still useful. However, in the last decade, what with the profit in poverty for educational entrepreneurs, the most sweeping generalizations have been drawn by those who would assert African or creole substrata and deny that features of British or Irish dialects of the seventeenth century might be better preserved among American Negroes than among their white counterparts, or indeed among Southern Americans of all races than among speakers of other regional varieties of American English.

Part of the difficulty has risen from the practical nature of most recent research, e.g. the attempt to provide better teaching materials in the expanded Black Belts of northern and western cities. Investigators have assumed "Standard English" to be the prestigious local varieties in such metropolitan areas, and have largely ignored the existence of Southern varieties of standard speech, some of which, as in Richmond, Charleston and New Orleans, antedated even the founding of Chicago. The delay in obtaining funds for editing the Linguistic Atlas materials, where a certain amount of comparable evidence is available, makes it difficult to evaluate the more extreme statements; and indeed, the situation in which the Linguistic Atlas records were made in the 1930's, before the days of lightweight high fidelity recording apparatus, curtailed the amount of syntactic evidence that could be recorded. In many discussions of varieties of nonstandard English spoken by Negroes, it appears that the grammatical details -- especially the syntactic -- provide the most striking contrasts to the standard English spoken by educated whites in northern metropolitan areas. But it is far from clear that these stigmata are reliable for determining the race of the speaker when one exa-

mines the casual speech of educated upper-class white Southerners, let alone their lower-class compatriots. Most of the recent large-scale investigations were conducted by Northerners in terms of the needs of Northern constituencies.

Along with more intensive investigations of Southern white speech, on all social levels, the suggestions of Labov that one must investigate a range of personal styles, for each informant, could be profitably followed. In his biographical study of George Wallace (1968) and in his more recent portrait of Congressman L. Mendel Rivers for *Life* (1970), Marshall Frady presents his subjects as using in their informal speech (and for Wallace, even from the platform) a wide range of grammatical features putatively associated with "Black English," such as the lack of inflections for noun plural and genitive, for verb preterite and participle and third-singular present indicative, and the absence of the present of the copula *to be* where standard English would expect it with participles, predicate nouns, and predicate adjectives. I myself have observed these features in radio broadcasts of interviews with Wallace.[30] In fact, my wife and her professional colleagues have observed that the absence of the copula is very common in my own speech when I am talking informally to my peers. I have also observed the same phenomena among my contemporaries in South Carolina and in the speech of my Tennessee-reared daughter. Furthermore, though this is as yet only intuitive (and thus properly suspect), there seems to be a greater difference between formal and casual speech in the South than there is in other regions.

In informal conversation at a conference at Tuskegee Institute (1968) James Sledd remarked on the difficulty of reaching a definitive solution on the extent of creole language influence on the dialects of Negro Americans. A person would need a detailed knowledge, not only of African languages and creoles and pidgins, but synchronic and diachronic variations of English and several Romance languages as well. And one cannot overlook the definite evidence from Early Modern English, from more recent Irish English, and from other dialects (such as Newfoundland[31] and the Upland American South) where creole influence is improbable. Some of this comparative evidence has been made available in recent work by Lawrence M. Davis (1970, 1971); more of it will be found in the M.A. thesis of Solveig Greibeslund (1970), a detailed comparison of the field records of three pairs of Negro and white informants of comparable education and economic status, and in the dissertation of Raymond K. O'Cain (1972), a sociolinguistic study of Charleston, South Carolina.[32] Also one must take very seriously the evidence gathered by Juanita Williamson and her colleagues and students in Memphis. A Negro American who has spent two decades in studying the speech of her community, Miss Williamson is extremely skeptical of the possibility that "Black English" has any peculiarities other than what might be explained by the normal processes of cultural lag. Although in her dissertation on Negro speech in Memphis (1968), and since, she has systematically looked for the Africanisms which Turner found surviving in Gullah, she has found none so far.

As William M. Austin suggested, many of the significant differences between the speech of Negroes and that of whites may not be linguistic at all. But the experience of white Southerners in Northern communities suggests that even paralanguage may not be a completely reliable marker. Austin and others also suggest that some of the more accurate intuitive judgments depend on resonances caused by anatomical differences. All of these possibilities, and more, must be looked into before the record can be adequate.

Whatever the final scholarly conclusions, one is, of course, faced with the fact that in many American communities, including most of the metropolitan areas of the North and West, there are large bodies of Negroes, poor and uneducated, whose speech patterns differ strikingly from those of local upper-class whites. Regardless of the ultimate origin of these dialectal differences, school systems are faced with the practical problem of providing better education, including better programs in reading and writing. Indeed, teachers and administrators and local molders of opinion could almost always profit from greater respect for speechways different from their own, whether the speaker is a Harlem junkie or a Texas president.[33]

NOTES

[1] The most widely publicized arguments for the alledgedly childlike mentality of the Negro and of his general inferiority are Dowd 1926 and Tillinghast 1902. Even so sympathetic a student of the Negro as Howard Odum accepted the stereotype of Negro inferiority in his early work, *Social and Mental Traits of the Negro* (1910).

[2] Myrdal 1944:965, "There is absolutely no biological basis for it [Negro dialect]; Negroes are as capable of pronouncing English words perfectly as whites are . . . ."

[3] Allen Walker Read, drawing from the advertisements for runaway slaves, throws a clear light on the process of the Negroes' learning of English (1939). He concludes, p. 258: "The present study shows that during colonial times there were Negroes in all stages of proficiency in their knowledge of English: a constant stratum of recently arrived ones without any English, those who were learning English during their first years in the new country, and a group who had learned successfully. The Negroes born in this country invariably used, according to these records, good English. The colored race were faced, against their will, with a huge problem in adopting a new language in a strange country, and their success, in the light of their opportunities, was equal to that of any other immigrant body."

[4] The generation after the Confederate War also witnessed the last period of European colonial expansion at the expense of the nonwhite races, the period in which the Nordic myth was so widely publicized by Gobineau, Chamberlain, Madison Grant in his *The Passing of the Great Race* (1916), and Homer Lea in his *The Day of the Saxon* (1912), and in which European imperialism was rationalized by Kipling and others as benign paternalism -- "the white man's burden."

[5] Much of what has been popularly labeled as "Southern speech," such as the dialects of the southern Appalachians, is properly not Southern at all, but South Midland, derivative from Pennsylvania. "The common notion of a linguistic Mason and Dixon's Line separating "Northern" from "Southern" speech is simply due to an erroneous inference from an oversimplified version of the political history of the nineteenth century . . . ."(Kurath 1949:vi). See also R. McDavid 1950a,b.

[6] Gullah is the creolized variety of English spoken by the descendants of Negro slaves in the area of rice, indigo, and Sea Island cotton plantations along the South Carolina and Georgia coasts. The term *Geechee* is sometimes used, either as a synonym for Gullah or as a designation for the Gullah spoken in Georgia.

[49]

[7] To some extent it has been used by elocutionists and their satellites to shame cultured Southerners -- into giving up their own dialectal patterns in favor of Southern British, Eastern New England, or whatever dialect the elocutionist speaks or sets up as a model of elegance. For the same motive -- a desire to depart from the regional patterns of the other race -- plus the identification of eastern New England with abolitionism and other efforts to break the caste system in the South, educated Southern Negroes sometimes model their own speech on that of eastern New England. Likewise, some Negro school systems are inclined to favor such New England speech characteristics as the [ɑɪðɚ, nɑɪðɚ] forms of *either*, *neither*, and the so-called 'broad a' [a, ɑ] forms of *half past*, *dance*, *grass*, etc.

[8] One must always use Wright with caution, since a large part of the evidence on which both the *Grammar* and the *Dictionary* are based was collected by amateurs with uneven training and without any systematic procedure. The unevenness of the results can readily be perceived if one attempts to chart for the British Isles the vocabulary variants which Kurath's *Word Geography of the Eastern United States* (1949) indicates as significant for the Atlantic Seaboard. For instance, of the variety of terms for the earthworm which Kurath has found representative of major or minor American dialect areas -- and of which most must have been found in the British Isles -- only *angledog* and *eaceworm* are recorded in Wright.
In selecting his American sources Brooks likewise shows a lack of discrimination. The part of Georgia in which Harris grew up was not near the Alabama line but in the eastern part of the state. Both Alabama and inland Georgia were areas of tertiary -- or at best secondary -- settlement, whose settlers came from areas where dialect mixture already had occurred. Finally, the informant whose speech is represented in Harris's stories may not have been representative of any variety of Georgia speech since Uncle Remus speaks of himself as having been raised in Virginia, or "Ferginny" as he would say it.

[9] "Slovenly and careless of speech, these Gullahs seized upon the peasant English used by some of the early settlers and by the white servants of the wealthier colonists, wrapped their clumsy tongues about it as well as they could, and, enriched with certain expressive African words, it issued through their flat noses and thick lips as so workable a form of speech that it was gradually adopted by the other slaves . . ."(Gonzales 1922: 10). "Simple language concepts of the unseasoned slaves . . . with their simple dialects . . ." (Crum 1940:113).

[10] We encountered this reaction in Dresden, Ontario, in the summer of 1950. In the spring of 1949 there had been local controversy over discrimination against Negroes in restaurants and barber shops, a situation which was widely publicized by the Canadian press and utilized by Communist front organizations for their own ends. Although some of the younger leaders of the Negro community were sympathetic to the purposes of the Atlas, efforts

to interview older Negroes were unsuccessful, because the community was sensitive about the type of publicity it had already received.

[11] Lorenzo D. Turner reports that his earlier Gullah records contained far fewer Africanisms -- especially the African-derived personal names -- than his later ones. See Turner 1949:12.

[12] I found among Negro informants a somewhat greater willingness than among whites to accept as authentic the responses suggested by the field worker, no matter how deliberately far-fetched some of these suggestions might be. On the other hand, I found at least one Negro informant who conformed to the traditional stereotype of Negro speech during the part of the interview conducted in the presence of his white patron, but who abandoned that role when we were alone [RIM].

[13] Myrdal was chosen as director of the project because Sweden is a nation without colonies, and therefore without institutionalized attitudes toward the nonwhite races. The Negro problem is summarized in *An American Dilemna* (1944); no person unfamiliar with this book can claim to 'know the Negro.' Herskovits's *The Myth of the Negro Past* (1941) is one of the special studies prepared for the project.

[14] Greenberg 1941, 1955; Hodge 1944, 1947; Welmers 1946, 1949a, 1949b, 1950a, 1950b; Welmers and Harris 1942. [Since 1951 such studies have multiplied.]

[15] The availability of accurate data on the actual speech of the Atlantic Seaboard has enabled scholars to make intelligent approaches to the problems of 'literary dialect' -- to interpreting the devices through which poets and novelists attempt to represent regional or local speech by respellings in the conventional alphabet. Four recent doctoral dissertations treat this problem, making use of Atlas data to discover the kind of dialect the writer was trying to represent: by James N. Tidwell (Ohio State, 1948), on literary representations of Southern speech; by Sumner Ives (Texas, 1950), on the dialect of the Uncle Remus stories; by James W. Downer (Michigan, 1958), on the dialect of the *Biglow Papers*; and by Charles W. Foster (Alabama, 1971), on the stories of Charles W. Chesnutt.

[16] Evidence that the American Negro stems from an advanced cultural background in Africa and has managed to preserve significant traits from that background does not help the case of those who attempt to rationalize discriminatory practices as justified by Negro cultural and psychological inferiority.

[17] This uniformity is attested both in Turner's own field records and in corroborative recordings made for Kurath by Dr. Guy S. Lowman, Jr., principal field investigator for the Linguistic Atlas.

[18] William Gilmore Simms, whose representations of dialect are rather accurate, regularly indicates quasi-Gullah characteristics of the speech

of Negro huntsmen, stable-boys, and field hands. But in *Katherine Walton* (1850-51), in which most of the action takes place in Charleston, he properly indicates no 'dialect' forms in the speech of a Negro butler and major-domo, who would normally speak the standard English of Charleston.

[19] The sentences here following are closely paraphrased or quoted from R. McDavid 1950a. See also Kurath 1972.

[20] *Pinto* is used chiefly for the old-fashioned hexagonal coffin (occasionally pentagonal, with the omission of the footboard); informants often explain the name by commenting that the narrowness of the coffin pins the corpse's toes together -- a spurious etymology which was seldom questioned prior to Turner's investigations.

[21] Turner does not list *takky*, 'horse,' generally recorded along the South Carolina coast in the form *marsh takky*, and often supposed to be of African origin. Presumably the proposed African etyma are dubious.

[22] It would have been very useful if Turner had indicated the geographical distribution within the Gullah country of each lexical item, including personal names. In an earlier report (Turner 1941:73), he suggested that groups of words and names traceable to particular African languages were found clustered in particular Gullah communities, and that this geographical distribution can be correlated with the pattern of slave settlement.

[23] An onomatopoetic variant /budidəŋk, -duŋk/ seems to be confined to the Georgetown area.

[24] Such phrases as *put the mouth on*, 'hex,' are also frequently heard, and are considered to be of Negro origin.

[25] Nearly every cultivated informant interviewed in South Carolina and Georgia used *ain't* at some time during the interview. In fact, one of the touchstones often used by Southerners to distinguish the genuine cultured speaker from the pretenders is that the latter are too socially insecure to know the proper occasions for using *ain't*, the double negative, and other such folk forms, and hence avoid them altogether.

[26] Welmers reports many speech forms in Americo-Liberian that have been recorded for the Linguistic Atlas in the South Atlantic States.

[27] Mathews 1948 attempts to derive the folk term *doney*, 'sweetheart,' through a Gullah personal name from the latter's suggested African etymon,

Bambara [doni] 'a burden.' However, the Linguistic Atlas records *doney* most frequently in areas where there is least reason to suspect Negro influence: the Shenandoah Valley and central and western North Carolina. Similarly, despite the absence of an attested Middle English etymon, it seems improbable that *tote*, 'carry,' is exclusively of African origin, since *tote*, 'haul,' is well attested in areas of New England and the inland North outside the area of probable Negro influence, along with such compounds as *tote-road*, *tote-sled*, *tote-wagon*, and *tote-team*.

[28] Mencken 1936:112-13 accepted the earlier theory of the paucity of African survivals in American Negro speech. However, by 1945, Turner's work had enabled him to revise his judgment.

[29] This Addendum was prepared especially for the reprinting of the article in Wolfram and Clarke 1971.

[30] Conversely, Southern connoisseurs of platform oratory have remarked that the rhetorical style of my *Landsmann* Jesse Jackson is ironically reminiscent of that of the late Eugene Talmadge and Theodore M. Bilbo.

[31] The study of the speech of Carbonear, Newfoundland, by Harold Paddock (1966) reveals a systematic inflectional difference between the present and the timeless non-past; he reports to me that essentially all of the stigmata in Fasold and Wolfram 1970 are found in Newfoundland folk speech, though of course not every feature occurs in every village. The hundreds of taped interviews, on folklore and local history, in the archives of Memorial University of Newfoundland constitute a priceless if relatively unexploited resource.

[32] O'Cain does not ignore the existence of upper-class speech, both white and Negro, representing well-established cultural traditions in the community.

[33] As custodian of the Linguistic Atlas archives for the Atlantic Seaboard, I offer a *mea culpa* for not having made the data generally accessible; but perhaps I am exculpated by the lack of funds or clerical assistance. I hope for better things, and meanwhile intend to produce the evidence on all points where the Atlas can speak. [With support from the National Endowment for the Humanities for both the *Linguistic Atlas of the Middle and South Atlantic States* (Kurath *et al.* 1979-) and the *Linguistic Atlas of the North-Central States* (Marckwardt *et al.* 1980-), the situation may soon be remedied.]

In a recent communication to *Language* (1960), my friend Professor Whatmough of Harvard expresses his qualms about this conference, lest it simply duplicate the operations of the already established Congresses of Linguistics. Sharing his concern that learned organizations, to retain their integrity, must not simply emulate the Parkinsonian habits of government bureaus and multiply with more than amoeban fertility but must demonstrate some fundamental purpose and communtiy of interest, I feel that it is incumbent upon us to define our aims and purposes so rigorously as to convince even the most skeptical. And since our aims and purposes and methods have been often called into question in the recent past, as unsuited to the complex urban society in which many of us already live and toward which the world is obviously moving, it behooves us to reexamine not only the nature of our discipline but the nature of the society in which we must find ourselves working in the future, to see both how we can continue to do effective work and what our discipline may be able to contribute toward making our society better for ourselves and for those to come.

Our point of reference here, as in so many other instances, is the basic definition of a language, as formulated by Sturtevant and Herskovits and others: "A language is a system of arbitrary vocal signals, by means of which a social group cooperate and interact and transmit their culture." This is a definition which, without disparaging the humanistic affiliations of linguistic study, clearly asserts for linguistics its position as the most scientific of the social sciences -- those disciplines which deal with the behavior of human beings in their relationships to one another. Starting from this, it takes no involved casuistry to reach the conclusion that dialectology is the branch, or application, of linguistics where the affiliations with other social sciences can be most clearly demonstrated. For dialectology is the study of the dynamics of language -- of the variations in the details of patterns, and ultimately in the patterns themselves, in response to population movements, political organization, economic growth, family relationships, educational opportunities, new habits of diet and medical care and entertainment, and all the other complex human activities. It is the corrective, if you will, for the neat and elegant but often sterile formulae which ignore the fundamental truth that a living speech is bound to be undergoing constant change, and in the process to be exhibiting areas of tension and uncertainty symptomatic of impending reformulation of the system. Of this, with its particular applications to American dialectology, I have spoken in the past and will speak again in the future; here, let it suffice that as dialectologists we must take as given the changes in a language in response to the changes in the culture in which the language is used, and set out to record those changes.

Our problem, then, is to define the nature of the society in which we are destined to live and work, to indicate the ways in which changes in this society may affect the phenomena with which we deal, to assess the charges that have been made recently against the traditional procedures of dialectologists, to reappraise our methods, and -- having done that -- to point out directions in which we may encourage our students to go.

The first characteristic of our society that we must recognize is *industrialization*: the application of large-scale power sources to the large-scale efficient production of means of sustenance and of both capital and consumer goods. It is not a new force, for it goes back at least as far as the development of the steam engine, but it has been enormously accentuated in recent years. Its most spectacular manifestation is the gigantic heavy-industry complex of Detroit or Essen or Magnitogorsk, but it permeates the whole system of production, through the light-industry manufacture of textiles and toys to the mechanization of agriculture, under whatever economic system. In every society the trend is toward the employment of a smaller proportion of workers in sustenance work -- in the provision of basic food and clothing and shelter requirements -- so that more can be occupied in producing the instruments of a higher standard of living and in providing the administrative and educational and professional services that such a higher standard will in turn demand. The automation of a factory that turns out automobile parts is a more spectacular manifestation, but only another manifestation, of the same process by which a steel plowshare replaces a wooden one, enables one plowman to do the work which two formerly did, and releases the other one for work in a factory.

The second characteristic of our society is *urbanization*. Urbanization proceeds from industrialization, and in turn creates the opportunities and demand for more of it. The modern foundry or factory, no matter how well provided with labor-saving machinery, demands the work of thousands of minds and bodies, to bring raw materials, to tend the machines, and to dispatch the finished products on their way. And no matter how successful we are in moving people from their homes to places of work -- a problem that the rush-hour traffic congestion in the metropolitan areas of the United States suggests we are far from solving completely -- it is still more convenient for the workman to live relatively near his place of work. And as new residential areas develop around new centers of industry, new service areas develop to provide the residents with shopping, educational, medical and entertainment facilities; the expanding population attracts new industries, and the process goes on. The superficial statistics of the decline in the population of the central cities should not distract our attention from the general expansion of urbanized areas. After all, the process of urban dispersal is not a new one; for New York City it began more than a century ago, for London and Paris even earlier. Not all of these urbanized areas will be earthly paradises -- the extent to which the amenities of our civilization are generally available will depend upon the technological advance of the region where these urban areas are located -- but the conscience of the world and the political alertness of the peoples concerned make it unlikely that the unhealthy slums of the early part of the Industrial Revolution can ever be recreated with impunity.

This brings us to the third characteristic of our society: *mass education*. It is abhorred by the conscious heirs of the genteel tradition, who find the schoolrooms concerned with matters beneath the dignity of a gentleman; it is undoubtedly abused by many of its proponents, who confuse the social custody of hordes of young with the process of providing intellectual stimulation for everyone according to the limits of his ability. But it is here to stay; it springs from the needs of an industrialized and urbanized society, and it provides in turn the stimulus for more industrialization and urbanization. The amiable and intelligent illiterate (often the leader in the older rural community), the strong back and weak brain that characterized the typical laborer sought by the early organizers of heavy industry -- these are now obsolete. The complexity of the new machinery of production and distribution and communication, from the corn-picker to the television camera, requires not only the practical experience

and intuitive intelligence that have always been the marks of skilled labor, but the disciplined knowledge of the craft, and the ability to keep up with further advances. Furthermore, the skilled laborer will not only become more skilled, but must constitute a larger proportion of the working force, as the traditional unskilled and menial occupations take less and less of the time of a smaller and smaller proportion of the population. The typical worker of the future, we can imagine, must be able to read well, to think in scientific terms, and to understand the implications of his work and thought and feelings in terms of his community, which will no longer be a village or even a nation, but the world at large. It is not sheer utopianism that leads us to foresee the possibility of a society beyond the dreams of Plato, where the philosopher class will embrace the entire citizenry and the machines will be the efficient and obedient serfs of everyone.

As we move hopefully toward such a world -- something neither Huxleyan nor Orwellian nor even Wellsian -- what will we find happening to the phenomena of dialect, to the features of pronunciation and grammar and vocabulary that distinguish one variety of a language from another? As Patrick Henry once said in other connections, we can judge what may happen only in the light of what has happened, and it is well to recapitulate the kinds of changes we have all seen taking place, from the beginning of time.

First, a society such as we envisage will inevitably be one in which geographical and social mobility are the norm rather than the exception. The history of such mobility is one of blunting the sharpness of dialect differences, as we see by comparing the dialects of North American English with those of British English, the dialects of the western United States with those of the Atlantic Seaboard, the dialects of twentieth-century Germany with those of the nineteenth. We can look to the disappearance of many relic areas, the attrition of the others, to a blurring of all kinds of dialect boundaries, and a diminution of differences.

Second, an urbanized and industrialized society will see the gradual disappearance of many items of the traditional folk vocabulary. As butchering, meat processing, canning and cheese-making, for instance, shift from the home kitchen to the factory, fewer people will know the language of the craft, and most people will be acquainted with only the commercial names of the finished products. As processes undergo a fundamental change, whole areas of activity will disappear from the everyday vocabulary. The mechanization of agriculture is a typical example. The introduction of the tractor has eliminated the whole vocabulary of harness and horse-drawn vehicles, to say nothing of materially altering the terminology of fertilizing the land; the combine has eliminated the sheaf and the stock, the haybaler has done the same for the haycock and the stack. The commercialized forms of mass entertainment have wreaked havoc on popular amusements, and not even the rites of passage have escaped the interference of the professional entrepreneur. As any American field worker knows, the investigation of some parts of the traditional folk vocabulary will even now, and from even the oldest informants, often provoke the comment: "This is something I haven't talked about for twenty years." And we can foresee only an accentuation of this process in the future.

Finally, the dissemination of education is bound to have its effect. This will be felt most sharply in the field of grammar, as the forms most definitely associated with the uneducated folk become replaced by those with a greater aura of real or imagined social prestige. This effect is already in evidence in the United States, where the folk verb forms are rarely encountered, even from the least educated, in the neighborhood of New York or Boston or Philadelphia. But it is also manifested, not only in the elimination of folk grammar but also in the loss of homely words and their replacement by general ones, and in the disappearance of many old-fashioned pronunciations such as /dɪf/ 'deaf.' And we can expect the same trend everywhere, from Iceland to Indonesia, as our world draws closer together, as education becomes more widely disseminated, and as new national states develop their standard languages from prestigious dialects.

As we stand facing the probable changes in the status of dialects, we find ourselves confronted with two mutually contradictory criticisms of our work, especially of the linguistic atlases recently published or currently in progress.

Both of these, I feel strongly, ignore the ends of a linguistic atlas, as I shall point out later; but it is well that we take both points of view into account.

The first point of view is that the atlases, and by inference all the work of scientific dialectology, ignore the heart of the folk speech -- that by using a selected questionnaire, selected informants, and selected communities, we do not get the really colorful dialect materials. From almost every community investigated the essentially justifiable complaint arises that we have omitted some of the most pertinent expressions of the local idiom, or that we have failed to consider a whole species of locally important discourse, such as that of sheep-herders, hard-rock miners, salmon fishers, or used-car salesmen. For these critics, our questionnaires are too short, and our em-phasis on the folk environment is insufficient.

The second point of view is that of the modernist, whether high-church structuralist or sociological statistician. These critics would discard the evidence of the linguistic atlases because most of them are phonetic rather than phonemic in their notation, because they include too many items from a pre-industrial rural culture, because they include representatives of too few social groups, and because they ignore the dynamics of population movement by insisting on native-born speakers of the communities whose speech is being recorded.

To this audience, it were tediously repetitious to engage in a detailed refutation of such diametrically opposed criticisms. But since we are speaking not merely to each other but to the larger audience concerned with our discipline and its implications, there can be no better place to assert that we accept these criticisms, and their implications, on the part of dialectology as a whole, while denying their necessary validity for the aims and methods of a linguistic atlas *per se*.

In actuality, as we know, there is a vast difference between the methods of the oldest and the newest linguistic atlases, and their methods have been constantly refined to take care of increasing knowledge about the complexities of linguistic processes and about the social and cultural forces behind them. From simple inquiries as to the nature and location of dialect boundaries whose existence had been previously recognized, we have progressed to the search for unknown boundaries and to the explanation of boundaries hitherto known and unknown. Older touchstones turn out to be invalid, and hitherto unsuspected differences appear. But throughout the process of refinement it has always been clear that even the most elaborate linguistic atlas can only provide a frame of reference against which further questions may be asked, and not the answers to everything.

Thus a linguistic atlas, as a frame of reference, must be historically oriented. To take the situation in the United States as an example, the American atlas project aims to trace the affiliations of American dialects with each other, and with the dialects -- standard and folk and intermediate -- of the British Isles. Since historical affiliations are often shown most clearly by relic areas, old and uneducated informants, and the parts of the vocabulary reflecting the Wordsworthian concern with humble and rustic life, it is not surprising that these parts of the inquiry should be represented beyond what might be suggested by a coldly random statistical analysis. But no linguistic atlas can sanely hope to discover all relic forms surviving everywhere among all classes of speakers. Similarly, the American situation being what it is, we need to search for regional differences in cultivated speech, to examine the intermediate types of speech between uneducated and cultivated, and to formulate some general statements about the relationships between the three types. But because no two communities will have exactly the same social structure, we cannot hope to take care, simultaneously, of all the kinds of social differences in language that may be found in every conceivable community: a fixed number of types will be unrealistically small for some communities but as unrealistically large for others. And by the same token, though the notations of pronunciation in an atlas can probably sort out the distribution of the important structural types of dialects that have already been discovered, they cannot be depended on to to discover new ones, since the critical contrasting pairs may not be included in the questionnaire. But even here the traditional methods may be more useful than their critics will allow: an impressionistic phonetic transcription can permit the discovery of areas of uncertainty which may be probed for new structural contrasts, but (once defined) a rigorously structured phonemic notation -- whether a tragerization or anything else -- will not permit the *discovery* of new contrasts in new dialects, but only the *assignment of incidence* for the contrasts it recognizes.

Let us then concede the incompleteness of any conceivable linguistic atlas, and the necessity of repeating the survey every generation or so, to discover new trends of linguistic change and to test the progress of the trends made evident by an earlier survey. It should surprise no one if cataclysmic economic and political and social and cultural changes, like those of the first half of this century, should have blunted the force of earlier trends, and set entirely new ones in motion. As scientists and as perceptive human beings, we should be prepared for changes like these.

But in any event, a general linguistic atlas, no matter how often it goes over the ground, is but the first stage of dialect work, the general frame of historical reference for the interpretation of future work. To rest content with it would be only a degree less naive than the observation of the Georgia lady who assured me that no investigation of Southern speech was necessary, since it had been definitively recorded in Margaret Mitchell's historical novel *Gone with the Wind* (1936). A linguistic atlas, a whole series of linguistic atlases, is but the first stage of the dialectology of an area. It is in the performance of the second stage that our discipline must

prove itself, by turning to its advantage the objections of our critics and by seeking to chart systematically the regional and social differences in linguistic phenomena (and other phenomena of communication as well) as they become identified. What I say will be most apposite to the situation in the United States, where primary settlement was completed only at the close of the last century and where our tradition of scientific dialectology is a very recent one, with nothing to show for itself like the long series of German monographs. But if our work in the United States takes its models and inspiration from our European predecessors, it may have something to repay in terms of suggestions for future investigations, particularly in those countries which like the United States have changed recently and rapidly from an agrarian to an industrial society.

1. The first priority, to complement the charting of dialect developments over wide areas, would necessarily be the intensive study of relatively small areas. Until very recently, most such studies have been organized in *diachronic* terms, with something like the sounds of Chaucerian English, British Received Pronunciation, or alleged 'General American' as the norm against which the phonology of the particular dialect is compared. The current need is for *synchronic* orientation, with each dialect or group of related dialects described as a system -- true, an open-ended and evolving system, with many areas of uncertainty, but a system nevertheless -- in terms of its own phenomena. There are few such local studies, and many more are needed.

Just what kinds of areas should be investigated in such studies? As Leonard Bloomfield once said in another connection, it really doesn't matter, since we have so few systematic local studies of any kind. But naturally one thinks of the opportunities for investigating in detail such relatively large but backward areas as the Ozarks or 'Egypt' in southern Illinois, where upland Southern settlement has undergone the traditional decay of small-scale American agriculture, within 'Egypt' another cycle of prosperity and decay as the small farms gave way to coal mining, and new possibilities of prosperity with the discovery of oil and the industrialization of the Ohio Valley. Such an investigation might be different in scale and scope, but hardly different in aim from the investigations one would like to see conducted in such smaller relic areas as the Irish fishing community on Beaver Island (Lake Michigan), Cape Ann in Massachusetts, the peninsulas of Chesapeake Bay, the Outer Banks islands of eastern North Carolina, or the Negro communities of southern Ontario, originally settled by fugitive slaves from the South. Almost any dialectologist in any country can think of his favorite relic areas with an interesting cultural background but a precarious future as the automobile, television, and the mail-order catalog threaten to eradicate the last vestiges of their traditional isolation. Nevertheless, the emphasis on relic areas should not deter other students from investigating the rise of new prestigious dialects in focal areas, whether the older metropolitan centers of Europe and Asia, the traditional centers of American colonial culture along the Atlantic Seaboard, the new industrial centers such as Manchester or Cleveland or Atlanta, or the most recent by-products of rapid industrialization like Akron or Magnitogorsk. Furthermore, we need detailed studies of transition areas -- such as those classical models by German dialectologists -- to help us sort out the isoglosses of established dialect boundaries and to estimate the direction of shift. Little has been done of this kind in the United States, in comparison with the number of problems posed by the recent settlement and the repeated changes in trading practices and in avenues of communication. It is probable that proposed investigations in the Mississippi Valley will show as great a spreading of the isoglosses as those in the Rhineland. Would perhaps the same be true in the lower Danube or Dnieper? Nor should we confine our attention to monolingual communities alone. In the United States we have models in the studies of Pennsylvania German, Wisconsin Norwegian, Texas Spanish, and American Czech bilingual communities; in Canada, the plotting of vestiges of bilingualism in so-called 'Lunenburg Dutch,' the variety of English spoken by the descendants of eighteenth-century German colonists. But opportunities for bilingual research exist among us in such metropolitan centers as Montreal, entrenched peasant societies like the Acadian French of Louisiana, isolated immigrant enclaves like the older Canadian French settlements in northern Illinois or more recent Ukranian communities in western Canada. We can even produce interesting, if elusive and vanishing, developments like the gemeinslavische *koiné* (popularly known as 'Slahvish') that has developed in our heavy-industry areas as a means of intercommunication among Poles, Czechs, Slovenes, Serbs, Croats, and Ukranians; we know that it exists and have vague ideas about its structure, but we have not yet studied it. How much more varied and complicated must be the multilingual dialectology of Europe and Asia!

2. Another type of second-stage investigation is the intensive geographically-oriented investigation of particular aspects of the language. Under Cassidy's inspiration we are just beginning the serious investigation in depth of the American dialect lexicon. Cassidy's own investigations of the folk vocabulary of Wisconsin are probably the furthest advanced, with publication probable within a few years;[1] a good study has been made of the eastern Alabama Negro vocabulary; the investigations in Newfoundland are also well along, and similar areas -- where a single investigator can hope to do a reasonably competent study in a reasonable time -- have been marked out for detailed surveys in various parts of the United States. Intensive examinations of grammatical differences have been proposed, though one can readily see problems in organizing and directing them. C. K. Thomas has shown what can be done with the massive accumulation of data on a relatively few phonological items; Robert Stockwell has proposed a scheme for investigating structural differences in phonology, and several critical phonemic oppositions have been recently investigated for their social significance in metropolitan Paris. Whatever the defects of these projects, as so far conducted, they provide a kind of data we have never had before, and suggest in new ways the complexity of the phenomena we are dealing with. Perhaps all these depth phenomena would be best started on a regional or local basis, but any of these should be capable of indefinite expansion, as it proves itself and as others become interested.

3. As our society becomes more urbanized, it would seem desirable for dialectologists to pay more attention to the urban vocabulary, and to the innovations that arise in urban centers. Too often we wait until an urban innovation has become almost a relic before we notice it; but alert dialectologists should be able to notice some of these innovations as they arise. In fact, it should not be impossible to develop a lexical investigation of peculiarly urban aspects of the vocabulary and with cultural aspects of the machine age, including such items as these:

a) As petroleum products and the internal combustion engine play an ever greater role in our society, local differences have developed, even in the face of mass-media advertising. Alongside such familiar contrasts between British and American usage as *petrol* and *gasoline*, *paraffin* and *kerosene*, we have such well-defined American regional terms for kerosene as *coal oil* (also the prevailing Canadian term), *carbon oil*, and *lamp oil*. The *shoulder* of a highway may be the *berm* (or British *verge*). The *limited-access highway* (as legislation has it) may be a *superhighway* or a *parkway* or (if a fee is required for using it) a *turnpike*, *thruway*, *tollway*, or a *toll road*. The *center strip* dividing the lanes of such a highway may be a *boulevard*, a *berm*, or a *median*. A highway *underpass*, under railroad or road, may become a *subway*. The clustering of garages, restaurants, gasoline stations and public toilets on such a highway becomes a *service plaza*, *service area*, or *oasis*, and highway patrolmen and their vehicles operate under various local designations, many of them not generally known.

b) Within cities there has developed a bewildering variety of terminology in addition to the traditional *street*: *avenue*, *boulevard*, *drive*, *place*, *parkway*, *circle*, *court*, *crescent*, and the like; sometimes these terms are applied haphazardly, at the whims of local politicians and real-estate entrepreneurs, but at other times they may reflect a real hierarchical difference. The paved walkway alongside a street is generally a *sidewalk* in the United States, but in the Philadelphia and Savannah areas a *pavement*, reflecting British usage, and in the New Orleans area a *banquette*. At least in residential areas, it is customary to have a grass strip between the sidewalk and the curb of the street; such a strip may lack any designation, or it may be known as a *parking strip*, *treelawn*, *boulevard*, *parkway*, or *neutral ground*. The distance between two parallel streets, or the area bounded by four streets, may be a *block* or a *square*; in Chicago a *block* (or, more specifically *long block*) is canonically an eighth of a mile, a *short block* just half as long. In Chicago, the traditional American *vacant lot* is still often called a *prairie*.

c) The designations of kinds of buildings also differ from city to city. A small *neighborhood store*, somewhat like a *delicatessen*, is a *confectionery* in Savannah. Houses built side by side, with each adjacent pair sharing their sidewalls, are called *row houses*, *attached houses*, *town houses* (apparently an innovation in the Chicago area) or a *Baltimore block*. An *office building*, if not more than four stories high, is often called a *block* in small Northern cities.

d) Even leaving out differences prescribed in enacting legislation, municipal services have various designations. The lowly *garbageman* has become a *sanitary engineer* in many ambitious municipalities, but in Chicago is still unabashedly a *public scavenger*. A policeman's *club* or *truncheon* is generally a *nightstick*, but in Baltimore glories in the title of *espantoon*. The fire department may keep its apparatus in an *engine house*, a *fire house*, a *fire station*, or a *fire hall*. And the convenient extra-legal connections that help in getting prompt attention from public officials may be summarized as *influence*, as *pull*, or -- as in Chicago -- as *clout*.

e) And despite the commercialization of the preparation and distribution of food, there are still definable local distinctions. Cuts of meat, and their designations, vary so widely from place to place that even the most sophisticated housewife has difficulty in explaining the differences between *filet*, *tenderloin*, *sirloin*, *porterhouse*, *T-bone*, *New York cut*, *Boston cut*, *English cut*, and their hundreds of congeners. The soda fountain is a very recent institution, and ice-cream products are increasingly manufactured in bulk and distributed through large commercial organizations, but a little investigation will reveal that a *milkshake* in eastern New England contains only milk and falvored syrup but no ice cream, and that a westward journey reveals ice cream in larger and larger proportions. The English *perambulator* or *pram* appears in various parts of the United States as a *baby-cab*, *baby-carriage*, *baby-coach*, or *baby-buggy*. Even funeral customs, despite the unctuous efficiency of American *undertakers* (who prefer *mortician* or *funeral director*), retain local differences in terminology. The household watch with the dead, whether Irish *wake* or Southern Negro *setting up*,[2] is less common than in the past, but in its place the public display of the *prepared patient* at the undertaker's workshop is known in some places as a *viewing*, in others as a *reviewal*. It is statistically improbable, of course, that all of these variant innovations in American English should be exactly duplicated in any other language community, but it is inconceivable that some analogous developments should not have arisen.

4. In the last generation there has been a great deal of research, and even more debate, about the suprasegmentals of a language: stress, intonations, transitions, and terminals. Without committing ourselves to a decision as to whether these phenomena are *phonemic* or *prosodic* in any given language, but with the concession that the status of any or all may differ from one language to another, we need systematic evidence for almost every language on how these phenomena vary regionally and socially. Since the phonetic qualities of vowel and consonant phonemes are recognized as having definable variations from place to place and class to class, it is only reasonable to suspect that such variations exist in the significant suprasegmentals, whether we call them phonemes or not; in fact, differences in the relative intensity of stresses (however intensity is defined), within the same accentual system, have been recognized intuitively as regionally significant within the United States. We have enough evidence to know that the analysis of these phenomena, within any language, is extremely complicated; to convert heat into light on the subject, we need less rhetoric and much more data of a systematically comparable kind. To secure systematically comparable data without distortion will naturally tax our skill and ingenuity, but the potential reward is worth the effort. Nor should we stop

here, but we should extend our research to the comparative study of paralanguage -- the extralinguistic modifications of the speech stream by rasp, drawl, and the like -- and of kinesics, the system of gestures and other communicative body movements. In their own right, as contributions to pure knowledge, such studies are naturally desirable; but they could also have far-reaching implications as diagnostic tools for the social anthropologist and the psychiatrist, enabling them to distinguish between the regionally different and the socially or psychically perturbed, just as the more familiar evidence of dialectology on pronunciation and grammar enables the teacher to differentiate the regionally different from the socially inferior.

5. As we embark on interdisciplinary projects, we need a larger number of more delicately articulated studies of social differentiation in language and of the dynamics of change. American sociologists have undertaken scores of community studies, but have never systematically correlated dialect differences with class differences; the only two partial exceptions are the Putnam-O'Hern study of the "alley people" of Washington (1955), and Ives's unpublished research for the Urban Life Research Institute of New Orleans. In our society of the future, such dialect differences are likely to become even more significant than they have been in the past, as overt pressures toward social equality and the increasing availability of the material means of social status make the less mutable dialect touchstones more important diagnostically. The best motivated legislation and judicial rulings can do little to alter the status of unpriveleged minorities, of whatever origin, if they leave unchanged the subtler characteristics by which prejudice and discrimination are rationalized. In urban centers of the northern United States comparative studies of Negro and white speech could provide valuable, if sometimes embarrassing, evidence on the extent to which official integration of the schools is nullified by segregated associations -- or none -- between students off the school grounds. Studies like this will naturally call for something like random sampling, rather than the traditional selected sampling of linguistic atlases, for the inclusion of recent immigrants along with lifetime residents, and for younger informants as well as older ones.

6. Last, we must not rigidly restrict ourselves to any one method of gathering the data. The postal questionnaires of Wenker were not invalid in themselves, but only insofar as they attempted to gather the data for which they were least suited -- impressionistic phonetics -- from an impersonal entity called a village. Restricted to specific evidence of lexicon and grammar and even phonemic contrasts, and distributed to specific and identifiable informants, the postal questionnaire has been able to gather -- at relatively low cost -- much of the essential data for many of the American regional atlases and for the Linguistic Survey of Scotland (McIntosh 1952; Mather and Speitel 1975-:1.10-15). Among technical innovations, the portable tape recorder cannot ask the questions for the field worker, but it does provide a permanent record of the interview, against which the field worker can check his transcriptions, and evidence of conversational usage, which can be compared with the informant's direct responses under questioning. For certain types of interviews in depth, including the study of kinesics, a sound camera is likewise more useful than the naked eye. In the laboratory, we can make profitable use of the sound spectrograph, the reverse playback, and the speech-stretcher, to determine the actual acoustic components of speech sounds. And as further technical aids are developed, we should be happy to make use of them. Our past work can never be truly obsolete, but we should not limit our future work by the precedents of the past.

Finally, whatever we do, we should approach our discipline with proper humility toward the complexity of the phenomena we are investigating. The forces of urbanization and industrialization and mass education can, it is true, operate more widely and more rapidly now than analogous forces have ever operated in the past. But we should remember that languages are always changing, and that no pure dialects can really exist as long as communities are in contact. In fact, even the social flux of our own day has its precedents in the past -- in the first urban revolution of about 4000 B.C., as well as in the bourgeois revolution of the late Middle Ages. We cannot recreate the linguistic situations that existed in those times of change, but by studying our own age with the resources at our disposal, we may be able to better understand the past as well as to determine our future. A serious and scientific dialectology is one of the best instruments of cooperation with other social sciences for developing an appreciation of the complex behavior of this interesting animal called man.

[1] The Wisconsin materials are not yet published; but this investigation has served as a model for the more extensive *Dictionary of American Regional English* (*DARE*; 1981–) now nearing completion.

[2] But *wake* as a transitive verb is prospering in Chicago, in such contexts as 'she died Tuesday and will be *waked* Thursday at Piner's Chapel.'

When kings have become philosophers and philosophers have become kings, when the average American citizen becomes less intensely competitive with his neighbors and more willing to give each one a chance to do to his fullest capacity the work for which he has the greatest aptitude and interest, then -- as class markers lose significance -- it will hardly be necessary to talk about social dialects. But until that time, while a person's social standing will be assessed in terms of the way in which his use of English measures up to what the dominant culture consider the marks of educated speech, it will be important to understand the linguistic indicators of social difference in any given community. Everyone knows from his own experience that such indicators exist, though he may misjudge the actual significance of a particular item. As an example of the kind of mistake one can make, until I was nearly thirty I could not imagine that a truly educated and cultivated person would fail to distinguish between such pairs as *horse* and *hoarse* or *dew* and *do*, or such triads as *merry*, *marry* and *Mary*.[1]

But in compensation for such limits, I learned intuitively that in my native community (Greenville, South Carolina) one's vowels were clear markers of one's social standing. This experience prepared me for what I encountered in teaching in a wide spectrum of other communities -- Charleston, South Carolina; Lafayette, Louisiana; Cleveland and Chicago -- where complex social dialect situations could be readily observed.[2]

The intuitive and informal observations in these situations have been reinforced by some three thousand hours of field interviewing for the Linguistic Atlas project, and by the more intensive studies that younger investigators have undertaken -- some of them, I am proud to state, students of mine. This paper presents a synthesis of some of the evidence gathered in these investigations; if any specific remark impinges on a sensitive corn, say that of a metropolitan school superintendant, the corn-bearer should not blame the evidence but the society in which the evidence was gathered.

A dialect, in the sense in which American scholars use it, is simply an habitual variety of a language, set off from other such varieties by a complex of features of pronunciation (/drɪn/ vs. /dren/ 'drain'), grammar (*I dove* vs. *I dived*) or vocabulary (*doughnut* vs. *fried cake*). Dialects arise through regional or social barriers in the communications system: the stronger the barrier, the sharper the dialect differences. Most often we think of a dialect as the way some stranger talks; we generally assume that we speak 'normal English' -- or French or Russian or Burmese or Ojibwa, as the case may be.

The most obvious dialects, to most of us, are the regional varieties -- the Eastern New England type, of the late President Kennedy; the Southwestern variety, of President Johnson; or the Charleston variety, which everyone in the Up-Country of South Carolina used to mock in something like the following:

[wi·l hav ə le·ᵊt de·ᵊt ət e·ᵊt and go·ᵊ əut
tənəit ɔn ðə bo·ᵊt ənd rɔid bɔi ðə batrɪ ənd
θro·ᵊ brɪkbats ət ðə batlʃɪps]

"We'll have a late date at eight and go out tonight on the boat, and ride by the Battery and throw brickbats at the battleships."

Other regional varieties may be less conspicuous than these, but we generally do fairly well in sorting out the stranger from the person who grew up in our home town.

In addition to regional dialects, however, we have social dialects. A social dialect, as I define it, is an habitual sub-variety of the speech of a given community, restricted by the operation of social forces to representatives of a particular ethnic, religious, economic or educational group. By and large, the more that any one sub-variety is esteemed above all others in a given community, the sharper will be the distinction between it and its less-favored competitors. No community is without social dialects; but in general, the fewer the locally sanctioned class barriers, the more difficult to find the true class markers, in speech as in anything else. Since it is impossible to give in detail all kinds of social dialect situations, my discussion here is confined to two examples -- Greenville and Chicago. Both illustrate the traditional pattern of urban growth from in-migration, though the scales and the details are different. For Greenville I draw on years of intuitive observations as a child and adolescent (observations the more likely to be objective since as a child I felt no identity with any local class or clique or cult), followed by field investigations for the Atlas. For Chicago I rely on conscious observations, especially on the dissertation of Lee Pederson (1965a).[3]

Greenville, like most of the Upland South, was originally settled by Ulster Scots and Pennsylvania Germans, who came southward along the Shenandoah Valley and the eastern slopes of the Blue Ridge. A few of the most adventurous drifted northwest with Daniel Boone and his associates, to colonize the Ohio Valley; another group, fiercely individualistic, infiltrated the Appalachians, where they made some of the best whiskey in the world (illegal, of course) until the industrialization of moonshining during the unlamented Noble Experiment. Most, however, settled down to family farming in the Piedmont. The town of Greenville, in the geographical center of the county, developed out of a village that grew up around a grist mill established by a local trader during the American Revolution. Here the county seat was located, with the establishment of counties in the 1790's; and a small professional elite, partly from the cultural focus of Charleston, partly from the other focus of eastern Virginia, founded law firms, banks and other businesses. Early in the nineteenth century the village became a summer resort for rice planters and their families during the malaria season (roughly May 1 - November 1); a few of these summer people became permanent residents and members of the local elite. Others from the Charleston area, including representatives of humbler families, refugeed in Greenville during the Civil War. From the house servants of these Charleston-oriented families are descended many of the present-day leaders in the local Negro community.

With the spread of cotton culture following Eli Whitney's invention of the gin, the plantation system -- and its concomitant, Negro slavery -- spread to the southern half of the county, and the Negro population increased by 1860 to about one third of the total. But the plantation interests never dominated the county. In particular, the mountainous northern half was unsuited to plantation agriculture, and the mountaineers were particularly resentful of Negro slave competition. The county was a stronghold of Unionist sympathy before and during and after the Civil War; contrary to the official myth, the percentage of desertions from the Confederate Army was high, and there were many echoes of the popular designation of the Lost Cause as "a rich man's war and a poor man's fight." A Greenvillian, Benjamin Perry, was governor of South Carolina during the short-lived period of reconciliation before Congress established the Reconstruction government. With emancipation, most of the plantation slaves became tenant farmers, and many Negroes continue in that status today, despite the drift from farm to city and thence to the North.

During the period of industrialization that set in toward the end of the nineteenth century, the county in general and the city of Greenville in particular became one of the centers of the Southern textile industry. The mills maintained the traditional segregated employment patterns of Southern industry extablished by William Gregg, at Graniteville, S.C., in the 1830's. Gregg had looked to the textile industry as the salvation of the poor white farmers crowded off the land by the spread of the plantation system, and as a refuge where they would be protected against the unfair competition of slave labor. The continuing pattern has been for new mills to be staffed by displaced or unsuccessful farmers from the mountains and other unproductive areas, though by now textile employment has become a hereditary way of life for the fourth generation, who may move from mill to mill over a hundred-mile span, but who remain tied to the industry, basically one for low-skilled and low-paid labor, susceptible to long periods of depression and unemployment and bitter competition from the newer mills in the Deep South. Except for menial tasks, Southern cotton mills hire few or no Negroes, and the traditional threat of Negro employment is cannily exploited by mill management whenever the unions launch organizing drives.[4] As a result, the cotton mills around Greenville, as elsewhere in the South, remain essentially un-unionized. Until recently, most mill operatives lived in company villages with company stores furnishing long-term credit on terms sometimes little short of peonage. These villages, like the mills, were set up outside the city limits to avoid city taxes. However, since World War II the company villages have begun to disappear, as the mills have sold off the mill-village houses to operatives and others.

The mill schools were rather poor at first, thanks to a district school system that till the 1920's received little help from the state.[5] About 1920, when the population of the mill belt had reached some twenty thousand, little less than that of the city proper, the management of the various mills joined to support a united and segregated school district, largely restricted to the children of mill operatives. This school system was independent of that of the city proper, which at that time provided a competent traditional education for local whites and a separate and inferior one for Negroes. So strong were the economic and social barriers setting off the mill district from the town that it used to be said, not altogether in jest, that Greenville was a community of three races -- whites, Negroes and cotton-mill workers. The mill hands and the city people were as mutually distrustful as either group of whites and the Negroes -- and the former distrust was

[61]

repeatedly exploited by low-grade demagogues. Within the Negro community, there
were also competing groups; but of those
the local whites were largely ignorant.

Negro speech, like educated white speech
of the town, generally had loss of constriction of postvocalic /-r̃/; rural
white, cotton mill and mountain speech
generally retained constriction. Educated
speech had [raɨt] but [ra·d]; uneducated
speech normally had [ra·t]. Thus *nice
white rice* became a social shibboleth;
for Negro, cotton mill, mountain and rural
uneducated white speech most commonly had
[na·s hwa·t ra·s], while a few speakers
with Charleston or eastern Virginia connections (or pretensions) had [nəɪs hwəɪt
rəɪs]. A very few Charleston- and
Virginia-oriented speakers (mostly women)
affected the so-called 'broad *a*' in such
words as *half past* and *dance*. This pronunciation had no prestige; in fact, it
was often an excuse for ribald humor. The
Charleston intonation and vowel qualities
would be tolerated in elderly distinguished citizens, but cruelly ridiculed in
the young. Folk verb forms were common on
all levels of speech in all styles, except
in the most formal situations for the most
cultivated. An educated speaker who would
not use *ain't* in familiar conversation
with his social equals was looked on with
suspicion, as if attempting to cover up an
unsavory past. Local and regional lexical
items were used in everyday speech as a
matter of course; a child might read
about the *chipmunk* Nurse Jane in the Uncle
Wiggly stories without identifying it with
the *ground squirrel* in the city park.

From this microcosm it seems a far cry
to the macrocosm that is Chicago. Yet
here too we may trace the chain of influence from the historical background to the
sources of local speech patterns and the
relationships of those speech patterns to
the social order.
Northern Illinois -- like northern Indiana, southern Michigan and southeastern
Wisconsin -- was first settled from the
Inland Northern dialect region: western
New England, by way of upstate New York.
In many of the small towns in Chicago's
exurbia, the older families still show
distinctly New England speech traits, such
as the centralized diphthongs [əu] and
[əɨ] in *down* and *ride*, or /ʊ/ in *spoon* and
soon. But the city of Chicago developed a
more polyglot tradition from the beginning. The city was established at the
time when the Erie Canal made it easy for
the economic and political refugees from
western Europe to reach the American
heartland. The Irish brought reliable labor for the new railroads and a continuing
tradition of lively politics; the Germans
contributed their interest in beer, education, art, music and finance. Almost immediately Chicago also became a magnet for
the younger sons of the agricultural settlements in southern Illinois and southern
Indiana -- Midlanders, whose speech patterns derived from western Pennsylvania.
Scandinavians followed Germans and Irish;
toward the end of the nineteenth century
the population of the metropolitan area
was swelled by mass peasant immigration
from southern and eastern Europe -- the
strong backs and putatively weak brains on
which Chicago's mighty steel industry was
built. When this immigration tailed off
during World War I, a new supply of basic
labor was sought in the Southern Negro.
Negro immigration has increased until Chicago is possibly the largest Negro city in
the world. More recently the Negroes have
been joined by Latin Americans (Mexicans,
Cubans, Puerto Ricans), and last by rural
whites from the southern Appalachians. In
response partly to the pressure of the increasing non-white population, partly to
easy credit and slick promotion, Chicago
whites like those in other cities have
spread into the suburbs, many of which are
at least informally restricted to a single
economic and social (sometimes even an
ethnic or religious) group (Pederson
1965a).

In Chicago as in most large cities, the
development of social dialects has been a
by-product of what might be called differential acculturation: differences in the
facility and speed with which representatives of various social groups develop the
ability to live alongside each other as
individuals, without stereotyped group
identification. In favor of the trend is
the traditional American principle of individual dignity, and the belief that each
man should be allowed to improve his lot
as far as his ability and his luck permit.
Against it is the tendency of people to
flock together according to their nature
and common ties -- whether Filipinos, Orthodox Jews, Irishmen, hipsters or college
professors -- a tendency abetted by those
with a stake in keeping the flock from
scattering and by the tendency of each
group to reject the conspicuous outsider.
In the early nineteenth century, the Pennsylvanians and downstaters, with a few
generations of Americanizing under their
belts, soon mingled freely with all but
the wealthiest and most genealogically
conscious Northerners. Acculturation was
more difficult for the "clannish" Irish,
Germans and Scandinavians.[6] The Irish
were usually Roman Catholics; the Scandinavians spoke a foreign language; many
Germans suffered from both handicaps, and
all three groups had broken with their native cultures only recently and maintained
many of their native customs. Nevertheless, all three of these groups had enough
in common with the 'Older American
Stock' -- all coming from northwestern
Europe -- to make some sort of symbiotic
assimilation easy, though all of these
older immigrant groups were to suffer

during the xenophobic hysteria of 1917-19 and after.[7] In general they managed to paticipate freely in the community, while retaining their cultural societies, newspapers and even foreign-language schools.

The later immigrants from southern and eastern Europe suffered, in general, from the twin disabilities of foreign language and Roman Catholicism. Moreover, they were largely peasants and illiterate, without the strong sense of their cultural tradition that the Germans and Scandinavians had brought.[8] All these groups found themselves at the focus of a complicated polyhedron of forces. In an effort to help their acclimatization -- and no doubt to avoid the erosion of traditional ecclesiastical allegiance -- the Roman hierarchy fostered the 'ethnic parish,' designed specifically for a single nationality or linguistic group. Whether or not this institution served its immediate purpose, it had the side effects of further identifying foreignness and Roman Catholicism, of separating the new groups from the American Protestants, from the 'native Catholics' (chiefly of German descent), and from each other, and of fostering ethnic blocs in local politics.[9] The blocs persist; but the common tendency of Chicagoans (as of Clevelanders) of southern and eastern European descent is to abandon their ancestral languages and turn their backs on their ancestral cultures, even in the first American-born generation. The notable exceptions are the Jews, with the attachment to the synagogue, to the synagogue-centered subculture, and to the family as a religious and culturally focused institution. But it is possible for an individual from any of these new immigrant groups to give up as much of his ethnic identity as he may wish, and to mingle relatively unnoticed in apartment building or housing development alongside members of the earlier established groups.

In contrast to both of these groups of European immigrants, the American Negro in Chicago is a native speaker of American English, normally of at least five generations of residence in North America (cf. R. and V. McDavid 1951b); little survives of his ancestral African culture, though undoubtedly more than American Caucasoids are generally willing to admit. Early Negro settlers in Chicago were able to settle as individuals -- whether freemen or manumitted or fugitive before the Civil War, or emancipated migrants afterward; furthermore, a large number of the earliest Negro immigrants were skilled craftsmen, who might expect to find a place in an expanding economy, and with some education to smooth off the rough corners of their dialects. However, even as an individual settler the Negro was more easily identified than any of the whites who had preceded him; and many Negroes exhibited traumata from slavery and mass discrimination. With the mass migrations of Negroes, other forces began to operate: the arrivals from 1915 on were largely a black peasantry, somewhat exposed to urban or small-town life but almost never actively participating in the dominant culture. Their own American cultural traditions -- gastronomic, ecclesiastical and everything between -- often diverged sharply from those of middle-class Chicago. Their speech, though American English, was likewise sharply different from that of their new neighbors. Even an educated Mississippian has a system of vowels strikingly different from the Chicago pattern. An uneducated Mississippi Negro would have had his poor sample of learning in the least favored part of the Southern tradition of separate and unequal schools; his grammar would differ more sharply from the grammar of educated speech in his region far more than would the grammar of any Northern non-standard dialect differ from the local white standard. Furthermore, the easy identification of the Negro immigrant would provoke open or tacit pressure to reinforce the tendency of living with one's kind -- a situation which, for the Chicago Negro, is likely to strengthen the linguistic and cultural features alien to the dominant local dialect pattern. Finally, the displacement of unskilled labor by automation has injured the Negroes -- less educated and less skilled, on the whole -- more than it has other groups. The specter of a permanently unemployable Negro proletariat has begun to haunt political leaders in Chicago as in other Northern cities, with inferior educational achievement and inferior employment opportunities reinforcing each other, and in the process strengthening the linguistic differences between whites and Negroes.

Of the Latin American, it can be said that he adds a language barrier to the problem of physical identification which he often shares with the Negro. Of the displaced Southern mountaineer, it has often been observed that he is even less acculturated to urban living than the Negro or the Latin; however, his physical traits will make it easy for his children to blend into the urban landscape, if they can only survive. [In the past decade, as Lawrence Davis has demonstrated (1971), the speech of Chicago's Appalachian community has actually diverged further from local norms.]

What then are the effects of this linguistic melting pot on the speech of metropolitan Chicago? And -- since I wear the hat of English teacher as well as that of social dialectologist -- what are the implications for the schools?

First, the speech of the city proper has apparently become differentiated from that of the surrounding area, as the result of four generations of mingling of Inland

[63]

Northern, Midland, and Irish, and the gradual assimilation of the descendants of continental European immigrants. The outer suburbs call the city /ʃikágo/, butcher /hagz/, and suffer from spring /fag/; to most of its inhabitants the city is /ʃikɔ́go/, quondam /hɔg/ butcher to the world, beset by Sandburg's cat-footed /fɔg/. To the city-bred, *prairie* and *gangway* and *clout* have connotations quite different from those they bear in the hinterlands (Pederson 1965a,b). Little if anything survives in the city of such Inland Northern speech forms as [əi] and [əu] in *high* and *how*, [u] in *soon* and *spoon*, or /éʲe/ as an oral gesture of assent. Even the second generation of Irish, lace-curtained or otherwise, have largely lost their brogue; such pronunciations as /ohɛ́rə/ for *O'Hare* Field seem to be socially rather than ethnically identifiable.[10]

Among the older generation with foreign-language backgrounds, one finds sporadic traces of old-country tongues, such as lack of certain consonant distinctions (e.g., /t/ and /θ/, /d/ and /ð/) that are regular in standard English. Among the younger generation of educated speakers some of the Jewish informants stand out, not only for the traditional American Jewish vocabulary, from *bar mitzvah* and *blintz* to *tsorris* and *yentz*, but for the dentalization or affrication of /t, d, n, s, z, r, l/. The former features have spread to other local groups, but the latter has not. The so-called Scandinavian intonation of English is rarely encountered, even among informants of Scandinavian descent; it has not been picked up by other groups as it has in Minneapolis.

Negroes born in Chicago before 1900 vary less from their Caucasoid contemporaries than the latter do among themselves, attesting to something like genuinely integrated residential patterns in the past. However, Chicago-born Negroes under 50 show many features of Southern and South Midland pronunciation, notably in the consistent use of /ʃikágo/ in outland fashion, in often having /griz/ and /grizi/ as verb and adjective (Atwood 1950a; Hempl 1896), in the frequent loss of postvocalic /r/ in *barn*, *beard* and the like, in contrasts between *horse* and *hoarse*, and in relatively greater length of stressed vowels. These Negroes also show distinctive extralinguistic speech traits. Like Southern Negroes they often display a quaver of ingratiation when speaking to someone presumably in authority -- a feature uncommon in white speech. Like all Southerners they show a wide interval between strongest and weakest stress, between highest and lowest pitch, intervals far wider than found in Inland Northern. In grammar the Chicago-born Negro who grows up in an environment of poverty and limited cultural opportunities -- as most

Chicago Negroes grow up -- has a tendency to use forms that identify him easily and to his disadvantage, in writing as well as speech. Most of these forms are common verbs -- absence of the third-singular present marker, as in *he do*, *it make*; old-fashioned preterites and participles, as *holp* 'helped'; or the appearance of an -s marker in unexpected places as *we says*, *they does* -- or in plurals of nouns, like *two postes* /-əz/. Many of these features of pronunciation and grammar, especially the lengthened stressed vowels, are also found among the recent immigrants from Appalachia, who have their own paralinguistic phenomena, such as strong nasalization, and a few grammatical peculiarities like the sentence-opening *used to*: "Used to, everybody in these-here hills made their own liquor."

As far as the teaching of English is concerned, the overt commitment of American education -- whether or not it is always recognized, let alone successfully practiced -- is that each student should acquire a command of standard English, the English of educated people, sufficient to enable him to achieve the social and economic position to which his ambition and intelligence and ability entitle him. This does not mean that everyone should talk like the works of Henry James or Walter Pater; it does mean that everyone should be aware that certain words or grammatical forms or pronunciations will tag them, justly or not, as unfit. We also have an American tradition -- again, one not always honored -- of respect for the dignity of the individual and the integrity of the family, no matter how deviant their behavior by the standards of Madison Avenue or *Better Homes and Gardens*. No educational program should aim at forcibly alienating the individual from his cultural background; if he must make a break, he must make it with understanding of all the forces involved.

It would therefore seem in order for a language program to start from an examination of the data, probably of a much more massive collection of data than we have access to as yet. In fact, the gathering of data should be recognized as a continuing responsibility, for the culture and the language -- and the values of cultural and linguistic traits -- will continue to change.

With the data collected, it should be possible to determine which words or grammatical features or pronunciations are typical of the various social groups in the community. Once this objective social identification of speech forms is established, it should be possible to compare such forms with the common subjective reactions in the community, both as to the accuracy of the subjective identifications and as to the pleasantness or unpleasantness of associations.[11]

Forms, words, pronunciations which are obviously characteristic of a disadvantaged minority and which produce unfavorable reactions in members of the dominant culture should be the systematic target of the early programs in the schools. The emphasis should not be negative, on error-chasing exercises, but positive, on habit-producing drill.

Where the home language is something other than English, or is a variety of English sharply removed from the local standard, it would probably be desirable to teach standard English as a whole, as a foreign idiom, to be used in certain situations where the culture demands it. We would thus produce many bilinguals and bi-dialectals, capable of communicating with ease in two or more different cultural worlds. We have ample precedent: Eugene Talmadge of MacRae, Georgia, was the son of a plantation owner and won a Phi Beta Kappa key at the state university, but knowing that plantation owners and Phi Betes have little voting power in Georgia statewide elections, he perfected his command of rural Georgia folk speech to induce the 'wool hats' to support him as their spokesman. Huey Long, on the contrary, was a 'red neck' (poor white) from northern Louisiana, who had educated himself to a command of standard English (when he chose to use it) comparable to that of the Lodges and Saltonstalls. And those of us who have grown up in the South can cite many examples of Negro house servants who -- operating intuitively according to the classical tradition of decorum -- could speak the folk dialect to the yard man and cultivated English to the quality without making a lapse in either mode. It should be possible through education to give a larger number the advantages that a few have acquired through intelligence or luck or both.

Where traces of a foreign-language pronunciation exist in a student's English, these should also be approached systematically by teachers who know the structure of the English pronunciation system, and if possible the system of the home language as well.[12] To linguists and other cultural anthropologists it is superfluous to remark that the problem is cultural, not physiological. Yet too often in the schools it is not recognized that the child whose parental language lacks the contrast between /s/ and /z/ constitutes a different kind of problem from one with a cleft palate.

English classes for speakers of other languages should be organized under professionally competent direction, with knowledge of what has been done recently to improve techniques and materials.[13] If there are many children from homes where a language other than English is spoken, special programs in English must be provided from the beginning of the child's school experience. Instruction toward reading English might be deferred until speaking and auditory comprehension are developed; instruction in reading the home language might be given instead. Conceivably, the Latin-American child could, by the fourth grade, be reading in Spanish two years ahead of what his Anglo competitors are doing in English and then could be more rapidly phased into reading English than if he had had reading thrust upon him before he had any competence in speaking or comprehension. Here, however, the design of programs is complicated, and the need for cross-disciplinary cooperation is particularly great.

An obvious difficulty in setting up special reading programs in the home language -- perhaps in the long run more important than the lack of trained teachers or imaginative administrators -- is the shibboleth of 'segregation.' But it is an established policy for the schools to provide special programs for children suffering from physical handicaps: the blind, the deaf, the lame. It would be equally humane to provide special programs for children suffering from cultural handicaps -- a foreign language or a sharply divergent variety of English -- which have some chance of being eliminated by intelligent diagnosis and purposeful instruction; no amount of taking thought can restore sight to the blind. Furthermore, there is a great difference between genuine integration and mere physical juxtaposition; the earlier in the school career a positive language program is adopted, the sooner students will be able to perform as equals, regardless of race or ethnic background -- the only situation in which true integration can be said to have been achieved.

Once the schools become aware of the need for specific programs to cope with the problems of social dialects, two by-products for the school curriculum could develop naturally. First, the most obviously 'culturally deprived' are those whose parents and grandparents, in the heat of the melting pot and the passions of war, were alienated from their native cultures and led to think of everything foreign as inferior. Depending on the size of the school system, there should be room in elementary programs for a broad spectrum of foreign languages, not merely those with the snob appeal of French, German, Italian, Spanish and now Russian, but little discussed tongues like Croatian, Hungarian, Lithuanian and Ukranian. To develop such a program would require cultural sensitivity and some intricate arrangements for shared time, but the cost would be relatively low and the potential gain in self-respect would be high.

The second by-product, even more easily achieved, and I like to think even more significant, is a deeper understanding of the meaning of dialect differences. Too many students, too many parents, too many teachers, shy away from alien varieties of English as from the plague; they feel that any variety different from their own is *ipso facto* inferior. In Detroit, even superior students have undergone the brainwashing of courses in 'corrective speech' if their native pronunciation has been that of Oklahoma. But once the problem of social dialects is honestly faced, it should be possible to explain that differences arise not from mental or moral inferiority but from differences in cultural experience, and that the most divergent dialect, however ill-suited for educated middle-class conversation, has a dignity and beauty of its own. Faced in this way, the social dialects of a metropolitan area become not a liability but an asset, a positive contribution to educating our students in understanding the variety of experience that enriches a democratic society.

NOTES

[1] Such distinctions are characteristic of the Southern and South Midland dialect areas of the Atlantic Seaboard (Kurath and R. McDavid 1961). A summary of features of the principal areas of the Atlantic Seaboard was prepared by E. Bagby Atwood, from the Atlas archives (1950b); it has been freely adapted as a general reference, as in Chapter 9 of Francis 1958.

[2] Phonetic summaries of cultivated Charleston and Greenville speech are in Kurath and R. McDavid 1961. Lafayette, a bilingual community (English-Acadian French), has been studied by Wallace A. Lambert, of MacGill University; Chicago by Pederson (1965a,b), Cleveland by Drake (1961), and Akron by Udell (1966).

[3] In addition to his dissertation, Pederson has been actively involved in R. McDavid and Austin 1966, and has collected a massive quantity of lexical evidence from the metropolitan area.

[4] This was evident during the fiasco 'Operation Dixie,' a widely publicized but poorly planned drive of the Textile Workers Union, CIO, following World War II. For evidence I am indebted to Earl Taylor, then of the Greenville TWU office.

[5] There was no constitutional commitment to public education in South Carolina before the Reconstruction Constitution of 1868. With public education a much more recent commitment than, say, in the old Northwest Territory, it is not surprising that some spokesmen for the 'Southern Way of Life' have talked casually about abandoning the public school system, as an alternative to desegregation.

[6] It is obvious that only outsiders are clannish; in-groups are merely closely knit.

[7] Since the Germans were the largest functioning foreign-language group, and their position in the cultural life of the community was so high, it is impossible to calculate to what extent the teaching of languages and literature, and the position of the scholar, suffered as a result of these witch-hunts. The abolition of Germanic studies in Texas, as a gesture of patriotism, was only one of many such acts.

[8] Paradoxically, one of the most successful adaptations of native cultural traditions to the opportunities of the American setting -- that of the South Italians of Chicago to public demands during Prohibition -- tended to stigmatize the whole group, whether or not they actively participated in the Syndicate's version of venture capitalism.

[9] Fishman *et al.* 1966:333-37 attacks the heavily Irish American hierarchy of the Roman church for discouraging the ethnic parish in the past generation. In contrast, Msgr. John L. O'Brien, director of parochial education in the Charleston diocese, was outspoken in his belief (based on his home community in Pennsylvania) that the ethnic parish tended to prevent the development of a truly Catholic church in the United States. The Irish, after all, had found their ethnicity one of their greatest obstacles to full participation in American Society.

[10] The pronunciation /ohɛ́rə/, definitely substandard in Chicago, was however the normal one for Mayor Richard J. Daley, probably the most powerful municipal politician in the United States. To urban Chicagoans a *prairie* is a vacant lot; a *gangway* is a passage between two apartment buildings; *clout* is access to political power.

[11] An instrument to evaluate such reactions has been prepared by Vernon S. and Carolyn H. Larsen (1966). For pronunciations of single words, Middle Westerners of the middle class could not distinguish between Negro and Southern white speech. Apparently the stereotype is to equate anything 'Southern' with 'Negro,' 'rural' and 'uneducated,' for the Southern white whose voice was included in the instrument was the most highly educated and had lived only in urban areas.

[12] A series of contrastive studies, for English and specific other languages, has been published by the University of Chicago Press.

[13] The problem of preparing materials for special groups demands continuous experimentation and interdisciplinary cooperation. The needs of elementary school children in urban areas are least satisfactorily met so far, but any special group needs attention to the peculiarities of its learning situation.

In my boyhood -- more years ago than I care to remember -- we used to define an expert as "a damned fool a thousand miles from home." Since I am considerably less than a thousand miles from where I grew up, and stand but a few minutes from my residence in Hyde Park,[1] it behooves me to avoid any claim to expertness about the problems faced in practical situations where the dialect of the school child is sharply divergent from what is expected of him in the classroom. For many of these situations, neither I nor any other working dialectologist knows what the local patterns actually are; for some, there has been no attempt, or at best a partial and belated one, to find out the patterns. Nevertheless, the implications of dialectology for the more rational teaching of English in the schools -- and not only in the schools attended by those we currently euphemize as the culturally disadvantaged -- are so tremendous that I am flattered to have John Fisher ask for my observations. The problems are not limited to Americans of any race or creed or color, nor indeed to Americans; they are being faced in England today, as immigrants from Pakistan and the West Indies compete in the Midlands for the same kinds of jobs that have drawn Negro Americans to Harlem and the South Side, and Appalachian whites to the airplane factories of Dayton. In fact, such problems are faced everywhere in the world as industrialization and urbanization take place, on every occasion when people, mostly but not exclusively the young, leave the farm and the village in search of the better pay and more glamorous life of the cities. In all parts of the world, educators and politicians are suddenly realizing that language differences can create major obstacles to the educational, economic, and social advancement of those whose true integration into the framework of society is necessary if that society is to be healthy; they are realizing that social dialects -- that is, social differences in the way language is used in a given community -- both reflect and perpetuate differences in the social order. In turn, the practicing linguist is being called on with increasing frequency to devise programs for the needs of specific groups -- most often for the Negroes dwelling in the festering slums of our northern and western cities; and generous government and private subsidies have drawn into the act many teachers and administrators -- most

of them, I trust, well meaning -- who not only have made no studies of dialect differences, but have ignored the studies and archives that are available, even those dealing with their own cities.

Perhaps a data-oriented dialectologist may here be pardoned an excursion into the metaphors of siegecraft, recalled from the time when under the tutelage of Allan Gilbert I learned something of the arts of war and gunnery, if not all their Byronic applications. In confronting our massive ignorance of social dialects, the professional students of the past generation have been a forlorn hope -- burrowing into a problem here, clawing their way to a precarious foothold of understanding there, seizing an outwork yonder. Like many forlorn hopes, they have been inadequately supported, sometimes ignored, even decried -- not only by their literary colleagues -- with the usual patronizing attitude toward anything smacking of affiliation with the social sciences, but also by their fellow linguists who are interested in international programs for teaching English as a second language, in machine translation, in formulaic syntax, or in missionating to convert the National Council of Teachers of English. It is small wonder that some students of dialects have withdrawn from the assault to participate in these better-heeled campaigns; it is a tribute to the simple-minded stubbornness of the survivors that they have not only persisted but advanced. Today their work, their aims, are embarrassingly respectable, as legions spring from the earth in response to the golden trumpet sounding on the banks of the Pedernales. It is inevitable, perhaps even fitting, that the practical work in social dialects should be directed by others than the pioneers in research. But it is alarming that many of those now most vocally concerned with social dialect problems not only know nothing about the systematic work that has been done, about the massive evidence (even if all too little) that is available, but even have a complete misconception about the nature and significance of dialects. At the risk of drawing the fire of the House Un-American Activities Committee, I would agree with my sometime neighbor James H. Sledd that our missionaries should at least know what they are talking about before they set out to missionate.

I have a particular advantage when I talk on this subject: I am one of those who speak English without any perceptible accent. I learned to talk in an upper-middle-class neighborhood of Greenville, South Carolina, among corporation lawyers, bankers, textile magnates, and college presidents, among families with a long tradition of education and general culture. Many of my playmates, like myself, represented the sixth generation of their families in the same county. It never occurred to any of us to tamper with our language; our only intimate acquaintance with non-standard grammatical forms in writing came from stories in literary dialect or from the quaint and curious exercises that infested our textbooks -- though we knew that less privileged forms of speech than ours were found in our community, and were not above imitating them for rhetorical effect. Not a single English teacher of an excellent faculty -- our superintendent had his doctorate, not from Peabody or from Teachers College, Columbia, but from the University of Berlin, 1910 -- made a gesture of tampering. Nor have I heard anything in the exotic dialects of the Northeast or the Middle West that would make me feel less content with a way of speaking that any educated person might want to emulate. And yet, a few years ago, my younger sister, who has remained in the South Carolina Upland, told me over the telephone: "Brucker, you've been North so long that you talk just like a Yankee." Even though I doubt if I would fool many real Yankees, I know that something has rubbed off from my travels and teaching to make me talk a little different from the boys I grew up with. Still, whenever I go back and start talking with them again, I find myself slipping into the old ways; it is natural for us to shift our way of talking, according to the people we are talking with. In fact, it is the people we talk with habitually who give us our way of talking. Here, in essence, is the way dialects originate. And until everybody lives in a sterile, homogenized, dehumanized environment, as just a number on the books of an all-powerful state, we can expect differences in environment to be reflected in those differences in speech that we call dialects.

An appreciation of this fact would avoid a lot of nonsense expressed in categorical statements in educational literture. Two amusing if distressing examples are found in *Language Programs for the Disadvantaged: Report of the NCTE Task Force* (Corbin and Crosby 1965). These statements, the more distressing because so much of the report is magnificently phrased, probably arose from the inevitable wastefulness of haste (the Task Force was in the field only last summer) and from the imbalance of the Task Force itself: there was only one linguist and not a single sociologist or anthropologist or historian in a group heavily loaded with supervisors and (to coin a term, which is probably already embalmed in educationese) curriculologists:

> Most disadvantaged children come from homes in which a nonstandard English dialect is spoken. It may be pidgin, Cajun, Midland, or any one of a large number of regional or cultural dialects. Many preschool teachers are concerned about the dialect of their children and take measures to encourage standard pronunciation and usage (70).

> . . . the general feeling is that some work in standard English is necessary for greater social and job mobility by disadvantaged students with a strong regional or racial dialect (89).

Among the bits of nonsense to be found in these two statements we may notice:

1. A belief that there is some mystical "standard," devoid of all regional association. Yet the variety that we can find in cultivated American English, as used by identifiable informants with impeccable educational and social credentials, has been repeatedly shown in works based on the American linguistic atlases, most recently and in greatest detail in Kurath and R. McDavid 1961.

2. A belief that there are "racial" dialects, independent of social and cultural experiences.

3. A snobbishness toward "strong" dialect differences from one's own way of speaking. Would Bobby Kennedy, politically disadvantaged after the Atlantic City convention, have run a better race in New York had he learned to talk Bronx instead of his strong Bostonian?

4. A glib juggling of terms, without understanding, as in the parallelism of "pidgin, Cajun, Midland." *Pidgin* denotes a minimal contact language used for communication between groups whose native languages are mutually unintelligible and generally have markedly different linguistic structures; typical examples are the Neo-Melanesian of New Guinea and the Taki-Taki of Surinam. However scholars may debate the existence of an American Negro pidgin in colonial days, speakers of pidgin constitute a problem in no Continental American classroom, though it would be encountered in Hawaii and the smaller Pacific islands. *Cajun* properly describes the colonial varieties of French spoken in southwestern Louisiana and in parts of the Maritime Provinces of Canada from which the Louisiana Acadians were transported; even if by extension we use the term to describe the varieties of English developing in the French-speaking areas of Louisiana and the Maritimes, the problems of teaching English in these areas are really those of teaching English as a second language. *Midland* is a geographical designation for those dialects stemming from the

settlement of Pennsylvania and embracing a broad spectrum of cultural levels. At one extreme, we may concede, are the impoverished submarginal farmers and displaced coal miners of the Southern mountains, at the other are some of the proudest dynasties of America -- the Biddles of Philadelphia, the Mellons of Pittsburgh, the Tafts of Cincinnati, and their counterparts in Louisville and St. Louis, in Memphis and in Dallas -- people it were stupid as well as impractical to stigmatize in language like that of the Task Force Report. So long as such glib generalities are used about social dialects, we must conclude that our educators, however well-intentioned, are talking nonsense.

And regrettably, such nonsense is no new phenomenon in American culture; it has long been with us. Much of it, fortunately, runs off us like raindrops off a mallard's back. But enough lingers in the schoolroom to do positive harm. My friend Bob Thomas, the anthropologist -- a Cherokee Indian and proud of it, though with his blond hair and blue eyes he looks far less like the traditional Cherokee than I do -- tells of his traumata when he moved to Detroit from Oklahoma at the age of fourteen. Although Cherokee was his first language, he had picked up a native command of Oklahoma English. Since he had always lived in a good neighborhood, and his family had used standard English at home, he had no problems in grammar; through wide reading and a variety of experiences he had acquired a large and rich vocabulary. But his vowels were Oklahoma vowels; and some benevolent despot in Detroit soon pushed him into a class in 'corrective speech.' The first day the class met, he looked around the classroom and noticed everybody else doing the same. As eyes met eyes, it became apparent that the class in 'corrective speech' contained no cleft palates, no stammerers, no lispers, no foreign accents, not even any speakers of substandard English -- for again, the school was in a good neighborhood. The only thing wrong with the boys and girls in the class was that they had learned English, not in Michigan, but in Oklahoma, Arkansas, Missouri, Kentucky, Tennessee, West Virginia, Mississippi, and Alabama. "We all realized immediately," Bob told me years afterward, "that they were planning to brainwash us out of our natural way of speaking; and it became a point of honor among us to sabotage the program." To this day, Bob flaunts his Oklahoma accent belligerently; if the teachers had let him alone, he might have adapted his pronunciation to that of the Detroit boys he played with, but once he felt that the school considered his home language inferior, nothing could make him change. The first principle of any language program is that, whatever the target, it must respect the language that the students bring with them to the classroom.

Another kind of nonsense was demonstrated by the head of the Speech Department at the University of Michigan during my first Linguistic Institute. Impelled by the kind of *force majeur* that only a four-star general can exert, I had compromised with my scientific interest in linguistics to the extent of enrolling in a course in 'stage and radio diction,' only to find myself bewildered, frustrated, and enraged from the outset. Typical of the petty irritations was the panjandrous insistence on the pronunciation /pradjus/, though all my friends who raised fruits and vegetables for market, many of them gentlemen with impeccable academic credentials, said /prodjus/. But far more distressing were the pronunciations advocated in the name of elegance. We were advised to reject the Middle Western and Southern /æ/, not only in *calf* and *dance* and *command*, but even in *hat* and *ham* and *sand*, for an imitation of the Boston /a/ in environments where Bostonians would never use it, so that we would say /hat/ and /ham/ and /sand/, pronunciations legitimate in no American dialect except that of the Gullah Negroes of the South Carolina and Georgia coast. A few departmental underlings even went all out for an equally phony British [ɑ], again in the wrong places, yielding [hat] and [ham] and [sand], and all of them plumped for replacing the Midwestern [ɑ] of *cot* and *lot* with an exaggerated [ɔ]. Of course, Midwesterners ordering [hɔt ham sandwɪtʃɪz] are as suspect as counterfeit Confederate $3 bills. It is possible that some compulsive aspirants to social elegance docilely lapped up this pap; but those of us who were seriously concerned with English structure and usage laughed the program out of court and left the course, never to return. A second principle can be deduced from this experience: to imitate a dialect sharply different from one's own is a tricky and difficult assignment. A partial imitation is worse than none, since the change seems an affectation to one's neighbors, and the imperfect acquisition seems ridiculous to those whose speech is being imitated. Any attempts at teaching a standard dialect to those who speak a nonstandard one should be directed toward an attainable goal, toward one of the varieties of cultivated speech which the student might hear, day after day, in his own community.

At this point, perhaps, some of you may be muttering, "But what do these experiences have to do with dialects? I always thought that a dialect was something strange and old-fashioned." Many will share your opinion, especially in such countries as France and Italy, where an academy accepts one variety of the language as standard and casts the rest into outer darkness. In such countries the

[69]

word *dialect* implies a variety of the language spoken by the rustic, the uneducated, the culturally isolated. To say that someone "speaks a dialect" -- as one Italian professor patronizingly described one of the best soldiers working with me on our Italian military dictionary -- is to exclude him forever from the company of educated men. For a dialect, to such intellectuals, is a form of the language they had rather be found dead than speaking.

True, there are other attitudes. Germans and Austrians make a distinction between the standard language -- literary High German -- and the dialects, local and predominantly rural forms of speech. But educated Germans do not always avoid dialect speech forms; in some areas, such as the Austrian Tyrol, an educated person will take particular pains to use some local forms in his speech, so as to identify himself with his home. The attitude may be a bit sentimental, but it does help to maintain one's individual dignity in a homogenizing world.

A more extreme attitude was prevalent in the Romantic Era. If the Augustans of the seventeenth and eighteenth centuries looked upon dialects as corruptions of an originally perfect language, the Romantics often alleged, in Wordsworth's terms, that people in humble and rustic life used "a purer and more emphatic language" than that to be met with in the cities. In this viewpoint, the dialects represent the pure, natural, unchanging language, unencumbered by the baggage of civilization. This attitude has long prevailed in Britain; even today the *Survey of English Dialects* (Orton *et al.* 1962-71) is heavily slanted toward archaic forms and relics and ignores modern innovations.

Nor are Americans wholly free from this attitude that a dialect is something archaic and strange. Time and again, a field worker for our Linguistic Atlas is told, "We don't speak no dialect around hyur; if you want *rale* dialect you gotta go down into Hellhole Swamp" -- or up into Table Rock Cove, or at least across the nearest big river. To many of us, as my student Roger Shuy put it, a dialect is something spoken by little old people in queer out-of-the-way places.

When we become a little more sophisticated -- as we must become on a cosmopolitan campus -- we realize that cities as well as rural areas may differ in the ways in which their inhabitants talk. Thus we next conclude that a dialect is simply the way everybody talks but us and the people we grew up with; then, by force of circumstance, we realize that we speak a dialect ourselves. But at this point we still feel that a dialect is something regional or local. When we notice that people of our own community speak varieties of English markedly different from our own, we dismiss them as ignorant, or simply as making mistakes. After all, we live in a democratic society and are not supposed to have class markers in our speech. It is a very sophisticated stage that lets us recognize social dialects as well as regional ones -- dialects just as natural, arising out of normal, everyday contacts.

By this time we have elaborated our definition of a dialect. It is simply a habitual variety of a language, regional or social. It is set off from all other such habitual varieties by a unique combination of language features: words and meanings, grammatical forms, phrase structures, pronunciations, patterns of stress and intonation. No dialect is simply good or bad in itself; its prestige comes from the prestige of those who use it. But every dialect is in itself a legitimate form of the language, a valid instrument of human communication, and something worthy of serious study.

But even as we define what a dialect is, we must say what it is not. It is different from slang, which is determined by vogue and largely distinguished by transient novelties in the vocabulary. Yet it is possible that slang may show regional or social differences, or that some regional and social varieties of a language may be particularly receptive to slang.

A dialect is also different from an argot, a variety of the language used by people who share a common interest, whether in work or in play. Everyone knows many groups of this kind, with their own peculiar ways of speaking and writing: Baptist preachers, biophysicists, stamp collectors, model railroad fans, Chicago critics, narcotic addicts, jazz musicians, safecrackers. But in the normal course of events a person adopts the language of such subcultures, for whatever part of his life it may function in, because he has adopted a particular way of life; he uses a dialect because he grows up in a situation where it is spoken. Again, some argots may show regional or social variations; the term *mugging*, to choose one example, is largely found on the Atlantic Seaboard; the sport has different designations in the Great Lakes region and on the Pacific Coast.

Nor are dialect differences confined to the older, pre-industrial segments of the vocabulary. Here European and American attitudes differ sharply. Eugen Dieth (1948) chided the editors of the *Linguistic Atlas of New England* (Kurath *et al.* 1939-43) for including such vocabulary items as window shades, the razor strop, and the automobile, such pronunciation items as *library* and *post office* and *hotel*, on the ground that these are not genuine dialect items. Yet if they have regional and social variants, as all of these have in North American English, they warrant inclusion. In my lifetime I have seen the *traffic circle* of the Middle Atlantic States become the *rotary* of Eastern New England; the *service plaza* of the Pennsylvania *Turnpike* become the *oasis* of the Illinois *Tollway*; the *poor boy* of New Orleans -- a generous sandwich once confined to the Creole Gomorrah and its gastronautic satellites -- appearing as a *grinder* in upstate New York, a *hoagy* in Philadelphia, a *hero* in New York City, a *submarine* in Boston. Nor will dialect terms be used only by the older and less sophisticated: a Middle Western academician transplanted to MIT quickly learns to order *tonic* for his children, not *soda pop*, and to send his clothes to a *cleanser*. And though some would consider dialect a matter of speech and not of writing, one can find regional and local commercial terms on billboards and television as well as in the advertising sections of local newspapers.

Finally, dialect terms are not restricted to sloppy, irresponsible usage -- a matter of personality type rather than of specific vocabulary items. And though regional and local terms and usages are likely to appear most frequently in Joos's casual and intimate styles, the example of William Faulkner is sufficient evidence that they may be transmuted into the idiom of the greatest literature.

All of these comments are the fruit of centuries of observation, at first casual and anecdotal, later more serious and systematic. The grim test of the pronunciation *shibboleth*, applied by Jephthah's men to the Ephraimites seeking to ford the Jordan, the comic representations of Spartan and Theban speech by Aristophanes, the aspiration of the Roman cockney Arrius-Harrius, immortalized by Catullus, the Northern English forms in the *Reeve's Tale* -- these typify early interest. With the Romantic search for the true language in the dialects came the growth of comparative linguistics, and the search for comparative dialect evidence in translations of the Lord's Prayer and the proverb of the prodigal son. The search for comparable evidence led, in the 1870's, to the monumental collections for Georg Wenker's *Deutscher Sprachatlas*, later edited by Ferdinand Wrede and Walther Mitzka (Wrede *et al*. 1927-56) -- 44,251 responses, by German village schoolmasters, to an official request for local dialect translations of forty sentences of Standard German. Designed to elicit fine phonetic data, the collections proved notably refractory for that purpose, but the sheer mass of evidence corrected the unevenness of individual transcriptions. More important, the discovery that questions designed for one purpose may yield a different but interesting kind of evidence -- as *Pferd* proved useless for the /p:pf/ consonant alternation in dialects where the

horse is *Roß* or *Gaul* -- was reflected in greater sophistication in the design and use of later questionnaires. Less happy was the effect on German dialectology, with later investigations, such as Mitzka's *Wortatlas* (Mitzka and Schmitt 1951-73), sticking to correspondence techniques, a short questionnaire, an immense number of communities, and an expensive cartographic presentation of the data. But the *Sprachatlas* and *Wortatlas*, and the Dutch investigations modeled upon them, provided us with the evidence on which to discover their own defects.

A valuable innovation was made at the turn of the century in the *Atlas linguistique de la France*, directed by Jules Gilliéron (Gilliéron and Edmont 1902-10). Correspondence questionnaires gave way to field interviews on the spot, in a smaller number of selected communities (some six hundred in this instance) with a longer questionnaire; a trained investigator interviewed a native of the community in a conversational situation and recorded his responses in a finely graded phonetic alphabet. As with the German atlas, however, the communities chosen were villages; larger places were first investigated in the *Sprach- und Sachatlas Italiens und der Südschweiz*, under the direction of the Swiss scholars Karl Jaberg and Jakob Jud (1928-40), who also introduced the practice of interviewing more than one informant in the larger communities. With certain refinements, then, the basic principles of traditional dialect study were established by World War I. Some subsequent investigations have followed Wenker, others Gilliéron; some, like the current Czech investigations, have combined both methods, relying primarily on field interviews but using correspondence surveys in the early stages, so that the selection of communities can be made most effectively. Only the British Isles have lagged, perhaps because Joseph Wright's *English Dialect Dictionary* (1898-1905), with its claim to have recorded *all* the dialect words of English, has erected a Chinese Wall worthy of Mr. Eliot's scorn. Not till the 1950's did any kind of field work get under way in either England or Scotland; in both countries it was handicapped by a shortage of funds and field workers, and in England by an antiquarian bias that over-emphasized relics, shunned innovations, and neglected opportunities to provide data comparable to that obtained in the American surveys. Yet both Harold Orton in England and Angus McIntosh in Scotland have enriched our knowledge of English.

Perhaps because American linguists have kept in touch with European developments, the *Linguistic Atlas of New England* (Kurath *et al*. 1939-43), launched in 1930, drew on the lessons of the French and Italian atlases. Although the transition from casual collecting to systematic study was not welcomed by all students, nevertheless -- even with the Hoover Depression, World War II, the Korean intervention, and the tensions of the Cold War -- a respectable amount of progress has been made toward a first survey of American English. The *Linguistic Atlas of New England* was published in 1939-43; scholars are now probing for the changes that a generation has brought. For five other regional surveys, field work has been completed and editing is under way: 1) the Middle and South Atlantic States, New York to central Georgia, with outposts in Ontario and northeastern Florida (Kurath *et al.* 1979-); 2) the North-Central States: Wisconsin, Michigan, southwestern Ontario, and the Ohio Valley (Marckwardt *et al.* 1976-78, 1980-); 3) the Upper Midwest: Minnesota, Iowa, Nebraska, and the Dakotas [publication is now complete, Allen 1973-76]; 4) the Pacific Southwest: California and Nevada [editorial work continues on interpretive studies; Bright 1971 is an early work]; 5) the Gulf States: Georgia, Florida, Alabama, Mississippi, Louisiana, Arkansas, and eastern Texas. Elsewhere, field work has been completed in Colorado, Oklahoma, Washington, Missouri, and eastern Montana; respectable portions have been done in several other states, Newfoundland, Nova Scotia, and British Columbia; with a slightly different method E. Bagby Atwood produced his memorable *Regional Vocabulary of Texas* (1962). In all of these surveys the principles of European dialect investigations have been adapted to the peculiarities of the American scene. Settlement history has been studied more carefully before field work, since English-speaking settlement in North America is recent, and its patterns are still changing. At least three levels of usage are investigated -- partly because cultivated American speech has regional varieties, just like uneducated speech, and the cultivated speech of the future may be foreshadowed in the speech of the intermediate group; partly because until very recently general education has been a more important linguistic and cultural force in the United States than in most of the countries of Europe. Urban speech as well as rural has been investigated in each survey, and intensive local investigations have been encouraged. The questionnaires have included both relics and innovations. All of these modifications were suggested by Hans Kurath, Director of the Atlas project.

Just as warfare is still decided ultimately by infantrymen who can take and hold territory, so dialect study still depends on competent investigators who can elicit and record natural responses in the field. The tape recorder preserves free conversation for later transcription and analysis, and permits the investigator to listen repeatedly to a response about whose phonetic quality he is in doubt; but the investigator must still ask the right questions to elicit pertinent data. He must remember, for instance, that *chicken coop* is both a vocabulary and a pronunciation item -- that the pronunciation in the American North and North Midland is /kup/, in the South and South Midland /kup/, that *coop* in the North designates the permanent shelter for the whole flock, in the South a crate under which a mother hen can scratch without an opportunity to lead the little ones off and lose them in the brush. The full record for such an item may require three or four questions, which only a human interviewer can provide.

But if the field worker remains essential, the objects of his investigation may change. Recent studies have turned increasingly to urban areas, urbanizing areas, and minority groups. To a long list of impressive early investigations one may now add such contributions as Lee Pederson's study of Chicago pronunciation (1965a) and Gerald Udell's analysis of the changes in Akron speech resulting from the growth of the rubber industry and the consequent heavy migration from West Virginia (1966). Among special groups investigated in detail are the Spanish-American bilinguals in San Antonio by Mrs. Janet Sawyer (1957), the American Norwegians by Einar Haugen (1953), the New York City Greeks by James Macris (1955), the New England Portugese by Leo Pap (1949), the Chicago Slovaks by Mrs. Goldie Meyerstein (1959), the Gullah Negroes by Lorenzo Turner (1949), and the Memphis Negroes by Miss Juanita Williamson (1968). In all of these studies the emphasis has been on the correlation between linguistic and social forces.

Another significant development has been the investigation of the way language attitudes are revealed by the choice among linguistic variants under different conditions. The most impressive work of this kind has been done by William Labov, in his study of the speech of the Lower East Side of New York (1966). Limiting himself to a small number of items -- the vowels of *bad* and *law*, the initial consonants of *think* and *then*, the /-r/ in *barn* and *beard* -- phonological details that can be counted on to appear frequently and in a large number of contexts during a short interview, Labov gathers specimens of linguistic behavior under a wide range of conditions. At one end of the spectrum is the reading of such putatively minimal pairs as *bed* and *bad*; at the other is the description of children's games or the recounting of an incident when the informant thought he was going to be killed. The difference between pronunciations in the relaxed situation and those when the informant is on what he considers his best linguistic behavior is an index of his social insecurity. Almost as revealing is the work of Rufus Baehr with high school students in the Negro slums of the Chicago West Side (1964). It is no surprise that in formal situations the students with greater drive to break out of their ghetto reveal striking shifts of their speech in the direction of the Chicago middle-class norm. This kind of discovery should give heart to all who believe that a directed program of second-dialect teaching can make at least a small dent in our problem of providing a wider range of economic and educational opportunities for the aspiring young Negro.

Out of all these investigations two patterns emerge: 1) a better understanding of the origin and nature of dialect differences; 2) a set of implications for those who are interested in providing every American child with a command of the standard language adequate for him to go as far as his ability and ambition impel him.

No dialect differences can, as yet, be attributed to physiology or to climate. Perhaps anatomists will discover that some minor speech differences arise from differences in the vocal organs; but so far there is no evidence for any correlation between anatomy and dialect, and the burden of proof is on those who propose such a correlation. As for climate: it is unlikely that nasality could have arisen (as often asserted) both from the dusty climate of Australia and the dampness of the Tennessee Valley. And though it is a favorite sport among Northerners to attribute the so-called 'Southern drawl' to laziness induced by a hot climate, many Southerners speak with a more rapid tempo than most Middle Westerners, and the Bengali, in one of the most enervating tropical climates, speak still more rapidly. For an explanation of dialect differences we are driven back, inevitably, to social and cultural forces.

The most obvious force is the speech of the original settlers. We should expect that a part of the United States settled by Ulster Scots would show differences in vocabulary, pronunciation, even in grammar from those parts settled by East Anglians. We should expect to find Algonquian loans most common in those regions where settlers met Algonquian Indians, French loans most frequent in Louisiana and in the counties adjacent to French Canada, Spanish loans most widespread in the Southwest, German loans clustering in cities and in the Great Valley of Pennsylvania, and indubitable Africanisms most striking in the Gullah country.

Speech forms are also spread along routes of migration and communication. The Rhine has carried High German forms northward; the Rhone has taken Parisian forms to the Mediterranean; in the United States, the same kind of dissemination has been found in the valleys of the Mississippi, the Ohio, and the Shenandoah.

If speech forms may spread along an avenue of communication, they may be restricted by a physical barrier. As Kurath has observed, there is no sharper linguistic boundary in the English-speaking world than the Virginia Blue Ridge between the Potomac and the James. The tidal rivers of the Carolinas, the swamps of the Georgia coastal plain, have contributed to making the Old South the most varied region, dialectally, in the English settlements of the New World.

The economic pattern of an area may be reflected in distinctive dialect features. *Fatwood*, for resin-rich kindling, is confined to the turpentine belt of the Southern tidewater; *lightwood*, with a similar referent, to the Southern coastal plain and lower Piedmont. *Case weather*, for a kind of cool dampness in which it is safe to cut tobacco, occurs over a wide area, but only where tobacco is a money crop. *To run afoul of*, a maritime phrase in the metaphorical sense of 'to meet,' seems to be restricted to the New England coast.

Political boundaries, when long established, may become dialect boundaries; in the Rhineland, pronunciation differences coincide strikingly with the boundaries of the petty states of pre-Napoleanic Germany. In the New World, on the other hand, political boundaries have seldom delimited culture areas. Yet *county site*, for the more common *county seat*, is common in Georgia but unknown in South Carolina, and Ontario Canadians speak of the *reeve* as chief officer of a township, the *warden* as chief officer of a county, and a *serviette* instead of a table napkin -- terms unfamiliar in the United States.

Each city of consequence may have its distinctive speech forms. The grass strip between the sidewalk and the curb, undesignated in South Carolina, is a *tree belt* locally in Springfield, Massachusetts (and hence unlabeled in *Webster's Third New International Dictionary*), a *tree lawn* in Cleveland, a *devil strip* in Akron, and a *boulevard* in Minneapolis and St. Paul. And only Chicagoans naturally refer to political influence as *clout*, or to a reliable dispenser of such influence as a *Chinaman*.

Nor are differences in the educational system without their effect. Where separate and unequal education is provided to particular social groups, we can be sure that a high-school diploma or even a college degree will be no indication by itself of proficiency in the standard language. That this problem is not confined to any single racial or cultural group has been shown by institutions such as West Virginia State College, which have undergone the process of reverse integration. This particular school, which once drew an elite Negro student body, is now eighty percent white, with the white students mostly from the disadvantaged mountain areas along the Kanawha. Since the teachers in the mountain schools are not only predominantly local in origin, but often have had little education beyond what the local schools offer, and then, since most of them habitually use many non-standard forms, it has been difficult for the college to maintain its academic standards in the face of increasing white enrollment, however desirable integration may be.

Most important, perhaps, is the traditional class structure of a community. In a Midwestern small town, it is still possible for one brother to stay home and run a filling station, and another to go off and become a judge -- and nobody mind. But in parts of the South there is a social hierarchy of families and occupations, so that it is more respectable for a woman of good family to teach in an impoverished small college than to do professional work for the government at twice the salary. Here, too, an aristocratic ideal of language survives, and the most cultivated still look upon *ain't* as something less reprehensible than incest -- but use it only in intimate conversation with those whom they consider their social equals. Here too we find we find the cultural self-assurance that leads an intelligent lawyer to ask the linguistically naive question: "Why is it that the educated Northerner talks so much like the uneducated Southerner?"

If social differences among the WASP population are reflected in linguistic differences, we should not be surprised if similar differences among later immigrants are reflected in the extent of linguistic borrowing from particular foreign-language groups, or even from the same foreign-language group at different times. Our longest continuous tradition of borrowing, with probably the largest and most varied kinds of words, is that from various kinds of German. Even the bitterness of two world wars cannot prevent us from seeing that of all foreign-language groups the Germans have been most widely distributed, geographically and socially, throughout the United States -- as prosperous farmers, vaudeville comedians, skilled craftsmen, merchants, intellectuals. In contrast, the hundreds of thousands of Italian- and Slavic-speaking immigrants of the last two generations have left few marks on the American vocabulary; most of them were of peasant stock, often illiterate, and settled in centers of heavy industry as basic labor.

Even more striking is the change in the incidence of Texas borrowings from Mexican Spanish. In her study of the bilingual situation in San Antonio (1957), Mrs. Sawyer has shown that although early Spanish loans were numerous, quickly assimilated, and widely spread -- *canyon*, *burro*, *ranch*, *lariat*, *bronco*, *silo* are characteristic examples -- there have been few such loans in the last seventy years. The explanation is the drastic change in the relationships between Anglos and Latins. When English-speaking settlers first moved into Texas, they found the hacienda culture already established, and eagerly took over culture and vocabulary from the Latins who constituted the local elite. Anglo and Latin, side by side, died in the Alamo March 4, 1836, and conquered at San Jacinto seven weeks later. But since 1890 the Texan has encountered Mexican Spanish most often in the speech of unskilled laborers, including imported braceros and illegally entered wetbacks; derogatory labels for Latins have increased in Texas English, and loans from Spanish have declined. We borrow few words from those we consider our inferiors.

We can now make a few clear statements about the facts of American dialects, and their significance:

1. Even though much work remains to be done, we can describe in some detail most of the principal regional varieties of American English, and many of the important sub-varieties; we can indicate, further, some of the kinds of social differences that are to be found in various dialect areas, and many of the kinds that are to be found in some of the most important cities.

2. We can be sure that in many situations there are tensions between external norms and the expectations of one's associates. These tensions, most probably, are strongest in the lower middle class -- a group anxious to forget humbler backgrounds but not sure of their command of the prestige patterns. Since the teaching profession, on all levels, is heavily drawn from the lower middle class, we can expect -- as Marjorie Daunt found years ago -- that anxiety is the characteristic attitude of the English teacher toward variations in usage. There is a strong urge to make changes, for the sake of making changes and demonstrating one's authority, without stopping to sort out the significance of differences in usage. This attitude is reflected in the two most widely known programs for teaching better English to the disadvantaged: a socially insignificant problem, such as the distinction between *Wales* and *whales*, is given the same value as the use of the marker for the third singular in the present indicative. Future programs should use the resources of the dialect archives, at least as a start, even though more detailed and more recent information may be necessary before one can develop teaching materials. The inevitable prescription in a pedagogical situation can be no better than the underlying description.

3. There is evidence that ambitious

students in slum areas intuitively shift their speech patterns in the direction of the prestigious local pattern, in situations where they feel such a shift will be to their advantage. Some actually achieve, on their own, a high degree of functional bidialectalism, switching codes as the situation demands. In any teaching program it would seem intelligent to make use of this human facility.

4. The surest social markers in American English are grammatical forms, and any teaching program should aim, first of all, at developing a habitual productive command of the grammar of standard English -- with due allowance for the possibility that the use of this grammar may be confined to formal situations in which the speaker comes in contact with the dominant culture.

5. Relatively few pronunciation features are clear social markers, though in many Northern cities there is a tendency to identify all Southern and South Midland pronunciations as those of uneducated rural Negroes. How much one should attempt to substitute local pronunciations for those which are standard in regions from which migrants come would probably depend on the extent to which variations in standard English are recognized and accepted in the community: Washington, for instance, may be more tolerant than New York City. In any event, programs to alter pronunciation patterns should concentrate on those pronunciations that are most widely recognized as substandard.

6. Few people can really identify the race of a speaker by pronunciation and voice quality. In experiments in Chicago, middle-class Middle Westerners consistently identified the voice of an educated urban white Southerner as that of an uneducated rural Negro, and many identified as Negro the voice of an educated white Chicagoan. Similar experiments in New York have yielded similar results. And many white Southerners can testify to personal difficulties arising from this confusion in the minds of Northerners. In Ithaca, New York, I could not get to see any apartment advertised as vacant until I paid a personal visit; over the telephone I was always told that the apartments had just been rented; James Marchand, a Middle Tennessean once on the Cornell faculty, carefully identified himself as "Professor Marchand," if he wanted a garageman to come and pick up his car. And the telephone voice of my Mississippi-born chairman, Gwin Kolb, is racially misidentified with alarming regularity.

7. There can be no single standard in programs for the disadvantaged; the target dialect must vary according to the local situation. In Mississippi, the same program can be used for Negroes and whites, because they share most of the same grammatical deviations from the local standard, and share phonological patterns with that standard; in Cleveland, grammatical features in writing are sufficient to distinguish Negro college applicants from white better than ninety percent of the time, and deviations from local standard pronunciation are far more striking and numerous among Negroes than among locally-born disadvantaged whites.

8. To the suggestion that Southern Negroes should not be taught local standard pronunciation, but some external standard -- the hypothetical variety some call 'network English'[2] -- there is a simple answer in the form of a question: "Do you want integration in the South?" The Southern patterns of race relations have suffered too long from too many separate standards for Negro and white; it would be ironical if those speaking most loudly in behalf of the aspirations of the Southern Negro should create new obstacles to those aspirations. The language problems of the uneducated Southern Negro are the language problems, even to fine detail, of the uneducated Southern white in the same community; the South may well solve the language problems in its schools before Detroit does. Once the races are brought into the same classroom, a community will need only one intelligent program based on a solid body of dialect evidence.

9. While we are planning language programs for our disadvantaged, we must educate the dominant culture in the causes and significance of dialect differences; it is particularly urgent that we educate teachers on all levels, from kindergarten through graduate school. The disadvantaged will have enough to do in learning new patterns of language behavior; the dominant culture must meet them part way, with greater understanding, with a realization that dialect differences do not reflect intellectual or moral differences, but only differences in experience. Granted that this reeducation of the dominant culture is bound to be difficult, we should not be so cynical as to reject it, on the ground that it cannot take place. In an age when we are turning the heat off under the melting pot and accepting the cultural contributions of Americans with ancestral languages other than English, in an age when we are learning the art of peaceful coexistence with a variety of economic and political and cultural systems, it should not be difficult to extend this acceptance to fellow Americans of different cultural backgrounds and linguistic habits, and especially to recognize that cultured American English may be found in many regional and local varieties. It is a poor cultural tolerance that would accept all cultivated speech except that in other parts of our own country.

With my deep-ingrained horror of patent-medicine salesmen, I would not leave you with the impression that we already have all the answers, or even all the evidence we need to arrive at those answers. We need many more kinds of investigation, and we should like to think that John Fisher, with his unlimited license to stalk money-bearing animals, might help us conduct some of them. We are still to do even the preliminary surveys in such parts of the country as Tennessee and Arkansas [by 1977 covered by Pederson for the Atlas of the Gulf States]; we need many more studies of the actual patterns of social dialects in most American cities. We really have no serious evidence on regional and social differences in such prosodic features as stress and pitch and juncture. The recognition of paralanguage -- the non-linguistic modulation of the stream of speech -- is so recent that we have no idea as to the kinds of regional and social differences that may be found in tempo and rhythm, in range of pitch and stress, in drawl and clipping, in rasp and nasality and mellifluousness. We have not even begun to study regional and social variations in gesture and other kinds of body movement. But we do have a framework which we can fill in detail, continually building our teaching programs on solid research into the ways in which Americans communicate in various localities, and into the attitudes of specific speakers toward those whose usage differs from their own. In comparison with the immensity of our social problems, our linguistic knowledge is as a little candle in the forest darkness at night; let us not hide that candle under a basket, but put it in a lantern and use it to find our way.

NOTES

[1] This essay is the text of an address given at the MLA General Meeting on English, in Chicago, December 28, 1965.

[2] [The fate of the most notable example of 'network English' -- Richard Nixon -- should induce caution in those advocating this variety.]

Part II
Applied Dialectology

The *Linguistic Atlas of New England* (LANE) is the first published section of the Linguistic Atlas of the United States and Canada, directed by Hans Kurath and sponsored by the American Council of Learned Societies.[1] Besides substituting evidence for previous conjectures about many problems of New England speech, it is the first linguistic atlas of English. It is also the first published linguistic atlas of an area where industrialization, rapidly following settlement, has been a major influence in the creation and dissemination of everyday speech forms.[2]

LANE consists of three large folio volumes, bound as six (Kurath *et al.* 1939-43), and the *Handbook of the Linguistic Geography of New England* (Kurath *et al.* 1939).[3]

The *Handbook* contains six chapters: I. The dialect areas of New England: a discussion of innovations, relics, patterns of distribution, and means of dissemination of linguistic forms. II. Methodology: the selection of communities and informants; evaluation of the field records; instructions for field work; differences between the field workers; the make-up of the maps; a bibliography of linguistic geography. III. The settlement of New England: a summary of the settlement history of the area investigated, with a bibliography of New England history. IV. Phonetic alphabet and other symbols. V. The work sheets (questionnaire). VI. Communities and informants: brief analyses of the communities investigated, with short summaries of local history and bibliographical notes; biographies, family histories, and character sketches of the informants. There are twenty-four charts and a table of linguistic distributions, a table of informants by types, two phonetic tables and eight diagrams, a map of New England population distribution in 1930, and two maps showing settlement history. Chapters II, IV, and V thus help interpret the data recorded by the field workers; chapters I, III, and VI facilitate understanding the patterns of distribution.

A few of the most significant features of LANE are: 1) the use of several field workers; 2) the investigation of several levels of speech; 3) the content of the work sheets.

1. Nine field workers were used: Kurath, Miles L. Hanley, Guy S. Lowman, Jr., Bernard Bloch, Rachel S. Harris, Cassil Reynard, Martin Joos, Marguerite Chappal-laz, and Lee S. Hultzén.[4] Of the 416 records, Lowman made 158, Bloch 87, Miss Harris 49, and Hanley 45, with 77 records by the other five investigators. Differences in handling the questionnaire and in phonetic notation are recorded, the former on the maps where differences in interviewing may be relevant, the latter in the discussion of the phonetic alphabet.

The multiplication of field workers always creates *personal boundaries* distinct from true linguistic boundaries. Whoever uses LANE must face this problem. Yet differences among the field workers actually enable one to evaluate each group of records more accurately than if only one field worker had covered the whole territory. For, say, Edmont's consistent but unmeasured personal bias throughout the *Atlas linguistique de la France* (Gilliéron and Edmont 1902-10), LANE has a series of of personal biases which help correct each other. Actually the personal differences rarely cause trouble in interpretation; even the apparently complicated differences in transcribing the low-back vowels (*Handbook* 126-27) create no insuperable difficulties in phonetic analyses, and almost no difficulty in analysing phonemes.[5]

2. The need for interviewing more than one informant in each community, thus providing information on more than one level of usage, arises from the nature of American society. From the earliest settlements, Americans have been characterized by both geographic and social mobility.[6] Consequently standard American English is not sharply different from other social varieties; furthermore, the standard language is not uniform and there has been little accurate information about its variation. Thus an investigation of American English involves both social and regional varieties; it must seek to record both the relics of the past and the tendencies of the present, including the great body of common speech which is neither standard English nor extremely rustic or proletarian. Our knowledge of other languages is defective when investigators have neglected these intermediate varieties; our knowledge of American English would be inadequate without them.

Investigators for LANE were thus instructed to interview three types of informants: 1) wherever possible, a member of the oldest living native generation, with a minimum of travel, reading, and formal education; 2) in most communities, a second informant, younger, somewhat better educated, or both; 3) in about twenty percent of the communities, a cultured informant, generally college educated and from an old and distinguished local family.[7] The informants vary from community to community, depending on the personality and judgment of the field worker and the persons who might be available for interviewing; but in two hundred communities, individual variations probably cancel each other. With a difference in age or sophistication always represented, the direction of linguistic change, if there is any, should be readily apparent.

3. The work sheets measure not only survivals of British dialect usage but innovations that have arisen in North America through contacts with speakers of non-English languages or through the development of new metropolitan culture centers. Everyone realizes that such terms as *chipmunk* and *skunk* might be established in New England as borrowings from Algonquian, while in other regions the English terms *ground squirrel* and *polecat* were transferred to North American animals. One less often recognizes that by 1700 such cities as Philadelphia, Boston, Charleston and New York were not only the ports through which British vocabulary innovations, such as *piazza* 'porch' or *pavement* 'sidewalk' were introduced, but centers of commerce and culture in their own right; in 1776 Philadelphia and Boston were the second and third most important cities in the English-speaking world. Such cities as these, and the newer commercial and industrial centers which arose in the nineteenth century, have influenced American English, not only by determining the local or national status of existing forms but by creating new ones. A regional term for non-alcoholic carbonated beverages or the baby carriage or kerosene -- cultural innovations of the nineteenth century -- is as significant as a regional name for a frying pan or a haystack; a true record of regional differences must consider both innovations and relics.[8]

In selecting items for the LANE work sheets, Kurath followed these principles: 1) they should fit naturally into a conversational interview; 2) they should be familiar to most informants, both urban and rural; 3) they should promise to reveal regional or social differences in vocabulary, grammar, or pronunciation. The selection drew on the experience of many scholars, particularly C. S. Grandgent, J. S. Kenyon, G. P. Krapp, and George Hempl, especially Hempl's short questionnaire (1894). For comparing British and American pronunciation, Kurath incorporated many items from A. J. Ellis's Comparative Specimen, Dialect Test, and Classified Word List (1869-89:V.7*-31*). Like any work sheets, these are selective, not exhaustive; the questions were distributed over many of the common aspects of human behavior, and the total length was kept at about 750 items, to provide for interviews averaging from eight to twelve hours in length.

The data of LANE is presented by hand-lettered overprinting on colored base maps. The base map indicates political boundaries (national, state, and county), principal cities, significant topographical features (coastlines, rivers, and mountains), and -- in a table -- the communities investigated by each field worker.

The overprinted data includes:

1. The responses of each informant for the item presented on the map -- normally the full impressionistic phonetic record as made by the field worker, so that anyone who wishes may make his own phonemic analyses.

2. Informants' observations about the status of linguistic forms, and notations of the conditions under which forms were recorded. *Reported forms* the informant has heard from others but does not use himself; they may be obsolete or archaic or innovations. *Suggested forms* the informant admits he uses when the field worker mentions them, but did not offer during the interview. Reported and suggested forms are not as strong evidence as forms offered by the informant. *Conversational forms*, on the other hand -- recorded by the field worker as they occur spontaneously during the interview -- representing informants' unguarded usage may be more valid than forms obtained by direct questioning.[9]

3. A commentary -- sometimes a simple statement of the item presented on the map, sometimes also an indication of the contexts in which the item was obtained, a discussion of the item, and incidental comments by informants. For the maps dealing with the outdoor toilet (#354) and the noisy burlesque serenade after a wedding (#409), the commentaries are very detailed.

Some maps contain less information than others, but even the rather simple map for *girl* (#377) furnishes information for at least three charts -- one for the variant *gal*, one for palatalization of initial /g-/, and one for vowel quality and loss of /-r/.[10]

When one charts items from LANE and examines the settlement history, he finds several clear-cut patterns of distribution. A few of these appear on the maps accompanying this article.

Map 1 shows items reflecting settlement history and migration. *Horning* 'burlesque serenade after a wedding' was carried by Rhode Islanders to western Massachusetts and southern Vermont. *Great-beams, high-beams* 'barn loft' spread with settlement from Worcester County, in central Massachusetts, northward along the Connecticut

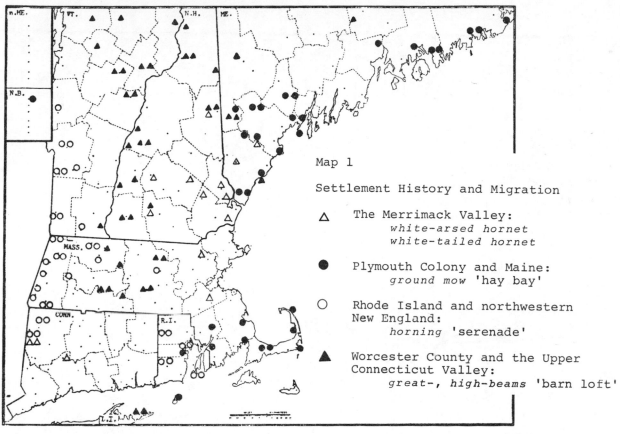

Map 1

Settlement History and Migration

△ The Merrimack Valley:
     white-arsed hornet
     white-tailed hornet

● Plymouth Colony and Maine:
     ground mow 'hay bay'

○ Rhode Island and northwestern
   New England:
     horning 'serenade'

▲ Worcester County and the Upper
   Connecticut Valley:
     great-, *high-beams* 'barn loft'

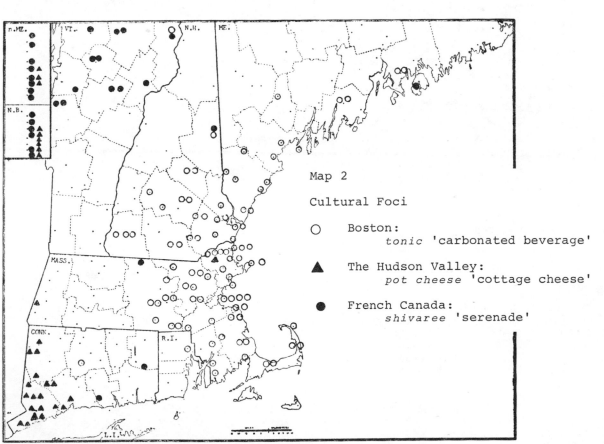

Map 2

Cultural Foci

○ Boston:
     tonic 'carbonated beverage'

▲ The Hudson Valley:
     pot cheese 'cottage cheese'

● French Canada:
     shivaree 'serenade'

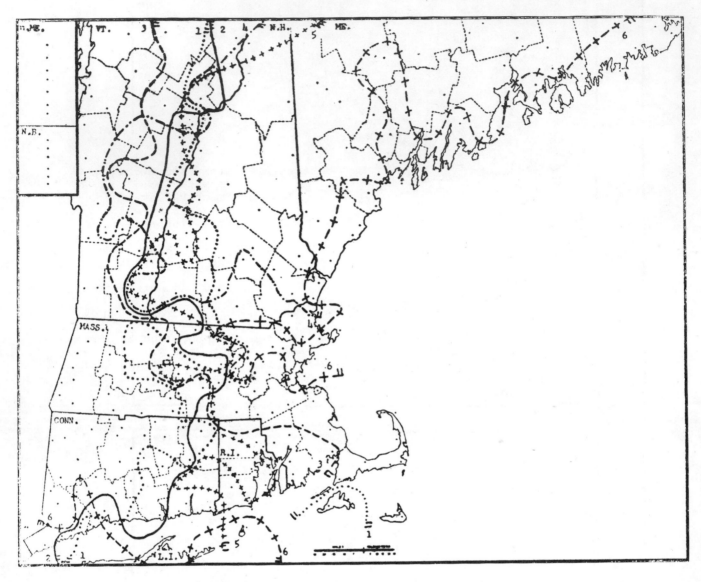

Map 3

Eastern New England Pronunciation

Limits of Predominance

.....	1)	loss of /-r/ in *barn*
————	2)	/u/ in *tube*
- - - - -	3)	/ɔ/ in *hog*

Limits of Occurrence

··-···	4)	/ʊ/ in *gums*
+++++	5)	/a/ in *can't*
+-+-+	6)	loss of /h-/ in *whip*

/u/ in *tube*, the loss of /-r/ in *barn*,
and the loss of /h-/ in *whip* are also
typical of the New York City Metropolitan area.

[82]

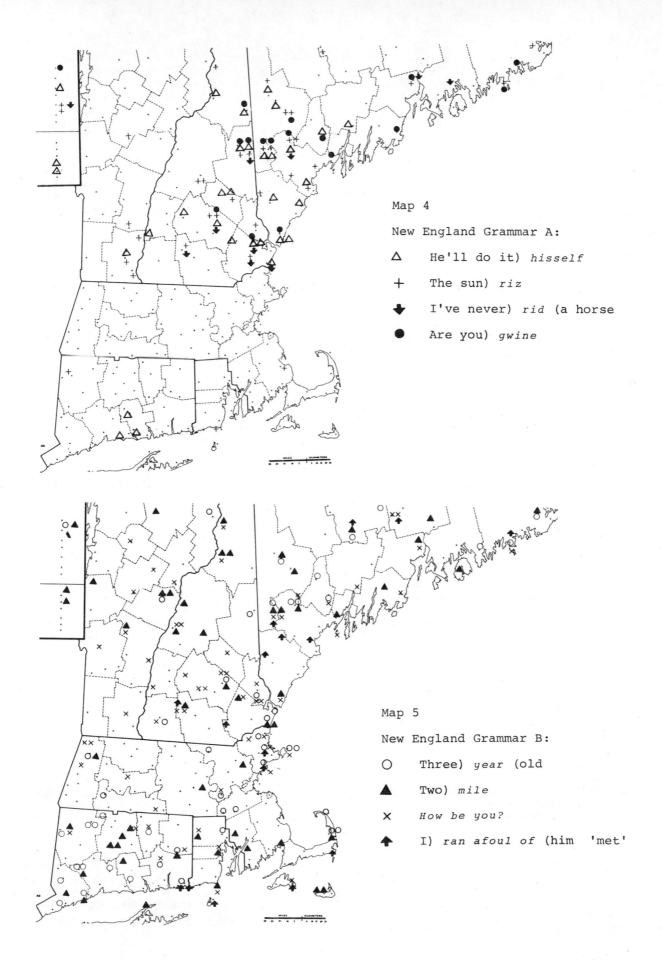

Map 4

New England Grammar A:

△   He'll do it) *hisself*

+   The sun) *riz*

⬇   I've never) *rid* (a horse

●   Are you) *gwine*

Map 5

New England Grammar B:

○   Three) *year* (old

▲   Two) *mile*

✕   *How be you?*

⬆   I) *ran afoul of* (him 'met'

River. *Ground mow* 'hay bay' was taken to the coast of Maine by colonists from the Plymouth area in southeastern Massachusetts. *White-arsed hornet* is largely confined to coastal communities in New Hampshire and their derivative settlements.

Map 2 shows terms spreading from culture centers. In eastern New England *tonic* is the name for non-alcoholic carbonated beverages throughout the Boston wholesale trading area. In southwestern New England, economically dependent on New York City, the Hudson Valley Dutch term *pot cheese* 'cottage cheese' has spread as the New York City trade name. In northern New England, sparsely populated, adjacent to French Canada, and with many recent settlers of French-Canadian descent, *shivaree* (<Fr. *charivari*) has become the usual term for a burlesque wedding serenade.[11]

Map 3 shows isoglosses for pronunciation features characteristic of eastern New England. For three of these features -- /u/ in *tube*, the rounded vowel /ɔ/ in *hog*, and the loss of post-vocalic /-r/ in *barn* -- the isoglosses represent *limits of predominance*: these features are shared by nearly all informants in eastern New England and sometimes also appear in western New England. For the other items the isoglosses represent *limits of occurrence*: the 'broad *a*' in *can't*, a social shibboleth, is favored by younger and more sophisticated informants; the loss of /h-/ in *whip* is largely confined to coastal communities (cf. R. and V. McDavid 1952b); *gums* with /ʊ/, the vowel of *foot*, has been recorded sporadically from older speakers in areas settled from New England, but only in northeastern New England is it very common and used on all cultural levels.

Maps 4 and 5, showing nonstandard grammatical forms, dispel the myth of a uniform 'American Vulgate' grammar, differing consistently from the standard language. True all these forms are rare in Massachusetts. But four forms -- the reflexive pronoun *hisself*, *riz* as the preterite of *rise*, *rid* as the past participle of *ride*, and *gwine* as the present participle of *go* -- are seldom found outside the very conservative area of northeastern New England. *Ran afoul of* 'met,' a nautical metaphor, is limited to communities on or near the coast. The old-fashioned greeting *How be you?* and the uninflected plurals *two mile* and *three year old* are very widely distributed; other uninflected plurals such as *two pound*, *six foot*, *forty rod*, and *thirty bushel* are even more common, the last two being used by a majority of New Englanders.

In a short article one can only suggest the usefulness of LANE, which becomes more impressive as each scholar discovers its resources. When other regional atlases appear, one may interpret the relation between New England speech and other varieties of American English; the new linguistic surveys of the British Isles may provide comparable data for interpreting all forms of American English in their historical perspective.

NOTES

[1] This account used Kurath 1949, Atwood 1953a, and data for two works then in preparation: Kurath and R. McDavid 1961 and V. McDavid 1956.

[2] For other accounts see Pop 1950:914-23, Dieth 1948, and reviews by Marckwardt (1940b) and Menner (1942). [The most detailed evaluation of LANE is O'Cain 1979, which also contains an excellent account of the negotiations which led to support by the ACLS.]

[3] Kurath was director and editor of LANE and principal author of the *Handbook*, Miles L. Hanley was associate director and Guy S. Lowman, Jr. principal field investigator. Bernard Bloch, assistant editor, prepared the chapter of the *Handbook* dealing with the phonetic alphabet. Marcus L. Hansen, historian, prepared the summary of settlement history and assembled the data on the history of individual communities. Mrs. Julia Bloch compiled and edited the sketches of communities and informants.

[4] Kurath became Editor of the *Middle English Dictionary*, and is now Professor Emeritus of English at the University of Michigan, as well as director of the Atlas project. Hanley [died 1954] and Joos [died 1978] held professorships at the University of Wisconsin; Bloch [died 1965] became Professor of Linguistics at Yale University; Hultzén [died 1968] held a professorship at the University of Illinois; Miss Harris (now Mrs. Kilpatrick) was at the University of Iowa as Director for Iowa of the *Linguistic Atlas of the Upper Midwest* (Allen 1973-76), and later moved to Eastern Carolina University, Greenville, North Carolina. Lowman died in an automobile accident in 1941, during field work in upstate New York; he had investigated the Atlantic Seaboard states from central New York to the southern boundary of North Carolina.

[5] In my analysis of American pronunciation I am struck by the agreement between Lowman's transcriptions and mine in areas where we both made records: New York, South Carolina, and Georgia.

[6] The 1940 census indicates that over ten percent of the U.S. population had moved from one state to another since 1935. Even in the relatively stratified slaveholding states before 1865, poor whites could rise to the affluence and prestige of the plantation class.

[7] Four New England communities -- Boston and Springfield in Massachusetts, Providence and Newport in Rhode Island -- have two cultured informants each. For the Atlantic Seaboard area there are more than 150, by far the largest available body of comparable evidence on standard American English.

[8] The items were chosen specifically for New England; in other regions some items have been dropped and promising new ones added. *Hoofs* has proved to be a consistently fruitful item in other regions, though it was not included in New England; on the other hand, *forty rods*, designed to record the uninflected plural, has been dropped, since the *rod* is not a common unit of measure outside the New England settlement area. See A. L. Davis, R. and V. McDavid 1969.

No questionnaire can be complete for a living language; new differences will develop or be discovered while scholars are recording old ones. No American regional survey has yet recorded such items as the stressed syllable of *apricot* (often /æ/ in the New England settlement area, normally /e/ elsewhere) or the phrase *stand in line* 'queue up,' for which many speakers in the New York metropolitan area say *stand on line*.

[9] Particularly for grammatical forms with a real or imagined social status, the informant may respond to direct questioning with the form he considers 'correct'; in conversation he may use without inhibition forms which he stigmatizes as characteristic of Negroes, poor whites, or other unprivileged groups.

[10] The *Handbook* (54) suggests methods of charting; one may obtain lithoprinted outline maps from the Atlas at cost. Atwood *et al.* 1948 is a useful index of words and phrases. [For the second edition of the *Handbook* (1973), Audrey Duckert prepared a map inventory and a complete word index.]

[11] For the spread of *shivaree* west of the Atlantic Seaboard, see A. L. Davis and R. McDavid 1949.

When the Linguistic Atlas of the United States and Canada was inaugurated in 1930, scholars envisaged a systematic survey of all English-speaking North America. A quarter century later, however, published data is available for only one section, New England.[1] The relative slowness with which the investigation has proceeded has disappointed many who are accustomed to expect miracles from American energy and efficiency. Nevertheless, work has continued, though at an uneven pace.[2] In fact, though most of the material is unpublished and some areas still uninvestigated, one may now draw much more accurate conclusions about the distribution of American dialects than were commonly drawn a generation ago, and still are drawn by those who have not familiarized themselves with the Atlas materials.

As field work in New England drew to a close, Hans Kurath, director of the Atlas, inaugurated plans for a similarly intensive investigation of the other Atlantic Seaboard states. This was a logical step, since the Middle and South Atlantic States, along with New England, constituted the area of original settlement, from whose speech patterns the dialects of the inland states -- a secondary settlement area -- would naturally be derived. Originally Kurath planned separate atlases for the Old South (Delaware, Maryland, Virginia, North Carolina, South Carolina, and Georgia) and for the Middle Atlantic States (New York, New Jersey, Pennsylvania, and West Virginia). Later, however, as he revised plans for editing and publishing, he decided to combine the data into one large atlas (LAMSAS).

Although nine field workers had participated in collecting the data from New England, the plans for the South Atlantic States called for only one, Guy S. Lowman, Jr. Aside from the recognized advantages (not without some compensating disadvantages) of having all the data collected by one investigator, the choice of Lowman was logical since he had done by far the largest share of the New England field work and excelled in the minuteness and accuracy of his transcriptions. After a year of preliminary investigations, testing revisions of the questionnaire to take care of the new cultural situation in the South, Lowman began field work in Virginia in 1934.

It was hoped that local institutions would bear much of the expense of field work in the South Atlantic States, as they had done in New England. In fact, enough such aid was available to enable Lowman to complete the field work in Virginia and North Carolina, but local support failed to materialize in South Carolina and Georgia. Thus field work was shifted to the Middle Atlantic area, under the sponsorship of the American Philosophical Society and several universities. With this help Lowman completed New Jersey, Pennsylvania, West Virginia, Maryland, the easternmost strip of Ohio, the New York City metropolitan area, and the Hudson Valley; he was working in upstate New York when he was killed in an automobile accident in the summer of 1941.

Shortly before Lowman's death, Raven I. McDavid, Jr., a student of Bernard Bloch (assistant editor of LANE), had obtained a Rosenwald Fellowship for the intensive study of the speech of northwestern South Carolina, and under Kurath's direction was engaged in supplementing Lowman's work. After a four-year interruption during World War II, McDavid -- with funds supplied by the American Council of Learned Societies -- completed field work in South Carolina and eastern Georgia in 1948, and by the following spring had also completed New York State and a few border communities in Canada.

Preliminary editing of the South Atlantic materials was begun while the Middle Atlantic field work was still under way. For much of this preliminary work, as for much of the preliminary editing of LANE, the Atlas relied on student assistance supplied under the college aid program of the National Youth Administration. With the abolition of the NYA during World War II, the summoning of linguists and their students to war work,[3] and the transfer of the Atlas archives from Brown University to the University of Michigan when Kurath assumed the editorship of the *Middle English Dictionary* (1946), editorial work was suspended and has not yet been resumed. Kurath has drafted detailed plans and cost estimates for editing and publishing the LAMSAS materials, but so far the ACLS has been unable to secure the necessary funds.

Whenever editing is resumed, one change is certain to be made from the format in which LANE was published, as well as the atlases of France and Italy: lithographed over-printing from hand-lettered phonetic data, on base maps. The high cost of professional hand-lettering has meant that LANE is priced so high ($180 when issued -- and today's higher costs for draftsman's

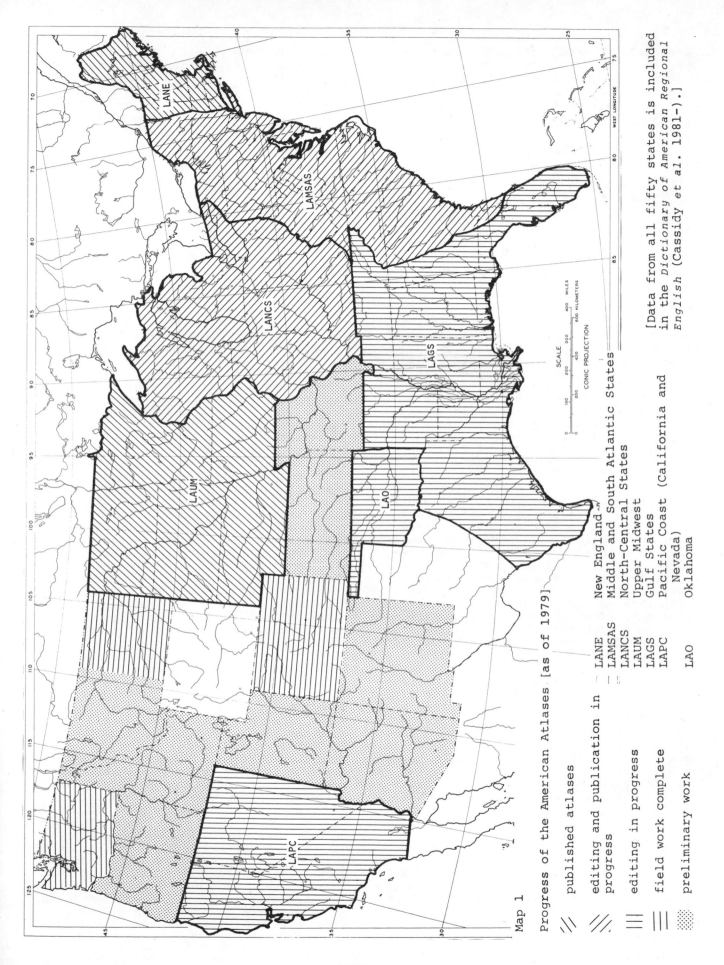

Map 1

Progress of the American Atlases [as of 1979]

published atlases

editing and publication in   LANE   New England
progress   LAMSAS   Middle and South Atlantic States
   LANCS   North-Central States
editing in progress   LAUM   Upper Midwest
   LAGS   Gulf States
field work complete   LAPC   Pacific Coast (California and
   Nevada)
preliminary work   LAO   Oklahoma

[Data from all fifty states is included
in the *Dictionary of American Regional
English* (Cassidy et al. 1981–).]

work and printing would entail a far higher figure) that few small institutions or individual scholars can afford it. Kurath has therefore decided to publish the LAMSAS materials in the form of tables, prepared from type and printed by photo-offset.[4] Not only will the cost be less than half that of hand-lettered overprinting, but the tabular presentation will permit a smaller page size, which will allow far easier handling than is possible with the large New England volumes. Furthermore, experience with the New England materials has demonstrated that charting of individual items can be done much more speedily and accurately from the tabular list manuscripts than from the maps.

If further investigation of American dialects had to wait for the editing and publication of the materials from the Middle and South Atlantic States, scholars would be severely handicapped. Fortunately, from the beginning Kurath has placed the Atlas archives at the disposal of competent scholars, and encouraged the publication of interpretive articles; in fact several such articles appeared during the early stages of editing the LANE materials. These interpretive and derivative studies, varying in dimensions from brief notes to complete volumes, have both demonstrated the complexity of American dialect patterns and suggested important modifications of method.

The first of a series of University of Michigan publications in American English, Kurath's *Word Geography of the Eastern United States* appeared in 1949. Copiously illustrated, not only does it delineate with isoglosses the major dialectal regions of the eastern United States and accurately picture their constituent areas,[5] but it also provides specific information on the regional and social distribution of the lexical variants for some 120 items from the Atlas questionnaires. The second volume in the series, Atwood's *Survey of Verb Forms in the Eastern United States* appeared in 1953; it discusses in detail the regional and social variations in these grammatical items, with particular reference to the relationship between these facts of distribution and the popular and pedagogical notions of what constitutes standard English. The third volume in the series is Kurath and R. McDavid's *Pronunciation of English in the Atlantic States* (1961). The Texas dissertation of Sumner Ives, on the dialect of the Uncle Remus stories of Joel Chandler Harris, completed in 1950, has yielded several significant articles (1950b, 1952, 1954).[6]

Aside from the obvious usefulness of a large body of comparable data, systematically collected over a wide area by competent investigators, the LAMSAS materials have so far rendered two important services:

1. They have pointed out the need for discussing social differences in any picture of dialect variations. Despite popular misconceptions, a dialect is not merely the most old-fashioned speech of uneducated informants in isolated communities, but the characteristic speech of any identifiable regional or social group. Properly, one should not contrast a standard language and local dialect, but must recognize that both standard and old-fashioned speech have regional variations, and that between the standard language and the most old-fashioned speech is a large body of common speech, differing more or less from the extremes according to the social structure of the particular region and community in which it is found. In all regions and communities, to be sure, the standard language exerts an influence on old-fashioned speech; but the extent of this influence varies from place to place, and only by including representatives of the common speech can linguistic geographers judge fairly the kinds of change that are taking place.

2. Moreover, it is already possible to draw a very different picture of the important regional differences than scholars customarily drew a generation ago. For a long time it was traditional to set up a three-fold division of American dialects into "Eastern" (New England or eastern New England, sometimes also including New York City), "Southern" (everything south of Pennsylvania and east of the Mississippi, plus Arkansas, Louisiana, and parts of Texas, Oklahoma, and Missouri), and "General American" (everything else).[7] Apparently two principal criteria were involved: 1) the so-called "General American" retained postvocalic /-r/ in *beard*, *barn*, *born*, in contrast to the supposed practice of the other two regions; 2) "Eastern" and a minority of "Southern" had /a/ (phonetically [a] or [ɑ]) in such words as *dance*, *half*, *pasture*, following the practice of British Received Pronunciation, while "General American" had /æ/. In short, "General American" was largely a negative term, depending on the absence of specific characteristics observed in the other two areas.

As the data came in from the Atlantic Seaboard, it soon became apparent that the older theory needed drastic revision. First of all, the presence or absence of postvocalic /-r/ was no longer a reliable criterion, since this feature was found to occur both in parts of eastern New England and in much of the South, though limited in the South to certain social groups. Furthermore, Pennsylvania usage, in both vocabulary and pronunciation, was frequently very different from that of New York State, though both states had been credited with speaking "General American," and Pennsylvania forms prevailed in many parts of the historical and political

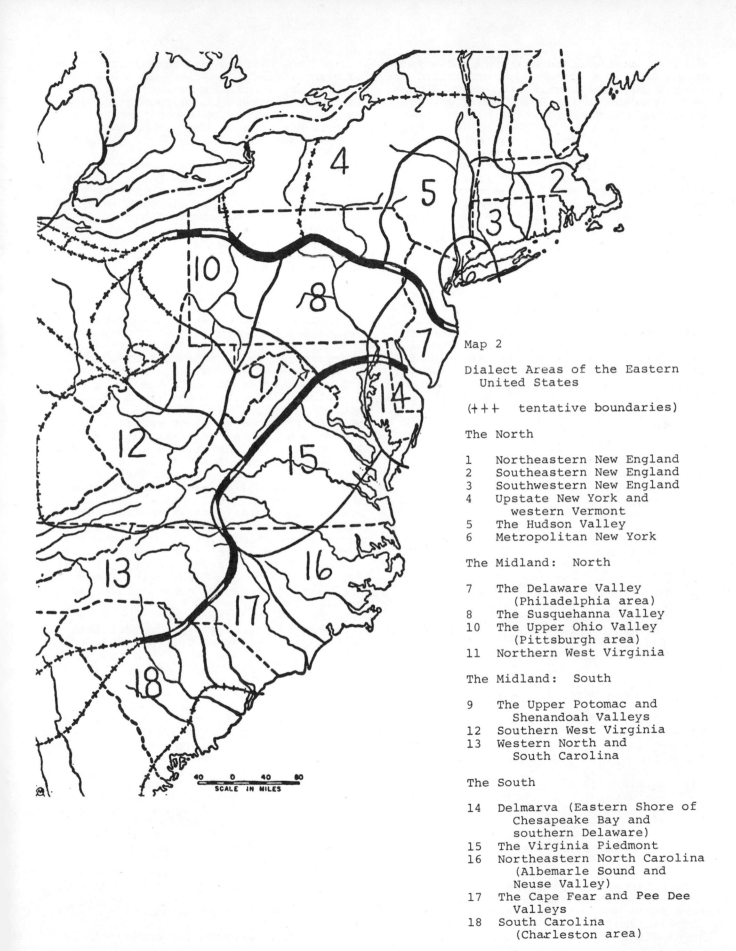

Map 2

Dialect Areas of the Eastern
   United States

(+++ tentative boundaries)

The North

1   Northeastern New England
2   Southeastern New England
3   Southwestern New England
4   Upstate New York and
        western Vermont
5   The Hudson Valley
6   Metropolitan New York

The Midland: North

7   The Delaware Valley
        (Philadelphia area)
8   The Susquehanna Valley
10   The Upper Ohio Valley
        (Pittsburgh area)
11   Northern West Virginia

The Midland: South

9   The Upper Potomac and
        Shenandoah Valleys
12   Southern West Virginia
13   Western North and
        South Carolina

The South

14   Delmarva (Eastern Shore of
        Chesapeake Bay and
        southern Delaware)
15   The Virginia Piedmont
16   Northeastern North Carolina
        (Albemarle Sound and
        Neuse Valley)
17   The Cape Fear and Pee Dee
        Valleys
18   South Carolina
        (Charleston area)

South.[8] On the basis of this evidence, Kurath set up a *Midland* dialect region, comprising Pennsylvania and Pennsylvania-settled areas in the South and West, restricting the term *Southern* to the older plantation settlements of the South Atlantic coast and to their derivatives, and establishing a *Northern* region including not only New York City and eastern New England but western New England, New York State, and their settlements to the west. As far as the South is concerned, these observations are supported by demography and social history. The Southern mountains, the Shenandoah Valley, and (in great part) the Piedmont areas of the Carolinas and Georgia were originally settled by Germans and Ulster Scots from Pennsylvania. These areas resisted the plantation system and the institution of chattel slavery, were strongholds of Union sentiment at the time of the Confederate War, and even today differ sharply from the coastal areas in their political attitudes.

In the *Word Geography* Kurath groups the American dialects of the Atlantic Seaboard as follows (see Map 2):

The North:

1. Northeastern New England
2. Southeastern New England
3. Southwestern New England
4. Upstate New York and western Vermont
5. The Hudson Valley
6. Metropolitan New York

The Midland:

North Midland:
7. The Delaware Valley (Philadelphia area)
8. The Susquehanna Valley
10. The Upper Ohio Valley (Pittsburgh area)
11. Northern West Virginia

South Midland:
9. The Upper Potomac and Shenandoah Valleys
12. Southern West Virginia
13. Western North and South Carolina

The South:

14. Delmarva (Eastern Shore of Maryland and Virginia, and southern Delaware)
15. The Virginia Piedmont
16. Northeastern North Carolina (Albemarle Sound and Neuse Valley)
17. The Cape Fear and Peedee Valleys
18. South Carolina (Charleston area)

Although Kurath established this scheme on the basis of vocabulary evidence, before field work was complete in South Carolina and New York State, it has been borne out by the grammatical and phonolo-gical data.[9] For some items, such as the homonymy of *horse* and *hoarse*, the Hudson Valley agrees with Pennsylvania rather than with the rest of the North;[10] for many items, including the differentiation of *horse* and *hoarse* and the pronunciation of *coop* (see Map 3), the South Midland agrees with the South, or parts of it agree with such Southern focal areas as the Virginia Piedmont and the South Carolina Low Country.[11] But taking the phenomena as a whole, the division into Northern, Midland, and Southern types seems well established. Furthermore, the division is very useful for interpreting the data from the secondary and tertiary settlement areas further west, although one readily concedes that the dialect areas are less sharply defined inland than along the Atlantic Coast, and many forms which were already relics in New England or the South simply do not appear.

The following table, then, serves to characterize the more outstanding regional speech types; in its present form this table summarizes not only the books and articles of Kurath, Atwood, and others, but many studies which have so far had only oral presentation at meetings of learned societies, or treatment in unpublished theses. The summary is admittedly incomplete, since for not all of the dialect areas -- even along the Atlantic Coast -- has there been equally thorough study of the collected data. For other areas, particularly the transition areas, no distinctive characteristics have been discovered; for still others the statement is brief, as that the Delmarva area (14) is characterized most easily by *caps* 'corn husks,' *lodge* 'bed on the floor,' and *mongst-ye* (second person plural pronoun).[12]

Outline of the Principal Speech Areas
of the Eastern United States

Numbers in parentheses after each area correspond to the numbers on the map of dialect areas (Map 2). The Roman numerals after each item indicate, insofar as it has been determined, the social distribution of the item in the areas where it has been observed; these numerals correspond essentially to the social classification of Atlas informants: I: old-fashioned, rustic, poorly educated speakers ('folk speech'); II: younger, more modern, better educated speakers ('common speech'); III: cultured, well-educated speakers ('cultivated speech'). Numbers in brackets ([I], etc.) indicate less currency in that group. *Phonetic* transcriptions are enclosed in square brackets; *phonemic* transcriptions are enclosed in slants.

The North (1-6), Pronunciation:

Distinction between /o/ and /ɔ/ in

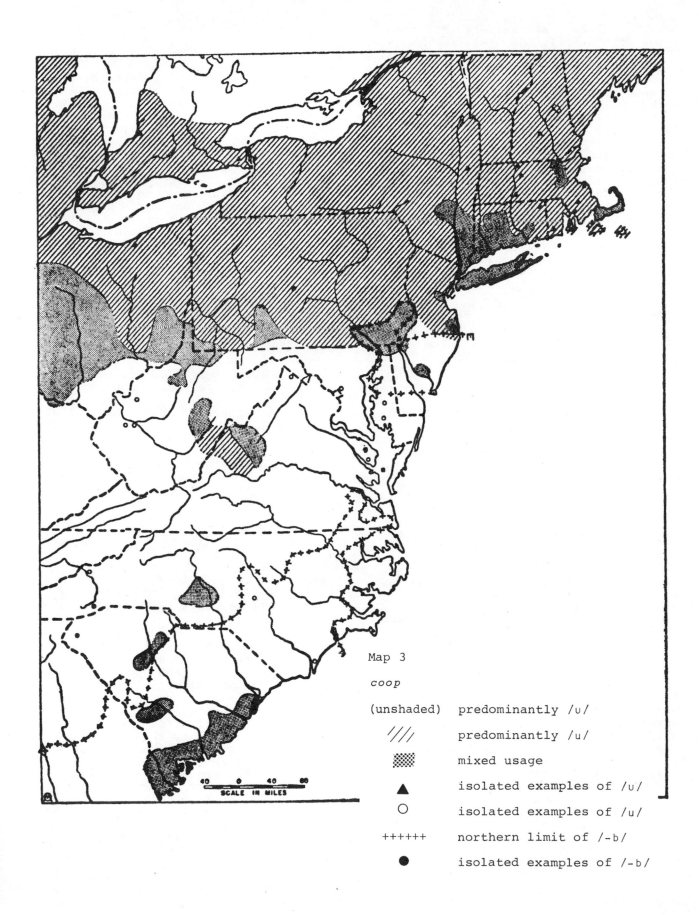

Map 3

coop

(unshaded)	predominantly /ʊ/
////	predominantly /u/
▦	mixed usage
▲	isolated examples of /ʊ/
○	isolated examples of /u/
++++++	northern limit of /-b/
●	isolated examples of /-b/

mourning:morning, hoarse:horse, fourteen: forty, etc. I, II, III. Also South. This feature probably receding in Inland Northern.

[ɨ] in unstressed syllables of *haunted, careless, pumpkin*. I, II, III. Also South.

[æ] sometimes in *stairs, care*. [I], [II], [III]. Also South.

Centralized first element in the diphthong of *fine* ([ʌɪ], [ɐɪ]). I, [II].

Centralized first element in the diphthong of *loud* ([ʌʊ], [ɐʊ]). I, [II].

/ð/ regularly in *with*. I, II, III. Possibly receding in Inland Northern.

/s/ in *grease* (v.) and *greasy*. I, II, III.

/ʊ/ in *roots*. I, II, [III].

/ʌ/ in *won't*. I, II, [III]. Not in New York City and lower Hudson Valley.

/u/, /ʊ/ in *gums*. I, [II]. Receding in Inland Northern.

/ʌ/ in *because*. I, II, III. Also South Carolina-Georgia Low-Country.

/a/, /ɔ/ in *nothing*. I, [II].

The North (1-6), Vocabulary:

pail. I, II, III. Midland and Southern *bucket*.

swill 'garbage.' I, II, III. Midland and Southern *slop*.

clapboards 'dressed siding' (on a house). I, II, III. Midland and Southern *weatherboards, weatherboarding*.

brook 'small stream.' I, II, III. Rare in Inland North.

cherry pit 'seed.' I, II, III.

angleworm 'earthworm.' I, II, III.

johnnycake 'cornbread.' I, II, III.

whiffletree, whippletree. I, II, III.

eavestrough 'gutter on roof.' I, II, [III].

spider 'frying pan.' I, II. Also South. Receding in Inland North.

fills, thills 'buggy shafts.' I, II.

quite (spry. I, II, III. Midland and Southern *right* (spry.

The North (1-6), Morphology and Syntax:

dove /doʋ/ (preterite of *dive*). I, II, III.

sick to the stomach. I, II, [III].

all to once. [I], [II]. Receding in Inland Northern.

he isn't) to home. I, II. Receding in Inland Northern.

hadn't ought 'ought not.' I, II.

it wa'n't me. I, II. Also South. Receding in Inland Northern.

see (preterite). I, II. Also South.

clim (preterite of *climb*). I, II. Also South.

be as finite verb (*How be you? Be I going to?*). I. Rare in Inland Northern.

/-θs/, /-ðz/ in *troughs*.

scairt 'scared.' I, II.

begin (preterite). [I], [II]. Also

South.

Eastern New England (1-2), Pronunciation:

[a] inconsistently in *afternoon, glass, bath, France*, etc.; consistently in *barn, yard*, etc. I, II, III.

/-r/ "lost" except before vowels: *barn, beard, four, Thursday, horse, father*, etc. Also New York City and South. Linking and intrusive /r/ are common: *idear of it*, etc. I, II, III.

[ɒ] in 'short o' words: *crop, lot, on, fog*. I, II, III. Often no distinction between these words and words like *fought, law, horse*, etc. Sometimes the latter group has a higher vowel [ɔ].

/u/ rather than /ju/ or /iw/ after /t,d, n/: *Tuesday, due, new*. I, II, III. Also North Midland.

Shortened and centralized [o] ([ð]) in *stone, coat*, etc. I, [II], [III]. Also sporadically in Inland North.

/i/ in *beard, car*, etc.

Eastern New England (1-2), Vocabulary:

pig-sty 'pen.' I, II, III.

bonny-clabber, -clapper 'curdled milk.' I, II, III.

sour-milk cheese 'cottage cheese.' I, [II], [III].

apple dowdy 'deep-dish pie.' I, II, III.

buttonwood 'sycamore.' I, II, III.

Eastern New England (1-2), Morphology and Syntax:

waked up. I, [II], [III]. Also South. Forms found in **Northeastern** New England:

riz 'rose.' I. Also South.

driv 'drove.' I. Also South.

div 'dived.' I. Also South.

gwine 'going.' I. Also South.

I was sitting) *agin* (him, . . . *against* (him 'next to.' I.

Inland Northern (4; usually includes all or part of New England settlement. Areas in Great Lakes Basin and Upper Mississippi Valley), Pronunciation:

/-r/ kept after vowels: *horse, four, father*, etc. I, II, III. Also Midland.

/a/ in *on, hog, fog, frog* (not *dog, log*). I, II, III. Also Eastern Virginia and Eastern North Carolina.

/a/ often fronted to [a‹] or [æ] in *hot, fog, on*, etc. I, II, III.

/iw/ sometimes in *Tuesday, due, new, music, beautiful*. I, [II], [III]. Receding in Great Lakes and Upper Midwest.

/æ/ in *bleat*. I, [II], [III].

Inland Northern (4), Vocabulary:

stoop 'porch.' I, II, III. Also New York City and Savannah Valley.

lobbered milk, loppered milk 'curdled milk.' I, II, III.
  Dutch cheese 'cottage cheese.' I, II.
  sugar bush 'maple grove.' I, II, [III].
  stone boat 'sled for hauling stones.' I, II, III.

Inland Northern (4), Morphology and Syntax:

  There are buttons) *onto* (the coat. [I].
  We burn coal) *into* (the stove. [I].

New York City and lower Hudson Valley (5-6), Pronunciation (usually confined to the immediate vicinity of New York City):

  /-r/ "lost" except before vowels. I, II, III (NYC only). Also New England and South.
  No distinction between *mourning:morning, hoarse:horse,* etc. Both usually have /ɔ/. I, II, III (NYC, HV). Compare North Midland.
  Adjourn:adjoin, curl:coil, etc. frequently not distinguished, [ɜɨ] or [əɨ] (less frequently [oɨ]) serving for both. I, II. Also occasional in New Orleans.
  /e/ in *Mary, dairy.* I, II, III. Also Eastern New England and South.
  /a/ in *foreign, orange, borrow;* also in *on, hog, frog, fog, log* (not *dog*). I, II, III.
  /i/ in *beard, ear,* etc. I, II, III. Also Eastern New England.
  Raised and lengthened [æˆ·] and [ɔˆ·] in *pan, lawn,* etc. I, II, [III].
  /u/ in *won't* (NYC, HV). Also Charleston.
  /w/ regularly for /hw/ in *wheelbarrow,* etc. I, II, III (NYC, HV). Also Eastern Pennsylvania and Charleston.
  Glottal stop [ʔ] for /t/ in *bottle, mountain,* etc. I, II (NYC).
  /d/ for /ð/ in *this,* etc. I, II. Chiefly in foreignized speech, NYC only.
  /ŋg/ for /ŋ/ in *Long Island,* etc. I, II. Chiefly in foreignized speech, NYC only.

New York City and lower Hudson Valley (5-6), Vocabulary (usually includes Hudson Valley):

  Dominie 'preacher.' I, II, III.
  pot cheese 'cottage cheese.' I, II, III.
  olicook 'doughnut.' I.
  hunk 'base' (in tag games). [I](NYC only).
  -kill 'small stream' (proper names only). I, II, III.
  barrack 'haystack.' I, II. Rural only.
  suppawn 'corn mush.' I, II. Rural only.
  skimmerton, skimmilton 'mock serenade.' I, II. Rural only.

New York City and lower Hudson Valley (5-

6), Morphology and Syntax:

  He lives) *in* (King Street. I, II, [III]. Also Charleston and Canada, possibly Baltimore.
  We stood) *on* (line. I, II, III.

Midland (7-13), Pronunciation:

  /r/ kept after vowels. I, II, III. Also Inland North.
  /ɔ/ in *on* (also South); in *wash, wasp;* in *log, hog, fog, frog.* I, II, III.
  /ɛ/ in *Mary, dairy.* I, II, III.
  /ə/ in the unstressed syllable of *haunted, careless, pumpkin.* I, II, III.
  [ɨ] in the unstressed syllable of *stomach.* I, II.
  /θ/ regularly in *with.* I, II, III.
  /r/ frequently intrudes in *wash, Washington, mush, judge,* etc.

Midland (7-13), Vocabulary:

  blinds 'window shades.' I, II, III. Also Canada.
  skillet 'frying pan.' I, II, III. Spreading in North-Central States and Upper Midwest.
  snake feeder 'dragon fly.' I, II, [III]. Competes with *snake doctor* in South Midland.
  poke '(paper) sack.' I, II, [III]. Not in Eastern Pennsylvania.
  sook! 'call to cows.' I, II, III.
  green-beans 'string beans.' I, II, [III]. Not in Eastern Pennsylvania.
  a little piece 'short distance.' I, II, III. Also South Carolina.

Midland (7-13), Morphology and Syntax:

  clum 'climbed.' I, [II].
  seen 'saw.' I, II. Spreading in North-Central States.
  you-uns (second person pl. pronoun). I, [II]. Not in Eastern Pennsylvania.
  all the further 'as far as.' I, II.
  I'll wait on you 'for you.' I, II, [III]. Also South Carolina. Receding in North-Central States.
  I want off. I, II, [III].
  quarter till eleven. I, II, III.

North Midland (1-8, 10-11), Pronunciation:

  /u/ after /t,d,n/ in *Tuesday, due, new,* etc. I, II, III. Also Eastern New England.
  No distinction between such pairs of words as *mourning:morning, hoarse:horse,* etc. Also Hudson Valley. Such pairs seem to have /ɔr/ in the Hudson Valley and Eastern Pennsylvania, /or/ in Western Pennsylvania.
  /ɪ/ predominant in *creek.* I, II, [III]. Also common in North, and spreading in Inland Northern.

North Midland (1-8, 10-11), Vocabulary:

  spouting, spouts 'roof gutters.' I, II,
[III].
  run 'small stream.' I, II, III.
  smearcase 'cottage cheese.' I, II,
[III].

North Midland (1-8, 10-11), Morphology and
Syntax:

  No forms observed.

Eastern Pennsylvania (7-8), Pronunciation:

  /ɔr/ in both *mourning:morning, hoarse:
horse*, etc. I, II, III. Also Hudson Valley.
  /w/ in *wheelbarrow*, etc. I, II, III.
Also Hudson Valley and Charleston.
  [ɒ] in *barn, marbles*, etc. I, [II],
[III].
  /a/ in *frog, hog, fog*. [I], II, III.
Also North.
  /i/ as [ɨi] in *me, be*, etc. I, [II],
[III].

Eastern Pennsylvania (7-8), Vocabulary:

  baby coach 'baby carriage.' I, II,
[III]. Philadelphia area only.
  pavement 'sidewalk.' I, II, III.
Germanisms (often scattered throughout the
North Midland):
  paper toot 'sack.' I, II.
  clook 'setting hen.' I.
  ponhoss 'scrapple.' I, II.
  fat-cakes 'doughnuts.' I, [II].
  thick-milk 'curdled milk.' I, II.
  spooks 'ghosts.' I, II, III. Also Hudson Valley.
  snits 'dried fruit.' I, II.

Eastern Pennsylvania (7-8), Morphology and
Syntax:

  sick on the stomach. I, II.
Germanisms:
  The oranges are) *all* 'all gone.' I, II.
  got awake 'woke up.' I, II.

Western Pennsylvania (10), Pronunciation:

  /ɔr/ in both *hoarse:horse, mourning:
morning*, etc. I, II, III.
  No contrast between such pairs of words
as *cot:caught, collar:caller*, etc. Informants have /ɔ/, less often /a/, in both
words.
  /ʊ/ in *food*. I, II.
  /u/ in *drought*. I, [II].

Western Pennsylvania (10), Vocabulary:

  hap 'comforter.' I, [II].
  cruds, crudded milk 'curdled milk.' I,
II.
  mind 'remember.' I, II, [III]. Also
South Carolina.

  hay doodle 'haycock.' I, II. Expanding
in North-Central States.
  grinnie 'chipmunk.' I, II.
  carbon oil 'kerosene.' I, II.
  baby cab 'baby carriage.' I, II.

Western Pennsylvania (10), Morphology and
Syntax:

  No distinctive forms observed.

South Midland (9, 12-13), Pronunciation:

  [a·], [a·ə] for /ai/ in all phonetic environments, as in *nice time*. I, II.

South Midland (9, 12-13), Vocabulary:

  french harp 'harmonica.' I, II, [III].
  pack 'carry, tote.' I, II.
  clabber milk 'curdled milk.' I, II,
III.
  redworm 'earthworm.' I, II.
  sugar tree 'sugar maple.' I, II, [III].
  fireboard, mantelboard 'mantel shelf.'
I, II.
  milk gap 'cow pen.' I, [II].

South Midland (9, 12-13), Morphology and
Syntax:

  dogbit 'bitten by a dog.' I, II. Also
South Carolina.
  The sun) *raised*. I, [II].
  drinkt (preterite and participle). I.
  shrinkt (preterite and participle). I.
  sot down 'sat.' I.
  swim (preterite). I.
  I ran on him 'met.' I, [II].

The South (14-18), Pronunciation:

  /r/ lost except before vowels. [I],
[II], III. Also Eastern New England and
New York City. Linking and intrusive /r/
usually do not occur in the South after
stressed syllables, but are very common
after some unstressed syllables, as in
swallow it /'swalər ɨt/.[13]
  /e/ in *Mary, dairy*. I, II, III.
  [ɨ] in unstressed syllables of *haunted,
careless, pumpkin*. I, II, III. Also
North.
  /e/ in *bleat*. I, II, III.
  /z/ in *Mrs.* (/'mɨzɨz/, /mɪz/). [I], II,
III.
  [-ɨl] in *towel, funnel*. I, II, [III].
Also Eastern New England.
  [-ɨn] in *mountain*. I, II, [III]. Also
Eastern New England.
  /k-,g-/ palatalized in *car, garden*, etc.
I, II, [III].
  [ɨ] in stressed syllables of *sister,
milk, dinner, ribbon*, etc. I, II, III.

The South (14-18), Vocabulary:

  lightwood /'laitəd/ 'fatty kindling.'
I, II, [III].

low 'moo.' I, II, III.
tote 'carry.' I, II.
carry 'take, escort, conduct.' I, II,
[III].
chittlins 'edible intestines.' I, II,
III.
co-wench! 'call to cows.' I, II, III.
hasslet 'liver and lungs.' I, II, III.
Also North.
snap beans, snaps 'string beans.' I,
II, III. Spreading.
harp, mouth harp 'harmonica.' I, II,
III. Not in Charleston area.
turn of wood 'armload.' I, II, [III].
fritters. I, II, III.
Confederate War 'Civil War'(1861-65).
I, [II], [III].

The South (14-18), Morphology and Syntax:

It wa'n't me. I, II, [III]. Also
North.
He belongs to be careful. I, II.
heern tell. I. Also Northeastern New
England.
He do 'does.' I.
What make (him do it? 'makes.' I.
Is I (going? I.
gwine 'going.' I. Also Northeastern
New England.
He fell) *outn* (the bed. I.
I like him) *on account of* (he's so
funny. I, [II].
all two, all both 'both.' [I], [II].

Eastern Virginia (14-15), Pronunciation:

[ʌu], [əu] before voiceless consonants:
house, out; against [æu] before voiced:
down, loud, etc. I, II, III. Similar alternation in the Charleston area, and in
Canada.
[əi], [ai] before voiceless consonants:
white, mice; against [a·ɨ], [a·ɛ], etc.,
before voiced: *time, ride.* I, II, III.
Similar alternation in the Charleston
area, and in Canada.
/a/ in *long, strong.* I, II, III.
[a,ɑ] in *pasture* and a few other words.
I.
[a,ɑ] in *stairs.* I.
/ʊ/ in *home.* I.
/ɛ/ in *afraid.* I, II, III.

Eastern Virginia (14-15), Vocabulary:

batter bread 'spoonbread'(soft cornbread). I, II, III.
lumber room 'store room.' I, II, III.
croker sack, crocus sack 'burlap bag.'
I, II, [III]. Also South Carolina.
corn house 'corn crib.' I, II. Also
South Carolina and New England.
hoppergrass 'grasshopper.' I.
goobers 'peanuts.' I, II, [III]. Also
spread into South Midland.

Eastern Virginia (14-15), Morphology and
Syntax:

clome 'climbed.' I.
see (preterite). I, II. Also North.
I ran) *up on* (him 'met.' I, II.
He did it) *for purpose.* I, [II].

South Carolina-Georgia Low-Country (18),
Pronunciation:

Centralized beginnings of diphthongs
[ʌu], [əu] and [ʌi], [əi] before voiceless
consonants in *house, night.* I, II, III.
Tidewater communities only. Also Eastern
Virginia and Canada.
[ɜɨ] occasional in *bird, curl, adjourn*;
not homonyms with *Boyd, coil, adjoin.*
[I], [II], [III].
Centering diphthongs [o·ʊ], [e·ə] in
road, post, and in *eight, drain.* I, II,
III.
Syllable nuclei of *beet, boot, bought*
monophthongs or in-gliding diphthongs,
very rarely up-gliding diphthongs.
/w/ in *whip, wheelbarrow*, etc. [I],
[II], [III]. Also Hudson Valley and Eastern Pennsylvania.
[ʊ] in *pot, crop, oxen.* I, [II], [III].
Also Eastern New England.
/u,ʊ/ in *won't.* [I], [II], [III]. Also
Hudson Valley.
Only one front vowel phoneme before
/-r/: homonymy of *ear:air, fear:fair*,
etc. I, II, III. Rare above tidewater.
/-b/ in *coop.* I, II. Also Eastern
North Carolina.
/θ/ in *with, without.* I, II, III. Also
Midland.
/æ/ in *pa, ma, palm, calm.* I, [II],
[III].

South Carolina-Georgia Low Country (18),
Vocabulary:

fatwood 'fatty kindling.' I, II, [III].
Tidewater in South Carolina, further inland in Georgia and Florida.
press, clothespress 'movable wardrobe.'
[I], [II], [III]. Chiefly in Santee Valley.
stoop 'small porch.' [I], [II], [III].
Chiefly in Savannah Valley. Also North.
cripple 'scrapple.' [I], [II], [III].
Savannah Valley.
spring frog 'small green frog.' I, II,
III.
groundnuts 'peanuts.' I, II, III. Also
Delaware Bay.
joggling board 'springing board anchored
at both ends.' I, II, III.
awendaw /ˈo-ɪn,dɔ/ 'spoon bread'(soft
cornbread). [I], [II], [III]. Charleston
neighborhood only.
savannah 'grassland.' I, II, III.
mutton corn 'sweet corn.' I, II, [III].
sivvy beans, seewee beans 'lima beans.'
I, II, III.
corn dodgers 'dumplings.' I, II.
Africanisms of various spread:
bloody-noun 'large bullfrog.' I, II,
III.

cooter 'turtle.' I, II, III.
pinders 'peanuts.' I, II, [III].
buckra 'white man.' I, II, III.
yard-ax 'untrained preacher.' [I].
Widely known, but generally labeled a Negroism.
pinto 'coffin.' [I]. Chiefly from Negro informants.

South Carolina-Georgia Low-Country (18), Morphology and Syntax (forms current in Negro speech, occasionally in old-fashioned white speech):

He come over) *for* (tell me. [I].
Uninflected preterites and participles. [I].

South and South Midland (9, 12-18), Pronunciation:

/ju/ after /t,d,n/: *Tuesday, due, new.* I, II, III.
[a·ᵋ], [a·], etc. in *five, my,* etc. I, II, III.
/o/ and /ɔ/ distinguished before /-r/ in *mourning:morning, hoarse:horse, fourteen: forty.* I, II, III. Also North.
/æʊ/ predominant in *mountain, loud,* etc. I, II, III. Not common in Charleston area.
/z/ in *grease* (v.) and *greasy.* I, II, III.
/æ/ in *stairs, care, chair.* I, II, III. Also North.
/o/ in *poor, your,* etc. I, II, [III].
/ʊ/ in *coop, cooper.* I, II, III.
/ʊ/ as a high-central rounded vowel. [I], [II], [III]. Not in Charleston area.
/u/ as a high-central vowel [ʉ] (monophthongal or diphthongal). I, II, III. This fronting somewhat less common in Charleston area.
/ʌ/ in *put.* I, [II].
/ʊ/ in *bulk, bulge, budget.* I, II, [III]. Not in Carolina-Georgia coastal plain, which agrees with North and North Midland in having /ʌ/.

South and South Midland (9, 12-18), Vocabulary:

light bread 'white bread.' I, II, III.
clabber 'curdled milk.' I, II, III.
corn shucks 'husks.' I, II, III.
pallet 'bed on floor.' I, II, III.
jackleg preacher 'unskilled preacher.' I, II, [III].
snack 'light lunch between meals.' I, II, III. Also New York City.
pully bone 'wishbone.' I, II, III.
snake doctor 'dragon fly.' I, II, III. Not on Carolina-Georgia coast, where *mosquito hawk* prevails.
ha'nts, haunts 'ghosts.' I, II, [III]. Receding north of Ohio River.
disremember 'forget.' I.
hay shocks 'haycocks.' I, II, III.
branch 'small stream.' I, II, III.

South and South Midland (9, 12-18), Morphology and Syntax:

you-all (second person pl. pronoun). I, II, III.
I might could. I, II. Also Pennsylvania German area.
I'm not for sure. I, II.
seed 'saw.' I.
I taken (preterite). [I], II.
tuck (preterite or participle of *take*). I, [II].
holp 'helped.' I, [II].
riz 'rose.' I. Also Northeastern New England.
div 'dived.' I. Also Northeastern New England.
mought 'might.' I.
[-ɪz,-əz] in *fists, posts, ghosts, costs.* I.
hisself, theirself, theirselves. I, [II]. Also Northeastern New England.
Inflected comparison of present and past participles when used adjectivally: *lovinger, growed-uppest,* etc. I, [II].
bought bread. I, II.
Perfective use of *done,* as *I ('ve) done told you that.* I, II.
use to didn't, use to wouldn't, etc. I, II.
half after seven. [I], [II].

Canada (principally Ontario), Pronunciation:

[əi], [əu] and the like before voiceless consonants, as in *nice, house.* I, II, III. Also Eastern Virginia and tidewater South Carolina.
/a,ɔ/ in *shone.* I, II, III.
/ʊ,u/ in *won't.* [I], [II], [III]. Also Hudson Valley and Charleston area.
Lack of contrast between /a/ and /ɔ/: homonymy of such pairs as *cot:caught, collar:caller.* [I], [II], [III]. Chiefly western Canada. Also in Western Pennsylvania and Eastern New England.

Canada (principally Ontario), Vocabulary:

chesterfield 'sofa.' I, II, III. Also northern California.
coal oil 'kerosene.' I, II, III. Also Eastern Pennsylvania, Maryland, and Shenandoah Valley; spreading in Ohio and Mississippi Valleys.
shivaree 'mock serenade.' I, II, [III]. Spreading into Ohio and Mississippi Valleys.
county town 'county seat.' I, II, III.
reeve 'township officer.' I, II, III.
warden 'county officer.' I, II, III.
dew worm 'large earthworm.' I, II, III.
tap 'water faucet.' I, II, III.
serviette 'table napkin.' [I], II, III.
stook 'pile of sheaves.' I, II, [III].

Canada (principally Ontario), Morphology and Syntax:

He lives) *in* (King Street. I, II, III. Also New York City, Charleston, and possibly Baltimore.

The first inland area to be investigated was the North-Central States (LANCS). Begun as an independent project under the direction of Albert H. Marckwardt of the University of Michigan, LANCS has retained its autonomy, though since the transfer of the Atlantic Seaboard archives to Michigan in 1946 it has been possible for Kurath and Marckwardt to cooperate closely. [With the Atlantic Seaboard materials and copies of those from the North-Central States at Chicago, R. McDavid also provided liaison between the two projects from 1964 to Marckwardt's death in 1975.]

Although Cassil Reynard, one of the New England field workers, had completed six field records in Ohio in 1933, systematic preliminary work towards LANCS really got under way in the summer of 1938, when the Horace M. Rackham Fund of the University of Michigan provided funds for Harold B. Allen and Norman Eliason to do eight records each, in Michigan and Indiana respectively. The purpose was to determine whether enough dialect differences existed in the traditional 'General American' area to justify a more detailed linguistic survey.[14] From these records and from a second group of records done the following summer (ten in Illinois by Allen, five in Ohio by Fred G. Cassidy) such sharp regional differences were discovered between the speech of Michigan and that of the southern parts of Ohio, Indiana, and Illinois that a more intensive linguistic investigation was felt not only justified but necessary.

With this evidence in mind, Marckwardt planned a slightly less extensive coverage of the North-Central area (Marckwardt 1940a, 1941, 1942b) than had been provided along the Atlantic Seaboard. Since the North-Central States constituted an area of secondary settlement (parts of northern Wisconsin and northern Michigan were not permanently settled till the 1890's), the network for each state was set at about twenty-five communities. As in the Pennsylvania German and Hudson Valley Dutch settlements along the Atlantic Seaboard, a number of the communities selected had been originally settled by foreign-language groups, and some of the informants, though native speakers of English, had grown up in homes where another language was also spoken. The choice was deliberate, so that LANCS might assay the occurrence of borrowings from such immigrant languages as Canadian French, various German dialects, Holland Dutch, Norwegian, and Swedish (Haugen 1950a). Administratively, it was decided that the field work in each state should be considered a separate project, to be supported financially by local institutions insofar as possible.

With Cassidy's appointment to the faculty of the University of Wisconsin, that state was the first in which field work was completed (1940; see Cassidy 1941). In 1948 a grant from the University of Michigan enabled R. McDavid to complete that state; in 1949-50 he completed Illinois with support from the state university, and in the following summer he and V. McDavid (formerly one of the field workers in the Upper Midwest) did border records in eight communities of southwestern Ontario. With support from Western Reserve University, the Ohio State University, and the Ohio Archaeological and Historical Society, R. McDavid and A. L. Davis (a student of Marckwardt, Kurath, and Bloch) have completed Ohio. Indiana and Kentucky have gone more slowly because of local problems: Indiana University has supplied field workers, but has not been able to keep any one in the field long enough to complete the state; and until 1955 Kentucky educational institutions could not find money for field work. [The last records were completed in 1977. R. McDavid did most of the work in eastern Kentucky; several investigators -- notably Byron Bender, George Motherwell, Robert Howren and Robert Thompson -- pieced out Indiana and central Kentucky.]

As a related project, A. L. Davis developed a new application of the old correspondence technique (1949). By carefully selecting the items for a multiple-choice lexical questionnaire and controlling the project at all stages, he showed that one can use correspondence technique to get valid dialect evidence. His techniques have been used, with slightly modified questionnaires, in later regional investigations; in Ohio they are now being used to supplement the field records, and Edward E. Potter has used them in a close-meshed survey as the basis for a dissertation on the complex transition area in northwestern Ohio (1955; see also A. L. Davis and R. McDavid 1950, D. Reed and Spicer 1952).

The editing of the North-Central records is in the preliminary stages. Duplicate archives are being set up at Michigan and Western Reserve, with Marckwardt working on vocabulary and R. McDavid (now associate director of the project) on pronunciation. Much of the grammatical evidence is treated in V. McDavid 1956 (see also R. and V. McDavid 1960). While the editorial work is being organized, scholars are encouraged to use the North-Central materials, as well as those from the Atlantic Seaboard, to prepare interpretive studies.

It is already apparent that when comparable evidence is systematically examined, the term 'General American' is as inapplicable in the North-Central States as it is along the Atlantic Seaboard (see Maps 4-6). From the Appalachians to the

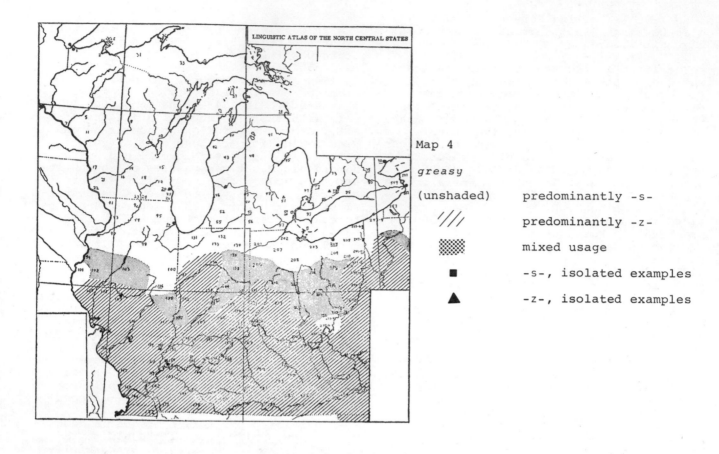

Map 4

greasy

(unshaded)　　predominantly -s-

///　　predominantly -z-

▦　　mixed usage

■　　-s-, isolated examples

▲　　-z-, isolated examples

Map 5

see (Preterite)

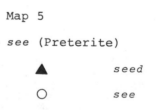

▲　　　　*seed*

○　　　　*see*

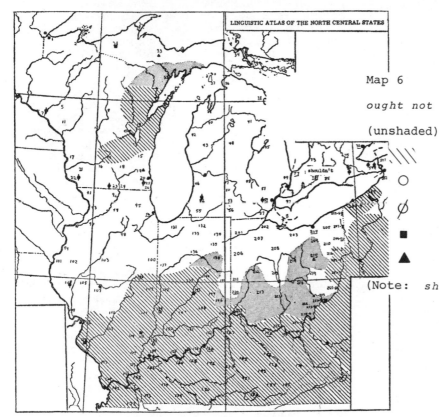

Map 6

ought not

(unshaded)   predominantly *hadn't ought*

                   predominantly *oughtn't*

○   *hadn't ought*, isolated examples

∅   *oughtn't*, isolated examples

■   *didn't ought*

▲   *shouldn't ought*

(Note: *shouldn't* predominates in Ontario.)

Mississippi, one may detect westward extensions of the North, Midland, and South. Northern forms spread from New England and New York State into Michigan, Wisconsin, and the northern parts of Ohio, Indiana, and Illinois. South Midland forms have spread from West Virginia, southwestern Virginia, and western North Carolina, through eastern Kentucky into southern Ohio, southern Indiana, and southern Illinois. North Midland forms have normally spread directly westward from Pennsylvania along the old National Road, while Southern forms are largely confined to the newer plantation areas of central and western Kentucky, but occasionally appear in Illinois and Indiana communities along the Ohio River.

The Atlas of the Upper Midwest (LAUM) has largely been the work of one man, Harold B. Allen, with the support of one institution, the University of Minnesota. Six field workers have assisted Allen; the University of Iowa supplied and supported two field workers, and institutions in the Dakotas supplied a small amount of financial assistance (Allen 1952).

Although the severe Upper Midwest winters confined field work to the summer months, the work progressed steadily from its beginning in 1947 to its completion in 1956. The archives include some 200 field records, supplemented by over a thousand lexical questionnaires.

Plans for publishing the LAUM materials have not been announced, but preliminary editing is already under way. [Publication is now complete: Allen 1973-76.]

In 1956 little had appeared in print about the distribution of particular linguistic forms in the Upper Midwest. As with the LANCS materials, most of the grammatical items are discussed in V. McDavid 1956.

So far, it appears that the division between Northern and Midland forms continues in the Upper Midwest, though the divisions are less sharply defined than in the North-Central States, just as the North-Central divisions are less sharply defined than those along the Atlantic Seaboard; it seems that the so-called 'standard' grammatical forms are more widely distributed, geographically and socially, in the Upper Midwest than further east. The explanation may be the large proportion of educated foreign-language speakers among the early settlers (so that there would be a tendency to learn English from books rather than from folk contacts), the early establishment of public education, or a combination of these influences. Finally, many of the isoglosses setting off Northern speech forms from Midland seem to lie further north in the Upper Midwest than they do in much of the North-Central area; Allen and Marckwardt have investigated this phenomenon, which may be explained by the influence of the Mississippi River on patterns of settlement and trade (see Marckwardt 1957, Allen 1964).

Another of the Upper Midwest field workers, Robert Weber, has studied the speech of the Minneapolis-St. Paul metropolitan area (1965).

The Linguistic Atlas of the Rocky Mountain States presents another set of problems for the investigators. Settlement history has been most uneven: although the basic settlement patterns in Utah were completed before the Civil War, other parts of the region were settled barely forty years ago. Two of the more colorful occupations of the region, stock-raising and speculative mining, did little to further the building up of permanent settlements. The very physical geography of the region renders impossible the relatively even distribution of population that one finds in many of the eastern states. Consequently one encounters special local problems in field work and interpretation of the data, or at least an accentuated form of the characteristic American dialect situation as contrasted with the European (Kimmerle, R. McDavid, and V. McDavid 1951). Moreover, the relatively sparse population of the region has inevitably meant that there are few institutions possessing traditions of research in the humanities and funds to support such research. Under these circumstances, work has proceeded slowly, though the project has received the general sponsorship of the Rocky Mountain Modern Language Association. Director of the project is Professor Marjorie Kimmerle of the University of Colorado, with T. M. Pearce of the University of New Mexico as associate director. Correspondence questionnaires of lexical items are being used to supplement the field records.

At this stage, field work is complete in only one state, Colorado, where Miss Kimmerle did most of the interviews, with some assistance from Allan Hubbell (then at the University of Denver) and Mrs. Etholine Aycock of the Colorado Agricultural and Mechanical College. John McKendrick of Brigham Young University completed most of the field work in Utah, as part of his progress toward a Ph.D. dissertation at the Johns Hopkins University, but received no encouragement to complete it. In New Mexico, Donald Dickinson conducted seven field interviews as part of the work toward his M.A. thesis; Pearce has since added several more field records, and continued the distribution of correspondence questionnaires and the investigation of special vocabulary projects. Dr. Klonda Lynn, of the University of Arizona, has completed about a third of the projected field work for her state. Several field records -- chiefly by McKendrick and Verne Dusenberry -- were made in

southwestern Montana in the summer of 1951, as a part of a special program at Montana State College; since that time, however, little or no work has been done. Wyoming investigations have been confined to the distribution of correspondence questionnaires.

Recognizing the difficulties involved in getting support for the Rocky Mountain project as a whole, Miss Kimmerle has begun editing the Colorado materials alone, in the hope that publication of them will stimulate the field work in states which have heretofore lagged. Because of ill health, she was not able to complete editing (her materials remain at Colorado), though her derivative studies (e.g., Kimmerle 1952) have served to maintain interest. Perhaps the completion of McKendrick's dissertation, which will then permit the comparison of data from two adjacent states, Colorado and Utah, with sharply contrasting patterns of settlement history,[15] will give other scholars the incentive to go ahead [see Hankey 1960].

Work on the Pacific Coast has been facilitated by the fact that the largest institution of that region, the University of California, has provided support for the project on a long-term basis, through the research funds of both the Berkeley and the Los Angeles branches.

Investigations into the dialects of the Pacific Coast were started in 1951 by David W. Reed of the University of California, another student of Kurath and Marckwardt. Confronted by both large areas and dense metropolitan populations, he has enlisted the cooperation of UCLA, with John Moncur as associate director for the southern parts of California and Nevada. For the northern part of the Pacific Coast, work is under the supervision of the co-director of the project, Carroll E. Reed of the University of Washington, a student of Kurath at Brown. David De Camp of Washington State College, a former student of David Reed, is associate director under Carroll Reed, with whom he shares supervision of work in Oregon, Idaho, and the westernmost parts of Montana. A few border points will be included from British Columbia.

The network of communities and informants is denser for the Pacific Coast Atlas than for any other region away from the Atlantic Seaboard. The goal for California and Nevada is 300 interviews, about 200 for the northern section of the project. Correspondence questionnaires have been used from the beginning, with a goal of 1500 for Nevada and California and probably twice that for the entire area. For the California-Nevada section, both collections are over half completed; for the northern section, somewhat less. Details still remain to be worked out about the exchange of information between Washington and California, to say nothing of plans for editing and publication. But with funds and competent direction assured, the Pacific Coast Atlas should be completed without undue difficulty.

Leaving out progress reports (C. Reed 1952, D. Reed 1954), two major works have already grown out of the Pacific Coast Atlas, De Camp's study, under David Reed's direction, on the speech of the San Francisco metropolitan area (De Camp 1954, 1958-59), and Elizabeth Bright's California-Nevada *Word Geography* (1971).

Work on the Pacific Coast has been complicated by the irregular pattern of settlement history. English-speaking settlements had been established on San Francisco Bay, the Columbia River, and Puget Sound before the territories were annexed to the United States. Population increase has been rapid but sporadic, with first one and then another part of the region growing as local industries boomed. All immigrant groups, European and Asiatic, have contributed to the increase, especially in California, where the highly mixed community is the rule rather than the exception. Population distribution is uneven, heavily urbanized and suburbanized areas such as greater Los Angeles and the San Francisco Bay area contrasting with desert and forest. Irrigation, migratory labor, and fruit and vegetable specialties have created an agriculture based on large-scale factory farming rather than the small individual holdings characteristic of most Eastern agricultural areas.

Little work has yet been done in Texas, despite the presence of Atwood at the state university, the well-advertised wealth of many Texans, and the flamboyant local patriotism of most. The delay has been due, principally, to a lack of competent field workers. So far, Atwood has distributed checklists (Atwood 1953b), and directed one dissertation, that of Arthur Norman (1955) on the speech of Jefferson County in southeastern Texas. Norman has also investigated the bilingual German settlement at New Braunfels. Although systematic field investigation of the whole state is still probably a few years away, prospects have grown brighter with the development of the University of Texas as a major center for the study of linguistics. [As yet, however, Atwood 1962 is the one major publication. Eastern Texas is included with the Gulf States project.]

Similarly, no systematic survey has been undertaken in the Gulf States and lower Mississippi Valley (Tennessee, western Georgia, Florida, Alabama, Mississippi, Louisiana, and Arkansas), nor in Missouri, Kansas, or Oklahoma. Most of these states, like most of those in the Rocky Mountain region, lack institutions with funds and research interests; where funds and research interests exist -- as in Florida, Louisiana, Missouri, and Oklahoma -- field workers have not been available. The largest body of data has been collected in Louisiana, where the students of C. M. Wise at Louisiana State University have done about a hundred field interviews; though obviously of uneven quality, this material will be useful to those planning more systematic investigations. At Tulane University Ives has cooperated with sociologists in developing dialect tests for indicating the social status of urban informants, with particular reference to the situation in New Orleans. In 1956 Norman completed several field records in New Orleans, toward the proposed South-Central Atlas. At the University of Missouri, parallelling the earlier work of Robert Ramsay on place names, George Pace is sponsoring a systematic correspondence study of local vocabulary items, and looks toward inaugurating field work. [Since 1968, however, Lee Pederson has organized the Linguistic Atlas of the Gulf States and directed the field work to completion. Editing is now under way.]

The investigation of Canadian dialects has generally been limited to border communities, in connection with regional surveys in the United States. From New Brunswick to Saskatchewan, thirty-four interviews have been completed in such communities, but nothing systematic has yet been completed, and little attempted, in Canadian speech as such. Before the outbreak of World War II, Henry M. Alexander of Queen's University (Kingston, Ontario) had completed about half the field work for a survey of the Maritime Provinces (New Brunswick, Nova Scotia, Prince Edward Island), but has not resumed work since the war. More recently, H. Rex Wilson of Augustana College (Rock Island, Illinois), a native Canadian, has completed an investigation of the speech of Lunenburg County, Nova Scotia (1959). [Murray Wanamaker has made a similar study of the Annapolis Valley (1965), and with Murray Kinloch he and Wilson have continued the investigations of the Maritimes.] The new Canadian Linguistic Association has expressed interest in a Linguistic Atlas of Canadian English, but has not reached the stage of systematic planning; the active role which Avis has played in the work of the Association, both as one of the founders and as associate editor of the *Journal*, augurs for the success of the project. Meanwhile, the Rev. Brother Pius is completing a correspondence survey of vocabulary items in eastern Ontario, as a master's thesis at the University of Toronto, and other scholars are making some experimental interviews on tape, to be incorporated in North-Central files for Ontario. Even with the limited data now available, the characteristics of Canadian English, and the relationships between the speech

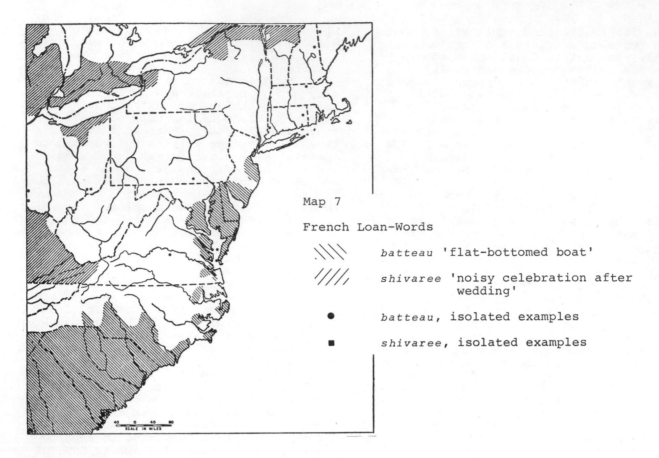

Map 7

French Loan-Words

⟍⟍⟍⟍ *batteau* 'flat-bottomed boat'

╱╱╱╱ *shivaree* 'noisy celebration after
        wedding'

● *batteau*, isolated examples

■ *shivaree*, isolated examples

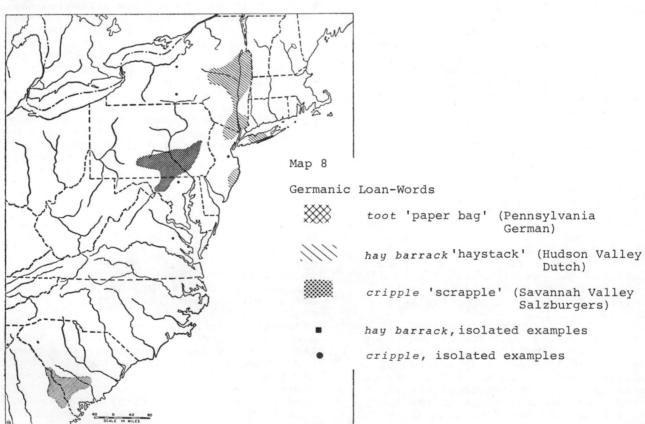

Map 8

Germanic Loan-Words

▨ *toot* 'paper bag' (Pennsylvania
      German)

⟍⟍⟍ *hay barrack* 'haystack' (Hudson Valley
        Dutch)

▒ *cripple* 'scrapple' (Savannah Valley
      Salzburgers)

■ *hay barrack*, isolated examples

● *cripple*, isolated examples

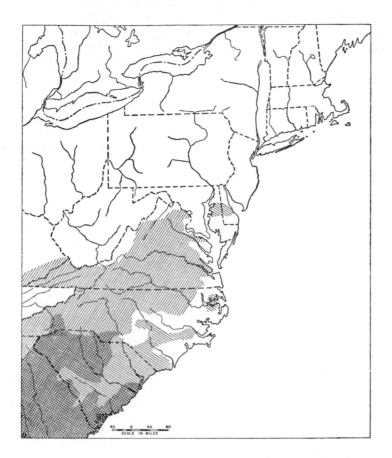

Map 9

African Loan-Words

///// *goober* 'peanut'

\\\\\ *pinder* 'peanut'

of the United States and that of Canada, have attracted the attention and piqued the curiosity of many scholars (R. Mc-David 1954a, Avis 1954-56, Allen 1959). Since the incorporation of Newfoundland into the Dominion of Canada as the tenth province, the provincial university has been interested in both a linguistic atlas and a dialect dictionary of Newfoundland speech; as the first English settlement in the New World, and long isolated from the rest of English-speaking North America, Newfoundland is a field of research deserving the best investigation modern linguistics can devise.

Of other English-speaking areas in the New World, only Jamaica has been investigated (Cassidy 1961, Cassidy and LePage 1967).

While the regional surveys have been making fair headway, less success has attended efforts to compile a dialect dictionary of American English, though in their inception these efforts antedate the Linguistic Atlas project by four decades. The reasons have been numerous: lack of financial support, concentration of scholarly attention on other projects (not only the Linguistic Atlas and the *Dictionary of American English*, but to a far greater extent the excellent research in American Indian languages and the recent emphasis on the theory of structural analysis and its application to particular

languages), and various financial and personal problems within the American Dialect Society. More important than all of these, however, has been the lack of any center to plan and direct such a project. Within the last decade, however, the Dialect Society has grown both in membership and in scholarly interests. Within the same period, there has arisen a new group of scholars interested in developing plans for systematically examining the American dialect vocabulary: Thomas Pyles of the University of Florida (secretary of the Society 1953-56),[16] James B. McMillan and I. Willis Russell (now secretary) of the University of Alabama,[17] and particularly Cassidy, who has worked out in Wisconsin a technique for getting usable lexical data by correspondence (Cassidy 1948, Cassidy and Duckert 1953). Cassidy's method has been utilized by Saunders Walker in a study of the folk vocabulary of the eastern Alabama Negro (1956). Further dissertations of this type are being planned, and the method has been endorsed by the 1954 meeting of the Dialect Society.

Along with the work in American English, this century has seen work in the New World developments of the other languages brought to the Western Hemisphere by settlers from Europe. For these languages, in addition to the geographical distribution of particular forms, and the Old World origins of New World dialects, scholars are concerned with the survival or disappearance of non-English linguistic forms in a bilingual situation dominated everywhere by English, and with the effects of English on these other languages while the bilingual situation still prevails.

A casual examination reveals that not all of these non-English immigrant languages have been investigated with the same thoroughness.[18] Whether or not a language has been seriously approached by scholars has depended not merely on the extent of immigration (by these standards American Italian, only casually investigated so far, would have had much more study than, say, American Portugese), but on the status of the immigrant language and -- most of all -- on the interest of competent scholars. To evaluate all works on foreign-American dialects and bilingualism would demand another article, by a specialist. One may cite, however, the investigations of Canadian and Louisiana French by Ernest F. Haden (1942, Haden and Joliat 1940) and Joseph M. Carrière (1939), and the *Atlas linguistique du Canada francais* (in progress; Dulong 1954); investigations of Pennsylvania German by Learned (1888-89), J. William Frey (1942a, 1942b, 1945), and Carroll Reed (1949) and Lester Seifert (C. Reed and Seifert 1954); Haugen's study of American Norwegian, with wider implications in its contribution to the study of bilingualism (1953); Leo Pap's treatment of American Portugese (1949); Rudnyčkyj's investigations of American Slavs (1952); and Lorenzo Turner's analysis of West African survivals among the Gullah Negroes of the South Carolina and Georgia coast (1949). These works have naturally differed in emphasis as in method. From all of them, however, the same picture emerges: of the steady pressure of English on all non-English languages, greatest in the areas of experience most closely identified with the American scene, least in those areas where older habits, customs, and beliefs have been most tenaciously retained. Yet even as the other languages have disappeared, they have left their mark on American English, most noticeably in the vocabulary (see Maps 7-9) but sometimes also in structural details. All of these works have been illuminated by Weinreich 1953; all may be appraised more accurately when British scholars complete their pending surveys of the English dialects of the British Isles (McIntosh 1952, Dieth and Orton 1952, Orton *et al.* 1962-71, Mather and Speitel 1975-). All might be helped by more intensive dialect work in American aboriginal languages, including studies of the impact of European speech forms.[19]

From this cursory analysis, it is apparent that much valuable work in American dialects has been completed, and much more undertaken, though the field will not be exhausted for a long time. Perhaps even more important than the details of the studies which have been published is the awareness, on the part of American scholars, of the importance of sound method -- an awareness that in practice has been translated into a sure adherence to methods that have proved fruitful, and a willingness to modify these methods so as to take care of new situations.

ADDENDUM

For the convenience of the profession, the following information on the 1979 state of the regional atlases is in order.

The *Linguistic Atlas of New England* has been reprinted (1972), and a second edition of the New England *Handbook* has appeared (1973), with a reverse index of maps to work sheets, a map inventory, and a complete index of words and phrases.

The *Linguistic Atlas of the Middle and South Atlantic States* (Kurath *et al.* 1979-), whose archives were transferred to the University of Chicago in 1964 and ten years later to the University of South Carolina, is well along in editing, with R. McDavid as editor-in-chief, Raymond O'Cain as associate editor and George Dorrill as assistant editor. Kurath continues as director. Two fascicles have gone to press.

Under a plan approved by Marckwardt in 1975, the *Linguistic Atlas of the North-Central States* (Marckwardt *et al.* 1980-) is being edited at the University of Chicago by a consortium of scholars, with R. McDavid as editor-in-chief. The *Handbook* and the *Grammar* (the latter by V. McDavid) should go to press late in 1979, the *Word Geography* (by Richard Payne, a student under Marckwardt at Princeton) somewhat later. For the convenience of editors scattered at several institutions, the complete field records have been microfilmed, and copies of the surviving taped interviews are also available (Marckwardt *et al.* 1976-78).

The *Linguistic Atlas of the Upper Midwest* has been edited and published (Allen 1973-76).

Except for a study of eastern Montana (O'Hare 1964), no further work has been done in the Rockies. Plans remain uncertain, as they do for the Pacific Northwest (Brengelman 1957 is a further study).

Editorial plans are under way for the Linguistic Atlas of the Pacific Coast (California and Nevada). David Reed and Allan Metcalf have drafted editorial plans similar to those for the North-Central States. Bright 1971 is a summary of the lexical evidence in the field records.

Field work has been completed for Oklahoma and a part of Missouri. Although the death of W. R. Van Riper, director of the Oklahoma project, is an irreplaceable loss, plans are under way to edit his materials after the pattern of the North-Central States.

For the Linguistic Atlas of the Gulf States, from central Georgia through eastern Texas, field work has been completed under the energetic direction of Lee Pederson, and editing has begun. Transcriptions ("protocols") of the taped field records will be published by microfiche. Other publications will include a handbook and summary volumes, and a complete dictionary of recorded forms. In the same region two independent studies have appeared -- Atwood's *Regional Vocabu-*

lary of Texas (1962), a lexical study based on interviews by students, and Gordon Wood's *Vocabulary Change* (1971), based on correspondence checklists. M. Barrett's Alabama materials are also nearing publication.

Wilson and his associates continue work toward a linguistic atlas of the Maritime Provinces.

Since 1965, Cassidy has moved energetically toward a *Dictionary of American Regional English* (Cassidy *et al.* 1981-), which should be completed in the early 1980's.

The civil rights movement of the 1960's led to an increased emphasis on the study of social dialects, particularly in urban areas, e.g., Pederson 1965a,b, Labov 1966, Shuy, Wolfram, and Riley 1968. For overall appraisals see Forgue and R. McDavid 1972 and R. McDavid 1979.

NOTES

[1] Hans Kurath *et al.* 1939-43 (LANE); Kurath *et al.* 1939 (*Handbook*). For a brief criticism see R. and V. McDavid 1951c, in this volume pp. 79-85.

[2] For previous studies of the progress of the regional atlases see R. McDavid 1949a, 1951c.

[3] For a popular but sound treatment of the wartime language program see "Science Comes to Languages," an article prepared by the staff of *Fortune* (1944). Since the conclusion of World War II, many American linguists have participated, directly or indirectly, in the language training program of the U.S. Department of State; until the summer of 1956 this program was under the direction of Henry Lee Smith, Jr. (one of the organizers, and for a time officer-in-charge of the wartime Army Language Section), later head of the new Department of Linguistics and Anthropology of the University of Buffalo. The growing popular recognition of the importance of linguistics has drawn other linguists from their orthodox academic interests into large-scale government, university, missionary, and industrial programs for teaching foreign languages to United States citizens, and American English to speakers of other languages.

[4] Kurath's experience as editor of the *Middle English Dictionary*, now being published by photo-offset from typed copy, indicates that this process also reduces the chances of error in publication, since the copy can be prepared in the editorial office, with only the mechanical processes of photographing and printing to be done by the printer. [Composition for LAMSAS is by IBM Selectric typewriter; a special phonetic element (Camwil 1873-M) was designed in 1974.]

[5] Kurath 1949 was in press before field work had been completed in South Carolina, Georgia, and up-state New York. However, preliminary analyses of the data from these areas show few divergences

from Kurath's scheme, and these chiefly in minor details. See R. McDavid 1951a,b, 1955a.

[6] Other dissertations based on Atlas materials include: Bloch 1935, Penzl 1934, Harris 1937, Hawkins 1942, Dearden 1943, Frank 1949 (compare an independent study, Hubbell 1950, which used both Linguistic Atlas materials and data collected by other means, principally phonographic recordings), Avis 1956, Downer 1958, Van Riper 1958, Wetmore 1959, Hankey 1960, and Williamson 1968.

[7] The term 'General American' owes its currency largely to its use in Kenyon 1924 and Krapp 1925. Kenyon was a native of the New England settlement area in northern Ohio, Krapp of Cincinnati, in southern Ohio; both called their own speech 'General American,' though one of the most important dialect boundaries in the United States crosses northern Ohio from east to west, just south of the area of New England settlement.

The term is still used by many phoneticians, especially by those who have not kept up with recent work in linguistic geography. However, the territory in which 'General American' is assumed to prevail seems to shrink as more accurate information is gathered about regional and local speech characteristics. In this more restricted sense, it is used in Thomas 1947. 'General American' thus seems to be a negative term, applicable to those areas (such as those of recent urbanization) too newly settled to have characteristic speech forms, or to those about which so little is known that local dialect varieties cannot be identified. [It was dropped in the second edition (1958) of Thomas 1947.]

Kurath was one of the first to question the legend of the uniformity of 'General American.' See Kurath 1927.

[8] Undoubtedly the traditional picture of both the extent and the uniformity of Southern speech

(as of 'Southern' attitudes) has been encouraged by the very vocal sectional consciousness of Southern politicians, especially on issues involving race relations.

[9] In New England and the South Atlantic States, pronunciation features characteristic of the culturally dominant areas (Boston and the Virginia Piedmont especially; Charleston to a less extent) have wide regional occurrence in cultured speech, though not in the speech of the less educated.

[10] The pronunciation /wunt/ won't is shared by the Hudson Valley and Charleston; sick to the stomach and hadn't ought by the North and the Albemarle Sound area of eastern North Carolina; /dov/ dove as the preterite of dive by the North and the Charleston area.

[11] This phenomenon is treated in R. McDavid 1953b, 1955a.

[12] In its original form, this summary was prepared by Atwood (1950b), from data available in Kurath's Word Geography (1949), his own charts for the Survey of Verb Forms (1953a), and other observations such as those found in the dissertations of A. L. Davis (1949) and Frank (1949). It has been expanded considerably as other scholars have systematically explored the Atlas data. Its present form is a modification of the table appearing in R. McDavid 1958a.

[13] The developments of /-r/ in the South Atlantic States are very complex, reflecting a complicated settlement history and changing social patterns. Not only is there a different development of /-r/ in stressed and unstressed syllables, with greater loss of /-r/ in the latter, but in stressed syllables the retention or loss of /-r/ seems to vary with the preceding vowel. Thus there is often /r/-like vocalic constriction in words of the type burn, heard, with a mid-central vowel, when /-r/ is lost in beard and barn; the converse also happens. For details see Van Riper 1958.

[14] The questionnaire for the North-Central States is basically the short questionnaire devised by Kurath in 1937 on the basis of the longer questionnaires for LANE and LAMSAS. To it have been added about fifty items, chiefly restorations from the longer questionnaires, that seemed to provide evidence for separating North Midland from South Midland, and South Midland from the South. Since even its expanded form can be covered by a skilled field worker in a long afternoon or evening, it lends itself admirably to the wide-meshed investigations.

The other regional surveys have also used Kurath's short questionnaire of 1937, with modifications and additions to take care of local conditions.

[15] Although the first settlement was made in Utah in 1846, by 1870 a majority of the American-born inhabitants were natives of the territory, and the population of Utah has continued to be much more stable than that of the other Rocky Mountain States. This stability has at least part of its roots in the strong patriarchal discipline of the Mormons, who established the first settlements in Utah as a refuge from the persecutions to which they had been subjected in New York State, Missouri, Illinois, and elsewhere. The 'peculiar institution' of polygamy was practiced by the Mormons in Utah until 1896; external hostility to this institution and other Mormon practices undoubtedly provoked a sense of cohesiveness among the Mormons themselves, and consequently a greater tendency to preserve both their social order and older traditions in self defense.

[16] Pyles 1952 is an excellent popular study.

[17] McMillan and Russell were editors of the Dictionary of Current American Usage, being prepared under the sponsorship of the National Council of Teachers of English [later published as Bryant 1962]. McMillan 1946 is also one of the few systematic studies of a local American dialect. Another is Barrett 1948.

[18] For work down to 1936, and a survey of foreign-language communities at that time, see Mencken 1936:661-97.

[19] A few studies have been made of bilingualism among the American Indians, e.g., Spicer 1943, Herzog 1941.

A linguistic atlas of the Ojibwa-Ottawa language, spoken by many independent tribal units in Ontario, Michigan, Wisconsin, and Minnesota, was proposed in 1941. However, the entrance of the United States into World War II caused linguists to put the project aside, and it has never been revived.

When the time comes to write the history of American dialectology in the twentieth century, the chronicler could hardly do better than consider it as the lengthened shadow of Hans Kurath. For this indefatigable Austrian-born American has not only given a new direction to the scholarly investigation of the popular speech of the United States and Canada, both by his own pioneer research and by his planning and directing of the Linguistic Atlas of the United States and Canada in its Atlantic Seaboard aspects, but has exerted a powerful impact on all other investigations, whether of English or of the immigrant languages, both by being available for consultation as to the directions such projects should take and by having contributed to the training and development of almost every other scholar of consequence in the field.

The record of the public personality is easy to trace. Born at Villach in Austria in 1891, he came to the United States in 1907 and became an American citizen in 1912 -- one of the hundreds of thousands of Americans of German and Austrian origin who have contributed not only to building the great metropolitan areas of the Middle West but to making them centers of intellect and culture. After beginning his college education at the German-American Teachers' Seminar in Milwaukee, he attended the Universities of Wisconsin and Texas, receiving his A.B. from the latter institution in 1914. He pursued his graduate education at the University of Chicago, in the Departments of German and Comparative Linguistics, and received his Ph.D. in 1920. His dissertation, on the words for the emotions, was one of the first dissertations to contribute to Carl Darling Buck's monumental *Dictionary of Selected Synonyms in the Principal Indo-European Languages* (1949).

Kurath's first teaching experience was as an instructor in German at the University of Texas, from 1914 to 1916 and 1917 to 1919. At Texas he became acquainted with Eduard Prokosch, whose daughter Gertrude (herself a distinguished anthropological scholar, who has devised a method for recording the movements of American Indian and other aboriginal dances) is now Mrs. Kurath. Here, too, he met one of the less pleasant phenomena of American culture -- the rampant xenophobia, of World War I and its aftermath, which led the state legislature to abolish all work in German at the University. Between his two

terms at Texas, and following the last one, he was a graduate fellow at the University of Chicago.

After completing his graduate work he accepted a post at Northwestern University, and four years later was promoted to the rank of Assistant Professor, which he held for five years. In 1929 he went to Ohio State University as Professor of German and Linguistics, and in 1931 moved to a similar post at Brown University, where the headquarters of the Linguistic Atlas of the United States and Canada were established. He remained at Brown until 1946, serving during the last five years of his stay as Chairman of the Division of Modern Languages -- one of the first such posts established in an American university, dignifying the teaching of languages in its own right rather than a mere ancillary to the teaching of literature. In 1946 he accepted an invitation of the University of Michigan to succeed Thomas A. Knott as editor of the *Middle English Dictionary* [a position he held till his retirement in 1962].

His interest in American dialects arose from his travels as a student and teacher, and from the traditional orientation of Germanic studies in the direction of the folk culture. While at Northwestern he began his series of field investigations and correlations with available data that led to the first clear statement about dialect areas of the United States, in a tract prepared for the Society for Pure English (1928a). It is characteristically ironical in our profession that the statements in the tract are still often cited as authoritative, though Kurath has long since abandoned them in the face of new evidence. The gathering of such evidence, during his tenure at Ohio State, marked him as the person whom the American Council of Learned Societies would call to direct their project of a Linguistic Atlas of the United States and Canada.

It is characteristic of Kurath that, despite his own brilliance, he insists on careful planning and precise method in whatever project he undertakes, rather than relying on intuitive improvisation. This characteristic is sometimes irritating to the bright young men of the profession, and sometimes the ironies of history have made it seem rather grandiose; but without a carefully disciplined view of the future we should accomplish nothing. In essence, the plan of the Linguistic Atlas was rather simple: to push the field work in New England to completion within a relatively short time, and then -- while the New England materials were being edited -- to gather the evidence for the rest of the country at the same pace, with the momentum obtained by the success of the New England work being sufficient to draw the support of foundations and university research funds to support work in the rest of the country. But the plans left out the possibility of domestic and foreign catastrophe. By the time field work was under way in New England, in the fall of 1931, the United States was in the grip of the Hoover Depression; sound investments evaporated, and only Kurath's devotion to the project enabled him to keep one field worker (Guy S. Lowman, Jr.) and two editorial assistants (Bernard and Julia Bloch) at work until the beginnings of World War II. Lowman died in an automobile crash in 1941; Bloch joined the Intensive Language program at Yale University and stayed to succeed Leonard Bloomfield as key man in the Department of Linguistics. Work on the Atlas from Brown was suspended for the duration, except for Kurath's personal research; and though funds were made available after the war for completion of the field work in the Atlantic Seaboard states, the collections remain unedited to this day. [With Kurath's retirement, the collections for the Middle and South Atlantic States were transferred in 1964 to the University of Chicago, where the first stage of editing was completed. Since 1974 the bulk of the final editing has been conducted by Raymond K. O'Cain, at the University of South Carolina.]

Nevertheless, the actual contributions of Kurath to the advancement of linguistic geography are more than sufficient to assure his place in the history of our discipline, even though they fall short of what he wanted to do and could have done had circumstances been more kind. The *Linguistic Atlas of New England* (Kurath *et al.* 1939-43) -- with its accompanying *Handbook* (Kurath *et al.* 1939), itself a model presentation of dialectological method -- stands in its own right as the first large-scale systematic study of dialects anywhere in the English-speaking world. The first derivative study based on the collections form the Atlantic Seaboard, Kurath's *Word Geography of the Eastern United States* (1949), forever disposed of the myth of a uniform 'General American' speech (presumably, according to its earlier proponents, bounded by the Connecticut, the Potomac, the Ohio, the Brazos, and the Pacific Ocean), raised the the Pennsylvania-derived Midland dialects to the position of one of the two most important forces in establishing the present patterns of American regional speech, and showed that many of the most highly publicized dialects of the political and his-

torical South were really Midland in origin, though sometimes modified by social and cultural forces. A second major derivative study, Atwood's *Survey of Verb Forms in the Eastern United States* (1953a) has demonstrated the effects of education and urbanization on popular grammar, but has likewise shown the survival of regional grammatical differences even in standard speech, such as *hadn't ought* 'ought not,' and *dove* /dov/ as the preterite of *dive*; the dissertation of V. McDavid, *Verb Forms in the North-Central States and Upper Midwest* (1956), shows the same kind of patterns persisting to the Mississippi and beyond, in the heart of the territory once assigned to 'General American.' The third work in this series, Kurath and R. McDavid's *Pronunciation of English in the Atlantic States* (1961) emphasizes social differences and the influence of focal areas, and indicates how the cultural prestige of the upper-class speech in an important center may profoundly modify the educated speech of an entire region. As other scholars consult the Atlantic Seaboard collections, we may expect further important derivative studies, pending the editing and publishing of the entire work.

In the meantime, moreover, the other regional surveys in the United States and Canada show the influence of Kurath, both directly through his generous and unobtrusive advice and indirectly through the work of his students -- as editors, directors, and teachers of new investigators. The following is but a partial list of Kurath's students who are active in promoting American dialect studies:

1) in the North-Central States, the Director Albert H. Marckwardt of Michigan, and the Associate Director, Raven I. McDavid, Jr., of the University of Chicago, and the Assistant Director, Virginia McDavid, of Chicago Teachers College, plus Cassil Reynard, Frederic G. Cassidy, Harold B. Allen of the University of Minnesota and Alva L. Davis among the field workers, and Thomas Wetmore of Ball State College on an associated project;

2) in the Upper Midwest, the Director Harold B. Allen, the Deputy Director for Iowa, Rachel Harris Kilpatrick, formerly of the University of Iowa, and field workers Virginia McDavid, Raven I. McDavid, Jr., and H. Rex Wilson;

3) in Texas, the Director E. Bagby Atwood, of the University of Texas;

4) in the Rocky Mountain States, the Director Marjorie Kimmerle of the University of Colorado, plus her former colleague Clyde Hankey, now of Western Michigan University;

5) on the Pacific Coast, the two Directors, David W. Reed of the University of California (Berkeley) and Carroll E. Reed of the University of Washington;

6) in other parts of the United States, Ann Shannon of the University of Kansas,

William R. Van Riper of Oklahoma State University, Rudolph Fiehler of Louisiana Polytechnic Institute, Nate Caffee of Louisiana State University (to say nothing of his emeritus colleague Claude M. Wise), Gordon Wood of the University of Chattanooga, and Juanita Williamson of Le Moyne College (Memphis, Tennessee);

7) in Canada, W. S. Avis and H. Rex Wilson, both of the Royal Military College, and active in the work of the Canadian Linguistic Association, with Wilson chairman of its committee on research in English dialects.

Add to these the activity of Kurath's students and colleagues (past and present) in the dialectology of other languages, and we have him influencing the whole stream of dialect work in the Western Hemisphere, and even outside it. His contributions to dialectology, through the Linguistic Atlas, are best summarized in the following statement, taken from an appeal for funds for editing which I prepared for the American Council of Learned Societies in 1950, but brought up to date in a few particulars:

The unpublished collections of the Linguistic Atlas from the Atlantic Seaboard consist of over 1050 field records from nearly five hundred communities in the area extending from upstate New York and border communities in English-speaking Canada to the Altamaha Valley in Georgia and the northeastern corner of Florida, distributed so as to be fairly representative of settlement history and population distribution.

Each field record contains the usage of an informant -- native to the community investigated and typical of an age or cultural group in that community -- on over 750 items of grammar, pronunciation, and vocabulary, built around such topics of ordinary conversation as the household, the farm, the weather, health, cooking, religion and superstition, business and sports, so as to provide comparable data for the area investigated. These records have been filed in the office of the Linguistic Atlas at the University of Michigan.

The Atlas collections represent by far the most comprehensive record of American usage. For future work in American English to be valid -- particularly where questions of regional or social distribution are concerned -- the Atlas materials must be made accessible to the greatest possible number of scholars. It is such scholars who will formulate new historical analyses on the basis of the descriptive evidence presented in the Linguistic Atlas. Such analyses may lead to new interpretations of particular details in the history of the language; or, applied to the study of dialect representations in literature, may throw light on the speech of particular periods or places. Already two ground-breaking analyses of literary dialects have been prepared from Atlas materials -- by J. W. Downer (1958), of the dialect of James Russell Lowell's *Biglow Papers*, and by Sumner A. Ives (1950a) on the representation of Negro speech in the Uncle Remus stories of Joel Chandler Harris.

The Atlas does not confine itself to folk speech or that of the partially educated; about a tenth of the records are those of cultured informants, and the major cultural centers of the Atlantic Seaboard -- such as Boston, New York, Philadelphia, Baltimore, Richmond, and Charleston -- are especially well represented in this respect. Thus the Atlas contains the fullest record of American cultured speech now available. No data is as satisfactory for the analysis of regional types of socially privileged speech as is that provided in the Atlas.

Such a work as the Atlas has many specific implications. For the student of American dialects, it is important to have definite criteria on which one can draw, with accuracy, the boundaries of dialect areas, so that one can now speak with some assurance of such major dialect types as Northern, Midland, and Southern -- or of such more localized types as Eastern New England, Metropolitan New York, the Virginia Piedmont, and the South Carolina Low-Country -- rather than the older division into 'Eastern,' 'Southern,' and 'General American.' The older interpretation -- apparently based chiefly on the pronunciation of /r/ in such words as *father*, *first*, *barn*, and *beard* -- must be discarded in the light of phonological and grammatical (as well as lexical) evidence setting off the northern tier of counties in Pennsylvania and Ohio from the rest of those two states, and the Shenandoah Valley of Virginia from the Piedmont.

On the basis of the Atlas we can now set up a division into dialect types on linguistic evidence, rather than one reflecting the somewhat arbitrary American political boundaries. In fact, the evidence of the Atlas substantiates many commonly recognized but not systematically analyzed economic and cultural subdivisions within particular states. Specifically, one can now no longer draw a linguistic Mason-Dixon Line along the southern boundary of Pennsylvania and label everything south of that as 'Southern.' Material already published clearly shows the linguistic effect of the southward migration of Ulster Scots and Germans through the Shenandoah Valley into the Piedmont of the Carolinas and Georgia -- a difference in settlement history reflected in differences in agricultural practices, in economic interests, in political adherence. Thus in Virginia there has long been a conflict of interests between the Shenandoah Valley and the eastern part of the state, separated from the Valley by the Blue Ridge Mountains, along which runs a major dialect boundary. In the Carolinas and Georgia, and presumably in Alabama, the chief dialect boundary roughly parallels the Fall Line, the shore line in an earlier geological period and the head of navigation in the period of settlement. The area below the Fall Line, the coastal plain, was the area of plantation agriculture and large slaveholdings; the Piedmont, above the Fall Line, was an area of small, independent farms and relatively few slaves -- and since the Civil War it has been rapidly industrialized, to gain spectacularly in population while the population of the early agricultural areas declined. The differences between the coastal speech of these states and the Pennsylvania-derived speech of the Piedmont reflect present and past conflicts of interest.

The Midland affiliations of the speech of the Peedee-Cape Fear Valleys in the Carolinas, reflecting both a difference in settlement history from the rest of the Carolina coast and an early trade route from the Midland settlements in the North Carolina Piedmont, illuminate the political history of South Carolina, explaining the fact that in state elections Horry County -- the northeasternmost county on the South Carolina coast -- until recent years traditionally voted with the counties of the Piedmont rather than with the Charleston area.

On the basis of the Atlas material on file in 1945, as interpreted in the *Word Geography of the Eastern United States* (1949), Kurath has divided the Atlantic Seaboard, from Maine to South Carolina, into eighteen fairly well-defined dialect areas, reflecting largely the areas of original settlement and routes of migration. In several of these areas, especially the Hudson Valley and central Pennsylvania, many words of foreign-language origin (and some phonological and syntactic features) have been found in the local varieties of English, reflecting languages that have either disappeared, like the Dutch of the Hudson Valley or the South German along the lower Savannah, or are still spoken alongside English in bilingual communities. Thus the Atlas may provide an index of what happens when two cultures come in contact. The problems of foreign-language survivals, dialect mixture within a surviving foreign language, and bilingualism have been analyzed in studies of the Gullah Negro dialect by Lorenzo Turner (1949), of Pennsylvania German by Carroll Reed and Lester Seifert (1954), and of American Norwegian by Einar Haugen (1953). As Haugen's pioneer study points out, one cannot fairly evaluate linguistic borrowing without accurate information about the varieties of both languages spoken in the area in which the contact occurred.

Furthermore, people do not carry their speech patterns to new communities and leave the rest of their culture behind. It is likely that many items of folk culture will be found distributed in patterns similar to those which the Atlas, along with its derivative studies, has found for details of American speech. One may expect to find differences in items of material culture, of diet, and of folklore. One notes that the shape of haystacks changes sharply when one crosses the Blue Ridge from the Virginia Piedmont to the Shenandoah Valley, that in the 'Dutch Fork' area of central South Carolina the chimneys of farmhouses are placed differently from elsewhere in the South, that -- although turnips are grown everywhere -- the tops (better known as *greens* or *sallet*) are apparently not an article of human diet north of the South Midland speech area, and that a number of folk songs have regional variants coinciding in distribution with dialect areas delineated by Atlas research.

Speech patterns so clearly reflect differences in local attachments that no study -- theoretical or paractical -- of regionalism can afford to ignore them. Regional boundaries indicated by speech patterns and similarly intimate cultural traits are much more real than those drawn, say, according to prevailing agricultural products. For instance, cotton will be grown wherever it promises to be a profitable crop; but it would be a mistake to lump together as a cultural unit the Sea Islands of South Carolina and Georgia, the Alabama Black Belt, the Mississippi-Yazoo Delta, the Texas plains, and the irrigated lands of Arizona and Southern California.

Similarly the Atlas provides evidence for examining social differences. The number of field records from the important cultural centers along the Atlantic Seaboard will permit a number of studies to be made of educational and class differences in speech, which then may be used by sociologists to facilitate the interpretation of data derived from other sources. Frank's dissertation on the speech of New York City was the first study of the social distribution of speech forms within a single community (1949); David De Camp's study of San Francisco (1954, 1958-59), based on field work for the Atlas of the Pacific Coast, Arthur Norman's of Orange County, Texas (1955), and Janet Sawyer's of San Antonio, Texas (1957), have added to our understanding of the problems of social differences in language, and we can expect new dimensions from similar projects, in progress or planned, like Robert Weber's study of the Minneapolis-St. Paul metropolitan area (1965) and projected investigations of Chicago and Akron. R. McDavid's articles have suggested the usefulness of dialect data as a criterion for determining caste and class differences within a community. Although this criterion has not appeared in the community studies hitherto conducted by American sociologists, it has appeared in the work of the Urban Life Research Institute of New Orleans, thanks to the participation of Ives, and is provided for in a proposed sociological study of metropolitan Detroit. Along with these contributions, the Atlas provides evidence for gauging the cultural domination of one area by a prestigious cultural center, whether within or without the area; phonology, lexicon, and grammar all will show this domination. The psychologist, too, could profitably make use of Atlas materials in studies of attitudes, especially of prejudices and taboos; R. McDavid's recent study of the pronunciation of *Negro* (1960b) is an example in point. In all investigations of these types, the linguistic geographer has the advantage over other investigators in that speech is habitual and culturally determined, and -- for most people -- much less subject to distortion by public opinion, current fashion, or advertising pressures than many other cultural details.

By systematically investigation the speech of various age and educational groups, the Linguistic Atlas of the United States and Canada has introduced into the science of dialect geography the principle of social differences and the dimension of time. This represents an advance in technique, building on the methods of Wenker and Wrede, of Gilliéron and Edmont, of Jaberg and Jud. It is therefore not surprising that the American collections have been consulted as a model by the German dialectologist Walter Fischer, the British scholars interested in dialectology -- such as J. R. Firth, Angus McIntosh, and Harold Orton --, by Chao and Grootaers for the study of dialect differences in China, and by J. K. Yamagiwa for Japan.

In English-speaking North America the implications of the Linguistic Atlas data from the Atlantic Seaboard have led to the initiation of regional studies, some of which have passed the completion of field work and are approaching publication. It is already apparent that these regional surveys will be as valuable for interpreting settlement history and social structure as the material from the Atlantic Seaboard.

Similarly, the information about American regional dialect divisions that has been gained from the Atlas project should prove very valuable for work on any dictionary of American dialects that may be undertaken. The recent revival of interest in such a dictionary has been due largely to the stimulus provided by the Linguistic Atlas. Conferences devoted to planning such a dictionary have drawn largely on the experiences of the Atlas staff; the committee of the Dialect Society concerned with regional speech has been headed for nearly a decade by a member of the Atlas staff; the subcommittee on plans for a dialect dictionary were thoroughly familiar with the principles of linguistic geography, and repeatedly affirmed adherence to those principles. The two systematic local investigations that have been undertaken -- Cassidy's *Wisconsin Words* [it remains unpublished], and Saunders Walker's dissertation on the folk vocabulary of the eastern Alabama Negro (1956) -- have profitably adapted the technique of systematic questioning of selected informants on selected items in a selected network of communities.

The Atlas has already shown its potential value to the makers of more general dictionaries. A dictionary of pronunciation or the consultant on pronunciation for a general dictionary can make use of the materials to indicate regional and social usage; the writer of definitions can attest regional or social occurrences of words or meanings. The scholar interested in Americanisms or Briticisms can work more effectively if he knows the patterns of regional and social distribution within the United States.

Likewise, the Atlas should be very useful to those concerned with improving the teaching of English. Because it has systematically investigated several levels of usage over a wide area, it enables one to replace the older normative and subjective judgments of 'correctness' by an evaluation of the actual social standing of linguistic forms. One may now make far better and more accurate judgments as to whether particular linguistic forms are in general colloquial use, acceptable in one region though not in another, old-fashioned, or simply substandard. Such evidence should enable English teachers, at whatever level, to devote less of their time to hunting for real or imaginary errors, and more to teaching the more effective use of language. Such evidence has already been drawn from the Atlas materials, especially in Kurath's *Word Geography* and Atwood's *Survey of Verb Forms*, the dissertations by Frank and V. McDavid, and a recent comparison of Atlas evidence and handbook judgments prepared under Allen's direction, as a Minnesota dissertation (1958), by Jean Malmstrom of Western Michigan University. The general value of the Atlas was appropriately recognized from the beginning by the National Council of Teachers of English, under whose auspices the first conference on planning the Atlas was held.

The Atlas project has created an increasing amount of interest in American English during the two decades it has been under way. Popular articles in newspapers and national magazines have drawn wide favorable attention, as did the treatment of the Atlas in the popular television feature *The Alphabet Conspiracy*, where Kurath played an important role -- that of himself. This increasing interest has naturally been reflected in college curricula: despite the notorious apathy of the literary groups that dominate most English departments, institutions with course offerings in American English have grown from three in 1930 to several times that number today. As the number of course offerings has increased, so has the demand for texts. Marckwardt and Thomas Pyles of Florida have each prepared general treatments of the subject; a survey of American dialects and dialectology is included in Francis's *The Structure of American English* (1958), and a detailed treatment of the subject under the editorship of R. McDavid and others is well on its way to completion. It is safe to assume that the publication of the materials from the Middle Atlantic and South Atlantic States would result in a larger number of of published books and articles on American English, and would stimulate related projects, by which the study of American English may be correlated with the study of other aspects of American culture.

To have instituted and directed a work of such significance should be more than enough to assure Kurath's place as a scholar. But the same energy that enabled him to keep the Atlas work going during the Depression led him, at the age of 53, to enter a new field of scholarship in which he has gained additional distinction.

Despite his dissertation, Kurath was not known as a lexicographer -- let alone a specialist in the lexicography of Middle English. Consequently, there was some severe criticism expressed when the University of Michigan selected him to succeed Knott as editor of the *Middle English Dictionary*. No detailed defense of the decision was made at the time, and none will be attempted here; but it was apparent that what weighed heavily with the selection committee was Kurath's proved reputation for organizing and directing a large-scale research project and bringing it to publication. As with the Atlas project, his first step was to examine the materials and to draw up a detailed plan of operations, which might hope to survive the mutability of any particular piece of human flesh. As with the Atlas, too, his plan has been incompletely fulfilled, for there have never been enough funds or editorial assistants to make the project move as rapidly as he would have preferred. Nevertheless, with a small staff he has already published the general plan and bibliography and two volumes of the *Dictionary* itself (Kurath, Kuhn *et al.* 1952-), and fascicles are now appearing at the rate of about one volume every two years. It will be more than another decade before the last volume is out, but already the *Middle English Dictionary* has won general acclaim. [In 1975 a generous grant from the Mellon Foundation provided funds which should assure completion of editorial work by 1985.] Nor has the *Dictionary* monopolized his time, though he puts in his full work week like everyone else on the staff. He maintains his interest in the advancement of dialect studies in the Western Hemisphere, has directed, or helped direct, a dozen dissertations in the field, and has kept abreast of innovations in method and new kinds of interpretations in dialect studies in all parts of the world. For several years he was director of the University Linguistics Program and of the Linguistic Institute in the summers. His influence is seen in the steady expansion of linguistics at Michigan, in the high intellectual ferment and general *Gemütlichkeit* among the students in the summer programs, and in the success of Michigan in maintaining a first-rate summer program in linguistics even in those summers when the official Linguistic Institute of the Linguistic Society has been located elsewhere.

So much for the official Kurath. But there is a personal Kurath, at least as important, reflected in the loyalty of his former students and those who have worked under his direction. And in view of our associations for the last twenty years, I feel that the portrait would be incomplete without a discussion of this part of the man.

The first time I met him, in the Michigan League building before the Ann Arbor conference of 1940 on non-English dialects in the United States, I did not know what to say to him. It was characteristic of him that he put me at my ease, and -- aware of the fact that I was then without academic connections -- remarked, "I wish I could find funds to put you to work on the Atlas, but we don't have any." Somehow, in that one sentence (entirely unsolicited by any requests on my part) he enabled me to see my own vocation, not as another teacher of English with a side interest in dialects, but as that of a serious professional student of language, with no need to be ashamed in the face of other such scholars, however great their distinction. I could hardly believe this, yet -- a year later, when I had received a Rosenwald Fellowship to work on South Carolina dialects -- at the first opportunity he invited me to participate in the Atlas project. I can imagine the difficulties I must have caused him with my own combination of timidity and brashness, not helped by personal tragedies and a break with the Southern ethos which had hitherto dominated my thinking, but he never reproached me for what I didn't do but rather gave more than full credit for whatever I had accomplished. The opportunity to collaborate with him on the *Pronunciation* meant much to me, but what meant more was his precept (and example) of continuing to work, regardless of the difficulties, and his gentle reminder that, for those who choose the road of scholarship, recognition may come more slowly than for those who choose the road of administration and propaganda, but it will come more surely and be more solidly established. This understanding was an unimaginable boon during the painful years of unemployment, marginal employment, and low-paid academic employment (which sometimes seemed worse than no employment at all); it is not to be forgotten in present prosperity.

It should therefore be no surprise that I welcomed the invitation from Dean Wilt of our Division of Humanities to propose candidates for honorary degrees, and that, when Kurath received the degree of Doctor of Humanities from the University of Chicago at the convocation of December 18, 1959, I was very happy to have a chance of participating in the ceremonies, and of reading the following speech of presentation:

Mr. Chancellor, I present as candidate for the degree of Doctor of Humane Letters, Hans Kurath -- Professor of English at the University of Michigan, Director of the Linguistic Atlas of the United States and Canada, and Editor of the *Middle English Dictionary*.

For many years, as scholar and teacher, he has advanced the scientific study of language -- the one essentially distinctive characteristic of man's humanity -- and particularly of the English language. His dissertation on the words for the emotions in the Indo-European languages was a significant contribution to Buck's great semantic dictionary. His early studies of dialect differences in the United States and their relationships to the dialects of Great Britain made him the inevitable choice for the directorship of the American Linguistic Atlas, which not only has revised all previous judgments, including his own, on patterns of dialect distribution in the United States, but has contributed new dimensions to subsequent dialect studies everywhere; the findings -- both for the monumental *Linguistic Atlas of New England* and for the unpublished collections from the Middle and South Atlantic States -- are clearly and elegantly summarized in his *Word Geography of the Eastern United States* and the forthcoming *Pronunciation of English in the Atlantic States*. Called to the editorship of the *Middle English Dictionary*, he has breathed new life into a seemingly moribund project and is producing a work indispensable to all students of medieval culture. And for more than forty years he has taught and inspired students -- in fields ranging from medieval textual criticism to American criminal argots -- not only to carry on his work but to make their own significant contributions to the study of language, especially of the vehicle of our culture, the English language. His colleagues in linguistics have recognized him, a founding member of the Linguistic Society of America, by making him its president; I now ask that we recognize him as one of our distinguished graduates by conferring on him the degree of Doctor of Humane Letters.

[In 1979, Kurath remains intellectually as vigorous as ever. He has contributed invaluable criticism of editorial plans and procedures (e.g., 1968); the edited LAMSAS and LANCS bear his impress on every page.]

When we compare varieties of American English, we generally assume that differences in grammar reflect social differences, and that differences in vocabulary or pronunciation reflect regional differences.[1] Yet we must often modify this useful practical rule. The word *bastard* occurs everywhere, but everywhere it seems to be a cruder term than *illegitimate child*. In all regions where *jacket* and *vest* are synonymous, *jacket* is apparently more rustic and old-fashioned. Conversely, Atwood's monograph (1953a) shows that the divergences in status between the preterites *dove* and *dived*, *woke up* and *waked up*, *sweat* and *sweated*, are more regional than social. Moreover, though /klɪm, kləm, klom, klæm, klam, klum/ all have less prestige as preterites than *climbed*, at least three of these forms occur in definite regional patterns: /klɪm/ in the North and South, /kləm/ in the Midland, /klom/ in Eastern Virginia.[2] Even /ɛt/ as the preterite of *eat* -- a social shibboleth to many speakers -- turns out to be the socially elegant for in Charleston, South Carolina, where the use of /ɛt/ (and of *ain't* in informal speech) sets off those who belong to the best Charletonian society from those who would like to belong but don't.

We should therefore not be surprised if some pronunciations carry connotations of social prestige or lack of it. We can discuss a few of these pronunciations by examining the evidence collected for the Linguistic Atlas of the United States and Canada. This evidence has been collected in the field by trained investigators using a finely graded phonetic alphabet and a questionnaire of selected items dealing with everyday experience. The persons interviewed are strongly rooted natives of their communities, typical of various age or social groups. Usually there is one person, as unsophisticated as possible, from the oldest generation, and another either younger or more sophisticated or both. Besides, there are enough cultured informants to indicate the local or regional standards. For the Atlantic Seaboard states alone, the field workers for the Atlas interviewed over 150 cultured informants -- a greater number of cultured informants than even the largest standard dictionary has utilized for the entire United States. [*Webster's New International*, second edition (1934). The *Third New International* (1961) has a wider range by far, thanks to the industry of its pronunciation editor, Edward Artin. Ironically, the greater evidence and more accurate statements on pronunciation proved to be one of the grounds on which the *Third* was assailed by journalists and belle-lettristes.]

Besides the relative status of informants in their own communities (indicated by the field worker after he has completed the interviews), one must evaluate communities, or groups of communities, against the whole body of American English. Previous work in linguistic geography, especially Kurath's *Word Geography* (1949), enables us to judge pronunciations by the type of dialect areas in which they occur. Focal areas are those areas whose economic, social, or cultural prestige has led to the spread of their linguistic forms into other areas. Examples are Eastern New England (Boston), Eastern Pennsylvania (Philadelphia), the Hudson Valley (New York City), the Virginia Piedmont (Richmond), and the South Carolina Low-Country (Charleston). Pronunciations characteristic of focal areas are likely to have prestige, especially when used by the younger and more sophisticated speakers.

Relic areas, on the other hand, are those whose geographical or cultural isolation, and relative lack of prestige, has caused the retention of older forms or prevented the spread of forms characteristic of these areas. Examples are Northeastern New England, the Eastern Shore of Chesapeake Bay, and Eastern North Carolina. Pronunciations characteristic of relic areas are likely to lack prestige, especially if they are chiefly used by the older and less sophisticated speakers.

A third problem we must consider is the attitude of speakers towards particular pronunciations -- whether we call them "secondary responses" with Bloomfield or "metalinguistic details" with Trager. Here, incidental comments of the informants are of great value. For instance, the American *vase* /ves/ is a /vaz/ in Southern British Received Pronunciation. We might expect /vaz/ to have prestige in the United States, especially in those areas of New England and the Old South where British customs are admired and British speech forms are often adopted into local cultured speech. However, not only is /vaz/ rare as a spontaneous pronunciation, but the frequent comments of informants that "if it costs over $2.98 it's a /vaz/" suggest that many people who say /vaz/ are judged as parvenus who have acquired the pronunciation during a recent exposure to culture and who wish to use it to impress their neighbors. Judgments that pronunciations are characteristic of less privileged social groups -- Negroes, unsuccessful farmers, recent immigrants -- indicate for such pronunciations a lack of prestige in the community, regardless of their status elsewhere or their occurrence in the informant's unguarded conversation.

Finally, some informants may deliberately stick to pronunciations they know are considered old-fashioned, unprivileged, or simply peculiar. New Yorkers generally consider it substandard to pronounce a *curl* of hair and a *coil* of rope the same way, yet I know at least one prosperous and well-educated New Yorker of colonial stock who does not distinguish such pairs. The most sophisticated informant interviewed in Charleston proclaimed that she personally said /təˈmætəz/, though she knew other people said /təˈmetəz/ or /təˈmatəz/ -- "because Grandmother H. always said /təˈmætəz/, and what Grandmother H. said is good enough for me." One cultured informant near Galt, Ontario consistently says /bul, pul/ for *bull*, *pull*, instead of /bʊl, pʊl/ because these pronunciations have come down in his Scotch-Canadian family. Such examples of 'rugged individualism,' family pride, or personal stubbornness do not give us patterns of prestige, but they warn us to go slow in condemning what we do not say ourselves.

As Kurath has often pointed out, there are three types of differences in pronunciation: 1) differences in the pronunciation of the individual phonemes; 2) differences in the occurrence of the individual phonemes; 3) differences in the system of phonemes.[3]

Differences in the pronunciation of the individual phonemes are hardest to detect and evaluate. Some of these pronunciations are fairly striking, and do denote social status:

1. The ingliding diphthongal pronunciation of *date* and *boat*, as [deˑət] and [boˑət], is generally confined to the Charleston area.

2. The fronted [ʉ] in *two*, *boot* is very common in the Midland and South.

3. The monophthongal or near monophthongal variety of /ai/ occurring finally and before voiced consonants in *high*, *hide*. This type of pronunciation is chiefly found in Southern and South Midland dialects. Though sometimes ridiculed by speakers from other regions, it is rarely considered an unprivileged form in the areas where it occurs -- and then only if the speaker does not differentiate *high* from *hah*, *blind* from *blond*, *hide* from *hod* or *hard*. [With increasing affluence and the spread of education in the South, the monophthongal [aˑ], in whatever position, is unquestionably

a feature of Southern cultivated pronunciation.]

4. The fronted beginning of /au/ ([æu, ɛu]) in such words as *cow* is found in northern New England and the New England settlement area, and in the South and South Midland. In the North they are generally considered old-fashioned or rustic, and are disappearing. They are very common in the Richmond area and seem to be spreading nearly everywhere in the South except in South Carolina.

5. The centralized beginning of /ai, au/ ([əɪ, əʊ]) in *rite*, *ride*, *lout*, *loud*. Sometimes this occurs only when the diphthong is followed by a voiceless consonant, sometimes in all positions. In the Inland North the centralized beginning may occur regardless of the consonant following the diphthong, but in this region the centralized beginning is often considered somewhat old-fashioned and rustic, though it is used by many cultured informants. The centralized beginning when the diphthong is followed by a voiceless consonant, but not otherwise, is characteristic of the speech of three well-defined areas: Canada (especially Ontario), the Virginia Piedmont, and the Atlantic Tidewater area from Georgetown, South Carolina, to St. Augustine, Florida. In view of the social prestige of the Richmond and Charleston areas, the pronunciations of *light* and *lout* as [ləɪt, ləʊt] probably have privileged status.

6. An ingliding vowel with a rather high beginning sometimes occurs for /æ/ in such words as *calf*, *bad* [æʌə, ɛə] or for /ɔ/ in *law* [ɔʌə, oʌə]. These pronunciations are most common in such cities as New York, Philadelphia, and Baltimore. They are especially common in families with a central or eastern European background, and the more extreme varieties are often considered substandard.[4]

There are relatively few differences in the system of phonemes that all students would agree upon:

1. For some speakers the 'New England short o,' /ɵ/, occurs alongside /o/ in such words as *coat*, *road*, *home*, *whole*. It probably is found everywhere in the New England settlement area since it has been recorded as far west as Montana. On the other hand, even in New England it is losing ground, since it is found chiefly in smaller and relatively isolated communities and in the speech of older and less sophisticated informants.

2. A falling diphthong /iu/ occurs alongside /ju/ (or /u/) in such words as *puke*, *beautiful*, *music*, *tube*, *due*, *new*, *suit*, *sumach*, *grew*, *blew*. It is found chiefly in the New England settlement area, but also occurs along Chesapeake Bay and the Carolina and Georgia coast. It is slightly old-fashioned, especially in the North (it occurs most frequently in *puke*, which does not have a 'schoolroom pronun-

ciation'); yet it still occurs in cultured speech.

3. In the Pittsburgh area the vowel /a/ occurs only before /-r/, with both *cot* and *caught*, *collar* and *caller* having /ɔ/. This feature also seems to occur frequently in western Canada and in the Minneapolis area. If anything, it seems to be spreading among younger and better educated speakers.

Differences in the occurrence of individual phonemes are most common and easiest to evaluate. They may be grouped according to several social types, though we must remember that these groupings are only tentative ones:

1. Some differences are purely regional:

In such words as *whip*, *wharf*, and *whoa*, some speakers have /hw-/, others /w-/ (R. and V. McDavid 1952b).

For *humor*, the pronunciation /hjumər/ occurs sporadically and chiefly in the Northern area, though elsewhere there are indications it is being sponsored by the schools as a spelling pronunciation. /jumər/ is far more common, at all levels of usage. For other words of this group, however (though the evidence is less adequate), the forms with /ju-/ seem to be less widespread and somewhat lacking in prestige.

For *without*, the middle consonant may be either /θ/ or /ð/ at any social level. In the North and eastern North Carolina /ð/ is overwhelmingly predominant; in Canada, the Midland area, eastern Virginia, South Carolina, and Georgia /θ/ is very frequent.

Ewe is /jo/ in most of the country where people have knowledge of sheep. Since this pronunciation is never heard from those who have not lived where sheep were raised, it may be considered an occupational pronunciation among sheep herders.

Bleat, the cry of a calf, is prevailingly /blæt/ in the North and /blet/ in the South, being replaced by *bawl* in the Midland; /blit/ is almost exclusively a city pronunciation.

Because is frequently pronounced /bɪˈkəz/ in the North and in South Carolina, but rarely in other regions. Where this pronunciation occurs it is used by speakers of all degrees of sophistication.

The unstressed vowel of *without* is always /ɪ/ in the North and the South, but usually /ə/ in the Midland.

Beside the usual /tʃu-/, *Massachusetts* is often /dʒu-/ in New England, but /tju-/ or /tu-/ in the South and South Midland.

Instead of /wɔnt/ (or the common Southern /wount/) *want* is very often /want/ in Massachusetts and Vermont, /wɛnt/ in New Jersey and western Pennsylvania. Both of these pronunciations occur sporadically in western areas settled ultimately from New England.

Words such as *orange*, *Florida*, *borrow*, and *tomorrow* may have either /a/ or /ɔ/ before /-r/. In the Atlantic Seaboard states /ɔ/ is most likely to occur in these words in northern New England, western Pennsylvania, and the Charleston area. For such words as *Florida* and *orange*, /ɔ/ is practically universal in the North-Central States and westward, but in these same areas /a/ or /ɔ/ may occur in *borrow* and *tomorrow*. [These conclusions are supported by the work of C. K. Thomas.]

For *bulge*, *bulk*, and *budget*, both /u/ and /ə/ occur: /ə/ in the North and North Midland, /u/ in the South Midland, eastern Virginia, and the Piedmont of the Carolinas and Georgia, /ə/ again along the southern coast south of Chesapeake Bay.

For *won't*, /wont/ occurs everywhere. In addition there are four forms with regional distribution: 1) /wɛnt/ in the North, outside of the Hudson Valley; 2) /wɔnt/ in North Carolina; 3) /wunt, wʊnt/ in Canada, New York City, the Hudson Valley, Chesapeake Bay, eastern North Carolina, and the Charleston area. All of these forms occur in cultured speech.

For many of the words derived from Middle English /oː/ -- and some borrowings that have fallen into the pattern -- both /u/ and /ʊ/ occur, without social distinction but with sharply differing regional patterns. This is true of *coop*, *cooper*, *hoop*, *goobers*, *room*, *broom*, *root*, *cooter*, *food*, *hoof*, *roof*, *spooks*, and probably others. For instance, I -- a native of upper South Carolina -- normally have /u/ in *root*, *cooter*, *food*, *roof*, *spooks*, and *goober*, /ʊ/ in *coop*, *cooper*, *hoop*, and either /u/ or /ʊ/ in *room*, *broom*, *hoof*.

For such words as *tube*, *dew*, *new*, we find /iu/ in the North and occasionally along the southern coast, although it is somewhat old-fashioned in both areas. In the South and South Midland, /ju/ is predominant. It occurs as a prestige form in some communities in the North and North Midland. In northeastern New England, the Hudson Valley, and the North Midland, /u/ is almost universal and is spreading in other parts of the North.

Such pairs as *horse* and *hoarse*, *morning* and *mourning*, *border* and *boarder* are usually distinguished in the North, the South, and the South Midland, but not in the North Midland. In many parts of the Inland North and in Canada the distinction is disappearing.

2. A few pronunciations seem to lack prestige everywhere. *Italian* as /ai + tæljən/ is generally looked down upon [as used by President Carter, it became an issue in the 1976 campaign]; /dif/ (instead of /dɛf/) for *deaf* and /waundɪd/ (instead of /wundɪd/) for *wounded* are generally considered old-fashioned.

3. Other pronunciations lack prestige, but occur in limited regions:

Along Chesapeake Bay, *fog* and *hog* occasionally have /o/.

Rinse is rarely /rɪntʃ, rɛntʃ/ in the North, but these pronunciations are common in the Midland and the South. They are slightly old-fashioned, but not uncommon in cultured speech. The hyper-form /rɪnz/ is less common, limited to the same areas, and chiefly found in the speech of the half-educated.

Coop occurs with /b-/ on Delaware Bay and along the southern coast south of Chesapeake Bay. This pronunciation is not common in cities, is slightly old-fashioned, but is used by many cultured speakers.

In parts of the South Midland and the South (but not in the Virginia Piedmont) *took*, *roof*, and *hoof* frequently have /ə/ in uneducated speech.

In much of the South and South Midland, the less educated speakers have /ə/ in *put*, to rhyme with *cut*.

For *loam* and *gums*, the pronunciations with /u,ʊ/ are confined to the New England settlement area, with /ʊ/ more common in Maine and New Hampshire than elsewhere. Although generally lacking in prestige, /gʊmz/ and /lʊm/ sometimes occur in cultured speech in Maine and New Hampshire. In other areas cultured speakers occasionally say /gʊmz/ and /lʊm/.

Two pronunciations of *can't* -- /kɛnt/ and /kæint/ -- occur chiefly in parts of the South and South Midland. Although both pronunciations seem to have spread from the Virginia Piedmont, /kɛnt/ seems to be the older and /kæint/ the more recent form. Consequently, although both forms occur in the speech of all types of informants, /kɛnt/ is often considered just a little more old-fashioned.

4. Several pronunciations may lack prestige in one region but be acceptable in another:

In the South and South Midland the pronunciation of *creek* as /krɪk/ is usually considered very quaint and lacking in prestige, since it is largely confined to the uneducated Negroes of the Carolina and Georgia coast. Even in the South, however, /krɪk/ may occur in the speech of cultured Charlestonians. In the North both /krik/ and /krɪk/ occur, with some pressure from the public schools to enforce /krik/ as a spelling pronunciation. However, /krɪk/ is very common in Northern cultured speech. In the North Midland, especially in Pennsylvania, /krɪk/ is practically universal.

In the Atlantic Seaboard states, *farm* and *form* are rarely homonymous, and where this homonymy occurs, as occasionally in South Carolina and Georgia, it is only in uneducated speech, and consequently frowned upon. In parts of Louisiana and Texas, however, this homonymy is normal among all classes of speakers.

Soot is most frequently pronounced as /sət/, except in Pennsylvania. In many parts of the country /sət/ is looked upon as old-fashioned, rustic, or uneducated. In the South, however, it is the pronunciation used by a majority of cultured speakers.

Many scholars, even Fries (1940:10), have labeled the pronunciation of *catch* with /ɛ/ as lacking in prestige. However, /kɛtʃ/ is overwhelmingly the normal pronunciation, for the nation as a whole and for all regions except southern New England, the Hudson Valley, Pennsylvania, and the city of Charleston, where /kætʃ/ is the majority usage. In the areas where /kætʃ/ is the usual pronunciation, it is naturally preferred by educated speakers. In Virginia, and to some extent in North Carolina, /kætʃ/ is a prestige pronunciation, used by a majority of the cultured informants but by few others. In other parts of the country, however, a majority of the cultured informants say /kɛtʃ/ (R. McDavid 1953a).

5. For some words, one pronunciation may have prestige in one region and another pronunciation have prestige somewhere else:

For *raspberries*, the 'broad a' pronunciation with /a/ seems to have some prestige in eastern New England, and to a lesser extent in New York City and eastern Virginia. In other parts of the country, however -- particularly in the Inland North -- the pronunciation with /æ/ is socially preferred, and the /a/ pronunciation considered old-fashioned or rustic.

For such words as *hog* and *fog*, pronunciations with /a,ɔ,ou/ have been recorded from speakers on all social levels. The /a/ pronunciations seem to have social prestige in Boston, New York City, Philadelphia, Charleston, Richmond (but not in smaller communities in the Virginia Piedmont), western North Carolina, northwestern South Carolina, and northern Georgia. In other Southern communities the cultured informants have /ɔ,ou/. It is probable that /ou/ is an older prestige pronunciation that has spread from the Virginia Piedmont, with /a/ replacing it in cultured Richmond speech and in the cultured speech of other metropolitan centers.

Almost everyone knows that the two pronunciations of *greasy* sharply divide the eastern United States, with /-s-/ more common in the North and North Midland but /-z-/ usual in the South and South Midland. In some areas where both pronunciations occur, they are associated with different social levels or social contexts. Trager has frequently pointed out that among his boyhood playmates in Newark the /-z-/ pronunciation was confined to such derogatory phrases as a *greasy grind*. In South Carolina and Georgia the /-s-/ pronunciation is regular among the Gullah Negroes but almost never occurs in the speech of whites.

6. Occasionally a pronunciation may

have social prestige in one area but elsewhere be only one of several acceptable pronunciations. For instance, *office* with /a/ has social prestige in eastern Pennsylvania and eastern Virginia; in other areas /a/ or /ɔ/ or /ou/ may occur without any implication of social distinction.

7. Some pronunciations have prestige in the limited areas in which they occur:

The pronunciation of *can't* with /a/ is the socially preferred form in eastern New England, and to a lesser extent in New York City, Philadelphia, and eastern Virginia. Elsewhere it is extremely rare.

The pronunciation of *soot* as /sut/ is largely confined to the Northern areas. Wherever it occurs, it is likely to be found in the speech of the moderately or better educated.

The lack of constriction of post-vocalic /-r/ (the so-called 'loss of /r/') in *burn*, *barn*, *beard* occurs mostly in eastern New England, New York City, and the South Atlantic States. In the areas where it occurs, it is most likely to appear in the speech of the younger and better educated informants. In some communities in the South Atlantic States the rustic and uneducated white speakers preserve the constriction of /-r/, while Negroes and the more sophisticated whites lack constriction. In such communities visitors from the Inland North or the North-Central States, where the constriction of /-r/ occurs in the speech of all classes, are likely to be at a social disadvantage. Conversely, in some Inland Northern communities, the only residents who lack constriction of /-r/ are the Negroes who have come from the South in the last generation. In these communities, Southern students have had difficulty securing rooms. In telephone conversations, landladies may identify the lack of constriction of /-r/ as a Negro characteristic and announce that no rooms are available.

8. A few pronunciations are always somewhat prestigious since they occur most frequently in cities and in the speech of the younger and better educated informants. However, if the group of informants using such a pronunciation is very small, the prestige of the pronunciation may be lost since the pronunciation will be interpreted as a mark of conscious snobbery.

The pronunciation of *soot* as /sut/ always has social prestige, not only in Pennsylvania where /sut/ is the usual pronunciation but in the North where /sut/ is a common pronunciation among educated speakers and in the South where /sət/ is the usual pronunciation among speakers of all classes.

The pronunciations of *vase* as /vez/ (less frequently /vaz/), and of *nephew* as /nɛvjə, -ju/ (much less commonly /nɛvi/) are largely confined to cultured informants -- chiefly in southern Ontario, Bos-

ton, New York City, Philadelphia, Richmond and Charleston, where British speech forms are likely to have prestige. Inland informants who say /vez/ or /nɛvjə/ usually have strong family or cultural ties to one of those centers.

The pronunciation of *sumach* with /su-/ instead of the more common /ʃu-/ is also largely confined to the larger coastal cities and to a relatively few inland cultured informants.

Such words as *suit*, *blew*, *threw* are normally pronounced with /u/. Although the pronunciations with /ju/ have social prestige in England they are extremely rare in this country, occurring almost exclusively in the North. Most Americans consider them unnatural and affected.

9. Sometimes the pronunciation of a word may involve a number of intricately related cultural, historical, and political facts. One of the most complex of these is *Negro*, where the pronunciations involve not only the status and the attitudes of those who use them, but the reactions of those the pronunciations designate. The historical pronunciation /nɪgər/ is by far the most common, and in many communities it is the normal pronunciation used by speakers of both races. However, since it is used by many people as a term of contempt, it is actively resented by Negro spokesmen -- regardless of the intent behind it. The spelling pronunciation /nigro/ is comparatively new, but it has been actively sponsored as a polite pronunciation and is so used by most cultured speakers of the North and North Midland. However, /nigro/ is very rare south of the Mason-Dixon line, partly because it is recognized as a Northern pronunciation of a word about which most Southerners have strong prejudices, partly because it violates the normal Southern tendency to have /ə/ in unstressed syllables. The pronunciation /nɪgro/ is also a common polite form in the North and North Midland, but relatively uncommon in the South. The normal polite form in the South (and occasionally in other sections) is /nɪgrə/. Most cultured informants in the South do not use /nɪgər/, which they feel is both derogatory to the Negro and characteristic of poor white speech. The difference in status and implication of /nɪgrə/ and /nɪgər/ is very sharply maintained in the South, though frequently outsiders do not understand the distinction and wonder why the Southerner does not say /nigro/, which to the Southerner seems unnatural.

Even such a limited approach to the problem of social differences in pronunciation indicates that it is very complex and that the person who attempts to label the status of a pronunciation must have information about such social forces as trading areas, educational practices, and community structure. Nor will it be a simple matter for teachers to apply the knowledge gained from studies such as this. Yet one may suggest certain procedures.

Those who teach English in the public schools should be fully aware of the socially preferred pronunciations in the communities in which they are teaching. They should not waste time or energy attempting to force exotic pronunciations upon their students, regardless of how desirable or elegant such pronunciations seem. They should also be aware that other types of pronunciations may be acceptable in other communities. Such awareness will not only make it easier for teachers to deal with the student who has moved to the community from another region, it will also make it easier for them to teach in communities outside their own dialect area.

Teachers of English to foreign students must also recognize this problem. In universities with a cosmopolitan student body, the instructors and drillmasters may speak any one of several varieties of American English. Even if it is possible to choose instructors and drillmasters from one dialect area, or require them to use something like a uniform dialect in their classes, as soon as the foreign student goes into his regular classes he will hear other types of pronunciation from the professors and his fellow students. The problem would be less difficult at smaller colleges where the faculty and the student body are predominantly from one region. Even here, however, the students will occasionally encounter other varieties of English. The longer they are in the United States and the broader their contacts -- by travel, movies, radio, or television -- the more frequently they will hear other pronunciations than those they have learned. How much attention the teacher should pay to variant pronunciations is a matter of practical pedagogy, depending on circumstances -- it is much more important for the student to master one American pronunciation of *can't* than to learn a little about several pronunciations -- but certainly the advanced students should know that speakers may differ markedly in the details of their pronunciations and yet all speak socially acceptable American English.

NOTES

[1] This paper was originally presented at a meeting of the Michigan Linguistic Society, December 8, 1951. Most of the information on which it is based comes from the Atlantic Seaboard records of the Linguistic Atlas of the United States and from the records of the Linguistic Atlas of the North-Central States. Occasional examples come from the records of the Linguistic Atlas of the Upper Midwest, the Linguistic Atlas of the Rocky Mountain States, and from other research in American English. Professors Hans Kurath and A. H. Marckwardt of Michigan, H. B. Allen of Minnesota, and Marjorie Kimmerle of Colorado have made it possible to use these records.

The American Council of Learned Societies provided a scholarship for 1951-52 to make it possible for me to investigate the relationship between dialect differences and social differences. Many of the details in this paper have been expanded in Kurath and R. McDavid 1961.

[2] The regional designations are those found in Kurath 1949, and in articles by Kurath, Atwood, R. McDavid, and A. L. Davis. Linguistically, the North includes New England, the Hudson Valley (including New York City) and derivative settlements in upstate New York, Pennsylvania, and further west. The Inland North is the northern area exclusive of the Hudson Valley and eastern New England. The Midland includes most of New Jersey and Pennsylvania, with derivative settlements to the west and south. The North Midland includes most of New Jersey and Pennsylvania, plus northern West Virginia. The South Midland includes the Shenandoah Valley, southern West Virginia, southwest Virginia, and the mountain and upper Piedmont areas of the Carolinas and Georgia. The South includes the older plantation areas of eastern Virginia and the coastal plain and lower Piedmont of the Carolinas and Georgia. The boundaries between these sections are much less sharp west of the Appalachians than along the Atlantic Seaboard.

[3] The particular type of analysis one favors will often determine the category to which he assigns these differences. The analysis here used is basically that of Kurath and R. McDavid 1961. Phonetic symbols are enclosed in brackets, phonemic symbols in slanting lines. Phonemic equivalents are as follows:

Vowels:

/i/ as in *beet*
/ɪ/ as in *bit*
/e/ as in *bait*
/ɛ/ as in *bet*
/æ/ as in *bat*
/a/ as in *hot*, *father*
/ɔ/ as in *bought*
/o/ as in *boat*
/ə/ the New England 'short *o*' as in *coat*, *road*, *home*
/ʊ/ as in *put*
/u/ as in *boot*

Diphthongs:

/ai/ as in *write*
/au/ as in *rout*
/ɔi/ as in *oil*

/æi/ as in the common Southern and South Midland *bag*, *half*

/ɔʊ/ as in the common Southern and South Midland *law*, *hog*. This diphthong also occurs in New Hampshire.

/iu/ as in the common New England *beautiful*, *music*. This diphthong also occurs along the South Atlantic coast.

[4] These differences in the pronunciation of the individual phonemes are sometimes analyzed as phonemic or systematic differences, e.g., Trager and Smith 1951, Labov 1966.

One of the more interesting by-products of my recent work on *The American Language*[1] has been an appreciation of the changes in Mencken's attitude toward the NCTE from the first edition of 1919 to the final supplement of 1948. Almost as illuminating has been the process of observing, in the public press of the past five years, the contrapuntal change in the public image of the NCTE. So far as linguistic attitudes are concerned, it would seem that the emblematic caricature of the English teacher is no longer Miss Fidich, but Irma LaDouce.[2]

The only mention of the NCTE in the first edition (1919) was a modest one:

> Of late the National Council of Teachers of English has appointed a Committee on American Speech and sought to let some light into the matter, but as yet its labors are barely begun and the publications of its members get little beyond preliminaries (11).

This statement survived into the third edition (1923), to be joined by a note on what seemed a distressing state of affairs among the illuminati:

> *The Saturday Review*, which is certainly not deficient in English spirit, lately declared that Dr. [Brander] Matthews "minimizes the natural differences in language to an absurd degree," and sets down his curious notion that American novelists do not use Americanisms as "obviously a war hope, like hanging the Kaiser." But he is supported by various other Gelehrten of the Sunday supplement species, and to some degree, by the National Council of Teachers of English. This organization of pedagogues, following the drive managers of the war time, conducts an annual Better Speech Week. The documents it issues offer but one more proof of the depressing fact that schoolmasters, at least in America, learn nothing and forget nothing. Its whole campaign seems to be centered upon an effort to protect the grammar books against the living speech of the American people (viii-ix).

It was, fortunately, not till his mellower years, when he had seen the later work of the NCTE in investigating the nature of American English, that Mencken observed that in the 1916 presidential address, one of his favorite personal devils, Fred Newton Scott, observed that "almost everyone who touches upon American speech assumes that it is inferior to British speech" (Supplement II:24; Scott 1917).

But in whatever Valhalla he now adorns, HLM must be chuckling at the torrents of abuse spewed at the NCTE by the self-appointed guardians of the national linguistic chastity. To hear their moans, the NCTE, captured by a band of white-slavers known as structural linguists, has sold our language into a fate worse than death and celebrated this deed of infamy in a contract of some 450,000 clauses, uttered at Springfield, Massachusetts, under the imprint of the G. and C. Merriam Company, in 1961. In vain does the NCTE dissociate itself from any commercial publication; in vain do the editors of the Merriam *Third* protest that structural linguistics (at least in its current state) has little or nothing to do with the art of lexicography; in vain do serious students of the language explain that labels of *usage* rarely concern even minor details of *structure*, and almost never its basic statements. The American public has to have a goblin to exorcise; and if in the palmy days of McCarthy I, one could find a communist behind every third Federal desk, today those who feel that the national literacy has declined can see a structural linguist in every little red schoolhouse, brainwashing the once doughty advocates of good English into peddling a gospel of permissiveness. From literary mandarins and from glib grabbers of the fast buck comes the same anvil chorus in the *New Yorker*, the *Saturday Review*, *Horizon*, the *American Scholar*, the leaflets of the Council for Basic Education and assorted syndicated columns, no doubt working off long-repressed resentments against the petty tyrannies of English teachers, long dead or retired. I hope that the secretariat of the NCTE will have time to compile and publish a *Schimpflexicon* of these diatribes, following the precedent of Mencken, so that we can all laugh at the absurdities and rejoice in the enemies we have made -- the surest badge of our professional maturity.

It is not my business to defend Phil Gove[3] and his associates; after two years enough of the dust has settled so that honest criticism by competent reviewers can be written and the real flaws in the Merriam *Third* (largely ignored in the hue-and-cry) pointed out for the guidance of those beginning to assemble material for the Merriam *Fourth*. It is not my business to thump a tub for linguistics; this discipline has come of age and can defend itself, even against the will of some of its most gaudy spokesmen, whose prose is almost as flatulent as that of the typical iconizer of Henry James. I can only say that it is inconceivable that the Linguistic Society of America, an organization of fewer than three thousand members -- not all of them structuralists, most of them concerned with other languages than English, nearly all of them busy with a dozen full-time projects and a majority of them blissfully ignorant of the existence of the NCTE -- could capture and dominate thirty times that number. When I informed Mencken that one of my informants in Sylvania, Georgia, had designated a bull, euphemistically, as a *preacher cow*, he acclaimed this as "the grandest tribute to the clergy in nineteen centuries of Christianity." The notion that the structural linguists have taken over the NCTE is the grandest tribute to the reasonableness of linguistics and to the rationality of English teachers that has ever been uttered in the history of either of my two professions. What I shall do now is to document the change in Mencken's attitude toward the NCTE, observe what our organization has done since he ceased writing, and then see what is being done and what might be done if our way of speech survives.

By the time of the fourth edition (1936) Mencken noted that in the NCTE there was already a strong party receptive to linguistic realism and willing to recognize American standards on their own merits. He quoted with approval the statement of Tressler 1934:

> Although thousands of English teachers [i.e., in the United States] with the blood of crusaders and martyrs in their veins have for decades fought heroically against the corruption and utter ruin of English, their warfare has had by and large slight effect on the language. . . . It's hardly wise for the National Council at this late date to attempt to confine it in a straight-jacket (66).

In this edition Mencken referred several times to specific findings of Leonard 1932 (published under NCTE auspices, let us remember) on such forms as preterite *begun*, preterite *dove*, preterite *drunk* (he lacked the findings of Avis 1953, Atwood 1953a, Allen 1957, and V. McDavid 1956 on participial *drank*), participial *proven*, object-slot *who*, and *it's me*.

In Supplement One (1945) he marked Noah Webster as a forerunner of "the innovations of the National Council of Teachers of English." He quoted with gusto Pooley's presidential address of 1941, an appeal to linguistic common sense, and cited Tressler again in defense of the most awful and most persistent of American four-letter words:

the only way for the schoolma'am to make headway

against *ain't* would be for her to set her pupils to "chanting in unison for five minutes a day for a month, 'I *ain't* going, you *ain't* going, we *ain't* going, they *ain't* going; in fact, nobody *ain't* going'" (406).

Supplement Two (1948) makes further reference to the Leonard report, and mentions with approbation Fries's *American English Grammar* (1940), also done under NCTE sponsorship. This is still the model study of usage: even if it has not yet satisfied the visceral reactions to particular items by the intellectually unwashed if intellectually arrogant, it indicates clearly, to those accustomed to using their cerebra, the way any objective study must be conducted. Although Mencken did not specifically recognize the part the NCTE has had in the Linguistic Atlas from its beginning, we can also take his frequent citations of Atlas evidence as approbation of the interest of the Council in our way of speech.

In the fifteen years since Mencken ceased writing, that interest has persisted. The number of linguistic papers presented at the national meetings and published in our various journals has steadily increased; the attendance at sessions devoted to the study of linguistic problems has been gratifyingly large. The workshops offered at national meetings, after hours during the school year, and in various summer programs indicate a serious concern with language as the most characteristic human activity and the vehicle by which our culture is transmitted. Often against the wills of the belletristic brahmins who dominate university departments, our profession is becoming aware of the need for teaching English to native speakers of other languages, and of the terrifying potentialities of this challenge for our national moral distinction if we succeed and our national political extinction if we fail. We are even responding to the ever more pressing need of effective programs in English for the culturally deprived in our great cities -- a more massive social mudsill than the most sanguine dream of Calhoun and the other slavocrats ever envisaged, the social converse of Madison Avenue's grey-flanneled dream of two cars on every parking space and a ballooning Park Forest mortgage for every white-collar worker. We are salving our conscience by planning programs for teaching standard English to the adult American Indian, so that he can make his problems and aspirations more clearly known to the noble white savage. We are calling on linguistics to help us solve our problems in teaching reading, from the kindergarten to advanced literary criticism. And we have, as the board of directors of our interlocking professional interests, an active Commission on the English Language.

But is this activity, this official lip-service, enough? If we accept linguistics as a valid part of our professional training as teachers of English, are we engaging in studies that will give this part of the training a solid intellectual basis? Or are we content to write formulas and glib adaptations of what was done a generation ago?

I raise these questions knowing that I risk lending aid and comfort to the literary lamas who oppose linguistics because it demands exact knowledge and the dirtying of our hands in partnership with the social and behavioral sciences. But no dilution of linguistics, no intellectual crawfishing, is going to make that group any easier to convince. Contrariwise, it is conceivable that a larger body of objective information, widely disseminated, will indicate that linguistics can provide an answer to some of the problems in which they are most deeply interested.

The other risk is that I may be misrepresented as supporting the ill-tempered attacks on the curriculum centers and research projects that have been set up under Project English. But my criticism is of another order. The design of Project English is getting its own evaluation, in massive doses, from a wide spectrum of observers; and whatever its faults, it does encourage our profession to plan a more systematic analysis of our problems. What I urge is recognition of past and present hasty optimism, and attention to long-neglected research that will give us at worst more content to talk about and at best the critical evidence for solving our problems.

Mencken commented more than once on our national capacity for seeking simple solutions to complex problems:

[The American] will resist dictation out of the past, but he will follow a new messiah with almost Russian willingness, and into the wildest vagaries of economics, religion, morals and speech. A new fallacy in politics spreads faster in the United States than anywhere else on earth, and so does a new fashion in hats, or a new revelation of God, or a new means of killing time, or a new shibboleth, or metaphor, or piece of slang (1936:92).

During the past quarter century we have seen wide publicity given to general semantics, usage studies, friesian syntax, trageremic phonology and chomskemic transformations; the self-appointed fuglemen and haruspices of each revelation (sometimes merely turning a coat to suit the occasion) have proclaimed each in turn as the panacea for all the ills of God, man, and English teachers, and teachers in turn have parroted the jargon of each new cult as eagerly as their female contingent grabs the latest Christian Dior creation or Lanvin man-bait. Yet while the diligent examiners of factual data, "extremely empirical" as they may be, are dismissed to limbo by the catechumens of the new dispensations, not one percent of the latter (including many of their most persuasive circuit riders) are acquainted with the foundations of the doctrines they are espousing. How many who have hailed the *American English Grammar* have digested the first four chapters and the last, which explain a method and an end destined to survive, regardless of what time and society do with the details in the intervening sections? How many who seize upon the typographical convenience of tragerian /-y,-w,-h/ are acquainted with the century of intellectual explorations which argue for the analysis of English syllabics as sequences of vowel plus semivowel?[4] How many know that Fries liked *noun* in 1952 as much as the American electorate apparently liked another monosyllable, but adopted numerical designation of parts of speech to avoid the confusion inherent in the older names? How many realize the intimate relationship between the rules of the transformationalists and the stages in programming computers for machine translation of Russian? In short (and to be viewed with alarm) how many who talk eloquently about descriptive methodology are simply laying down a new prescriptivism?

Our Council, directly and through its commissions and workshops, must concern itself with American English at all levels: 1) the training of scholars who can do basic research; 2) the sponsoring of basic research; 3) the interpretation of basic research in pedagogically viable materials; 4) the training of classroom teachers who can use those materials. In recent years we have done a great deal in the last category, and something in the third; demand will sooner or later achieve the first, if we do not use up all our seed corn. The second, the basic research, is lagging, and is our greatest challenge. In we view our language in anthropological terms as a system of arbitrary vocal signals by means of which a social group cooperate and interact and transmit their culture, the opportunities are endless.

We have a large number of theories of grammar; but not one of them has been fully developed, nor have there been enough dialogues to test these against one another to see where the strengths and weaknesses of each lie. As James H. Sledd has frequently remarked, we probably need several theoretical approaches, to suit our needs on various occasions; but lacking the necessary dialogue, confrontations become contests in adolescent debating rather than searches for the truth.

We likewise need dozens of grammatical studies based on clearly defined corpora -- whether spoken or written matters little, so long as we know that the material is genuine and not tortured by some editorial flunky. Since Fries published his *Structure of English* (1952), there has been one tolerable grammatical study of the syntax of spoken American, Bowman 1966, and none of the syntax of any American author, living or dead. Without such studies, discussions of style will continue to degenerate into gobbledygook.

We need more data on the ways in which the varieties of American English differ from each other, regionally and socially. A generation after the Linguistic Atlas project was inaugurated, we still have incomplete evidence on the regional variation within our speech community. And even in this survey the speech of Negroes, American Indians, and other culturally divergent groups is drastically underrepresented. We have few studies in social dialects, whether rural or urban, and only a handful dealing with problems of bilingualism. And these studies skimp the critical areas of syntax, of pitch and stress and juncture, or paralanguage and kinesics.

In lexicography, we need continuing projects. The *Dictionary of American English* (Craigie and Hulbert 1936-44) ceased operations when it went to press; and though Mitford Mathews is struggling heroically to bring out a supplement to the *Dictionary of Americanisms* (1951), it is hardly likely that he will be able to continue to produce supplements beyond this century. The Wentworth-Flexner *Dictionary of American Slang* (1960) is stimulating enough to be banned by the California Superintendent of Education, but it is far from definitive; the Dictionary of Occupational Terms folded with the WPA; no comprehensive dictionary of criminal argots is in sight; the Dialect Dictionary is still a dream.[5] Not one of these projects should be allowed to languish, or to cease with publication; since they reflect the living part of the language, they need continuous revision. Of equal concern to us are dictionaries of such other varieties of English as Briticisms (gallantly pursued by Allen Walker Read), Canadian (Avis *et al.* 1967), Jamaican (Cassidy and LePage 1967), and Australian; and to provide us with a baseline for judging the development of American English, we need the resuscitation and speedy completion of the Dictionary of Early Modern English.[6]

Even these studies leave uninvestigated many fascinating historical problems. Almost any author, great or small, Puritan divine or frontier storekeeper, provides us with a wealth of unsifted evidence -- not on vocabulary alone,[7] but on morphology, syntax, and even on pronunciation. We can probably do some extrapolation of the history of American pronunciation from the existing treatises like Krapp's *English Language in America* (1925), from the Linguistic Atlas, and from the English and Scottish dialect surveys, when they see the light of day (Orton *et al.* 1962-71, Mather and Speitel 1975-); but we should provide what further evidence we can, from whatever sources.

Perhaps most in demand (if we observe the reviews of the Merriam *Third*) is an adequate and continually revised treatment of usage. So far, the only reasonably dependable materials are those from the Linguistic Atlas, which represent samplings not only of informants but of forms. We have to devise techniques of getting data that will not only give us wider range but escape the petty tyranny of the copy editor.[8] And here, as everywhere, we must have the means of altering our judgments as the facts change.

This jeremiad would almost give the impression that the whole of Mencken's infernal labor, as he put it, was in vain, for in 1919 he reminded American academe (much to the distress of its official spokesmen) that he too often had to run the lines himself, because scholars had neglected to provide the basic materials on Americanisms, historical phonology, dialects, grammar, and a host of other topics. Actually, as Arthur Kennedy says, we have come a long way since 1919.[9] We have a considerable body of specific information, and some creditable major works. But we need better works and more evidence. The cost of all the projects outlined in this paper would come to considerably less than that of a single rocket aborted by a misplaced comma in the control tape; an organization of 86,000 members -- and still growing -- can provide all the manpower, even without the certain cooperation of other groups. This basic research is a relatively small gesture by way of demonstrating that the NCTE, the only national organization solely concerned with the national tongue, believes that the study of American English is, in Mencken's terms, "interesting -- and more than interesting, important."

NOTES

[1] Mencken 1963. Page references to particular versions of *The American Language* are inserted in parentheses following specific quotations; the particular version appears in these parentheses where it would not be apparent from the context.

[2] Miss Fidich was a favorite cartoon character in the old *Life*; primly dressed, she invariably appeared in embarrassing situations, with the caption, "Why, if it isn't Miss Fidich, my old schoolteacher!" She is frequently cited by Henry

Lee Smith, Jr., and his disciples as the epitome of hidebound prescriptivism. She is likewise attacked, under an alias, in Lloyd 1954. She is treated sympathetically in Joos 1962.

[3] Philip B. Gove, editor-in-chief of *Webster's Third New International*, was probably the most widely known and most viciously attacked American lexicographer since Noah Webster. [Regrettably, the unenlightened reaction is still common; witness the success of the *American Heritage Dictionary* (1969) and of Morris and Morris 1975.]

[4] Trager himself freely admits that his analysis derives from the work of Henry Sweet and of Prince Nicholas Trubetzkoy.

[5] Since 1965 Frederic G. Cassidy of Wisconsin, with generous support from his institution and from funding agencies, has been realizing that dream through the *Dictionary of American Regional English* (1981-).

[6] Under Sir William Craigie's plan for a series of period dictionaries to supplement the *OED*, the Early Modern English Dictionary was launched by Fries at Michigan, circa 1930. Because of the chronic poverty of scholarly dictionaries and the diversion of Fries's energy to the teaching of English as a second language (a wartime necessity) it suspended activity, though its basic reading program is complete and some preliminary editing has been done.

[7] With computer printers it is now possible to produce concordances very rapidly, without the need to drop the little words (articles, auxiliaries, and the like) so important for syntactic studies.

[8] In Joos's personal archives is interesting correspondence from well-known writers (whose names I am not at liberty to mention) expressly objecting to the practices of copy editors in changing their well-considered grammatical constructions.

[9] He observed that the number of items on American English appearing between 1919 and 1945 had considerably exceeded what had previously appeared (Mencken, Pound, Malone and Kennedy 1945).

For nearly three thousand years many observers, both lay and professional, have recognized that no speech community lacks the subdivisions that we call *dialects*.[1] For a century, now, serious students of languages have been collecting systematic information on the dialects of the principal European languages; many of their findings have been published in a series of *linguistic atlases* and related monographs, of which the *Linguistic Atlas of New England* (Kurath *et al.* 1939-43) is one of the most notable examples.[2] Most of these investigations, heretofore, have looked toward the past, toward the historical and cultural forces that have produced these divisions. Now, however -- and particularly in the United States -- the serious students of dialects are thinking in terms of the future: they see, in an increasingly urbanized society, dialect differences as marking potentially troublesome lines of social division, and they seek to apply their knowledge so as to reconcile the diverging groups and to provide the wider understanding of each other that a mature political community must gain to endure. The experience of dialectologists is reminiscent, in a way, of that of nuclear physicists two decades ago; long considered impractical dreamers, they suddenly find that they have in their hands awful potentials for the survival or the destruction of their way of life.

That this new emphasis in dialectology should have arisen in the United States reflects both the peculiarities of the American dialectal situation and the consequent new methods that students of dialects have developed to cope with that situation. In most of the European countries there is one prestigious variety of the national tongue, fostered by schools, by mass media of communication, and by tradition: Standard High German, Parisian French, Moscow Russian, Castilian Spanish, Florentine Italian, or British Received Pronunciation (otherwise known as Public School English, since it is systematically imposed on the inmates of such reputable and expensive academies as Eton, Harrow, and Rugby). In these nations, in consequence of the cultural situation, scholars traditionally assume a polar opposition between *standard language* and dialect, and their investigations of dialect show traces of the Wordsworthian syndrome that somehow "humble and rustic life" reveals most purely and accurately the nature of the speech community. In both the German and French atlases, the investigators sought representatives of the 'local dialect' as something sharply different from educated French or German, which they assumed to be uniform, and contented themselves with a single representative specimen in each community surveyed. In both of these studies, moreover, the speech of larger communities was ignored in favor of that of country villages. It is true that there was some modification in the Italian atlas directed by Jaberg and Jud (1928-40), with larger communities included and more than one speaker interrogated in such centers. But the emphasis was largely the same, and it has continued in the recent *Survey of English Dialects* (Orton *et al.* 1962-71). It is really not unfair to state that the conventional European definition of a dialect is a form of the language that an educated man had rather be found dead than speaking.

For many reasons, adequately rehearsed elsewhere, the American situation is quite different from the European one, though it has respectable precedent, notably in classical Hellas before the preeminence of Athens. Even in colonial times there was no single focus for the culture of the colonies; Boston, New York, Philadelphia, Charleston, and the Virginia Fall Line ports (Alexandria-Georgetown, Fredericksburg-Falmouth, Richmond and Petersburg) served as centers of a local culture, each with its own standards of prestige and its characteristic forms of pronunciation, grammar, and vocabulary. With the coming of independence and the expansion westward, further local centers arose -- Cincinnati, Chicago, New Orleans, St. Louis, Atlanta, Nashville, and San Francisco -- each with its own criteria for distinguishing cultivated and uneducated speech. Despite intense rivalries, humorous or otherwise, the cultivated speech of any American community has long been recognized as being as good as that of any other. For this reason, when Hans Kurath organized the American linguistic atlas project in 1929, he could not simply set off standard speech from dialects and investigate only the latter; he had to assume that standard speech as well as folk speech had local varieties, and that between these two extremes there was an intermediate stage, *common* or *popular speech* -- hitherto not studied and often not even assumed in dialect investigations -- sometimes closer to the cultivated, sometimes closer to the folk. Thus, instead of the single type of speech represented by a single informant that most European investigators had studied, Kurath insisted on three basic types of informants, with the understanding that a full investigation of the social differences in any community would require a far finer screening than would be feasible for a survey aimed at the entire United States and Canada. Preliminary analyses have not only justified this procedure but reemphasized the need for many new and intensive studies of specific kinds of communities.[3]

In the postwar period, many specific communities have been investigated.[4] As these investigations have proceeded, accompanied by studies of popular reactions to linguistic variants, scholars have likewise seen the need for amplifying both the range and the intensity of investigations. Syntactic evidence is notably difficult to get by direct interviewing; yet syntax is that part of language with the greatest potential significance for the teacher of English. The role in language of such suprasegmental features as stress, pitch, transition, and terminals has been redefined; such features -- as well as vowels, consonants, grammatical forms, phrase structures and vocabulary -- probably have significant regional and social variants, but investigators have had difficulty obtaining minimal contrasts in natural situations. As promising, and as difficult to handle, are the variations in *paralanguage* (non-significant modulations of the stream of speech, such as drawl, clipping, nasality, rasp, abnormal loudness or softness, abnormally high or low pitch, and the like), and in *kinesics*, the study of gestures and other bodily movements. Although these features are not represented in writing (save in suggestions by the writer), they are important in face-to-face communication, but their regional and social variants are yet to be sorted out.

In the meantime, the social differences in modes of communication have been accentuated by the speeding up of some of the traditional forces in American society -- industrialization, urbanization (and specialized suburbanization) and the lengthening of schooling for larger proportions of the population. As new groups of workers have invaded the metropolitan areas and many city dwellers have fled to suburbia, a greater proportion of our urban school population has come from the less privileged groups in society. Not only are these groups so large and politically potent that they can no longer be ignored by the magnates of urban society, but conscience, court decisions, an eye on international repercussions, the increasing demand for skilled technicians in automated industry, and alarm at the growing relief rolls of the unemployable have led to concern with the problems of the underprivileged and consequent reassessment of English programs. Segregated schools and segregated housing patterns are on their way out; but physical juxtaposition does not create integration, and specific attention to the communication problems of the minorities must be a part of any curriculum that aims at providing equivalent educational and economic opportunities for all students. Although the most intense problems, for a variety of historical and cultural reasons, are those of the Negroes of rural Southern background who have congregated in the Black Belts of Northern cities, similar attention must be given the problems of rural whites migrating to cities in their own regions, to rural whites leaving their regions for metropolitan areas elsewhere (notably the rural Southerners -- hillbillies, Arkies and Okies),[5] the colonies of foreign-language speakers, the Puerto Ricans and other Latin Americans,[6] the new urban colonies of American Indians, and such old Asian groups as Chinese and Japanese. A little casual investigation is enough to show that the language problems of these groups bear no resemblance to those of the middle-class White Protestant Gentiles in whose interests our curricula are largely drawn.

Although linguists had noted some years ago that social dialects could create serious educational problems, reactions in the public school systems came tardily, sporadically, and -- as too often happens -- largely without drawing on the systematic evidence already available. It was argued, plausibly, that the classroom teachers had to do something right away; it was not recognized that hasty programs might even compound the problems. Above all, it was not understood that the old item-correcting exercises were particularly fruitless in the face of established systematic habits, and that the notion of changing a whole system of speech and eradicating the old habits would run up against the cruel facts that the intentions of the English teachers would seldom be reinforced by the practices of other teachers, let alone the environment of the playground and the home. As linguists were drawn into these programs, a new emphasis gradually developed: instead of a new dialect, a new mode of communication, being offered as a replacement of the habitual home patterns, it was suggested that it be presented as an alternative mode, expressly suited for the classroom, the department store, the clerical office, and other places where a nonstandard variety of speech (and writing) would put a person at a disadvantage; if he chose to use the old mode in the home, on the playground, at camp, or in other relaxed situations, it was to be recognized that such modes, too, have their proper uses. The aim, in other words, was to foster conscious *bidialectalism*, with a great deal of code switching permitted, just as in bilingual states like Switzerland or Luxembourg children learn at an early age to switch freely from one language to another, as the situation demands.

In view of the dialect situation in the United States, no single set of materials could work equally well in New York, in Chicago, in St. Louis, and in Memphis, but each major school system must think in terms of its local problems. Nowhere else, for instance, is there anything like the problem of the Puerto Ricans in New York City; for the Spanish-Americans of the Southwest are of their own region if not in its dominant cultural group. However, from discussions of interested research linguists, classroom teachers, and school administrators some common principles seem to be emerging:

1. First of all, a social dialect profile must be developed for the community. For many major cities the Linguistic Atlas archives provide at least a framework, and for some, a fairly detailed body of preliminary evidence. But in each community some supplementary work must be done, to sample more deeply the speech of the underprivileged minorities, to provide more detailed evidence on particular problems, and to offer a body of evidence from which problems as yet uninvestigated may be approached. Where most of the evidence is available in phonetic transcriptions, there must be tapes, especially of free connected discourse, from which scholars may derive evidence on syntax, suprasegmentals, and paralanguage. Ideally, there should be sound films for evaluating kinesics, but up to now even the scholars capable of transcribing and analyzing kinesic data are so few that the added expense of sound films might be hard to justify.

2. The next stage is that of establishing comparisons of the data, to see which features of speech seem to be identified with particular ethnic or social groups.

3. A third stage is to see how the racial and social occurrences of particular linguistic forms coincide with popular conceptions. Here one could envisage a series of instruments by which respondents are asked to evaluate particular utterances on a scale of pleasantness or unpleasantness, and to assign each utterance according to the racial and social group of the speaker. Here is an interesting testing ground for folk beliefs, *e.g.*, that one can 'always' identify a Negro voice on the telephone. The correlations between actual usage, popular identification, and emotional evaluations are not known, and until we have evidence we may be neglecting some of the most significant if subtle aspects of communication.

4. Finally, when the correlations have been established, it will be possible to set up a rational teaching program to emphasize those features of speech most strongly disapproved by the dominant culture and most correctly identified as characteristic of an underprivileged minority. Naturally, systematic features have a higher priority than incidental ones; a consistent lack of the third-singular present indicative inflection yielding such forms as *she have, he do, it make*, etc., is much more significant in the picture than the use of *I seen* instead of *I saw*.[7] We are here simply following the advice of Fries (1940): that any rational teaching program must be based upon an examination of the evidence, and constantly reappraised as new evidence is provided and new situations arise.

One can imagine a variety of situations in which variations on these procedures will be introduced. A few examples may provoke the appraisal of other kinds of social interaction for which special materials would be needed:

1. In a community like Greenville, South Carolina, the integration of the rural and cotton-mill schools into one system came approximately at the time of the Supreme Court decisions on racial segregation. The tradition of cultural isolation in the textile villages has reinforced habits of grammar and pronunciation that set the mill children off from both Negroes and urban whites.

2. In Southern and border communities like Cincinnati, St. Louis, Memphis, and Atlanta, the local whites and Negroes are likely to share the same phonological systems and the same social range of grammatical variations, though the scale is skewed by the traditional caste system of the South. In all of these communities, however, the white working class is likely to be under constant reinforcement from the Southern uplands, where a different set of phonetic values is found and a somewhat different set of stress and pitch patterns. But here phonology is in general less of a problem than grammar.

3. In Akron, basically an Inland Northern community deriving its pronunciation patterns from western New England by way of upstate New York, the rubber factories have drawn their basic labor principally from the impoverished farms and coal-mine villages of West Virginia, where strikingly different vowels are heard, as well as many nonstandard grammatical forms.

4. In Chicago, Inland Northern in origin but strongly influenced by the Irish and German immigration of the nineteenth century, the heavy migrations of Deep South Negroes have provided both a striking contrast of phonetic values and one of grammatical details. Hill Southerners have more recently appeared in Chicago to further complicate the dialect patterns, but in nothing like their numbers in Detroit and Cleveland.

5. In New York, striking differences between privileged and proletarian speech have long been recognized. These have been further complicated by heavy migration from Southern and Eastern Europe, by heavy Negro migrations, and most recently by the Puerto Ricans. It may be that the phonetic values of the old elite are no longer emulated by the emerging lower middle class, so that there is a consequent accentuation of class cleavage.[8]

6. Washington has become a predominantly Negro city, with white government workers largely withdrawn to the suburbs. There has been a Negro elite, but its children are so outnumbered by the recent and poorly educated migrants that its speech patterns may disappear within a generation.

In each community the initiative must come locally. But the local groups can be more effective if they exchange information, and if they can draw on a body of experienced consultants who have worked with a variety of dialects. The problem is too grave to be left to fragmentary approaches, and the NCTE and the Center for Applied Linguistics have already taken steps toward coordination of effort, with more to come.[9]

Nevertheless, identifying the overt stigmata of underprivileged dialects and providing an opportunity to learn a privileged local variety of speech is not going to solve the problems of these minorities by itself. In 1940 Fries pointed out that the most striking characteristic of his "Vulgar English" was its impoverishment, in grammatical structure as well as in vocabulary. The social dialectologist is needed, but so are practical rhetoricians who can draw on the resources of all objective grammarians to produce more effective materials for progressively enriching the syntactic experience of the students -- something no current materials can do. Along with the experience in the language must come a richer experience in the culture which our language transmits -- a more substantial body of content in all academic subjects. And the dominant culture must take positive action both to break down overt and covert barriers against minorities and to understand them as human beings with normal human feelings and aspirations.

And here, too, the dialectologist can make his contribution. He knows that whatever their prestige, all varieties of a language are equally normal in their origins, and are transmitted by normal social and cultural forces. A person who speaks a divergent dialect, one of low prestige, does so not because he is intellectually or morally inferior but because he grew up in an environment where such a form of speech was used. It is the business of American education to provide the speakers of such dialects with alternative modes by which they can secure educational and economic and cultural advantages commensurate with their abilities; it is also the business of American education to provide an understanding of dialectal as well as religious minorities. To provide this understanding the linguist must be willing to work to help educate the public at large, and before that the parents' and citizens' groups who support the schools, but first of all the teachers who first meet the members of the minorities in the lower grades, in a situation that can be either a bane or a blessing.

NOTES

[1] The research on which this paper is based was supported in part by Grant No. 2107 from the Cooperative Research Branch of the U.S. Office of Education to the University of Chicago. This aid is gratefully acknowledged, as well as the work of my colleagues related to the project: William M. Austin, A. L. Davis, and Melvin Hoffman of the Illinois Institute of Technology; Lee Pederson of the University of Minnesota; Virginia McDavid, William Card, and Thomas Creswell of Chicago Teachers College South; and Robert Hess, Sol Tax, John P. Willis, John Dawkins, Vernon Larsen, Carolyn Larsen, and Gerald Udell of the University of Chicago.

[2] A good short survey of dialectology is to be found in Chapter 19 of Bloomfield 1933; a more detailed survey is Pop 1950. A bibliography of important works in the field down to the New England *Atlas* is to be found in Kurath *et al.* 1939. Later bibliographical evidence is in Allen 1973-76. The most detailed evaluation of the New England *Atlas* is O'Cain 1979.

[3] Large-scale derivative studies are Kurath 1949, Atwood 1953a, Kurath and R. McDavid 1961, and V. McDavid 1956. Surveys of American dialects and dialect research are to be found in Chapter 9 of Francis 1958 and Chapter 7, Section 4 of Mencken 1963. The parallel between the American situation and the early Hellenic one is presented in Martinet 1962.

[4] Notable are Frank 1949, Hubbell 1950, Sawyer 1957, Howren 1958, DeCamp 1958-59, Pederson 1965a, Udell 1966, Labov 1966, Williamson 1968, O'Cain 1972, Hopkins 1975, Herndobler 1977, Miller 1978.

[5] Where 'reverse integration' occurs -- that is, where whites are admitted to institutions formerly reserved to Negroes -- a special variant of this situation sometimes occurs, since the Negroes may be better prepared and use more prestigious speech forms than the incoming whites, particularly if

the latter come from the depths of the Southern mountains.

[6] In the American Southwest, where English speakers have come to dominate areas long held by rural speakers of Spanish, the cultural contact may be especially traumatic for the latter.

[7] That there are important structural differences between white and Negro speech in some of our metropolitan centers does not mean that we must necessarily postulate either a generalized Afroamerican pidgin in the past or a generalized substandard Afroamerican *koiné* at present, though one may arise in the future if the fault lines in our society continue to widen. Both of these are interesting theoretical problems, and the former has been defended eloquently by Beryl Bailey of Columbia University and by William Stewart of the Center for Applied Linguistics. With our current knowledge it is safest to assume that in general the range of variants is the same in Negro and in white speech, though the statistical distribution of variants has been skewed by the American caste system. For a summary, see R. and V. McDavid 1951b [in this volume, pp. 43-51].

[8] The range of variation and the accepted underlying linguistic norms on the New York Lower East Side have been investigated intensively by Labov (1966). He has not included in his sampling, however, any representatives of the old line Upper-Upper New York class (see Uskup 1974 on elites).

[9] Problems in social dialects have been discussed at a variety of meetings and conferences, beginning with the Chicago CCCC of 1962. A special conference devoted to the subject was held at Bloomington, Indiana, August 3-5, 1964, under the chairmanship of A. L. Davis and the sponsorship of the NCTE and the U.S. Office of Education; see Shuy 1965.

Although linguistics is one of the most rapidly developing of the social sciences, its position among them is not generally recognized, either by the layman, by the other social scientists, or even by some of the linguists themselves.[1] The concealment of this relationship is due to several circumstances, not the least of which is the traditional modesty of science, which too often contents itself with recording and measuring, and leaves to others the derivation of broad conclusions from its findings.

But perhaps the most important block in the way of fully understanding the proper position of linguistics is that the teaching of language in our compartmentalized university curricula is almost exclusively done by departments of literature -- English, Romance, Germanic, Slavic, and the like. English grammar is taught as a tool to enable the student to write acceptable literary essays; French or German or Russian grammar, as a tool to prepare the student for reading *Les Miserables* or *Faust* or *Anna Karenina*. These ends are not unworthy in themselves, but the emphasis upon them in our academic system prevents students from realizing that the command of a language is necessary not only for facile reading and fluent conversation but for the understanding of the culture in which the language is spoken. And the historical connection and superficial resemblances between the Indo-European languages most commonly taught in our universities often leads students to lose sight of basic differences in the grammatical systems of these languages -- to say nothing of the existence in other societies of varying types of grammatical structure, as well as the types which we are accustomed to associate with the languages of Western Europe.

The great advances in the techniques of linguistics as a science have come since it became recognized as a social science by the anthropologists of the Boas-Sapir school. When the study of American Indian languages and cultures was systematically undertaken, it was soon discovered that just as the patterns of Indian culture could not be scientifically appraised by assuming the categories of Western European civilization as the norm from which everything else was a deviant type, so the sound types and grammatical categories of American Indian languages could not be appraised by assuming as universally normal the patterns of pronunciation and grammar

found in Indo-European languages. From this realization came the beginnings of modern linguistics as a descriptive science, with the grammar of each language worked out according to the observations of trained field workers without distortion by the patterns of the field worker's native language.[2] Along with this advance in linguistic techniques came the realization by cultural anthropologists that language is the medium through which the cultural relationships of a people are expressed, and that without the knowledge of linguistic principles by which an understanding of the native language may be attained, the anthropologist can attain only the most superficial description of a culture.

The way in which cultural patterns and attitudes are reflected in the language of the culture has been pointed out by many linguists -- perhaps most brilliantly in the articles on Hopi by Benjamin L. Whorf (1941a, 1941b). It has been experienced by the linguists who prepared the textbooks on Far Eastern languages for the War Department and by the students who learned those languages. But it can also be found in the English language as spoken in various parts of the United States. Leaving out the fact that the wide range of economic and military and political contacts between speakers of English and the speakers of other languages has resulted in the borrowing by English of a wide variety of foreign words for new things encountered in foreign cultures, the importance of language as a mirror of culture can be demonstrated by dialect differences in American English, as observed in field work for the Linguistic Atlas of the United States and Canada.[3]

As in any discussion in the social sciences, it is necessary to dispose of a few myths -- to show what simply is not so before we discuss what is so. It is untrue that climate itself has any influence on pronunciation. Southerners do not speak slowly because the climate makes them lazy. Midwesterners do not talk through their noses because they have long damp winters and lots of cloudy weather. New Englanders do not talk rapidly because the climate is bracing. As a matter of fact, many Southerners -- especially the Gullah Negroes -- talk very rapidly (as do Burmans and Bengali, in an even hotter climate), and many New Englanders drawl. Pronunciation and rapidity of speech in a given dialect area have nothing to do with the climate but are a reflection of other forces, such as the kind of speech used by those who settled in the area and the subsequent contacts of the inhabitants with speakers of other dialects.

In any dialect area of the United States the field worker will observe the growing tendency toward uniformity and standardization arising from increasing ease of transportation and communication, radio and movies, and the extension of public-school education. Under the impact of these influences the old folk words tend to disappear and are replaced by the commercial words for the same things. *Porch* replaces *piazza*, *veranda*, or *gallery*; *window-shades* has displaced *curtains* and *blinds* as a designation for the shades on rollers; and *dope* as a folk term for Coca-Cola (the common folk term in South Carolina and Tennessee as late as fifteen years ago) has given way to the commercially-sponsored *Coke*.

With the spread of public education has come a certain linguistic snobbery and a tendency to assert spelling pronunciations as the norm. That is, many common pronunciations, historically sound and normal in the pattern of a local dialect, are looked down upon because they are associated with illiteracy and the inability to spell, and new spelling pronunciations are fostered as 'correct' by teachers ignorant of the nature and development of the language but convinced (because they possess the skill) that the relatively recent and infrequent skill of writing is the norm to which the far older universal skill of speaking must be made to conform. Thus along the Atlantic Seaboard the younger generation is taught it must sound the /h/ in *wheelbarrow* and *whetstone*;[4] the rhyming of *hearth* and *earth*, of *soot* and *cut*, of *creek* and *sick*, of *ewe* and *dough*, of *bleat* and *gate*, of *roil* and *tile* is discountenanced; and *sumach* is not allowed to begin with the sound everybody uses at the beginning of *sugar*. The snob appeal of not using the same pronunciation as the uneducated or rustic people of one's own community reaches the limits of absurdity in the insistence of some teachers on the pronunciation of *either* and *neither* with the diphthong of *die*, or the attempt to force the 'broad a' in words of the *ask*, *chance* type on students in areas where those words normally have the vowel of *hat* or a diphthong based upon it (Trager 1940). Fortunately these attempts generally have little influence, and the normal pronunciation pattern of the community reasserts itself. Sometimes, also, a speaker masters a few shibboleths but reverts to type when off guard, as the man in the subway whom Bernard Bloch heard say, ". . . and she didn't drop *eyether* one of them, *eether*," or the Negro informant in Charleston, South Carolina, who told me about his "ahnt," but in the next sentence spoke of "Aunt Susie," using the vowel of *hat*.

The tendency to abandon local folk pronunciations and substitute pseudo-elegant or spelling pronunciations is most characteristic of the newly-risen middle class, who are anxious to differentiate themselves from the illiterate and less fortunate in their community. The uneducated person knows only the folk usage; the person sure of his social position in the community feels under no necessity to change the pronunciation normal to him and his family. Thus in Charleston, upper-class speakers, even of the generation now in college, still use the palatal consonants in *car* and *garden* (conventionally transcribed *kyar* and *gyarden*), still say *whetstone* and *wheelbarrow* without an /h/, and many upper-class speakers unblushingly rhyme *earth* and *hearth* or pronounce *palm*, *calm*, and *tomato* with the vowel of *hat*.

From the extent of local dialect areas one can form an accurate picture of the extent of early settlements. Even if we did not know that Up-Country and Low-Country in South Carolina were settled by people from different parts of the British Isles, we might suspect it from the way they talk. The characteristic Charleston diphthongs in *date* and *boat* are found along the Carolina coast from Savannah to Georgetown, and reach inland to Sumter and Aiken and the neighborhood of Columbia -- where the slow movement in from the coast ran up against the inundation of the Piedmont by the Scotch-Irish moving down from Pennsylvania. The term *bloody-noun* for a big bullfrog is another feature of coastal dialects, as is the term *mosquito-hawk* for *dragonfly*, where the Up-Countryman normally says *snake-doctor*. In the Providence area in New England, and in a small area in western Massachusetts settled from Providence, *eaceworm* is the local term for the *earthworm*. In Rhode Island one also hears the term *horning* for a burlesque serenade of newly-married couples -- a term that has been carried by settlers from Rhode Island to the Berkshires and southwestern Vermont, and thence to western New York. In the Middle West the settlers from the South carried with them the /z/ sound in *greasy*, and *corn-shuck* and *singletree*, where the settlers from the North brought *corn-husk* and *whiffletree*. The area settled predominantly from the South follows an irregular line a little south of parallel 40 in Ohio and Illinois, a little north of it in Indiana. Likewise local dialects preserve evidence of non-English-speaking settlers though the languages those settlers spoke may have disappeared. *Stoop* is a Dutch word for *porch* that has been taken into the English of the Hudson Valley and carried wherever settlers from that area have gone. In the South, *pinder* and *goober* for *peanut*, and *cooter* for *terrapin* (or sometimes for *turtle*), have spread far beyond the communities to which they were originally brought by West African Negroes. *Smearcase*, a Pennsylvania German word for *curd* or *cottage cheese*, has been found as far south as Greenville, South Carolina; in the English of the Middle Atlantic Seaboard will probably remain the pronunciation of *Long Island* as *long-guyland* long after the descendants of immigrants to that area have forgotten their ancestors from southeastern Europe.

Similarly, trade and communication are reflected in the perpetuation of some words and pronunciations. In the Boston wholesale trading area, *tonic* is the common name for what is elsewhere known as *pop*, *soda pop*, *soft drinks*, or *cold drinks*. Around New Haven *callathump*, originally a slang term at Yale, is the designation of a burlesque serenade. The substitution of an *ee* glide for *-r* in such words as *bird*, *work*, and the like -- a type of pronunciation commonly associated with Brooklyn and New Orleans -- is also an old upper-class pronunciation in Manhattan and in the cotton-planting area of the Deep South. It is found in the plantation area from north of Charleston to South Georgia, along the Gulf Coast to the mouth of the Mississippi, and up the Mississippi and its tributaries along the fertile bottom lands as far inland as Decatur, Alabama. Thus the fact that the Tennessee River Valley in North Alabama is, like the Black Belt from Montgomery southward, historically an area of cotton culture, is reflected in the persistence of plantation-type speech in both sections, with the Up-Country type in between, in the hill country around Birmingham.

Similarly, the isolation of a community is demonstrable by speech forms quite different from those of neighboring communities. In Eastern New England *-r* is generally not pronounced in such words as *hard* and *car*, except in Marblehead, Cape Ann, and Martha's Vineyard -- all relatively isolated communities. On Block Island, at the eastern end of Long Island Sound, *tippety-bounce* survives as the local name for *seesaw*, but nowhere else in New England. Among the mountain people of the Carolinas one still hears *fought* rhyming with *out*, or *search* rhyming with *starch*.

Although, as we have seen, climate has no effect on pronunciation, yet climate, topography, flora, and fauna are all reflected in the vocabulary of a community. In a flat country there will be none of the specific names for types of mountains -- such as *pinnacle*, *bald*, *dome*, *knob* -- that one finds in the Smokies. The Up-Countryman who has never seen a *salt marsh* would hardly be expected to have a name for it, nor would a Low-Countryman normally know the term *gully-washer* for a very heavy rain. In the Deep South one should not expect to find everyday words for kinds of snow, for kinds of sleds, or for coasting. The native of the Delta would not build *stone walls* around his cow lot, nor would he have any need for a *stone boat* to carry rocks out of his fields. The Charlestonian knows almost nothing of the *sugar maple*, the northern Vermonter at least as little about the *sycamore*. To the inlander who has never seen a *sea turtle*, *turtle* and *terrapin* are likely to be synonyms.

The interrelationships between urban and rural life are also seen in the vocabulary. Where the city dweller has no contact with the farm, he will not know many of the more obvious parts of the vocabulary of farm life. And, conscious of a social difference which he interprets as his own superiority, he is likely to have in his vocabulary terms of contempt for the farmer more biting than those where there is free exchange of rural and urban population. The city dweller everywhere is unlikely to know the taboos of farm life -- that the *bull*, *ram*, *stud*, and *boar* are rarely called by those names among farmers and almost never when women are present. And if he speaks of castrating animals, the urbanite will usually say *castrate* (or possibly *geld*), never *cut*, *change*, or *alter*. Many city dwellers have even said they thought a *boar* was an entirely different animal from a *hog*. And only a person who had had some experience with animals would certainly know what a *shoat* is, or would refrain from using *pig* and *hog* synonymously.

The traditional economy of a region is brought out in little suggestions in the vocabulary. The farmers of South Carolina consistently have polite terms for the *bull*, the *stud*, and the *boar* -- but a *ram* is never called anything else. The explanation is simple: sheep raising was never an important occupation on the Carolina farm. In some parts of the South *potatoes* still means *sweet potatoes* (as in the favorite rural dish of *possum and potatoes*), the others being designated always as *Irish potatoes* or *white potatoes*; elsewhere in the South *potatoes* out of context is ambiguous and has to be qualified; in the North, *potatoes* normally means *Irish potatoes*. Where corn meal is the basic flour, there will be many kinds of *corn bread* in the diet. The farmer who stacks his hay in the field and leaves his cattle out of doors during the winter will hardly know of a *hay mow* or a *cow barn*. A society with a rural orientation might divide the day into *morning* and *evening*, with the dividing point a one o'clock or two o'clock *dinner* followed by a rest in the heat of the day. This orientation may be carried over into the daily routine of the upper classes in a conservative place like Charleston, where a relative abundance of cheap servants perpetuates the custom of a heavy midday *dinner* and a relatively light *supper* after which the servants (or the mistress, if the servants customarily go home when they have finished cleaning up after *dinner* and preparing the food for *supper*) find it a simpler chore to clean up. In the relatively servantless big city, the white-collar worker will eat a midday *lunch* somewhere near his office and wash the dishes after *dinner* when he gets home; the steelworker may carry his *dinner pail* with him, and eat *supper* at home. In rural South Carolina a *lunch* is something one eats between regular meals.

One's language also reflects the change in the size and organization of the family. The rural farmhouse -- to say nothing of the larger city house -- customarily had both a *parlor* and a *living room*. The *parlor* was shut tight except for important events -- weddings, funerals, the minister's calls, and the Sunday-dinner visits of grandparents, aunts, and uncles. Now there is less awe of grandpa and grandma and the minister; so they are invited to sit down with the family in the *living room* and talk informally; and with smaller families, smaller homes, and higher rents, it would be foolish to set aside one room for infrequent 'state' entertainments.

Nor does the everyday vocabulary fail to reveal the political, social, and religious structure of the community. The New England farmer hardly knows the term *county seat*; the *county* hardly enters into his political thinking, for all the important business of local government is handled by the *township* or *town*, in its annual *town meeting*. In the South and West, however, the township -- if it exists at all -- is little more than a surveyor's unit, and all the important records are kept by the *county* at the *county seat* or *courthouse* -- in the South a carryover from the days when voting was limited to the large property owners, when a plantation covered as much area as a New England *town*, and the plantation owners would get together in a committee meeting at some central point, the *county seat*, and choose the county officials. That the county system and county consciousness prevails even in parts of the South where plantations and slavery never flourished means only that the prevailing patterns of local government were fixed by those persons who dominated the early settlements.

The less democratic social organization of the South is also revealed in the local fondness for military titles, earned or honorary, and in such caste-conscious terms as *poor white trash*, used by both Negroes and whites. Where emphasis is less on family background and more on individual merits, as traditionally in rural New England, a person may be spoken of with contempt -- but rarely as a member of a contemptible class. Nor, where rich and poor attend churches of the same denomination, should one expect to find terms like *jackleg preacher*, *yard ax*, or *table tapper*, which in the South are often applied to the untrained ministers who work at other occupations and devote their spare time to congregations of the less formally organized denominations to which most of the poorer and uneducated whites and Negroes belong. Similarly, a person who doesn't know the term *Mass* has probably had few contacts with Roman Catholics. And among the less sophisticated, the custom of *taking on* at funerals, of making a great outward show of grief as a form of respect for the deceased, is more likely to be known and approved than among the educated.

And one's language reveals the prejudices in one's background. In rural New England *the Civil War* is generally known as *the Rebellion*, except by those cynics who still refer to it as *Abe Lincoln's War* or *the Nigger War*. In the South the usual folk name among the older generation is *the Confederate War*; *the War Between the States* and *the War for Southern Independence*, both of which have been sponsored by the Daughters of the Confederacy and sectionally-minded schoolteachers, have not caught on very much; in fact, the younger generation normally speaks unblushingly of *the Civil War*. Naturally, where there is frequent contact and at least potential economic competition, there will be more nicknames, derogatory and otherwise, for religious, racial, or immigrant minorities than where such contacts are few. The Southerner would normally have more such names for the Negro, the New Yorker for the Italian or Jew. A curious reflection of such prejudices is the fact that around Beaufort, South Carolina (and to a lesser extent elsewhere in the South), *schoolma'am*, for *schoolteacher*, is a term of contempt, or at least of mild opprobrium. In the folk speech, especially in the phrase *Yankee schoolma'am*, it is commonly restricted to those teachers from the North who came down after the Civil War to educate the Negroes, and who still staff the Mather vocational school for Negro girls of Beaufort County.

Finally, there is fad language. The fad may be associated with a particular occupation, or it may be concerned only with the pronunciation of a single word. Of the first type are the elegant terms that have grown up with the attempts of the undertaking business to acquire social respectability -- the substitution of *casket* for *coffin*, *box*, or *pinto*, and of *cemetery*, *memorial park*, or *burial estate* for *graveyard* or *burying ground*; of the latter the fluctuating pronunciations of *iodine*, *quinine*, and *mayonnaise*, for each of which I have heard at least two different pronunciations from the same person at intervals of a few years. If something is fashionable, one must keep up with fashion, not merely to avoid the stigma of the rustic pronuncaitons already referred to.

These are only a few samples from the experience of one linguist in the field. For the social scientist interested in understanding social behavior, differences in local dialects have further significance. It is not improbable that the iteration of terms does much to fix the attitude of speakers toward social issues and social problems of which those terms are a manifestation. A social scientist must be careful in the terminology he uses in discussion with speakers of a dialect area different from his own. A classic example is the unfavorable Southern reception of Henry Wallace's "century of the common man," for to the average Southerner *common* is a term of contempt. The more one investigates American dialects, the more impressive is the evidence that linguistic phenomena are an essential part of the data that must be considered in the analysis of problems involving the social sciences.

NOTES

[1] [This article was suggested by Gordon W. Blackwell, a classmate of mine at Furman University 1929-31, later Professor of Sociology at the University of North Carolina and President of Furman. So far as I know, he was the first American sociologist to be aware of possible linguistic cues to social problems. All the recent educational applications of the study of social dialects derive from his interest; to say that my own career was likewise influenced by his interest would be an understatement.]

[2] Descriptive linguistics is much older. The Sanskrit grammarians, especially Panini (*circa* 400 BC), consistently approached language problems on the basis of what the language actually said. But their work was not known in Western Europe and had no influence upon the development of linguistic thinking until the nineteenth century. Even today the language thinking of most teachers is in the normative tradition, deriving from the unrealistic metaphysics of the Greek grammarians and followed with more or less ludicrous results by Roman, medieval, Renaissance, and modern arbiters of usage. Their attitude reaches its ultimate absurdity in the publication of lists of 'words everybody mispronounces' and 'grammatical mistakes everybody makes.'

[3] Field work in the South Atlantic States was made possible for the writer, first, by a fellowship from the Julius Rosenwald Fund in 1941, and later by an honorary fellowship from Duke University and a grant by the American Council of Learned Societies. Observations on the distribution of linguistic forms in New England are based on the records of the *Linguistic Atlas of New England* (Kurath *et al.* 1939-43), in the Middle West on the preliminary survey of the Great Lakes and Ohio Valley regions conducted by A. H. Marckwardt, otherwise on the writer's own experiences in the field.

[4] Where the fashion is to ape British Received Standard Pronunciation, teachers do try to force their students to drop the /h/ in *wheelbarrow* and the like. The snob appeal is of course the same.

The relationship between speech forms and
the cultural configurations and prestige
values within a civilization has been indicated by linguistic scientists, but so
far most of the study of that relationship
has been directed toward languages outside
the Indo-European family (Whorf 1941b).[1]
It is, however, just as proper to utilize
the data of linguistics, as derived from a
study of dialects of our own language, in
analyzing some of the problems within our
own culture (R. McDavid 1946; in this
volume, pp. 131-35).

As an example of a situation in which
linguistic data and other cultural data
must be correlated, one may examine the
distribution in South Carolina and the adjacent parts of Georgia of postvocalic
/-r/ as constriction in such words as
thirty, *Thursday*, *worm*, *barn*, *beard*,
father (in popular terminology, speakers
lacking constriction in words of these
types are said not to pronounce their
/-r/).[2] A social analysis proved necessary for this particular feature, because
the data proved too complicated to be explained by a merely geographical statement
or a statement of settlement history. In
this particular problem, moreover, the social analysis seems more significant than
it might seem in others, because the presence or absence of postvocalic /-r/ as
constriction becomes an overt prestige
symbol only on a very high level of sophistication. With little experience a
speaker learns that the folk forms
[laɪtəd], *lightwood*, and [faəboəd], *fireboard*, do not have the prestige of the
corresponding standard forms *kindling* and
mantelpiece (the transcriptions are for
the type of dialect in which these lexical
items generally occur) -- that the folk
forms are generally recognized as 'coun-
trified' or 'common.' Folk verb forms,
like *I seen what he done when he run into
your car*, are under a strong social taboo,
and as a rule may be used by highly cultured speakers only for deliberate, humorous effects. Even some pronunciations,
such as [aɪðə(r], [naɪðə(r], instead of
[iːðə(r], [niːðə(r], *either*, *neither*, or
the so-called 'broad a' pronunciation
[haf past] instead of the more common
[hæf pæst], *half past*, are fairly generally known as symbols of real or fancied
elegance. But there is little or no direct concern with a person's postvocalic
/-r/ except as a part of the occupational
training for such highly sophisticated
crafts as elocution, pedagogy, concert

singing, acting, radio announcing, and
some branches of the ministry. Since the
traditions of these professions generally
require that their practitioners tinker
with their speech in other ways, persons
deliberately concerned about the presence
or absence of constriction in their postvocalic /-r/ would not be used as representatives of natural local usage on any
cultural level. In short, constriction --
or lack of it -- in the speech of Atlas
informants may be considered due to the
normal operation of social forces and not
to any conscious notions of elegance.

Map 1 shows the geographical details essential to an understanding of the distribution of postvocalic /-r/ in South Carolina. The tidewater area, extending inland about thirty miles through a network
of islands and peninsulas and tidal
creeks, except along the beach front of
Horry County, was the area in which the
first cultural centers were planted:
Georgetown, Charleston, Beaufort, and Savannah. About thirty miles inland is a
belt of pine barrens, which have never
been suitable for large-scale plantation
agriculture, and where small-scale farming
is the prevailing pattern.[3] Above the
pine barrens the rich coastal plain
spreads inland for about seventy miles, to
the infertile sand hills along and just
below the Fall Line. Above the Fall
Line -- the old head of navigation on the
rivers, and the shore line in an earlier
geological period -- the rolling Piedmont
begins, gradually becoming more broken until in the northwestern corner of the
state it merges into a fringe of the Blue
Ridge Mountains. From the coast to the
Fall Line is generally known as the Low-
Country; above the Fall Line, as the Up-
Country.

The conventional statement about the
Southern postvocalic /-r/ is that it does
not occur as constriction in words of the
type here under examination. The fact
that in every Southern state one may find
locally-rooted native speakers with constriction in at least some of these words
has been either overlooked or deliberately
ignored.[4] The usual statement is still
that Southern and New England speech differs from so-called 'General American' in
that the two former types do not have constriction of postvocalic /-r/ (Krapp
1925:1.38, Baugh 1935:444-49, Ekwall
1946:13).

However, records made for the Linguistic
Atlas of the South Atlantic States showed

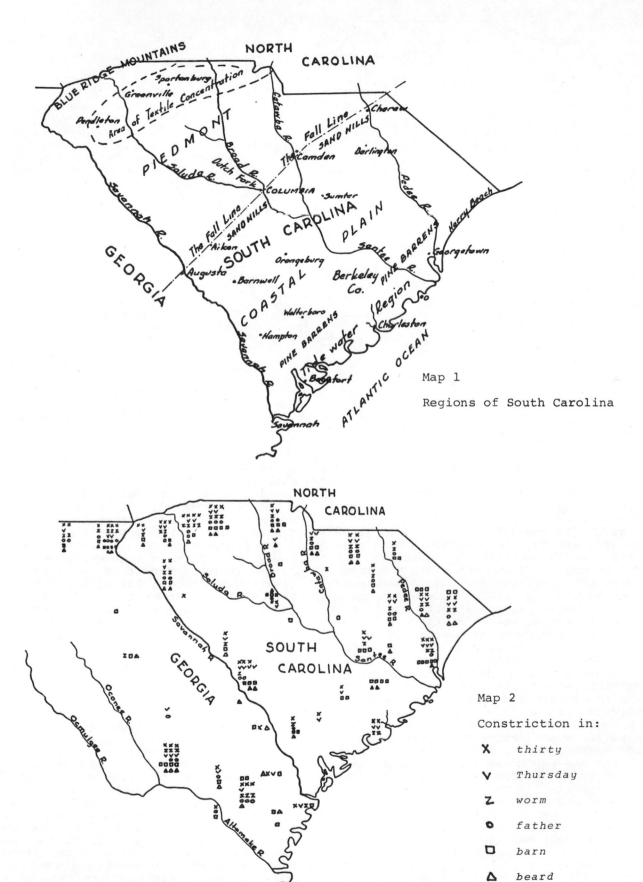

Map 1

Regions of South Carolina

Map 2

Constriction in:

𝘟 thirty

𝘝 Thursday

𝘡 worm

∘ father

⬠ barn

△ beard

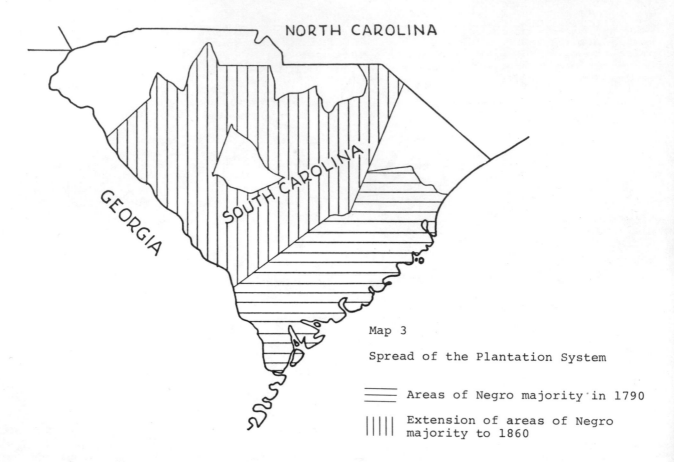

NORTH CAROLINA

GEORGIA

SOUTH CAROLINA

Map 3

Spread of the Plantation System

≡≡≡ Areas of Negro majority in 1790

||||| Extension of areas of Negro majority to 1860

very early that postvocalic /-r/ does occur with constriction in many Southern communities, including several of those first investigated in South Carolina by Guy S. Lowman, Jr. These data led Hans Kurath, director of the Atlas, to set off tentatively two areas in South Carolina within which constriction occurred: the middle and upper Piedmont, and the area north of the Santee River.[5] A simple explanation of the evidence seemed possible at that time: the area north of the Santee was settled predominantly by Scotch-Irish planted from the coast, was adjacent to the Highlander settlements in the Cape Fear Valley of North Carolina, and could be looked upon generally as a cultural continuation of the Cape Fear settlements. The northwestern corner of the state was settled originally by the main Scotch-Irish migration southward from Pennsylvania, and would naturally represent a southward prong of the Midland area that Kurath has set up as stemming from the Pennsylvania settlements.[6] The explanation was still on the basis of geography and the area of original settlement.

But if a geographical interpretation of the postvocalic /-r/ was the proper one, it might have been expected that further field work would substantiate and simplify the picture. Instead, with further research the picture has become more complicated, as Map 2 indicates. Many speak-

ers -- even whole communities -- are found with constriction of postvocalic /-r/ in the area where the 1941 evidence did not indicate constriction to exist, and many speakers lack constriction in areas where constriction seemed indicated as normal. A purely geographical interpretation of the distribution is likely to be meaningless: it is difficult to see how, in a geographical sense, Barnwell and Orangeburg counties can be less Midland than Hampton and Berkeley, where constriction occurs. It is therefore necessary to make a statement of other social phenomena in order to explain the distribution of postvocalic /-r/ in South Carolina.

In the communities where postvocalic /-r/ occurs with constriction, it has been noticed that three variables operate toward decreasing the amount: normally, the more education an informant has, the less constriction; and within the same cultural level, younger informants generally have less constriction than older ones, and urban informants less than rural.

Moreover, the communities in which constriction occurs have in common a proportionately large white population -- generally a majority, even in 1860, when the proportion of Negroes in South Carolina was largest (see Map 3).[7] These communities are counties or parts of counties where farming, often scratch-farming, was the rule, and where the cultural orientation was toward the county seat and the local religious congregation. They comprise the pine barrens, the hinterland of the Horry beach, the sand hills, and the mountain margin -- lands where the plantation system could not be even temporarily profitable -- and the Dutch Fork between the Saluda and Broad rivers, where a cohesive, religious-centered Lutheran community with a tradition of self-sufficient farming was able to resist the lure of alleged money crops. Constriction in the speech of textile workers in Piedmont metropolitan areas is only superficially an exception to the observation that constriction is a mark of cultural isolation: the textile workers were originally recruited from the culturally peripheral areas, and the paternalistic company village that characterizes the Southern textile industry has created a pattern of cultural segregation as real and almost as strong as that setting off whites from Negroes.[8]

When one studies both the early settlement history and the current distribution of speech forms other than the postvocalic /-r/, it is apparent that the original area without constriction was only a small part of the state.[9] The area settled by Southern British speakers hardly reached above tidewater; further inland, whether the settlers came in the great migration from Pennsylvania or first landed at Charleston or other ports, the early population was made up almost entirely of Scotch-Irish and Germans, who might be expected to retain their postvocalic constriction of /-r/, just as they have retained much of their characteristic vocabulary.[10] Only in the Beaufort, Charleston, and Georgetown districts -- and only in the tidewater riceland sections of those districts -- were the southern British settlers, in whose dialect constriction would have first been lost, the dominant group in 1790; and in those same sections plantation agriculture and large slave majorities prevailed (see Map 3). Clearly, the spread of the loss of constriction accompanied the spread of the plantation system, both representing the imposition on the majority of the patterns, if not the will, of a minority.

The spread inland of the minority speech pattern, so far as constriction is concerned, naturally involved several types of social readjustment. The following social forces are known to have operated; given the established prestige of the original group that lacked constriction, the tidewater plantation caste,[11] each of these forces would have tended to reinforce the prestige of the constrictionless type of speech as a model:

1. Following the establishment of American independence, the reopening of the slave trade,[12] and the invention of the cotton gin, plantation agriculture spread inland from the coast, displacing many of the small farmers, who in turn moved west into the frontier communities (Petty 1943: 70-81).

2. Some successful Up-Country farmers became planters, and intermarried with the older plantation caste (Cash 1941:14-17).

3. As inland towns arose, they tended to become cultural outposts of Charleston. The original Fall Line trading posts -- Augusta, Columbia, Camden, and Cheraw -- were financed by Charleston capital for the Indian trade (Meriwether 1940:69-71). As the trading posts grew into towns, the local business and financial leaders had an increasing number of contacts with the group in Charleston that has always controlled the financial life of the state. Sometimes, Charlestonians even migrated to the Up-Country to establish offshoots of their family banks or business houses. The cotton of the Up-Country was marketed through Charleston factors until well into the twentieth century.[13]

Not only financial ties attached the Up-Country townspeople to Charleston. Both health and fashion contrived to make the Low-Country planters migrate inland during the malaria season to such health resorts as Aiken, Pendleton, Greenville, and Spartanburg (Brewster 1942). Some of the Low-Country visitors settled permanently, to become the local elite. Even the Civil War did not disturb this trend; in fact, the siege of Charleston caused many Charlestonians to become refugees in the Up-Country, and some did not return with the cessation of hostilities. For the Charlestonian not completely above the salt in his home town, the Up-Country provided a greater sense of social prestige than he could have known between the Ashley and the Cooper. Even Irish Catholics transplanted to the Up-Country, though remaining exotic in the Protestant environment, found that a Charleston origin and a trace of a Charleston accent helped them to become accepted as part of the socially preferred group.[14]

Charleston long continued to dominate the cultural and professional life of South Carolina. The state medical college is still located in Charleston, and apprenticeship in the office of a Charleston lawyer has long been considered the best type of legal training, even if, as with James F. Byrnes, the career is made in the Up-Country. The moving of the state capital to Columbia, and the setting up of the state university there, did not change the picture materially; from the beginning, the dominant group in Columbia society was the plantation caste, the rulers of South Carolina.

The many Protestant colleges in the Up-Country did little to counteract the trend -- partly because after 1830 (and almost all the Up-Country colleges were established after that date) there was but one approved social system and no room for competitors; partly because a rising educational institution tended to conform by way of showing its cultural legitimacy; partly because many of the founders and early faculty members of these inland institutions were themselves from tidewater areas, or at least educated in institutions located in these areas.[15]

None of these influences operated alone; they make up a complex, rooted in the desire of every ambitious South Carolinian to be accepted by, and, if possible, taken into, the ruling caste. Politically, this same desire was manifested in the ardor with which many Up-Country leaders adopted and championed the cause of Charleston and the interests of the large slave holders.[16] In any event, the prestige of the old plantation caste has meant the spread inland of many of their speech ways, including the lack of constriction of postvocalic /-r/, and the trend toward the loss of constriction continues. It even serves to reinforce Southern xenophobia, for among the phonetically sophisticated the lack of constriction has become a point of caste and local pride.[17]

It is true, of course, that prestige values can change. It should not be surprising, therefore, that indications already exist that constriction of postvocalic /-r/ may some day become respectable in South Carolina. The presence in local military posts of many Northern and Western servicemen, with strong constriction of their /-r/, as well as with a different and more sophisticated line of conversation, has led many Southern girls to the conclusion that a person with constriction can be acceptable as a date for the daughter of generations of plantation owners, or even possibly as a husband. Even in the heart of the Low-Country, a number of girls in their late teens or early twenties are still speaking with a newly acquired constriction of postvocalic /-r/,

long after the training camps have closed.[18] Perhaps the trend is about to be reversed.

In the meantime, since practical applications of scientific information are always sought, there are some ways in which this analysis of the social distribution of postvocalic /-r/ in South Carolina might be put to use by other social scientists. Just as in South Carolina, so probably in most of the other states of the Deep South, constriction is a linguistically peripheral feature found in culturally peripheral communities, generally on poor land among people who were driven onto that land -- or, as with the textile workers, into their occupation -- by the pressure of competition from the plantation system and Negro labor. It is among those people, whose cultural situation was originally brought about by Negro competition, that the fear of continuing Negro competition is keenest, and is most easily exploited by demagogues. It is from those people that the Ku Klux Klan, the Bleases and Talmadges and Bilbos, and the lynching mobs have tended to draw their strength.[19] Consequently, a Southern official whose job dealt with interracial problems might screen with a little extra care those native applicants for, say, police jobs whose speech showed strong constriction. And those interested in changing the racial attitudes of the whites might well concentrate their efforts on those areas where constriction has survived in greatest strength. Perhaps this suggestion is extreme, but it shows the possibilities.[20] For language is primarily a vehicle of social intercommunication, and linguistic phenomena must always be examined for their correlation with other cultural phenomena -- as for the correlation between the spread of the unconstricted postvocalic /-r/ in South Carolina and the rise of the plantation system.[21]

NOTES

[1] This paper was presented at the symposium on linguistics and culture sponsored by Section H (Anthropology) of the AAAS at Chicago, December 27, 1947.

The data for this study have been derived from the field records collected for the Linguistic Atlas of the South Atlantic States prior to 1941 by Guy S. Lowman, Jr., and since that time by R. McDavid. The latter field work was made possible first by a fellowship in 1941 from the Julius Rosenwald Fund and later by an honorary fellowship from Duke University and grants from the American Council of Learned Societies.

[2] The term 'constriction' includes turning up of the tongue tip (retroflexion, perhaps the rarest type of constriction in English), retraction of

the tongue, spreading of the tongue, and other tongue movements providing friction during the articulation of a vowel. Traditionally, 'retroflexion' has been used where this paper uses 'constriction.'

[3] The difference between a farm and a plantation is not merely one of size, but rather of the attitude of the owner toward participation in the work of farming. Even on the largest farms, in the Up-Country and north of the Santee, the farmer and his family normally did a great deal of the manual labor; on the plantations, the work of the planters was almost exclusively managerial.

[4] It is a tradition among some schools of scientific investigation not to insist on facts and

[140]

examples, and to ignore them when they conflict with previously formulated theories.

[5] Chart accompanying talk before the annual meeting of the Linguistic Society of America, New York, 1944.

[6] The concept of the Midland group of dialects, spreading westward and southward from the Philadelphia area, is perhaps the most fruitful contribution Kurath has made to the study of American dialects. The division into Northern, Midland, and Southern types is generally a better explanation of the historical facts and the present distribution of vocabulary items than the older grouping of Eastern, Southern, and 'General American,' and is at least as good a framework for an analysis on the basis of phonetic types.

[7] Since the available statistics are for counties, the large slaveholdings on the Sea Islands and the river ricelands obscure the presence of the many small farmers in the pinelands of the Beaufort and Charleston districts.

[8] The mill villages, regardless of size -- some are over ten thousand in population -- are usually unincorporated, with all municipal functions handled by the mill management. The company store, with bills deducted from millworkers' wages, has existed on a scale unparalleled in any other industry, except possibly coal mining. Separate schools are provided for mill children -- at Greenville, even a separate high school -- and each mill village has its separate Protestant churches (Pope 1941).

In South Carolina, the paternalistic textile village dates from the founding of the Graniteville mill, in Aiken County, by William Gregg, in 1845. Gregg is also traditionally responsible for the pattern of employing only white labor in production operations in Southern textile mills. He advocated the building up of a textile industry as a philanthropic enterprise which would provide the poor whites with a means of livelihood secure from Negro (slave) competition.

[9] The loss of initial /h-/ in *wheelbarrow*, *whetstone*, *whip* -- a feature of Southern British Received Pronunciation today -- hardly occurs outside the immediate vicinity of the coastal centers, and is by no means universal even there. Such Midland vocabulary items as *a little piece* ('a short distance'), *jacket* ('vest'), *coal oil* or *lamp oil* ('kerosene'), and *quarter till* (the hour) may still be found in many Low-Country communities.

Original settlement from southern Britain does not necessarily imply a tendency toward loss of constriction. Field records made in England by Lowman show constriction in many southern British folk dialects today (Viereck 1975). It does not, of course, weaken the argument for the influence of prestige factors to assert that the loss of constriction occurred principally in American communities which maintained close cultural contacts with the city of London; in fact, this assertion only reemphasizes that influence.

[10] Expansion inland from the coast in the eighteenth century was not the work of groups within the older communities as it was in New England. Instead, frontier townships were laid out, and groups of immigrants settled directly upon them. As a rule, the townships north of the Santee were settled originally by Scotch-Irish, those south of the Santee by Germans and German-Swiss (Meriwether 1940).

[11] Although by the time of the American Revolution the bulk of the white population of South Carolina was to be found in the frontier townships and in the new settlements made by the immigrants from Pennsylvania, political power was held by the plantation group around Charleston. All the delegates to the Continental Congress and to the Constitutional Convention came from this group.

The tidewater planters and merchants kept up their ties with England after the American Revolution, and a fair number of their sons were educated in England. Even today the socially elite in Charleston and Savannah tend toward uncritical admiration of things English, at least of the practices of the English upper classes.

[12] Under the royal government several efforts were made to restrict the importation of slaves, generally by imposing high import duties, but profits from rice and indigo plantations kept these efforts from being very effective (Petty 1943:50-57).

[13] Interest rates were usually very high. For Up-Country resentment toward Charleston, especially toward the symbols of Charleston influence, the merchant and the banker, see Robertson 1942:81-84, 91-107.

To my paternal grandfather, an Up-Country farmer, Charleston was a symbol of sharp business practices, if not outright dishonesty.

[14] Refugees from Charleston contributed particularly to the growth of Greenville. The Roman Catholic group in Greenville dates from the Civil War. Paradoxically, although the Roman Catholic Church has repeatedly served as a whipping boy for Up-Country Ku Klux Klan organizers, demagogues, and Protestant ministers, Roman Catholics as individuals have achieved far more complete cultural integration in Greenville than in the outwardly more tolerant culture of Charleston.

Even today, Charlestonians not fully accepted in their native city have found their origin a password to social acceptance in the Up-Country. Typical of the colonial attitude of the older families in Up-Country towns is their reverence for the exclusive balls given by the St. Cecilia Society of Charleston. In Greenville, for instance, there is much more talk of the possibilities of being invited than one would hear in Charleston from people of the same social standing.

[15] This was true even among the Baptists, the most loosely organized of the major Protestant sects (McGlothlin 1926).

[16] John C. Calhoun, the most eloquent orator for slavery and nullification and Southern separatism, was born on the South Carolina frontier, and in

the early stages of his political career was a spokesman for the frontier philosophy represented nationally by Andrew Jackson. After marrying into a Charleston family, he became the spokesman for the plantation interests (Robertson 1942:101-02).

[17] A former student of mine, the son of a Darlington County informant, explained, "The reason we Southerners resent the way the Yankees roll their /-r/ is that it reminds us of the way the crackers talk." In South Carolina the term *crackers* is used (though less than formerly) by the townspeople, the plantation caste, and the plantation-reared Negroes as a derogatory designation for the poor whites -- nonslaveholders, or descendants of nonslaveholders -- in areas where large slaveholdings once prevailed.

[18] This phenomenon has been observed particularly in such constrictionless Low-Country towns as Walterboro and Sumter. The radio and the movies will probably reinforce this new trend. Similar effects may be expected from the recent and continuing migrations of Negroes northward and of Up-Country whites to coastal towns.

An apparent tendency to replace the Low-Country ingliding diphthongs in *date*, *boat* [de·ᵊt, bo·ᵊt] with the Up-Country upgliding type [de·ɪt, bo·ʊt] also suggests a reversal of the trend in prestige values. One must remember, however, that in linguistic geography each phonological or lexical item must be judged on its own merits, and nothing could be more dangerous than to predict the fate of postvocalic /-r/ in South Carolina from the fate of the Low-Country diphthongs in *date* and *boat*.

[19] South Carolina political observers have noticed that Horry County, the northeasternmost coastal county, has generally voted the same way as the upper Piedmont in state elections, and always gave a heavy Blease majority. Linguistic evidence -- not only the preservation of constriction, but of many lexical items as well -- indicates the cultural tie between the two sections.

[20] It is not necessarily true that only persons in the Deep South lacking postvocalic constriction of /-r/ would be likely not to mistreat Negroes. Many of the plantation caste would resent the notion of equality, much as they would resist anti-Negro mob violence by poor whites. But since the revision of racial attitudes is largely a matter of education, it can hardly be without significance that in South Carolina the postvocalic /-r/ loses constriction among the group with the greater amount of education. It is also worthy of note that almost every lynching in South Carolina in the last twenty-five years occurred in counties where the field work for the South Atlantic Atlas has disclosed strong constriction of postvocalic /-r/.

[21] [As pointed out in other essays in this volume, the status of /-r/ in the South is changing. Levine and Crockett 1967 shows that it is in wide use among the younger generation in Hillsboro, North Carolina, and O'Cain 1972 finds it appearing in greater strength in Charleston. One doubts, however, that represents a triumph of 'national norms' over regional ones, much less the spread of a so-called 'network English.' The latter solution would suggest a greater Southern admiration and emulation than can yet be demonstrated for Richard Nixon, the outstanding public example of this type of speech. A far simpler explanation is that increasing affluence and a wider spread of educational opportunities are bringing into the group of cultivated speakers a larger proportion of those who naturally had the postvocalic constriction; and with economic and cultural security, they feel less need to emulate any other model.]

R. McDavid 1946 (in this volume, pp. 131-35) suggested that the study of American dialects, as in the Linguistic Atlas of the United States and Canada, might be profitably coordinated with investigations in the other social sciences. The purpose of this paper is to suggest one direction in which such coordinated effort might be directed: toward the practical end of diagnosing potential inter-group tensions in American communities before they reach a critical stage.[1]

The premises upon which this suggestion is based are derived from the nature of language and of language learning:

1. Language is a social phenomenon. The common definition of a language, as accepted by linguistic scientists and other anthropologists, is a set of arbitrary acoustic symbols by means of which a social group cooperate and interact and transmit their culture (Sturtevant 1947:1-3, Herskovits 1948:440). It is inconceivable that a language could exist in the absence of a social group; it is as inconceivable that any social group could exist without a language through which the division of tasks can be arranged and the greater part of the learning conducted. The more complex the social group, the greater its dependence on language.

2. The type of language or dialect which one speaks is determined not by physical type or by climate but by one's social contacts. Any person without a physical deformity is potentially able to make any of the speech sounds in any language; which sounds he does make depends on the language spoken by those persons with whom he habitually associates. Although many Texans drawl, many coastal South Carolinians and Georgians -- both white and Negro -- speak very rapidly, as do the Burmans and Bengali; conversely, a drawl is not an uncommon feature of New England speech; thus any explanation of Southern drawl as due to laziness induced by the hot climate is purely fanciful.[2] An American child growing up in an Indo-Chinese or Liberian village will speak Annamese or Kpelle as a native, and have no difficulty with the tones or consonants that his elders find so formidable; the sons of Chinese storekeepers in Augusta, Georgia, speak the English of the community without a trace of a Chinese pronunciation; Canadian-born Nisei speak like other Canadians in their community.

3. The language patterns of the individual speaker are determined only slightly by the speech of his parents, but principally by his social contacts in his community outside the home. Where the speech patterns of the parent and those of the community differ, it is to be expected that details of the parent's speech will be most clearly reflected in the speech of very young children, gradually disappear as the children grow older, and be essentially lost by the time the children reach maturity. This process is to be expected whether the parents speak a foreign language or a dialect (in the United States, a dialect of English) different from the dialect spoken in the community.

4. The normal tendency toward increasing cultural uniformity in a Western industrial civilization is shown, linguistically, in an increasing uniformity of speech and the disappearance of the most divergent local dialects. Sharply local features of speech, or those derived from a foreign-language background -- whether such features are found in grammar, pronunciation, or vocabulary -- tend to be replaced by features of the regional standard. Even features of speech indicative of educational differences -- as, in the South, the difference between the cultivated past tense *I saw*, the common *I seen*, and the folk *I seed*[3] -- tend to disappear as the average educational level is raised.

5. Therefore, the appearance of new dialect differences between speakers of the same age and educational background in a community suggests the development of inter-group tensions. In particular, the occurrence of more such differences in the speech of the younger generation than in the speech of their elders may be taken as a warning that something is developing contrary to the normal (and by the values of our society, the desirable) social trend.

One may assay this hypothesis by taking a limited number of well-known situations in which such inter-group cleavages have been noticed, and examine the extent to which dialect differences reflect the cleavages:

1. The relatively small participation of educated Negroes in the organized cultural life of Southern cities.

2. The development of Negro-white tensions in Middle Western cities, such as Detroit and Chicago.

3. The development of tensions between Lutherans and Roman Catholics of German origin, and between Roman Catholics of

German, Italian, and Polish origin in many large cities, such as Buffalo.

Many excellent sociological community studies deal with these situations and others where one might test correlations between dialect differences and caste and class lines within a community. Several of the better-known community studies -- such as Dollard's *Caste and Class in a Southern Town* (1937) and Warner's *Yankee City* series (1941-59) -- deal with communities where one might expect to find significant social dialects. Yet in none of these studies has any systematic effort been made to record and analyze the local varieties of speech.[4] Therefore, observations on these correlations are those which were made incidentally in the course of field work for the Linguistic Atlas; they are far from definitive but illustrate the possibilities for coordinated research.

In each of these situations the inter-group cleavage is reflected in observable dialect differences:[5]

1. In Southern cities many educated Negroes abandon the normal patterns of cultivated speech in the community and attempt to imitate the socially privileged speech of other areas, particularly that of Eastern New England. Such imitation is found, specifically, in the pronunciation of *either*, *neither*, as /ayðər, nayðər/, and in the use of the so-called 'broad *a*' [a·,ɑ·] pronunciations of *aunt*, *grass*, *half past* as /ahnt/, /grahs/, /hahf pahst/. There are indications that such imitation is not only found in the speech of educated Negroes but encouraged by the teachers in Negro public schools.[6]

2. In Detroit, older generation native-born Negroes normally speak a type of Michigan speech (generally derived from that of Western New England and Upstate New York, as one might expect from settlement history [see A. L. Davis 1949]) like that of native Michigan whites of the same age and educational attainment. However, regardless of how many years their parents have been living in Michigan, or how much education they have had themselves, many Michigan-born Negroes of the age group from twenty to thirty-five speak dialects exhibiting many Southern or South Midland characteristics,[7] especially in the pronunciation of the diphthongs in *grass*, *mine*, *cow*, and *law* /græys, mahn, kæw, lɔw/.

The social cleavage may even be indicated by the retention of lexical items, which are much more easily supplanted than phonological patterns. As an exercise in method, students in a course in American English at the University of Illinois were asked to get their friends to fill out multiple-choice check lists of items found by the Linguistic Atlas to have regional variants along the Atlantic Seaboard. An examination of these check lists revealed that some students native to the Chicago area but with Southern-born parents normally used Southern or South Midland regional terms which could not have been learned from books, such as *crocus sack*, *croker sack*, instead of the more common Chicago terms *gunny sack* and *burlap bag*. A check revealed that every native Chicago student in whose vocabulary these Southern terms persisted was a Negro.

3. In Buffalo the first generation of immigrants naturally spoke the language of their native countries by habit and preference, and English only imperfectly. The second generation seem to have become fairly well assimilated to the dialect patterns of the community. In the third generation, however, with the institution of parochial schools segregated according to ancestral national origin and often heavily staffed with teachers (especially nuns and celibate clergy) whose native language is not English, the mastery of English is less complete and new fractional dialects are apparently developing.[8]

Overt manifestations of inter-group tensions, as in race riots, do not develop overnight. They take a long time developing, and considerably before a critical stage is reached a linguistic scientist could detect the symptoms of social cleavage -- in the development or abnormal persistence of social dialects within the community -- and direct the attention of the authorities toward the conditions responsible for this situation.

The recording and analyzing of dialect differences in a community is not a panacea, but merely a diagnostic device. Nor is the knowledge of the symptoms any guarantee that the proper remedial steps may be taken. Axiomatically, all social phenomena should be studied and the data utilized as a basis for action. Nevertheless, the use of dialect data has certain definite advantages: 1) much of this data can be gathered relatively unobtrusively, and people are in general less emotional about the words they use than about their playground experiences as children; 2) as the Linguistic Atlas and its derivative studies are completed,[9] social scientists should have information available from which sharply graded social diagnostic tests may be devised. In the future, it should be taken for granted that no community study can be considered adequate unless it includes a survey of local speech patterns under the direction of a linguistic scientist; it is not without significance that such a survey has been included in the preliminary plans of Wayne State University sociologists for a study of Detroit.[10]

[1] This paper is based in part on the Goldwin Smith Lecture -- "Dialect: Settlement History and Social Structure" -- delivered at Cornell University, November 22, 1949. Transcriptions follow Trager and Smith 1951.

The linguistic data on which the conclusions are based were gathered during field work for the Linguistic Atlas of the United States and Canada; funds for this field work were provided by the Julius Rosenwald Fund, the American Council of Learned Societies, the University of Michigan, the University of Illinois, Western Reserve University, and the Ohio State Archeological and Historical Society. Suggestions of social implications were made by C. F. Hockett of Cornell and N. A. McQuown of Chicago [see also R. McDavid 1958a, Marshall and Vlach 1973].

[2] Nevertheless, in a recent widely syndicated 'popular science' newspaper column (1949), A. E. Wiggam explained that the Negro cannot pronounce postvocalic /-r/ in *beard*, *bird*, *bard* because his lips are too thick. And in a Rocky Mountain university, the professor of pedagogics in charge of training English teachers explained the pronunciation patterns of Minnesota on the ground that the climate induced endemic sinusitis.

[3] For the meaning of the terms *cultivated speech*, *common speech*, and *folk speech*, see Kurath 1949.

[4] John Gillin, of the University of North Carolina, recognized the desirability of obtaining linguistic data to correlate with the other data obtained in communtiy studies; unfortunately, however, he lacked funds and facilities for including linguistic research in the studies under his direction.

[5] Speakers of the types here discussed were not included in the records made for the Linguistic Atlas, whose emphasis is on the normal speech patterns of a community in terms of locally-rooted informants. The discovery of these divergent types, however, resulted from the experience of field work.

[6] The attempts of educated Negroes to assimilate their speech to the speech type of Eastern New England is understandable. From the Abolitionist movement to the present day, New England has symbolized -- to Southern Negro and Southern white alike -- attitudes sharply opposed to the institution of slavery and to the subsequent Southern caste system. Moreover, many Negro schools in the South were originally staffed with white teachers from New England.

[7] *Southern*, so far as the Atlantic Seaboard is concerned, refers to the speech of the Southern coastal plain and the lower Piedmont; *South Midland* to the speech of the upper Piedmont and the southern Appalachians. The boundary between Southern and South Midland is sharpest in Virginia, where it follows the crest of the Blue Ridge from the Potomac to the James; it is less sharply defined in the Carolinas and Georgia but it is still one of the sharpest dialect boundaries in the English-speaking world. See Kurath 1949.

[8] The observations on the situation in Buffalo were suggested by conversations with local newspapermen in my search for informants.

[9] The most extensive study of the dialect of a community based on the Atlas is Frank 1949. A similar social analysis, using different materials of inquiry, is Hubbell 1950. Both of these treatments emphasize the class cleavages in the speech of the metropolitan area. [Labov 1966 is a more detailed study of a small part of the area.]

[10] [The survey of Detroit was undertaken much later, and under other auspices: Shuy, Wolfram, and Riley 1968, Wolfram 1969.]

This paper is a venture into the often forbidden domain of meaning. It accepts the basic assumption that no complex of phonemes has an inherent power for good or ill. It insists, however, that an important part of the record of any linguistic form is the attitude of the people who use that form, and the attitude of those about whom that form is used. Consequently, when two mutually antagonistic social groups seem to associate good and evil with particular words or pronunciations, it becomes the business of the linguist to find out as much as he can about the actual use of the disputed forms. In making such an investigation, the linguist does not assume that the mere recording of the facts will by itself resolve the tensions; he insists, however, that a framework of fact will be useful to those who seek objective discussion of the problem at issue.

The evidence for this paper is derived from the collections of the linguistic atlases of North American English. As part of the record of usage, investigators have assembled evidence on designations for racial and cultural minorities, including neutral and opprobrious designations for the Negro. In 1952, during the early stages of working with Hans Kurath on *The Pronunciation of English in the Atlantic States* (1961), I charted pronunciation variants of *Negro*, but discovered that the distribution of these variants was too complicated to be described in full in the limited space available in the book. Subsequently, as court decisions intensified the feelings associated with particular pronunciations, my interest in the problem was renewed. Finally, in the spring of 1957, William D. Workman, Jr., at work on his defense of the traditional Southern position, *The Case for the South* (1960), posed the linguistic and anthropological question of why the colored people -- or at least their spokesmen -- insisted on [nɪgro] in preference not only to [nɪgər], but to the "polite Southern pronunciation" [nɪgrə] as well (46-49). The attempt to frame an intelligible, accurate, and judicious statement led to re-examination of the atlas evidence and hence to this paper.

Before examining the atlas evidence on *Negro*, we need to recognize two other kinds of evidence: historical and sociological.

Historically, *Negro* is a borrowed word -- from Spanish or Portugese or both. Early

spellings suggest either that it was borrowed several times with several different phonemic shapes, or that it developed these phonemic shapes rather early during its career as an English word. The pronunciation [nɪgər], first cited by the Oxford Dictionary from a poem by Burns, written in 1786, was probably in use much earlier than that. A variety of pronunciations was probably known in the American colonies. Noah Webster recommended the spelling *neger*.

Sociologically, all pronunciations except [nigro], but especially [nɪgər], have become a focus of resentment to the Negro press and to most leaders of Negro opinion. As Mencken (1945:626) points out, the resentment has placed this particular variant in the status of a taboo word for many educated Negroes, who refuse to write it out but indicate it, when such indication is inescapable, as *N-----*, *N----r*, *n----r*.

In interpreting the evidence of the atlas collections, we must bear in mind certain facts about these collections:

1. The responses are obtained from natives of particular communities, about 770 communities and 1632 informants from the Atlantic Seaboard, 229 communities and 564 informants from the North-Central States. About ten percent of the informants are cultivated speakers; of the rest, half are old and uneducated, the others middle-aged with approximate high-school educations.

2. Since the files for the Atlantic Seaboard were completed in 1949, there may have been some shifts in the incidence of particular pronunciations, or in attitudes toward them. However, the most recent field records from the North-Central States suggest that such changes, if any, have been relatively slight, and have not altered the basic fact that certain pronunciations tend to arouse certain psychological responses.

3. Every informant was asked what designations he used for the particular group, a task which tested the field worker's power of innocent circumlocution. The field worker attempted to record the informant's normal or neutral terms, then any derogatory ones he used or might know of. The informant's comments on particular terms were often relevant, as were the terms he used freely in conversation. Field workers differed in the extent to which they recorded conversational responses or informants' comments, and the

circumstances of interviews varied so much that no field worker could be completely consistent in his practice. Nevertheless, these differences average out over the large number of interviews conducted for the atlases, so that our sample is adequate for generalizations.

The most widespread pronunciations, in order of frequency, are: [nɪgər], [nɪgrə], [nɪgro] (with a subvariant [nɪgəro]), and [nigro] (with a subvariant [nɪgrə]). Other recorded variants, none of frequent distribution, are: [niger], [negər], [negrə], [negər], [nɪgərə], [nɪgru], [nɪgru], [nɪgru], [nɪgru]. There may be other variants, as yet unrecorded.

Of the pronunciations recorded in the eastern United States, [nɪgər] is by far the most widely distributed, occurring in the speech of all classes and all regions. It occurs as the normal or neutral pronunciation in most of northern New England, southwestern Pennsylvania, the South Midland,[1] most of Virginia and North Carolina, and northeastern South Carolina. It is indicated as a derogatory pronunciation in southern New England, metropolitan New York, New York State, northern and eastern Pennsylvania, New Jersey, Delaware, Maryland, the older plantation areas of Virginia and North Carolina, most of South Carolina, and the Georgia coastal plain.

In many communities [nɪgər] is accepted as a normal or neutral pronunciation by the more old-fashioned informant, but considered as derogatory by the younger. This is especially true in Virginia and North Carolina and New York State, somewhat less true in New England and the lower South. To this trend there are relatively few exceptions, chiefly in New England, Pennsylvania, and West Virginia. Almost nowhere in the South does the old-fashioned informant condemn [nɪgər] as derogatory and the younger informant accept it as normal or neutral.

The pronunciation [nɪgrə] is very common in South Carolina and Georgia, only slightly less common in Virginia and North Carolina. It is considerably less common in Maryland, where it occurs only west of Chesapeake Bay, in West Virginia, and in western New York State. It occurs occasionally in New England (three times in Maine, twice in eastern Massachusetts), once in southern New Jersey. It is otherwise lacking in the North Midland, in metropolitan New York, in the Hudson Valley, and in Delmarva north of the Virginia line.

In the areas in which [nɪgrə] is commonest -- the Potomac to northeastern Georgia -- it is used by whites of all cultural levels, with somewhat greater frequency among the cultured and middle group than among the uneducated. By white informants it is usually considered a polite, or at worst a neutral, term, which educated

Southerners are taught to use rather than the derogatory [nɪgər].

The pronunciation [nɪgro] is very common in northern New England, New Jersey, eastern Pennsylvania, the Chesapeake Bay area, and northern West Virginia. It is less common in southern New England, metropolitan New York, New York State, western Pennsylvania, the Shenandoah Valley, and the tidewater South Atlantic States south of the Potomac; it is uncommon in the uplands of the South Atlantic States. Like [nɪgrə], it is used by speakers on all social levels, and often occurs in the speech of the middle group and the cultured, as a polite form, in communities where [nɪgər] is the normal uneducated usage.

The subvariant [nɪgəro] occurs alongside [nɪgro] in seven communities along the New England coast, three on Chesapeake Bay and at the mouth of the Neuse River in eastern North Carolina. Every occurrence of [nɪgəro] but one is in the speech of the uneducated, white or Negro.

The variant [nigro] is the dominant form in the North, except for conservative northeastern New England, and in eastern Pennsylvania. It is less common in western Pennsylvania, West Virginia, and New Jersey, and is very rare in the South, with its only noticeable Southern concentration in the Charleston area. This somewhat surprising concentration of [nigro] in and near Charleston is susceptible to two explanations. First, the Charleston area -- in contradistinction to to other parts of the South Atlantic States -- shares other linguistic features with parts of the North, such as *mouth organ* for 'harmonica' or [dov] as the preterite of *dive* or [wunt] for 'will not.' Second, the acceptance of [nigro] may be an indication of the way in which an aristocratically oriented society preserves a tradition of good manners by compromising on things indifferent while leaving the essentials untouched.

From Baltimore north, [nigro] is heavily favored in cultivated speech, especially in the larger centers of population. North of the Ohio River and the Mason-Dixon Line, it is generally the form favored by the younger and better-educated informants when community usage is divided. On the other hand, in West Virginia communities of divided usage, [nigro] is usually the old-fashioned term, yielding to [nɪgro] in more modern speech. In parts of West Virginia and Pennsylvania, furthermore, [nigro] is apparently considered more derogatory than competing pronunciations.

So far we have confined ourselves to the responses from white informants. We may now turn to the forms and remarks obtained from Negro informants, bearing in mind that the atlas data was recorded by white field workers, and that in the course of his long and intensive education in applied human relations, the Southern Negro has become keenly aware that his success -- even his survival -- may depend on his ability to guess the answer the Southern white man wants him to make.[2]

For the Atlantic Seaboard, thirty-four Negro informants were interviewed. Further inland, there were two interviewed in Kentucky and one in Minnesota. Six of these records were incomplete or abbreviated, so that no response -- or only partial data -- was obtained from these informants for this particular item. Regrettably, among these incomplete records are two of the field records obtained from New England Negroes. The full tabulation of responses from the others is as follows:

[nɪgər]: acceptable (inferred from informants' conversational use) 3; derogatory 11 (3 qualify by saying that it may be friendly if used by one's own group, 1 by accepting it in joking relationships); no comment 9; "old-fashioned" 1.

[nɪgrə]: acceptable 5; "used to be derogatory" 1; no comment 2.

[nɪgro]: acceptable 5; "modern" 1; derogatory 1; no comment 3.

[nɪgəro]: no comment 1.

[nigro]: acceptable 6; "modern" 1.

We are thus confronted with a complex of regional distributions and social evaluations, in which phonemes become symbols of status, subject to different evaluations on the two sides of the color line.

It is now necessary to discuss the metalinguistics of the four main pronunciation variants.

1. It is clear that [nɪgər] is considered socially reprehensible by a majority of Negroes and by a growing number of white Americans in all parts of the United States. Furthermore, this pronunciation is used by only a small minority of cultured informants: one fifth of those in New England, one tenth of those in the South Atlantic States, one thirtieth of those in the Middle Atlantic States. That it is still considered a normal or neutral term by many white informants, in all parts of the country, is not likely to lessen the offense; to such informants, a normal or neutral society is one in which the Negro is in his place and does not seek to change it.

2. It is understandable that the Negroes themselves should favor the Northern 'polite' pronunciation [nigro] over the Chesapeake Bay [nɪgro] and the Virginia-South Carolina [nɪgrə]:

a. Both [nɪgro] and [nɪgrə] are associated with the usage of Southern whites. Although the Southern whites themselves may look upon these pronunciations as courteous, Negroes may interpret them as condescending to those of inferior status.

b. Conversely, [nigro], generally Northern and speicfically New England and heavily favored in urban centers, would be associated with the region from which the Negroes have traditionally expected aid and understanding, and with the kind of social environment to which they have looked for their greatest opportunities.

c. The Negroes as a group have only recently attained literacy. Like other groups that have recently come to literacy in English, whether from total illiteracy or from literacy in another language, they will likely show the tendency of the newly literate to emphasize relatively artificial spelling pronunciations rather than easy cultivated usage -- to pay greater attention to the sound associations of the written symbols *per se* than to the actual speech sounds which the symbols represent (see Pyles 1952:245-53).

3. In turn, one may understand why the white Southerner often resents the Negroes' adopting the pronunciation [nigro] as a favored designation for themselves.

a. He correctly interprets this pronunciation as symbolizing a desire on the part of the Negroes to change their status.

b. If a Northern, especially a New England, pronunciation symbolizes understanding and opportunity to the Negro, to the Southern white it often symbolizes a tradition of misunderstanding, if not overt hostility, toward Southern institutions and attitudes.

c. The educated Southerner, usually coming from a well-established tradition of easy cultivated speech, is largely unsympathetic toward spelling pronunciations and is known to look with disfavor upon the too precise articulation of unstressed syllables. In Virginia and South Carolina, the foci of [nɪgrə], we normally have *borrow*, *barrow*, *tomato*, *tomorrow*, *wheelbarrow* with final [-ə], *Wednesday* and *yesterday* with final [-ɪ], *nephew* and *Matthew* with final [-jə]. To single out *Negro* for special phonetic treatment with final [-o] would actually be a new mode of discrimination. And many Southern whites, on all cultural levels, show their resentment of [nigro] by accompanying this pronunciation with sarcastic paralanguage probably more offensive, because deliberate, than the contemptuous vocalizations that often accompany [nɪgər].

We thus have a tendency for the current racial tensions to be expressed in phonological terms. One of the less pleasant aspects of the situation has been the observable fact that some white Southerners who condemned [nɪgər] as derogatory a generation ago, have adopted it as their normal pronunciation today.

Here one might stop. But a sermon should end with a moral, if only an obvious one.

1. Whether one says [nɪgər] or [nɪgro] or [nɪgrə] or [nigro] actually makes no

difference in the cosmic picture. But if people believe it makes a difference, it will make it -- to them.

2. Any move toward reducing the importance of this metalinguistic barrier would be helpful, if difficult. Probably the Southern white should be the one to start breaking down this barrier, because he is the dominant person in the Southern cultural pattern, and the adoption of [nigro] as an everyday alternative, if not a consistent replacement, might cost him a little rearranging of phonetic sequences but would be repaid by a considerable increase in understanding. Conversely, Negro leaders should realize that traditional pronunciations are simply traditional pronunciations and not in themselves deliberate insults.[3]

3. Even in times of tension, deep-rooted linguistic taboos can be approached rationally, in terms of historical developments and sociological distributions. And so approached, they may lose much of their terror.

NOTES

[1] As defined by vocabulary evidence in Kurath 1949, and confirmed by later grammatical and phonological sutdies, the North comprises New England, the Hudson Valley, and derivative settlements to the west; the Midland comprises New Jersey, Pennsylvania, and their derivatives to the west and south; the South comprises the older plantation settlements from Chesapeake Bay to Florida. Within the Midland, the North Midland comprises Pennsylvania, New Jersey, and northern West Virginia; the South Midland includes the Shenandoah Valley, southern West Virginia, southwest Virginia, and the Piedmont and mountain areas of the Carolina and Georgia. The South Midland has been under political and cultural domination of the plantation areas, so that its speech is heavily interlarded with Southern forms, especially Southern pronunciations.

[2] A partial control exists, in some thirty field records from the Gullah country of South Carolina and Georgia, made by Lorenzo D. Turner of Roosevelt University in the early stages of the work that yielded *Africanisms in the Gullah Dialect* (1949). These informants consistently indicated [nigro] as a neutral pronunciation and [nigər] as derogatory.

[3] [The past two decades have seen this ethnic linguistic problem change its focus, with the increasing use of *black* -- often to the discomfort of those who had painfully become used to saying [nigro]. Whether the fashion will continue is problematical -- after all, for a long time *black* was the most derogatory of terms -- but at least it transfers the problem from phonology to lexicon.]

The recent tragic events, in Los Angeles and other American cities, have been all too eloquent testimony to the fact that the American Negro is far less integrated into the framework of American society than the good of that society demands.[1] As we examine the role which each citizen may need to play in achieving a greater measure of true integration, the dialectologist must not be overlooked. To be sure, he can play only a small part in the solution of a great and too-long-persisting problem. Confronting the upstirrings of wrath in Watts and other ghettos, any dialectologist who asserted that he could solve the problems of integration through his science alone would be as naively optimistic as a hunter attempting to stop a charging rhinoceros with a popgun. Nevertheless, the dialectologist does have the means of discovering major linguistic breaks in the network of relationships that characterizes a speech community -- breaks that derive from fault lines in the society itself and that may in turn contribute to the widening of those fault lines. He has the skills with which to investigate the linguistic structure of a community, and to determine which linguistic features correlate most clearly with measurable social differences. Furthermore, in collaboration with colleagues in other fields, he may use these investigations to determine which kinds of linguistic differences are identified with social differences by the various groups who actually live in the community. Finally, he may collaborate with practical educators and editors in devising materials which may be used to help the various depressed groups acquire the linguistic features identified with the groups that fully participate in the various activities of the society.

Since too many of the programs designed to deal with changes such as those in the ethnic or religious composition of the schools are improvizations, thrown together after a state of tension has developed, it is important that future programs be devised as early as possible in the sequence of events that mark a change in racial or religious or ethnic relationships in a given community. Informally, I would distinguish three principal stages in the process of change.[2]

First, we have the stage of *desegregation*, the removal of old barriers, in which two or more groups are physically juxtaposed in new relationships. In some communities this may be accomplished by legislative decree or by judicial decision; in others it may be accomplished less formally by the action of a few individuals in moving to a community or participating in relationships where their group had never been known before.

Second, we have the stage of *accommodation*, in which members of various groups -- as individuals, as families, and as larger aggregations -- learn to live and work and study and play alongside each other, to respect each other's traditions and mores, to coexist peacefully. This is the crucial stage, the one which exercises all the talents of those who lead each group. The behavior of the hitherto dominant group is crucial at this stage, when old patterns have been set aside and new ones not yet established. An inability to act at this time may even result in what could be called *negative accommodation*: if the old inhabitants reject their new neighbors and join the *sauve qui peut* to mortgaged suburbia or to the parochial schools,[3] the neighborhood can rapidly turn into another extension of the ghetto, with those who have broken old barriers now confronted with new ones and embittered at having broken the old ones in vain. The scandalous decay of our central cities is a monument to the failure of accommodation.

Finally, we have the stage of *integration*, when identification of the individual as a person replaces identification of the individual as a member of his racial, ethnic, or religious group. In this stage, each person participates -- according to his interests and on his own merits -- in all kinds of activities, whether cooperative or competitive. In the school situation, this involves all aspects of the program, but particularly the academic part -- the real justification for any schools. It is necessary to emphasize academic attainment, because members of various minority groups are traditionally accepted (in schools and elsewhere) as athletic performers or other public entertainers long before they are conceded equality in other respects, or have demonstrated it.

Judged by this last criterion, genuinely integrated school situations are far too few in the United States. Members of hitherto depressed minority groups tend to drop out of school earlier and in greater numbers than do their contemporaries from the dominant culture. Where they continue at school, fewer of them take -- or succeed in -- the program for academic advancement.[4] The rest advance at a slower pace and have, in statistically disproportionate number, difficulties and deficiencies in the basic academic skills, most noticeably in the command of the standard language.[5] This lag in academic achievement is particularly distressing when one remembers that technological advances are eliminating most of the low-skilled jobs at which members of such minorities have traditionally worked during the period of accomodation. Steel making, meat packing, even street cleaning are mechanized if not actually automated. It is true that these same technological advances are also creating many new jobs, perhaps more than they are eliminating. But unfortunately (from the point of view of a depressed minority) these new jobs normally demand competence in precisely such academic disciplines as mathematics and the standard language. An amiable and strong illiterate may have had his place in the old-time steel mill or coal mine; he has no place as a receptionist or the minder of automated machinery, let alone as a secretary or computer programmer. Yet until the members of our depressed but aspiring minorities have fair opportunities to succeed at such employment, we cannot say that we have achieved integration.

The difficulties in achieving integration, in coping with the changing relationships between social groups, thus essentially arise from a failure to anticipate the problems of accomodation. To cope with all these problems demands the use of all the intellectual and moral resources of our society and is far beyond the scope of a single paper. More specifically, the crises in the schools -- as in Chicago or New York -- seem to arise from a failure of educators and administrators to understand that such periods of accomodation create basic problems which demand different approaches from those which the schools have inherited from a less complicated society. Too many raw teachers are still being assigned to so-called 'hardship schools,' without any awareness (or any attempt to make them aware) of the kinds of environments from which their students come; too many 'standard textbooks' are routinely administered to all students, without any attempt to find out whether the student's previous experience makes any meaningful reaction possible. Fortunately, however, this is far less true than it used to be. In many localities, citizens' committees and groups of scholars -- most often independent of the school administration but in such places as Wilmington, Delaware, actively cooperating with such school leaders as Dr. Muriel Crosby -- have assessed the problem. Out of these assessments has arisen a feeling that a teacher in urban schools needs special training in

psychology, in social anthropology, and in language structure and variation, far beyond what is conventionally provided in teacher-training courses. Some programs to provide such training are actually under way, especially the parts of such programs concerned with language.[6]

Needless to say, the first stage in devising a language program for a particular group is to place the language practices of that group in a particular social setting. Here we have a start in the recent investigations of social differences in a number of urban communities. Some of these -- for example, Pederson 1965a, Udell 1966, or Strang 1968 -- are, in essence, more intensive applications of the traditional methods of dialectology, adapted to an urban situation. Some, like Labov 1966, are concerned with the status of particular linguistic variants in a particular community; some, like Basil Bernstein's in London or Fred Strodtbeck's in Chicago, are concerned with differences in the matrix in which language is acquired and habitually used by particular social groups.[7] Each approach has its value; taken together, these studies provide massive evidence on the peculiar language problems of the underprivileged, especially of the Negro in the urban slums of the United States.

First, the socio-cultural environment is one which at worst actually inhibits rather than encourages the normal processes of language development,[8] and which at best produces a poverty of vocabulary, of syntax, and of style. This last situation is but a special case of the conclusion of Fries (1940) that the principal difference between so-called 'Standard English' and so-called 'Vulgar English' is the relative impoverishment of the latter. To enrich the language variety of such groups it is first of all necessary to enrich their cultural experience, notably through such instruments as special nursery school programs which give particular attention to language.[9] These programs, by and large, are outside the province of dialectology, though a dialectologist might be called on to evaluate the language models to which the children are exposed in such programs.

Second, the grammar of the underprivileged often shows striking differences from that of the standard language, to the point where some observers insist that we are dealing with separate grammatical systems. Whether or not this is true -- and we lack any adequate serious descriptions on which to base a conclusion -- these differences are so numerous and so widespread that it is futile to use the conventional classroom approach of treating them as 'errors' for the students to 'correct.'[10]

Finally, because of patterns of segregated housing, the Negro child in many cities of the northern United States acquires a pronunciation sharply divergent from that of the local middle-class white, not only in such phonic details as the quality of /e/ and /o/, or in such matters of incidence as /grizi/ instead of /grisi/ for *greasy*, but sometimes even in the system of phonemes. These differences, again, are of too large an order to be treated -- as they have too often been treated -- merely as 'mispronunciations' subject to remedy by classes in 'corrective speech.' Problems of this kind are less common in the South than in Northern cities, where any variety of Southern speech is at first blush popularly identified as 'Negro speech.'[11] In many Southern communities, especially the smaller towns, the pronunciation of uneducated Negroes differs from the local standard in the same ways as does the pronunciation of uneducated whites, and both share most of the features of that standard. In parts of the South, actually, the pronunciation of urban Negroes, of whatever degree of education, is closer to the local white standard than is the speech of uneducated whites.

In coping with these diverse problems we are repeatedly brought back to the fact that not only is there a difference between the home dialect of the average slum Negro and the dialect of the dominant local middle-class whites, but that the former is reinforced by the patterns of segregated housing. Any attempt to eradicate the home dialect, any attempt to stigmatize it, may produce serious traumata. Instead, the standard language should be taught as a system, as a mode of communication especially appropriate for school and the better employment situations to which it is hoped education may lead. It should never be taught as a series of discrete items. It should be taught by adaptations of the techniques that have been found useful for the teaching of foreign languages -- but with awareness that the students have at least some passive familiarity with it. What the child does about other situations -- and ultimately about any use of the neighborhood dialect at all -- should be left to him and his family; for it is conceivable that he might find it useful to have two or more modes of speech, each for a particular range of environments. Such a situation we might call one of functional bidialectalism, analogous to the functional bilingualism so common in such nations as Switzerland and Luxembourg, with the speaker switching codes as occasion demands.[12] Such functional bidialectalism has, in fact, been achieved informally and intuitively in some degree by many Negroes and whites in various American communities

(Baehr 1964). In the end, as ghettos disappear, the need for such special programs will also vanish; but that time is still distant.

Since the local situation presents its own problem, the development of a rational teaching program requires the cooperation of the dialectologist from the beginning.[13] His primary role is that of specifying the social differences in language that exist in the particular community, and of helping to ascertain the relative importance of such differences as social markers. The investigations he will conduct in this role will be on a larger scale and will use informants of many more types than have customarily been interviewed for the classical dialect atlases. Nevertheless, any such investigation must build on the work of its giant predecessors, from Georg Wenker to the present, and in the American scene particularly on the magnificent archives assembled by Hans Kurath and his associates.

But such a program is only part of the picture. Since the cultural understanding that leads to an integrated society involves both the underprivileged and the dominant culture, it is unrealistic to expect that the former should bear all the burden of accomodation by simply learning the language of the latter. It is at least as important to educate the members of the dominant culture -- particularly as represented by parents, educators, administrators and members of school boards -- as to the nature and origin and significance of dialect differences. Here again the dialectologist must be called upon; since his habitual work is to record dialects and to sort out the facts and significance of their distribution, it should be his responsibility to see that any popular statements about dialects are based on fact. It is particularly important that the public come to understand that differences in dialect do not arise from differences in intellectual or moral stature, but simply from differences in cultural experience.

As was emphasized at the beginning, the contributions of the dialectologist alone will not cure deep-seated ills; along with other students of human behavior, he should have been consulted before local situations became so obviously desperate. Nevertheless, both for remedying old situations and preventing others from developing -- or at least from becoming worse than they already are -- the dialectologist, along with representatives of many other disciplines, has work to do -- work so important that it deserves the best efforts of our profession.

[1] Many of the statements in this paper are based on R. McDavid and Austin 1966. Other participants in the project were Alva L. Davis, Melvin Hoffman, Lee Pederson, Thomas Creswell, Virginia McDavid, Carolyn Larsen, Vernon Larsen, and John Willis.

[The viewpoint of this paper is perhaps not as fashionable now as it was in 1965, nor is the notion of non-violent adjustment. Apostles of 'black nationalism' and 'Black English' not only urge separatism but emphasize differences in speech modes, even when the facts argue otherwise.

One might comment sardonically on some of the ironics of the new pose such as the preference among some *soi-disant* spokesmen for *black* rather than *Negro* -- though *black* has a long history as a derogatory term -- and for the identification with Islam and pan-Arabic political causes, forgetting that the African slave trade was run by Arabs. Touching everyone -- since I use the word frequently in this paper -- is the vogue use of *ghetto* as a general term for any area, slum or otherwise, inhabited predominantly by one ethnic group. In the spring of 1968 a candidate for a position in the student government of the University of Chicago was described as having grown up in the *Icelandic ghetto* of Phoenix.]

[2] This informal classification has no claim to scientific validity. But it does provide a basis for discussion, and does avoid the rhetorical trap of confusing *desegregation* and *integration*, the initial and final stages, of assuming that physical juxtaposition has solved the problem. As careful observers are too painfully aware, it merely confronts the community or neighborhood with the problem.

[3] In Chicago the Negroes are less than twenty-five percent of the total population but a good half of the enrollment of the public schools [a much higher proportion in 1978]; parochial schools, with something over half as many pupils as the public schools, have relatively few Negroes -- not because of discrimination but because few Chicago Negroes are Roman Catholics, accustomed to the presence of parochial schools, or able to afford even the modest tuition the parochial schools charge.

In many Southern communities, it should be pointed out for the record, parochial schools desegregated earlier and with far less difficulty than the public schools, simply because they were independent of local political pressure and able to prepare for the change. In 1946, eight years before the Supreme Court decisions on segregation, my friend Msgr. J. L. O'Brien, director of parochial education in the Charleston diocese, calmly told me that he knew desegregation was coming, that for two years he had been preparing his teachers for the change, and simultaneously he had brought the Negro parochial schools to full professional accreditation -- so that a smooth change could take place on a day's notice.

[4] In private schools, where achievement is the chief criterion -- the University of Chicago Laboratory School is an example I am intimately familiar with -- genuine integration is better achieved than in the public schools. But such schools enroll a minuscule share of the U.S. school population.

[5] In the last three or four decades, the public schools of the United States have generally adopted a policy of 'social promotion' -- that is, every fourth grade child is automatically advanced to the fifth grade, regardless of how well or how poorly he has mastered fourth grade work. European observers are pardonably confused at the notion of children being in the tenth grade but reading at the third-grade level.

[6] An informal sequence of courses, devised by faculty members concerned with the local schools, is offered by the Extension Division of the University of Chicago; a more elaborate program has been drawn up at Chicago State University. During the summer of 1965 several workshops concerned with problems of urban education were conducted at various colleges and universities in the United States.

[7] For several years Strodtbeck has conducted an experimental nursery school for small groups of children from homes supported by Aid for Dependent Children. Although he claims no magic, he reports that in the ten weeks of this environment there is a rise of over fifteen points in the average Intelligence Quotient.

[8] The average domicile is an apartment -- crowded, often dirty, always noisy, and constantly threatened by physical violence. Often there is no legal father in the household; the mother is away much of the daytime, entrusting the children to an elderly grandmother, aunt, or neighbor. Such a custodian normally discourages the processes of curiosity by which children develop language proficiency: she has no time to spend in language play and -- because of the external menace -- discourages the children from playing outside or from talking to neighbors. The television -- which, properly used, might be an instrument of language enrichment -- is generally left on at full blast to become merely another bit of background noise.

[9] In the United States, nursery schools (for children from three to five years old) have heretofore been private enterprises, attended chiefly by middle-class children -- the very group that needed them least. A number of experimental nursery schools were included in Operation Headstart, a 1964-65 program for children in slum areas; the success of these schools has led to an expansion of the program under the new federal campaign against poverty and deprivation. No reports are available yet on what language programs, if any, have been included or contemplated in such schools.

[10] Most noticeable, perhaps, since it is found in writing up to the college level, is the distribution of the {-Z} morpheme of verb inflection in

the present indicative. In standard English this appears as a regular marker of the third singular and only as such a marker; in the South, in uneducated speech of all races, it may be omitted in the third singular (as it is in southern England); it may also, in the same speakers, appear in the first singular or in the plural, as well as in the third singular, the conditions of presence or absence for a given speaker not being fully worked out as yet. In Northern urban areas, however, this distribution is identified with uneducated Negro speech.

A second feature concerns the pattern of auxiliaries. The copula may be omitted in such sentences as *He dead*, where standard English would have *He is dead*. *Done* is used as a perfective, indicating that an action has been completed, and usually suggesting emphasis, as *I done told you*. *Been* with verbs of motion may indicate departure and return. The following paradigm may occur:

He gone (no longer here).

He done gone (already gone, and you should have expected this).

He been gone (gone and returned).

He done been gone (already gone and returned, and you should have expected this).

Such forms, again, are to be heard in the South from both Negro and white uneducated speakers -- including whites of groups that have limited or no contacts with Negroes. In Northern cities, however, they are almost never heard except from Negroes.

A third set of differences is a higher incidence of such folk forms as uninflected plurals of measure (*two mile*, *six pound*) and nonstandard preterites and participles: *I seen*, *he come*, *we done*, *you clum*; *have wrote*, *have holp* /hop/ 'helped,' etc. Some of these forms are generally distributed; some, like *holp*, are characteristically Southern and South Midland. In the Northern urban environment, nearly all of these may be heard from uneducated whites, but not nearly as often as from uneducated Negroes.

[11] The prevalence of this identification was demonstrated at Chicago in the fall of 1964, when a class consistently attributed to unidentified pronunciations by the instructor (a white Southerner by birth) the same qualities they ascribed to the unidentified pronunciations of two Negro speakers on the same tape: "rural, uneducated, Negro." Informally, I had noticed at Cornell University (Ithaca, New York) in the fall of 1950 that townspeople would not discuss over the telephone the renting of an apartment; I had to show my Caucasoid features before I talked. [In two decades in Chicago my voice has often been racially misidentified over the telephone and on tapes, perhaps oftener by blacks than by whites.] Other whites from the South have had similar experiences in Ithaca as late as 1965. Ethnocentric reactions are not the peculiar property of any one region. During field work in South Carolina and Georgia for the Linguistic Atlas of the United States and Canada (1945-48) I was often asked, "Why is it that the educated Northerner talks like the uneducated Southerner?" This reaction probably stems from the fact that in the old South postvocalic /-r/ is preserved chiefly in uneducated white speech.

[12] The Center for Applied Linguistics has received a grant for developing a language program for the city of Washington, D.C., where over eighty-five percent of the children in the public schools are Negroes. Scholars at the Center consider that no functional bidialectalism should be imposed on the students, since many of them come from homes where standard, middle-class English is the normal mode of communication. I would agree, and emphasize that the standard language would always be the vehicle and the model in the classroom, but presented as a system, not negatively as the substitution of discrete items.

[13] Without the cooperation of the dialectologist, fantastic judgments may be made as to what to teach. Programs in the Detroit schools have heretofore been based on *ad hoc* prejudices of individual teachers, without any reference to the local standard. And a recent drill program for Negro students at Claflin University (Orangeburg, South Carolina) included among its goals the establishment of the *wail/whale* contrast, although this contrast is lacking in many varieties of standard English, including British Received Pronunciation and the South Carolina Low-Country, and nowhere seems to be a social marker.

When I face an audience of this kind,[1] I find myself smitten with deep feelings of responsibility and humility. Nothing is more irritating than the performance of the self-styled expert, who glides majestically down from his ivory tower and condescends to tell the workmen in the shop how to do more effectively the task to which they have been devoting their lives. If what I say here has any relevance to the problems which the classroom teacher daily encounters, it arises not from any mysterious expertise but from two simple facts. First, in my field work with the Linguistic Atlas I have spent something like five thousand hours eliciting from socially classifiable speakers of American English the linguistic forms which they habitually use (and sometimes eliciting them against their will, or at least in spite of deeply ingrained social taboos), and in my editorial work about as much time classifying such forms according to regional and social patterns of distribution; and second, and perhaps more significantly for your purposes, I too have read a share of freshman themes, twenty thousand or more. Most of these themes, I freely confess, I have read in that state of blissful arrogance that comes from a traditional English major and a doctorate in literature, and from the traditional humanistic contempt for all who profess education and the social sciences; the rest I have read in the bewilderment of one striving to learn something new but guilt-ridden at the thought of having to abandon once-cherished knowledge and racked by the tensions between divergent forces in an academic environment where the aims of higher education have been far from clear even to the oldest and wisest hands. It is perhaps also true that some of the validity of these remarks derives in part from a realization of my own indifferent success as a teacher of composition, and from the consequent realization that this vocation is a complex one, not to be sneered at by the academic elite, a vocation demanding the mastery of a variety of skills and yielding to no panacea, however eloquently proclaimed. The most I will claim for a knowledge of dialectology is that it can reinforce other skills and permit their more effective use; it certainly cannot supplant them.

It is now fashionable to repeat the truism that writing well demands practice in writing, a great many assignments carefully and intelligently read by a sensitive but hard-boiled instructor.[2] Such a mastery through practice is most easily achieved if the students come from an upper-middle-class environment in a community of a relatively homogenous if complex culture, and have parents who are interested in the skillful use of words and who provide home libraries well stocked with models of good writing. In such an environment, with recruits from the less privileged groups kept at a minimum, the social norms are so evident that they alone can do much of the basic teaching. But today, despite the one-class suburb, the pressures of increasing industrialization and urbanization, of lengthening school attendance, and of the elimination of many instruments of cultural segregation, make such a homogenous and sterilized environment ever harder to find, even if it were desirable. The teacher of English composition[3] must deal with students whose homes show a wide range of economic and social positions, racial and religious and linguistic backgrounds, reading habits, and degrees of experience with writing as a vehicle of social communication. To deal with this complex situation the teacher needs to understand the varieties of social experience reflected in varieties of linguistic behavior; and to achieve this understanding he needs an appreciation of the achievements and potentialities of dialectology,[4] the branch of linguistics that deals systematically with variations in linguistic practice within a given speech community.

It has often been said that language is the characteristic that taxonomically most clearly differentiates man from all other forms of life.[5] We may add a corollary: that dialectology is that branch of linguistics that most clearly touches the relationships between human beings in their complex social behavior. The study of dialect differences, in what may be considered the American sense of the term *dialect* -- that is, a variety of a language, regional or social or both, set off from all other varieties of that language by a complex of features of pronunciation, grammar, and vocabulary -- has implications for an understanding of regional cultures, of social cleavages, and even of psychological adjustments within and without the bounds of what is conventionally adjudged as normal. Dialectology does not conflict with descriptive linguistics, of any shade of churchmanship, or with the newer generative grammar; rather, it seeks to test, to elucidate, to exemplify and to specify contrasts in structure or in permissable transformations. If sometimes the dialectologist seems fiercely opposed to theories widely held at the moment, this apparent opposition springs only from the fact that a knowledge of many regional and social varieties of a language will provide the critical data for putting a generalization to the test so that the generalization is either laid aside or restated to take care of the newly presented evidence.

We must concede that the dialectology of American English is far from complete. Even with the limited questionnaire of the Linguistic Atlas, and with its selective sampling of communities and informants, there is recorded evidence from only about three-fourths of the United States, and of this, only one regional survey, that for New England, has so far been published. Even in phonological materials, where the Atlas provides the greatest amount of evidence, there are areas of uncertainty.[6] Inflectional morphology is touched on only selectively, with some of the most interesting verb forms not yet investigated;[7] derivational morphology, syntax, and the suprasegmentals -- stress, pitch and pause -- are hardly touched. In fact, for syntax and suprasegmentals we have not even worked out satisfactory techniques for investigation. Dialectology demands comparable data, with consistent frames in which the data may be spontaneously elicited; yet the rigorous direct eliciting of syntactic and suprasegmental evidence through rigidly defined frames may produce unnatural responses, such as the displacement of stress or the use of phrase-final sequences of pitches that would never occur in normal conversation. The tape recorder has not solved these problems: like all instruments, even the most elaborately designed computer, a recording device cannot of itself elicit information, but can only receive and preserve what the investigator has obtained in the particular bio-social environment. In another domain of criticism, the dialectologist has rarely concerned himself with the speech of the heavily urbanized areas in which most Americans now live. I have spoken primarily of the Linguistic Atlas, but similar comments can be made about other projects. For example, the archives of C. K. Thomas contain massive quantities of evidence, from all parts of the United States, on the low-back vowels, such as those in *horrible Florida oranges* or *borrow tomorrow's sorrow*, but have less to say about other phonological problems and nothing about grammar or vocabulary.[8]

But a concession that something has not yet been done is not an assertion that it cannot be done. If differences exist or can be postulated, techniques can be found for measuring them. Even in the most delicate area of comparison, that of the suprasegmentals, linguists and psychiatrists and cultural anthropologists have been profitably pooling their experience and techniques. This collaboration is already beginning to show how psychic distress is reflected, in its grosser manifestations, in distortions of vowels and consonants, and even in minor or incipient disturbances, in abnormal juncture phenomena and in deviant distributions of vocal gestures and qualifiers such as drawl, clipping, rasp, nasality, or mellifluousness.[9] For these problems see Pittenger, Hockett and Danehy 1960 and McQuown 1971.[10]

For American pronunciation, at least in the most populous regions, we have some reliable statements on the structure of phonemic systems, on the nature and distribution of the phonic variations of the phoneme, and on the incidence of particular phonemic entities in particular words (Kurath and R. McDavid 1961). We even know something about the distribution of certain consonant clusters, such as initial /tʃ-,dʒ-,nʃ-,stʃ-/ in *tube*, *due*, *new*, and *student*, or final /-sts/ in *posts*, *fists*, *costs*, with the reasonable probability of extrapolating to other forms in which such clusters may occur. We know a great deal about many details of verb inflection (Atwood 1953a, V. McDavid 1956), including problems of concord and negation, and about a few syntactic problems such as the structure of relative clauses. What is more, for wide areas of the United States, we have recorded not only the regional but the social distribution of variants, so that (at least for the colloquial style) we can make more accurate statements than ever before about what is standard everywhere (e.g., *like* as a conjunction), what is standard in limited areas (e.g., *dove* as the past tense of *dive*), what is generally nonstandard (e.g., *clumb* for *climbed*), and what is restricted to the folk speech of cultural backwaters (e.g., *gwine* for *going*). Such information is not always welcome: even the professional journal of American scientists has recently decried the laxity of standards in the latest edition of our largest-scale dictionary. But the principle of finding out what occurs in what environments, and indicating it, is still a valid one for linguistics, as for any other science, even though the findings may not please our personal tastes.

For urbanized areas, we have many excellent investigations: for New York City Frank 1949, Hubbell 1950, Labov 1966; for San Francisco De Camp 1958-59; for Chicago Pederson 1965a, L. Davis 1971, Herndobler 1977; for San Antonio Sawyer 1957; for Detroit Wolfram 1969; for Louisville Howren 1958; for Akron Udell 1966; for

Savannah Hopkins 1975; for Augusta, Georgia, Miller 1978. The urban Negro has been investigated in Memphis (Williamson 1968), to a less degree in New Orleans and Washington, and there is a fundamental work on isolated rural Negro speech (which underlies the dialect patterns of our black ghettos) in Lorenzo Turner's *Africanisms in the Gullah Dialect* (1949). As Haugen 1956 shows, we have begun to understand the problems of bilingualism, through studies of such groups as those of Norwegian, German, Portugese, Spanish, Greek, and Czech ancestry. There are even some perceptive studies of the ways authors may use dialect materials for literary effect (Ives 1950a,b, Downer 1958).

How this material may be used by the classroom teacher will differ from situation to situation. Only a few of the applications can be presented here. But they may be summed up under the rubric that student linguistic behavior differing from the socially approved dialect of the teacher's community may be diagnosed not in terms of degeneration from a universal grammatical standard but in terms of the student's linguistic and social background. Consequently, the measures directed toward altering those practices may be presented, not in terms of correctness but in terms of the economic and social desires which appear to motivate most people in our culture.

The student from a German-speaking community may sometimes carry over into English composition the German habit of inserting a participial or prepositional phrase between determiner and noun. The student of Eastern European background may have grave difficulties with the use of the English definite article. The American Negro, especially one recently arrived from the South or reared in a black ghetto, may not use in his speech the conventional inflectional suffixes on nouns or verbs, so that he may omit them in writing where they belong or write them in the wrong places.[11] The rural Louisianian from the Cajun country, whether or not he is a native speaker of French, may have the same problem.

Even where there is no foreign-language background in the home, the student's linguistic behavior may include forms which strike the teacher as aberrant. Even an educated Southerner may use such combinations of auxiliaries as *might could*, *used to could* or *ought to could*, reflecting the familiar cultivated usage of his own region. He may even forget to write such consonant sequences as *-sts*, which do not normally occur in his speech. The Northerner, on the other hand, may say *sick to the stomach* or *hadn't ought*, or speak of his receding /gumz/, rhyming with *dooms*, as a former president of the University of Michigan did -- to the horror of the half-educated dental technician who

cleaned his teeth. The eastern Kentuckian may convert *used to* into an adverb, as previous generations converted *maybe*, and transfer it to the beginning of the sentence, as in "*Used to,* everybody around here would bake their own bread." The student who lacks the phonemic contrasts which I have between *horse* and *hoarse*, between *former* and *farmer*, between *do* and *due*, and between *cot* and *caught*, may have spelling problems with which his classmates are unconcerned. The student with a system of stress and pitch sequences different from those of the instructor will probably have his peculiar problems of word division and punctuation, or of avoiding linguistic sequences which are clear as he says them but ambiguous as he writes them. For such students the remedy is not to decry their native dialect or to attempt to alienate them from their habitual linguistic behavior, but to recognize that in their situations the problem of fit between speech and writing, never a simple matter for any speaker of English, has special complications which are best attacked in terms of the student's own desire to communicate to the widest possible audience.

Since the composition teacher, whether he likes the role or not, usually has more intimate association with the student, and consequently a deeper insight into the student's personality than the teachers of other academic subjects, or even the professional administrative advisers, a familiarity with the range of normality within various regional and social dialects may help him in dealing with psychological problems. Occasionally this knowledge may enable the teacher to refer the student to professional treatment before the problem becomes too complicated; more often, it may enable him to understand that what is different for the majority of the class may be normal for the subculture from which the student comes -- and is thus to be treated as a pedagogical problem, not as a psychiatric one.

But perhaps the most important is the broader knowledge that a familiarity with dialectology may offer both student and teacher, in terms of the relationships between linguistic practices and social affiliations. This knowledge will not obstruct the mastery of the socially approved dialect that every student must achieve if he is to fulfill the traditional American dream of participating more fully in the blessings of our society than his father did; indeed, a knowledge of dialectology should further this mastery, by providing a more accurate description of the socially approved dialect, and of its relation to other dialects. And beyond this, a familiarity with the principles and findings of dialectology may yield an enriched understanding of the complex cultural heritage we Americans all enjoy, may demonstrate in dramatic fashion that one may be different without being inferior, and thus lead -- from simple curiosity through a more sophisticated understanding of language -- to a deeper appreciation of the complexity and potentiality of this interesting animal called man, for whom language is the most peculiar attribute.

NOTES

[1] This paper was presented originally at the NCTE Annual Meeting, in Philadelphia, November 1961.

[2] Few schools, at any level, have been as intelligent and courageous (as well as humane) as the University of Michigan in limiting the number of composition sections per teacher and the number of students per section, so as to permit effective teaching.

[3] Here, as throughout, composition is emphasized because it is the most important task of the classroom English teacher and the touchstone by which the effectiveness of an English department is most commonly evaluated. But the same problems face teachers of reading, from the elementary stages through advanced criticism of literature.

[4] The development of this discipline is treated in Pop 1950; the methods employed in the American Atlas are presented in Kurath *et al.* 1939. An overview of American dialects is found in Chapter IX of Francis 1958.

[5] This concept originated with John Kepke, Brooklyn, N.Y., about 1948, but to my knowledge has never before been attributed to him in print.

[6] As Jules Gilliéron, director of the *Atlas linguistique de la France*, once put it, the perfect questionnaire can be devised only after all of the evidence has been recorded and analyzed. For instance, some speakers of American English have one kind of /l/ in the proper name *Billy*, another in *billy* 'policeman's club.' New contrasts such as this are always appearing, or being discovered, and it is impossible to anticipate them.

[7] The lists included in Chapter IX, Section 2 ("The Verb") of Mencken 1936 are far longer than those in any American regional survey.

[8] Thomas 1947 contains the text he uses for eliciting evidence and refers to his previous studies.

[9] The systematic investigation of such features was first proposed by Henry Lee Smith, Jr.; it has since been essayed by many other linguists, notably Charles F. Hockett and Norman A. McQuown.

[10] Meanwhile, cooperation in the clinical situation has begun, notably at Eastern Pennsylvania Psychiatric Institute, Philadelphia; during a visiting consultantship it became apparent how a disturbed son could use nonstandard pronunciations to express his resentment toward a socially pretentious mother, and how the mother's social insecurity was betrayed by her use, during excitement, of vocalizations characteristic of the class from which she had come rather than of the class to which she was attempting to belong.

[11] If one may intrude on territory shunned by angelic feet, it seems logical that those concerned over the imperfect participation of minorities in our culture should urge a thorough study of the linguistic features by which a given minority is stigmatized in the eyes of the ignorant majority. But the self-proclaimed fuglemen and haruspices of minorities have often prevented the making of such studies or their publication when made.

Dialect associations of phonemes and graphemes may vary strikingly from one part of the culture to another. English patterns of phonemic-graphemic correspondences involve several layers of cultural convention, and some of the practices of some subcultural subdialects may be sharply at variance with the normal practices of a speaker. These complexities of association make it difficult for someone not only to spell a word he normally confines to the spoken informal style, but to pronounce a word which he is accustomed to meeting only in print. And if the words of the last group are frequently mispronounced in oral reading, there is a reasonable supposition that they will be as frequently misapprehended in silent reading. This supposition, like many others, needs to be tested, but pending disproof I shall continue to assert it.

More important than this, and amusing examples may be drawn from anyone's recollections,[1] is the basic problem: to what extent do dialect differences in American English complicate the task of teaching in American schools the reading of matter written or printed in English? I shall here use *reading* in its widest sense, to include not only simple literacy but the skill -- the art, in fact -- of understanding materials of increasing complication, whether scientific or aesthetic in their essential bent.

Here we have to ask ourselves a few questions, some of which, like jesting Pilates, we cannot expect to have adequately answered in this life: 1) What is the process of learning to read, in linguistic and sociolinguistic terms? 2) What is dialectology? 3) What is the general dialectal situation in American English? 4) How does this situation affect the problem of the classroom teacher, as a teacher of reading? 5) How much do we know about various kinds of dialect differences in American English? How much more can we hope to know? 6) How do these differences, as we know them, affect the problem of the classroom teacher of reading in the American dialectal situation?

What is the process of learning to read, in linguistic and sociolinguistic terms? On this question I gladly yield to the greater expertise of the professionals. There are many forces converging to a point when a teacher guides a student into the ability to understand the graphic representation of the language the student can already manipulate orally and understand aurally. But even here a few propositions can be restated.

A reading program, in any language, at any stage in a student's career, is likely to be effective in proportion to its use of the language habits that the student has acquired in speaking.

All children by the age of six use extremely complicated syntactic patterns; furthermore, children's vocabularies are frequently underestimated, rarely overestimated.

Our culture demands a high degree of reading skill of anyone who hopes to participate adequately in its benefits; but conversely, more than any other culture ever known, it provides frequent opportunities for children to develop at an early age associations between the language and its graphic representation. It is an ironic fact that the culturally most deprived groups actually make the greatest use of the entertainment medium that provides the greatest opportunities for developing these associations -- television.

All instructional programs which are concerned with developing skills might learn from the intensive language programs of World War II and develop drill materials based on functional situations and substitutions in patterns. Admittedly limited in my knowledge of the subculture of professional teaching of reading, I find none of the so-called basal readers that has yet done this.

What is dialectology? Dialectology is the study of language differences within a speech community, with a *dialect* simply defined as a variety of a language, generally mutually intelligible with other varieties of that language, but set off from them by a unique complex of features of pronunciation, grammar and vocabulary. Dialect, thus used, is not a derogatory term but a descriptive one; it is equally applicable to the Gullah of Edisto Island (locally /edɪsto ɔɪlənt/) and to the quaint and curious subspecies of cultivated Eastern New England speech employed by the senators from Massachusetts. These differences are often apprehended intuitively or informally, but they can always be classified objectively provided comparable data have been elicited. The methods of eliciting such data and the techniques of classification have been described on many occasions: the handbooks of the linguistic atlases of Italy (Jaberg and Jud 1928-40) and of New England (Kurath *et al.* 1939-43) present rather detailed accounts of methods and procedures.

What is the general dialectal situation in American English? Dialects in American English are less sharply set off from each other than those in British English or in any of the better known languages of Western Europe. With few exceptions, an American from one region can understand one from another region without difficulty. The more recently a part of the country has been settled, the less sharp are the dialect differences; in the Rocky Mountain and Pacific Coast states there are no differences as great as those between Boston, New York, and Albany.

Second, there is no single regional variety of speech that has established itself as prestigious, and therefore to be imitated more than all others. In Italy the educated speech of Florence has been preferred since the fourteenth century; in France the French of Paris; in England, the upper-class speech of London, now half embalmed in the guise of Received Pronunciation. But in the United States the educated speech of Boston, New York, Atlanta, Chicago, San Francisco or Seattle stands on a par with that of Richmond or Charleston or St. Louis or any other cultural center. The time is largely past when a teacher attempts to impose on his students a dialect from another region.

Third, there is extreme mobility, both regional and social, epitomized by the fact that the great-grandson of an Irish common laborer was president from 1961 to 1963, and was succeeded by the son of a Southern marginal farmer. The son of an Italian immigrant is Secretary of Health, Education and Welfare, and the rolls of Congress are studded with those whose ancestors were the humblest of people, who rose by their own merits. And the records of internal migration are at least as complex, as any linguistic geographer can tell us. The movements of Daniel Boone from Virginia to North Carolina to Kentucky and finally to Missouri typify the search of Americans for new frontiers, physical or economic. The migrations of children of servicemen or Methodist ministers have always been proverbial; today the children of corporation executives and junior executives are also likely to change schools every few years. And teachers themselves, from all over the nation, are drawn westward by California gold, or to the large metropolitan areas by higher salaries and pensions and better working conditions. The typical kindergarten or first-grade classroom today is likely to show a wide range of regional or social dialects, or both.

How does the dialectal situation affect the teacher of reading? This dialectal situation means that the teacher must accept a multi-valued conception of standard English, with a consequent variety of phonemic-graphemic associations. He must also be ready to face the problem of introducing to reading materials in the standard language children for whom standard English is an alien idiom and the dominant culture an unknown culture.

How much do we know about various kinds of dialect differences? Fortunately, we have at our disposal a large body of evidence on regional and social differences within American English. Such broad-gauge studies as the Linguistic Atlas are largely unpublished as yet, but several significant derivative books and monographs and a spate of articles have appeared. Other more specialized studies, such as C. K. Thomas's investigations of the low-back vowels before /-r/, have given valuable information on particular problems. Several specific communities have been investigated, with emphasis on social differences in dialect; especially notable are the study of New York's Lower East Side by William Labov (1966) and that of metropolitan Chicago by Lee Pederson (1965a). Viewed in terms of linguistic phenomena, we have the following kinds of information:

1. A delineation of most of the significant dialect areas east of the Mississippi, and of those in several states farther westward.

2. As far as segmental phonemes are concerned, rather detailed information on differences in the phonemic systems of these dialects, on the incidence of the phonemes in particular words, and on the phonetic qualities of the phonemes.

3. Rather good sampling of variations in verb forms; less adequate sampling of other matters of inflection and of most matters of syntax.

4. Rather detailed information on representative selections of the folk vocabulary of older America, particularly of the folk vocabulary of rural areas; less adequate information about regional and social differences in the lexicon of more recent aspects of culture, especially of the characteristic vocabulary of urban areas. Enough information, in any case, to permit tentative generalizations about the regional differences in culture, somewhat more accurate than the impressionistic feelings we all have. Certainly enough to realize the complexity of urban culture, where chitterlings and bagels may be sold in the same store, and the daughter of two white Anglo-Saxon Protestants (WASPs, familiarly) may come home from kindergarten talking of dreidels.

5. Very little about regional or social variation in the suprasegmentals: stress, intonation, transitions, and terminals. Almost all the evidence on such variations is to be found in nontechnical observations, such as Mencken's summary of the intonation patterns of English in the Pennsylvania German areas (1948:204). Exceptions to this generality are a few

pages in Pike's *Intonation of American English* (1945) and such incidental comments that in such words as *nonsense* James Sledd and I, like many Middle Westerners, have the sequence /ˊ+ˆ/, but the phonetic qualities of our stress phonemes are such that to Middle Westerners like Martin Joos we seem to be saying /ˊ|ˊ/. The whole range of regional and social variation in these complex phenomena needs detailed investigation.

The same observation can be made about the dialectology of paralanguage and kinesics; again, as with the dialectology of suprasegmentals, there has been no systematic research, but a number of shrewd intuitive guesses. For these fields, as with the suprasegmentals, we can all concede that the phenomena have only recently been considered systematically structured as a part of human communication, so that the techniques of dialectal investigation would take some time to develop. However, our objective appreciation of the delay in no way mitigates the urgency of the investigation, nor lessens our appreciation of such pioneering work as has been conducted by Basil Bernstein at the University of London or by Rufus Baehr at the University of Chicago (1964), limited as their conclusions may be.

6. Again, there is little systematic evidence available about regional and social differences in children's speech, or differences in the speech of equivalent social groups in the same region but residing in cities, suburbs, small towns, and rural communities. This in no way detracts from the value of Strickland's magnificent study (1962), or of the Loban study at California (1963), or of the work just beginning on the Chicago South Side. It simply recognizes the need to learn far more than we have yet learned. [Howard Dunlap's Atlanta study (1974) is an important recent work.]

How do these differences affect the teacher of reading? The implications of this current state of our knowledge of American dialects for the practical work of teaching reading will demand the cooperation of several kinds of scholars and the devotion of skilled teachers. What follows represents the thinking of one person who feels that it is important to put the resources of dialectology, regional and social, at the service of society, and who is willing both to offer his mite and to listen to suggestions as to how that mite can be most profitably invested. Some observations follow.

Whatever the disadvantages of our current system of writing down English, we are not likely to find a better one generally adopted. We must assume that students in our schools are going to have to use the conventional English alphabet when they read. While we should not discourage the experimental use of such devices as the Pitman Augmented Alphabet, we must remember that they are strictly interim devices, and their use must allow for a systematic phasing out, and the mastering of the conventional system. Furthermore, any such interim device must be tested in terms of its adequacy in representing the units of the sound system that contrast in the various standard dialects of American English.

The regional differences in children's speech are probably diminishing, though undoubtedly there are differences in experience that might be considered in any program. On the other side of the coin, however, television now brings a wide assortment of vicarious experiences to most children in most areas; one might think in terms of a reading program that would enable the children to investigate more widely on their own the worlds of Robin Hood, the cowboys, the spacemen -- or the wide range of materials offered by Garfield Goose -- when the television is being repaired or repossessed.

Social differences present a more complicated problem. Under the older demographic pattern, most phonological and lexical details were shared throughout a community, and the social differences were largely matters of grammar -- differences in particular morphological or syntactic features (e.g., *seed* vs. *saw*, *all to once* vs. *all at once*). It was assumed that newer immigrant would have peculiarities of speech, but that assimilation to the normal patterns of their communities would gradually take place; and by and large this expectation has been fulfilled, as one may observe from listening to any presidential news conference. However, in recent years the prevailing pattern in American cities has been altered to something once restricted to the rural areas of the Southeast, and what had been the ideal of a humanistically oriented plantation culture modeling itself on its interpretations of the classical societies is now fulfilled as the nightmare of a technologically determined urban and suburban civilization, where a high degree of literacy is essential for any true participation in the benefits of society. The mudsill of happy slaves on which Southern apologists erected their myth of an Aristotelian-oriented society has now become a frustrated and properly resentful, low-skilled and often unemployable proletariat, potentially threatening the stability of urban society. Set off by skin color, by ignorance of the values of the dominant culture, and by a dialectal cleavage which contrasts the pronunciation, grammar, and vocabulary of Southeastern folk speech and North-Central common and cultivated speech, they find integrated schools, fair employment, and open occupancy a cruel mockery, as working-class whites, themselves anthropologically unsophisticated, join the *sauve qui peut* in search of a suburban haven.

The usual teacher, compulsively in pursuit of middle-class norms, has no conception of the environment of deprivation, exploitation, frustration, and violence in which the lower-class urban Negroes live. The normal curiosity of children about the world is inhibited by properly fearful parents; absence of mothers means the lack of anyone for the children to talk to; books are nonexistent; and in a cacophonous world the television -- potentially a powerful instrument for acculturation -- becomes just another source of background noise.

The educational advancement of this new urban group -- which means basically the improvement of their ability to read -- constitutes the greatest challenge to American education. It is likely that teaching some form of standard English as a second language will be necessary; and it might be easier to start this second language in the kindergartens or earlier, and use this as the vehicle of reading, and hence of introduction to the values of the dominant culture.

Paralanguage and kinesics are largely cued into reading materials by lexical devices, e.g., such verbs as *sauntered*, *gesticulated*, *simpered*, and *whined*. Some of this comes into oral reading in the early grades; relating to it is important for silent reading in the advanced grades and in college, to say nothing of later life. Whether these cues can be grasped informally -- as is the usual procedure today -- or should be formally indicated is something that needs exploration. Where regional and social differences occur, some accounting may be necessary, but we need to discover those differences first.

Suprasegmentals, like segmentals, are not adequately represented by the conventional writing system, but have been conventionalized over some four centuries by generations of editors and printers. Where regional and social differences occur -- especially in the same classroom -- so that the same gross phonetics may signal different meanings or different gross phonetics signal the same meaning, one may hope that in the future teachers will be sophisticated enough to recognize what is going on and to explain the differences to the student (and one is unrealistic if he thinks that children in the early grades cannot detect such differences and wonder about them). In most cases, it is unlikely that there will be serious differences in the positions of the terminals (Trager and Smith's single-bar, double-bar, double-cross [1951]), and there seems to be no reason for failing to order line breaks in elementary reading materials according to the positions of the terminals. (This, I am told by some experienced teachers of reading, is frowned upon, as interfering with the development of a wide eye-span; but what profiteth a man to span whole lines at a glance and miss the structural cues to meaning? It would seem that there is really no basic conflict, but only a question of ordering materials.)

The problems of general differences in the regional and social vocabularies have been approached in the analysis of the potential regional and social differences in children's speech. But there will always be a problem of relating visual signal and speech signal in words that are associated primarily with either the spoken or written side of the language. A legendary episode in my childhood concerns a time in 1914 when I brought in the evening paper and remarked from the headline "/dʒepɨn/ (Japan) enters the war" (less heinous in my community perhaps than elsewhere, since a local tobacconist was named Gapen /gepɨn/). And I still recall my first attempts to render *negotiations* and *cooperate* (respectively /nɨgətèʃənz/ and /kúpərèt/), or a rather good second-grader's /vɛləkəsi/ and /mæŋgi/ for *velocity* and *mangy*. Conversely, familiar childhood words like *fice* or *rinktums* or *larrows* (to pull a few out of my own recollection) may lack an established orthographic form altogether. Because a dialect is associated with some kind of subculture, there may be differences in the most feasible words to introduce in a given set of reading materials.

In the early grades, it would seem that the grammatical problems, generally social rather than regional, can be handled as matters of selection, careful allocation to context, and pattern drill. The forms *saw* and *seen* are both a part of the language experience of every American child; the problem is to make sure that he regularly selects the forms *I saw* and *I have seen*. This may be related to the problem of teaching the standard usage as a second language, and of associating all reading materials with this usage. Problems like associating the /-s,-z,-əz/ allomorphs with the third singular present indicative, where the home dialect has /φ/, must certainly be handled in this fashion.

Perhaps the most important -- and certainly the most systematized -- impact of dialectology on the teaching of reading will come in the area of phonemic-graphemic associations in the segmentals. (Several scholars, notably Charles F. Hockett of Cornell, are investigating the relative frequency of certain kinds of phonemic-graphemic associations.)

There are two problems to be considered: 1) structural differences, presence or absence of such contrasts as *do/dew*, *cot/caught*, *morning/mourning*, *have/halve*; 2) differences in the incidence of phonemes, as found in the variant pronunciations of *coop*, *on*, *fog*. These must be related to the necessity of introducing at the earliest possible moment such forms as *a*, *the*, and the like, the desirability of proceeding from grosser to finer graphic distinctions, and the distribution of the learning load so that too many sound-symbol associations are not thrust upon the student at once. (Leonard Bloomfield, C. C. Fries, and other linguists have recognized the importance of getting into the program, as early as possible, the high-frequency function words.) And somehow, not too late, the student must be conditioned to the morphographic side of the English orthographic system, so that he can assoicate *history* and *historical* and so on.

A complex dialectal problem develops when there is another language in use at home, whether Acadian French, Milwaukee German, Yiddish, or Puerto Rican Spanish. This is often further complicated when the students or the parents first encounter English of a nonstandard type. However, these are best treated here as differences in degree and not in kind.

A student of dialectology is not, *per se*, an authority on all problems of reading, or necessarily on any of them. His role is, rather, that of a consultant, to collaborate with the others involved in this most important problem in American education -- to be a devil's advocate if necessary -- by attempting to anticipate some of the problems teachers and students may have in using materials in a different cultural situation from that for which they were originally designed.

NOTES

[1] Humorous anecdotes can be documented from such sources as, for example, Mayor Collins of Boston who, on meeting the aristocratic Senator Hoare at a social gathering, asked, "And how is Mrs. W?"

The problem of producing better writers, from the humblest level up, is the most important problem facing English departments today; in fact, it is bigger than English departments, in ways I hope to indicate later, and it is the operation by which the effectiveness of English departments is most commonly judged.

The successful teaching of composition is an art, not a science -- though we hope that science will help. In this way it is analogous to medicine, where the principal obligation of the practitioner is also to the patient. Research, experiment, and controlled tests are all required before a scientific discovery may be incorporated in the healing arts. And in the end the effectiveness of any new treatment will depend on the successful interaction of the patient and the clinician, and on the willingness of the clinician to choose eclectically from all the schemes that promise to help, according to the situation and the condition of the patient.

In both the practice of medicine and the teaching of composition the clinician must be like the councilor at Edwin's court -- willing to draw on anything that promises to throw a little light into our ignorance, but wary of letting innovation successful in one part of the treatment ossify into prescribed ritual for the entire process.

The fact that a 'traditional' program exists is itself argument that a better program is possible, and the more eloquently the tradition is defended the more convincing the argument that change will lead to improvement. Contrariwise, the more loudly a new panacea is proclaimed, and the sharper the dichotomy its adherents would set up between it and all that went before, the more likely it is simply another gadget, destined to be thrown on the junk pile as soon as the new model rolls off the academic assembly lines.

In the hope that we can achieve a multi-partisan composition policy centered on the students' needs, I should like to describe a general framework in which such a policy must operate. I must disclaim any expertise in running a composition program. I never had any administrative authority over one, and only indifferent success in the eight or ten disparate programs in which I taught up to June 1957. But in the swamps of South Carolina, the bayous of southern Louisiana, the Tennessee Valley, the hills of West Virginia, and the asphalt jungles of Cleveland I have met a wide spectrum of academic pathology in freshman composition sections; and along with my colleagues and students I have helped investigate regional and social differences in many parts of the English-speaking New World. Such anthropological experience may be relevant. I also qualify as an 'authority' -- or, did -- as a freshman English student who in his previous schooling and in his home and community had not learned to write satisfactory standard English. That I did learn is indication that freshman English can be effective, if the teacher is good and the assignments are numerous enough.

From my experience one can derive little comfort for the tub-thumpers for any school of linguistics. A. T. O'Dell, my teacher, knew what linguistics was available to the composition teacher of 1929; yet he never introduced it systematically or even overtly into the classroom, but only where a particular composition called for it. One can add, however, that there is also little comfort in my experience for the handbook salesman. We bought a handbook, as the college required, but never opened it. Nor is there much in my own experience to hearten those who would make of the freshman course and the general humanities offerings a farm system for developing graduate students in literary criticism. Our models for writing were largely essays, rarely devoted to aesthetic topics (an exception is Stephen Leacock's "Homer and Humbug," which I still quote joyously on occasion), but principally to social and political problems; and when we did get into the short story, in the last quarter, we approached our models seldom as style, often as structure, and most often for new ideas designed to awaken culturally and intellectually deprived young males of white Protestant Anglo-Saxon nativistic persuasion. In short, it was a course in composition and nothing else, with the assumption that the first need of the student was to learn to think on his own. It was probably the most shattering and beneficent intellectual experience I have ever had; and I have never ceased to thank the caprice of circumstance that led me into that particular section at that particular time.

But to return to our issue. Let us examine the problem of teaching English composition today, not only from the point of view of various linguists, but from that of the cultural anthropologists (to whose ranks all linguists belong in some degree

or other), and from that of the historian
of American society. The college composition class of today *is* different from that
of an earlier time. The reasons for the
differences are many, and they are the inevitable result of three interrelated
threads in our tradition.

First of all is the thread of industrialization, starting from the time when the
Puritans, a town-centered group, put their
intelligence to work on the conquest of
the wilderness by devising such simple but
revolutionary tools as the American ax-
handle. Somewhat later, Eli Whitney, most
notorious for devising the cotton gin and
thereby preserving chattel slavery two unnecessary generations, founded the assembly line by developing a system of inter-
chageable parts. In large-scale competitive industry there is little room for going by native intuition; there is every
need for devising more efficient machinery
that requires more highly skilled operatives. The strong backs and weak brains
of primordial Gary are happily obsolete;
we pour more steel with fewer men, but
those few must be able to read more intricate sets of directions. And we can expect this trend to continue, whether we
like automation or not.

With industrialization comes urbanization, with its sub- and ex- varieties.
People live in larger communities, with
more intricate rules governing their interactions. But lest we fall prey to the
Wordsworthian syndrome, we should remember
that *civil*, *polite*, and *urbane* generally
have more favorable connotations than *pa-
gan*, *rustic*, *heathen*, and *boorish*. The
economic opportunities of the city life
provide increased leisure and means for
indulging in education, and the desire to
participate more fully in those economic
opportunities provides greater incentives
to obtain education. Urban colleges and
universities have grown even faster than
the populations of urban areas, and their
quality has more than kept pace.

Here we are led to our third thread --
the American commitment to the greatest
possible amount of education for the
greatest number, which C. P. Snow described as the most generous the world has
ever known. Beginning with the Northwest
Ordinance of 1787, this commitment has
grown in scope and intensity, if with uneven participation of regions and social
groups and with uneven standards of the
product. We could perhaps devise a far
more rational system if we had the chance,
but we won't have it. What with humane
reasoning and the fears among the craft
unions, our schools must keep their inmates for a larger portion of their lives;
what with new philosophies of education,
which it is certainly not my business to
discuss in detail, and with the demand for
a high-school diploma as a secular equivalent of a confirmation certificate, stu-

dents are no longer flunked as they once
were, but sooner or later will get some
sort of diploma from some sort of high
school. And with growing affluence, and
the increasing emphasis on the affluent
value of a college diploma, larger numbers
of those who might have been content with
less are looking for some sort of college
that will take them in. Today any high-
school graduate can find some sort of college that will accept him and, if he is
reasonably diligent, award him some sort
of baccalaureate. As a graduate of a
small college, I cannot label this as necessarily a bad thing. But it complicates
the task of the curriculum planners, and
nowhere more than in English.

In English departments, we boast justi-
fiably of our role as continuing the
classical tradition -- a tradition re-
shaped by the Puritan demand for an educated ministry and by the professional
scholarship of nineteenth-century Germany.
This tradition was designed for an elite,
not for the larger groups that have been
drawn towards our colleges by the American
way of industrialization, urbanization,
and mass education. It was still less designed for the partially assimilated
groups from outside the center of our culture who are just beginning to enter colleges in large numbers -- immigrants from
Southern and Eastern Europe; Louisiana
Cajuns, Puerto Ricans, and other Latin
Americans; and most notably those American Negroes who are the product of generations of enforced illiteracy and deprivation. As the uneasy stirrings of our con-
sciences are strengthened both by court
decisions and by the power of these groups
to exercise disciplinary action at the
ballot box, we can expect that more of
their representatives will appear in college classrooms, perhaps to our ultimate
enrichment but certainly to the present
augmentation of our burdens.

The truth of the proposition is thus
manifest: as we enlarge our college enrollments, we will entrap a larger proportion of those fitted by nature and experience to benefit from the kind of education
English departments prefer to administer,
but those will become a decreasing proportion of the college population. We are
facing nothing new, only the acceleration
of old trends. This in no way means a necessary decline in education, any more
than the wider dissemination of printed
trash among those whose parents read nothing means a necessary decline in literary standards. But it means that we have
a different clientele from our old one,
and need to adjust our practices accord-
ingly.

The impossibility of the task is further
complicated by the fact that any solution
attempted at the college level comes after
ten to twelve years (or more) of classroom
experience. Like legislated planned

[165]

parenthood, what we might contrive would be more effective if we could make it a couple of generations retroactive. If, as seems to be the case, even the well-supported school systems of the great cities of America have not been able to come up with adequate preparation in language skills, we can't expect to work miracles overnight in the colleges. We can only try.

Perhaps the first thing to do is to recognize that most of the new clientele will have little taste for or interest in literary values. This does not mean that we should give them over to pap; it rather means that we should work harder to find material of quality -- however unfashionable in the current critical scene -- that somehow can be related to their interests and abilities. If we can seduce a small fraction into the habit of reading something better than their wont, if only into supplementing the *Chicago Tribune* with the *New York Times*, we can count ourselves lucky. In fact, the development of any habit of serious reading will be an achievement.

But if the new clientele are somewhat lacking in literary interest, they are desperately concerned with learning to write well enough to fulfill the demands of their potential jobs. Among the cash-valued assets of a college education is the ability to handle business correspondence, to describe laboratory procedures, to write reports (or Army field orders), to develop (or to abstract) technical manuals, to fill out accident forms. None of these assignments is likely to result in eternal prose; but students will be paid well for them in the outside world. We may say, if we wish, that these are not the business of college English departments; but these are what people increasingly go to college to learn -- and where English departments reject responsibility, they will be provided somewhere else in the organization.

What remains to be noted are the various subspecies of grammatical study that the principal types of culturally deprived freshmen in the colleges can expect to receive, and the kinds of fit between grammatical study and student that can be provided, at least in part.

First, there is a great deal of talk about so-called traditional grammar, as if it were a monolithic and well-established point of view. It is neither; what is commonly meant is the school grammar of the nineteenth and early twentieth centuries, later than some of the other types of grammatical study, and only partially supported by the actual writings of the prescriptive grammarians of the eighteenth. Such an elementary observation by linguists, but so likely to set off emotional explosions in the more naive classroom teacher, as the fact that English verbs

have and have always had only two tenses was a commonplace in the days of Lowth and Priestly. Since the school grammar approach is generally viewed as prelinguistic, it need not concern us here.

For practical purposes, we need pay about as little attention to the descriptive-historical school, which with the findings of Jones and Rask and Grimm and Bopp launched our traditions of historical and comparative grammar even before the ossification of the school grammarians. It is unfortunate that the excitement of the new historical perspectives drew off many of those who would normally have been drawn to English grammar and left the making of school texts to hacks, but there is no point in mourning.

The principal contribution of the historical grammarians is their emphasis on the fact of inevitable change, and their indications that many so-called corruptions -- say, the preterite *clumb* -- were actually more legitimate than their standard competitors -- or, like the conjunctive *like*, have always been a part of standard syntax. But the teacher rarely needs to draw on this legitimizing; he needs more often the corollary doctrine of usage -- that words, structures, affixes, and pronunciations must be judged according to who uses them in what situations in place or time and with what attitudes -- a far more complex matter than is appreciated in the simple popular assumptions on either side of the barbed wire. Here is where the dialectologist operates, both regionally and socially -- and I have several tons of material on American dialects to offer as evidence to the skeptic who visits the Atlas archives at the University of Chicago or the University of South Carolina.

We finally come to the descriptive-synchronic or structural linguists, with two major camps today, which we may call the descriptive analytic and the descriptive synthetic. The first seeks to show what are the constituents of larger structures; the second, how larger structures may be made out of smaller ones. Each of these camps has its various cubicles and cell-blocks. Despite the publicity given to special groups, none of these special groups has a monopoly on either approach. There could be no more disastrous mistake than to equate structural grammar with the teachings of Trager and Smith or generative grammar with those of Chomsky and his school. Trager and Smith represent only one group of American structuralists whose inspiration was Leonard Bloomfield; there are students of Bloomfield not wholeheartedly sympathetic to Smith and Trager, non-Bloomfieldian American structuralists, and structuralists from other lands like the Swiss Saussurians, the Prague school of Trubetzkoy, Jakobson and others, and some syncretists like the Americanized Czech

Paul Garvin; and the descriptive tradition goes back to the Sanskrit grammarians of 500 BC.

Among the generative groups -- besides the Chomskyans -- are the schools of Zellig Harris, of Sidney Lamb, of the Englishman Michael Halliday, and several circles in Russia largely unknown in this country. All share the desire of being able to produce larger structures from smaller ones, by a series of explicit procedures often misnamed 'rules'; in this aim they have more in common with the traditional rhetoricians than with grammarians as generally recognized, though the rhetoric may be of such a low order as the production of comprehensible English prose from a mechanical translation of a Russian essay on lunar topography. Some people, like Kenneth Pike and his tagmemic group, switch from analysis to synthesis at will.

We must consider what part of all this rapidly growing body of linguistic theory and technique can be of value to our students. To do this, it seems to me, we must direct our attention to two groups of students. The two kinds of students we will find in ever-larger numbers in college composition classes are the overtly different and the superficially assimilated. And it is likely that each will need a different selection from the growing body of linguistic knowledge.

The first group is the obvious cultural minority: the Spanish-Americans of Texas, the Cajuns, the in-migrants from the Southern mountains, the Puerto Ricans, and above all the Negroes. Each of these groups not only has a distinct way of speech that sets it off from the host population among which it is trying to find a way of life, but accompanies it by a series of easily identifiable social and even physical traits. The grammatical problems in these groups are often so gross that they must be approached, at first in any event, by techniques similar to those of good foreign-language teaching -- including contrastive analyses and pattern practices -- until a series of new linguistic habits becomes established for certain communication situations. Structural analyses -- like the patterns of subject-verb concord -- and dialectology systematically directed to the particular minority group in relationship to its host are going to be in demand here. These matters have been discussed in detail at various conferences (e.g., Shuy 1965) and in a continuing flood tide of publications.

The other type, the superficially assimilated, are harder to detect, and much harder to do anything with. At least the conspicuous minority have a ghetto to escape from, and can soon get a knowledge that such forms as *he do* and *she have holp* are going to tag them as belonging to the ghetto. But the superficially assimilated have already attained many of the creature comforts in such tight little islands of respectability as, say, Marynook. They have brick bungalows, well-kept if small lawns, late-model cars, a houseful of appliances and the appropriate mortgages and installment loans. But they are not accustomed to linguistic communication on an intellectual level; they have read little and written less; they may have little reading matter except a newspaper, a slick magazine or so, a Bible, some battered textbooks and perhaps a set of *Compton's* or the *World Book*. This, I confess, was my own problem despite some social and economic advantages not enjoyed by most of this group. Their themes are neat, relatively free of gross misspellings or grammatical errors, and hopelessly dull -- the inevitable C-. Here the generative approach may have something to offer, by way of a progression from simple to more complex sentences -- or, as Chomsky has sometimes put it, from kernel sentence to embedded clause. I do not know what other generative groups besides Pike's are specifically working on this problem, but here it seems is a fair testing ground for their theories -- always with the qualification that a determined and inspiring teacher can make the worst approach work, and that a dull and diffident one can bring disaster upon the best.

The problem is with us, inescapably; we might as well accept it as inevitable and see what we can do with it. For some aspects of the problem one linguistic approach may help; for others, some other. But we will be deceiving ourselves if we attempt to use a simple-minded set of linguistic gimmicks, of whatever school, in attempting to solve the most important problem of English departments, and indeed of American education.

The true worth of a scholar depends not only on his own performance and that of his students, but also on the influence he has exerted on his colleagues, both in his institution and elsewhere. This influence, however, is often difficult to assay, because it is seldom a matter of record. Bibliographies and academic biographies can be put together without much trouble; but few of us bother to make note of the occasions when a voluntary reading of a manuscript, a friendly conversation, or a chance comment directed our research and teaching into a new field. It is because my great indebtedness to Harold Thompson is of this kind that I am happy to participate in this volume dedicated to him.[1]

Our friendship goes back ten years, to the time when I was completing the field work in New York State for the *Linguistic Atlas of the Middle and South Atlantic States* (Kurath *et al.* 1979-). As I had learned in my investigations in the South, where I had friends or family connections in almost every community I studied, successful field work is impossible without the cooperation of local people who can help the field worker meet good informants and gain their confidence. Consequently, I was very happy to be introduced to the author of *Body, Boots and Britches* (1939), who could so ably acquaint me with the folk culture of New York State. Actually -- and such generosity and enthusiasm are characteristic of him -- he did much more. County by county, he sent me to personal friends among the local historians and antiquaries, who not only cooperated in the work but often entertained me; he helped me select the townships and villages that might be most typical of each county, and indicated some of the local topics and traditions that might unlock the lips of reluctant informants. In return, he asked only that I keep my eyes open for people who might also have something to say to his folklore students in their local investigations. So little onerous was this request that I not only enjoyed fulfilling it, but began keeping my eyes open for ways in which the distribution of dialect features might correspond to the distribution of other features in the folk culture, and to look forward to the time when interdisciplinary cooperation of linguists and folklorists might be developed in the United States to the enrichment of both studies and the education of the public.

The relationship of linguistics to folklore is very old and respectable, though many American structural linguists of the younger generation seem to lose sight of it in their desire to establish a rapport with cultural anthropology, statistics, psychiatry, communication theory, and symbolic logic. But the beginnings of linguistics and of folklore as serious disciplines go back to a common origin -- the seventeenth- and eighteenth-century assertion of the dignity of the popular cultures of Europe, especially of Northern Europe, against the dominant neoclassical tradition. This assertion had many facets: the rise of national states against the vestiges of the medieval dream of a universal church-state dominated by Emperor and Pope; an increased interest in the English common law, as legitimizing the aspirations of the people and their representatives in Parliament against the claims of royal divine right; the collection of Old English and Icelandic literary monuments; the Wordsworthian choice of humble and rustic life as the subject for serious literary expression; the descriptive grammatical study of the vernaculars on their own merits as opposed to the latinate tradition of normative grammar; and the dethronement of Greek and Latin from linguistic preeminence to the position of sister languages to early Germanic, Sanskrit, Albanian, and Balto-Slavic. The interrelationships of these interests and their affiliations with the Romantic Movement are dramatically brought home when one recollects that Jakob Grimm, who summarized systematically the developments of the Indo-European consonant system in the various languages of that family, was one of the brothers who published the collections of *Kinder- und Hausmärchen*.

From the Grimms' time to the present, the mutual interest of linguistics and folklore has been maintained in various ways. In Europe, the collaboration has been especially fruitful in Germany, in Scandinavia, and among the specialists in Finno-Ugric culture; in the last field we may point particularly to the studies in Cheremis folklore which Sebeok and other linguists are now publishing at Indiana University (Sebeok *et al.* 1952-68). But as far as the American scene is concerned, this collaboration has revealed itself chiefly through the interest of folklorists in the local dialects of the areas whose folklore they are investigating. Such an interest has stimulated an awareness of distinctive dialect features, but the awareness -- like the interest in the folk culture -- has often been an uncritical amateur concern, with the defects of its virtues. If the amateur is often able to catch a dialect word, or the formula for a folk remedy, which the scholar has not had the chance to observe, he as often does not distinguish between the truly local and the general; if the amateur is able to saturate himself in the speech and culture of a limited area and study it exhaustively, he often is unaware of the affiliations of his favorite community to the culture as a whole. And it may often happen that the personal habits of amateurs will result in intense investigations of a few areas and neglect of other areas of equal or greater intrinsic importance. For instance, before the days of the Linguistic Atlas project, the two areas in which most studies of dialect had been made were Cape Cod and the southern Appalachians. New England professors normally spent their summers on the Cape, and their Southern colleagues in the mountains. But at the same time there had been almost no studies of some of the oldest areas of settlement, such as Chesapeake Bay and the Albemarle Sound area of eastern North Carolina.

In American folklore, similarly, sporadic rather than systematic investigations, as well as an emphasis on collecting the strange rather than discovering the pattern, have made it difficult to evaluate the evidence. Moreover, uncritical collecting for collecting's sake may result in the collection's being useless. Three years ago I found among the effects of a late colleague half a ton of miscellaneous clippings on the backgrounds of various American historical novels, a collection which he himself had never put in order and which no one else knew what to make of. And the valuable *Frank C. Brown Collection of North Carolina Folklore* (White *et al.* 1952-64) would have been much more valuable had Brown spent more time in arranging and preediting while he was alive.

Yet, as European and American scholars alike have shown, both dialect and folklore research, carefully conducted, can yield valuable evidence on the complex interrelationships of various ethnic, economic, and social groups. The two disciplines have much in common in the problems of obtaining and evaluating evidence, in the most fruitful methods of investigation, and in the ways in which the findings of a preliminary survey may be utilized in other research.

The best evidence is that obtained from the natural conversation of living informants, rather than from hearsay. But the investigator has no easy problem finding good informants and using them effectively. Often, in the most highly diversified speech areas, a local contact, convinced

that *dialect* means quaint oddities, will assure the investigator that there is no dialect spoken in the county, and that if he wants to find any, he should look on the other side of the river. Nor will a good informant necessarily know what the investigator means by such terms as *dialect*, *superstitions*, or *proverbs*; the mother of a friend of mine had an inexhaustible store of Swedish proverbs, which she told freely at the slightest excuse or just to accompany her household chores; but on occasion when he invited her to "tell some more proverbs," she gave him only a blank stare. The significance of the evidence -- even the fact that it is evidence -- is likely to be apparent only to the trained investigator.

Besides, even the cooperation of a willing informant does not mean that the investigator is relieved of the problem of interpretation. Some informants are notorious prevaricators, anxious to supply the information the investigator is looking for; consequently, prompted responses, actually suggested by the investigator, are of relatively little value. On the other hand, a cautious informant may hesitate to admit as his own a folk grammatical form or a folk belief that he actually uses. On one of my earliest field trips, an old gentleman in the South Carolina mountains labeled as the usage of "ignorant folks and niggers" grammatical forms which he regularly used in his own anecdotes; and it is almost traditional that buckeyes and rabbits' feet will tumble out of the pockets of the village skeptic while he is eloquently proclaiming his own contempt for superstition. For this reason the investigator must be alert for evidence of unguarded usage, for hints that beliefs and practices attributed to the older generation or to the uneducated may not have died out but are very much alive in the community.

Both the linguistic geographer and the folklorist must also realize that words and beliefs may spread in several ways. It is easy to imagine transmission by migration or by borrowing from neighboring communities, less easy to imagine transmission by leaps from major cultural center to subsidiary center, with the intervening countryside untouched. Yet this pattern of dissemination is very common in American dialects; in New York State, for instance, the Genesee Country and the old whaling community of Hudson show rather frequent loss of /-r/ in *barn* and *beard*, in common with New York City and eastern New England but contrary to the prevailing usage in the Hudson Valley, the Adirondacks, and the Finger Lakes. The explanation lies in the cultural ties of Rochester and Hudson to Boston, New York City, and the New England whaling ports. Even more familiar is the experience of the York Stater who acquired a taste -- and the word -- for *hominy grits* at an army post in the deep South, and continued to eat them after his discharge. It is often alleged that experiences of this kind are peculiar to our generation and will end by obliterating all folk cultures and regional distinctions. But these experiences (and alarm at them) are nothing new. Prosperous North Country wool merchants, moving into London in the fourteenth century, introduced the pronouns *they*, *their*, *them* into standard English; and the potato itself, along with its name, came to Ireland from the American Indian.

In assaying dialects or folk culture, there seem to be three stages of research, though the progress of investigation does not necessarily proceed in orderly fashion from one stage to the next.

I. More or less random observation of the peculiarities in a somewhat restricted area, such as folk remedies in the Smokies or the surviving archaisms in the speech of the Gullah Negro.

II. Selected sampling, over a wide area, to determine regional and social patterns of distribution. The various linguistic atlases, European and American, are the best-known projects of this kind, but similar projects exist in place-name study and in folklore.

III. More intensive studies based on the patterns of distribution revealed by wide-area sampling. Such studies may concentrate on a few features in a large number of communities, or on a great many more features in a more restricted area.

Stage I, pioneering, is indispensible for both folklore and dialect study. Effective systematic surveys or intensive investigations require careful preliminary work, noting features that should be more widely explored, their probable distribution, and the interrelationships of local social groups. But since the pioneer investigations are usually undertaken by amateurs, the findings are too often unsystematic and loaded in the direction of oddities, things recorded because the observer considers them different. Even a local antiquary, steeped in the culture of his environment, may not be completely reliable, because he may not realize that what he is familiar with every day is uniquely local; for instance, the Hudson Valley *hay barrack* -- a haystack protected by a sliding roof on poles -- is distinctively local (outside the area having shown up only once in the United States, in Duluth, in the speech of an elderly woman of Flemish descent), but a person whose knowledge of haymaking was confined to the Hudson Valley might not suspect that the *barrack* is at all unusual. And until I studied the speech of regions outside the South, I assumed that everyone knew the term *jackleg preacher* to describe an amateurish, uneducated minister, without a regular charge, who made his living doing something else and preached here and there on Sundays to congregations that could not find anyone better qualified to fill their pulpits.

The techniques of Stage II, systematic surveys by selected sampling over a wide area, have been worked out in detail by linguistic geographers, students of place names, and European folklorists. In the United States, under the sponsorship of the American Council of Learned Societies and the general direction of Hans Kurath, this procedure has yielded the published *Linguistic Atlas of New England* (1939-43), complete though unedited records from the rest of the Atlantic Seaboard and most of the Midwest, and a great deal of field work in the Rocky Mountain and Pacific Coast states.

1. In the area investigated, a network of communities is drawn up. The choice of particular communities reflects a complex process of reasoning. The density of the network should in some way correspond to the density of population; yet allowance must be made for the fact that the more sparsely settled areas are likely to show greater local diversity. Furthermore, older settled areas need more study than do recent ones, because again the local diversity is probably greater. Several kinds of communities need to be included: earliest settlements in an area (Plymouth, Massachusetts); cultural foci (Boston, New York City, Charleston); decaying communities, once more important than they are now (Nantucket); isolated settlements (the Outer Banks of North Carolina); communities originally settled by closely knit groups from other parts of the United States (Mormon Nauvoo, in Illinois), from the British Isles (Albion, Illinois), from Canada (Rosebush, in central Michigan), or from continental Europe (the Danish settlement at Askov, Minnesota).

2. Selected questions covering the types of information in which the investigators are interested. For the Linguistic Atlas projects typical questions involve

a. Whether the vowel of *pool* or that of *pull* or that of *cull* is used in such words as *coop*, *cooper*, *hoop*, *goober*, *hoof*, *roof*, *soot*, *root*, *cooter*, *food*, *spoon*, *spook*.

b. Whether the past tense of *climb* is *climbed*, *clim*, *clam*, *clom*, *clome*, *clum*, or *cloom*.

c. Whether the dragonfly is popularly known as a *devil's darning needle*, *sewing needle*, *spindle*, *snake feeder*, *snake doctor*, or *mosquito hawk*.

d. Whether *corn dodgers* refers to small loaves ('pones') of corn bread, corn dumplings, corn griddle cakes, or spheroids of corn meal cooked in the grease in which fish have just been fried.

3. A trained investigator, who knows the purpose of the investigation, has

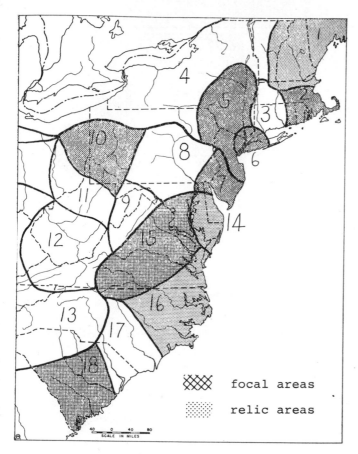

Map 1

Dialect Areas of the Eastern United States

The North

1 Northeastern New England
2 Southeastern New England
3 Southwestern New England
4 Inland North (western Vermont, upstate
     New York and derivatives)
5 Hudson Valley
6 Metropolitan New York

The Midland: North Midland

7 Delaware Valley (Philadelphia)
8 Susquehannah Valley
10 Upper Ohio Valley (Pittsburgh)
11 Northern West Virginia

The Midland: South Midland

9 Upper Potomac and Shenandoah Valleys
12 Southern West Virginia and Eastern
     Kentucky
13 Western Carolina and Eastern Tennessee

The South

14 Delmarva (Eastern Shore)
15 Virginia Piedmont
16 Northeastern North Carolina (Albe-
     marle Sound and Neuse Valley)
17 Cape Fear and Peedee Valleys
18 South Carolina Low-Country
     (Charleston)

⧉ focal areas

∷ relic areas

studied the cultural history of the area, is skilled in writing minute transcriptions at high speed, and is able to control the interview so as to obtain the greatest possible cooperation from the local informants.

4. Selected informants, native to and representative of their communities. Since one of the obvious forces in American society is the pressure toward uniformity, toward eliminating local and individual peculiarities, the American linguistic atlases have tried to measure this force by using at least two types of informants in each community: an unsophisticated representative of the oldest living native generation, and a middle-aged person with up to a high-school education. In many communities, including the major cultural centers, educated representatives of the older families are also interviewed; in communities where foreign-language groups have long been important, at least one informant comes from those groups.

5. Normally a conversational situation, with the interviewer writing down the responses on the spot. The investigation may be supplemented by correspondence materials, especially vocabulary check lists, and by tape recordings which can preserve the material of the interview. But the success of the investigation depends on the skill of the investigator in

choosing qualified informants and obtaining their cooperation.

After the field work is completed, the patterns of distribution are charted for a large number of items. Where a feature is geographically restricted, its outer limit is indicated by an imaginary line called an *isogloss*; where a number of isoglosses essentially coincide, one establishes a *dialect boundary*, between two *dialect areas*. Dialect areas are of three principal types: a *focal area* (like the Hudson Valley), with a well-defined center, is one whose economic or cultural prestige causes its words or pronunciations to spread into other areas; a *relic area* (like Northeastern North Carolina), lacking a well-defined center, is one whose isolation has encouraged the preservation of words or pronunciations that have been lost elsewhere; a *transition area* (like the Carolina Piedmont) is one which lacks many distinguishing features of its own, but in which the features of other dialect areas are intermingled (see Maps[2]).

If this commentary so far emphasizes dialect rather than folklore, it merely represents the relative state of American research in the two disciplines, the fact that dialect research has so far produced better cooperation among groups of scholars for the execution of large-scale projects. But as the experience of German and Swiss scholars indicates, an atlas of

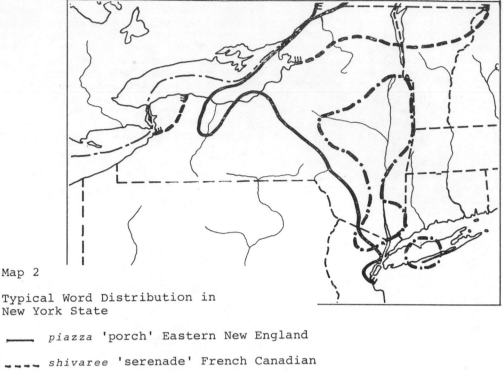

Map 2

Typical Word Distribution in
New York State

——— *piazza* 'porch' Eastern New England

▬ ▬ ▬ *shivaree* 'serenade' French Canadian

▬ . ▬ *hay barrack* 'haystack'
Hudson Valley Dutch

American folklore is just as feasible as one of American dialects.

Stage III is the exploitation of the patterns of regional and social distribution that large-scale projects have revealed. An atlas, of dialects or of folklore, does not close the door to other research; it is but a framework, indicating the most profitable directions for future studies.

From the point of view of the student of dialects, the next stage is a dictionary of popular speech. At present, a test project is under way in Wisconsin, where Frederic G. Cassidy is investigating the vocabulary in depth, in fifty communities, with a questionnaire much longer than that used by the Linguistic Atlas. A slightly different technique was suggested in 1941 by Hans Kurath in order to utilize most effectively the findings of the Linguistic Atlas. In his judgment, the relative uniformity of a focal area like the Hudson Valley suggests that one sampling point would be sufficient for the dialect dictionary; in contrast, the relative diversity of a relic area like Northeastern New England or a transition area like Upstate New York would call for sampling at several points. This scheme of Kurath's assumes that dialect is not restricted to the quaint eccentricities of older-generation illiterates; it assumes additions as well as losses in everyday speech; it is

concerned not merely with Celtic or Old Norse survivals, say, but with innovations due to the industrialization and culture contacts of the nineteenth and twentieth centuries. [Cassidy's *Dictionary of American Regional English* (1981-) draws on both Kurath's experience and his own: 1002 long interviews, supplemented by a diversified reading program.]

It would seem that Kurath's scheme might be adapted to a large-scale survey of American folklore. It would assume, necessarily, that not all superstitions or good-luck charms have been handed down from our ancestors, but that adaptations and innovations may occur. It would assume that folklore is found not merely in isolated rural areas, among the unsophisticated, but may appear in our largest and most sophisticated cities, and may be associated with activities only a few decades old. Whether or not baseball players still believe that one who sees a wagonload of empty beer barrels is likely to break out in a rash of base hits, this superstition in its classic 1900 version could not antedate the game of baseball. Nor could one expect to find before 1890 the belief that a young man out riding with his girl is entitled to a kiss when he passes a car with one headlight out. Both of these superstitions may go back to other institutions in earlier periods; but their existence shows that folklore may still develop in the industrial age.

One of the most interesting projects would be to determine the extent to which dialect boundaries and folklore boundaries correspond. So far as popular material culture is concerned, there are striking hints of this correspondence. As Kurath has repeatedly stated, few dialect boundaries are as sharp as that constituted by the crest of the Blue Ridge from the Potomac to the James, setting off the Pennsylvania-derived Shenandoah Valley settlements from the plantation culture of the Virginia Piedmont. And even the most casual tourist can see an equally striking difference in the shapes of the haystacks: in the Valley, the large, square stack or the Pennsylvania *rick*; in the Piedmont, the small, round 'Southern' stack, built around a center pole.

A second application could be the study of occupational vocabulary or occupational lore. The area would be smaller, and the scope of the inquiry less extensive, but within that range the details could be more thoroughly covered. For instance, cotton is the same plant, wherever grown, but there are regional and social differences in the techniques of producing the crop. It would be useful to get an inventory of these differences, of the words associated with them, and of the accompanying beliefs. Going further, it would be interesting to see to what extent vocabulary varies from one kind of farming to another. Nor need we confine ourselves to the vocabulary of folklore of rural occupations; highly specialized and technical crafts, both legal and illegal, photography and safe-cracking, have their own terms and lore, as David Maurer has shown in his perceptive studies of criminal argot (1950, 1951, 1955, 1963, 1974, Maurer and Vogel 1954, and others).

A hundred lifetimes could be spent in the study of the vocabulary and folklore of racial and cultural minorities, both in their own right and for their impact on the dominant groups. The most striking cultural minority is the American Negro; characteristics of his speech and folklore have been examined in greatest detail in the old plantation country of the South Carolina and Georgia coast, notably in Lorenzo Turner's *Africanisms in the Gullah Dialect* (1949). Yet no one has seriously studied the extent to which Negro speech or Negro folklore has affected the Southern whites. It is interesting that the Africanism *cooter* 'turtle' has spread from South Carolina Negroes not only to the whites but to the Catawba Indians, who have zealously kept themselves apart from the Negro. Many Negro communities exist in the North as well, varying in character from old agricultural colonies like the one near Dowagiac, Michigan, to close-packed slums like those in Harlem and the Chicago South Side. Apparently the older colonies have been assimilated in all but race; when Dorson was collecting his *Negro Folktales in Michigan* (1956), he found no storytellers near Dowagiac except recent arrivals from the South, and practically all of his best informants in the state were Southern born. On the other hand, mass immigration into metropolitan areas seems to have produced cultural isolation between Negro and white comparable to that in the South; many middle-aged or younger native-born Chicago Negroes have Southern speech characteristics like /-z/ in *greasy*, like *croker sack* as a designation for a burlap bag. Among such groups one might well expect to find survivals of Southern Negro folklore, with interesting modifications in the metropolitan environment.

The appearance of French-Canadian *shivaree* in northern New England and the northern Adirondacks is not surprising to those of Harold Thompson's students who have found French lore in Essex, Franklin, and St. Lawrence counties. There is still room for much more work on the speech and culture of both the French Canadians and the Louisiana Cajuns.

Among the German groups, the Pennsylvania colonies have been well studied, and so have some of their offshoots in the Great Lakes area, but much remains to be done with other groups like the Palatines in the Mohawk Valley or the urban colonies in New York City and Buffalo. In South Carolina, the Dutch Fork Lutherans northwest of Columbia preserve a few loan words from German, an architectural peculiarity of setting the chimneys a few feet forward of the ridgepole rather than centering them on the peak, and a tradition of self-sufficient family farming that has enabled them to escape the hazards of mortgaged cotton crops and installment credit; intensive research in language and folklore should be profitable there, as well as in the Savannah Valley, where old Salzburger settlements have contributed to the local culture *cripple*, an Anglicization of a South German word for what Pennsylvania Germans call *ponhoss* and Philadelphians call *scrapple*. Especially promising, and to now almost universally uninvestigated, are the speech and folklore of such mixed-blood groups as the 'Jackson whites' of Bergen and Rockland counties, the 'Croatans' of southeastern North Carolina, the 'Turks' and 'brass ankles' of the South Carolina Low-Country, the 'creoles' of southern Alabama (not to be confused with the Louisiana Creoles, of pure French or Spanish ancestry), and the 'redbones' of western Louisiana. And for each of these minority groups, the investigator must solve the question of its status: Is it envied, respected, accepted, tolerated, or despised?

Although we have much reliable information regarding the regional distribution of dialect features in the United States, we know relatively little about their social distribution, beyond the studies of verb forms by Bagby Atwood (1953a) and Virginia McDavid (1956). Similarly, although we have considerable knowledge about the folklore of the uneducated, we do not know how far up the social ladder particular items of folklore are current, or whether certain kinds are restricted to particular social levels. Here the investigator will wonder whether the social distribution of folk speech and folklore will be the same in stratified areas like eastern Virginia and the Carolina Low-Country as it is in unstratified areas like central Ohio, in closed social systems like that of the South Atlantic states as in open social systems like that of rural New England. One would want to know in what areas it is important for the local upper class to know the local folkways; it is hardly conceivable that someone from outside the South could fully appreciate the implications of the following story:

An elderly Negro witness was being cross-examined by a young white lawyer who had come from a poor white background and was anxious to prove himself by demonstrating his professional skill to the judge and the rest of the community. The Negro stood the ordeal with good humor, and a tolerant understanding of everyone's place in the social system. Finally the young lawyer snapped at him, "Just what do you do for a living?"

"Well," he answered, "I farms a little and I fishes a little and I cuts wood a little, and I wuhks for Cap'm Frank up at the big house [plantation]; and on Sundays I's a kinda jackleg preacher."

"A jackleg preacher, you say?"

"Yes, suh. A jackleg preacher."

"Well, what do you mean by a jackleg preacher?"

"Well, suh, I ain't aimin' to show no disrespect; but since you done ax me, I reckon a jackleg preacher like me is to a rale preacher like what you is to a good lawyer."

Finally, is it not even possible that in some regions the local upper classes have their own folk traditions? Certainly the circulation of stories derogatory to Franklin Roosevelt, however they may have originated, was pretty well restricted to the upper-middle classes. And a shrewd knowledge of the mores of white-collar suburbia was revealed by the Connecticut businessman who bemoaned, "Here it is Saturday night again; and I've got to get drunk again; and God! how I dread it!"

Heretofore, studies of dialect and folklore have concentrated on rural areas, in keeping with an interest in relics of older traditions. But today a majority of Americans live in urban areas, and future studies might profitably be directed to these areas. To cite a few studies, Allan Hubbell (1950), Yakira Frank (1949) and William Labov (1966) have independently analyzed the pronunciation of New York City English; David DeCamp has made a similar study in metropolitan San Francisco (1958-59); Lee Pederson (1965a) and others in the Chicago area; Ray O'Cain in Charleston, South Carolina (1972). In folklore less has been accomplished, though Moritz Jagendorf (1953) and Ben Botkin (1953) have published some valuable material. So far most of the evidence suggests that developments in urban speech are in the direction of loss of what the countryside has to offer: simplification of pronunciation systems, loss of nonstandard grammatical forms, and disappearance of much of the folk vocabulary. Yet certain new local expressions seem to have arisen in cities: *bodega* 'food and liquor store' in parts of New York City (especially the Puerto Rican settlements in East Harlem) and occasionally in other urban areas; *confectionery* 'neighborhood food store' in Savannah; *tree lawn* 'grass strip between sidewalk and curb' in Cleveland -- this strip is known as the *devil strip* in Akron and as the *boulevard* in Minneapolis; and *prairie* 'vacant lot' in Chicago. It is probable that similarly localized urban folklore would also be found if investigators searched it out.

This finally introduces the problem of the innovation and diffusion of folklore and folk speech. It is a commonplace that slang spreads and fades very rapidly, though some local differences survive. The same is true of occupational jargon, including that of the schools: in the South and parts of the Midwest, high-school and college students call a literal or interlinear translation a *pony*; in metropolitan New York, it is often called a *trot*. Criminal argots are professionally rather than regionally identifiable, though regional differences occur even there: according to Maurer, the technique employed by robbers or rapists (*muggers* in the New York City press) in overpowering their victims from behind is known on the Atlantic Seaboard as *the mug*, in the Midwest as *the arm*, and on the Pacific Coast as *the gilligan hitch*. But what slang, jargon, and argot have in common is a volatility, a tendency to change rapidly, over a wide area, as soon as the inner group suspects that outsiders ahve caught on to the usage of the cognoscenti.

In the same way, folklore can spread rapidly, whether it is truly spontaneous or merely planted by a clever press agent (like much of the lore about Paul Bunyan and the steel man Joe Magarac). Two stories will illustrate this process.

This story, with half a dozen variants, was heard from as many independent informants over a two-week period in the summer of 1956, obviously inspired by the controversy over the desegregation of the public schools in the South:

Two South Carolina Negroes made a lot of money and went to Washington to celebrate. They checked in at the Willard, ordered several bottles of good whiskey, and then asked the bell captain to send up a couple of women.

A few minutes later came a knock at the door, and when they opened it, there stood two white girls. The first Negro was aghast: "Man, we are sure in trouble now!"

"Shut your mouth, man!" called the other. "We ain't trying to go to school with them."

The second, rather widely circulated in Great Lakes industrial cities during the current economic recession, apparently sprang up during the similar slump of 1954, possibly with the acquiescence of local Democratic organizations:

Two farmers in eastern Kentucky were discussing the coming election. "Who are you going to vote for?"

"Cain't make up my mind. Times is mighty hard."

"Times is hard for me, too, but I still like Ike. He brung my boy back from Korea."

"Well, I like Ike, too. He brung both my boys back from De-troit."

Purists, perhaps, might be unwilling to accept these stories as folklore. Nevertheless, whatever their origins, once they get into the channels of popular transmission, they are the property of the folk. And so it has been since the days of Menes and Hammurabi.

In short, the linguistic geographer and the folklorist who take their work seriously realize that their task is not merely to recover the relics of ancient traditions, but to catch the changes in traditions as they occur. Folklore, folk speech, and folk culture are living and evolving reflections of human activity. It is this attitude that Harold Thompson has inculcated in his students; it is in this spirit that future linguistic geographers and folklorists must continue to work, if they are to make their disciplines meaningful.

[An atlas of American folk life is now in the advanced planning stage, with food to be the first topic of investigation.]

NOTES

[1] This article was contributed to a special issue of *New York Folklore Quarterly* in honor of Harold W. Thompson, late professor of English at Cornell University and a pioneer in the study of the folklore of New York State. Few teachers have generated so much enthusiasm among their students, or induced so many of them to continue their work, whether as professional scholars or as spare-time local historians.

[2] The maps were prepared by Virginia Glenn McDavid of Chicago State University, Associate Editor of the *Linguistic Atlas of the North-Central States*. Map 1 is adapted from Kurath 1949:fig. 3.

The student of linguistic geography and that of toponymics might well consider how they can cooperate with each other somewhat more effectively than they have done in the past. Basically, these disciplines are much alike. Neither is a pure science, but both are bridges through which many branches of learning are brought together for their mutual enrichment. Both of them draw on and contribute to the work of the social historian, the student of population origins and distributions and movements, the geographer (physical, economic, political, and cultural), the historical linguist, the structural linguist, and the like. Like almost every other discipline, only more so, these fields can be most effectively exploited by the investigator working with the materials in the field, obtaining the data from live informants and writing down the responses on the spot. Working conditions sometimes do not approach the ideal, especially when one is dealing with the geographical distribution of linguistic forms -- whether verb inflections or place-name elements -- at some time in the past. Under these circumstances the only evidence available may be documentary: interlinear glosses, charters, deeds, or maps. But as indispensable as documentary evidence may be under these conditions, or as helpful as it can be as supplementary evidence when an investigation is conducted in the field, the investigator should not stop with the documents when he has other ways of getting at the evidence. One smiles rightly at the attitude of one of the county officials in Georgia when I was doing the field work for the Linguistic Atlas in 1947. This functionary insisted that I need only read *Gone with the Wind* to discover what Georgia speech was actually like; and it took half an hour of my most patient explaining to make the point that Margaret Mitchell's knowledge of Southern speech and culture, though undoubtedly broad, detailed, and generally accurate, was neither encyclopedic nor infallible. Yet students of dialect have sometimes tried to use novels as primary sources, and students of place names have sometimes contented themselves with the scented nomenclature of a Chamber of Commerce map, to the neglect of the more vigorous, if often less easily printable, names actually used by the public.

Furthermore, the cultural situation in the United States -- one by which cultural borrowing may operate at a distance, through such intermediaries as the newspaper, the returned war veteran, the tourist, or simply the reader of novels or history -- introduces complications beyond the experience of the more stable rural areas in Europe. On the one hand, *piazza* as an architectural term was introduced into England by the architects of Covent Garden, was transferred to the columned porches of Georgian houses in eastern New England, Chesapeake Bay, and the South Atlantic coast, and has become a folk synonym for porch as far west as the Mohawk Valley in New York and the Appalachian foothills in the Carolinas and Georgia (Kurath 1949:45, figs. 35, 43), and new architectural fashions have established *patios* in areas far removed from any contact with Spain or Spanish colonies. On the other, the map of the United States is liberally sprinkled with *Rome*s and *Troy*s, with *Jalapa*s (/ɟuwlæpə/ in South Carolina [transcriptions here follow Trager and Smith 1951]) and *Buena Vista*s (normally /byuwnə + vistə/), and even an occasional *Sans Souci*.

The investigation of linguistic geography or place-name distribution may serve so many purposes that the planners of such a project have the problem of limiting themselves to certain obtainable objectives. In theory, at least, a project in either field is almost unlimited in its scope: the investigator of place names would like to record all such names, and all pertinent information about them; the investigator of dialects would like to have evidence on the complete phonemic system (with occurrences of every phoneme in every possible phonemic context), a full inventory of all grammatical forms in everyday use, and a nearly complete vocabulary of the everyday language, including all the usual meanings of all the words. In practice, however, the investigator must settle for something less than the ideal; even the most abundantly endowed university or foundation has limits to the funds it can place at the disposal of a particular project. Competent investigators are scarce, and have many other demands on their time; and even the most cooperative and talkative informant ultimately finds his information and his patience exhausted. The annals of research bear witness to the numerous ambitious projects that broke down because they attempted too much. Two such projects were begun in Italy: the 1947 project to revise the toponymic map of the republic by

Map 1

creek

○   i y

●   i

including every place name, no matter how trivial, still seems far from realization; earlier (1928-43) there were nationalistically-inspired plans for a natively organized linguistic survey to put to shame the *Atlas* of Jaberg and Jud (1928-40) by employing a finer graded network (1000 communities) and a larger questionnaire over 7000 items) than the Swiss dialectologists had used, but they collapsed upon the death of the field investigator, Hugo Pellis, with less than two-thirds of the peninsula covered.

Consequently, the interrelationships between linguistic geography and toponymic research may be limited in a particular instance by the restrictions each investigator imposes upon the scope of his project. For some particular projects the interrelationships may be very tenuous. For instance, an inquiry limited to regional distinctions in intonation patterns and terminal junctures may derive little assistance from an investigation into the names of county seats and market places, even if (as rarely happens) the investigator of place names faithfully records pronunciation. Nevertheless, other types of phonological investigations could be aided by an accurate record of a number of place names, since such names often expand the corpus of contexts in which particular vowels and consonants may occur.

More practicable, however, for testing the relationships of these two disciplines is the assumption of neither exhaustive nor narrowly restricted projects, but rather general investigations of selected phenomena, the examination of major place names in a restricted area on the scale they would be included in, say, the Merriam *Webster's Geographical Dictionary* and a general preliminary survey of dialects, like one of the regional surveys in the Linguistic Atlas project. And instead of listing each discipline's contributions to the other, it is more fruitful to examine several types of linguistic phenomena to demonstrate how for each type the evidence derived from one discipline is related to the work of the other. We must make only one fundamental preliminary observation: the data of the linguistic geographer can usually be analyzed in detail for regional and social distribution, while the work of the place-name investigator cannot; on the other hand, the place-name investigator, like Raup (1957), may bring to the immediate problem a mass of detailed evidence on a restricted number of items, so as to provide the answers to questions the linguistic geographer can only pose.

For phonology, the contribution of the place-name investigator to linguistic geography is somewhat restricted. Even where the pronunciation is faithfully recorded, the place-name study can rarely contribute much by way of phonetic detail on the pronunciation of the various phonemes in various contexts. More often, even a very broad notation of pronunciation will give important evidence as to the incidence of particular phonemes and the structure of the phonemic system in a particular dialect. Even conventional spelling of place names can be useful; true, it will conceal such regionally significant distributions as /krik/ and /kriyk/ for pronunciations of *creek* in the Middle West (see Map 1), but it may suggest the kinds of consonant clusters that occur or adduce the critical environment on which a structural statement depends.

As an example of the value of place-name evidence for structural statements, we may summarize one part of the discussion at the 1956 Texas conference on problems in English phonology (Hill 1962). Among the participants in the conference were several speakers of Southern and South Midland dialects who for some time had questioned whether all the phonological contrasts in their region could be handled by the Trager-Smith analysis of nine vowels and three semivowels (/y,w,h/, representing respectively an offglide toward high-front position, an offglide toward high-back position, and either length or an offglide toward mid-central position). In particular, it was suggested that certain dialects might have the length factor and the centering offglide in contrast; and evidence of this contrast was offered from the dialect of Atlanta, Georgia. However, most of the words in which the length factor occurred revealed it in the sequence [æ·v] as in the common nouns *salve*, *valve*, and the surnames *Cavan* and *Davin*; and in the Atlanta dialect no one could find an example of /æw/ (as in the Atlanta pronunciation of *house*) before /v/. Thus there were grounds for insisting that the phonetic sequence [æ·v] might be interpreted phonemically as [æwv]. But the place name *Lowville* (county seat of Lewis County, New York) was sufficient to overcome the objection, since it would normally be pronounced /læwvəl/ in Atlanta as well as in the Adirondacks.

In many other ways phonological evidence may be supplied by place names. In the superfixes, the patterns of stresses and internal junctures, there may be evidence from the word division of names; for instance, *Pee Dee*, the official spelling of the Board of Geographic Names (not the spelling preferred by South Carolinians, I hasten to add), undoubtedly reflects the local pronunciations of the type /piy + diy/, with the word division representing the internal juncture. And in general, synchronic evidence from phonology may supply clues for place-name etymologies, which in turn will supply evidence for phonological history.

There is relatively little that toponymic research can contribute to the study of grammar, and most of that is concerned with the problems of place-name syntax. These problems are overtly concerned with the relative position of the generic and the specific, covertly with the patterns of stress and juncture. But overtly or covertly they lead ultimately to interesting facets of cultural history. *River*, for instance, nearly always follows the specific, as in *Santee River* and *Fraser River*; in the neighborhood of Detroit, however, *River Rouge* and *River Raisin* testify to the period of French sovereignty. In southern Louisiana, the stream designations *bayou* and *coulée* (both proximately, the latter ultimately as well, of French derivation) regularly precede the specific; in other parts of former French territory, however, the order has been Anglicized, as in the community name *Mound Bayou*, Mississippi, the streams *Cypress Bayou*, *Plum Bayou*, and *Bakers Bayou* in Arkansas, and *Nezpique Bayou* in western Louisiana. *Lake* may precede or follow, the former being slightly more likely in territories once controlled by France. But we have among large lakes *Great Salt Lake* and *Lake Superior*; among small artificial lakes in the Carolinas, *Stone's Lake* and *Lake Summit*; among lowland lakes in southern Louisiana, *Lake Pontchartrain* near New Orleans and *Calcasieu Lake* to the west, near the city of *Lake Charles*. There is some evidence that the antecedent generic is becoming slightly more fashionable than the following one. A small lake in western North Carolina, in resort country, was known as *Kanuga Lake* forty years ago, now more commonly as *Lake Kanuga*; and perhaps a majority of the large artificial lakes created for irrigation and power developments follow the same pattern -- *Lake Mead*, above Hoover Dam (sometime Boulder Dam) on the Colorado; *Lake Murray*, *Lake Marion*, and *Lake Moultrie* in South Carolina. Yet to this trend the area of the Tennessee Valley Authority is an exception, with *Kentucky Lake*, *Pickwick Lake*, *Norris Lake*, and *Hiwassee Lake*, to mention a few. Are these differences matters of chance, or are there underlying cultural forces which the linguistic geographer and the toponymist might discover?

Most of the relationships between linguistic geography and toponymic research, however, concern the vocabulary. Among stream names there is the problem of number and rank in the hierarchy of stream sizes in an area; some regions distinguish only the *river* and the *creek*; others the *river*, the *creek*, and the *branch* (or some semantic equivalent for a small stream); still others may have a hierarchy of four or five sizes. Where there are three or more sizes, it is not to be assumed that the name of each type will appear with equal frequency as a common noun and as an element in place names: *branch* and *brook*, for instance, are widely

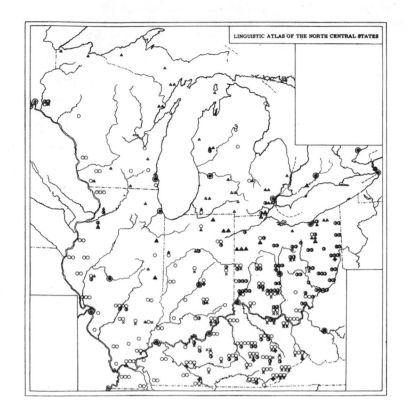

LINGUISTIC ATLAS OF THE NORTH CENTRAL STATES

Map 2

stream

○	*branch*
△	*brook*
◑	*run*
✕	*fork*
▲	*ditch*
♠	*lick*

known as general terms, but local informants often have difficulty naming a single specific stream of this size; *kill*,
in the old Holland Dutch settlements in
New York and New Jersey, is fairly common
in place names but almost never occurs as
a separate word (nor does the place-name
element *pol* 'tidal marsh,' as in *Canarsie
Pol*); *run* occurs both as a common noun
and as an element in place names, but more
commonly as the latter. There may be
clear regional distinctions in the distributions of these elements, as we find both
along the Atlantic Seaboard and in the
North-Central States (see Map 2). *Brook*
is largely confined to the New England
settlement area; *run* is a North Midland
term, with some occurrences in Virginia,
which has been taken down the Ohio Valley
from Pittsburgh as far as the neighborhood
of Louisville; *branch* is characteristically Southern and South Midland. Terms
largely restricted to the North-Central
area are *ditch*, as a designation for a
running stream in flatlands, whether re-
claimed marsh or prairie; *lick*, principally in the Ohio Valley between the Big
Sandy and the Salt; *fork*, mostly in the
knobs and mountains of Kentucky. Moreover, there is a striking correlation between the southern limits of the lexical
form *run* and those of the pronunciation
/krik/, not surprising to one who knows
that both of these items are characteris-

tic of the North Midland as opposed to
South and South Midland.
Similarly, there are significant regional differences in the names for elevated
points. Probably in most parts of the
eastern United States, people are content
with two terms, *mountain* and *hill*, except
for occasional local features of striking
shape. In much of Kentucky, however,
there is an intermediate size, the *knob*.
In more broken terrain, as in western
North Carolina or the Rockies, there are
more specialized terms for particular
shapes: *bald*, *dome*, *peak*, *pinnacle*,
butte, *mesa*. Needless to say, the significance of each of these terms depends to
some extent on the character of the surrounding terrain; *Little Mountain*, near
Columbia, South Carolina, would be a very
modest hill in the Blue Ridge and unnoticed in the Rockies.
When we go from generic terms to specific names we have rich sources for studying linguistic relationships of various
tribal or nationality groups. Sometimes
we have hidden generics in specific names:
the *lac* in *Lake Mille Lacs* (Minnesota),
the *bogue* in *Bogue Falia River* (Mississippi), the *kill* in *Fishkill Creek* (New
York), or *Brook Run* outside Richmond, Virginia; in fact, *Mississippi* itself simply
means Big River, and *Michigan* Big Lake.
But as a language dies out in a locality,
place names from it cease to have meaning-

ful significance in themselves, and become merely sequences of phonemes designating particular places or things.

Finally, problems of semantics of origin may bring together the linguistic geographer, the toponymist, and the local historian for their mutual benefit. In northern West Virginia, a hypothetical *Spider Creek* would almost certainly owe its name to associations with arachnids; in the Adirondacks or near the Dismal Swamp, however, it might have some association with a frying pan. Or conversely, if *Whippletree Pass* should appear on an old travel map through the Rockies, almost certainly there were some Yankees in the original party of explorers and surveyors. In short, then, the linguistic geographer and the toponymist have many common areas of interest. They often work with different kinds of material, with differing degrees of intensity, and toward different goals; it would be foolish to ask one to do the other's work. Nevertheless, each would do well to recognize the other's field as a legitimate scholarly discipline, and be ready to utilize the answers obtained in one field as an aid toward solving the problems of the other.

As one of the younger branches of linguistic science, dialect geography has provided valuable evidence by which the student of languages can explain the apparent exceptions to phonetic laws or indicate the directions in which phonetic, grammatical, or lexical innovations have spread. To the social scientist, for whom linguistics is properly a branch of cultural anthropology, dialect geography is potentially a very useful tool for examining the cultural configurations and prestige values operating in a speech community (R. McDavid 1946 [in this volume, pp. 131-35], 1948 [in this volume, pp. 136-42]). Both of these functions of dialect geography may be suggested by the study of the distribution of the form *shivaree* [ʃɪvəriː], 'a noisy burlesque serenade, used chiefly as a means of teasing newly married couples' in the North American English speech community.

The term is of interest to the student of dialect geography for several reasons. Its occurrence was noted early in several areas by many students of American dialects, and it has continued to draw attention (Hanley 1933, Meredith 1933, Flanagan 1940). Its pattern of distribution is peculiar, with the isogloss setting off its area of prevalence generally running from north to south.[1] Without any commercial or social prestige to aid in its dissemination -- such as undoubtedly helped the spread of *sauerkraut* or *spaghetti* -- it has become one of the most widely distributed folk terms borrowed by American English from any European language.[2] Finally, the accent pattern [ˌʃɪvəˈriː], in the speech of many informants, is atypical for nouns in American folk speech, which predominantly have the primary stress on other than the final syllable.[3]

The etymology of *shivaree* has been satisfactorily established. It is derived from French *charivari* (compare Picard *caribari*), in turn a derivative of the Medieval Latin *c(h)arivarium*; its ultimate origin is unknown (Littré 1863-72), but its occurrence in French goes back at least to the fourteenth century. In some form the word occurs everywhere in France, generally designating a mock serenade following a wedding slightly divergent from the normal pattern in a community -- such as that of an old maid, an old bachelor, a widow, or a widower.[4]

Although raucous celebrations are common in rural England following unpopular or atypical weddings or as a form of social censure,[5] the French term does not seem to be part of the British folk vocabulary. It was not recorded in the collections for Wright's *English Dialect Dictionary* (1898-1905) nor in Lowman's field records from southern England (1937-38, Viereck 1975). Furthermore, all British citations in the *OED* indicate literary rather than folk usage; the earliest occurrence given is 1745, in a translation of Bayle's dictionary of French; the best-known British occurrence is still in the subtitle of the magazine *Punch: or, The London Charivari*, which began its career in 1841 as a British analogue to the earlier *Charivari*, a humorous magazine in Paris.

In contrast with its literary occurrence in the British Isles, the word -- whether in the etymological orthography *charivari* or in something approximating a phonemic spelling -- had been domesticated in (English-speaking) North America as a folk word for a folk custom sometime before 1805. A Pittsburgher transplanted to New Orleans, a city already considerably Americanized by the heavy river traffic, thus commented on the custom (Watson 1843:229):

Masquerades have ceased here since eight or nine years past; but *sherri-varries* are still practiced. They consist in mobbing the house of a *widow* when she marries; and they claim a public donation as a gift. When Madame Don Andre was married, she had to compromise by giving to the outdoor mass three thousand dollars in gold coin! On such occasions the mob are ludicrously disguised. In her case there were effigies of her late and present husband in the exhibition drawn in a cart: there her former husband lays in a coffin, and the widow is personated by a living person and sits near it. The house is mobbed by thousands of the people of the town, vociferating and shouting with loud acclaim; hundreds are seen on horseback; many in disguises and masks; and all have some kind of discordant and noisy music, such as old kettles, and shovels, and tongs, and clanging metals can strike out. Every body looks waggish, merry, and pleased. Very genteel men can be recognized in such a melee. All civil authority and rule seems laid aside. This affair, as an extreme case, lasted *three entire days*, and brought in crowds from the country! It was made extreme because the second husband was an unpopular man, of humble name, and she was supposed to have done unworthily. Their *resistance* to yield *any homage* to the mob, caused the *exaction*, and the whole sum was honorably given to the orphans of the place. At a later period, Edward Livingston, esq., was *sherri-varried* here; on which

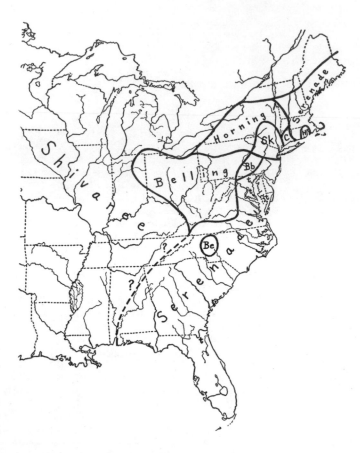

Map 1

shivaree

Bb   *bull-band*

Be   *belling*

C   *callathump*

H   *horning*

Sk   *skimmilton, skimmerton*

t   *tin-panning*

occasion the parties came out promptly to the balcony and thanked the populace for their attention, and invited them to walk into the court-yard and partake of some of their prepared cheer. The compliment was received with acclamations and good wishes for many years of happiness, and the throng dispersed, none of the genteel partaking of the refreshment. When a *sherri-varrie* is announced, it is done by a running cry through the streets, as we cry, fire! fire! and then every man runs abroad, carrying with him any kind of clanging instrument, or any kind of grotesque mask or dress. All this comes from an indisposition to allow ladies *two chances* for husbands, in a society where so few single ladies find even one husband! a result, it is to be presumed, of the concubinage system so prevalent here.

The present distribution of *shivaree* and other terms for the custom is shown on the accompanying map. It is common to all of Canada and much of the United States. Only in the Eastern seaboard states and parts of the South is the word seldom encountered.[6]

On the seaboard there is a multiplicity of words: *serenade*, which is general in the coastal South and in eastern New England; *tin-panning*, restricted to the Chesapeake Bay area and the neighborhood of Jacksonville, Florida; *bull-band(ing)* in the Pennsylvania German sector; *skimmilton* or *skimmerton* in the Hudson Valley; *belling* in most of Pennsylvania, West Virginia, Ohio, and the mountain districts of North Carolina; *salute* in eastern Nova Scotia; *callathump*, possibly a Yale College word, confined to Connecticut, with a few instances in the Yankee settlement area of New York; and *horning*, found in Rhode Island and in derivative settlements in western New England and upstate New York. *Shivaree* is extremely rare in these Eastern states, occurring only in those parts of New York and northern New England which are adjacent to Canada, where it is known from New Brunswick westward, and in the southwest corner of Virginia.[7]

In the secondary settlement areas -- the Great Lakes region and the Mississippi Valley -- *shivaree* is the dominant term. Of the words which were brought to the interior by the westward movement, only *belling*, *horning*, and *callathump* seem to have survived. The first of these is common in Ohio and parts of Indiana, but rare elsewhere; *horning* has become established in most of the Yankee settlement area of New York State and Michigan -- where it is used beside *shivaree* -- and *callathump* is occasionally found in the expression *callathumpian band* or *callathumpian parade*, generally used of a children's procession with false faces, especially on the Fourth of July.[8] *Serenade* was occasionally given by Midwestern informants, but usually for a rather dignified celebration.

In the entire Mississippi Valley from Minnesota and Wisconsin to the Louisiana Gulf *shivaree* is the ordinary term for the custom. Only in southeastern Alabama is the word rare, and this is adjacent to the Georgia *serenade* area. West of the Mississippi to the West Coast *shivaree* seems to be prevalent with only sporadic occurrences of any of the other terms. It is interesting to note that the term is more widely known in the northern part of the Pacific Coast than in California, possibly because the area was settled by a more homogeneous population, predominantly rural. Further evidence of the extent to which the term has been domesticated is the fact that *shivaree* has been borrowed into some of the American-Scandinavian dialects (Flaten 1900, Stefansson 1903, Flom 1926). [As with many other words in other situations, there is a good deal of useful evidence in loans from English into immigrant languages. *Horning*, brought to Wisconsin by early settlers from New York State, was borrowed very early by the Norwegians (Haugen 1953:88). Wisconsin Norwegians have later borrowed *shivaree* but consider it a 'Yankee' word, while *horning* is now felt as native Norwegian.]

Though the custom of wild horseplay to haze the bride and groom seems to have been common to all areas of the country so that we do not have to deal with any important change in the culture patterns of the settlers, the term *shivaree* has been borrowed on the folk level by all groups which moved west of the Appalachians. The reasons for this wholesale borrowing of a foreign word seem to be evident in the geographical extension of the native terms. In the secondary settlement areas those native words were in competition with each other as a result of the mixture of Easterners in new lands, and the borrowing seems to have been a compromise. Furthermore, the most widely spread folk terms of the Eastern United States, *horning* and *belling*, are of a makeshift nature; while *serenade* frequently has a more dignified and nonspecialized meaning. *Skimmilton*, *bull-band*, and *callathump*, which might have had an appeal because of their distinctiveness, are highly local-ized in the East.

Other conditions favorable to borrowing were present. There were early settlements of French scattered throughout the area, especially along the waterways, which served as the avenues of approach for the English-speaking frontiersmen and remained the ordinary avenues of commerce until the building of the railroads. In addition, the area was buttressed to the north and to the south by large French communities. In the North the early lake trade with Canada, and the continuing migrations from Canada to the northern parts of the region, served as a constant reinforcement of French influence. In the South the port of New Orleans became the most important outlet for the products of the interior of the country. The flatboat laden with pork and lumber brought the Hoosier, the Sucker, and the Puke to that fascinating city; the river steamer plying the Mississippi, the Ohio, and the Missouri catered to those who could afford a more comfortable kind of transportation. The preceding account of the elaborateness of the New Orleans *sherri-varrie* indicates that it must have had a great appeal to the exuberant spirit of the woodsmen, rivermen, and early farmers; and the elite -- or sedate -- could not have failed to be aware of it.

Dialect geography with its careful techniques of investigation again bears out the shrewd guesses made by some of the earlier scholars who interested themselves in American English. John S. Farmer (1889:140) supplies a fitting conclusion:

> *Chiravari*, a noisy serenade to which the victims of popular dislike are subjected; a custom universally known but bearing different names according to locality. Discordant sound-producing instruments, such as tin pots, kettles, drums, etc. are employed. The custom is known under the name *chivaree* (pronounced chevaree) in all parts of Canada and the States originally colonized by the French.

We would need only to augment the phrase 'victims of popular dislike' to 'wedding couples and occasionally victims of popular dislike.'

NOTES

[1] Both phonologically and lexically, American dialects seem to be divided into three main types -- Northern, Midland, and Southern -- with the isoglosses (lines setting off the zones of occurrence of forms characteristic of each area) running roughly east and west. For instance, in the Northern area, the vessel in which water is carried is generally called a *pail*; in the Midland and Southern areas, a *bucket*. The conception of a division into Northern, Midland, and Southern dialect types -- supplanting the older and less accurate division into Eastern, Southern, and so-called 'General American' -- has been enunciated and validated most clearly by Kurath 1949.

Dialect areas are less sharply divided in the Mississippi Valley, a secondary settlement area, than along the Atlantic Seaboard. Nevertheless, the isoglosses still generally follow an east-west direction, as for the areas of occurrence of *pail* and *bucket*, or for the pronunciations [gri:si] and [gri:zi].

[2] The term *bateau* 'flat-bottomed rowboat' is practically universal in South Carolina and Georgia, but is rare in the Middle West. *Clook* 'setting hen,' *rainworm* 'earthworm,' and *snits* 'dried sliced fruit' are normally found only in areas where the earliest settlers were predominantly German; *to cook coffee* 'make coffee' only in areas with a heavy Scandinavian settlement.

[3] On the basis of our present information, we are unable to make any definitive regional statements about the accent pattern; such a statement will not be possible until field records are available for the entire Mississippi Valley.

[4] Marriage, as one of the critical acts in the life cycle indicating a change in social status, has always been a matter of public concern, through statute or mores or both (Sumner 1940: 370, 391-92, 409).
Even in our loosely organized industrialized urban society a marriage is an occasion for friends of the bridegroom and bride to harass them. For instance, the bacchanalian and priapic ribaldry of the stag supper for the bridegroom, deflating the tires of the bridegroom's automobile, decorating the bridegroom's car with tin cans and old shoes, and impeding the consummation of the marriage by telephoning the newlyweds' hotel room at frequent intervals (Tucker 1949). The importance of such outlets for the aggressive tendencies of a cultural group has been pointed out by many social scientists (Kluckhohn 1949:277-78, Chase 1948:83).

[5] For example, the *skimmington*, *skimmington ride*, by which the citizens of Casterbridge expressed their disapproval of the behavior of Lucetta (Hardy 1886:Chapter 39).

[6] The data on which this study is based has been gathered from the files for the *Linguistic Atlas of New England* (Kurath *et al.* 1939-43) and the *Linguistic Atlas of the Middle and South Atlantic States* (Kurath *et al.* 1979-); from the records collected under the direction of Albert H. Marckwardt for the North-Central States (Marckwardt *et al.* 1980-), under the direction of Harold B. Allen for the Upper Midwest (Allen 1973-76), and by Henry M. Alexander for the Maritime Provinces; from field records made for local studies by Madie W. Barrett in southeastern Alabama (1948), by

James B. McMillan in east-central Alabama (1946), by C. M. Wise and graduate students under his direction in Louisiana, and by Lorenzo D. Turner in the Gullah Negro communities of the South Carolina and Georgia coast (1949); from studies of regional vocabulary such as A. L. Davis 1949 and Atwood 1962; from Wentworth 1944; and from additional information furnished by McMillan, Wise, E. F. Haden, Louise Pound, Ben W. Black, R. L. Ramsay, Carroll E. Reed, David W. Reed, and John G. Mutziger.

[7] Whatever the local term, one may observe certain common features of the practice. It is now not confined to second marriages or to unpopular persons, but is a normal procedure in the community; in fact, the absence of such revelry may indicate that the couple is not fully accepted in the community. The celebration is no longer associated with consummation of the marriage, but is often deferred until the return of the couple from their honeymoon. Open resentment of the practice on the part of the newly married couple intensifies the noisemaking and other teasing. The noisemakers are customarily placated by an invitation to an informal supper, often prepared in advance in anticipation of the revelry, gifts of beer and cigars, or a money contribution (usually the price of a keg of beer).
Noisemaking apparatus utilized for the celebration includes dishpans, cowbells, horns, and other bits of household and farm hardware, muskets and shotguns and other firearms (in the South, where rural houses usually lack basements and are built on pillars, the firearms are often emplaced and discharged at a position calculated by the revelers to be directly underneath the nuptial bed), suspended circular saws, homemade cannon (often fashioned of old anvils), and long strands of catgut stretched over barrel tops or between tree limbs and the house.

[8] The use of the term *callathump* for a procession with false faces may indicate that the wearing of masks was formerly a part of the merrymaking. The use of masks is noted only in the description of the New Orleans celebration.
Phillips 1856-60:III, 29-35 gives an exhaustive treatment of the custom of medieval France, listing the following characteristics: 1) the participants wear masks; 2) the masked people make a great deal of noise; 3) the couple must pay for their release; 4) the custom was forbidden under threat of excommunication and fines.

Linguistic geography may simply present the facts about a linguistic detail on which there has been speculation; it may enable a speaker to judge the social acceptability of a linguistic form on the basis of usage rather than prejudice; or it may throw light on the history of the language, and suggest the forces that have led to the prestige of linguistic forms. Conclusions of all these types can be drawn from an examination of the occurrence or loss of initial /h-/ before semivowels in the states of the Atlantic Seaboard, as recorded in the field records for the Linguistic Atlas of the United States and Canada.[1]

The emotional attitudes toward the preservation of /h-/ in these words are associated with those toward the pronunciation of /h-/ before vowels -- or, rather, toward the phonemic contrast between vowels preceded by aspiration and those not so prededed, as *hail:ail*, *howl:owl*, a contrast which in southern England generally distinguishes standard from nonstandard speech.[2] As a rule, in words of Old English or Scandinavian derivation, the /h-/ is preserved in standard speech but lost in southern English folk dialects (Wright 1905).[3] In words of Romance derivation, the orthographic *h* has probably not been pronounced since the time of Vulgar Latin (Jespersen 1909-49:1.2.942); but during the last century there has been a tendency to insist on the pronunciation of orthographic *h* as a badge of superiority, though the socially preferred pronunciations of such words as *heir*, *hour*, and *honor* indicate that the innovation is by no means complete.[4]

Although the pronunciation of /h-/ before vowels does not constitute a social shibboleth in the United States, there is evidence that the presence or absence of /h-/ in words like *whip* and *humor* is often considered a test of social acceptability.[5] Thus when Pyles (1949:393) remarked that in his dialect (of Frederick, Maryland) the cluster /hw-/ does not occur, despite the efforts of well-meaning schoolteachers to impose it on generations of students,[6] a Utica reader immediately commented that nowhere had she observed a person of true culture who did not possess that cluster.[7] Such responses are not confined to laymen. Thomas Lounsbury and William Dwight Whitney,[8] and more recently C. K. Thomas and A. G. Kennedy,[9] have insisted that there is a social stigma attached to those who do not pronounce /h-/

in words of these types. H. L. Mencken, on the other hand, considers the pronunciation of /h-/ in *whip*, etc., an affectation (1948:95).[10]

Dictionaries give little information on the geographical or social distribution of the forms of these words with and without /h-/. *WNID-2* (1934) states that *humor* generally has /hj-/, and that words like *whip* generally but not always have /hw-/.[11] Kenyon and Knott 1944 essentially follows *WNID-2*.[12] The *ACD* (1947) indicates both /hj-/ and /j-/ for *humor* but only /hw-/ for the *whip* type. Needleman 1949 cites *humor* with both /hj-/ and /j-/, and indicates that both /hw-/ and /w-/ are acceptable in *whip*. The *OED* is more detailed in its statements of geographical and social distribution: it characterizes the /h-/ in *humor* as a recent spelling pronunciation, and for words of the type of *whip* gives /w-/ as the general British form, with /hw-/ usual in Scotland, Ireland, and North America.[13] Both Michaelis and Jones 1913 and Jones 1917 indicate a preference for /hj-/ in *humor* and for /w-/ in *whip*.[14] H. W. Fowler recognizes /hj-/ and /j-/ as socially acceptable in *humor*, /hw-/ and /w-/ in *whip*.[15]

Many general and local studies of American pronunciation deal with the /h-/ in words like *whip* and *humor*. Hempl 1891 observes that he, and presumably others, have /w-/ in unstressed *what* and the like, and in *wharf* when stressed, though /hw-/ is far more common.[16] On a more ambitious scale, Grandgent 1893 attempts to ascertain regional patterns of distribution; he finds an overwhelming preponderance of /hw-/.[17] Krapp[18] and Kenyon[19] observe that both /hw-/ and /w-/ occur, without commenting on regional or social distribution. Kurath twice indicates a preponderance of /hw-/ in American usage,[20] and Marckwardt merely states that Southern British speakers are more likely than Americans to replace /hw-/ by /w-/.[21]

The distribution of /hw-/~/w-/ and of /hj-/~/j-/ has been incidentally or specifically observed in many local studies published during the last sixty years -- among them studies by Primer,[22] O. F. Emerson,[23] W. A. Read,[24] Shewmake,[25] Greet,[26] Ayres,[27] Cleanth Brooks,[28] Oma Stanley,[29] C. K. Thomas,[30] Argus Tressider,[31] H. L. Mencken,[32] and Allan F. Hubbell.[33] In addition, the pronunciation of *wheelbarrow* is charted by Kurath *et al.* 1939:9, where the form with /w-/ is indicated as one of the characteristic pronun-

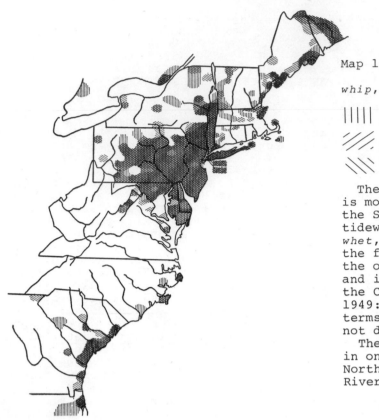

Map 1

whip, whetstone, wheelbarrow

||||| *whip*, without /h-/

/// *whetstone*, without /h-/

\\\ *wheelbarrow*, without /h-/

The implement for sharpening a scythe is most commonly called a *whetrock* in the South Atlantic States outside the tidewater area. The terms *whetseed*, *whet*, and *whetter* occur sporadically -- the first chiefly on Albemarle Sound, the others on the Delmarva peninsula and in eastern North Carolina between the Cape Fear and Neuse Rivers (Kurath 1949:60, fig. 83). Since all these terms have the same initial, they are not distinguished on this map.

The word *whip* was recorded as [hup] in one coastal community of eastern North Carolina, just north of the Neuse River.

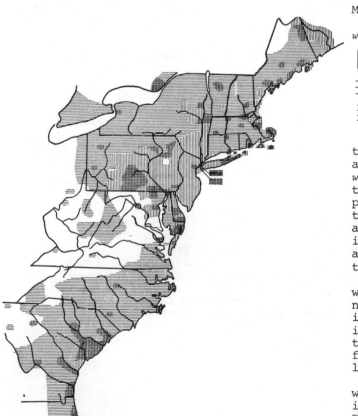

Map 2

whinny

||||| /w-/

≡ /hw-/

▦ divided usage

The sound made by a horse at feeding time, or on recognizing his owner or another horse, is frequently called *whicker* in eastern New England and in the southern coastal plain from Chesapeake Bay south. In Southern communities close both to the coastal *whicker* area and to the inland *nicker* area, it is occasionally called *whinker*. Since all these terms have the same initial, they are not distinguished on this map.

Blank areas on the map are those in which a horse's *whinny* is called by names with different initials: *laugh* in the Pennsylvania German area, *nicker* in the Virginia Piedmont and in areas to the northwest and the southwest influenced by the Virginia Piedmont (Kurath 1949:62-63, fig 97).

The pronunciation *hinny* or *hicker*, with /h-/ but without /w/, was recorded in three widely separated communities: Beaufort and Chester, South Carolina, and Milledgeville, Georgia.

ciations of eastern New England.[34] These studies are of uneven quality and were prepared in various ways, from simple anecdotal treatment to systematic examination of comparable material. In general, these studies indicate 1) that the areas in which /ǰ-/ is prevalent in *humor* do not necessarily coincide with areas in which /w-/ is prevalent in *whip*; 2) that the forms without /h-/ are most likely to occur in coastal communities, especially from the head of Chesapeake Bay to the Hudson Valley; and 3) that these coastal communities -- at least for the /w-/ forms -- do not constitute a continuous area. This is probably as much as one can hope to obtain without a systematic investigation of comparable data.

The principles governing the collection of data for the Linguistic Atlas are those generally followed in linguistic geography since Gilliéron and Edmont (1902-10): 1) selection of a network of communities in the area to be investigated; 2) choice of representative native informants -- in this country normally two for each community, differing in age or education or both; 3) use of a prepared questionnaire containing carefully selected items; 4) interviews conducted on the spot by trained field workers; 5) interviews conducted as far as possible in a conversational situation; 6) recording of the informants' responses in a finely graded phonetic alphabet. By observing these principles, the American Atlas makes every effort to secure natural responses and comparable data.[35] As a result, we now have reliable observations (within the limits of the questionnaire) from selected points on the Atlantic Seaboard from the St. John's Valley in New Brunswick to St. Augustine, Florida, or almost the entire area settled by English-speaking colonists before the Revolution[36] -- a framework which allows us to draw more definite conclusions than earlier scholars.

The material for determining the regional and social distribution of /h/ before /ǰ/ and /w/[37] is provided by the Atlas informants' recorded pronunciation of the following words: for /hǰ-/, *humor*,[38] usually in the context *good humor*, occasionally in *sense of humor*; for /hw-/, *whip*, *wheelbarrow*, *whetstone*, *whinny*, *wharf*, and *whoa*.[39]

To interpret the data it is necessary to make arbitrary decisions. There is no sharp boundary, phonetically, between what might be interpreted as /w-/ and what might be interpreted as /hw-/, or between /ǰ-/ and /hǰ-/; that is, there is no sharp opposition between a fully voiceless and a fully voiced bilabial frictionless continuant, but rather a series of sound types ranging from [ʍ] with lip-rounding or palatalization to [w] or [ǰ], as the initial voicelessness progressively decreases. For practical purposes, any

voicelessness or murmur accompanying or preceding the semivowel is here interpreted as belonging to the phoneme /h-/; only those transcriptions where the field worker has written fully voiced [w,ǰ] are interpreted as indicating the loss of initial /h/. Where /v-/ and /w-/ have fallen together in a bilabial fricative or a labiodental frictionless continuant, these sound types are interpreted as /w-/ without a preceding /h-/.[40]

The five maps which accompany this paper require some words of interpretation.

Map 1 indicates by three kinds of shading the areas in which the Atlas field workers recorded the words *whip*, *whetstone*,[41] and *wheelbarrow* without /h-/. It is very difficult to represent on one map the responses of 1500 informants, especially since the areas of divided usage a are precisely those in which early settlement or density of population necessitated the greatest number of interviews. Thus, the single occurrence of /w-/ in *wheelbarrow* among the four informants in Rabun County, in the northeastern corner of Georgia, is more conspicuous on the map than the unanimous usage of the thirteen informants in Manhattan. It is apparent from the map that there is some difference in the distribution of forms without /h-/: initial /w-/ seems to occur most frequently in *whip* and least frequently in *wheelbarrow*;[42] but in general the three territories coincide.[43]

Pronunciations of these words without /h-/ occur in three different types of distribution.

1. There is, first, an area where forms with initial /w-/ predominate, extending from the neighborhood of Albany south to Washington, Annapolis, and the Maryland-Virginia line on the Eastern Shore of Chesapeake Bay, and from the eastern end of Long Island west to the confluence of the Shenandoah and the Potomac, and to the headwaters of the Ohio. This area thus embraces the Hudson Valley, metropolitan New York, the Delaware and Susquehanna Valleys in Pennsylvania, the greater part of the Delmarva peninsula, and part of the Piedmont area of Virginia and Maryland -- essentially the two eastern portions of Kurath's North Midland, with adjacent territory to the north and south (Kurath 1949:fig. 3).[44] The forms with /w-/ are thus established in three of the active *focal areas* of the Atlantic Seaboard (i.e. areas whose economic, political, or cultural prestige has helped spread their speech forms to other areas): the Hudson Valley (including metropolitan New York City), the Philadelphia area, and the Pennsylvania German area.

2. Next we find a predominance of pronunciations with initial /w-/ in two discontinuous coastal areas: the New England coast from Boston north to the Canadian border, and the South Atlantic coast from

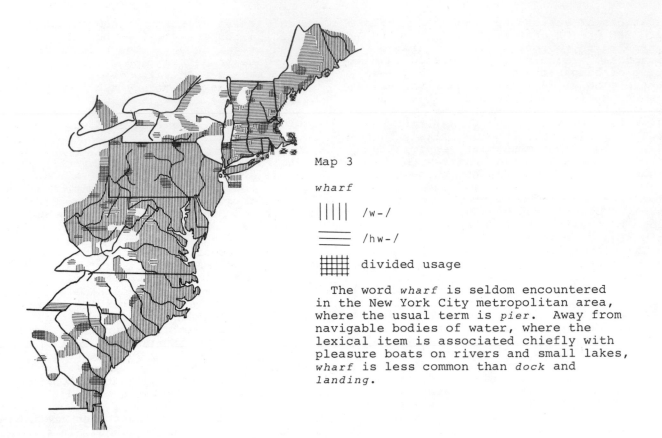

Map 3

wharf

||||| /w-/

≡ /hw-/

▦ divided usage

The word *wharf* is seldom encountered
in the New York City metropolitan area,
where the usual term is *pier*. Away from
navigable bodies of water, where the
lexical item is associated chiefly with
pleasure boats on rivers and small lakes,
wharf is less common than *dock* and
landing.

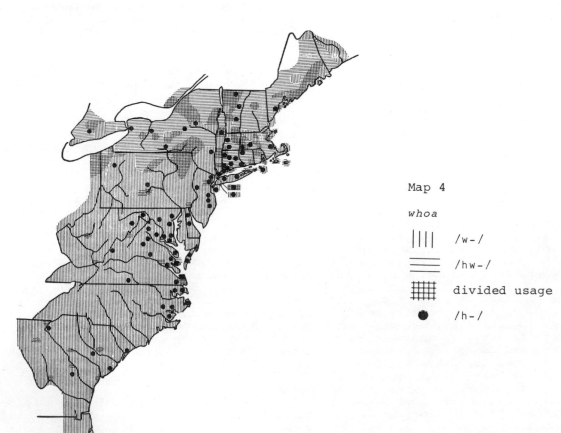

Map 4

whoa

||||| /w-/

≡ /hw-/

▦ divided usage

● /h-/

Georgetown, S.C., to St. Augustine, Florida.

3. Finally, pronunciations of this type occur in scattered communities, chiefly along the coast.

In New York State the boundary of the area with predominant loss of /h-/ coincides with the bundle of isoglosses setting off the Hudson Valley from upstate New York; in Pennsylvania it roughly follows a west-east line from the crest of the Alleghenies to the forks of the Susquehanna, essentially following the bundle of isoglosses setting off the North from the Midland.

It is difficult to decide whether forms without /h-/ are spreading or becoming less frequent in the Middle Atlantic States. In communities of divided usage at the edge of this area, such as Washington and a number of points in central and western Pennsylvania, it is usually the younger and more sophisticated informant who uses the form without /h-/. On the other hand, in metropolitan areas nearer the center of this area, it is the forms with /h-/ that are likely to occur in the speech of cultured informants. This is true in New York City and its suburbs, in Philadelphia, and in Baltimore. Thus, in Baltimore, all three of the cultured informants have /hw-/ in *whip* and *wheelbarrow*, and two of them have it in *whetstone*. It may be that in this area we are witnessing two trends: an earlier spreading of forms with /w-/ through the prestige of the New York and Philadelphia foci, and a later restoration of /h/ in those foci in spelling pronunciations arising under the influence of the public schools.

In the narrow coastal areas from Boston north and from Georgetown south, clear trends seem to be even less evident than in the central Atlantic area. In neither area is there any evidence that the forms without /h-/ are spreading inland. In both Boston and Charleston -- the old economic and cultural centers of the two areas -- the most sophisticated informants use /hw-/, though occasionally /w-/ also occurs in their speech.

Map 2 shows the presence or absence of initial /h/ in *whinny* or *whicker*. The latter form is frequent both in eastern New England and along the South Atlantic coastal plain, from the southern end of Chesapeake Bay to Florida. The analysis of the pronunciation with /w-/ is complicated by the occurrence of two rather common lexical variants with different initials: *laugh* (possibly of German origin) in eastern Pennsylvania (Kurath 1949:62-63), and *nicker* in the Virginia Piedmont and in areas strongly under Virginia influence: Maryland, West Virginia, and the Piedmont and mountain areas of the Carolinas and Georgia.

The distribution of forms without /h-/ largely agrees with that of *whip*, *whet-stone*, and *wheelbarrow*. There seem to be a few more communities in which *whinny* or *whicker* shows loss of /h-/: in South Carolina and Georgia, the area with /w-/ in *whinny* or *whicker* spreads up the Santee Valley as far as Columbia, and within this area such forms are used by a relatively larger number of cultured informants. If one seeks reasons, one may suggest that *whinny* or *whicker* is a homely word, seldom learned from books except in the larger cities, and is thus less likely to develop a spelling pronunciation than the words shown on Map 1.

Three informants in the South Atlantic States (at Beaufort and Chester, S.C., and Milledgeville, Georgia) use forms of the types *hinny* or *hicker*, where the /h-/ is retained but the following /w/ is lost.

Map 3 shows that *wharf*, like *whinny*, occurs in only part of the Atlantic Seaboard area. In the Hudson Valley and Greater New York, the usual word is *pier*; in inland communities, away from navigable waters, where local experience with boating is confined to pleasure craft on rivers and small lakes, the words most usually recorded are *dock* and *landing*.

Pronunciations of *wharf* without /h-/ are much more widely distributed than such pronunciations of the other words we have examined. In New England they occupy more of the coast and occur more frequently inland. They are found in New York State in the upper Susquehanna Valley and throughout Pennsylvania; and they predominate in West Virginia and in the South Atlantic States. The difference in distribution is most striking in Virginia and North Carolina; whereas *whip*, *wheelbarrow*, *whet-stone*, and *whinny* rarely show loss of /h-/, *wharf* occurs without /h-/ almost everywhere in the South Atlantic States where it is recorded at all.

The wider distribution of /w-/ in *wharf* may be explained by the social status of the word. Speakers who use the word most frequently are likely to know it as part of an occupational vocabulary dealing with the sea or with seaports; and inland speakers who acquire the word are most likely to acquire it from contacts with the sea and with seaports. Since the area in which /w-/ is more common in other words lies along the seacoast, it is not surprising that the seacoast pronunciation of a typical seacoast word should have been accepted rather far inland.[4][5]

Map 4 shows the word *whoa*, used as a cry to stop a horse. This has a still different distribution of the forms without /h-/. Whereas *whip*, *wheelbarrow*, *whet-stone*, *whinny*, and *wharf* generally have coastal forms with /w-/ and inland forms with /hw-/, the division for *whoa* is in terms of latitude rather than of distance from the coast. The isogloss marking the southern limit of /hw-/ in *whoa* coincides with the line that Kurath has established

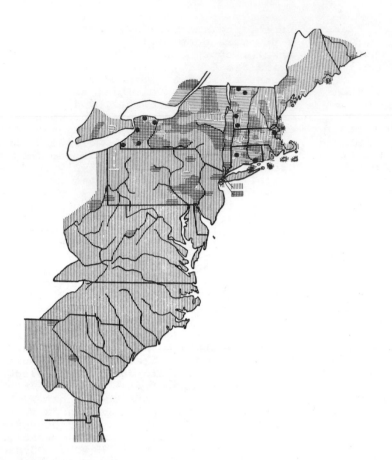

Map 5

humor

||||| /ɟ-/

≡ /hɟ-/

▦ divided usage

● /h-/

as the southern limit of the Northern
speech area, running roughly east and west
across Pennsylvania on the latitude of the
forks of the Susquehanna. South of that
line /hw-/ occurs in *whoa* barely twenty
times, and never predominates in any community. It is thus clear that /hw-/ in
whoa is characteristically Northern. But
even in the Northern area /hw-/ is not
universal. In Maine, Vermont, central
Massachusetts, the Adirondacks, eastern
Ohio, and the Plymouth Colony area from
Plymouth to Cape Cod, the word very commonly has /w-/; this is the usual form,
in fact, in the Hudson Valley and on all
of Long Island except the eastern end.

Beside /hw-/ and /w-/ in *whoa*, one also
finds /ho/, with retention of /h/ but loss
of /w/. This form is most frequent in
western Connecticut, in the New York metropolitan area, and along the South Atlantic coast from the head of Chesapeake Bay
to the Neuse River. It also occurs sporadically in Massachusetts, upstate New
York, and South Carolina (Kurath 1949:16,
66, fig. 108).

Of the major cultural foci along the Atlantic Seaboard, only Boston has a majority of informants who pronounce *whoa* with
/hw-/. However, all three forms -- with
/hw-', w-, h-/ -- are well established; and
in view of the lessening importance of
horse-drawn vehicles, the chances are that
none of these terms will ever attain na-

tional currency at the expense of the
others.

Map 5 shows the pronunciations of the
word *humor*. These also have a regional
distribution of north against south. The
forms with /h-/, however, occur both in a
smaller territory and, in communities
where they occur at all, more often alongside forms with /ɟ-/. On the other hand,
there is evidence that /hɟ-/ is being introduced in some of the eastern focal centers, probably through orthographic influence.

Areas in which *humor* always has /hɟ-/
are relatively small: most of the Connecticut Valley and the Lake Champlain watershed, plus scattered communities in eastern New England, western New York, eastern
Ontario, and eastern Pennsylvania. In
most of Maine, New Hampshire, New Jersey,
and the lower Hudson Valley, *humor* has
only /ɟ-/, as it has in Manhattan and most
of Long Island; but Brooklyn and Queens,
the Philadelphia, Boston, and Portland
areas, and the Merrimack and Delaware Valleys show divided usage. In Pennsylvania
west of the Susquehanna and in the entire
area south of the Mason-Dixon Line, forms
with /hɟ-/ are rare, occurring always
alongside forms with /ɟ-/ in the usage of
the community and often (as with both occurrences in Georgia and one in West Virginia) in the usage of the same informant.
It should be noted, however, that in many

communities with divided usage -- Portland, Boston, Providence, Springfield, New Haven, and the lower Delaware Valley -- the forms with /hj-/ occur in the speech of the younger and more sophisticated informants. This suggests that we may see the /hj-/ type becoming more common, perhaps as a spelling pronunciation encouraged by the public schools.

A few occurrences of forms with /h-/ but without /j/ are recorded.[46] A third of them occur in Vermont, and another third in upstate New York west of the Genesee River, an area whose original settlers came predominantly from western New England.[47] One Negro informant in coastal Georgia has initial /nj-/. The substitution of /nj/ for /j/ is a common feature of the speech of the Gullah Negroes (Turner 1949:27, 243).

Our examination of the Atlas materials from the Atlantic Seaboard shows that the distribution of forms with /h-/ before /w, j/ is much more complex than previous investigations had indicated -- that we must consider, in fact, not one pattern but four, of which two are complicated by the fact that the word in question does not occur in all parts of the area. It is also apparent that the distribution is geographical rather than social. The question then arises how this distribution is to be explained.

One is first tempted to examine the situation in the British Isles. In southern England today, speakers of the Received Standard favor /hj-/ in *humor*, as in all other words of its class, and consider the /j-/ pronunciation a little old-fashioned; but they prefer /w-/ in *whip*, and consider /hw-/ characteristic of Scottish or American speech. The occurrence of /w-/ in *whip*, *wheelbarrow*, *whetstone*, and *whinny* on the Atlantic Seaboard, chiefly along the New England and Southern coast and in the hinterlands of New York City and Philadelphia, may be partially explained by the commercial and social ties between London and the American ports, but it is not the whole story: the Virginia Piedmont, despite the economic, cultural, and social ties of the Virginia planters to London and the English university towns, uses /hw-/ in these words.

Our present knowledge of British folk speech is likewise of little help. The only systematic investigation so far -- fifty-two interviews conducted in 1938 by Guy Lowman, Jr. -- reveals that /h-/ is uniformly lost in southern England in all the words under examination.[48] Wright's *English Dialect Grammar* and *Dictionary* (1905, 1898-1905) show /hw-/ and /hj-/ only in Scotland and the northernmost communities of England; grammars of local dialects, including Wright's grammar of his own Yorkshire dialect (1892), show consistent loss of /h-/.[49] For Scotland and northern Ireland, as important as

southern England for the study of American English, there is little information.

There is always a temptation to ascribe a dialect pattern to the influence of a foreign-language group. The areas in which the loss of /h-/ before semivowels is most complete are the Hudson Valley and eastern Pennsylvania. Since neither German nor Dutch has initial clusters of the types /hw-,hj-/ one might ascribe the loss of /h-/ in these areas to the foreign-language substratum.[50] But the most that one can validly say is that in communities with dialect mixture -- and every community on the Atlantic Seaboard spoke a mixed dialect from the beginning -- Dutch and German speakers learning English would learn the forms without the initial clusters lacking in their native language. This explanation is supported by the rather high frequency of forms with /w-/ for /hw-/ in Middle Western cities with large groups of German, Italian, or Slavic immigrants. But it finds little support in South Carolina above tidewater between the Santee and the Savannah: here, even though the original eighteenth-century population was mostly German (Meriwether 1940), pronunciations of *whip*, *wheelbarrow*, *whetstone*, and *whinny* without /h-/ are exceptional.

Perhaps the best -- though only a partial -- explanation of the differences in distribution is arrived at by considering the two clusters separately. It is apparent that /j-/ in *humor* is far more widely current in standard speech in the United States than in England, while for all words but *wharf* (for which the American pattern is explained by the economic and social backgrounds in which the word is used) and *whoa* (for which we have no British material except in Lowman's records), /w-/ is more prevalent in England. Moreover, the judgment of lexicographers and other recent observers is that in England the prestigious forms are /hj-/ and /w-/, both of which are gaining under the influence of the prevailing London pronunciations. We may conclude that in England the /hj-/ in *humor* indicates a spelling pronunciation which has gained favor in the last century, while the spread of /w-/ in *whip* reflects the ascendancy of one dialectal type over another.[51]

Studies in English historical phonology emphasize that the two clusters must be considered separately. In the early seventeenth century, initial /h-/ was generally not pronounced in words of Romance derivation, presumably including *humor* (Zachrisson 1927:107; Zachrisson's word lists do not suggest any loss of /h-/ in *whip* and the like). During the eighteenth century, orthoëpists increasingly insisted on the pronunciation of orthographic initial *h* in such words, but only Johnston 1764 listed *humor* as requiring /h/ (Jespersen 1909-49:1.2.943). Ellis reported the nineteenth-century pronunciation of *humor* as generally lacking the /h/ (1869-89:4.1145).

For words like *whip*, pronunciations without /h/ have apparently existed for over five centuries; it is generally agreed that they spread from the London area throughout southern England. Luick finds evidence for such pronunciations in the London dialect of about 1400 (1921-40: 1.704, 753). Kökeritz cites fifteenth-century Suffolk spellings suggesting the loss of a phonemic contrast between initial /hw-/ and /w-/.[52] Wyld finds evidence for the change from /hw-/ to /w-/ in the correspondence of Queen Elizabeth (1920:138-39, 180; 1927:§286). It is first noticed as a phonological feature in Jones 1701. In Johnston 1764 the loss of /h-/ in these words is reported as common. William Kenrick's *New Dictionary of the English Language* (1773; Ellis 1869-89:4. 1050-55) and Perry's *Royal Standard Dictionary* (1775; Krapp 1925:2.245-46) both indicate /w-/ in *whine*, etc. In his work *Propriety Ascertained* (1787), James Elphinston, a Scot, labels pronunciations of *whip* and the like with /w-/ as bad practices noticed in England. Walker 1791 terms the loss of /h-/ in these words a London peculiarity (Jespersen 1909-49:1. 13.51). Ellis calls attention to the fact that in the nineteenth century /hw-/ was retained in northern England but was not common in the south, where there seemed to be a definite trend toward /w-/, most evident in the London area (1869-89:1.188; 2.573, 605; 4.1145). Sweet 1874 suggests that the disappearance of the cluster /hw-/ will soon be complete.[53] Fifteen years later, however, he predicts that it may be restored as a spelling pronunciation[54] -- a prediction which has not yet been fulfilled. By the turn of the century Skeat reported the change to /w-/ as accomplished in standard British English.[55]

Predictions concerning the extent of such a change are hazardous; but a series of observations by competent observers can indicate a trend, especially if they take into account the cultural forces operating in favor of one or more of the competing forms.

By the time of the American Revolution neither the restoration of /h-/ in *humor* as a spelling pronunciation nor the simplification of /hw-/ to /w-/ had been carried out in the cultured speech of southern England. Consequently it is easy to understand both the overwhelming preference of American speakers for *humor* with /j-/, and the fact that the areas with /w-/ in *whip*, *wheelbarrow*, *whetstone*, and *whinny* center around the ports, where contact with England was longest maintained by the mercantile class. Probably the social prestige of British pronunciations -- as among the older families in Charleston and among some of the socially privileged groups in New York City -- has kept the pronunciations with /w-/ in the status of cultured forms. It is likely, furthermore, that this status, rather than a foreign-language background, is responsible for the fact that these forms are city pronunciations; socially prestigious speech forms often spread from city to city without affecting the intervening rural areas.[56] That /w-/ is more widely distributed in *wharf* than in the other words of this group is satisfactorily explained by the fact that *wharf* is associated with the coast: the pronunciation is usually acquired with the word itself by inland speakers through contacts with coastal people. *Whip*, *wheelbarrow*, and *whetstone*, on the other hand, designate objects typical of everyday life in any rural or small-town community. There is no reason for inland speakers to borrow the coastal pronunciation.

The history of *whoa* is less adequately documented than that of any other word in this set. Though *ho* as an interjection dates from the fourteenth century, *who(a)* from the fifteenth, and *woa* from the eighteenth, the cry to stop an animal does not appear in literary citations before the nineteenth century; the *OED* citations of *whoa*, *woa*, and the dialectal variant *way* all appear between 1828 and 1850. *Ho* occurs much earlier, with citations from the Middle English period; but again the first citation as a cry to stop an animal is dated 1828. This is a typical word from the sphere of humble life; it would scarcely appear in literature before the era of romantic realism, and would not be influenced by orthographic traditions or the doctrine of correctness. As a consequence we can expect several variants to exist side by side in the dialects over a long period, and to enter the American colonies together (Kurath 1949:16, 41, 66, fig. 108).

But even on this basis we cannot explain the fact that *whoa* occurs with /hw-/ only in the New England settlement area. We must recognize, to be sure, that dialect mixture has been the rule rather than the exception in all American communities from the beginning (A. L. Davis and R. McDavid 1950). Even though /w-/ did not completely replace /hw-/ in prestigious British speech until the end of the nineteenth century, forms with /w-/ were current in colonial New England and probably in the other colonies (Orbeck 1927:9). That the process of leveling out the original dialect mixture in New England should result in a preponderance of /hw-/ in *whoa* is no more surprising than that the same process should favor such characteristically Northern words as *pail* and *swill* (Kurath: 1949:12-13, 48, 56, fig. 67). Systematic investigation of British dialects[57] may provide the basis for more detailed conclusions; for the present we can only summarize the recorded facts. The methods of linguistic geography exemplified in the American Atlas have generally confirmed the previous observations of competent scholars, and have provided us with a framework for interpreting these observations more accurately.

[The simplification of the initial /hw-/ cluster in *whip*, etc., and the recognition of the simplification by the Merriam *WNID-3*, was one of the examples of linguistic degeneracy mentioned in the attack on the *Third* by the professional defenders of the good, the true and the beautiful. It has been most recently deplored by Morris and Morris 1975. But however distressful the change may be to someone who regularly has /hw-/, there is no question that the simplification has been spreading recently and is now characteristic of educated speech in most metropolitan areas of the northern United States.]

NOTES

[1] The Linguistic Atlas project was initiated in 1930, under the sponsorship of the American Council of Learned Societies and the direction of Hans Kurath. So far only the New England section and its handbook (Kurath *et al.* 1939-43, 1939) and the Upper Midwest section (Allen 1973-76) have been published. Field work for the *Linguistic Atlas of the Middle and South Atlantic States* was completed in 1949 and *LAMSAS* is now being published (Kurath *et al.* 1979-); the records were consulted for this article with Kurath's permission. The records from southwestern Ontario, essentially contiguous to the Canadian communities investigated in connection with the work in New York State, are included in the *Linguistic Atlas of the North-Central States* (Marckwardt *et al.* 1980-).

The authors appreciate the assistance of J. W. Downer in checking data in the files of the Linguistic Atlas.

[2] In general, the intrusive [h] before a vowel seems to be most common before stressed syllables, especially before extra-loud stress. In such dialects [h] is not phonemic; non-significant preaspiration of initial vowels is a common function of loud stress (Proctor 1885).

[3] An important exception is the pronoun *it* (which usually occurs with weak stress), where the historical form [hɪt] is associated with lack of social prestige; compare stressed [hɪm] but weak-stressed [ɪm]. Recent investigations have found exceptions to the traditional picture of preaspiration as a non-distinctive feature of initial vowels in southern British dialects (Kökeritz 1932:§221, Widén 1949:§93). This modification is probably due less to recent influence of the standard language than to the fact that recent investigations have been more systematic than those on which Wright based his observations. Thus the 1938 survey of southern England by Guy S. Lowman, Jr. (Viereck 1975) disclosed that dialects west of London largely retain postvocalic /-r/ in *first*, *barn*, *beard*, etc., although it has been traditional to state that this sound was lost everywhere in southern England (cf. Widén 1949: §7).

[4] Dickens' representation of Uriah Heep as saying *'umble* indicates that by 1850, the date of *David Copperfield*, the pronunciation of initial /h-/ in such words had become for some people a badge of social respectability. Conversely, the practice of representing the pronunciation without /h-/ as 'dialectal' and typical of an unsavory character such as Uriah Heep may have increased a tendency to look upon the pronunciation of these words with /h-/ as socially preferred (Ives 1950b). The mixture of attitudes toward these pronunciations is shown in a series of letters to *Notes and Queries* (1853), prompted by the appearance of *David Copperfield* and Dickens' representation of *'umble* as a substandard form. In a debate among amateurs over the propriety of pronouncing initial /h-/ in English words of Romance derivation, pronunciations without /h-/ were variously described as a mark of culture, a vulgarism, and an affectation assumed by younger members of the clergy. *Humor* was frequently said to be one of the words where the pronunciation without /h-/ was acceptable in cultured speech.

[5] Except for a few dialects, chiefly in the southeastern United States, where *here* and *hear* have /hj-/, this cluster occurs only before /u/, mostly in words of Romance derivation.

[6] "To this day 'the baby whales' and 'the baby wails' sound exactly alike in my pronunciation, as they do in the pronunciation of many speakers in all parts of the country, cultured and uncultured alike."

[7] Spears 1949. Yet the cultured informant interviewed for the Linguistic Atlas in the Utica area has no /h-/ in *whip* and *humor*.

[8] Lounsbury (1904:23, 194, 197) insists that the pronunciation of /hw-/ rather than /w-/ in words like *whip* is overwhelmingly predominant 'in polite society' in the United States, but concedes that there is 'wavering' in the usage for *humor*.

Whitney (1874:268-70) is even more prescriptive. "That those who say *hwen* and *hyu* have preserved an earlier and fuller sound, which has suffered corruption and abbreviation in the mouths of the other party, admits no serious question. . . . With a great part of the vulgar speakers of English, the tendency is toward eliminating the surd instead of the sonant of the combination which ought to contain both, converting *when* into *wen*."

A. J. Ellis (1869-89:4.1125) suggests that Whitney's attitude was perhaps influenced by the

way he had heard people pronounce his own name:
"Mr. Whitney is an incontrovertible authority as
to the way in which he pronounces, and wishes
others to pronounce, the initial sounds of his
own name, but . . . he must have met with many
who disputed it. Possibly he is often called .
. . [i.e. a pronunciation with /w-/ for /hw-/],
as he certainly would be generally in London."
Whitney's conclusions were also disputed by E.
S. Sheldon (1890), a native of Maine: "*Humor* I
think I used to pronounce [yʊ̃] without the [h].
The *wh* question I cannot here discuss fully, but
I should regularly write [hw] in the words concerned, and not [w]. But some Americans do say
[w], especially in the word *wharf*, common in New
England at least, as [wɔəf] or [wɔf]. Compare the
dialect of the *Biglow Papers*. I remember a college classmate of mine, some twenty years ago, who
came from Cincinnati, and who regularly said [w]
for the written *wh* as in *where*, *when*, etc. Perhaps the [h] now common was introduced or at least
assisted by the schoolmasters."

[9] Thomas 1947:102, "In all English dialects the
substitution of [j] for [hj] . . . is considered
substandard, though common in most large cities.
Similarly, the substitution of [w] for [hw] is
usually considered substandard in America, though
this also is common in most large cities. In the
South of England, on the other hand, the substitution of [w] for [hw] is normal."
    Kennedy 1935:209, "Some people regularly simpli-
fy this combination to [w] alone, saying *wen*,
were, *wy*, and so on, and everyone does it to some
extent in hasty and careless speech. Some speakers, it is true, intensify the diphthong [ɪu]
after initial [h] so as to produce a combination
[hj] in such words as *Hewlett*, *huge*, *human*, *humor*,
and then, just as in the case of [w] above, the
[h] is lost, and such pronunciations as [jumr] and
[jumən] result."

[10] Mencken asserted that the attempt to enforce
the pronunciation of /h-/ in such words was an affected imitation of the British, "The majority of
Americans seem to have early abandoned all effort
to sound the *h* in such words as *when* and *where*.
It is still supposed to be sounded in England, and
its absence is often denounced as an American bar-
barism, but as a matter of fact few Englishman actually sound it, even in their most formal discourse. . . .The Americans do not sound the *h* in
heir, *honest*, *honor*, *hour*, and *humor* and their
derivatives, and frequently omit it in *herb*, *humble*, and *humility*"(1936:350). It is difficult to
understand how Mencken could have got the picture
of British and American usage reversed.

[11] S.v. *humor*: "The *h*, formerly silent, is now
generally pronounced, both in England and the
United States, although many good speakers, following the older orthoëpists, as Smart, omit it,
esp. in the senses referring to mental states."
In the synopsis of opinion and disputed points of
pronunciation -- a feature carried over intact
from earlier Merriam-Webster dictionaries -- all
dictionaries except that of the Rev. James Stor-
mouth are indicated as recognizing both /hj-/ and
/j-/ pronunciations of *humor* (Introduction §277).

In another passage (Introduction §258) we read:
"*wh* as *when*, *what*, *which*, is, in America, usually
pronounced as *h* + a voiceless *w*, no voice being
heard until the beginning of the following vowel.
In England, and by many American speakers, it is
usually pronounced simply as a voiceless *w*, although still often, especially in the South of
England, as an ordinary *w*."

[12] Three pronunciations are given: with [hju-,
hɪu-,ju-]. The [ju-] type is indicated (Introduction §210) as "most likely to occur in 'sense of
humor,' 'mood,' and the verb." Words of the *whip*
and *whoa* types are cited only with [hw-], but with
the notation that [w-] pronunciations are common.

[13] S.v. *humour*: "The pronunciation of the initial *h* is only of recent date, and many still omit
it, esp. in the senses under II," which deal with
feelings. S.v. *wh-*: "/w-/ is now universal in
English dialect speech, except in the four northernmost counties and north Yorkshire, and is the
prevailing pronunciation among educated speakers.
/hw-/ is general in Scotland, Ireland, and America, and is used by a large proportion of educated
speakers in England, either from social or educational tradition, or from a preference for what is
considered a careful or correct pronunciation."
    Cf. Jespersen 1909-49:1.13.51, "In order to in-
dicate the retention of the old sound as an Irish-
ism B[ernard] Shaw has recourse to the spellings
hwat and *hwy* (*John B[ull's Other Island]* 9.77)."

[14] The /ju-/ form of *humor* is labeled 'dialectal' by Michaelis and Jones, 'old-fashioned'
by Jones. Michaelis and Jones has no entries
under [hw-]; Jones gives [hw-] as a secondary
(i.e. less frequent) pronunciation for words of
the *whip* group, except for *whoa*, which is given
only with [w-].

[15] Fowler 1926:240, "*Humour* is still often or
usually pronounced without the *h* sound; the derivatives now being rarely without it, *humour*
itself will probably follow suit." "The broad
principles [of socially acceptable pronunciation]
are: pronounce as your neighbors do, not better;
for words in general use, your neighbor is the
general public"(466-67).

[16] Hempl suggested that the large proportion of
Scotch and Irish settlers may have helped American
pronunciation to retain the /hw-/. He noted that
/w-/ regularly occurred "only in Maryland and in
certain circles in New York City." Cf. Jespersen
1909-49:1.13.51.

[17] Grandgent's observations were based on
answers to a mailed questionnaire. "My correspon-
dents are nearly unanimous in favor of *hw* in all
the examples except *wharf*, *whoa!*, and the interjection *why*."

[18] Krapp 1925:2.245-46, "The pronunciation . . .
varies . . . both pronunciations occurring in all
regions and at all levels of speech, though the
former [i.e. the one with /hw-/] is the more common. Especially when relatively lightly stressed,
initial *wh* is likely to be pronounced as *w*."

Krapp observes that the pronunciation with /w-/ has been opposed by early American grammarians and other authorities. It was, however, regarded as standard by the *Royal Standard Dictionary* of the Londoner Perry (1775) and was taken over in the early American editions of that work. In his *Travels* (1821-22:1.468), Timothy Dwight reported, without disapproval, that Bostonians often omit /h-/ in words written with *wh*.

Noah Webster (1789) spoke of /w-/ in *whip* and the like as a fault. He asserted that the "pure English stock" in the United States keeps /h-/ in these words, and that its loss is a foreign corruption (Ellis 1869-89:4.1068).

[19] Kenyon 1924:§227, "The distinction between [hw] and [w] by which, e.g., *whether* is distinguished from *weather* is still standard usage in America, though there are a great many speakers who do not make the distinction. Reliable statistics are lacking as to whether the substitution of [w] for [hw] is increasing here. It has probably been frequent for many generations." Kenyon cites (§348.2) several pronunciations of *humor*, suggesting a semantic difference between the forms with and without /h-/, but does not indicate their relative distribution.

[20] Kurath 1928a:284, "In *white, wheat, whale,* etc., the [w] is always preceded by a voiceless fricative; only in the exclamatory *why!* and in weakly stressed position, as in *somewhat, whatever, whenever,* and unstressed *when, what, where,* this voiceless sound is slighted." Kurath 1928b: 386-87, "Among the retarded sounds one might mention . . . the first consonant in *wheat* [ʍiːt] which with us is still generally pronounced as a voiceless labial fricative followed by a voiced glide (except in parts of the South; elsewhere rather commonly in unstressed *whatever, whenever, wherever,* and the exclamatory *why!*), while it became fully voiced in Southern English."

Stuart Robertson (1934:227) observes that, contrary to Kurath's statement in Kurath 1928a, initial /w-/ in words like *whip* does occur in New York City and Philadelphia.

[21] Marckwardt 1942a:46, "Like [h] the sound [ʍ] tends not to appear in unstressed situations, where [w] is frequently substituted for it. . . . There is also some difference between British and American practice in respect to [ʍ] in such words as *whine, whether, whale,* Southern British tending to employ [w] to a greater extent."

[22] Primer 1888:91, "In the combination *wh* the *h* is always silent [in Charleston]." Primer 1890: 199, "[In Fredericksburg] the *h* never disappears in the combination *wh* as in Charleston, S.C."

[23] Emerson 1891:168, "In [the Ithaca dialect] the sound [i.e. /hw-/] is regularly preserved, though /w-/ for /hw-/ is occasionally heard as an individual peculiarity. In unstressed syllables /hw-/ is sometimes reduced to /w-/, sometimes lost."

[24] W. A. Read 1911:530. Using a written check list, he found, for informants in the Gulf States,

69 examples of /hj-/ in *humor*, 172 of /j-/. Wise 1933:39 states that in the South /hw-/ is usual in *white,* etc., but that /w-/ sometimes occurs in New Orleans.

[25] Shewmake 1920:31, "The omission of the [h] sound in words like *white* and *where* is not characteristic of the Virginia dialect except in one word, *why,* and not in this one except when it is used with exclamatory or expletive force."

[26] Greet 1931a:170, "[ʍ] stressed is stable on the coast as well as elsewhere in the South." Greet 1931b:401, "There is some uncertainty in the employment of [ʍ] [in Maine]. I believe that normally [w] for [ʍ] is more common than the retention of [ʍ]. This is not true, I think, of polite speech in Boston and Cambridge." Greet 1933:62, "[ʍ] is commonly replaced by [w] except in the word *wharf,* which is very common . . . [w] for [ʍ] in stressed syllables occurs rather often in the speech of coastal Virginia and South Carolina, and I am told that it is current in Philadelphia, as it is in New York City, particularly in Brooklyn and elsewhere on Long Island. Generally in the United States [ʍ] is stable in stressed syllables, though usually modified to [w] in unstressed syllables." Greet does not cite the evidence that led him to revise his judgment of two years before.

[27] Ayres 1933:9 reports that /hw-/ is normal in Bermuda in *which* and *while,* though *whaling* has initial [v].

[28] Brooks 1935:41 is in doubt about the interpretation of spellings like *w'ich, w'y, w'at* in the Uncle Remus stories of Joel Chandler Harris -- since he had himself done no field work in the dialect area which he attempts to compare with British speech.

[29] Stanley 1937:56, "The initial [h] has not been restored in *herb, humble, humor* . . . in East Texas speech; that is, they have not acquired the spelling pronunciations which they have in some sections." Stanley reports (71) that in East Texas /hw-/ is normal in words like *whip* and *wheelbarrow.*

[30] C. K. Thomas 1935-37, 1942. Thomas obtained most of his data from readings of a prepared text, which would probably yield more occurrences of /hw-,hj-/ than would be found in normal speech. Most of his informants are college students.

For upstate New York he reports 27 occurrences of *humor* with /hj-/, 5 with /j-/. The proportions of /hw-/ to /w-/ vary from 4:3 for *wheeze,* to 28:1 for *when.* For the three words on which he has the most information, the figures are 321:84 (*wheelbarrow*), 293:58 (*while*), 224:58 (*what*). For subdivisions within the upstate area, the percentages of occurrences of *wheelbarrow* with /w-/ are: 'Southern' (lower Hudson) 57; 'Eastern' (Mohawk and upper Hudson) 35; 'Northern' (Adirondacks and St. Lawrence) 3; 'Central' (Finger Lakes) 16; 'Western' (Genesee to Lake Erie) 15. He concludes that there is a trend toward /w-/ in the southern and eastern sections, the forms lacking /h-/ being most common in the neighborhood of large cities.

For the downstate New York area -- New York City, Long Island, and suburban Rockland and Westchester Counties -- Thomas finds a relatively higher proportion of forms without /h-/. For *humor* he has 10 examples with /hj-/, 7 with /j-/. Only one word (*where*, with a non-significant proportion of /hw-/ in 6 records to /w-/ in 5) has /hw-/ more often than /w-/. The ratio of /w-/ to /hw-/ is generally about 3:2 -- *wheelbarrow* has 52 /w-/ to 46 /hw-/; *white* 159:113; *while* 112:104; *whale* 89:25; *whistle* 63:15.

[31] Tressider 1943:271. Tressider's informants were girls, students at Madison College, a state teacher's college in Harrisonburg, Virginia. He reports /j-/ more common than /hj-/ in *humor*, though occurring only twice in *huge*. Most informants have /hw-/ in *where*, etc., but forms with /w-/ appear occasionally, especially among students from the counties on the Eastern Shore of Chesapeake Bay; out of six informants from this area, three have /w-/.

[32] Mencken 1948:203, 209. The pronunciation of words like *whip* with /w-/ is twice noted as characteristic of the Philadelphia area.

[33] Hubbell (1950) bases his conclusions on phonographic recordings of both prepared texts and free conversation. He distinguishes both age levels and cultural levels among his informants, and recognizes the limitations of read material (cf. Frank 1949).

Of /h-/ Hubbell writes (42): "So far as its phonetic distribution is concerned, metropolitan speech differs from that of much of America in that the initial cluster /hw-/ (in words like *when* and *white*) does not occur in the speech of most New Yorkers. . . . Furthermore, the initial cluster /hj-/ (in words like *huge* and *humorous*) is very frequently lacking on the uncultivated and intermediate levels. . . ." Again (54): "On the uncultivated and intermediate levels of New York speech the cluster /hj-/ does not occur, all words like *huge* being pronounced with /j-/ alone. (Such pronunciations are very common in the speech of Columbia undergraduates who come from the city.) The distinction recorded in our dictionaries between /j-/ as a variant in *humor* and its derivatives, and /hj-/ alone in other words of this group appears in the speech of [five informants]. But more commonly New Yorkers are consistent in pronouncing all these words with /hj-/ or /j-/." And again (52): "In words of the type of *whale*, *wheel*, *when*, the cluster /hw-/ may occur, but the most common pronunciations on all levels of metropolitan speech are [those without /h-/]. Speakers who employ /hw-/ consistently in all words of this historical class are rather rare. In uncultivated speech /w-/ is universal; on the intermediate and cultivated levels, /hw-/ may not infrequently be heard, but its use is more often than not sporadic -- the speaker will employ it only in a restricted number of words or will pronounce the same words now in one way and now in the other. . . . There can be little doubt that the /hw-/ pronunciations are for the most part consciously adopted ones, adopted because of the widespread

notion that pronouncing *whale* and *wail*, *whet* and *wet* as homonyms is 'incorrect.' New Yorkers of Irish birth usually employ /hw-/ or some variant of it in these words, but the pronunciation rarely survives in the speech of the second generation."

[34] "The loss of [h] in *wheelbarrow*, *whetstone*, etc., is common on the coast from Marblehead to Machias, and occurs in scattered points elsewhere. . . . In *wharf*, a seashore term, the loss of [h] is much more widespread. It seems that the conservative coast towns from Long Island Sound to New Brunswick have preserved in this word a type of pronunciation that was widely current in New England in Colonial times and that this coastal pronunciation has been retained in the upland through contact with the seashore"(cf. Kurath *et al.* 1939:23, chart 8).

[35] Field workers were encouraged to record *conversational* responses, i.e. forms which occurred spontaneously in the informants' conversation while discussing a particular topic suggested by the field worker. These are especially significant when they differ from answers to direct questioning.

[36] [Comparable data is now recorded for all of the United States east of the Mississippi, for all of the two next rows of states except Kansas and West Texas, and for Colorado, eastern Montana, Washington, Nevada, and California.]

[37] The distribution of /h-/ before vowels does not appear to be significant for American English. For words of Old English or Scandinavian derivation, the absence of /h-/ seems to be confined to sporadic foreign-language settlements. For words of Romance derivation, where there seems to be some variation in British usage, *hotel* (which is stressed on the first syllable by perhaps a majority of American speakers) always has /h-/, and *hostler* is only a book word except among railwaymen; *humble* and the proper name *Humphrey* or *Humphries* seem to have geographical variants, the forms without /h-/ being apparently more common in the South Atlantic States than elsewhere, but are very difficult to elicit in a conversational interview.

[38] Most of the other words in which some speakers have /hj-/ and others have /j-/, such as *huge* and *human*, are difficult to elicit in a conversational situation. Moreover, of this group *humor* seems to be the word occurring most frequently with /j-/ (Thomas 1935-37, 1942).

[39] *While* was systematically recorded only in New England; stressed *what* was not investigated in New England. *Wheel* (*the baby*) was also not investigated in New England; in the Midland and the South, the verb for this action is generally *roll* or *ride*. *What time is it?* was recorded throughout the Atlantic Seaboard; but in this phrase, *what* has reduced or weak stress, and is thus not comparable with the other words (cf. fnn. 20 and 21).

[40] This procedure is not strictly phonemic, since conceivably some speakers may have weak

murmur onset before semivowels or vowels, and strong aspiration for /h-/. However, in the absence of a phonemic analysis for each informant, the assumption that murmur is an allophone of /h-/ is at least a working hypothesis by which the data can be interpreted.

[41] No attempt has been made to identify the communities in which the variants *whetrock*, *whetseed*, *whetter*, and *whet* occur, since all these have the same initial.

[42] Explanations of the facts are risky. Nevertheless, *whip* does occur often with secondary or tertiary stress in conversation and in compounds -- situations where the /h-/ might be weakened; and the common practice of moistening a whetstone with water or spittle may occasionally tend to an association with *wet*.

[43] In two communities in southern Ontario, the field workers recorded *wheel* in conversation with /w-/, though *wheelbarrow* was offered as a response to direct questioning with /hw-/.

[44] In his radio program *Where are you from?* Henry Lee Smith, Jr. set up an undelimited dialect type which he called Central Atlantic Seaboard; it probably coincides with the area where /h-/ is lost in these words. As a derivative of Smith's area we may include the St. John's Valley in southern New Brunswick, which was settled at the end of the eighteenth century by Loyalists from the New York City area (see Kurath *et al.* 1939:17, 23, 33, 238-40).

[45] Possibly the loss of /h-/ in *wharf* began earlier in England, since two of the four earliest examples cited in the *OED* (including the earliest) lack the /h-/. On the basis of the New England evidence alone, Kurath labels *wharf* a "seashore term" (Kurath *et al.* 1939:9). The contrast between the distributions of /w-/ in *wharf* and in *whip* is, however, much more spectacular in the South than in New England.

[46] Instances in which field workers recorded a falling diphthong with an unrounded first element are included with /hju-/.

[47] In two Vermont communities, the field worker recorded *music*, *beautiful*, and *bureau* with /mu-, bu-/, with a diphthongal but fully rounded syllabic.

[48] Under direct questioning, one informant used /hw-/ in *wheelbarrow* and another did so in *whetstone*. Each of these, however, also offered conversational instances of the same word with /w-/ (cf. Viereck 1975).

[49] Wright 1905:§240 reports that /hw-/ is preserved in the Shetlands and Orkneys, most of Scotland, Ireland, Durham, Northumberland, Cumberland, Westmoreland, northern Yorkshire, and the Isle of Man; elsewhere in England it has become /w-/ (see also Wright and Wright 1924:§284). Neither Wright 1905 nor Wright 1898-1905 includes *whoa*, whose pattern of distribution in the United States is

markedly different from that of *whip*, *wharf*, or *whinny*.

Kruisinga 1905:§246, §315 finds *humor* with /j-/ in Somerset, *whip* and the like with /w-/. Occasionally *what* and *when* appear with /h-/ and no /w-/.

Kökeritz 1932:§223 reports that in Suffolk the phoneme /w/ has a voiceless allophone in the neighborhood of voiceless sounds; but there is no evidence of a phonemic contrast between the two kinds of [w].

[50] The peculiarities of Charleston pronunciation have been attributed to the Huguenot settlement in the early eighteenth century (Primer 1889). Untrained observers have frequently asserted Negro influence to be responsible for those features of Southern white speech which are not found in their own dialects. For an evaluation see R. and V. McDavid 1951b (in this volume, pp. 43-51) and R. McDavid 1950a. The subject of borrowing has been treated by Haugen 1950a,b, 1953.

[51] Compare Jespersen 1909-49:1.2.943, "*Humour* and *hotel* are now pronounced with [h] by some educated speakers, without [h] by others." /w-/ for historical /hw-/ "is not . . . nowadays regarded as nearly so 'bad' or 'vulgar' as the omission of [h], and is, indeed, scarcely noticed by most people. In fact, a great many 'good speakers' always pronounce [w] and look upon [hw] as harsh or dialectal. In some schools, however, especially girls' schools, [hw] is latterly insisted on" (Jespersen 1909-49:1.13.51). See Robertson 1934:242.

[52] Kökeritz 1932:§370; especially significant are such hyperforms as *where* for *were*. See also Whitehall 1935:70 and Wyld 1920:311-12.

[53] The loss of /h-/ in the Old English clusters /hr-,hl-,hn-,hw-/ "is at the present moment being carried out with the only remaining member of the group" (525-26) -- i.e. /hw-/.

[54] Sweet 1888:§917, "Toward the close of [the eighteenth century] . . . [hw] began to be levelled under [w], and in the present cent. the change was carried out universally, even among those who still retained [h] as a mark of gentility. But of late years it has begun to be restored in Southern [British] educated speech, partly by the influence of the spelling, partly by that of Scotch and Irish pronunciation, so that in another generation it will probably be completely restored. It is now pronounced in unstrest words, where it was probably weakened into [w] in the period when it was a natural sound."

[55] Skeat 1901:452, "It is in the South that [hw] has become a mere [w], whilst in the Northumbrian district it is still fairly maintained."

[56] Thus, in the South Carolina Piedmont, urban informants -- like the mercantile and plantation caste of the coastal plain, especially Charleston -- generally lack the constriction of postvocalic /-r/ in *barn* and *beard*, though rural speakers often have it (R. McDavid 1948; in this volume, pp. 136-42).

[57] When we try to plot on a map of the British Isles what we learn from Wright 1898-1905 about items that have a clearly defined regional distribution in the United States, we discover how exceedingly fragmentary our knowledge of British dialects actually is. Thus, of the many names current in this country for the earthworm, only *eaceworm* and *angledog* are recorded in Wright's *Dictionary*. [Many of these gaps have been filled by Orton *et al.* 1962-71, by Kurath and Lowman 1970, by Viereck 1975, and by Mather and Speitel 1975-. But there is still much to be done.]

Among the significant differences between Standard English and Vulgar English which Fries indicated in his *American English Grammar* (1940), one of the more interesting is the occurrence of the uninflected plurals of nouns of measure. We may use Fries's summary of the evidence from written materials as an introduction to the problem of the regional and social distribution of these plurals in the spoken language (43-44; numbers in parentheses are references for Fries's corpus of letters):

> The *s*-less form of nouns for periods of time or measures of distance after numerals appears in a wider range of constructions in [Vulgar English] than in [Standard English]. The following examples are typical of uses that do not appear in . . . Standard English:
>
>   he has been in . . . 18 *month* (8168)
>   my husband left me 3 *month* ago (8012)
>   he only served about 3 *month* (8401)
>   havnt herd from him for two *month* (8118)
>   he is only 16 *year* of age (8040)
>   a 8 *month* old baby (8211)
>   about five *foot* away (8402)
>   five *foot* eight inches tall (8460)
>
> Even in [Vulgar English], however, this wider and older use of the *s*-less form after a numeral is not very frequent, for it appeared in only 11 percent of the situations in which it was possible.

The writers of grammars and composition manuals have long considered these uninflected plurals of nouns of measure as a regular feature of vulgar or illiterate English. They have consistently warned against the low social status of such a phrase as *nine foot high* -- and *foot* is usually the form selected as a social shibboleth. Mencken expresses the same judgment (1936:462): "The common indicators of quantity seldom add *s* for the plural in the vulgate. Especially when preceded by a numeral, such words as *mile*, *bushel*, *dozen*, *pound*, *pair*, *foot*, *inch*, *gallon*, and *peck* retain their singular form." In short, Fries, Mencken, and the compilers of handbooks agree in considering the use of these uninflected plurals a social rather than a regional matter. If these generalizations were true, we might expect to find these plurals equally common in the folk speech of all regions, from the north woods of Minnesota to the swamps of Georgia, and from the Maine seacoast to the Bad Lands of the Dakotas.

Actually, each of these forms has its own distribution, limited geographically as well as socially.

The origin of these plurals is a complicated story. The records of the Linguistic Atlas include evidence on eight of them: *rod*, *year*, *foot*, *mile*, *head*, *pound*, *bushel*, and *yoke*. In Old English as now, *foot* had umlaut in the nominative and accusative plural. *Bushel* was borrowed into English from French in the thirteenth century, bringing an -*s* plural with it. None of the others was of the Old English strong masculine declension, from whose -*as* nominative-accusative plural the Modern English -*s* plural came. *Pound* and *year* had zero inflection in the nominative and accusative plural. In Old English, *head*, *rod*, *mile*, and *yoke* had nominative and accusative plurals that ended in a vowel; by Middle English these vowels would have all weakened to [ə] and then disappeared, leaving the plural unmarked. Moreover, certain numerals in Old English took the genitive plural, whose inflectional ending -*a* would disappear like the other vowel endings, and the dative plural -*um* would suffer the same fate. Thus the uninflected plural could have developed from the nominative, dative, genitive or accusative plural; the regular -*s* inflection, which was established by spreading from the nominative-accusative of the strong masculine declension to other cases and other declensions, would have probably encountered strong resistance from such frequently used nouns as those of measure. At any rate, for all of these uninflected plurals except *bushel* there are very early citations in the *OED*, and in the files of the *Middle English Dictionary* citations for *bushel* become common by the middle of the fifteenth century.[1]

The method of the Linguistic Atlas is well known. In the area to be investigated, a network of communities is set up, fairly evenly spaced with regard to geographic and population distribution and selected so as to reflect the ethnic and cultural history of the region. In each community selected for investigation, two representative informants are normally chosen for interviewing -- persons who have lived in the community all their lives and whose families reflect the population origins of the community. Generally, one is of the oldest native generation, with little travel or formal education; the other is somewhat younger and better educated. In some places --

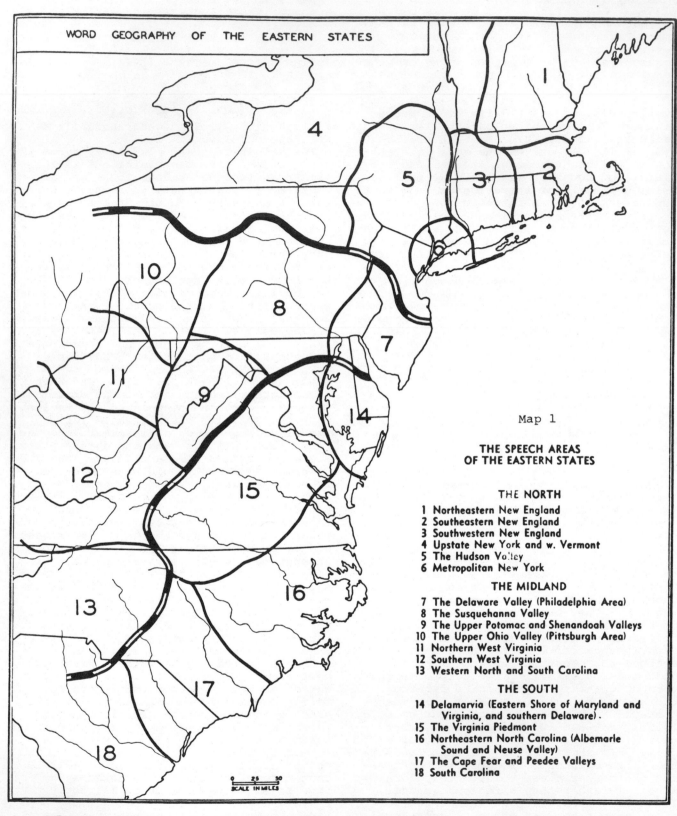

WORD GEOGRAPHY OF THE EASTERN STATES

Map 1

**THE SPEECH AREAS
OF THE EASTERN STATES**

THE NORTH

1 Northeastern New England
2 Southeastern New England
3 Southwestern New England
4 Upstate New York and w. Vermont
5 The Hudson Valley
6 Metropolitan New York

THE MIDLAND

7 The Delaware Valley (Philadelphia Area)
8 The Susquehanna Valley
9 The Upper Potomac and Shenandoah Valleys
10 The Upper Ohio Valley (Pittsburgh Area)
11 Northern West Virginia
12 Southern West Virginia
13 Western North and South Carolina

THE SOUTH

14 Delamarvia (Eastern Shore of Maryland and
   Virginia, and southern Delaware).
15 The Virginia Piedmont
16 Northeastern North Carolina (Albemarle
   Sound and Neuse Valley)
17 The Cape Fear and Peedee Valleys
18 South Carolina

0 25 50
SCALE IN MILES

From *A Word Geography of the Eastern United States*, by Hans Kurath (University of Michigan Press, 1949).
Reproduced by permission.

possibly a fifth of the communities investigated -- a third person is selected, a college-educated representative of a prominent local family. Each informant is interviewed by a trained field worker using a questionnaire of specific items, and the responses are recorded in minute phonetic transcription.

This particular study makes use of three bodies of Atlas materials:

1. The records from the Atlantic Seaboard States, collected under the immediate supervision of Hans Kurath, director of the Atlas project. The file comprises about 1500 records from Maine to eastern Georgia, plus the easternmost row of counties in Ohio and representative border points in New Brunswick, Ontario, and northeastern Florida. About 150 of these records are of cultivated speech.

2. The records from the *Linguistic Atlas of the North-Central States*, directed by Albert H. Marckwardt. This collection contains nearly 400 records from Wisconsin, Michigan, southern Ontario, Illinois, Indiana, Ohio, and Kentucky; about 30 are records of cultivated speech.

3. The records from the *Linguistic Atlas of the Upper Midwest*, directed by Harold B. Allen. This collection contains over 200 records from Minnesota, Iowa, the Dakotas, and Nebraska, plus a few border points in Canada; 15 are records of cultivated speech.[2]

In all, therefore, the conclusions for this paper are based on some 2100 field records from contiguous territory, including nearly 200 cultured informants -- the largest body of comparable data for American cultivated speech. Similar evidence is being collected along the Pacific Coast, in several of the Rocky Mountain States, and in parts of Texas, but it has not been consulted.

Because the questionnaires have varied somewhat from region to region, we do not have equally complete evidence on all of the plural forms that have been studied:

1. *Rod* was sought systematically only in New England, in the context *a hundred rods from here*. Outside New England, Guy S. Lowman, Jr., the principal field investigator for the Atlantic Seaboard States, made a systematic effort to elicit the form during his first year of Southern field work (1933-34), but when he found that the item was not generally known, he quit asking for it, and it was dropped from the questionnaire for the Middle and South Atlantic States. Other field workers, however, have recorded the form sporadically in upstate New York and elsewhere, when it occurred spontaneously in conversation.

2. Four items were investigated throughout the Atlantic Seaboard area, but were not included in the shorter questionnaires used for the North-Central States and the Upper Midwest:

year, in the context *three years old*
foot, in the context *nine feet high*
mile, in the context *ten miles*
head, in the context *two heads of lettuce*

3. Three items were investigated in all regions:

pound, in the context *two pounds*
bushel, in the context *forty bushels*
yoke, in the context *two yokes of oxen*

These contexts are by no means invariable. Most of these items are easily picked up in free conversation, and it makes no difference if the informant says a recipe calls for *two pounds* of flour, volunteers that he used to buy flour in barrels that held *two hundred pounds*, or indicates that a shoat becomes a hog when it weighs *a hundred pounds*.

The data for these plurals will be found summarized on both maps and tables. Map 1 is copied from Figure 3 in Kurath's *Word Geography of the Eastern United States* (1949), which indicates the speech areas of the Atlantic Seaboard as determined by lexical evidence. Some dotted lines mark tentative subareas suggested by a preliminary examination of the evidence from upstate New York, South Carolina and Georgia, Kentucky, and Ohio; these areas may well be modified as the evidence is more systematically analyzed. Other maps indicate the occurrences of the uninflected plurals, except the last group, where the distribution of the uninflected plurals of *yoke* and its synonyms seems to provide the more significant picture.

The first eight tables show the distribution of these plural forms by states. To be sure, the state is a linguistically irrelevant unit; nevertheless, for purposes of comparison, state-by-state totals are suggestive, and in regions where the dialect areas have not been determined (and where each state has been investigated as a separate administrative project), state distributions are the only ones we have to go on. Since the questionnaires have undergone revisions and some records are incomplete, the number of informants in each table is that of those who responded for the particular item; the percentages are of responses. The ninth table shows the relative incidence of these forms in the speech areas of the Atlantic Seaboard.

Rod

The plural *rod* is most common in Maine, New Hampshire, eastern Vermont, and northeastern Massachusetts -- the highly conservative area of Northeastern New England. Within this area, gaps appear in the Merrimack Valley, and in the northern part of York County, the southernmost county in Maine. Outside this area, *rod*

Table 1

rod(s

State	# inf.	% uninfl.	% both	% infl.	# cult. inf.	% uninfl.	% both	% infl.
New Brunswick	6	50	–	50	1	–	–	100
Maine	67	58	2	40	3	–	–	100
New Hampshire	42	45	10	45	3	67	–	33
Vermont	42	24	5	71	1	–	–	100
Massachusetts	108	19	7	74	15	–	7	93
Rhode Island	20	20	–	80	5	–	–	100
Connecticut	57	25	17	58	11	9	9	82
Long Island	2	100	–	–	–	–	–	–

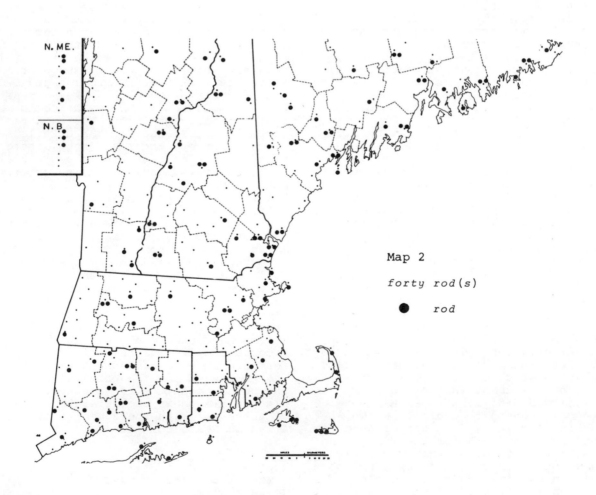

Map 2

forty rod(s)

●   rod

occurs only occasionally in the rest of Massachusetts, except for Nantucket (which was settled from Essex County, in northeastern Massachusetts) and Martha's Vineyard, where it is regular. It is fairly common in western Connecticut, and follows the Connecticut Valley north from Hartford. There are only two examples of *rod* in western Vermont, the source of much of the population of upstate New York and of the New England settlements in the Great Lakes Basin. Presumably *rod* was once considerably more common in western New England than it is now, for it has been recorded sporadically throughout the Northern settlement area as far west as southern Minnesota.

Year

Year is the least frequent of the uninflected plurals. It is quite common in Connecticut and in northeastern New England, but rare in the rest of Massachusetts and in Rhode Island. Again there are gaps in the Merrimack Valley and York County, and also in northeastern Maine. Although there are no examples of *year* in western Vermont, metropolitan New York, or the Hudson Valley, a few occur along the St. Lawrence Valley and in western upstate New York.[3] This leapfrogging across eastern New York State to the Genesee country in the west is characteristic of other linguistic features as well: the absence of constricted postvocalic /-r/ in *barn*, the fronting of /u/ in *two*, *piazza* 'porch,' *ketcht* as the preterite of *catch*, and *waked up* as the preterite of *wake up* (Atwood 1953a, R. McDavid 1951a).

In the Midland area, *year* is most common in southern New Jersey, which had a considerable body of early settlers from New England, and in western North Carolina, where it is the regular plural. There are a few examples in western Pennsylvania, West Virginia, Maryland, and the northernmost counties of South Carolina, and a string of occurrences following the Shenandoah Valley, one of the major routes of migration from Pennsylvania south to the Carolinas. There is also a scattering of examples in the region between the Cape Fear and Pee Dee Rivers, a linguistic corridor reflecting the Highland Scots settlements of the mid-eighteenth century, and an important trade route from the North Carolina Piedmont to the coast.

In the Southern dialect region, *year* occurs occasionally in Delaware, but not in the rest of the Delmarva peninsula. There are a few examples in the Virginia Tidewater region, more along the North Carolina coast and in South Carolina. The Virginia Piedmont lacks *year* entirely, and it is probably the expansion of the Virginia Piedmont to the west that is responsible for the absence of the form in southwestern Virginia.

Foot

Foot as a plural is common throughout all the Northern region, including greater New York City, but is present only on the periphery of the Hudson Valley. Like *year*, it does not occur in northeastern Maine. In the Midland region, *foot* occurs frequently in southern New Jersey and eastern Pennsylvania, less frequently in western Pennsylvania and West Virginia, but it is found in western North Carolina. *Foot* also occurs generally in the South, except that -- like *year* -- it is strikingly absent in the center of the Virginia Piedmont; it is also lacking in the Orangeburg area in the South Carolina Low-Country. Thus, in the South Atlantic States, *foot* occurs in a belt stretching from the North Carolina and South Carolina coast northwestward through Virginia and West Virginia to the Ohio. The areas in North Carolina and southern South Carolina where the plural *foot* does not occur are areas of heavy German settlement, but this may be merely coincidence.

Mile

Mile occurs almost everywhere in the Midland and the South, and is by contrast rare in the North. There are a few examples in Maine, New Hampshire, and Connecticut, but not many in Massachusetts, western Vermont, and eastern upstate New York. Again we find the uninflected plural, absent in eastern New York, occurring in the area west of the Genesee. Perhaps the examples here have been reinforced by Pennsylvania influence along the Genesee Valley; Midland vocabulary items are found in this part of New York State (R. McDavid 1951b).

Except near the Susquehanna, the northern limit of the Midland form *mile* seems to follow the boundary between New York and Pennsylvania, rather than -- as with most vocabulary items -- the southern boundary of the northern tier of Pennsylvania counties.

The Hudson Valley and New York City have practically no examples of *mile*. This item is very useful for indicating the area of New York City influence, since *mile* is common both in Connecticut to the east and New Jersey to the west.[4]

Head

The plural *head* is predominantly New England and Southern. It is the regular form in Maine, New Hampshire, and eastern Vermont; it is a little less common in Massachusetts, Rhode Island, and Connecticut, and rarely occurs in western Vermont and upstate New York. Although practically nonexistent in the Hudson Valley, it is fairly common in greater New York -- four examples in Manhattan and one in Brooklyn.

Table 2

year(s

State	# inf.	% uninfl.	% both	% infl.	# cult. inf.	% uninfl.	% both	% infl.
New Brunswick	5	–	–	100	1	–	–	100
Maine	66	12	6	82	3	–	–	100
New Hampshire	43	11	8	81	2	–	50	50
Vermont	49	4	2	94	1	–	–	100
Massachusetts	129	6	4	90	15	–	–	100
Rhode Island	26	4	–	96	3	–	–	100
Connecticut	56	13	13	74	10	–	–	100
New York	172	4	4	92	25	–	–	100
New Jersey	47	17	–	83	5	–	–	100
Pennsylvania	154	5	–	95	15	–	–	100
Ohio	26	8	–	92	4	–	–	100
West Virginia	107	8	–	92	7	–	–	100
Delaware	13	31	–	69	2	–	–	100
Maryland	58	9	–	91	7	–	–	100
Virginia	141	7	2	91	14	–	–	100
North Carolina	148	25	–	75	12	–	–	100
South Carolina	116	5	6	89	22	–	–	100
Georgia	58	15	11	74	8	–	–	100
Florida	7	–	29	71	2	–	–	100

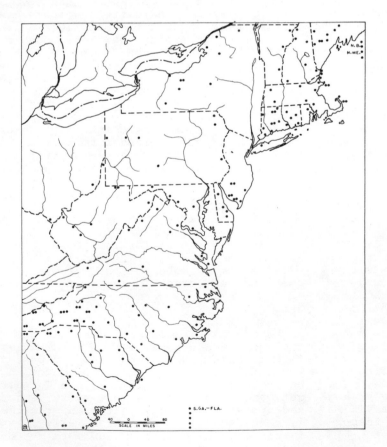

Map 3

three year(s) old

●   *year*

[204]

Table 3

foot, feet

State	# inf.	% uninfl.	% both	% infl.	# cult. inf.	% uninfl.	% both	% infl.
New Brunswick	7	86	–	14	1	100	–	–
Maine	48	75	6	19	2	50	–	50
New Hampshire	49	53	13	34	3	–	–	100
Vermont	48	39	20	41	1	–	–	100
Massachusetts	131	20	9	71	13	8	–	92
Rhode Island	23	5	22	73	5	–	–	100
Connecticut	65	12	18	70	11	10	–	90
New York	174	27	8	65	25	–	–	100
New Jersey	48	37	4	59	5	–	–	100
Pennsylvania	162	19	1	80	15	20	–	80
Ohio	28	4	–	96	4	–	–	100
West Virginia	110	14	1	85	7	–	–	100
Delaware	12	50	–	50	2	–	–	100
Maryland	62	27	2	71	7	–	–	100
Virginia	151	24	2	74	14	8	–	92
North Carolina	154	26	2	72	12	–	–	100
South Carolina	132	14	19	67	24	–	12	88
Georgia	63	23	14	63	8	–	–	100
Florida	6	–	17	83	2	–	50	50

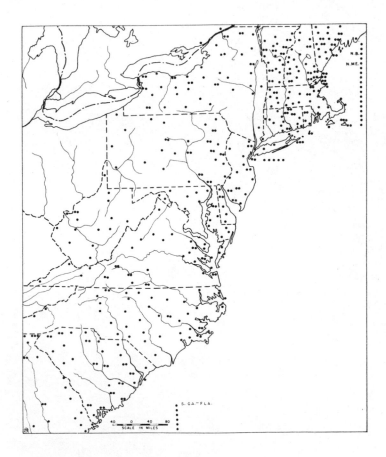

Map 4

nine feet high

● *foot*

Table 4

mile(s

State	# inf.	% uninfl.	% both	% infl.	# cult. inf.	% uninfl.	% both	% infl.
New Brunswick	5	40	–	60	1	–	–	100
Maine	74	20	–	80	3	67	–	33
New Hampshire	47	18	8	74	1	100	–	–
Vermont	51	10	–	90	1	–	–	100
Massachusetts	128	3	5	92	15	–	–	100
Rhode Island	23	13	–	87	3	–	–	100
Connecticut	66	11	9	80	11	–	–	100
New York	165	7	3	90	25	–	–	100
New Jersey	48	33	5	62	5	–	–	100
Pennsylvania	166	42	2	56	15	20	–	80
Ohio	32	44	6	50	4	25	–	75
West Virginia	110	40	–	60	7	–	–	100
Delaware	14	50	7	43	2	–	–	100
Maryland	62	46	–	54	7	–	–	100
Virginia	151	52	5	43	14	28	–	72
North Carolina	155	51	6	43	11	18	–	82
South Carolina	132	20	13	67	22	–	13	87
Georgia	63	23	19	58	8	–	12	88
Florida	7	–	–	100	2	–	–	100

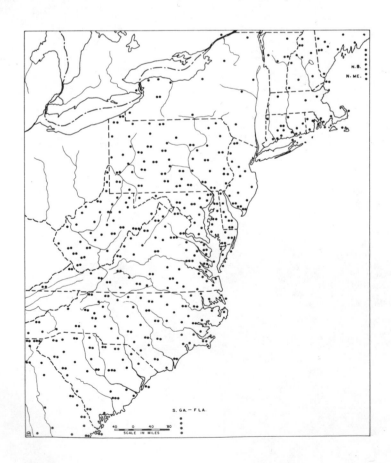

Map 5

two mile(s)

● *mile*

Table 5

head(s

State	# inf.	% uninfl.	% both	% infl.	# cult. inf.	% uninfl.	% both	% infl.
New Brunswick	7	100	–	–	1	100	–	–
Maine	70	77	3	20	4	–	25	75
New Hampshire	46	67	–	33	3	67	–	33
Vermont	45	30	3	67	1	–	–	100
Massachusetts	129	24	4	72	14	21	–	79
Rhode Island	23	13	4	83	5	–	20	80
Connecticut	65	15	3	82	11	18	10	72
New York	174	8	1	91	25	8	–	92
New Jersey	47	8	–	92	5	40	–	60
Pennsylvania	162	1	–	99	15	–	–	100
Ohio	27	7	–	93	4	–	–	100
West Virginia	110	4	–	96	7	–	–	100
Delaware	13	8	–	92	2	–	–	100
Maryland	59	13	–	87	6	33	–	67
Virginia	133	41	–	59	14	7	–	93
North Carolina	142	20	–	80	13	–	–	100
South Carolina	109	22	2	76	25	12	–	88
Georgia	50	18	2	80	9	12	–	88
Florida	5	–	–	100	–	–	–	–

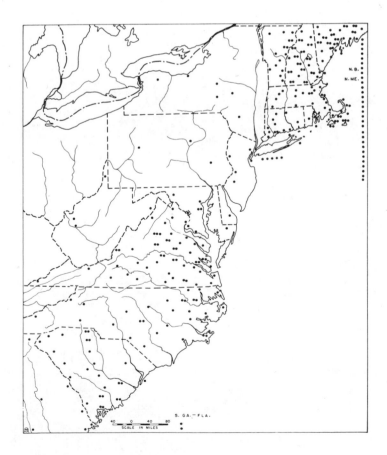

Map 6

two head(s) of lettuce

●   *head*

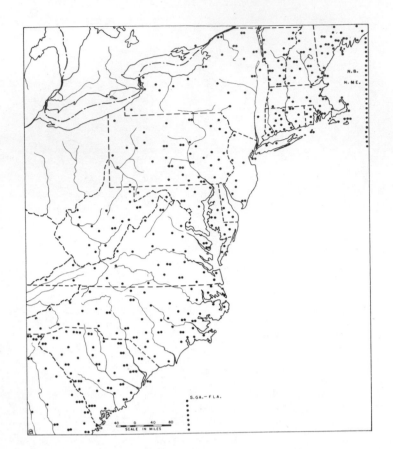

Map 7

two pound(s)

● *pound*

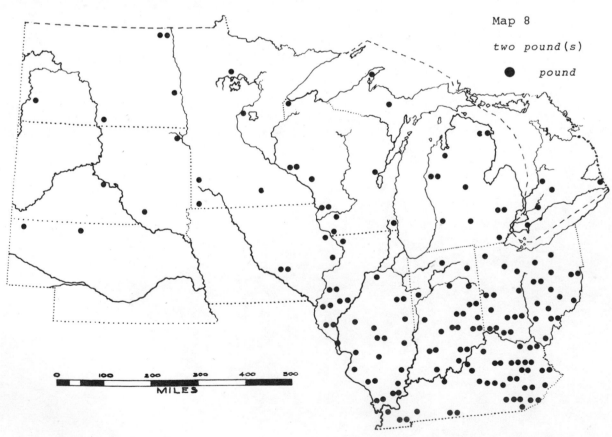

Map 8

two pound(s)

● *pound*

Table 6

pound(s

State	# inf.	% uninfl.	% both	% infl.	# cult. inf.	% uninfl.	% both	% infl.
New Brunswick	8	88	–	12	1	100	–	–
Maine	70	57	–	43	4	–	–	100
New Hampshire	42	42	6	52	2	–	–	100
Vermont	47	34	9	57	1	–	–	100
Massachusetts	127	12	8	80	14	–	–	100
Rhode Island	24	12	12	76	1	–	–	100
Connecticut	65	21	9	70	11	9	9	82
New York	162	15	5	80	24	4	–	96
New Jersey	48	18	–	82	5	20	–	80
Pennsylvania	162	26	–	74	15	–	–	100
West Virginia	110	20	–	80	7	43	–	57
Delaware	13	30	–	70	2	–	–	100
Maryland	60	23	2	75	6	–	–	100
Virginia	151	25	4	71	14	–	–	100
North Carolina	154	37	2	61	12	–	–	100
South Carolina	132	30	13	57	23	–	9	91
Georgia	63	42	9	49	8	12	12	76
Florida	7	–	29	71	2	–	50	50
Wisconsin	44	16	5	79	1	–	–	100
Michigan	62	11	10	79	5	–	–	100
Ontario	20	20	10	70	5	–	–	100
Illinois	65	34	8	58	4	25	–	75
Indiana	41	51	5	44	3	67	–	33
Kentucky	62	50	13	37	5	–	–	100
Ohio	91	24	14	62	9	–	11	89
Minnesota	63	9	–	91	6	–	–	100
Iowa	49	6	2	92	3	–	–	100
North Dakota	26	19	–	81	2	–	–	100
South Dakota	26	12	–	88	2	–	–	100
Nebraska	37	5	–	95	2	–	–	100

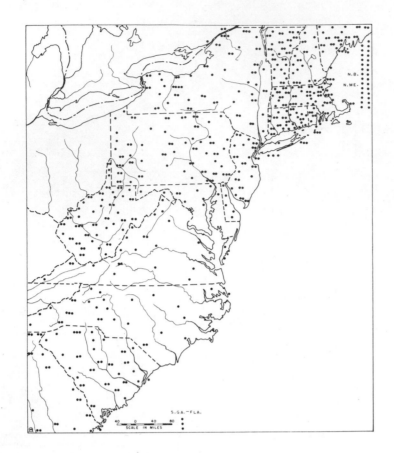

Map 9

forty bushel(s)

● *bushel*

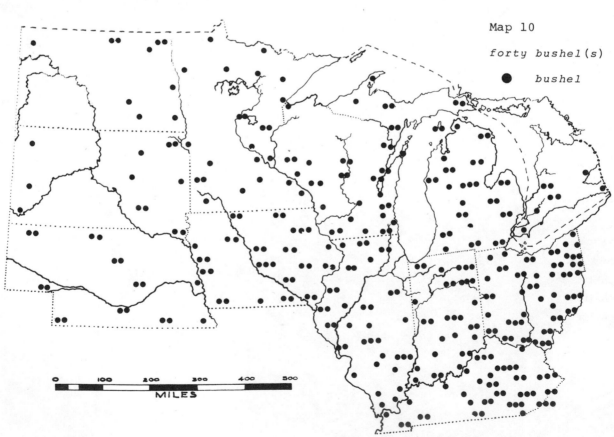

Map 10

forty bushel(s)

● *bushel*

Table 7

bushel(s

State	# inf.	% uninfl.	% both	% infl.	# cult. inf.	% uninfl.	% both	% infl.
New Brunswick	8	62	–	38	1	–	–	100
Maine	74	67	5	28	4	25	50	25
New Hampshire	47	48	–	52	3	67	–	33
Vermont	51	65	6	29	1	–	–	100
Massachusetts	128	46	3	51	15	33	–	67
Rhode Island	24	29	26	45	5	20	20	60
Connecticut	65	44	7	49	11	10	27	63
New York	163	44	6	50	25	16	8	76
New Jersey	48	58	2	40	5	40	–	60
Pennsylvania	162	44	–	56	15	13	–	87
West Virginia	108	58	–	42	7	43	–	57
Delaware	13	38	–	62	1	–	–	100
Maryland	62	16	–	84	7	–	–	100
Virginia	150	17	2	81	14	8	–	92
North Carolina	153	20	–	80	12	9	–	91
South Carolina	130	18	13	69	22	–	9	91
Georgia	63	23	12	65	9	12	–	88
Florida	7	29	–	71	2	–	–	100
Wisconsin	51	49	12	39	1	–	–	100
Michigan	60	65	7	28	4	–	–	100
Ontario	23	39	9	52	5	20	–	80
Illinois	66	52	8	40	4	–	–	100
Indiana	43	70	2	28	4	50	–	50
North Dakota	25	40	–	60	2	–	–	100
South Dakota	25	48	–	52	2	–	–	100
Nebraska	34	50	3	47	2	–	–	100

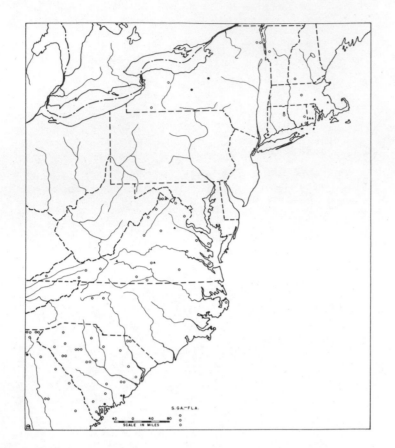

Map 11

two yoke(s) of oxen

○   *yokes*

●   *teams*

▲   *pairs*

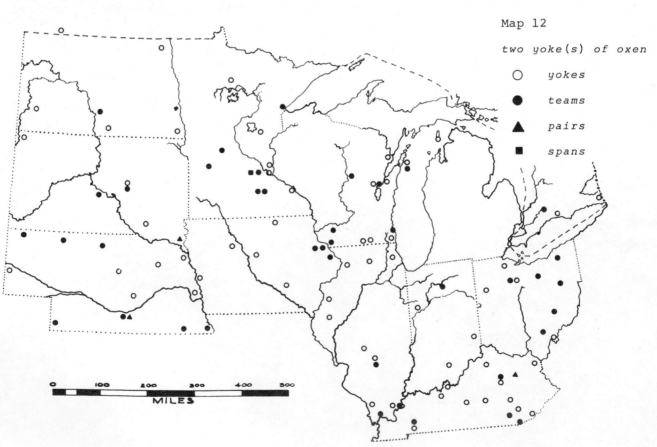

Map 12

two yoke(s) of oxen

○   *yokes*

●   *teams*

▲   *pairs*

■   *spans*

Table 8

yoke(s

State	# inf.	% uninfl.	% both	% infl.	# cult. inf.	% uninfl.	% both	% infl.
New Brunswick	8	100	–	–	1	100	–	–
Maine	47	100	–	–	4	100	–	–
New Hampshire	43	100	–	–	1	100	–	–
Vermont	33	97	3	–	1	100	–	–
Massachusetts	105	97	–	3	11	100	–	–
Rhode Island	13	77	–	23	2	100	–	–
Connecticut	35	94	–	6	8	100	–	–
New York	66	94	–	6	6	83	–	17
New Jersey	27	100	–	–	3	100	–	–
Pennsylvania	118	100	–	–	13	100		
West Virginia	103	100	–	–	6	100	–	–
Delaware	12	100	–	–	2	100	–	–
Maryland	53	100	–	–	6	100	–	–
Virginia	144	87	–	13	13	100	–	–
North Carolina	142	98	–	2	12	100	–	–
South Carolina	72	68	–	32	11	100	–	–
Georgia	37	65	–	35	4	100	–	–
Florida	3	67	–	33	–	–	–	–
Wisconsin	28	75	4	21	1	100	–	–
Michigan	6	83	–	17	–	–	–	–
Ontario	17	88	6	6	4	100	–	–
Illinois	33	73	–	27	2	100	–	–
Indiana	25	88	8	4	3	33	33	33
Kentucky	52	79	8	13	4	100	–	–
Ohio	51	92	–	8	5	100	–	–
Minnesota	37	86	–	14	3	100	–	–
Iowa	23	78	–	22	–	–	–	–
North Dakota	16	69	–	31	–	–	–	–
South Dakota	14	72	7	21	1	100	–	–
Nebraska	14	50	14	36	1	100	–	–

Table 9

Frequency in Atlantic Seaboard Speech Areas

Key: # very common; x fairly common; - rare

Area	rod	year	foot	mile	head	pound	bushel	yoke
NORTH								
1. Northeastern New England	#	x	#	x	#	#	#	#
2. Southeastern New England	x	-	x	-	x	x	#	#
3. Southwestern New England	x	x	#	x	x	#	#	#
4. Upstate New York and western Vermont	-	-	#	x	-	x	#	#
5. Hudson Valley			-	x		-	x	#
6. Metropolitan New York	-		x		-	-	x	#
MIDLAND								
7. Delaware Valley (Philadelphia area)	x	#	#		-	x	#	#
8. Susquehanna Valley (Pennsylvania German area)		x	#		-	x	x	#
9. Upper Potomac and Shenandoah Valleys	x	-	#		-	x	x	#
10. Upper Ohio Valley (Pittsburgh area)	-	-	#		-		#	#
11. Northern West Virginia	-	-	#		-		#	#
12. Southern West Virginia	-	x	#		-	x	#	#
13. Western North and South Carolina and North Georgia	#	x	#		-	x	x	#
SOUTH								
14. Delmarva (Chesapeake Bay)	-	#	#	-	#		-	#
15. Virginia Piedmont	-	x	#	#	x		-	#
16. Northeastern North Carolina (Albemarle Sound and Neuse Valley)	-	#	#	#	#		-	#
17. Cape Fear and Pee Dee Valleys	x	x	#	-	#		-	#
18. South Carolina and Georgia Low-Country	x	x	x	x	#		x	x

[214]

New Jersey, Pennsylvania, West Virginia, and western North Carolina have only occasional examples. In the South, *head* is very common in the Virginia Piedmont, from which it has spread into western Virginia. There are also a few examples in southern Maryland, eastern North Carolina, and South Carolina south and west of the Santee River. Interestingly, *head* is found not only in relic areas, where one might expect it as an archaism, but also strongly in focal areas, those whose economic, political, and cultural prestige has helped their speech forms to spread into other areas. Thus *head* is present in and around Boston, New York City, Charleston, and the cities of the Virginia Piedmont, though not Philadelphia.[5]

Pound

With a few exceptions, *pound* is distributed almost evenly throughout the three major dialect regions of the Atlantic Seaboard. Very common in northeastern New England, it is somewhat rare in central Massachusetts, the Hudson Valley, and southern upstate New York. The greater frequency with which it occurs in western New York is probably due to the influence of western New England rather than that of Pennsylvania, since *pound* also appears in the Adirondacks and along the St. Lawrence Valley.

In the North-Central States, *pound* occurs -- in general -- about as frequently as it does along the Atlantic Seaboard, but with some striking differences from state to state. Wisconsin, Michigan, and Ontario show an incidence of *pound* comparable to that in New York and Pennsylvania, Illinois and Ohio a somewhat higher incidence, and Indiana and Kentucky a very much higher one, so that on the basis of preliminary evidence Marckwardt selected *pound* as one of the critical items for defining the area of Midland influence.[6] With more information available, it seems better to suggest that the higher incidence of *pound* in the Ohio Valley is a reflection of South Midland influence; not only were South Midland settlers very numerous in Indiana, Kentucky, and southern Illinois, but along the Atlantic Seaboard *pound* is somewhat more common in the South Midland than it is in Pennsylvania.

West of the Mississippi, the incidence of *pound* drops off sharply, and there is no apparent differentiation between North and Midland. In fact, *pound* is slightly less common in Iowa and Nebraska than it is in Minnesota and the Dakotas.

Bushel

Bushel as a plural is most characteristic of the North and the Midland, with every Atlantic Seaboard state north of the Mason-Dixon Line showing at least forty-four percent of uninflected plurals, and no state in the Old South having as much as twenty-five percent. In Virginia, examples are scattered, most noticeably in a line marking the migration from Pennsylvania southward through the Shenandoah Valley. There are a few examples in eastern North Carolina, more in western North Carolina and throughout South Carolina and Georgia.

No striking regional distinctions appear in the North-Central States or the Upper Midwest, since these sections received relatively few settlers from the plantation South, and *bushel* is about equally common in Midland and North. The slightly lower incidence of *bushel* in the Upper Midwest, as compared with that in the North-Central States, may be explained by the later settlement, with public education established simultaneously with the land offices, and by the large proportion of literate settlers with a foreign-language background, who would often go directly to standard English through books instead of through the folk speech of earlier English-speaking settlers.[7]

Yoke

Yoke is by all odds the most common of these plurals, so common that on the relevant map we have indicated examples of only *yokes*, the inflected plural. For purposes of comparison, we have likewise indicated inflected plurals of common lexical variants: *pairs*, *teams*, *spans*. We have not included these lexical variants in the statistical tables, since one cannot assume that a person who offers the inflected form *pairs* would say *yokes* if he used the word.

The plural *yokes* occurs most frequently in South Carolina and Georgia, but even there in only about a third of the responses. Interestingly, there are no examples of *yokes* in western North Carolina, where draft oxen were used much later on the marginal mountain farms than on the cotton lands of South Carolina. In fact, there are only three occurrences of *yokes* in the entire state of North Carolina, somewhat more in Virginia (where oxen disappeared early in the Piedmont plantation area), none in the Midland, and only sporadic examples in the North.

In the North-Central States and the Upper Midwest the incidence of inflected forms rises sharply, reflecting less familiarity with the use of oxen, which have been largely replaced by tractors in both agriculture and lumbering, and which were never used in some parts of these sections. In fact, many informants in both these regions simply could not be induced to give a plural form; many had never seen an ox.

Previous judgments, like those of

Mencken, have been so insistent on the social distribution of the uninflected plurals that one is tempted to find a special explanation for their heavier incidence in some regions than in others. Automatically, one first suspects that there may have been a difference in the practices of different field workers. This suspicion must be reckoned with, because there were nine field investigators in New England alone and a total of twenty-four for the whole area under examination. But even allowing for some difference in training and procedure, the effect of field worker bias has been relatively small. For one thing, three quarters of the field records were made by two investigators, and within the area covered by each investigator there are more variations in the incidence of these plurals (or in any linguistic data) than one may find between the areas of any two investigators. For example, one may find rather clear differences even within such a relatively small area as northeastern New England, where Lowman worked, to say nothing of the territory he covered in the Middle and South Atlantic States. Perhaps a change in field workers is responsible for some of the sharp differences between eastern and western Vermont; almost certainly the high incidence of South Carolina, Georgia, and New York State informants using inflected and uninflected plurals of the same noun was at least partially due to the insistence of the field investigator in these areas on collecting as much data as possible from free conversation;[8] likewise, in New England, the areas investigated by Hanley, Harris, and Kurath show many conversational variants.

Another possible explanation is a difference in regional usage in England. Here we should like to have the data from the surveys now being conducted by Orton at Leeds (Orton *et al.* 1962-71) and McIntosh at Edinburgh (Mather and Speitel 1975-); for the moment, though, we must content ourselves with the evidence from Lowman's wide-meshed survey of southern England in 1937-38 (cf. Kurath and Lowman 1970, Viereck 1975). In the questionnaire used for this survey, Lowman included three of these plurals: *pound*, *bushel*, and *yoke*. However, the evidence is not very helpful: *pound* is the folk plural all over the area; *yoke*, *pair*, and *team* are used without any regional patterning; and the *bushel* is far less common as a measure of grain than the *comb* (four bushels) or the *quarter* (eight bushels). Actually, the complete British evidence would probably not solve our problem, since population history suggests that every one of the American colonies was an area of dialect mixture from the beginning.

One may find a partial explanation for some of the differences by examining the farming practices of the various areas. *Bushel* is absent from the Virginia Piedmont and eastern North Carolina, where tobacco, the traditional money crop, has been measured by hogsheads or hundredweight; if the word *bushel* were rarely used in everyday life, the standard form might gradually come to prevail. But in western North Carolina, where corn is a principal crop, we find *bushel* again; ignoring what corn is distilled and sold by the gallon (and, at least jocularly, older Carolinians often estimate the yield of a mountain cornfield as so many gallons to the acre), the crop would normally be reckoned in bushels. And along the South Carolina coast and in the Santee Valley, we find *bushel* again, because the staple crop was rice.

The most adequate explanation has already been suggested as the evidence was unfolded: the interpretation in terms of population history, settlement areas, trade areas, transportation, and culture. We should not be surprised to find, as we do find, that each of these plurals has its own history and geographical distribution.

This distribution is summarized in Table 9, where the relative incidence of the uninflected plurals is indicated for each of the speech areas which Kurath set off in his *Word Geography* on the basis of lexical evidence. The greatest incidence of uninflected plurals is to be found in Northeastern New England and Eastern North Carolina, two of the most striking relic areas along the Atlantic Seaboard. Next in incidence are Southwestern New England, the Delaware Valley, Delmarva, and the South Carolina Low-Country; three of these areas have important cultural centers. Next are Western North Carolina, Southern West Virginia, and the Cape Fear-Pee Dee corridor. The lowest incidence of the uninflected plurals is found in the Hudson Valley and Metropolitan New York.

On a regional basis, we can say that *pound* and *yoke* are about evenly distributed in North, Midland, and South. *Foot* and *head* are most common in the North and South, *bushel* in the North and Midland, *mile* in the Midland and South, and *year* in the South Midland and Northeastern New England. Thus no region lacks a concentration of one of these plurals.

An interesting social footnote is the distribution of these plurals in the speech of Negro informants. One of the most common devices used to give a literary stereotype of Negro speech is the uninflected plural; but the consistent use of uninflected plurals is found in the speech of only two Negro informants, one from the Gullah area of South Carolina and the other from the Gullah area of Georgia. An educated Negro of Charleston said *yoke*, and *year* as well as *years*, but inflected all the rest. In the Virginia Piedmont the Negro informants have about the same number of inflected plurals as the white informants of comparable social class, perhaps more.

Our maps do not show the trend in an area. If the instances of the inflected plural were also indicated, it would be apparent that where a community has divided usage, it is practically always the older and less educated informant who has the folk plural, and the younger and better educated who has the inflected one. This demonstrates that the uninflected plural is certainly receding, and where it is found at all -- with the exception of *yoke*, the item itself being a cultural relic -- it is a feature of folk speech. And with this same exception -- only two cultured informants use the inflected plural *yokes* -- the cultured speakers almost invariably have the standard inflected plurals. To be sure, even though the uninflected plurals are receding,

their occurrence is not limited to relic areas, since some of them are common in such focal areas as the Delaware Valley, the Virginia Piedmont, and the South Carolina Low-Country. Nevertheless, while recognizing that the facts are more complicated than Fries presented them, we are driven inexorably to the same conclusion he reached: that the uninflected plural of measure is not a feature of standard English. For, again making an exception of *yoke*, it is almost certain that those few cultured informants who use some of the uninflected plurals in speech would mark the inflection in writing.[9]

Confronted with such evidence as the Atlas presents, we may wonder if it is even necessary to mention these plurals in composition books. The chances are overwhelming that any native American college student who reads a composition book does not need to read that he should inflect his plurals.

NOTES

[1] See also Ekwall 1912. Compare Curme 1935: 23.4, "This old type of [uninflected] plural lingered into the modern period with nouns denoting measurement: 'Some of them weie fiue hundred *pound*' (Pory, *Leo's Africa*, A.D. 1600). In older English this plural spread in measurements to words originally masculine: 'The indigo plant grows about two *Foot* high' (*Pomet's History of Drugs*, A.D. 1712). In certain expressions this plural is still employed: 'ten *hundredweight*;' 'a German liner having 9000 *horse power*;' 'five *brace* of birds;' 'ten *gross* of buttons;' 'a gross = ten *dozen*;' often 'forty *head* of cattle;' ten *yoke* of oxen.' 'These lamps must be at least 40 *candle power*.' We often hear 'He is *five foot ten*.' The spread of this plural with measurements shows that a new idea had become associated with it, namely, a collective idea. With measurements this plural has in general passed out of the literary language. It still lingers, however, in colloquial and popular English: 'a couple of *year*' (dialect in the mountains of Kentucky)."

[2] Only the New England and Upper Midwest materials have been published: Kurath *et al.* 1939, 1939-43; Allen 1973-76. Permission to use the unpublished field records has been granted by the American Council of Learned Societies, sponsor of the Atlas project, and by Kurath, Marckwardt, and Allen.

Both R. and V. McDavid have participated in Atlas field work. Their experience covers all regions treated in this study except New England.

[Since the original publication of this article *LANCS* field work has been completed and editing is well under way at the University of Chicago (Marckwardt *et al.* 1980-). The materials for the Middle and South Atlantic States, now housed at the University of South Carolina, are in the final stage of editing (Kurath *et al.* 1979-).

When this article was written, in the fall of

1956, some of the field work still remained to be done in the North-Central States and the Upper Midwest. Since these recent records and the publication of Allen 1973-76 do not alter the basic pattern of distribution, no effort has been made to redraft the maps or recalculate the tables. A detailed appraisal of the North-Central evidence will be found in the grammatical volume of Marckwardt *et al.* 1980-, by V. McDavid.

[3] 'Upstate New York' includes all of New York State outside of Long Island, metropolitan New York, and the Hudson Valley.

[4] Although this item was not systematically investigated in the North-Central States, one may deduce that the uninflected plural is at least tolerated in standard usage, since it appears on road signs, e.g., "Ann Arbor 2 Mile," on U.S. 23.

[5] The distribution of *head* thus parallels the distribution of the loss of constriction of postvocalic /-r/, as in *barn*.

One may suspect that other contexts might show a somewhat different distribution of the uninflected plural of *head*. For *six head of children*, sought only in the South Atlantic States, the evidence is inconclusive, since relatively few informants used *head* or *heads* in this context. *Ten head of cattle*, where one feels the uninflected plural may be nearly universal, was not included in the questionnaire.

The appearance of *two head of lettuce* in focal areas may be partially explained by the fact that head lettuce is a relatively sophisticated article of diet, more familiar to urban than to rustic informants.

[6] Marckwardt 1940a; Marckwardt based his report on evidence from thirty-five communities, all from Michigan, Indiana, Illinois, and Ohio. No evidence

was available from the Middle Atlantic States, since field work in that region had just got under way.

[7] The incidence of folk verb forms drops off sharply from the North-Central States to the Upper Midwest. See V. McDavid 1956.

[8] Most rural informants base the differentiation between *pig*, *shoat*, and *hog* on their weight, a context in which the uninflected plural would naturally tend to occur spontaneously. Since R. McDavid was somewhat more thorough than most other field workers in investigating the nomenclature of swine, he probably caught more conversational examples of *pound* than other investigators. A similarly thorough exploration of swine nomenclature in Iowa and Nebraska might have produced somewhat different figures.

[9] As frequently as *ain't* occurs in popular speech, it is rarely written. It is apparently rare in the materials for Fries 1940, since it is nowhere treated in that work. Similarly, though three-fourths of the cultured informants from the Atlantic Seaboard say *he don't*, they would normally write *doesn't*.

The collections of the Linguistic Atlas of the United States and Canada, on which this paper is based, contain some 180 field records from New York State, about a ninth of the material collected along the Atlantic Seaboard from southern New Brunswick to northeastern Florida. Slightly over half of these were made by Guy S. Lowman, Jr., principal field investigator for the Atlas until his death in an automobile accident in 1941, while investigating the Finger Lakes region; most of the others -- plus a few records from border communities in Ontario -- I made during the academic year 1948-49. Material collected from other areas has of course been used where it throws light on the speech patterns of New York State.[1]

In examining the dialects of this country, a network of communities -- in New England by towns, in the rest of the country by counties -- is laid out according to the known facts of settlement history and population distribution. In each community a number of natives deeply rooted in the local culture are interviewed by a trained field worker; in most communities there are two such persons, or informants, one representing the oldest living native generation and having a minimum of formal education and contacts outside the community, the other being somewhat younger or better educated or both. In larger centers there are more informants, including one or more cultured informants with a college education or the equivalent in general cultural background; some cultured informants are also included from small-town or rural communities.

The interview is conducted with the help of a standard questionnaire of about 750 items, designed to obtain a representative sampling of pronunciation, grammar, and vocabulary. The items chosen deal with topics of everyday conversation -- the time of day, the weather, the household and furniture, the farm, tools and vehicles, clothing, topography, farm animals and calls to animals, crops, cooking, fruits and vegetables, wild animals, insects, trees and shrubs, kinship terms, body parts, states of health and illness, religion and superstition, social activities, business, and sports. The search is always for the common everyday term in use in the community now and in the past, rather than for the freak item or spectacular individual coinage -- for the bone and blood of the language that most accurately reflects the folk culture of the community. The interview is conducted in as close an approximation to ordinary conversation as the field worker is able to achieve, and the responses of the informants are recorded on the spot in phonetic notation, using a very finely graded alphabet.

The relative uniformity of American culture always strikes a European observer accustomed to the sharper regional and local differences of the older-settled nations. All Americans have in common most of their grammar and vocabulary, even when dealing with the simple things of everyday life that are learned from contacts within one's own community rather than from books. Even though local terms exist side by side with the general ones, a York Stater is likely to be understood in any English-speaking community in the United States if he talks of a *sawhorse*, a *vest*, a fresh-water *creek*, a *sidewalk*, a *ram*, a *bundle* of wheat, *doughnuts* (with slight reservations), *pancakes*, *cottage cheese*, a *sugar maple*, a *midwife*, or one's *best man*. Any normal horse will move forward if told *get up!* and no normal human being will be offended if saluted in late December with *Merry Christmas!* Even if some other local term is most frequently used in the community, the general term is recognized.

Another large part of the New York State vocabulary is shared both by the whole North and by at least part of the Midland sections which get their speech patterns from Pennsylvania settlements. In the North and parts of the Midland hay may everywhere be gathered into *haycocks* and stored in the *mow*; a field may be enclosed by a *stone wall* or a *stone fence*; a farmer takes a *grist* of wheat *clear across* the mountain to the mill, buys his commercial fertilizer in *burlap sacks* or *burlap bags*, and sharpens his scythe on a *whetstone*. The left-hand horse of a team could be described as the *near horse*, and would *whinny* or *whinner* at feeding time. After school *lets out* a farm boy *husks* the corn and summons the hogs to the trough with the call *pig!* or *piggie!* He will eat *bacon* with his eggs for breakfast; at Sunday dinner, if he has eaten his *string beans* and *greens*, he may have the *wishbone* to play with. And peaches are pickled or canned according to whether they are *clingstone* or *freestone*.

Where a term occurs throughout the Northern area, it may be found in all parts of New York State. A boy throwing *stones* across a *brook* may be frightened at the sight of a *devil's darning needle*; he may have *johnnycake* for supper and sleep under a *comfortable* or a *comforter*. A farmer will summon his cows to the tune of *co-boss!* or *come-boss!*, carry *swill* in a *pail*, and see that the traces are fastened to a *whiffletree* or *whippletree* -- on a two-horse rig the whiffletrees will be joined by an *evener*. A baby is *wheeled* in a *baby carriage* and *creeps* before it walks; a calf *blats* and a house is covered with *clapboards*. And after too much of a good time, a person is likely to feel sick *to* his stomach.

Where the Hudson Valley and western New England have the same term but eastern New England lacks it, the term is usually found throughout the area of northern settlement as far west as Lake Erie, and often to the Mississippi. So, throughout New York State a farmer may *draw* stone from the fields in a *stoneboat*, sit on the *stoop* after supper, look across the river *flats*, and wonder what to do with the *loppered* (or *lobbered*) milk and the hog's *pluck*. As far west as the Finger Lakes he may make rollers out of *buttonball* logs; beyond, he will use *buttonwood*, if the tree occurs.

The occurrence of a word in all of New England and in the Hudson Valley does not guarantee that it will be used in all of New York State. As far west as Oswego, Utica, and Cooperstown (but not in Syra-cuse, Norwich, or Binghamton) -- and occasionally in the Genesee Valley -- a house may have a *piazza* instead of a *stoop*, and sometimes both (Map 1).

A few words characteristic of eastern New England have filtered west. In the Genesee Valley oxen are -- or were -- driven with a *goad*. Here and there hogs are kept in a *pigsty*, plain flour is made into *white bread* or *yeast bread*, and when a lamb is raised on a bottle it becomes a *cosset*.

Where a word is limited in distribution in New England, or is regarded as old-fashioned where it is found, it will most likely occur in New York State only sporadically, if at all. There are only two apparent exceptions: outside the Hudson Valley it is a fairly common practice to tell a cow to *histe!* (only a few very sophisticated cows understand *hoist!*) to get her to assume the proper stance for milking; and salt-rising bread is frequently leavened with *emptins*, though the old York State term *kunell* is also heard. One farmer on Long Island has a calf that *blares*, as a few calves do in southwestern Connecticut, and many in the Merrimack Valley. One informant in Schuylerville -- very proud of his Nantucket ancestry -- calls a thunderstorm a *tempest*, as people commonly call it in southeastern New England. One man in Franklin County has helped put up posts and a roof to make a *hay cap*, like the people of Narragansett

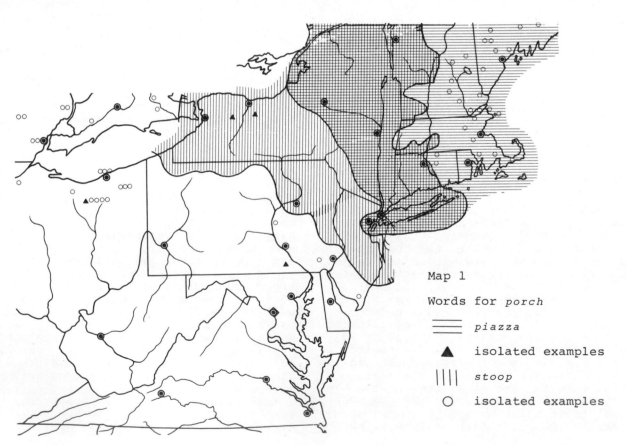

Map 1

Words for *porch*

≡ *piazza*

▲ isolated examples

|||| *stoop*

○ isolated examples

Bay; and like Narragansett Bay house-wives, one Cattaraugus County housewife prepares *apple slump* in a deep pan.

Outside the Hudson and Mohawk Valleys, one may still encounter traces of the New England taboos -- perhaps of Victorian origin -- against mentioning the names of male animals. Possibly because the dairy-ing industry is so important in New York State, the bull is the most widely recog-nized symbol of masculinity. Many infor-mants report, generally with a twinkle in the eye or a snicker in the voice, that before women one was supposed to call him an *animal*, a *critter*, a *sire*, a *toro*, a *male*, a *male cow*, an *ox*, a *steer*, a *top ox*, a *gentleman cow*, a *gentleman ox*, a *gentleman animal*, or just a *gentleman*. However, they consistently gave the word *bull* -- almost always as the first natural response, and rarely with voice or manner indicating that the informant felt he was taking an awful name in vain. Only one informant suggested a *ram* might be called a *gentleman sheep*, and all accepted a *boar* under that name.[2]

Of terms generally used in the Midland and South but rarely in the North, one finds a few occurrences of *firedogs* for *andirons*, *weatherboards* instead of *clap-boards*, *spicket* or *spigot* for the faucet on the kitchen sink (oftener for that on a barrel), many of *singletree* and *double-tree* (oftener the latter), respectively, instead of or alongside the Northern *whip-pletree* (or *whiffletree*) and *evener*, and one instance each (both in the Lake Erie area) of *comfort* instead of *comforter* or *comfortable*, and *ground squirrel* alongside the universal Northern term *chipmunk* (a word derived from the Algonquian Indians). A number of informants likewise know the *skunk* (another word of Algonquian deriva-tion) by his Midland and Southern (and probably earlier English) name of *polecat*. Of terms used througout the Midland, one finds a few instances of *blinds* for *shades*, *skillet* for frying pan, a *load* or *armload* of wood (beside the usual Northern *armful*), *quarter till* the hour, and *bawl* as the noise of a calf.

Of terms restricted to parts of the Mid-land, even fewer are found. Of all the terms peculiar to the West Midland, which extends southward from western Pennsylva-nia to the Carolina and Georgia mountains, only *green beans* occurs in New York State, ans its spread there may be due both to its occurrence in the Hudson Valley and to its adoption as a commercial term. From the North Midland, extending from West Jersey to Ohio, we have examples of *piece* for a lunch between meals, all over New York State except the Genesee Valley and the Finger Lakes. We also have occasional examples of *worm fence* for the ordinary crooked *rail fence*, *run* for a small fresh-water stream, *smearcase* (undoubtedly rein-forced by the German immigrants of the

nineteenth century) for cottage cheese, and *side meat* (plus the blend form *side pork*) alongside the prevailing Northern term *salt pork*. The predominance in western New York of *stone fence* over *stone wall*, which is more common to the east, may be due to the fact that *stone fence* is the usual North Midland term. Of words that have not generally spread out of Pennsylvania, *overhead* for the barn loft is very common in western New York; *fire-bug* (probably a blend of *firefly* and *lightning bug*) and *cluck* or *clook* for a setting hen occur sporadically; there are single examples of *ponhaws* for *scrapple* and *flitch* for a side of pork.

Of terms common in eastern Pennsylvania and on Chesapeake Bay, *coal oil* for *kero-sene* has the widest distribution in New York State, being used or known from the Finger Lakes west. There are a few spo-radic instances of *flannel cakes* for *pan-cakes* and *rick* for a long haystack; since *rick* occurs in the lower Hudson Valley and far upstate, Pennsylvania influence here is not likely. *Scrapple* is known by many informants, but since most of those who know the word are moderately sophisti-cated, they may have learned it as a com-mercial term. Of terms typical of the Pennsylvania German area, only *thick milk* for curdled milk (which also occurs as a relic in the Hudson Valley Dutch and Mo-hawk Valley German settlements) is found in New York State; it is the only term for this item in the Pennsylvania settle-ment on the Welland Peninsula. From west-ern Pennsylvania *gunny sack* for a *burlap bag* and *baby buggy* for a *baby carriage* have attained some currency in New York State, especially the western portion; trade channels have probably furthered the spread of both terms. Other terms from western Pennsylvania occur only occasion-ally: *doodle* for *haycock*, *sugar camp* and *sugar grove* beside the more usual *sugar bush*.

As would be expected, local folk words which New York State has in common with areas south of Pennsylvania are few. The only general Southern term occurring at all is *snap beans*, alongside *string beans*, chiefly in the Genesee Valley and Finger Lakes, but also in the Adirondacks and the St. Lawrence Valley. In the former area its occurrence may be partially explained by settlement history, but its occurrence in northern New York is likely due to its adoption as a commercial term, since it is not found in Canada. Three terms charac-teristic of the Virginia Piedmont are found frequently in the Genesee Valley and the Finger Lakes, occasionally elsewhere: *waistcoat* or *weskut* as an old-fashioned name for one's vest, *potato lot* for a po-tato field, and *nicker* for the cry of a horse. However, one must be cautious about attributing the presence of these terms to Virginia influence: *potato lot*

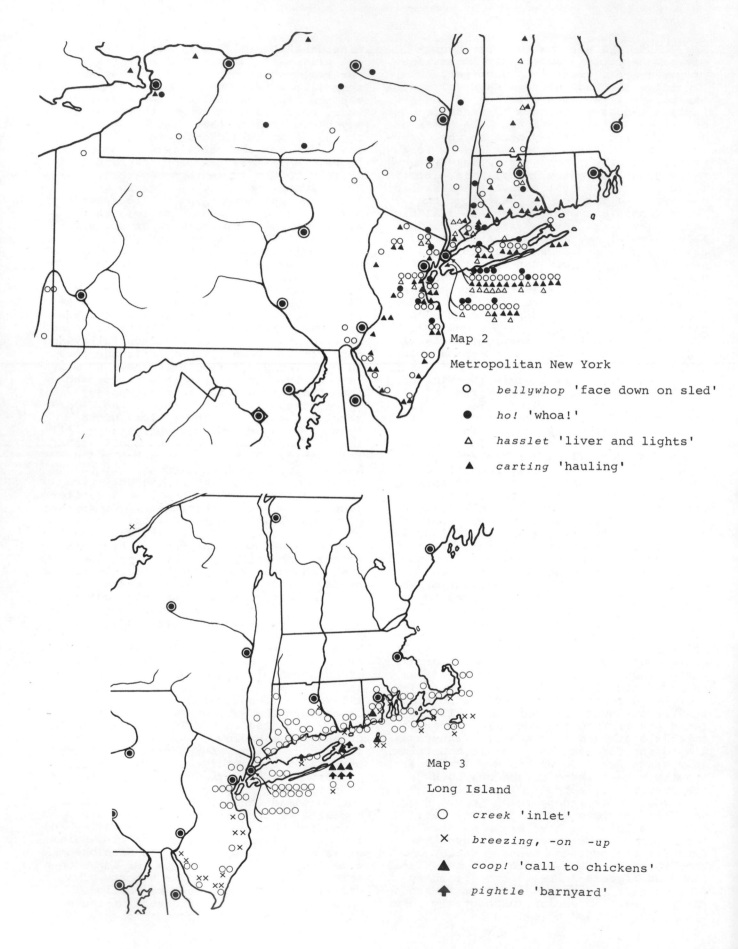

Map 2

Metropolitan New York

○   *bellywhop* 'face down on sled'

●   *ho!* 'whoa!'

△   *hasslet* 'liver and lights'

▲   *carting* 'hauling'

Map 3

Long Island

○   *creek* 'inlet'

✕   *breezing, -on -up*

▲   *coop!* 'call to chickens'

⬆   *pightle* 'barnyard'

is fairly common in Connecticut, *nicker* is not unknown in New England, and since terms for the vest were not recorded for the New England *Atlas* (Kurath *et al.* 1939-43), *waistcoat*, *weskut*, may also be old-fashioned there.

Four words suggest Canadian influence, since they were offered by all Canadian informants and occur in New York chiefly in areas near the border: *coal oil* for *kerosene* (where Canadian influence reinforced that from Pennsylvania), *dew worm* for the large earthworm, and *shivaree* for a mock serenade after a wedding. To be sure, *stook* -- widely distributed in England -- also occurs in eastern Massachusetts and in the upper Connecticut Valley (in the latter area Canadian influence may at least have helped its spread); as in England, one sometimes encounters the form *shook*, probably a blend of *shock* and *stook*.

The investigator who expects to find very sharp dialect boundaries in New York State will be disappointed. There is no division so sharp as that between the Yankee strip of northern Pennsylvania and the Ulster Scots and German settlements to the south, nor even so sharp as the divisions between the English, Germans, and Ulster Scots within Pennsylvania itself. Topography offers fewer obstacles to travel and communication; from the beginning the Hudson, Mohawk, and Champlain water routes provided relatively easy transportation between inland areas and the port of New York.

The general situation in New York State is a familiar type to students of linguistic geography. The early settled Hudson Valley, with what is now the largest city in the world as its core, has economically and culturally, if not politically, dominated the State. Primary settlement of the upstate area was chiefly from western New England, but because of the economic and cultural prestige of the Hudson Valley, its linguistic forms -- where different from those which the upstate region derived from New England -- have generally tended to spread. The Catskills and Adirondacks, especially the latter, constitute the only major barriers to travel. The ruggedness, thin soil, and short growing season of the central Adirondacks prevented permanent settlement until the end of the nineteenth century, when the coming of the railroads opened a resort area. These facts, plus the abutment of the northern counties on Canada -- an area with different economic and political foci -- probably explain the occurrence in the North Country of forms which have not been found in the central part of the state, including those which spread across Lake Champlain from Vermont.

For purposes of comparison, we will discuss the distribution of the folk vocabulary of New York State under Kurath's

three main divisions: Greater New York City, the Hudson Valley, and Upstate -- the last a continuation of Northwestern New England (Kurath 1949). All three of these divisions, especially the last, have more or less well defined local subareas. It is possible that when the *Linguistic Atlas of the Middle and South Atlantic States* is edited (Kurath *et al.* 1979-), the North Country may be set off as a fourth subdivision, but at this stage we cannot reach such a conclusion.

Greater New York City (Maps 2-3)

Only four vocabulary items seem characteristic of Greater New York City: *hasslet* for the edible organs of a hog, sheep, or calf, *burr* for the soft outer covering of a walnut, *ho!* to stop a horse (also found in Buffalo), and *school gets out*. Greater New York City and Long Island have the term *bellywhop*, rare elsewhere in the state, for coasting face down on a sled, and *carting* beside *hauling*. Probably the greatest influence of New York City on the vocabulary of the state has been in helping to spread, as trade names, the terms of the Hudson Valley. That *pot cheese*, a term with a Dutch background, is a New York City trade name for cottage cheese has certainly helped the term to spread into the dairying sections upstate which are dependent on the New York market.

On Long Island, a barnyard is sometimes called a *pightle* (rhyming with *title*), and *coop!* (with the vowel of *book*) is a common call to chickens. Along the Sound a kind of minnow is called a *killie* or *killiefish*. The commercial terms of the New York fish markets -- such as *menhaden* for a kind of herring, *porgy* or *poggy* for a salt-water catfish, and *round clam*, *hard clam* for the large clams used in chowder -- have spread eastward into New England. As in coastal communities from Maine to Florida, the shallow salt-water inlets along the Atlantic, the Sound, and the lower Hudson are known as *creeks* (usually with the vowel of *sick*); and when the wind is getting stronger it is frequently said to be *breezing*, *breezing up*, or *breezing on*.

The Hudson Valley (Maps 4-6)

Since the Hudson Valley, including East Jersey, is the oldest-settled portion of New York State, we are not surprised to learn that it has many characteristic words. Many of these are of Dutch origin, but the century and a quarter of English political control left its record also. The importance of the Valley in the life of the state and nation is shown in the spread of many of its words into the entire Northern speech area of the Great Lakes Basin and westward; many others are characteristic of New York State as a whole, or of large portions. But there

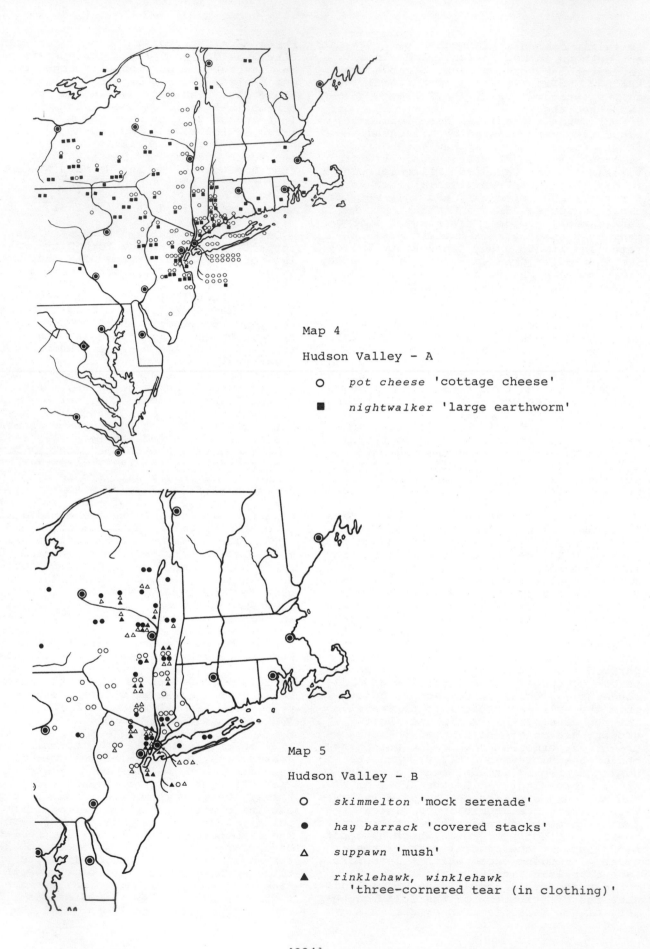

Map 4

Hudson Valley - A

○   *pot cheese* 'cottage cheese'

■   *nightwalker* 'large earthworm'

Map 5

Hudson Valley - B

○   *skimmelton* 'mock serenade'

●   *hay barrack* 'covered stacks'

△   *suppawn* 'mush'

▲   *rinklehawk, winklehawk*
    'three-cornered tear (in clothing)'

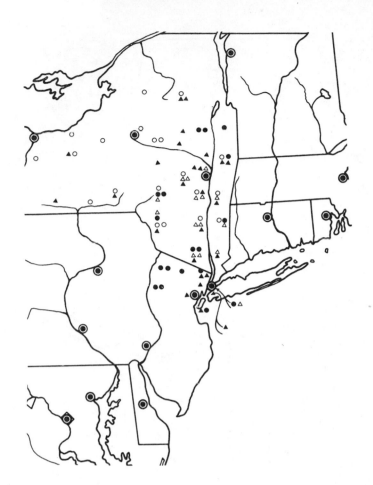

Map 6

Hudson Valley - C

o   *sap bush* 'maple grove'

●   *kill* 'small stream'

△   *clove* 'valley, pass'

▲   *kip!* 'call to chickens'

are some words which have hardly spread
north or west of Albany, some which are
confined to the lower reaches of the Hudson, and some which persist only as isolated relics.

Among the Hudson Valley words that have
spread far beyond its confines are *cherry
pit*, *stoop*,[3] *sawbuck* (probably with the
assistance of a similar Pennsylvania German etymon), *coal scuttle*, *teeter-totter*,
sugar bush, *snack* for a lunch between
meals, played *hookey*, and possibly *shuck*
for the soft outer covering of a walnut.
Wo! to stop a horse is not only the Valley
term but is almost universal in the Midland and South. The fact that *shades*,
gutters, and *shafts* -- the normal forms in
the Hudson Valley -- have been adopted as
commercial terms has undoubtedly facilitated their spread into other areas at the
expense of the New England *curtains*, *eaves
troughs*, and *fills* or *thills*. Three apparent Valley names for the deep-dish
apple pie -- *apple pudding*, *bird's nest*,
and *crow's nest* -- are widely known in New
York State, often labeled as newer names
which are supplanting the variety of names
by which this pie is known in New England.

A number of Hudson Valley words occur
widely within New York State, but rarely
beyond its boundaries. *Pot cheese*, for
cottage cheese, and *cruller*, for doughnut,
have spread north to the Canadian boundary
but are little known in the western part

of the state. *Nightwalker*, for the large
earthworm, is found as far west as the
southern end of the Finger Lakes region.

A number of terms are essentially confined to the Hudson Valley. Among these
are *barrack*, for a sheltered haystack,
suppawn or *spawn* for corn-meal mush, *winklehawk*, *rinklehawk*, for a tear in one's
clothes, *right* good (alongside the common
Northern *quite* good), *skimmelton* (familiar
to the reader of Hardy's *Mayor of Casterbridge* as a *skimmington ride* or *skimmety
ride*) for a mock serenade, *sap bush* beside
the more common *sugar bush*, *fishworm* for
earthworm, *kill* (with one possible exception, always in place names) for a small
fresh-water stream, and *kip!* as a call to
chickens. Throughout the Valley, *quarter
of* is more common than *quarter to*, and
sheaves of wheat are more common than *bundles*. The blend form *side pork* -- from
New England *salt pork* and Pennsylvania
side meat -- is very common. *Maple grove*
occurs as an old folk word; in most
places it is only literary. *Souse* as an
article of food is common in the Hudson
and Mohawk Valleys, only sporadic elsewhere, as is *come-by-chance* as a name for
an illegitimate child. In both the Hudson
and Mohawk Valleys *buttonball*, the Western
New England term, is the usual designation
for the sycamore.

The food terms *olicook* for doughnut,
rollichies for ground beef rolled in tripe

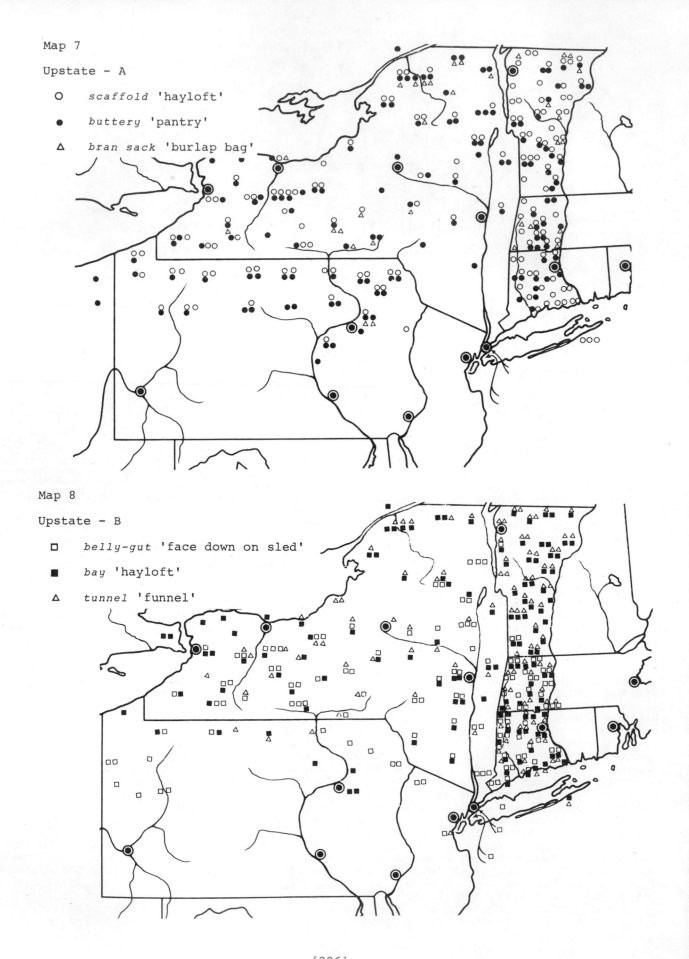

Map 7

Upstate - A

   O   *scaffold* 'hayloft'

   ●   *buttery* 'pantry'

   △   *bran sack* 'burlap bag'

Map 8

Upstate - B

   □   *belly-gut* 'face down on sled'

   ■   *bay* 'hayloft'

   △   *tunnel* 'funnel'

and pickled, and *thick milk* for curdled milk are confined largely to scattered families of Dutch descent. Several animal calls survive as local relics: the cow calls *kush!* sporadically and *co!* in East Jersey, the former Dutch, the latter English in origin; for quieting at milking time, the call is *sto!* in the Albany area, *kushie!* in East Jersey, and *tytie!* in Bergen County; the calf calls *tye!* in East Jersey and *keece!*, *kish!*, on the upper Delaware; and in the Albany area *come up!* to urge horses forward. Throughout the Valley sheep calls are very rare, as is the designation *buck* for a ram.

Upstate (Maps 7-8)

The Upstate area is possibly more uniform in its usage than any other major area along the Atlantic Seaboard except the Virginia Piedmont. The general pattern of the vocabulary is like that of Western and Northwestern New England, from which most of the early settlers came, with strong evidence of Hudson Valley influence, and in particular sections indications of influence from Eastern New England, the Midland, and Canada. In speaking of subdivisions, one must remember that Upstate New York is not like Eastern New England or the Carolina coast, where the lines are sharp, but that the particular sections blend almost imperceptibly into one another.

So far only one vocabulary item has been found which seems to be characteristic of New York State outside the Hudson Valley but not found outside the state -- *bed sink* (with one instance of *sink bedroom*), for a small, often windowless alcove, generally off the kitchen, in which the grandparents or other old people can sleep warm on winter nights.

Other words which are in more or less general use throughout the Upstate area are *chamber* for bedroom, *curtains* for shades, *clothes press* for closet, *buttery* for pantry, *scaffold* and *bay* for hayloft, *eaves trough* for gutter, *spider* for frying pan, *tunnel* for funnel, *jag* for a part load, *fills* or *thills* for *shafts*, *bellow* as the loud noise a cow makes when her calf is taken away, and occasionally *loo* (very frequently *low* -- the normal Southern term) for the soft noise the cow makes when she is hungry; the calls *histe!* to get a cow's leg back, *bossie!* to call the calves, *co-nan!* and *co-day!*, *co-dack!*, to sheep, and *hwo!* to stop a horse; *dutch cheese* for cottage cheese, *fried cakes* for doughnuts, *apple dumpling* for the deep-dish pie, *cherry stone* beside the more common *cherry pit*, *nightcrawler* for the large earthworm, *firefly* alongside the general American *lightning bug*, *school closes*, *skipped school*, and recollections of considering *bull* the unutterable name. *Horning* for a mock serenade occurs every-

where upstate except in the counties directly bordering Canada, and *belly-gut* is by far the most general term for coasting face down.

The Western Arm (Maps 9-10)

No student of New York State history needs to be reminded of the importance of the Erie Canal in the development of the western part of the state. Linguistically as well as economically it helped unite the state and prevent the formation of sharply defined dialect boundaries or isolated speech islands in the watersheds of the various Finger Lakes.

Only one word seems characteristic of the Mohawk Valley -- *ketch-colt* for an illegitimate child. The term occurs elsewhere, but chiefly as a recollected old-fashioned word. In the Mohawk Valley *second cutting* is a commoner term than *second crop*. From the Mohawk west many informants remember the Western New England *gad*, for the long whip used in driving oxen.

From the Finger Lakes westward, Midland forms began to appear in competition with those derived from New England and the Hudson Valley: *bawl* for the noise of a calf or the loud noise of a cow, and *side meat* for *salt pork* (plus the blend form *side pork*, so common in the Hudson Valley). The recurrence of the Eastern New England *buttonwood* for sycamore, instead of the Western New England and Hudson Valley *buttonball*, may be explained partly by the influence of Yankee settlements in northern Pennsylvania, partly by the occurrence of *buttonwood* in eastern Pennsylvania. The Hudson Valley *teeter-totter* is very common. *Rind* occurs with the vowel of *skin* (perhaps a blend, perhaps partially influenced by German *Rinde*); *earthworm* (generally a book word in the North) is heard from folk informants, and *waistcoat*, *weskut*, is the old-fashioned name for a vest.

The Finger Lakes area has *teeterboard* (with a few occurrences of *teeter*) as the prevailing term for a seesaw, the Pittsburgh and New Jersey hog call *poo-ig!* or *pwig!*, *saw bench* as the designation for a carpenter's horse, *syrup* as the sweet sauce eaten on puddings, *critter* and *animal* as polite names for the bull, relic occurrences of *rubstone* for whetstone and *snake fence* for the rail fence, and very few occurrences of *brook* (even in proper names) as a stream designation. The Susquehanna Valley and the Finger Lakes show several occurrences of *bottom lands* or *bottoms*, *gunny sack* for burlap bag (only south of Ithaca), *slop pail* beside the Northern *swill pail*, and relic occurrences of *spicket* for water faucet, *load* or *armload* for an armful of wood, and *firedogs* or *irons* for andirons.

The Genesee Valley and the Finger Lakes

show a marked infiltration of Hudson Valley terms: *souse*, *snack*, *maple grove*, and *played hookey*. *Sheaf* is common alongside *bundle*. The Midland *singletree* and *doubletree* frequently occur, less commonly the Midland and Southern *bacon skin* instead of *rind*. Paradoxically, *piece* for a light lunch -- the Midland term most widely spread in New York State -- is lacking; the New England *bite* occurs very frequently. There are several occurrences of *apple grunt* for the deep-apple pie, of *corn house* beside *corn crib*, of *nicker* beside *whinny*, *whinner*, and of *clabber*, *clabbered milk*, and *bonny-clabber* for curdled milk. And frequently *school closes*. From the Genesee Valley west one often finds *fritters* cooked in deep grease (a comparatively rare item in the New England cuisine, but common from Pennsylvania south), the Pittsburgh *baby buggy* for a *baby carriage*, and *teeter* as the normal designation for the seesaw.

The Genesee Valley proper has its characteristic infiltrations from other sections, notably the widespread use of the Pennsylvania *overhead* for the hayloft, and slightly less common use of *skillet* for frying pan. The New England *coal hod* is widespread; *piazza* occurs occasionally. The living room may also be called a *front room*, the outdoor toilet simply an *outhouse*, a potato field a *potato lot*, and the whip for driving oxen a *goad*. *Trim* is an occasional euphemism for castrate, and *bottom lands* occurs beside the usual New York State *flats*. The normal sheep call is *co-day!*; *co-nan!* is rare. *Curds* is an occasional relic name for cottage cheese. In the Rochester area, to coast lying down is to go *belly-whack*; in Rochester proper, also *belly-flop*. Along the Ontario watershed from Sodus to Welland, one often finds *green beans*, and *tap* for the water faucet. Possibly these terms reflect Canadian influence.

On the Niagara frontier one finds *blood sausage* and *liver sausage* as products of home butchering (possibly a cultural influence from German settlers) and *gravy* as the sweet sauce on a pudding. From the southern suburbs of Buffalo to Lake Ontario, *shivaree* is the only term for the mock serenade. In Buffalo *ho!* is the call to stop a horse; in Buffalo and on the Welland Peninsula across the border, one lies down on a sled to coast *belly-flop*.

The southwestern corner of the state shows the influence of western Pennsylvania in the occurrence of Midland *eavespouts* along with Northern *eaves troughs* in Erie, Cattaraugus, Allegany, and Chautauqua Counties, possibly in the absence of *comfortable* in these same counties, in frequent occurrences of *run* in stream names of Cattaraugus County, and of *sugar grove* beside *sugar bush* in Chautauqua. *Bottom lands* occurs in Cattaraugus and Chautauqua Counties, as does *apple*

john as a name for the deep pie.

The North Country

The North Country includes the uppermost reaches of the Hudson River, the New York portions of the Lake George and Lake Champlain watersheds, the St. Lawrence Valley, and the Adirondacks. The valleys on both sides were important avenues of communication and trade, even in aboriginal times, and were settled early; but the central Adirondacks did not receive permanent settlement till the end of the nineteenth century. It is not surprising that some Vermont forms have spread across New York State north of the main body of the Adirondacks, and that in this same region -- but seldom or never south of the mountains -- forms occur that reflect the culture of French Canada.

In the North Country one frequently finds *blood pudding* for *blood sausage*, less frequently *liver pudding*; the French-derived term *boodan*, for *liver sausage*, is also found. *Eavespouts* -- the Connecticut Valley and northern Vermont term -- is the normal term for *gutters*; *eaves trough* is practically unknown north or east of the central Adirondacks in New York State. *Stook* is the usual name for a pile of wheat sheaves; *tumble* frequently occurs alongside *haycock*, and *June bug* as a name for the *lightning bug*. New England *coal hod* and *piazza* are widespread, Hudson Valley *coal scuttle* and *stoop* extremely rare. Oxen are usually driven -- or remembered as driven -- with a *lash*, and the second crop of hay is the *aftergrass*. *Snap beans* is found sporadically throughout the area. The prevalence of *fishworm* in the North Country is probably due to the spread of this term from Middlesex and Worcester Counties, Massachusetts, up the Connecticut River to Vermont, but it was undoubtedly reinforced by the fact that *fishworm* is also widespread in the Hudson Valley. In the North Country *belly-bunt*, *belly-bump* are the usual names for coasting face down; the deep-apple pie is *apple grunt* or *apple (pan) dowdy*, and the sauce eaten with it is a *gravy* or a *dressing*. The bull is respectfully known as a *toro* or a *gentleman cow*. One finds as relic forms *gunny sack*, *jacket* for vest, *rock maple*, and *thick milk*. The presence of *shivaree* [charivari] everywhere north of the mountains again suggests Canadian influence. The St. Lawrence Valley has *neap* for the wagon tongue and *afterfeed* as a relic term for the second growth. Contrary to popular superstitions, but quite in keeping with the findings from the Carolina mountains, the Adirondacks seem to have no characteristic vocabulary, but are noted chiefly for the preservation of occasional relics, some not found elsewhere: *ha'nts* for ghosts (from both Warren County infor-

Map 9

Western Arm - A

○   *gad* 'goad'

◑   [ɪ] in *rind*

▲   *ketch-colt* 'illegitimate child'

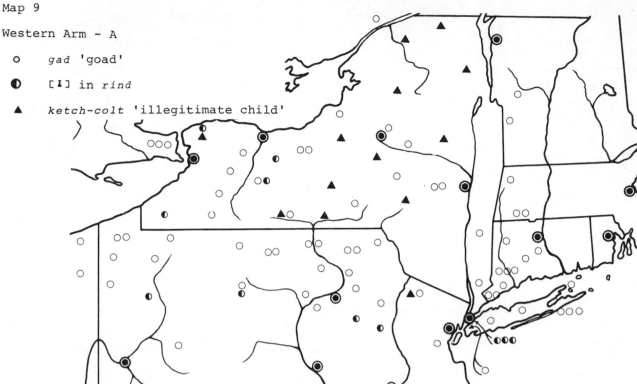

Map 10

Western Arm - B

○   (potato) *lot* 'small field'

●   *front room* 'living room'

△   *gravy* 'sweet sauce'

▲   *applejohn* 'deep-dish pie'

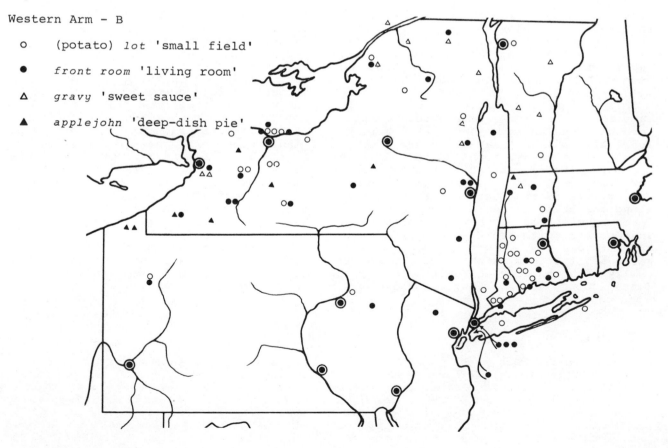

Map 11

The North Country

○   *neap* 'wagon tongue'

●   *tumble* 'haycock'

△   *June bug* 'lightning bug'

▲   *ha'nts* 'ghosts'

□   *afterfeed* 'second crop'

■   *aftergrass* 'second crop'

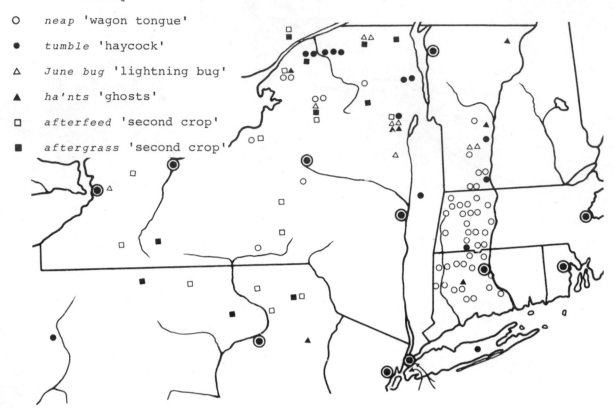

mants), *quarter till* the hour, *fire irons* for andirons, *chamber* for the barn loft, *snake fence* for the rail fence, and *nagel-hawk* for a tear -- probably from German *Nagelloch*, a reminiscence of the time when German was spoken in the Mohawk Valley.

This preliminary report on the folk vocabulary of New York State merely confirms Kurath's conclusion, based on the evidence available in 1941, that there are three major speech areas in the state: Greater New York City, a metropolitan area with few local terms of its own; the Hudson Valley, one of the most active focal areas along the Atlantic Seaboard, some of whose forms have spread far beyond the state; and Upstate, with great local variety but a remarkable basic homogeneity. Such obvious affiliations as those of the Hudson Valley with the Genesee Valley, or the North Country with New England and French

Canada, and the infusion of Pennsylvania terms into the basically Yankee vocabulary in the area from the Finger Lakes to the west, may -- even in the tentative form in which they must now be presented -- suggest directions in which students of other aspects of folk culture may profitably pursue their research, since people do not carry their speech along with them and leave the rest of their folk culture behind. When the *Linguistic Atlas of the Middle and South Atlantic States* is published (Kurath *et al.* 1979-), it should give many more leads to the students of all the social sciences, since language is the most obvious characteristic of man as a social animal, the characteristic that most clearly differentiates him from all other forms of animal life; a study of the way language functions and linguistic phenomena are disseminated is basic to the proper understanding of man.

NOTES

[1] The Linguistic Atlas of the United States and Canada, under the direction of Hans Kurath, formerly of Brown and now of the University of Michigan emeritus, is the product of the collaboration of many scholars, universities and colleges, and foundations, under the sponsorship of the American Council of Learned Societies since the inception of the project in 1930. Kurath has assumed direct responsibility for the New England and Middle and South Atlantic sections. Only the New England materials have been published, six volumes of maps and a handbook (Kurath *et al.* 1939-43, 1939); editorial work on the Middle and South Atlantic materials was interrupted by World War II. [On

Kurath's retirement in 1962, the files for the *Atlas of the Middle and South Atlantic States* were transferred to the University of Chicago, where R. McDavid resumed editing. In 1974-76, with the first stage of editing complete, they were transferred to the University of South Carolina, where greater support for editing was available. The University of Chicago Press began publication in 1979. The *Linguistic Atlas of the Upper Midwest* has now been published (Allen 1973-76).]

I am indebted to Professor Kurath not only for his generous interest in my career and his careful direction of my research, but for permission to examine and use for this paper the manuscript of Kurath 1949, from which the general framework of dialect areas and much of the particular evidence has been taken.

Several studies have been made of various aspects of New York State speech. The first systematic examination of an American dialect was Emerson 1891. For recent studies, see Thomas 1942, 1935-37. Independent dissertations on the speech of New York City are Hubbell 1950 and Frank 1949 [Labov 1966 is a more intensive study].

Funds for the completion of my field work were provided by the American Council of Learned Societies, and headquarters for the field worker by the Division of Modern Languages, Cornell University. For advice on the choice of communities and informants, and for local contacts without which the field work could not have been done nearly so speedily or effectively, I am indebted to Harold W. Thompson, of Cornell; to Louis C. Jones, Director of the New York State Historical Association; and to Albert Corey, State Historian of New York, and his organization of county and local historians.

[If the accompanying maps, which were lacking in the original article, do not fully confirm the statements in the article, one can only point out that it was an informal presentation prepared on the basis of the items selected for Kurath's *Word Geography*, during a few weeks after the completion of the field work. More detailed examination of the evidence, over the last two decades, makes new observations possible -- such as the wide distribution of *bran sack* 'burlap bag.' However, the statements in the article have been left in their original form.]

[2] Taboos have survived much more strongly in the South and South Midland, and are not to be tampered with lightly. To show the difference between the attitudes of the two sections, New York State informants consistently expressed incredulity over the fact that Lowman was once forcibly ejected from a Virginia farmhouse for using the naughty word *bull* in mixed company; one St. Lawrence County farmer fairly snorted, "What good would it do to call him a *roaring heifer*?" The study of sectional differences in linguistic taboos should be undertaken by a social psychologist.

Possibly because hog-raising is more important to the Southerner than to the Northerner, taboos on the mention of *boar* are about as strong in the South as those on *bull*. In contrast, no New York State informant ever had a parallel of the Southern folk definition of a *barrow*, which informants throughout the South regularly define as "a boar who has lost his prestige in the community."

[3] *Stoop* has been recorded for the Savannah River Valley in Georgia and South Carolina. The similarity between the older town houses in Savannah and New York suggests trade connections. Possibly New York architects, or Georgia architects trained in New York, designed the Savannah houses.

The student of dialect geography is interested not only in indicating the major dialect divisions within a speech community, but in interpreting apparent exceptions to the major patterns. Moreover, when two major dialect types have been found separated by a rather sharp boundary, it is important to examine just what speech forms have crossed that boundary, and to discover or suggest the reasons. This paper is concerned with the extent to which the folk vocabulary of Upstate New York[1] reflects linguistic influences from outside the Northern speech area of the Atlantic Seaboard states; specifically, it is concerned with the occurrences of words of Midland or Canadian origin.[2]

Kurath's analysis of the vocabulary of the Atlantic Seaboard (1949) sets up eighteen dialect areas between southern New Brunswick and the Savannah River, grouped into the three regional divisions of Northern, Midland, and Southern. Admittedly on incomplete data,[3] Kurath included all Upstate New York in the Northern area, and specifically indicated it as derivative from Northwestern New England (Kurath 1949:fig. 3). Since the indicated boundary between the North and the Midland runs somewhat south of the New York-Pennsylvania line almost due west from the forks of the Susquehanna, so that the northern tier of Pennsylvania counties is included in the Northern area, one might assume that it was not necessary to check within the Upstate area for Midland influences. Nevertheless, the physical geography of the region suggests the need for caution: the Delaware, Susquehanna, and Allegheny Valleys were natural routes of migration from Pennsylvania into upstate New York, and later routes of trade for the upstate area with Philadelphia, Baltimore, Pittsburgh, and Cincinnati; and the port of Buffalo would be the natural Great Lakes outlet for trade from western Pennsylvania. Finally, since no evidence has previously been available from either side of the Niagara and St. Lawrence Rivers, it is necessary to judge to what extent the international political boundary is actually a linguistic boundary.

The evaluation of the Midland contributions to the speech of upstate New York -- which we will roughly define as the area outside the limits of Dutch colonial settlement -- cannot be made without a knowledge of the patterns of settlement history. In general, the original settlers of this area came from western New Eng-

land, chiefly from Massachusetts and Vermont. In the post-Revolutionary adjudication of the territorial claims of New York and Massachusetts to the area by the treaty of Hartford (1786), the latter state was given title (though not sovereignty) to the area west of Seneca Lake -- a total of about six million acres -- which was opened to settlement through the efforts of a series of land promoters, many of whom went broke in the process.[4] A military tract of 1,500,000 acres east of Seneca Lake was set aside as allotments to Revolutionary veterans; settlement here was complicated by confusion of titles, squatting, and the usual fraud and maladministration that have characterized the handling of veterans' benefits. In both areas many of the earliest settlers were Revolutionary soldiers who had served in the Sullivan-Clinton campaign against the Iroquois in 1779, and settled on bounty land allotted to veterans. The predominant group of settlers from western New England was joined by considerable numbers from the Hudson Valley, and -- particularly in the region of the Finger Lakes and the Genesee Valley -- by many from Pennsylvania and some from further south. As a notable example, Colonel Nathaniel Rochester, the founder of the city of Rochester, was a Marylander who moved north as a conscientious objector against the institution of Negro slavery. The nineteenth-century migrations from Europe brought in groups with various foreign-language backgrounds; the German colony was especially large and influential in Buffalo. The Canadian border communities investigated for the Atlas were settled primarily by Loyalists expelled from the United States after the Revolution: those settling on the Niagara Peninsula came chiefly from Pennsylvania, those settling in the St. Lawrence Valley from New York and New Jersey; in both localities there was later settlement from New York State as well as from the British Isles.

The examination of data from upstate New York and the Canadian border communities emphasizes the accuracy of Kurath's dialect boundary between the North and the Midland, setting off the Yankee settlements in the northern tier of Pennsylvania from the rest of the state. Throughout upstate New York, and in the Canadian communities investigated, the regional words encountered are basically Northern; furthermore, where vocabulary differences are found within the Northern area, the items found in upstate New York reflect chiefly the usage of western New England, with a few additions -- such as *cherry pit* and *sugar bush*, both of Dutch origin[5] -- from the speech of the Hudson Valley.

In considering items outside the dominant pattern, it is particularly important, though sometimes difficult, to dissociate items representing the influence of another region from those that represent the survival of an earlier stage of dialect mixture. Thus both *pail* and *bucket*, both *slop* and *swill*, are found in New England and South Carolina; although west of the Hudson *pail* and *swill* are characteristically Northern, *bucket* and *slop* characteristically Midland and Southern, occasional occurrences of the latter forms upstate may not mean Midland influence. From the beginning of English-speaking settlement, it is likely that dialect mixture has been the rule rather than the exception in almost any American community (cf. A. L. Davis and R. McDavid 1950; in this volume, pp. 238-44). It is the pattern of distribution over a more or less wide area that proves or disproves regional influence.[6]

In emphasizing the difference between a regional contribution and scattered occurrences, which may possibly be relics from earlier settlement, we note that some words whose occurrence in New England is restricted do occasionally appear in upstate New York. For instance, one finds sporadic examples of such Eastern New England words as *goad* 'ox whip,' *pigsty* 'pig pen,' *white bread, yeast bread* 'ordinary bread,' *cosset* 'pet lamb,' *rock maple* 'sugar maple,' *apple dowdy* 'deep apple pie,' *bonnyclabber* 'curdled sour milk,' and *curds* 'cottage cheese.' Similarly, there are examples in upstate New York of such definitely old-fashioned words -- rare even in New England -- as *emptins* 'homemade leaven for salt-rising bread,' *rifle* 'emery-coated paddle for sharpening a scythe,' *lowery* [ˈlauɚɪ] 'cloudy,' *breezing up* 'increasing' (of the wind, a coastal term), and such localized terms as the occasional Western New England *tempest* 'thunderstorm,'[7] *hay cap* 'haystack,' and *apple slump* 'deep apple pie.'

For the same reason, a person evaluating the Midland contribution to the Upstate vocabulary should separate occurrences of those words characteristic of the Midland and South together, the whole Midland, and portions of the Midland adjacent to upstate New York, from occurrences of items normally found in more remote parts of the Midland or South. The latter group -- sporadic examples unless specifically discussed -- are summarized in the following table:

West Midland: *green beans* 'string beans'

South Midland: *jacket* 'vest,' *corn shucks* 'husks,' *hoe cake, corn dodger* 'corn bread,' *light bread* 'ordinary white bread,' *butter beans* 'lima beans'[8]

South Midland and South: *clabbered milk* 'curdled sour milk,' *see-horse* 'seesaw,'[9] *haunts* [hænts] 'ghosts'

Western North Carolina: *hickory* 'ox whip'

Southern: *snap beans* 'string beans'

Virginia Piedmont: *potato lot* 'potato field,' *nicker* 'noise by a horse at feeding time,' *waistcoat, weskit* 'vest'

Southern Coast: *mosquito hawk* 'dragonfly'

For none of these words is it necessary to assume Midland or Southern origins when we find them in upstate New York. *Green beans* is found in the Hudson Valley; both *green beans* and *snap beans* have recently spread as commercial terms, following the introduction of stringless beans, probably as having less unpleasant associations than the older (and perhaps less specific) term *string beans*. *Jacket*, probably an early Pennsylvania item (Kurath 1949:36), is found only in isolated communities, as is [hænts]; it is possible that *jacket* also occurs in New England, but the item was not recorded for the New England *Atlas* (Kurath *et al.* 1939-43). The occurrences of *clabbered milk* in the northern counties of the state are probably explained as a sporadic relic; where *clabbered milk* and *clabber* occur in the Genesee Valley and Finger Lakes region, one may suggest both the tradition of early Southern connections[10] and some carry-over of Eastern New England *bonnyclabber*. *Potato lot* -- common in the Genesee Valley -- is as often recorded in western Connecticut as in the Virginia Piedmont; *nicker* is not unknown in New England; *waistcoat, weskit* would probably have been recorded in New England had the item been investigated; and *mosquito hawk* has been found in some areas where Southern influence is improbable, such as Beaver Island at the northern end of Lake Michigan.

The terms typical of the Midland and South, the whole Midland, or portions adjacent to upstate New York, are also found as sporadic examples which may or may not reflect actual Midland influence. They also occur in patterns which suggest early settlements and later commercial and cultural ties. Most commonly they are found in three areas:

1. The Niagara Peninsula in Ontario, first settled by Pennsylvania Loyalists.

2. The Upper Susquehanna Valley, Finger Lakes, and Genesee Valley, where tradition and the recollections of older informants indicate a large early settlement from the Midland and South, and later connections through logging on the rivers.

3. The Niagara frontier and the Lake Erie shore, with Buffalo the natural lake port for the Pittsburgh area, and with the Allegheny River providing a route for

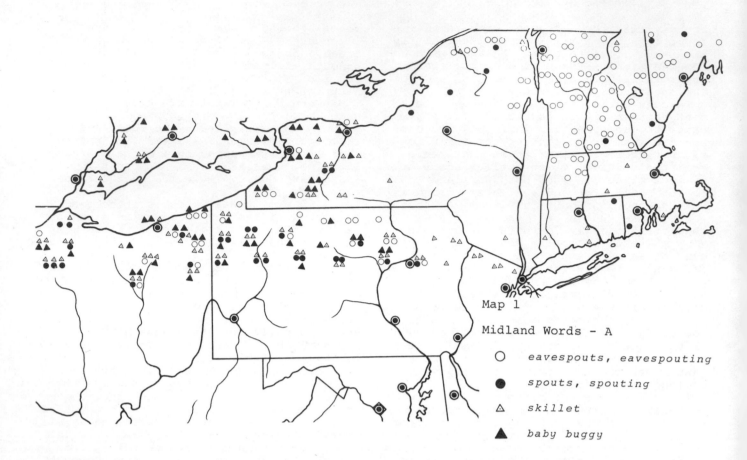

Map 1

Midland Words - A

○   *eavespouts, eavespouting*

●   *spouts, spouting*

△   *skillet*

▲   *baby buggy*

loggers to Pittsburgh and Cincinnati.

Midland and Southern: *firedogs* 'and-irons,' *weatherboards* 'clapboards,' *spicket, spigot* 'faucet' (less often for one on a sink than for one on a barrel), *singletree* 'pivoted crossbar behind a single horse,' *doubletree* 'pivoted crossbar behind two horses,' *comfort* 'tied quilt,' *ground squirrel* 'chipmunk,' *polecat* 'skunk,'[11] *walnut hull* 'soft outer skin,' *crawl* 'to creep, as a baby,' *slop* 'kitchen garbage'

Midland: *blinds* 'window shades,' *skillet* 'frying pan,' *load, armload* 'armful' (of wood), *sookie!* 'call to calves,' *quarter till* 'quarter of' (the hour), *bawl* 'noise made by a calf'

North Midland: *piece* 'lunch between meals,' *worm fence* 'rail fence,' *run* 'small freshwater stream,' *smearcase* 'cottage cheese,' *side meat* 'salt pork' (with the blend term *side pork* also frequent)[12]

Pennsylvania: *overhead, overlays* 'barn loft,' *firebug* 'lightning bug,' *cluck* [klʌk, kluk] 'setting hen,' *ponhaws* 'scrapple,' *flitch* 'bacon'

Eastern Pennsylvania: *coal oil* 'kerosene,' *flannel cakes* 'pancakes,' *rick* 'haystack,' *scrapple* 'cornmeal thickened with pieces of meat and the juice from liver sausage'

Pennsylvania German area: *thick milk* 'curdled sour milk'

Western Pennsylvania: *gunny sack* 'bur-lap bag,' *baby buggy* 'baby carriage,' *doodle* 'small pile of hay raked up in the field,' *sugar camp, sugar grove* 'maple grove'

The total number of items on this list is not impressive when one considers that it is derived from an examination of the lexical variants recorded in about 175 field records of over seven hundred items each. It is even less impressive when one notes that few of them are at all widely distributed. The only ones whose patterns obviously suggest Midland influence are *singletree, doubletree, skillet, overhead, coal oil, thick milk, gunny sack, baby buggy,* and *piece.* Of these, *thick milk* is of certain Midland derivation only on the Niagara Peninsula, since it occurs as a relic form among the Hudson Valley Dutch and Mohawk Valley Germans; *overhead* -- very common in the Genesee Valley -- has probably been helped in its spread by the variety of terms found in New England (Kurath 1949:53-54; Kurath *et al.* 1939-43: maps 102-03). The terms *baby buggy, coal oil,* and *skillet* (as indicated on Maps 1 and 2 -- as well as *gunny sack, singletree,* and *doubletree,* which were not charted) occur most frequently from the Finger Lakes westward. It should be noted that in the Great Lakes and Mississippi Valley all these terms have spread northward; in fact, *coal oil, gunny sack,* and *baby buggy* are practically universal in

Map 2

Midland Words - B

○   *coal oil* 'kerosene'

×   *side meat* 'salt pork'

▲   *side pork* 'salt pork'

△   *piece* 'lunch'

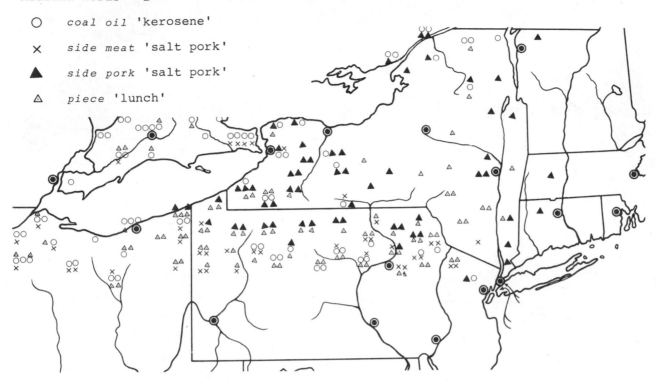

Illinois, and *gunny sack* and *baby buggy* in Minnesota, with *coal oil* very common in the speech of older informants.[13] These items have undoubtedly been spread by the importance of Pennsylvania as a manufacturing center, whose folk terms would often become trade terms, especially where steel and petroleum products were involved. Leaving out these terms, we have only *side meat* (plus *side pork*) and *piece* as widely distributed Midland borrowings; and *side meat* might have been spread as an old Midland commercial term. Thus *piece* seems to be the only folk word that has spread from the Midland to the North without being used as a commercial term (cf. Kurath 1949:32, 39, 71-72).

The evidence for Upstate borrowings from Canada is much easier to assay. Four words occurred in the speech of every Canadian informant and were also found in New York State: *shivaree* 'mock serenade after a wedding,' *stook* 'pile of bundles of grain,' *dew worm* 'large earthworm,' and *coal oil*. New York State occurrences of *shivaree*, *dew worm*, and *stook* (plus the blend form *shook*) are found predominantly in communities near the border, where it is reasonable to suspect Canadian influence (see Map 3).[14] The frequency of *coal oil* in the Buffalo area is probably due to the fact that it is both a Canadian term and a Pennsylvania one. Few Canadian terms have not been found in upstate New

York; such political terms as *county town* 'county seat,' *warden* 'chief county official,' and *reeve* 'township official' are not found -- but neither are the New England *shire town* 'county seat' or *selectman* 'township official.'[15] The only common terms which seem peculiar to Canada are *chesterfield* 'large overstuffed sofa' and *coil* 'pile of hay raked up in the field.'

A clear example of the introduction of a lexical item from two different directions is *eavespouts*, *rain spouts*, *spouts* 'gutters along the edge of the roof,' which appears in two widely separated parts of the state (see Map 1): 1) the Champlain Valley and the Adirondacks, where it most likely spread from Vermont; 2) the southwestern corner of the state, where it occurs as a variant of the Midland *spouting*, perhaps blended with the common Northern term *eaves troughs* (Kurath 1949:29, 53, fig. 54; A. L. Davis and R. McDavid 1950). Occurrences of *fishworm* 'earthworm' in western New York might represent any of three sources: it is the most common Midland term; it is also the usual term in the Hudson Valley; and in New England it has spread from Middlesex County, Massachusetts, west to the Connecticut Valley, up the Connecticut River to Vermont, and across Lake Champlain to the Adirondacks.[16]

On the basis of this preliminary examination of the Atlas' lexical data from

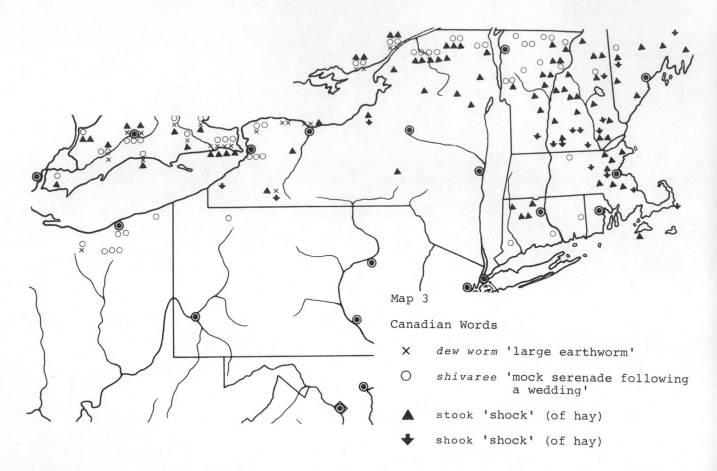

Map 3

Canadian Words

✕   *dew worm* 'large earthworm'

○   *shivaree* 'mock serenade following a wedding'

▲   stook 'shock' (of hay)

↓   shook 'shock' (of hay)

upstate New York, it is obvious that indubitable Midland forms of wide distribution in New York State are very rare. Most of the items that do occur seem to owe their occurrence to their use as commercial terms, and the areas in which such forms are most frequently found bear out what one would expect from a knowledge of settlement history and of nineteenth-century trading areas. Kurath's location of the boundary between the North and the Midland, and his statement of the sharpness of that boundary, has been verified beyond question -- as it will probably be verified by an analysis of the phonological and grammatical data in the Atlas records.

NOTES

[1] The data on which this paper is based were derived from the field records for the Linguistic Atlas of the United States and Canada, especially from the records for the *Linguistic Atlas of the Middle and South Atlantic States* (1979-), with the permission of Hans Kurath, director. For a more extended discussion, see R. McDavid 1951a (in this volume, pp. 219-31).

[2] 'Northern' includes New England, the Hudson Valley, and their derivative settlements to the west; 'Midland' includes Pennsylvania and derivative settlements to the west and south; 'Southern' includes the coastal plain and lower Piedmont plantation country in the Old South.

[3] Field work in New York State was interrupted in 1941 by the death of Guy S. Lowman, Jr., principal field investigator, who had just completed Long Island, metropolitan New York, the Hudson and Mohawk Valleys, and part of the upper Susquehanna

watershed. He had completed only four scattered interviews between the Finger Lakes and the Niagara River, none in the Adirondacks, in the St. Lawrence Valley, or on the Canadian side. In 1948-49, through funds from the American Council of Learned Societies, I was able to complete the field work in New York State, plus a few border points.

[4] In 1788 Oliver Phelps and Nathaniel Gorham acquired an option on the entire Massachusetts tract, and took up the land east of the Genesee River, plus 200,000 acres on the west bank -- a total of 2,600,000 acres. Two years later they sold 1,200,000 acres to Robert Morris of Philadelphia, who resold them to the London Associates, a British company headed by Sir William Pulteney. Phelps and Gorham later went bankrupt. Colonel Charles Williamson, the agent for the Pulteney interests, lost over a million dollars in lavish promotion and was dismissed.

In 1791 Morris bought the rest of the Massachusetts land, and immediately resold all but a Genesee River tract to the Holland Land Company, a Dutch corporation, which in 1801 began the sale of land from its office in Batavia, New York. See WPA Writer's Program 1940b:67, 434-35, 665, 668-69; Thompson 1939:62, 476-77.

[5] Kurath 1949:18, 24-25, 76, fig. 145. It must be emphasized that dialect differences in the United States are by no means as sharp as those in European countries, that throughout North America even the least literate speakers have in common the greater part of their vocabulary, their grammatical system, and even most of their phonemic patterns (though not necessarily the phonetic details).

[6] Increasing the number of informants increases the opportunity for isolated occurrences of atypical forms, relic or otherwise, whether from chance occurrence in the community or from tapping the particular memories and heritages of individuals or families. Where an area is known to be recently settled and rather highly mixed, increasing the number of informants will emphasize the mixture. The supplementary check lists distributed in Minnesota have revealed a far more highly mixed dialect situation in the northern part of the state -- a far higher incidence of non-Northern terms -- than the field records showed (Allen 1973-76). Thus doubling the total number of field records from New York State, with the new records (and few of the previous ones) in the area of most recent settlement, might show many more Midland words in the area without disturbing the fundamentally Northern nature of the Upstate folk vocabulary.

[7] *Tempest* was recorded from a Schuylerville (Saratoga Co.) informant, definitely conscious of his Nantucket ancestry. Many other isolated occurrences of words outside the normal pattern of the area may be family heirlooms, though perhaps not as consciously preserved.

[8] In New York State, as in its derivative settlements in Michigan, *butter beans* is normally a designation for the yellow wax string beans.

[9] *See-horse*, a blend term, occurred in the speech of a single Southern Tier informant, who also offered the other blend term, *teeter-horse*. It is difficult to explain the occurrence of either of these terms in New York State: *see-horse* otherwise does not occur in the Atlantic Seaboard states north of South Carolina; *teeter-horse* is a rare term in the Marietta section of southern Ohio; the forms *hicky-horse*, *ridy-horse*, *cockhorse*, which would have helped give rise to such blends, are all South Midland and Southern. See Kurath 1949:36, 59, fig. 79. Did the informant -- or one his elders -- pick the term up while log-rafting down the Ohio? Or did a child's rocking horse have something to do with the blend?

[10] For the tradition of Southern settlement around Bath, in Steuben County, see Thompson 1939: 477.

[11] The terms *chipmunk* and *skunk*, derived from Eastern Algonquian languages, were adopted in the North; in the Midland and South the older terms *ground squirrel* and *polecat* were, like *robin*, transferred to American fauna.

[12] It is possible that the prevalence of *stone fence* in western New York (except for Rushford, in Allegany County), in contrast to the greater frequency of *stone wall* in the eastern part of the state, is due to the fact that *stone fence* is also the North Midland term.

[13] This data is taken from a preliminary examination of the records for the *Linguistic Atlas of the North-Central States* (Marckwardt et al. 1980-), and for the *Linguistic Atlas of the Upper Midwest* (Allen 1973-76).

[14] *Stook* and *shook* were frequently recorded in the survey of southern England by Lowman (Viereck 1975). They also occur in New England, both in western Connecticut and in the upper Connecticut Valley; their presence in the latter area may be at least partially due to Canadian influence. For the distribution and spread of *shivaree*, see A. L. Davis and R. McDavid 1949 (in this volume, pp. 181-84).

[15] It seems axiomatic that political terms do not cross political boundaries; in the South, *county site* 'county seat' is common in Georgia but never heard in South Carolina.

[16] Kurath 1949:14, 26, 74, fig. 139. An example of apparent New York State borrowing from Pennsylvania is that of *jag* 'part load' (Kurath 1949:31, 46, 57, fig. 72), which occurs in most of the field records made in 1948-49. The case for this as a Midland borrowing breaks down, however, when it is noticed that Lowman did not systematically ask for this part of item 19.8 in the work sheets (the two questions normally asked were for 'a load taken to the mill,' and 'a load of firewood, etc., carried in one's arms') in New York State, though he did in Pennsylvania. Similarly, I did not regularly ask for, or get, the item *tool shed* 'place where tools are kept' for item 11.8, but asked only for the place for storing firewood. The full story of the distribution of such terms -- discovered to have a pattern only after a great deal of the Atlantic Seaboard field work had been done -- will be told by those who prepare a dictionary of American folk speech (Cassidy et al. 1981-); one would suspect, however, that *jag* would have been found in New England had the field workers asked for it. [For the pattern of *jag* see Marckwardt et al. 1980-.]

Students of dialect geography recognize, in general, three types of speech areas. A *focal area* is one whose economic, cultural, or political prestige has caused its speech forms to spread into surrounding areas. A *relic area* is one whose geographic or cultural isolation has permitted the preservation of older forms that have been lost elsewhere and has prevented the spread of local terms. A *transition area* is one which has undergone influence from two or more directions, so that competing forms exist in it side by side. Focal areas are studied because they set the patterns for standard types of speech;[1] relic areas because they are able to throw light on earlier stages of the language;[2] transition areas because they may help us to see what happens when population spreads from an area of early settlement to one of later settlement, or when arteries of communication are developed between areas of different cultural backgrounds. The speech patterns of a transition area are likely to be more complex than those of the other two types. For this reason there have been comparatively few studies of transition areas;[3] this paper is a preliminary study of such an area. It attempts to find out what problems a linguist may expect to encounter in investigating transition areas, and to suggest what further studies might be desirable.

The completion of field work for the linguistic atlases of the eastern states, the publication of Kurath's *Word Geography of the Eastern United States* (1949), and Atwood's analysis of the verb forms in that area (1953a), as well as the increasing number of studies correlating the eastern data with data from the secondary settlement areas in the Middle West (e.g., Marckwardt 1941, 1942b; A. L. Davis 1949), combine to make possible an interpretation of some of the features of midwestern dialects, even though much field work remains to be done in the region.[4]

As a settlement area, the northwestern quarter of Ohio is much newer than the rest of the state. Although it is at present a plain with no visible hindrance to free movement of population, it was formerly dominated by the 'Black Swamp,' the marsh lands of the Maumee River, which proved to be nearly impenetrable to land travel and could not be settled until extensive drainage had been undertaken. Nor was dampness the whole problem: the dreaded 'Maumee Fever' or malaria caused

epidemics among the pioneers and gave the region a bad reputation (Winter 1917:318; WPA Writer's Program 1940a:536, 560). The swamp and the fever diverted some of the Yankee population to the more easily cultivated lands of Michigan, and checked expansion of settlements from southern Ohio. As a result the area was nearly empty until the middle of the nineteenth century.

Canal transportation gave a great impetus to the settlement of the region. The Wabash and Erie Canal, connecting Toledo and Fort Wayne, was completed in 1843; the Miami and Erie Canal, linking Toledo with Dayton and Cincinnati, in 1845. Thus early in its history the area had east-west and north-south communications of great commercial importance. The coming of the railroads in the following decade brought about the obsolescence of the canal systems and increased the mobility of the population.

According to the U.S. Census of 1870, the first to give adequate information concerning the origins of the population, the northern counties show a high proportion of settlers from New York State, the remainder a far greater number from Pennsylvania. The actual ratios for these counties is as follows; the number for Pennsylvania is given first: Defiance 9:5, Putnam (Ottawa) 4:1, Van Wert 5:1, Wyandot (Upper Sandusky) 8:3, Wood (Perrysburg) 1:1. Lucas County, in which Toledo is located, shows a preponderance of New York settlers over those born in Pennsylvania by a ratio of 3 to 1. Since Perrysburg is on the edge of Lucas County, these figures may reflect the settlement of Perrysburg more accurately than do those for Wood County itself. Of the foreign population, the Germans have been the most important, followed by the Irish, the English, and the Welsh.

The five communities investigated in the area are a geographical sample: Perrysburg in the vicinity of Toledo, Defiance at the edge of the Black Swamp on the Maumee River, Ottawa a late settlement in the center of the area, Van Wert in the southwest corner, and Upper Sandusky in the southeast corner (see Map 1). These are all typical small communities of the area. To the north, Dundee, Michigan, shows almost without exception forms derived from New England and upstate New York.[5] The informants interviewed represent the oldest living generation of their communities; one informant in each community is

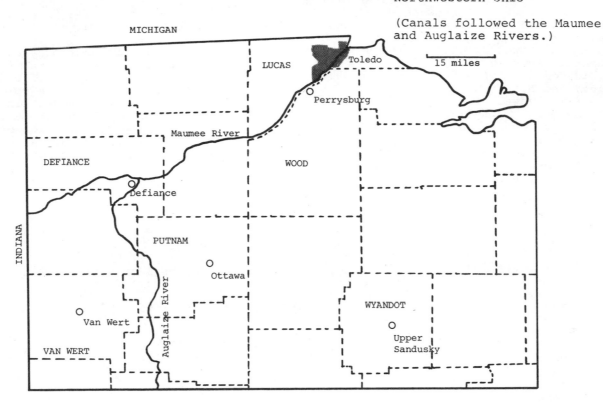

Map 1

Northwestern Ohio

(Canals followed the Maumee and Auglaize Rivers.)

extremely limited in education and social contacts, the other usually better educated and with a more extensive social life. The range in age is from 73 to 94; the educational range from second grade to normal school. These informants, in general, represent different cultural groups within the community; in no instance were the two informants intimately associated, and in only two communities were they even slightly acquainted.[6]

The tabulations given below show the distribution of certain words, pronunciations, and grammatical items. The terms 'Northern' and 'Midland,' as used in these tabulations, reflect the usage of Hempl 1896 and Kurath 1944, 1949. 'Northern' refers to the speech of New England -- especially Western New England -- and New York State, and of their settlement areas; it includes in addition the northern tier of counties in Pennsylvania, the Western Reserve, and Michigan. 'Midland' refers to the speech of most of Pennsylvania, and of the Pennsylvania-derived settlements in the interior of the South and in the Middle West.

Table 1 shows the distribution of thirty-nine vocabulary items; terms grouped together under the same number are synonoymous. Several terms and sets of terms in the list require a gloss: 3, large oblong pile of hay outside the barn; 4, small pile of hay in the field;

6, garbage; 7, frying pan; 8, paper bag; 9, harmonica; 12, double whippletree (for two horses); 14, implement for smoothing plowed land; 18, creek or brook (occurring also in place names); 19, quoits, the game of horseshoes; 20, cry of a calf; 22, setting hen; 23, call to cows; 24, call to horses in the pasture; 26, doughnut made with baking powder; 27, meat trimmings mixed with corn meal; 31, the green outer covering of a walnut; 32, dried apple slices; 35, dragonfly; 38, noisy celebration after a wedding.

Table 2 shows the distribution of a number of variant pronunciations; the first three affect relatively large groups of words, the rest affect only a single word each.

1. The vowel of *fog, hog, frog, on, pa, ma*: the symbol 'r' denotes a rounded vowel, the symbol 'u' an unrounded vowel; 'b' means that both pronunciations are used.

2. The stressed vowel of *wash, water*: symbols are the same as in Table 2.1. An asterisk after a symbol means that in at least some utterances of the word the informant used a diphthong with a retroflex (r-colored) second element.

3. The vowels of *horse, morning, forty,* and of *hoarse, mourning, four(teen)*: the symbol 's' means that the vowels in each pair of words are the same; the symbol 'd' means that they are different (lower

for words of the first group than for those of the second). Where there is a difference, it is usually greater between *horse* and *hoarse* or between *morning* and *mourning* than it is between *forty* and *four(teen)*.

4. The vowel of *won't*: the generalized phonetic symbols [o,u,ʌ] denote the syllabics of the types that occur in *boat*, *boot*, and *but*.

5. The vowel of *nothing*: the symbol [ʌ] denotes the syllabic of *but*; the symbol [a] denotes some variety of low central vowel.

6. The vowel of *room*: the symbols [u] and [ʊ] denote respectively the syllabics of *pool* and *pull*.

7. The vowel of *loam*: the symbols [o,u] have the same values as in Table 2.4.

8. The vowel of *gum(s)*: the symbols [ʌ,u,ʊ] have the same values as in Table 2.4 and 2.6.

9. The medial consonant of *greasy*.

10. The spirant of *with*: the first line shows the pronunciation of *th* in *with* before a word beginning with a voiced consonant or a vowel; the second line shows the pronunciation of *th* in *without*.

Table 3 shows the distribution of several grammatical forms and idiomatic combinations; again, expressions grouped together under the same number are synonymous.

Table 1. Vocabulary

x - usage of term by informant

(M) - Midland   (N) - Northern   unmarked - general or restricted usage

	Term	P1	P2	D1	D2	VW1	VW2	O1	O2	US1	US2
1.	sunrise		x		x			x	x		x
	sunup (M)	x		x		x	x			x	
2.	eaves troughs (N)	x	x		x						
	eavespouts			x							
	spouting (M)		x			x			x	x	x
	rain troughs							x			
3.	hay rick (M)			x	x	x	x	x	x	x	x
4.	hay cock (N)		x	x	x			x			
	hay doodle (M)			x		x	x	x	x	x	x
5.	pail (N)	x	x		x			x		x	
	bucket (M)			x		x	x		x	x	x
6.	swill (N)	x	x		x						
	slop (M)			x		x	x	x	x	x	x
7.	spider (N)	x	x								
	skillet (M)			x	x	x	x	x	x	x	x
8.	poke (M)					x			x	x	x
9.	mouth organ (N)		x	x	x					x	x
	(mouth) harp			x			x		x		
10.	fills [on a buggy] (N)	x		x	x			x			
	shafts		x	x	x	x	x	x	x	x	x
11.	whippletree (N)							x			
	singletree (M)	x	x		x	x	x	x	x	x	x
	swingletree			x							
12.	doubletree	x	x	x	x	x	x	x	x	x	x
13.	draw (N)				x						
	haul	x	x	x	x	x	x	x	x	x	x
14.	drag (N)	x	x	x							x
	harrow			x	x	x	x	x	x	x	
15.	(wooden) horse		x		x						
	trestle (M)			x		x			x	x	x
16.	kerosene										x
	coal oil (M)	x	x	x	x	x	x	x	x	x	x
17.	comforter (N)	x	x	x				x			
	comfort (M)	x				x	x	x		x	x
	coverlid								x		
18.	run (M)				x				x	x	x
19.	quates (N)		x								
20.	blat (N)		x								
	beller [bellow]	x					x		x		x
	bawl				x	x	x	x		x	
21.	whinny, whinner		x	x	x				x		x

[240]

Table 1. Vocabulary (Continued)

Term	P1	P2	D1	D2	VW1	VW2	O1	O2	US1	US2
21. whinker									x	
nicker (M)					x	x	x	x	x	x
22. clook (M)					x	x		x	x	
23. come boss! (N)	x	x	x							
so boss! (N)				x						
sook boss!			x				x		x	
sook!					x	x		x		x
24. cope! (M)			x		x	x				x
25. johnnycake (N)	x	x	x	x						
corn bread			x		x		x	x	x	x
corn pone (M)					x	x	x		x	x
26. fried cake (N)	x	x	x	x	x		x			
cruller (M)							x	x		
27. ponhoss (M)			x		x		x		x	x
scrapple				x						
28. thick milk (M)	x						x			x
clabbered milk (M)			x	x			x			
clabber (M)					x	x			x	
bonny clabber (M)										x
29. Dutch cheese (N)	x									
smearcase (M)		x	x	x	x		x	x		x
sour cheese									x	
white cheese						x				
30. cherry pit (N)	x	x		x	x		x	x		x
cherry seed (M)			x			x	x		x	
cherry stone							x	x		
31. walnut shuck (N)	x									
walnut hull (M)			x	x	x	x	x	x	x	x
32. snits (M)			x	x	x		x		x	x
33. shell [beans]			x		x	x	x		x	
shuck [beans]	x	x								
hull [beans] (M)				x						x
34. angleworm (N)	x						x			
fishworm (M)			x	x	x	x		x	x	x
fishing worm (M)					x					
groundworm			x							
garden worm			x							
35. darning needle (N)	x	x								
snake feeder (M)			x	x	x	x		x	x	x
snake fly						x				
36. hard maple (N)	x		x							
soft maple		x								
sugar maple								x		
sugar tree (M)			x	x	x	x	x		x	x
37. maple grove						x				
sugar grove	x			x		x				
sugar camp (M)		x	x		x		x	x	x	x
38. belling (M)	x	x	x	x	x	x	x	x	x	x
39. the baby creeps (N)	x		x	x					x	
the baby crawls (M)			x	x	x	x	x		x	x

Table 2. Pronunciation

Item	P1	P2	D1	D2	VW1	VW2	O1	O2	US1	US2
1. fog, foggy	r	u	r	r	r	r	r	r	r	r
hog	r	r	r	u	r	r	r	r	r	r
frog	r	r	r	r	r	r	r	r	r	r
on	b	u	r	r	r	r	r	b	r	r
pa, grandpa	b	u	r	r	r	r	r	r	r	
ma, grandma	b	u		r	r		r	r	r	
2. wash, washing	b	r	r*	r*	b	r*	r*	b*	r*	r*
water, watermelon	b	u	b*		r	r	r	u	u	b
3. horse:hoarse	d	s	s	d	s	s	d	s	d	s

[241]

Table 2. Pronunciation (Continued)

Item	P1	P2	D1	D2	VW1	VW2	O1	O2	US1	US2
3. morning:mourning	s	s	d	s	s	s	d	s	s	s
forty:four(teen)	d	d	d	d	d	d	d	d	d	d
4. won't	ʌ	ʌ	o,u	o	o	o	o	o	o	o
5. nothing	ʌ	ʌ	a	ʌ	ʌ	ʌ	ʌ	a	ʌ,a	ʌ
6. bedroom	u	u	u,u	u	u	u	u	u,u	u,u	u
room, storeroom	u	u								
7. loam	o	o	u	o	u	o	u	o	u	u
8. gum(s)	u,ʌ	ʌ	u	ʌ	u	ʌ	u,ʌ	ʌ	u	ʌ
9. greasy	s	s	s	s	z	s	s	s	s	s
10. with	ð	θ,ð	ð	ð	ð	θ	ð	θ	ð	ð
without		ð	ð	θ	θ,ð	θ	θ	ð	ð	ð

Table 3. Grammar

Item	P1	P2	D1	D2	VW1	VW2	O1	O2	US1	US2
1. hadn't ought (N)			x		x	x			x	
2. dived [past tense]	x				x	x		x	x	x
dove (N)		x	x	x			x			
3. clum [= climbed] (M)						x	x	x	x	x
4. woke (up)	x	x			x	x	x	x		x
waked (up)			x	x					x	
awakened			x		x	x			x	
got awake (M)					x					x
5. quarter till eleven (M)			x		x	x	x	x		x
6. sick to his stomach (N)	x	x						x	x	x
sick at his stomach			x	x	x		x			
sick in his stomach						x				
7. wait for me	x	x				x				
wait on me (M)			x	x	x				x	x

In vocabulary, the Northern items are concentrated in Perrysburg. They occur occasionally in Defiance, and are rare in the other three communities. Of the words marked Northern, only *pail*, *mouth organ*, *whinny*, *fried cake*, and *cherry pit* occur more than once in records from Van Wert, Upper Sandusky, and Ottawa. Of the Midland items, *sunup* (also found in the North as a relic), *skillet*, *singletree*, *doubletree*, *coal oil*, *comfort*, *smearcase*, *sugar camp*, *belling*, and *crawls* are found both in Perrysburg and Defiance. The sample is not large enough to determine whether trade could have been a determining influence. The Northern terms *evener* and *horning* (for *doubletree* and *belling*) are completely absent; the Midland terms *coal oil* and *belling* were offered by every informant.

As often happens in transition areas, several forms have been found which may be interpreted as blends: *eavespout* (D) = *eaves trough* × *spouting*; *mouth harp* (O, VW, D) = *mouth organ* × (French) *harp*; *whinker* (US) = *whinny* × *nicker*; *sook boss* (US, O, D) = *come boss* or *co-boss* × *sook*.

In pronunciation, the distribution of Northern and Midland variants in the Great Lakes area has generally been found to be closely parallel to that of the vocabulary variants. The variation in the syllabics of *fog*, *frog*, *hog*, *on*, *pa*, *ma*, is one of the best dialect indicators for the Middle West: the unrounded vowel in these words is generally Northern, the rounded vowel Midland (Marckwardt 1941). In northwestern Ohio the forms with unrounded vowel are concentrated at Perrysburg but are rare elsewhere. It will be noted that there is little consistency in the usage of the two Perrysburg informants: P1 has *hog*, *fog*, and *frog* with [ɔ], but [an~ɔn, pa~pɔ,ma~mɔ]; P2 has [hɔg,frɔg,fag,an,pa, ma]. All speakers show a consistent difference between the syllabics of *four* and *forty*, although the Ottawa and Upper Sandusky informants pronounce vowels in these words which are rather similar, while P1 has both [o] and [ɔ] in *forty*. Only O1 makes distinctions in both of the pairs *horse:hoarse* and *morning:mourning* (cf. Kurath 1940). The patterns for *wash* and *water* are extremely complicated: nearly every speaker has more than one pronunciation of at least one of these words. P1, for example, may [waʃ] in [wotɚ], while P2 [woʃɨz] in [watɚ]. All four informants in Perrysburg and Defiance have [u] in *room*; the younger informant in Defiance has only [ʊ], the others have [u] as well.

The Northern form [wʌnt] *won't* patterns as might be expected from the restricted occurrence of such typical Yankee words as *spider* and *darning needle*. The pronunciation [lum] *loam* seems not to be restricted to any area. The forms [gumz,gumz] *gums* pattern according to educational type, only the less highly educated informants having the rounded syllabics. *Greasy* with [s] occurs in every community. This well-known item shows almost exactly the distribution found by Hempl in the 1890's. The [s] form and the [z] form are separated by an isogloss somewhat more southerly than those for most other Northern items.[7] The forms [wɪð,wɪðauɬ] are characteristically Northern.[8] In this area there seems to be no kind of regularity for these items.

In morphology and idiom, the Northern *dove* complements the Midland *clum*, setting off Defiance and Perrysburg from the rest of the area; but Northern *hadn't ought* and *sick to his stomach* are found in other communities (cf. Atwood 1953a). The Midland forms *wait on me* and *quarter till* are found in every community except Perrysburg.

Germanisms are well represented in the area: *clook, snits, ponhoss, smearcase, got awake*. These must be the result of Pennsylvania German influence, reinforced by the direct German settlement in the region.

This sampling of what happens in a transition area reveals the complexity to be found even in a limited section of the so-called 'General American' speech area. The distribution of forms closely reflects the settlement history, but one is at a loss to give convincing reasons for the restriction of some items and the spreading of others.

Such questions cannot be settled in summary fashion. It would be very desirable if a detailed study were to be made of the area, closely correlating the historico-cultural complex with the speech forms. In such a study a wider range of age and education would be needed to ascertain whether such an area is becoming more homogeneously Midland or Northern or is creating its own unique blend of Midland and Northern elements; whether there is any relationship between categories of meaning and rates of change; whether vocabulary, pronunciation, or grammatical items show the greatest tendency to be retained in making such a shift; and whether differences in age or differences in education are of greater importance. (On the Atlantic Seaboard, age levels are generally less significant than culture levels, but there is a possibility that the reverse may be true west of the Alleghenies, where class distinctions are fewer and less sharp.)

Finally, looking both forward and backward, a detailed analysis of such a transition area may shed some light on the problems of dialect formation in this country, where speech mixture must have been the rule from the earliest colonial times. A detailed study of a small transition area would be extremely helpful to those planning an extension of the Linguistic Atlas to the Rocky Mountain area and the Far West; for the lateness of settlement and the mixture of population oblige us to regard almost all the United States west of the Mississippi as a transition area. Finally, such an investigation -- and even this preliminary study -- may be helpful to those who would compare American and British dialects. The linguistic atlases of the eastern states provide excellent comparable data from which the student of dialects in the Great Lakes area can work; the U.S. Census reports provide reliable material on population origins. If under these favorable conditions we find Great Lakes transition dialects difficult to analyze, our scanty knowledge of present-day British dialects and even scantier knowledge of the origins of the American colonial population should make scholars extremely skeptical of those who would point out a single Old-World origin for any single American dialect.

NOTES

[1] Typical focal areas in the eastern United States are Boston and its environs, metropolitan New York, and the Virginia Piedmont.

[2] Typical relic areas are Cape Cod in New England and the Banks Islands off the North Carolina coast.

[3] The only American study of a transition area is J. S. Hall 1942. Hall's introductory study of the settlement history indicates that the Smokies are to be considered a transition area; but unfortunately his analysis seems to assume that the area is a relic area of considerable uniformity.

[4] Only eight field records have been made as yet in Indiana, and the parts of Ohio adjacent to this northwestern sector have not been completely investigated.

This paper is based on ten records made in northwestern Ohio -- nine by R. McDavid in June 1949, the other by Frederic G. Cassidy in 1939. Funds for field work in Ohio have been provided by the University of Michigan, Western Reserve University, and the Ohio Archaeological and Historical Association.

[5] The sixty-six field records made in Michigan reveal a remarkable similarity to the findings for western New England and upstate New York. This is especially true of the records from the southeastern part of Michigan.

6 The field worker must often make a judgment about the educational status of an informant. Home study and aggressive social life may cause an informant with relatively little formal schooling to be regarded as better educated than another with the same school background.

The ten informants are designated by letter-and-number codes; the letter, or combination of two letters, denotes the community (P, Perrysburg; D, Defiance; VW, Van Wert; O, Ottawa; US, Upper Sandusky); the numerals 1 and 2 denote respectively the more and the less old-fashioned informant interviewed in that community. Personal data on the informants are given here:

P1: retired merchant, 84; F[ather] b[orn in] Ireland, M[other] b Ohio; 7th grade; not much interested in reading; virtually untraveled.

P2: retired merchant, 85; F and M b Germany; 8th grade; considerable reading (president of local library board) and extensive travel in U.S. (as salesman in his younger days).

D1: laborer, 94; F b Scotland, M b Pennsylvania; 2nd grade.

D2: retired farmer, 80; F b Pennsylvania, M b Ohio; normal school.

VW1: farmer, 82; F and M b Ohio; 3rd grade.

VW2: farmer, 73; F and M b Wales; grade school; self-educated, well-read; extensive travel as cattle buyer.

O1: farmer, 76 (in 1939, when the record was made); F b New York State, M b Ohio; school till fifteen years old.

O2: retired restaurateur and saloon keeper, 77; F and M b Ohio; 6th grade; extensive social contacts.

US1: laborer, 79; F and M b Ohio; grade school.

US2: farmer, 85; F and M b Ohio; normal school.

7 *Greasy* with [s] is regular in the Pennsylvania German area.

8 In the *Linguistic Atlas of New England* (Kurath *et al.* 1939-43) there are only forty instances of the voiceless spirant, twenty-two of them in Maine and New Brunswick.

Descriptive linguistics, in its broadest aspects, tells us not only what forms occur and in what combinations, but also in what parts of the linguistic community and in the speech or writing of what social groups particular variants may be found.[1] By examining these regional and social differences within the generally uniform structure of a language, dialectologists are able to correlate linguistic data with patterns of settlement history, regional growth, and social structure; furthermore, they are able to provide a solid base of fact for the value judgments necessary in such applications of linguistics as lexicography and the teaching of English.[2]

These regional and social differences have been summarized, for the older settlement area along the Atlantic Seaboard, in Kurath 1949, in Atwood 1953a, and in Kurath and R. McDavid 1961. This article summarizes the grammatical evidence in the field records for the *Linguistic Atlas of the North-Central States*.[4] Besides the general interest of dialectologists in accurately delineating regional and social patterns of usage, there are several reasons why an examination of grammatical evidence from the North-Central area should be of interest to the student of American English:

1. Since the North-Central states are an area of secondary settlement, it is desirable to see whether regional dialect differences, established for the Atlantic Seaboard, persist inland, in the heartland of the traditionally uniform 'General American.'

2. More specifically, conceding that the well-recognized relic areas of the Atlantic states preserve characteristic grammatical forms, it is desirable to know whether secondary settlement areas also show regional differences in grammar, contrary to Mencken's theory of a uniform American vulgate.

3. Since the teaching of standards of grammatical usage is one of the most important tasks of our schools -- and is the touchstone by which teachers of English, at all levels, are most commonly judged -- it is imperative to know what are the grammatical practices which actually differentiate cultivated from uncultivated usage, so that the teacher -- whether dealing with native speakers of English or with those who come from other language communities -- may work on those practices which are most likely to stigmatize a

student in the judgment of his peers or of his future employers.[5]

Field work for the *Linguistic Atlas of the North-Central States*, under the direction of Albert H. Marckwardt, of Michigan, began in the summer of 1938, with a preliminary survey of Michigan and Indiana; further preliminary investigations the following summer, in Ohio and Illinois, indicated enough clear regional differences to warrant a full-fledged linguistic atlas of the region, but only Wisconsin was fully covered before the United States became involved in World War II. Field work was resumed in 1948 and completed in 1977. In their 1960 form the North-Central archives comprise approximately 450 field records [564 in 1977].

The principles upon which American linguistic geography is based have been discussed many times (cf. R. McDavid 1958a). The following summary indicates the modifications required by the practical situation in the North-Central States, where the director has had relatively little money for an organized project, and where the field work in each state has been conducted according to the conditions which local institutions have attached to their financial support:[6]

1. A network of communities, representative of the economic and demographic history of the region: twenty-five to forty communities, providing adequate coverage for a survey of an area of secondary settlement.

2. Informants native to their communities, representing at least two different groups in each community by age, education, and sometimes by ethnic origin. As in the Atlantic states, cultured informants are interviewed in most of the important cultural centers.

3. A questionnaire composed of items from the daily experience of most informants and designed to reveal regional and social differences in vocabulary, pronunciation, and grammar. Since the dialectologist is interested not only in describing the present dialect situation but in establishing the historical affiliations of the present-day dialects, the selection of items -- as well as of communities -- is weighted in the direction of rural and small-town life.

4. Field investigators, normally with intensive training under more experienced workers in: a) handling the informants; b) the purposes of the questionnaire; c) the phonetic alphabet devised for the

Linguistic Atlas of the United States and Canada. More than four fifths of the North-Central interviews were conducted by field workers trained by the original Atlas staff in common practices of eliciting and transcribing, so that their records provide comparable data even on the phonetic level. In a few areas, however, the field workers did not have adequate training in the use of the questionnaire or in transcription in the Atlas alphabet; as a result, their records not only differ markedly in the phonetic transcriptions but often skimp the grammatical and lexical data. Fortunately, the boundaries of these areas never coincide with probable dialect boundaries and always overlap the areas covered by more experienced investigators.

5. Impressionistic transcription on the spot in a finely graded phonetic alphabet.[7]

In the field records for the North-Central *Atlas* is evidence on the regional and social variants for some 125 items of grammar. Some of these were offered by informants as lexical variants (as *bought bread, boughten bread, brought on bread* for *baker's bread, store bread*, etc.) and hence would not be recorded from every informant. Some forms -- such as the preterites of *come, run*, and *take* -- might be recorded in several contexts; the same context, on the other hand, might provide data on several forms -- as he *became sick, took sick*, or *was taken sick*. The inventory of grammatical items covered by the questionnaire is as follows:

1. Verbs[8]
   a) Principal parts (preterites only, unless otherwise indicated): *become, begin, bite* (p. ppl.), *blow, boil* (p. ppl.), *bring* (pret., p. ppl), *buy* (attributive p. ppl.), *catch* (inf., pret.), *climb* (pret., p. ppl.), *come, dive, do, draw up, dream, drink* (pret., p. ppl.), *drive* (pret., p. ppl.), *drown* (p. ppl.), *eat* (pret., p. ppl.), *fetch, fight, fit, freeze, give, give out* (p. ppl.), *grow* (pret., p. ppl.), *hear* (p. ppl.), *heat* (p. ppl.), *kneel, learn, lie* (inf., pret.), *lie out, ride* (p. ppl.), *rise* (pret., attributive p. ppl.), *run, scare* (p. ppl.), *see, shrink, sit* (inf., pret.), *spoil* (p. ppl.), *sweat, swim, take* (pret., ppl.), *teach, tear* (p. ppl.), *throw, wake* (up), *wear* (out) (p. ppl.), *write* (p. ppl.)
   b) Personal forms of the present indicative: *I be* (etc.), *I'm going, am I going, he does, he doesn't, he looks like* (etc.), *she rinses, it costs*
   c) Number and concord: *we were* (etc.), *here are, oats are*
   d) Negative forms: *am not, are not, is not; have not, has not; was not; do not; will not; ought not; didn't use to;* multiple negatives
   e) Infinitive and present participle: *to tell, singing and a-laughing, going*
   f) Phrases: *all gone, get rid of,*

might could, I shall be, we shall be, I've been thinking, I've done worked, I want to get off
2. Noun plurals: *bushel,*[9] *fist, hoof, house, ox, post, pound, shaft, trough, eaves trough, yoke* (*span, pair, team*)
3. Pronouns
   a) Personal pronouns: *it, it wasn't me* (etc.), *you* (nom. pl., gen. pl.), *ours, yours, his, hers, theirs*
   b) Interrogative pronouns: *who* (nom. pl., gen. pl.), *what* (nom. pl., gen. pl.)
   c) Relative pronouns: *who, whose*
   d) Demonstratives: attributive plural
4. Adjective formation: *poisonous*
5. Article (sandhi-alternation): *an apple* (etc.)
6. Adverbs and adverbial phrases: *a little way, a long way, anywhere, at all, look here!, rather cold* (etc.), *this way*
7. Prepositional syntax: *run across him, not at home, all at once, sick at his stomach, behind the door, named for his father, wait for you, died of diphtheria, fell off the horse, half past seven, quarter of eleven*
8. Subordinating conjunctions: *as far as, as if, because, unless.*

For interpreting the regional and social distribution of these forms and their variants, one needs a brief sketch of settlement and social history, pending a detailed presentation in the published North-Central *Atlas*. The basic patterns of settlement represent extensions westward of the major dialect regions of the Atlantic Seaboard states -- Northern, Midland, and Southern[10] -- with the Northern and South Midland regions providing the bulk of early settlement. Wisconsin, Michigan, southern Ontario, and the northernmost counties of Illinois, Indiana, and Ohio were all settled primarily by New Englanders and by upstate New Yorkers of New England descent. New Englanders and New Yorkers also established enclaves further south in such communities as Worthington (now a suburb of Columbus) and Marietta, at the confluence of the Muskingum and the Ohio. In southern Ontario there were also many United Empire Loyalists who were refugees from the Middle Atlantic states; later came direct migrations from the British Isles. South Midlanders from the western counties of Virginia and North Carolina pushed across the Cumberland Gap and other passes into Kentucky, and from Kentucky infiltrated the bottom lands of southern Illinois, most of Indiana, and southern Ohio. Groups of Kentuckians settled further north, along the Mississippi and its tributaries, notably in the lead region where Illinois, Wisconsin, and Iowa join. The opening of the National Road provided an overland route for Pennsylvania settlement of the central parts of Ohio, Indiana, and Illinois -- a wedge progressively narrowing as it approached the Mississippi -- while other Pennsyl-

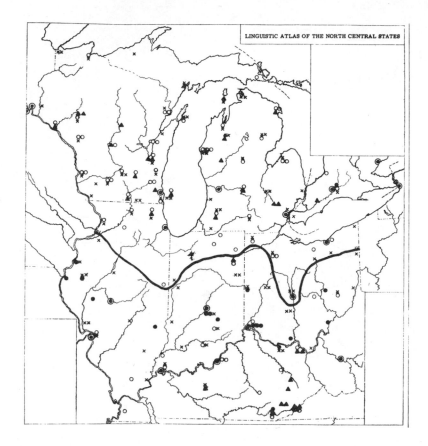

Map 1

Northern Forms

●   *sick to*   ——————

○   *scairt*

✕   *boughten*

▲   *clim*

vanians, chiefly from the Pittsburgh area, descended the Ohio Valley. These last migrations both introduced North Midland forms into the North-Central states and reinforced the general Midland contributions of the South Midland settlements.

The large-scale immigration from Northern Europe after 1840 brought fairly compact colonies into both urban and rural areas of the North-Central region, but fewest into Kentucky. Although these groups occasionally introduced loan translations of their native idioms, in the long run they probably accelerated the spread of Standard English grammatical forms, since -- placing a high value on education -- they appear to have often gone directly from their native language to Standard English, without learning the folk speech.

Direct migration from the Southern region proper -- the plantation settlements of the coastal plain and lower Piedmont of Virginia, the Carolinas, and Georgia -- was comparatively small. It seems to have been strongest in the westernmost counties of Kentucky, particularly the Jackson Purchase west of the Tennessee River, less strong in the Blue Grass area around Lexington and Louisville. However, thanks to the political and economic history of Kentucky, and the ties of cultured Kentuckians with the older plantation areas, the prestige of Southern institutions and

Southern speech forms has always been high in the Blue Grass State, and not ignored further north. With slavery forbidden north of the Ohio by the Northwest Ordinance of 1787, and economically unprofitable in the foothills and mountains that cover most of Kentucky, there were few Negroes among the early settlers, except in the Purchase and Blue Grass regions.

Alongside the pattern of settlement, and often disturbing the dialect areas that settlement had created, the North-Central region has witnessed the dramatic operation of three forces that have characterized American society from its beginnings -- industrialization, urbanization, and the spread of education. From the development of heavy industry near the end of the nineteenth century there has been a steadily accelerating migration from the farms and small towns to the cities and expanded metropolitan areas. The population of these expanded urban areas has been further augmented by new mass migrations, first of immigrants from Southern and Eastern Europe, later by Southern Negroes and poor whites. Each of these later groups has frequently established socially isolated colonies within urban areas, with the tacit or open cooperative blessing of industry, political machines, and churches, so that speech peculiarities of the group may tenaciously persist (R. McDavid 1951d; in this volume, pp. 143-

Map 2

Midland Forms

● *want off* ──────

○ *clum* ── ── ──

✗ *quarter till* ─ ─ ─

🠋 *got awake*

45). In compensation, popular education, inaugurated by the Northwest Ordinance, has been strongly supported north of the Ohio from the earliest settlements, so that there has been attrition of folk grammatical forms -- as well as of words and pronunciations -- under the impact of the standard language. The influence of popular education has so far been less significant in Kentucky, where industrialization came late, communications have been generally poor until recently, and the lack of funds and the proliferation of county governments have hindered the development of a strong state-wide school system.

Against this background we may examine the regionally distinctive grammatical features in the North-Central states. It should be remembered that in an area of secondary settlement the dialect regions -- Northern, South Midland, etc. -- are not so distinctly marked as they are along the Atlantic Seaboard. Furthermore, the occurrence of a particular form in a particular area does not mean that everybody in that area uses the form on all occasions.

Among the grammatical features characteristic of Northern speech (see Map 1), *trouths* 'troughs' (with /-θs/ or /-ðz/), *died from*, and *to* as a preposition of location -- in such contexts as *sick to the stomach*, (he isn't) *to home*, and *all to once* -- are well established throughout the area of Northern settlement. Less well established are *scairt* 'scared' and *het* 'heated.'[11] Except in Ontario, /wʌnt/ 'won't' predominates in the Inland North, as it does in New England and Upstate New York; in Ontario, however, /wʌnt/ is infrequent, but the Hudson Valley /wunt/, /wʊnt/ very common. Apparently expansive Northern forms are *dove* /dov/ as the preterite of *dive* and *hadn't ought* 'ought not'; *hadn't ought* is found as far south as the St. Louis and Cincinnati areas. On the other hand, *it wan't me*, *gwine*, and *be* as a finite verb -- old-fashioned in New England -- are very uncommon and seem to be rapidly disappearing.[12] On Beaver Island (an Irish fishing colony in northern Lake Michigan) and in scattered communities of northern Wisconsin is found the negative form *usen't to*, not uncommon in British English but rare in the Atlantic states.

Of characteristic Midland forms (see Map 2), *seen* as a preterite has spread widely throughout the North-Central states, except in cultivated speech. Occurring everywhere, without appreciable concentration in any single area, it is one of the few speech forms of the region that one may safely label as 'General American.' *Clum* 'climbed' is also an expansive form, except in cultivated speech, but has spread less than *seen*. *I want off* and *quarter till* occur throughout the areas of

[248]

Map 3

Southern and South Midland Forms

●   *done*   ───────

○   *dog-bit*

✕   *raised*

▲   *used to didn't, wasn't*

Midland settlement, though -- perhaps because of Southern influence -- *quarter
till* appears infrequently in the Blue
Grass and not at all in the Illinois communities near St. Louis. *Wait on* 'wait
for,' common in the Midland areas of the
Atlantic states, is relatively infrequent
in Illinois, and *all the further* 'as far
as' seems to be receding throughout the
area, but particularly in Illinois. *You-
uns* 'you' (pl.) is rare and old-fashioned;
such Pennsylvania Germanisms as *the
oranges are all* 'all gone' and *got awake*
'woke up' are extremely rare.

A few South Midland forms are fairly
well established in the areas of South
Midland settlement, though never to the
exclusion of competing forms: *dog-bit*
'bitten by a dog,' *used to didn't* 'didn't
use to,' *give out* 'tired,' and *sick in the
stomach.* Less well established are *drinkt*
'drank, drunk' and *the sun raised* 'rose.'
Receding are *shrinkt* 'shrank,' *I sot down*
'sat,' *swim* 'swam,' and the /-n/ forms of
the absolute genitive: *ourn, yourn, hisn,
hern, theirn.* *Drimpt* 'dreamed' is well
established in eastern Kentucky. Less
common, and usually confined to eastern
Kentucky, are *fit* 'fought,' *them there
boys*, and *e'er a, ne'er a* in such constructions as *he said ne'er a word about
it* (Map 3).

Although previous studies of the vocabulary of the North-Central states have not

disclosed any characteristic Southern lexical items (A. L. Davis 1949, Forrester
1954), several Southern grammatical forms
do occur. The most widely distributed of
these items is *waked up*, which is most
common in eastern Kentucky (sporadic occurrences of *waked up* in the Northern settlement area are probably explained by its
appearance in New England and in the Genesee Valley of New York). Southern forms
which are old-fashioned in the Atlantic
Seaboard are rare in the North-Central
states: *he do, the sun riz, I driv a
nail*, and *he div in* are definitely recessive, and largely confined to eastern
Kentucky (see Map 4). Of dialect areas
within the South, Eastern Virginia is represented by *I ran up on him* 'met,' which
is fairly common in Kentucky. However,
clome 'climbed,' another characteristic
Virginia item, rarely appears, and only in
northern Wisconsin and northern Michigan,
where Virginia influence is improbable.[13]

As with vocabulary and pronunciation,
some grammatical items are typical of two
of the major Eastern regions, or of parts
of them. *Forty bushel*, found throughout
the Northern and Midland regions of the
Atlantic Seaboard, is common everywhere in
the North-Central states. The Northern
and North Midland *boughten bread* 'baker's
bread' is moderately common north of the
Ohio River; south of the river it appears
only in Maysville, Kentucky, where fea-

Map 4

Southern and South Midland Relics

●   *he do*

○   *div*

✕   *hit* 'it'

▲   *heern*

tures of North Midland vocabulary and pronunciation are also found (Map 1). The Inland North (Vermont and New York State) and western Pennsylvania share *I ran onto him* 'met,' likewise common north of the Ohio. The Midland and South share *two pound*, one of the most characteristic non-Northern items in the North-Central states (Marckwardt 1940a); in Illinois and Wisconsin it follows the Mississippi (and presumably the migrations of Kentucky rivermen) from the lead region north to the neighborhood of Minneapolis. Outside the area of Northern settlement, the Midland and Southern *oughtn't* is well established, though yielding ground to the Northern *hadn't ought*.

As along the Atlantic Seaboard, there are a few items characteristic of the North and South but not of the Midland: *quarter to eleven*, *clim* 'climbed,' and the uninflected preterites *begin* and *see*; the high incidence of *see* in Kentucky and adjacent communities is probably due to its predominance in eastern Virginia. The Northern, Southern, and South Midland parts of our section -- but not the North Midland settlements[14] -- share *ketcht* (rarely *katcht*) 'caught,' *off'n* 'off,' the mistakenly labeled 'Common Americanism' *half after seven*, and *oxen* as a singular, with a new analogical plural *oxens*. The singular *oxen* and plural *oxens* seem to be more recessive in Wisconsin and Michigan

than in Kentucky and the Ohio Valley; better education, better communications, and the earlier disuse of oxen in agriculture are obvious explanations.

As we have mentioned, the Southern and South Midland areas of the Atlantic Seaboard have many items of vocabulary, grammar, and pronunciation in common, and Southern forms often infiltrate the South Midland -- a situation to be expected since not till the twentieth century did the South Midland develop cultural centers important enough to resist the pressure of plantation focal areas such as the Virginia Piedmont and the South Carolina Low-Country. A large number of grammatical items shared by South and South Midland are common in the North-Central states: *you-all* (dominant south of the Ohio, but sporadic and considered somewhat quaint further north), *a apple*, *taken* and *tuck* 'took,' *tuck* 'taken,' *sweated* (also occasionally in the North), *bought bread* 'baker's bread,' *look-a-here*, *this-a-way*, *drawed up* 'shrank,' *seed* 'saw' (in old-fashioned speech), the perfective *done* (as *I've done worked all I'm going to*), and apparently a greater tendency toward omission of the relative pronoun in such constructions as *he's the man owns the orchard* and *he's a boy his father's rich*. Less common, and practically restricted to eastern Kentucky, are *might could* and such recessive forms as *brought on bread* 'baker's bread,' *mout* 'might,' and the /-əz/ inflection in *it costes*, *fistes*, and *postes*.

Cutting across the patterns of regional distribution is the social distribution of these forms. This too follows in general the distribution found along the Eastern Seaboard. That is, forms characteristic of the oldest and least educated group in New York or Virginia continue to be found in the speech of that group; they do not suddenly appear in the speech of college graduates in Wisconsin or Illinois. However, as one goes west, the forms characteristic of the oldest and least educated group become much less frequent -- a testimony to the attrition of the rarer forms by dialect mixture, as well as to the efficiency of public education in eradicating characteristics of nonstandard speech. Throughout the North-Central states it is the less sophisticated speakers who use such forms as *blowed*, *growed*, *throwed*, *come* 'came,' *run* 'ran,' *eat* 'ate, eaten,'[15] *drownded*, *them boys*, he came over *for to tell me*, *he was a-singin'*, *he did it a-purpose*, and *I won't go without he goes*. Though *hain't* and *ain't* often occur side by side as negatives of both *have* and *be*, *hain't* is clearly the more old-fashioned, nearly always restricted to the most old-fashioned informants. Less clearly nonstandard, but certainly not predominant in cultivated speech, are *we was* and *he don't care*.[16] And as Avis 1953 and Allen 1957 have pointed out, *I have drank* is predominant in educated usage except in Kentucky; perhaps in Wisconsin and Michigan (where this predominance is clearest) there has been a confusion of meaning between the participle of *drink* and the adjective *drunk* 'intoxicated.'

Despite the disapproval of handbooks and other self-constituted authorities, certain other forms occur everywhere, in the speech of all social groups: *I been thinking* (with omission of *have*), *singin'* with the final alveolar nasal /-n/ rather than the velar nasal /-ŋ/, *like* as a subordinating conjunction in such contexts as *it seems like he'll win*, and *it wasn't me*.[17]

For a final group of forms, the status is indeterminate; that is, on the basis of our evidence we cannot classify the variants regionally or socially or predict the direction of change. Among these are *ran across* and *ran into* 'met,' *named for* and *named after*, *died of* and *died with*, *oats is thrashed* and *oats are thrashed*, *dreamed* and *dreamt*, *fitted* and *fit*, *learned* and *learnt*, *kneeled* and *knelt*, and the complex of *lie* and *lay*, with the infinitives *lie* and *lay* and the preterites *lay*, *laid*, and *lied*. Perhaps usage in this complex has been confused by associa-

tion with *lie* 'prevaricate.'[18]

On the basis of our evidence, then, we reach the following conclusions:

1. As in vocabulary and pronunciation, regional differences in grammar are less sharp in the North-Central states than along the Atlantic Seaboard. This is what one would expect in an area of secondary and relatively recent settlement, favored with a tradition of public education and leavened by large settlements of prosperous Germans and Scandinavians who might tend to approach English through books and the classroom rather than through the regional folk speech.

2. Nevertheless, many regional differences in grammar can be observed, on every level of usage.

3. As one would expect from the history of settlement, the regionally distinctive grammatical forms in the North-Central states normally reflect the usage of the Northern (especially Inland Northern) and the South Midland regions of the Atlantic Seaboard. Features from Eastern New England are very rare; features from the North Midland are highly recessive except when they also occur in the North or in the South Midland; features from the South appear only when they have infiltrated the South Midland areas of the Atlantic Seaboard or have been adopted in Kentucky -- originally a political subdivision and still to some extent a cultural dependency of Virginia -- but are more common than previous studies would have suggested.

4. Arteries of communication, especially the Mississippi and its tributaries, have facilitated the southward spread of Northern forms and the northward spread of forms from the South Midland.

5. The more spectacular relic forms are rare. Those that occur are most common in eastern Kentucky, still largely rural, with industry, communications, and education lagging behind those in the states north of the Ohio.

6. Finally, the social differences that actually occur in the speech of the North-Central region are not accurately reflected in the judgments of usage heretofore made by those who prepare teaching materials.

These general conclusions are likely to stand up, though some particular statements may be modified as the last records come in, intensive local studies are conducted, and the entire body of our evidence is compared with the data from the Atlantic Seaboard. As practitioners of the science of language, we must remember that all conclusions are tentative, the best we can reach with the evidence at hand, and subject to revision when we have more evidence.

[1] Preliminary versions of this study have been presented at the Linguistic Forum, Ann Arbor (July 1955), and at the Madison, Wisconsin, meeting of the Present-Day English group of the MLA (September 1957). The evidence on verb forms, as gathered to September 1955, is found in V. McDavid 1956.

Permission to utilize the North-Central field records has been given by A. H. Marckwardt, director of the *Linguistic Atlas of the North-Central States* (1980-), with whom the authors have worked closely for more than a decade.

[2] Like all studies of the social distribution of grammatical forms, this one owes much to the precept and example of Charles C. Fries, especially to his *American English Grammar* (1940).

[3] Kurath 1949 went to press before field work was complete in South Carolina, Georgia, and upstate New York. For these areas see R. McDavid 1951a, in this volume, pp. 219-31, and R. McDavid 1955a, in this volume, pp. 272-81.

[4] The archives of the North-Central field records are housed at the University of Chicago and have been published by microfilm (Marckwardt *et al.* 1976-78). Check list studies, which have been used in subsequent regional surveys to supplement the field records, were first employed in the North-Central region in A. L. Davis 1949. Subsequently, Kentucky was surveyed by check lists in Forrester 1954. Check-list archives have been gathered for Ohio, Indiana, and Illinois; as yet, all of these check-list collections are incomplete. Because literate Americans are self-conscious about grammatical propriety, check lists have not been used to sample grammatical differences.

[5] A comparison of handbook judgments and Atlas data on selected grammatical items is found in Malmstrom 1958.

No social scientist will be surprised to discover inconsistencies between the unguarded usage of informants and their reactions to direct questioning. Such discrepancies are a part of the record of usage, and should be recorded wherever possible.

[6] The principal support has been provided by the University of Michigan, through a series of grants from the Rackham Fund. Other institutions assisting the project have been Augustana College, the University of Illinois, Indiana University, the University of Kentucky, Michigan State University, the Ohio State Archaeological and Historical Association, Ohio State University, Western Reserve University, and the University of Wisconsin.

Support for the editing of the North-Central *Atlas* has been received from the American Council of Learned Societies, the National Council of Teachers of English, the University of Chicago, and especially the National Endowment for the Humanities.

[7] In some areas, to compensate for the inexperience of the field workers (and, theoretically, to save time in the field), interviews have been recorded on tape and transcribed later, by the interviewer or someone else. However, since the tape cannot record what the interviewer has not elicited, and since a transcriber incompletely familiar with the questionnaire will hardly recognize a form out of context, it is not surprising that the interviews on tape sometimes provide disappointingly little grammatical evidence, especially (and where the tapes should be most productive) alternative forms recorded from free conversation.

Differences among field workers, in experience and in practices in the field, naturally complicate the task of interpreting the data. The problem in the North-Central states is roughly analogous to that in New England, where nine investigators gathered the data but Guy S. Lowman, Jr., contributed nearly two fifths of the total, and Lowman's territory was contiguous to that of every other field worker.

[8] The classification of verb forms follows that in Atwood 1953a. Statements of the provenience of verb forms along the Atlantic Seaboard are based on Atwood.

[9] For a detailed study of the plurals of *bushel*, *pound*, *yoke*, etc., see R. and V. McDavid 1964, in this volume, pp. 199-218.

[10] This classification, first established in Kurath 1949, was originally based on vocabulary evidence but has since proved useful for grammatical and phonological evidence as well. For the Atlantic Seaboard, the North includes New England, the Hudson Valley, and their derivative settlements; the Midland, Pennsylvania and its derivative settlements; the South, the areas of older plantation culture from Delaware Bay to the Florida line. Within the Midland, the North Midland includes Pennsylvania and northern West Virginia; the South Midland, southern West Virginia, the Shenandoah Valley, and the upper Piedmont and mountains of the Carolinas and Georgia. Because of the cultural dominance of the plantation areas in the former slaveholding states, the South Midland is highly receptive to Southern speech forms.

For a preliminary examination of North-Central vocabulary, see Marckwardt 1957.

For the foreign-language groups, the most extensive study is Haugen 1953.

[11] Both *scairt* and *het* occur occasionally in Kentucky.

[12] *It wan't me* and *gwine* are also fairly common in the coastal South; they are found occasionally in Kentucky.

[13] For *clome* as an eastern Virginia form, see Atwood 1951.

[14] Kurath and R. McDavid have found many old-fashioned pronunciations -- e.g., /drin/ 'drain' -- are found in New York State, West Virginia, and

Maryland, but are practically lacking in Pennsylvania.

[15] In most parts of the United States, *eat* is far more common as a folk preterite than *et*, which (perhaps because it is Standard British) actually has some status in cultivated speech, notably in the Charleston area. Oddly enough, the handbooks often condemn *et* but never seem to mention *eat*.

[16] The cultured informants who use these forms in familiar conversation -- like the cultured Charlestonians who say *ain't* freely among themselves -- would never use them in writing or in formal speeches.

There is no systematic study of regional grammatical differences in written American English. Fries 1940 indicated that he had collected material toward such a study, but he has never published it. The conventions of edited English would make such a study, from printed materials, difficult but not impossible. See Eliason 1956.

[17] These forms are characteristic of informal conversation and would rarely appear in formal writing.

[18] An educated Kentuckian commented indignantly: "I know that some people tell us to say *lie down* and not *lay down*; but I also know some folks who can lie standing up."

There is a long and well-documented record of the desire of man to change a situation by thinking of a more beautiful -- or at least less unpleasant -- name; the term *Eumenides* 'gracious ones' for the Furies is a classical example. As far back as the Middle Ages there were a number of polite names for the outdoor toilet (and *toilet* itself is a euphemism): *privy*, which has survived, and *wardrobe*, which has not -- despite Chaucer's use of the term in the *Prioress's Tale*. For the same institution the Renaissance added *close stool*, which is still common in Britain, and *jakes*, immortalized by Sir John Harington's sixteenth-century treatise on plumbing (*The Metamorphosis of Ajax* -- probably pronounced /e dʒeks/) and a famous scene in Joyce's *Ulysses*; *jakes* is perhaps related to the Virginia *johnny house* or *jack house*, and to the popular *john*, originally a woman's epithet, which is threatening to displace all other polite synonyms. Whether it is Nancy Mitford or Harold Pinter -- frank as their discussion of sex and other forms of human behavior may be -- British authors still testify to human ingenuity at devising euphemisms.

But we yield little if anything to our cousins across the sea. The sixth chapter of H. L. Mencken's *The American Language* (1936, 1945, 1963) witnesses eloquently to the desire of American society to see that everybody wins and everybody gets prizes. It is perhaps most amusing when it deals with the attempts of the average citizen to upgrade the name of his occupation or institution, and thereby convince himself, if no one else, that he is more important as a personage than his work would indicate and that he is fit to play a far more gaudy role.

Some of the more familiar specimens have an interesting history. *Realtor* (not, we are reminded, related to the Spanish *toro*) was coined by the philanthropic Charles M. Chadbourn of Minneapolis, to distinguish the brethren of the Minneapolis Real Estate Board from more casual operators; offered to the National Association of Real Estate Boards, accepted, and duly registered, it cannot be legally used by anyone except a member of a local Board. There were rumblings when Sinclair Lewis applied it to George F. Babbitt of Zenith; but when asked for an official comment, Mr. Chadbourn observed that the designation was accurately applied, since Babbitt was presented as a prominent member of the Zenith Board and the State Association.

The undertaker, we all know, has likewise risen in ostensive public esteem, thanks to the ingenuity of the guild in devising necrophoric euphemy. "In my boyhood in Baltimore," Mencken once wrote me, "the undertaker stood on all fours with the garbage man. Now he has risen to the level of a chiropractor." Despite the creativeness of such pioneers as the Civil War embalmers who assumed the title of *Doctor* (in all justice, they probably knew as much about leechcraft as most of the Hippocratic brethren who provided their custom), there was little progress until 1895, when the *Embalmer's Monthly* coined the professional title of *mortician*. Unlike *realtor*, *mortician* is in the public domain, though the *National Selected Morticians* are as exclusive as the Society of Cincinnati. *Mortician* of late has given way to *funeral director*, but the activities of the honorable gentlemen have made almost every American familiar with such charming specimens as *slumber robe* for *shroud*, *service car* for *dead wagon*, *ambulance* for *hearse*, and *patient* for *corpse* -- and with the burgeoning *colleges of mortuary science*.

If we academicians smile at this addiction to euphemy among the subsaline, a glance at our institutions of higher learning will disabuse us. Even *Ball State Teachers College* is now transmogrified into a *university*, and the two *Illinois Teachers Colleges* (*North* and *South*) in Chicago -- once branches of the *Chicago Teachers College*, née *Chicago Normal School* -- have just become *Northeast Illinois State College* and *Chicago State College*, with university designation on the horizon. Except for the pedagogical Lhasa, *Teachers College, Columbia*, one is hard put to find a single confessed teacher's college in the new eruption of universities, though a cynic sometimes detects scant improvement in the faculties, students or curricula. Our public schools have afflicted us with the caucus-race known as *social promotion*, so that it is possible for high-school 'graduates' to have a third-grade proficiency in reading and ciphering. And even our most prestigious universities have inflated the craft of book reviewing into the awesome thaumaturgy of *literary criticism*, whose several competing sects are equally incomprehensible to the sober citizen.

As euphemy progresses, however, we find that many familiar terms fall into disrepute -- often, I suspect, because those on

the make lose their sense of humor and
proportion as they rise. Or perhaps they
think they can alleviate their frustra-
tions by proscribing a label, however
accurate or traditional it might be. In
the 1920's many Italian-Americans pro-
tested vociferously because Chicago newspapers referred to the successful minis-
trants unto the public thirst as *Italians*.
More recently the self-styled liberals
have fired a New York teacher for using
the counting rhyme "Eenie meenie"; the
Philadelphia School Board has emasculated
Huckleberry Finn (though the impact of the
novel depends on the contrast between
Jim's dignity as a man and his public label in a slaveholding society); and cor-
respondents have assailed the Merriam *Webster's Third New International Dictionary*
(1961) for including derogatory meanings
of *jew* and the blasphemous *n----r*, even
though they were clearly marked as offensive. (At the same time a Wisconsin As-
semblyman denounced what seemed to him a
communist-inspired definition of *McCarthy-
ism*.) Americans of German and Scandinavian descent -- the latter with some evidence from physical anthropology on their
side -- are still sometimes incensed at
squarehead; and in Louisiana, though both
groups are Caucasoids of French descent,
the *Creoles* despise the *Cajuns*, who return
the compliment with compound interest, to
the bewilderment of the outsider. It is
interesting that the recent epidemic of
Polack jokes has brought no outbursts from
the self-appointed spokesmen for the Polish-Americans; perhaps they realize that
there are worse problems than the stereotype of a public label -- and are showing
a maturity that other ethnic groups might
well emulate. [The maturity, alas, has
been short-lived. It is only a question
of time till Polish-Americans proscribe
Hamlet because it portrays Polonius (lit-
erally 'the Pole') unsympathetically.]

Our common regional, state and local
nicknames also have their offensive associations. I doubt if a Missourian today
would take kindly to *Puke*, or an Illi-
noisan to *Sucker*. *Michigander* originally
poked fun at the physique and political
ambitions of Lewis Cass; *Badger* at the
primitive living **accommodations** of the
transplanted Kentuckians who provided basic labor in the Tri-State lead mines and
holed up for the winter in the caves along
the Mississippi. Even outside the region
where it is traditionally preceded by
damn, *Yankee* has long been associated with
sharp business practices. *Tarheel* was derisive of North Carolinians, and was associated with the instability of their mili-
tia under fire in the Late Unpleasantness,
but it is now officially recognized, like
Wolverine and *Badger* and *Gopher*. Even
Cracker has been rehabilitated: in the
rural South the term has long meant and
still means a poor white -- a *redneck*, *po'*

buckra, or *poor white trash* -- and its application to Georgia testifies to the humble beginnings of people in that state.
But as Atlanta has grown into a center of
industry and learning and awareness of the
twentieth century, the epithet has lost
much of its sting, and urban Georgians are
even proud of it.

With this background we come to the special case of *Hoosier*. As applied to an
inhabitant of Indiana, it seems to be accepted almost everywhere in the state,
without resentment, as a neutral designation if not a compliment. For most Americans elsewhere, too, the term has only a
geographical association: a *Hoosier* is
somebody from Indiana. And it was in this
sense that I first came across the word in
the books I read as a child.

But *Hoosier* had another meaning at home.
To my mother -- who never visited Indiana,
and probably never knew anyone from that
state -- it was one of the most opprobrious epithets in her formidable armamentar-
ium of abuse, and was frequently used to
indicate her displeasure at my sisters and
me. If we took larger bites of an apple
than the canons of polite behavior dic-
tated, we were *eating like a Hoosier*. If
knife and fork were out of place on our
plates, we had *the table manners of a
Hoosier*. If our play became noisy and
quarrelsome, we were *acting like a bunch
of Hoosiers*. If my shirttail was out, I
was *going around looking like a Hoosier*.
But the connection between the word and
our real or fancied shortcomings remained
a mystery until I became a field worker
for the Linguistic Atlas, and discovered
that the term was often used in the uplands of South Carolina and Georgia to
refer to someone conspicuously rural and
usually at an economic or educational or
social disadvantage.

We are far from putting beyond conjec-
ture the origin of *Hoosier* in its current
geographical sense; nevertheless, we can
bring our conjectures a bit closer to
probability by examining the distribution
of the derogatory epithet along the Atlantic Seaboard, the evidence in Wright's
English Dialect Dictionary (1898-1905),
and the settlement history of the Northwest Territory.

As a social designation, *hoosier* is
found along the Atlantic Seaboard, from
West Virginia to Georgia (see Map 1); it
may well have occurred -- it may even
still occur -- in Alabama, Tennessee, and
Mississippi, but so far we have little
field work from those states. It is basically an upland term, characteristic of
the foothill and mountain sections, but it
occurs occasionally in the coastal plain
and even in the North Carolina tidewater.
It is heard more frequently from rural informants than from urban, from older
speakers than from younger, from uneducated than from educated. It is often

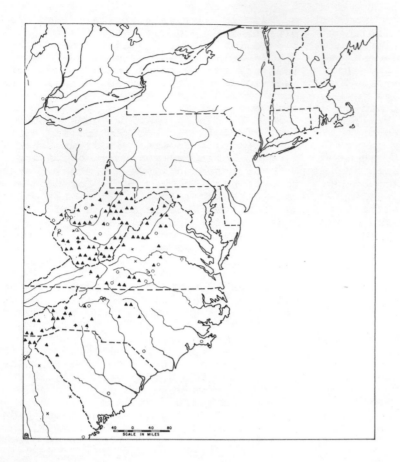

Map 1

hoosier

○   *hoosier*

▲   *mountain hoosier*

✕   *country hoosier*

⬆   *mountain hoover*

◑   *mountain boozier*

commented on as old, rarely as an innovation (R. and V. McDavid 1973, R. McDavid and Witham 1974).

It has several pronunciations, even leaving out the problem of the final /-r/. The standard Indiana pronunciation, with the medial consonant the same as in *measure*, is less common in the South than *hoojer*, with the consonant of *judge*; this may be a clue to the ultimate origin of the word. One informant made it *boojer*, probably a blend of *hoojer* and (*mountain*) *boomer*, another term for the rural mountaineer, and two informants, interviewed in the late 1930's, made it *hoover*, perhaps in freudian association with the oversold prosperity that turned sour.

The term most commonly occurs in phrases. *Hoosier* alone is just about as common as *country hoosier*; *mountain hoosier* is more common than both. Whether the association with the mountains always existed, or whether the mountain variety of the species was particularly vigorous and notorious, overshadowing all others, future scholars will have to determine.

The meaning is fairly constant: basically, an uncitified -- and by implication, uncivilized -- dweller in out-of-the-way communities; in other words, *hoosier* was synonymous with such familiar terms as *hayseed*, *hick* and *hillbilly*. But from this meaning it was only a short step to make *hoosier* become another name for the

poor white -- and like other names for him, less often neutral than disparaging. It was soon picked up by the Negroes as a term of contempt, like *cracker*, *peckerwood* and *poor white trash*. Whatever the associations of the term, they were not complimentary; and if one reads the works of Edward Eggleston with a sociologist's cold objectivity, he will likely conclude that in Eggleston's time the word still had its Southern meaning.

Unfortunately there is little solid evidence on *hoosier* before it was transplanted to North America. The pattern of its American distribution, however, suggests an origin in the north of England, Lowland Scotland, or Ulster -- the areas from which came the pioneer stock of western Pennsylvania and the Southern uplands. From Cumberland, the northwesternmost shire in England, Wright 1898-1905, regrettably incomplete, records *hoozer* 'something big, monstrous.' Possibly this indicates as association with *huge*; certainly it would suggest a relationship to *cracker* -- which in early records seems to have been synonymous with *boaster* or *braggart* -- and possibly with (*mountain*) *boomer*. It was a term suggestive of the raw strength of the frontier, of the yeoman farmers in contrast with the alleged refinements of plantation and mercantile society. And it was this group -- epitomized by Daniel Boone -- that thrust across the Appalachians into the Ohio Valley. One can reasonably suppose that the Southern *hoosiers* made up the bulk of the original population of Kentucky as well as in Indiana; the Southern upland origins of these areas are well attested in both census records and local oral tradition.

But Kentucky was originally a part of Virginia, was admitted to the Union as a slave state, and soon developed its own version of plantation culture. A few of the yeoman farmers, especially in the Blue Grass, themselves became slaveholders and planters. Others (like the Lincolns), whether morally scrupulous or economically unsuccessful, left slaveholding territory and crossed the river. The Ohio became a frontier between the Blue Grass, a new showplace of plantation opulence, and the small farms along the creek bottoms of southern Indiana. *Hoosier*, a term of derogation in the South, would naturally be extended to the inhabitants of southern Indiana, in origin Southerners of the despised class -- a label for those who could not make a go of it in Kentucky.

History, however, plays many tricks; the surest and shrewdest investments can turn sour. As elsewhere in the South, accumulated capital in Kentucky was reinvested in land and Negroes, and by 1850 the profit margin of the plantations was so small that in hard times the excess slaves were sold down the river to the new cotton lands of Mississippi. (Stephen Foster's "My Old Kentucky Home," however plaintively sung in a bourbon-soaked tremolo, is a bitter indictment of the traditional Kentucky past.) Tobacco depleted the soil; industry was slow to develop; and, except for Louisville, the Germans and Irish and other immigrants of the early nineteenth century did not provide in Kentucky the leavening influence they offered in the northern states; they felt they could not compete, as free men, with slave labor and the plantation economy. In the plantation-dominated society, despite its Jeffersonian background, education was the privilege of a few rather than the right of all. And as Emancipation wiped out the invested capital of the planters, Kentucky -- like other parts of the South -- became essentially a colony, whose agricultural and mineral wealth went to enrich the bankers of other regions.

Indiana, on the other hand, was a land of free men. With slavery forbidden by the Northwest Ordinance, it had no extractive plantation agriculture; instead, diversified family farming permitted the accumulation of investment capital and the adoption of labor-saving farm machinery like the McCormick reaper. Yankee settlements north of the Kankakee, Pennsylvanians along the National Road, foreign-born colonies throughout the state created a cultural diversity in which new ideas and new practices had an opportunity to prove themselves in fair competition. There was no single dominant metropolis, but a large number of middle-sized cities, each with its own kind of industry. The Northwest Ordinance committed Indiana and its sister states to public education in a way no Southern state has yet equalled (several of them had no constitutional commitment to education before the Reconstruction governments); the growth of industry and the urbanization of society meant that there was more taxable wealth to support education. Even by 1860 the average Indianian was far better off economically than his counterpart south of the Ohio -- to say nothing of having intangible advantages from living where freedom of thought was not constricted by the need to support a 'peculiar institution.' With the change in status the original derogatory connotations of *Hoosier* were no longer felt, even if they were remembered. In the three generations following the Civil War, the burgeoning economy of Indiana and the stagnation of the South drove out the last recollections of the origins of the state nickname. To be a *Hoosier* now is to be identified with the vigor and initiative one associates with the American Middle West. [The Southern attitude toward *Hoosier* is apparently not unknown in the Middle West. John Algeo and Emmett Lally point out that during their boyhood in St. Louis the term was generally used for a rustic, of whatever origin, and was always derogatory. Crinklaw 1976 suggests that it can still be a fighting word.]

And here there is a moral that other disadvantaged groups may remember -- though it is easy to be more objective about the problems of others than about one's own. The word -- the label of a group -- is not important in itself, only as it reflects a situation. In the long run, it is best not to waste energy in attempting to change one label for another; it is futile, if the real situation is unaffected. Though it is easy to make noisy protests about the use of a word, it is well to remember that the conduct and achievement of a group can make the harshest epithet innocuous, or even a matter of pride -- and make the blandest euphemism a term of contempt.

Forty years ago, I could imagine the arbiters of local elegance in South Carolina scornfully asking, "Would you want your daughter to marry a *Hoosier*?" Now that I have a daughter, I find she is about to marry one -- and I am delighted. Perhaps other labels will be worn as lightly in the next generation as *Hoosier* is worn now.

Even a decade ago it would have seemed academic to discuss the application of the techniques of linguistic geography to the study of American English in the Rocky Mountain area. At that time, much of the Atlantic Seaboard area of the thirteen original states was still unsurveyed, and only a tentative beginning had been made in the Great Lakes Basin. What dialect investigation was being conducted west of the Mississippi was chiefly in the form of scattered notes. Now, however, the situation has changed. Materials from the entire Atlantic Seaboard have been gathered and filed, and are ready for editing (Kurath *et al.* 1979-); by the end of the summer of 1951, the data from the North-Central states -- the Great Lakes Basin and the Ohio Valley -- should be in hand. [This optimistic prophecy was finally fulfilled in 1977. See Marckwardt *et al.* 1976-78, 1980-.] The publication of the *Linguistic Atlas of New England* (Kurath *et al.* 1939-43) and of Kurath's *Word Geography of the Eastern United States* (1949) -- an analysis of the correlation between settlement history and the distribution of vocabulary variants along the Atlantic coast -- has attracted wide attention and stimulated the development of new techniques of investigation. Although research in the Gulf Coast states and the Lower Mississippi Valley has lagged, in the Upper Midwest the energy of Harold B. Allen has brought the completion of field work in Minnesota, Iowa, and North Dakota, with Nebraska and South Dakota soon to come [published as Allen 1973-76].

Thus it is not surprising that within the last two years Atlas work has been extended to the Rocky Mountain region through the interest of the Rocky Mountain Modern Language Association, the Western Folklore Conference, and the Rocky Mountain Speech Conference. In the fall of 1950, the Rocky Mountain Modern Language Association became the official sponsor of the Rocky Mountain Atlas project. The University of Colorado offered summer training courses in 1950; Montana State College is offering similar courses in the summer of 1951. The Council on Research and Creative Work of the University of Colorado gave a grant toward Linguistic Atlas work in Colorado. Miss Marjorie M. Kimmerle and Mrs. Etholine Aycock have nearly completed the field work in Colorado outside the Denver area -- fifteen out of twenty-one proposed communities -- and Donald Dickinson is ready to begin work in New Mexico. With work in other states likely to begin next year, the time seems appropriate for discussing how the techniques of linguistic geography may be best applied to work in this new area.

Linguistic geography, as Bloomfield put it (1933:321), is the study of local differentiation in a speech area. For valid results a systematic examination is necessary, so that comparable data will be available. The framework for such systematic examination is best devised through a linguistic atlas -- a technique of investigation first attempted by Wenker and Wrede in Germany (Wrede *et al.* 1927-56) and later refined by Gilliéron in France (Gilliéron and Edmont 1902-10) and by Jaberg and Jud in Italy and southern Switzerland (1928-40), and by Kurath in this country. Such atlases employ five basic procedures for getting their data:

1. The use of a network of communities -- a limited number of communities in the area under examination. The community may be a village, as generally in Europe, a township, as in New England, or a county. These communities are chosen on the basis of settlement history, routes of migration and trade, and cultural significance within the area. That is, one should include as many as possible of the earliest English-speaking settlements, most of the major economic and cultural foci (such as Denver, Cheyenne, and Salt Lake City), some communities settled relatively early by homogeneous groups of foreign origin, and some -- such as Walden, Colorado -- that have been relatively isolated from the outside, whether by geographical inaccessibility or by local preference.

2. The interviewing of selected informants, a limited number of natives of each of the communities under examination, chosen so as to represent -- as nearly as possible -- a cross section of age groups and culture groups within the community.

3. The use of work sheets containing a limited number of specific items, designed to provide the basis for an adequate phonemic analysis -- a fairly complete statement of the facts of pronunciation -- and a cross section of usage in grammar and vocabulary. The work sheets are built around topics of ordinary conversation, such as the time of day, the weather, the household and furniture, the farm, tools and implements and vehicles, clothing, topography and roads, animals and calls to animals, crops, cooking, fruits and vege-

tables, wild life, trees and shrubs, family and social relations, body parts, sickness and death, religion and superstition, business and sports.

4. The recording of data in a finely graded phonetic alphabet. Supplementary data may be obtained by mailed check lists, or from electrical recordings; the latter are particularly valuable for determining stress, intonation, and juncture phenomena.

5. The use of a trained field worker to visit the communities in the network, choose the informants, and conduct the interviews. Preliminary or supplementary vocabulary material may be gathered by mailed check lists,[1] but for both grammar and pronunciation the interview on the spot is essential.

No serious scholar questions the last two procedures; however, a number have suggested that the first three might be reexamined and somewhat modified for work in the Rocky Mountains and for the Pacific Coast, on the theory that conditions are different. Although no one has as yet systematically summarized these conditions, they seem to fall into two categories: 1) conditions typical of all American dialect areas but more obvious in the Rockies than in the eastern part of the country; 2) conditions peculiar to the Rockies.

Arguments concerning the first category usually start from the premise that the Rocky Mountain area is too recently settled for techniques useful in the East to be applicable: nearly everybody living in a particular state was born somewhere else, most communities are too young to provide older-generation informants, communities are too mixed in origins to show the clear-cut dialect divisions one finds in the East, there are large settlements of foreign-language background, rural population is sparsely distributed, and cities have grown up without hinterlands -- that one finds, in short, a region of rootless, perpetually migrating people.

But these differences turn out to be differences of degree rather than of kind. An English observer once remarked that the oldest myth about the United States is the myth of its being a young country. Nevertheless, conditions of field work in any part of the United States are different from what one would normally find in Western Europe. It would be safe to go into almost any Dorsetshire or Breton village and interview the oldest inhabitant as a native informant; but without further verification, an American field worker might run the risk that the oldest inhabitant of an Iowa small town was born in New York, Pennsylvania, or Kentucky -- and even if a native of the town, such a person might have spent many of his formative years in another region. Stephen Vincent Benét aptly began his epic fragment

Western Star (1943) with the simple statement, "Americans are always on the move." The census reports for 1940 indicate that over ten percent of the United States population changed their residence in the preceding five years. Even in some Atlantic Seaboard states one finds communities with no native as old as the Biblical threescore and ten: Old Forge, in the central Adirondacks, had no permanent settlement till the New York Central opened that section to resort travel in the 1890's; Cadillac, in central Michigan, had its first settlement a few years earlier, in the wake of lumbering; there were almost no white men living on the Mesabi Range in Minnesota till the Merrits discovered the iron ore deposits; Atlanta, Georgia, was established barely early enough (1847) to get into the Civil War and *Gone With the Wind*. Dialect mixture may be assumed as the rule in almost every American community from the very beginning, not least in New England (Orbeck 1927). Communities of Spanish or Navaho speakers in the Southwest constitute the same type of problem for the student of English as the French in Louisiana, the Germans in Pennsylvania, or the Dutch and Finns in Michigan; the only difference is that the contacts of Spanish and Navaho speakers with speakers of English have possibly been less intimate and have begun more recently. Each of the states passed through a period of sparse rural settlement, and the pattern of cities in the wilderness has been typically American from the beginning (Bridenbaugh 1938). The differences in physical geography and social institutions between Massachusetts and Georgia are as great as those one finds between either of those states and, say, Colorado. For practical purposes, the Rocky Mountain area is -- as far as these conditions are concerned -- just passing through a stage through which the regions to the east have already passed. The linguistic geographer in the Rockies is therefore catching the process of dialect mixture and the formation of new dialect types at an earlier stage than in other areas.

There are, however, a few differences in kind between the social background of the Rockies and that of regions further eastward. Instead of the orderly spread of settlement inland from the coast, in even waves or up river valleys and outward from them, settlement in the Rockies progressed by leap-frogging across wide areas that were settled later and less securely. Thus the Mormons moved from Nauvoo, Illinois, to Utah, and other settlers from the Mississippi Valley to Oregon or the Colorado foothills without leaving any permanent intervening settlements. Because of climate and soil conditions, a very large part of the region has never had stable subsistence agriculture, with a predomi-

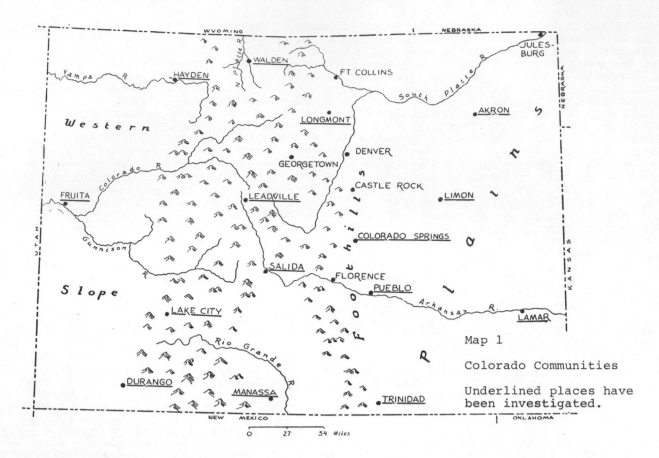

Map 1

Colorado Communities

Underlined places have been investigated.

nance of small farmers. Many communities have undergone the boom-and-bust cycle of speculative mining, leaving little behind.[2] Other parts have supported -- and can support -- only scattered ranches or small communities relatively isolated in mountain valleys; even agricultural communities tend to follow the pattern of factory farming, with a heavy dependence on migratory labor. Modern transportation influenced the Rocky Mountain area at an earlier date than it did the communities to the east, for railroads and even some motor highways preceded the settlement of many communities. Nevada, first state in the Rockies -- and granted statehood as a war measure, to assure a majority of states favorable to the Lincoln program -- was barely admitted to the Union before the first transcontinental railroad was built.[3] By the time the Rockies were settled, the system of American wholesale trade had developed to the point where many tools and implements which in the East had been made at home or in the village were more easily obtained commercially; consequently, one is likely to find trade names instead of the folk names current in the East. Finally, even the earliest English-speaking settlers in the Rockies were accustomed to public education, so that their communities had a rather high percentage of literacy from the start -- an environment in which items

of folk grammar might possibly not be retained. Thus the most significant difference between the dialect background of the Rocky Mountain states as a group and those to the east is that the culture of the English-speaking settlers in the Rockies had reached a more complex technological level when their earliest communities were established.

These differences in the economic and educational background -- what anthropologists might sum up as the cultural context -- suggest that certain modifications in details of the Atlas method may be necessary in the Rockies. In selecting communities, one should not expect any community to represent as much as it did along the Atlantic Seaboard. We may expect to find a number of pockets, of one or two communities, whose usage diverges sharply from that of the neighboring communities in the network. We will be confronted with the problem of reconciling an adequate geographical coverage over a large area to the facts of recent settlement generally and sparse population in some sections. We will have to face the problem of relic areas in the spectacular manifestation of the ghost town, where the cycle of wilderness-and-waste to waste-and-wilderness has gone through the brief florid prosperity of the mining town instead of the more protracted struggle of many small communities in New England and the Old South. None of this is new, since it has been faced already in Michigan and Minnesota; this time it must simply be faced for a whole area rather than for small parts.

In Colorado we have already faced these problems and have had to make certain modifications. Furthermore we have also had to face the usual problem of insufficient funds for a completely adequate coverage.[4] Only twenty-one communities were chosen for Colorado as against forty-three for South Carolina with a third the area. But the numbers are not quite so disproportionate when one considers that the population of South Carolina is somewhat larger than that of Colorado, thus providing a much greater density of rural population.[5] As Map 1 indicates, considerably more communities were chosen in the foothills area than in any other section of the state.[6] This is in line with Atlas practice in the East, where the communities chosen were much closer together along the Atlantic coast than in the secondary areas further inland. In Colorado the oldest English-speaking communities are in the foothills, which also constitute the area of densest population, most stable society, and greatest economic and cultural importance.

Since available funds permit only a limited number of communities to be investigated in Colorado, large areas are inevitably untouched. Some of the communities, such as Hayden, Fruita, and Durango are about 150 miles apart. On the eastern plains, such distances may make little difference, for there are no geographical barriers to hinder communication and make one section distinct from another. But on the Western Slope between Hayden and Fruita is range country, quite different from Hayden -- in a rich farming area -- or Fruita, in the Colorado Valley fruit-growing area. Between Fruita and Durango and just west of Lake City is an important hard-rock mining area, different from Fruita and Durango and lacking communication with Lake City. The selection of communities includes no mountain towns along the Colorado and Gunnison Rivers, though each of these upper river valleys is a distinct cultural area, and different from the lower fruit-growing valley near Fruita. Between Leadville and Walden is Middle Park, an extensive ranching, farming, and logging area. Walled in on all sides by high mountains, it is a distinct and separate unit. It would be desirable to have field investigation of communities in these areas, but the judicious use of a check list might help explain apparent anomalies in the distribution of lexical items that might be found by field investigation.[7]

In the East, the informants chosen for interviewing have generally fallen into two typical groups. To ascertain the roots of community speech, the field worker has attempted to interview a representative of the oldest living native generation -- usually seventy or over -- with a minimum of travel, reading, and formal education. To ascertain the normal pattern of community speech today, the field worker has interviewed someone in the middle-aged group (defined for Atlas purposes as 40 to 65), with about a high-school education. Occasionally college-educated informants are interviewed.

Manifestly some changes in the procedure for selecting informants will be necessary in the Rocky Mountains if the field worker is to obtain an accurate sampling of local speech. One cannot find eighty-year-old native informants in communities that came into being about 1890: any person of that age in such a community inevitably spent his formative years[8] somewhere else, and thus would not give a true picture of local native speech. Even the rarer example of the child of the solitary pioneer family living in the area before the community came into being is open to some objection, since linguistically such a person might be atypical in the community.

In view of the late settlement of Colorado, it is not surprising that it has been difficult to find natives over fifty. In 1900 only 31.8% of the population were natives. In the ordinary course of events, that percentage of natives of fifty or older is bound to have dwindled. But late settlement and the usual casualties do not wholly account for the difficulty of finding natives. Economic instability has had even more to do with depleting or at least shifting the native population. In mining sections, either the mining camps have gone bankrupt and left ghost cities behind, or the miners have died young from pneumonia or silicosis or moved away when mines were closed during the depression. In dry farming areas, many farms were abandoned during the periods of drought and dust storms. In fruit-growing areas, the hazards of inadequately controlled irrigation and insect pests like the coddling moth caused fruit farmers to abandon their orchards.

But despite the difficulties arising from recent settlement and economic instability, the basic principle for choosing informants in any community must still be that they are natives of the community, at least in the sense that they formed their speech patterns there. Certainly no one who came to the community as late as the age of eight or ten can be considered as representative of the speech of that community.[9] With this in mind, one will have to be content with somewhat less aged informants for the older group than one has found elsewhere -- and possibly with less nearly illiterate ones; but one should still try to get a representative of the oldest living native generation, as little contaminated as possible with outside influence. Moreover, with the average age of the older informants no longer over seventy, but nearer sixty if not under, choosing second informants in their fifties will no longer give an adequate age spread on the basis of which one could form judgments of dialect change. It would therefore seem advisable to lower the age of the second informants too, so that they would always be under fifty, and the nearer forty the better. It might also be desirable to have a third group of informants under age thirty, if one has time and funds. But the informants, of whatever age or cultural group, must always be locally rooted.[10]

The items in the field worker's questionnaire must likewise be reconsidered. To what extent should items be kept from the questionnaire used further east? To what extent must new items be added, to obtain an adequate picture of dialect divisions in the Rockies? Both of these questions can best be answered by finding the answer to a third: For what purpose will the data obtained from the questionnaire be used?

One should not force responses for items -- geographical or cultural -- which do not occur, such as the *sugar maple grove* in the Southern coastal plain, or the *salt marsh* in the Ohio Valley. But one can generally find out the absence of the item -- whether from the terrain or from the culture -- only by asking. And in a somewhat diversified area, of large geographical extent, one cannot be sure that an item which is missing in one state will be missing in all: the conditions that make for possible speech pockets make for possible culture pockets too. In general it seems advisable to include every item which has been productive of responses in the North-Central states and the Upper Midwest, except such as obviously are not a part of the physical environment. If the item does not provide vocabulary variants, it will at least provide evidence for checking on variations in pronunciation.

The items that will be added for the Rocky Mountains might fall into two groups. In one group are those which the experience of the field workers suggests might be regionally significant, but whose possible regional significance was discovered too late for the item to be used in the East. An example is the apparent Pennsylvania and Southern expression *the road is slick*, where New Englanders and York Staters would say *the road is slippery*. The other type of item is that which occurs widely distributed in the geography or the culture of the Rocky Mountain area but does not occur further east; one here thinks of such physical phenomena as canyons and alkali flats, or such institutions as the roundup. But

again a caution is necessary: one must not let one's enthusiasm for an institution or occupation lead him to ignore its possible lack of relevance for the total cultural experience of the people in a region.[11] To what extent, for instance, does the undoubtedly colorful vocabulary of the miner carry over into the experience of those who are not miners? Would there be any items of mining culture or sugar-beet culture with which the average speaker is familiar? Or do these happen to be specialized activities with specialized vocabularies? Few items from the fishing trade -- even such obvious ones as names of fish -- were productive for the New England *Atlas*; those informants who were not fishermen simply did not know them. In Colorado a preliminary vocabulary survey proved unequivocally that mining and sugar-beet terms were not familiar to the average person. And except for a few very general items like *cowhand* and *bronco*, even cowboy terms are proving to be unproductive. The only other new items that have been tentatively added to the questionnaire in Colorado are *adobe*, *go-devil* (a term designating various kinds of farm implements, often an especially sturdy cultivator necessary in dry farming), *corral*, *piñon*, *aspen*, *service berry*, and items of topographical features like *pass*, *park*, *gulch*, *arroyo*, *lagoon* (dry lake with no inlet or outlet, that fills up only after heavy rains). In the Rockies, it is not likely that many more items will be necessary. The field workers, and those helping the field workers plan their activities, must take into account the entire cultural context of the region, not the hobbies of the individual scholar.[12]

One cannot predict the patterns of distribution that the field work in the Rockies will reveal; if one could, then the field work would not be necessary. But one may predict the types of patterns that one will probably find. In general, one is likely to find a blurring of regional distinctions, with less clear bundles of isoglosses than scholars have found in the Mississippi Valley, just as the regional and local distinctions in the Mississippi Valley are less clear than those along the Atlantic Seaboard. One is likely to find that such regional and local distinctions as do occur are most evident in pronunciation, the most habitual feature of language, and less clear in grammar and vocabulary, where increasing education and cultural uniformity -- the increasing influence of state-supported schools and the Sears-Roebuck catalog -- may have leveled the differences that prevailed further east.[13] One might expect to find relatively less folk grammar surviving; or one might find differences in the educational and economic status of the various groups of settlers from the East reflected in a predominance of Rocky Mountain items

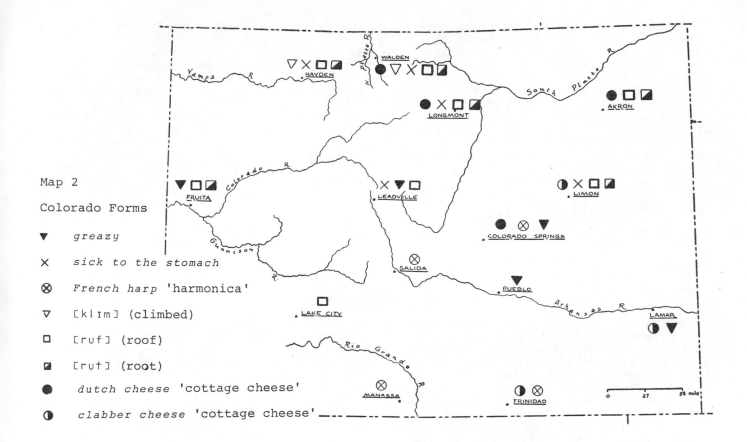

Map 2

Colorado Forms

▼   *greazy*

✕   *sick to the stomach*

⊗   *French harp* 'harmonica'

▽   [klɪm] (climbed)

◻   [ruf] (roof)

◩   [ruｔ] (root)

●   *dutch cheese* 'cottage cheese'

◐   *clabber cheese* 'cottage cheese'

of folk grammar derived from the region from which the least affluent, most poorly educated settlers came. One might expect to find that for many items only commercial terms are known, or that the relative survival of Northern, North Midland, or South Midland terms (there will probably be few Southern terms)[14] will vary from word to word, or from topic to topic, possibly in random fashion, possibly in patterns that reflect not only regional divisions in the Rockies but the habitual preference of certain groups of settlers for participation in certain activities.[15] And finally one may discover within the area regional variants for terms for some of the new items under investigation, or for items which do not show regional vocabulary variants in the East. One may expect to find relatively greater Canadian influence in the Rockies than further east; for there are no major American population centers -- like Calgary, Edmonton, or Regina -- anywhere near the border. In sum, there will undoubtedly be data from which one can set off regional and local speech areas; but one must not be disappointed if those areas are fewer and less clearly defined than those further east.

In spite of all the qualifications that one must make, the fact is that even a preliminary examination of the records done so far indicates that the speech of

Colorado is neither uniform nor randomly heterogeneous, but that items of vocabulary and grammar and pronunciation occur in patterns suggesting a correlation with places of origin and routes of migration.

A glance at Map 1 suggests that the valleys of the North and South Platte Rivers would be natural avenues of migration for settlers entering Colorado from Nebraska and Iowa -- states whose early settlers were predominantly from the North and North Midland. The valley of the Arkansas would be as logical a route for settlers coming from the South-Central states and southern Kansas. It is therefore reasonable to suspect that one would find Northern forms along the North and South Platte, and South Midland and Southern forms along the Arkansas.

Nor are we disappointed. Along the watersheds of the North and South Platte one finds such typically Northern items as *dutch cheese* 'cottage cheese,' [klɪm] as the past tense of *climb*, *sick to the stomach*, and the pronunciation of *roof* and *root* with [ʊ], the vowel of *put*.[16] Along the valley of the Arkansas one finds such South Midland and Southern items as *clabber cheese* 'cottage cheese,' *French harp* 'harmonica' (*mouth harp* and *harp* are more widely distributed, as in the East), and the pronunciation *greazy* (see Map 2).[17] Moreover, except in the northern part of the state, the usual folk preterite of *climb* is the Midland and Southern [klʌm].

These are not many items, to be sure, but that so many are obvious on a preliminary analysis should dispel once and for all the notion that Atlas methods are inapplicable in the Rockies.[18] That routes of migration into the northern and southern parts of Colorado are apparently reflected in the speech of those regions suggests that field work over a wider area -- and the more intensive examination of the evidence collected -- would reveal further correlation between speech and social forces (see R. McDavid 1946, in this volume, pp. 131-35; R. McDavid 1951d, in this volume, pp. 143-45). The results of field work done so far reinforce the argument for systematic collection and analysis of data: one cannot hope to find dialect boundaries if one does not use a method that will reveal them. But even if the field work had revealed no clear dialect boundaries, one need not be distressed -- a record of complete heterogeneity is as valuable, if validly made, as one showing clear regional boundaries. For one must not lose sight of the fact that the Rockies, however interesting themselves, are but a part of the North American English speech community, and that one of the most important problems in any large-scale study of the Rocky Mountain area is the way in which the various streams of culture from further east have met and intermingled against a new geographical background.

NOTES

[1] The use of a carefully devised mailed check list -- embodying items that have been shown to have regional patterns of distribution in the East -- for making the preliminary analysis of a region was suggested in A. L. Davis 1949. Similar check lists have been distributed by Allen to supplement the field work in the Upper Midwest. A check list based on Davis's was used in Colorado for a preliminary survey, the results of which may be found in G. H. Johnson 1950. Similar check lists for preliminary surveys have been used in Montana, New Mexico, and Wyoming. The most extensive use of questionnaires for analyzing the dialect vocabulary of an area is that by Cassidy in Wisconsin (1948).

[2] Such ghost communities are found in the East -- Jacksonboro, Georgia, for instance, or Valentown, New York (less than twenty miles from Rochester and almost within sight of the downtown section). But in the East, ghost towns are not so familiar a feature as they are in the Rockies. See Wolle 1941, 1949.

[3] The Union Pacific and the Central Pacific met at Promontory, Utah, in May 1869. The Southern Pacific completed its line from San Francisco to New Orleans in 1881, and the Northern Pacific its route to Portland in 1883. Additional routes were added in 1893 when the Great Northern finished its line to Seattle, and the Atchison, Topeka and Santa Fe reached from Kansas City to San Diego.

Nevada was admitted in 1864, Colorado in 1876, Montana in 1889, Idaho and Wyoming in 1890, Utah in 1896, New Mexico in 1911, and Arizona in 1912.

[4] The inability of a project like the Atlas to secure sufficient funds is somewhat bewildering to European scholars whose countries have considered the continuation of scholarly research indispensable even during the war and the postwar reconstruction. The contrast between the generous support which the governments of Sweden and Norway have given to investigations of folk speech in those countries, and the lack of such support in this country, must at least seem a little odd. [Since 1968 the National Endowment for the Humanities has partially redressed the balance.]

[5] Colorado total population (1940 census): 1,123,296. Total area: 103,948 sq. miles (10.8 persons per sq. mile). Urban population (cities over 10,000): 51% of the total population (50% in the foothills and only 1% on the Western Slope). Denver: 28.7% of the total population.

[6] The following towns were chosen on the basis of settlement history and cultural and economic significance: 1) Hayden, a small agricultural community in the Yampa River Valley, on a main highway leading into Utah. More stable than surrounding mining and oil towns. 2) Fruita, an old town in what was once the heart of the fruit-growing area. Very near Grand Junction, the most important trading center of the Western Slope. On a main highway leading into Utah. 3) Durango, trading center for surrounding farming and cattle-raising country. 4) Lake City, one of the first settlements in western Colorado. Once a hard-rock mining center. Isolated and almost abandoned by the old settlers. 5) Manassa, an agricultural town settled by Mormons from Utah, Georgia, and Alabama. In the Spanish part of the San Luis Valley. 6) Salida, on the upper Arkansas River, midway between the San Luis Valley and South Park. Founded when the Denver and Rio Grande Railroad was extended to the west. 7) Leadville, once the largest and most fabulous gold and silver camp in Colorado. 8) Walden, an almost isolated town in the North Platte Valley, one of the routes of migration. It has better communication with Wyoming than with Colorado. 9) Ft. Collins, the center of the north-central Colorado agricultural area. Along an early route to mining camps and stone quarries. 10) Longmont, a prosperous town in the sugar-beet area. Founded by the Chicago-Colorado Colony Company. 11) Denver, the state capitol, the most significant cultural and economic center. 12) Georgetown, at one time the most important silver camp in the state. 13) Castle Rock, midpoint between Denver and Colorado Springs, on the main foothills highway. 14) Colorado Springs, a

cultural center. At the foot of Pike's Peak, one of the first sites that attracted gold hunters. 15) Pueblo, manufacturing and trading center. The steel city of Colorado. 16) Florence, coal and oil town on the Arkansas River. 17) Trinidad, the center of a coal-mining region. An old Spanish town on the Santa Fe Trail. 18) Lamar, a prosperous town on the Arkansas River, one of the main routes of migration. A center for the surrounding dry-farming, irrigated-farming, and stock-raising area. 19) Limon, a shipping point for an extensive dry-farming area. Founded as a railroad camp. 20) Akron, a Burlington Railroad town, in the heart of a dry-farming area, the Dust Bowl of Colorado. 21) Julesburg, once a stopping point on the Overland Stage and the Pony Express route along the South Platte River, one of the main routes of migration.

[7] In addition, as Allen and Cassidy have discovered in the Upper Midwest, the use of the supplementary check list enables the investigator to dig a little deeper into the speech of the community, and uncover somewhat more lexical variants if the community is of mixed origins -- as most of the Rocky Mountain communities are likely to be. See Cassidy 1948.

Check lists and questionnaires cannot be sent out at random, especially in areas of recent and mixed settlement such as the Rocky Mountain states. Too often they get into the hands of people who are not natives, who have lived a great deal of their active lives in other areas, or whose interests and background are of the literary rather than the folk type. It is admittedly difficult to find the right kinds of informants by mail, when even a field worker has trouble locating them. It is more economical of the investigator's time and money to delay mailing out the check list until he is sure that the informant is a native, is likely to be a good informant, and is willing to take time to supply the information.

[8] The basic speech patterns are probably formed by the age of ten, if not earlier. It is sometimes necessary to interview informants who were as old as five or six when they came to the community. But one should be wary in evaluating such informants; one should certainly try not to interview informants who began to talk in a sharply different dialect region, or who had actually commenced their schooling before migrating to the community.

[9] The community need not be limited to the village or small town; in most of the rest of the country, the county has been considered the community unit. This definition will probably be adequate for the Rockies.

[10] It has been found desirable in the Atlantic Seaboard and Great Lakes areas to ascertain as much as possible about the settlement history and social structure of the community and to know at least by name the persons who might introduce the field worker to representative informants -- before going there to do field work. It would probably be even more advantageous to make such preliminary steps in the Rocky Mountain area.

Detailed county and local histories are not so often available as they are, say, in New York State or Illinois. Nevertheless, a careful investigation of the census figures can supply much of the evidence.

[11] The general principles on which items have been chosen are: 1) familiarity to the bulk of potential informants; 2) ease in eliciting during an interview. In other words, the emphasis is always on the every-day item, the blood and bone of the language. It is for these everyday items that one is likely to find the greatest number of significant variants -- both regional and social -- and the greatest perpetuation of folk terms.

[12] Some items in the work sheets have so far not yielded many responses: *sumac*, *firefly*, *crawfish*, *rowboat*, *wharf*, and some of the calls to animals. Naturally terms dealing with boats will not be as productive in Colorado as they would be in the parts of the region where river navigation or timber rafting has been more important. Naturally the types of calls used to farm animals will not be heard in the range country. But the occurrence or absence of these lexical items will be indicative of the prevailing culture in a locality.

The study of loan words and bilingualism in an area is an interesting problem in itself, but only partially related -- and subsidiary -- to the work of preparing a linguistic atlas. In fact, before studying the problems of bilingualism one essentially needs to make two linguistic atlases of the area -- say, one of English and one of Spanish -- being careful to select persons whose native and primary language is that for which the particular atlas is being compiled. With the data available for the two languages, then one can work with bilinguals and finally utilize a short check list to test the occurrence of items which may indicate the influence of one language upon another. See Haugen 1950a; Turner 1949; R. A. Hall 1950b; R. McDavid 1950a, in this volume, pp. 342-48; R. and V. McDavid 1951b, in this volume, pp. 43-51.

[13] On vocabulary as a criterion of dialect, Wyld observes (1920:15):
"The great factor which nowadays destroys the value of vocabulary as a specific characteristic of a given regional dialect, is the migratory habits of the population. Almost every village, even in districts remote from London or other great centres of population, contains several inhabitants who have come into it from some more or less distant county, either because they are in the service of local farmers or gentry, or the railway company, or because they were employed in the construction of the local railway line, and stayed on after it was completed. These persons bring with them alien habits of speech, and their families form so many nuclei whence these spread to a wider circle. This is certainly true of pronunciation and accidence, but probably to a less extent than of vocabulary, for this is far more readily acquired than new vowel sounds or a fresh grammatical system."
Scientific dialect geography, emphasizing the familiar item and the systematic use of comparable data, indicates that vocabulary may be a more

accurate index than Wyld suspected. See Kurath 1949. Nevertheless, phonological differences may persist long after vocabulary differences have disappeared.

A more serious flaw in Wyld's observation is the romantic assumption that there has ever been such a thing as a 'pure dialect,' or that dialect mixture -- in vocabulary and in pronunciation -- did not operate before the Industrial Revolution. The history of the standard English of London is contradictory evidence enough.

[14] The terms 'Northern,' 'Midland,' and 'Southern' were devised by Kurath as a more accurate indication of the facts of American regional speech than the older terms 'Eastern,' 'Southern,' and so-called 'General American.' As used by Kurath and others working with the Atlas, 'Northern' refers to the speech of New England, the Hudson Valley, and their derivative settlements in upstate New York and the northern tier of counties in Pennsylvania; 'North Midland' to the speech of the Pennsylvania settlements in the Delaware, Susquehanna, and upper Ohio Valleys; 'South Midland' to the speech of the Pennsylvania-derived settlements in the Shenandoah Valley, the southern mountains, and the upper Piedmont of the Carolinas and Georgia; 'Southern' to the coastal plain areas of plantation culture. As originally used, these terms designated areas along the Atlantic Seaboard; research in the North-Central states, however, suggests that they are accurately descriptive at least to the Mississippi.

[15] Range culture seems to have spread from Texas north. Thus it would not be surprising to find many South Midland lexical items, and even items of South Midland folk grammar, occurring in ranching communities as far north as Montana.

[16] The form [ru+] is practically nonexistent in the South Atlantic states, and in those states [ruf] is distinctly a minority pronunciation. See R. McDavid 1949b.

[17] These observations are based on various studies: A. L. Davis 1949, Atwood 1950a (amplified in Francis 1958), Atwood 1953a, Hempl 1896, and A. L. Davis and R. McDavid 1950 (in this volume, pp. 238-44).

[18] As the experience of the Linguistic Atlas has shown, field work and the analysis of the results of field work are two different processes. Not only is too much attention to what preceding informants have said likely to prejudice the field worker (even if unconsciously) in his next interviews, but the data is not immediately available in a shape that permits rapid comparison. Each field book must be fully coded, and the books separated so that data for each item can be filed together. This step is usually not taken till all the records are in from an area.

The completion of field work will facilitate further dialect studies -- whether the collection of data towards a dialect dictionary, or more intensive examination of a particular community for the correlation between dialect differences and class differences. The procedures developed in Atlas field work are especially useful in determining the number and location of check points for lexical collecting through picked local informants. See Cassidy 1948. [Hankey (1960) has edited the Colorado lexical material.]

THE UNSTRESSED SYLLABIC PHONEMES OF A SOUTHERN DIALECT:
A PROBLEM OF ANALYSIS   (1944)

Any phonemic analysis must adhere to two principles: 1) the same phonemic transcription cannot be used when there is phonetic contrast in similar phonemic surroundings; 2) the same phonemic transcription must be used where there is, within perceptual limits, phonetic identity in similar or closely parallel phonemic surroundings. Some analyses fail to adhere to these principles where such adherence would lead to conclusions at variance with previous notions of phonemics or with knowledge of other dialects or of the written form of the language. Linguists satisfied with lower (or more phonetic) levels of analysis find fewer of these problems; and essentially such analyses play fair, so long as they adequately describe the phonetic facts: it is possible for other linguists to take the data and carry it further. So long as one understands what type of analysis he is using, he can make the less complete analysis work, though perhaps not as efficiently as a complete analysis.[1]

This paper is an outgrowth of attempts to analyze the unstressed vowels of my own speech, a dialect spoken in Greenville, in the Piedmont section of South Carolina. Through various cultural influences, this Piedmont type of speech has been somewhat modified from other types spoken in the same community. In particular, my own speech and that of many of my generation are what is commonly called 'r-less'; that is, this dialect, unlike that of the older generation or that of many rural speakers of our generation, does not have /-r/ as retroflexion of a preceding syllabic (except /ə/ in stressed syllables) when /-r/ follows a syllabic and precedes pause, open juncture, or another consonant. In stressed syllables of the dialect, phonemic /-r/ occurs under these conditions as a centering glide [ə̯] or as length of the syllabic (often with some phonetic modification). Thus a hard man 'a cruel master' is distinguished from a hod-man 'one who carries a hod.' Whether or not phonemic /-r/ also occurs under these conditions in unstressed syllables of this dialect is a large part of the problem in analyzing the unstressed syllabics.

The stressed syllabics of this dialect have been previously discussed.[2] Briefly, there are six short vowels (the syllabics of pit, pet, pat, pot, putt, put /pit,pet, pat,pot,pət,put/), four diphthongs in /-y/ (the syllabics of bee, bay, hash, bite, /biy,bey,hayʃ,boyt/), and four diphthongs in /-w/ (the syllabics of cow, law, go, do /kaw,low,gəw,duw/). The phonetic values of some of these syllabics (especially the diphthongs of hash, baa /ay/ and of bite, buy /oy/) differ according to the phonemic surroundings, but these variations do not affect the soundness of the system. Unlike most other American dialects, this dialect has forms of the types boy, choice as disyllabic /bowi,tʃowis/. All of these syllabics may be found under conditions of loud stress, reduced loud stress, and medial stress.

As in other dialects, the syllabics found in unstressed syllables are less numerous than those found under other conditions of stress (Whorf 1943). One may distinguish three unstressed vowel phonemes, all characteristically lax and with a great amount of free variation in positions: 1) mid-central unrounded /ə/, sometimes retracted and occasionally raised or lowered, the unstressed syllabic of against, pedagogue, barracks,; 2) lower high-back, slightly rounded /u/, decidedly lowered and advanced, the unstressed syllabic of obey, genuflect, value;[3] 3) fairly high and somewhat front, unrounded /i/, with several easily distinguished allophones: a) final unchecked, lower high-central, raised and advanced, as in city; b) before nasals, lower high-front retracted to lower high-central advanced, as in fighting, women; c) in other positions, lower high-central advanced and lowered to upper mid-front raised and retracted, as in terraces, roses, added, exactly. Some additional contrasts which occur in other dialects are not found here: for example, when candid and candied are distinguished, as they are in my speech, the distinction is to be found in the stressed syllabics phonemically /a/ and /ay/ respectively, the unstressed syllables being identical.

This simple analysis, however, encounters complications when one attempts to extend it to all unstressed syllables. Going to morphophonemics or to other dialects, or both, is not evidence from the purely phonemic point of view. Moreover, one must ask whether a hypothetical linguist, encountering English for the first time through this dialect, would arrive at the same conclusions. What conclusions we can advance, however tentatively, must be those which seem most closely in agreement with the known facts of English structure, and must follow the principles already laid down.

Difficulty in the analysis of unstressed syllabics is found for several types of words.

It is frequently proposed that in English phonetically syllabic [m,n,ŋ,l,r] must be analyzed phonemically as /-əm,-ən, -əŋ,-əl,-ər/.[4] In contrast we have such forms as [reibən] *Rayburn*, [pætən] *pattern*, [eikən] *acorn*, in which the final nasal is not necessarily homorganic with the final stop on the stressed syllable, and in which the syllabic of the unstressed syllable is phonetically [ə]. We cannot transcribe *Patton* and *pattern* alike. We may say that in *pattern* the vowel [ə] is retained phonetically because /-n/ is preceded phonemically by a consonant; this consonant may be /-r/, which we know is a centering off-glide in stressed syllabics of this dialect, or /-h/, defined by Trager and Bloch 1941 as a postvocalic lengthening and centering element. Thus the contrasts already noted can be adequately explained. There are no contrasts for such forms as *woman, cannon, gingham, Traynham, hem 'em*; the unstressed syllabics of these forms are to be analyzed as phonemically /ə/, since the vowel in each of these is apparently somewhat shorter and obscurer than that of *pattern*. On the other hand, while it is easy to analyze *happen* as [hæpəm], where the unstressed syllable is phonetically syllabic [m], yet *weapon* (phonetically [wɛpən]) by this analysis would be phonemically /wepərn/ or /wepəhn/.

We have noticed that in certain inflectional syllables the syllabic is phonemically /i/, phonetically [ɨ̬]. Thus *batted, races*. We have, contrasting, *battered, racers*, where the unstressed syllabic is phonetically [ə]. If the latter is the same syllabic as we have previously found in *pattern, acorn* -- and there is certainly phonetic similarity -- then it too must be transcribed phonemically as /ər/ or /əh/. And if we transcribe *razors* as /reyzərz/ (or /reyzəhz/), we must likewise transcribe *Rosa's* as /rəwzərz/ (or /rəwzəhz/).

Similarly with such forms as *sofa* and *loafer*, where the final unstressed syllable is phonetically the same mid-central vowel [ə]. Morphophonemic observation, as to whether or not a sandhi consonant appears when the following word has a vowel initial, will not help us, for sandhi-r /-r-/ does not ordinarily occur in either *that sofa is here* or *that loafer is here*, or anywhere else. The unstressed syllabic might be phonemically /əh/ or /ər/, either of the possible analyses of the phoneti-

cally similar unstressed syllabics of *pattern* and *battered*.

If we are willing to be inconsistent in our analysis, we can perhaps evade some of these difficulties. But such action would not be scientific. If we wish to remain scientific, we have definite alternatives. By sticking to a lower, or more phonetic, level of analysis, we can set up for English -- or at least this dialect -- a series of syllabic consonants as unanalyzable units, neither vowels nor consonants; then we could write /ə/ phonemically where phonetic [ə] occurs. But this analysis is admittedly incomplete, and somewhat at variance with the rather clear vowel-consonant division we are accustomed to associate with English. The other analysis may lead to a few strange and surprising transcriptions, but it is more thorough. Either will probably work, so long as one states all the facts, but the more thorough analysis seems more in keeping with the aims of linguistics.

In conclusion, phonetically syllabic consonants are to be analyzed as /ə/ plus consonant. Thus *Patton* is /patən/; in *pattern, acorn, weapon* the unstressed syllabic may be either /ər/ or /əh/, likewise in *racers, battered, razors, Rosa's, sofa, loafer*. The somewhat shorter and less clear (but apparently slightly higher and retracted) unstressed syllabic of *woman* is /ə/, the statement being that /ə/ plus nasal does not become syllabic nasal following another nasal.

Choice between /əh/ and /ər/ might be difficult to make on the basis of the unstressed syllabics of this dialect alone. Comparison with other dialects in the same community might be facilitated by the analysis /əh/; thus the 'loss of /-r/' in unstressed syllables may be stated in terms of /-r/ becoming /-h/. In these other dialects *weapon* would be /wepəhn/ but *pattern* /patərn/, and similar distinctions would be made between *sofa* and *loafer, Rosa's* and *razors*. But if we analyze these unstressed syllabics of my dialect as /əh/ we should have to make a similar analysis of the stressed syllables, and there would be complications because there is a phonetic [-r], as retroflexion, in such forms as *bird*. For this dialect, then, it appears best to analyze the unstressed syllabics of *pattern, battered, Rosa's, sofa*, and the like as /ər/; comparison with other dialects of the community is not impaired, for the statement is that /əh/ falls together with /ər/ in unstressed syllables of my dialect, and that in this dialect -- except for such forms as *bird* -- /-r/ is always a lengthening and centering element.

[1] Delivered at the informal meeting of the American Philological Association and the New York Circle of Linguists, New York, January 1944. For the convenience of the reader, phonetic transcriptions are usually broad.

[This paper is another example of the difficulty in applying rigorously the concept of over-all pattern analysis, in this case the 6 × 3 pattern of Trager and Bloch 1941.]

[2] At meetings of the Linguistic Society of America, New York, 1938, and Chapel Hill, 1941. A summary of this analysis is found in R. McDavid 1943, in this volume, pp. 317-24.

[3] The unstressed phoneme /u/ seems to be less common than /ə/ or /i/; in such words as *obey*, *theologue*, *yellow*, it is often replaced by /ə/. The phonemic identity of /u/ in unstressed syllables is nevertheless clear, since there can be, and frequently are, such contrasts as *a bay* and *obey*.

[4] It has been remarked that the analysis of phonetically syllabic consonants as phonemically /ə/ plus consonant has not been established for this dialect. Evidence for such analysis exists, however, in 1) the general clear opposition of syllabic and nonsyllabic phonemes in English, and 2) the existence, in this dialect as elsewhere, of such contrasting pairs as *lightning* (phonetically [laɨtnɪŋ]) and *lightening* (phonetically [laɨtm̩ɪŋ]).

Many linguists have commented on the fact that in a number of American dialects -- such as of Metropolitan New York, New Orleans, and much of the plantation area of the Deep South -- the stressed syllabic in such words as *worm*, *Thursday*, *thirty* is /əy/ rather than the /ər/ or /əhr/ of such Central Western dialects as those described by Bloch and Trager or the /əh/ of British Received Standard.[1]

An examination of some of the field records made for the Linguistic Atlas of the South Atlantic States discloses that the replacement of /r/ by /y/ is not confined to words in which the stressed vowel phoneme is /ə/, but that this substitution may occur after almost any vowel phoneme which normally precedes /-r/. In some of the dialects here represented, postvocalic /-r/ often appears as a centering offglide; for those who prefer to speak in phonetic rather than phonemic terms, one may describe -- for such dialects -- the substitution treated in this paper as the substitution of a rising offglide for this centering offglide.

Preconsonantal substitution of /-y/ for /-r/ has been observed in several occurrences of the words *George*, *Georgia*, *porch*, *orchard*, *according*, *forty*, which would thus be phonemically /dʒɔydʒ,dʒɔydʒə, poytʃ,ɔytʃərd,akɔydiŋ,fɔytiy/. It is noticed that in a majority of these forms the stressed syllabic precedes the affricates /tʃ,dʒ/, but not in *forty* and *according*.[2]

The substitution of /y/ for /r/ has been observed in syllable-final position in the following words: *cur*, *chair*, *scar*, *stair*, and *Bear Creek* /kəy,tʃey,skay,stæy,bæy kriyk/.[3]

Probably related to this substitution is the occurrence of /y-/ for prevocalic /r-/ in *February*, *secretary*. So far as I have observed, the Southern records contain no examples of prevocalic /y-/ for /r-/ in stressed syllables.[4]

The converse substitution of /r/ for /y/ has likewise been observed. In areas where postvocalic /-r/ sometimes appears as constriction of the preceding vowel and sometimes as a centering offglide, the form /ɔrstərz/ frequently appears for *oysters*; and in an area of the South Georgia coast, where apparently no constriction of postvocalic /-r/ occurs, /arədayn/ was recorded for *iodine*.[5]

This paper makes no claim to have solved any major problems. It seems to suggest, however, that the records of the Linguistic Atlas, and other records of the English language as spoken in the United States and elsewhere, should be examined to see how widespread is the substitution of /y/ for /r/ and vice versa in specific morphemes or generally. If such substitutions should be fairly widespread, they may help linguists to formulate more efficient statements for comparing the structures of various dialects.

NOTES

[1] The phonetic transcription is of the general type used by B. Bloch, C. F. Hockett, H. L. Smith, G. L. Trager, and myself for the analysis of American English. In this system all syllabics of any dialect may be analyzed in terms of not more than nine vowels /i,e,æ,ɨ,ə,a,u,o,ɔ/ and four consonants /y,w,r,h/.

The evidence upon which this paper is based was taken from field records made in South Carolina and Georgia during the summer, fall, and winter of 1947-48. Since the process of distributing and filing these records has not been completed, a systematic examination and charting has been impossible at this time.

[2] The forms /skeys,skeyd/ for *scarce*, *scared*, are probably to be considered descriptively as examples of the same substitution since, for the South Atlantic area, in occurrences of these words with an /-r/ phoneme (whether constricted or not)

the vowel phoneme is usually /e/. Historically the substitution may have taken place earlier than the others of this type, but descriptively they should not be dissociated, since in adjacent communities, in different speakers from the same community, or even in different forms obtained from the same speaker, /skers,skerd/ (or perhaps /skehrs,skehrd/) may be observed as occurring alongside /skeys,skeyd/.

[3] It would probably be desirable, in dialects where *bird* is /bəyd/, to write the syllabic of *cur* as /kəy/ even if there were not a phonetically perceptible upglide, simply by reason of the principle of complementary distribution. By this principle, to cite an analogous example, the syllabic of *night*, *nigh* is to be analyzed phonemically as /ay/ in the standard dialect of Greenville, South Carolina, although *night* is phonetically [naɨt] and *nigh* phonetically [na·].

[4] John Kepke, however, reports that in the New York City area /byuriy/ has been a common substandard substitution for /bruriy/.

The substitution of /y-/ for /r-/ in *February, secretary*, has been pointed out as an example of dissimilation that occurs in many dialects. It would nevertheless seem relevant to treat this as a phenomenon related to the replacement of post-vocalic /-r/ by /-y/, because for many speakers the forms /febəweriy,sekəteriy/ are normal.

[5] That /ɔrstərz/ and /arədayn/ are generally to be considered as substandard forms only delimits the social distribution of this substitution, and does not invalidate it as a linguistic phenomenon.

The position of one dialect within a speech community may often be appraised intelligently by the layman, who recognizes that beyond a certain swamp or mountain the inhabitants talk differently. Many times, too, the layman may have a fair understanding of the ways in which that particular dialect differs from his own; he will notice the unfamiliar words or grammatical constructions, and may even be able to mimic passably well the pronunciation and intonation. The interest of the amateur in the strange details of neighboring dialects is often invaluable in suggesting where dialect boundaries may occur and which communities might most profitably be investigated.

Beyond this, however, the work of the lay observer needs at least consultation with the professional. Even though the layman may be well aware of the ways in which his county's speech differs most noticeably from that of an adjacent county, he ordinarily cannot evaluate the position of either dialect in reference to the whole body of American English. For instance, the average white Southerner may use the term *jackleg preacher* freely as a gloss for such more local terms as *chair-backer*, *stump-knocker*, *table-tapper*, and *yard-ax* -- designations for a part-time voluntary preacher, normally without formal seminary training and generally with a low degree of competence. To the native speaker from other regions, however, *yard-ax* and *jackleg* are equally strange, so that the Southerner speaking to a non-Southern audience must define in detail either *yard-ax* or *jackleg*. Conversely, a Low-Country South Carolina term like *haycock* or *mouth organ* may sound exotic to the man from the Up-Country but turn out to be the prevailing term north of the Potomac.

In other words, in identifying and characterizing a dialect it is necessary not only to indicate some of the more characteristic words, forms, and pronunciations in that area, but also to point out what other areas also share these features. To do this, the assistance of the trained scholar is necessary, whether he conducts the investigation himself or merely supplies advice for the lay investigator.

The Charleston area is an excellent example of a dialect area which is easily identified by the lay observer but whose position with reference to other dialect areas of American English cannot be indicated without reference to systematic evidence gathered from other parts of the eastern United States. For our purposes we will define the Charleston area as that dialect area of the South Atlantic coast whose center and main cultural focus is the port of Charleston. Its limits do not turn out to be the same for all features; in fact, these features seem to group themselves into three major geographical patterns, to be defined later. But all seem to center around the city of Charleston and seem to owe their persistence to settlement through that city or later cultural radiation from it.

The distinctiveness of the Charleston dialect has been long recognized by Up-Country South Carolinians. If someone from the Charleston area attends college at an inland institution or runs for state political office, he is readily identified, and his speech is often mimicked by his colleagues. This mimicry usually is confined to an imitation of the Charleston pronunciation of /e,o/ as in *date* and *boat*, to distortion of the [əu] diphthong in *out* toward [u], and to the replacement of /æ/ with /a/, especially in *Battery*.

Scholarly attention was first directed toward Charleston speech in a paper by Sylvester Primer, then of the College of Charleston, delivered at the Modern Language Association of America in 1887, and published in three different journals under the title "Charleston Provincialisms" (1888).[1] Ignoring vocabulary and grammar, he summarized the characteristics of Charleston pronunciation as follows:

1. homonymy of *fear* and *fair*, *ear* and *air*.

2. /e/ in *again*.

3. /æ/ in *pa*, *ma*; also in *calm*, *palm*, *psalm*, etc.

4. distinction of *morning*:*mourning*, *horse*:*hoarse*, etc.

5. /o/ in *poor*; also in *to*.

6. a tendency for /ʌ/ to replace /ʊ/ in *book*, *put*, *pull*, *pudding*.

7. coalescence of /v/ and /w/, with resulting homonymy of *wail* and *vail*, etc.

8. simplification of initial /hw/ to /w/ (see R. and V. McDavid 1952b, in this volume, pp. 185-98).

9. /tʃ/ retained in *pasture*, which remained distinct from *pastor*.

10. postvocalic /-r/ as [ə] or length in *war*, *hard*, etc.

11. initial /kj,gj/ (or palatalized /k, g/ in stressed syllables, as in *car*, *garden*, *girl*.

12. /θ/ in *with*.

However, this pioneer work -- one of the first attempts to describe the speech of an American community -- was not followed up. The economic blight which struck Southern educational institutions following the Confederate War greatly restricted the opportunities for research in such newer disciplines as linguistics, which only recently has won the attention of Southern universities and Southern scholars.

Neither the observations of the lay observer nor Primer's list takes into account the totality of the dialect in its relationships with other dialects. For such a complete picture it is necessary to have 1) a summary of the historical and cultural features that might make for a sharply differentiated dialect; 2) comparable data for several classes of speakers over a wide area. The first of these has been provided by the research of many historians; the second by the field records of the Linguistic Atlas of the United States and Canada.

Both historical and socio-cultural forces suggest that distinctive speech forms would develop in the Charleston area. Historical evidence indicates a sharp difference between the earliest settlers of coastal and inland areas in South Carolina and adjacent parts of Georgia. The tidewater area was settled first as mercantile plantations, with a quasi-feudal structure. The first settlers appear to have been predominantly from southern England (some by way of Barbados), though their precise origins have not been worked out. The original mercantile and planter groups were reinforced fairly early by other groups, notably Huguenots and Sephardic Jews; both of these increments were strongest in the immediate neighborhood of Charleston and in the Santee delta around Georgetown. From early in the colonial period there has been a small but steady amount of direct migration from other countries, particularly Ireland and Germany; as with other American cities, the peak of Irish and German migration was reached about 1850. The importation of Negro slaves as a labor force for indigo and rice plantations began rather early, reached a peak about 1800; although the slave trade was prohibited by law in 1820, illicit slave running continued till the eve of the Confederate War. Large numbers of Negroes were settled on islands and necks of land; partly through peonage, partly through lack of training for anything except agriculture, these Negro groups continued relatively undisturbed until far into the twentieth century. In the last thirty years, northern capitalists have bought up many abandoned plantations as winter homes, and many northern artists and writers have established studios in Charleston or neighboring communities.

Inland South Carolina, on the other hand, was settled by two distinct movements, in neither of which the tidewater plantation settlements played a prominent part. The coastal plain, from Conway and Queensboro near the North Carolina line to Ft. Moore on the Savannah, was planted with frontier townships designed as military outposts to protect the tidewater settlements; north of the Santee the townships were settled predominantly by Ulster Scots and Welsh Baptists, south of the Santee by Germans and German-Swiss. As a rule, the first settlers of each of these townships were recruited and transported in a body to their new homes, generally but not always by way of Charleston. The Piedmont and mountain areas were settled by two southwestward movements, one of English, Irish, and Ulster Scots from the Virginia Piedmont, the other of Ulster Scots and Pennsylvania Germans by way of the Shenandoah Valley; the documentary evidence does not always distinguish between these two movements (Meriwether 1940).

Over this rather diverse population the city of Charleston early established economic and cultural domination that has hardly been challenged down to the present day. A colonial capital and until the end of the eighteenth century the most important city south of Philadelphia, Charleston exerted over South Carolina and Georgia an influence equaled in the South only by that of New Orleans in the lower Mississippi Valley. During the colonial period it was the center of the Indian trade, both with the Cherokees in the southern Appalachians and with the Creeks and Choctaws in the Gulf States. It was the port through which the Carolina plantation owners generally bought and sold, and the business center through which they financed their operations; as plantation agriculture and cotton culture spread inland, the financial domination of Charleston was extended over the entire state. Even the economic changes of the last century have not destroyed this dominant financial position; until fairly recently it was easy for demagogues to rally the voters of the inland counties by appealing to their hatred of Charleston bankers and brokers.

The early feudal pattern of Charleston society has been perpetuated in the form of a select social upper class, based primarily on ancestry and connections, secondarily on education and cultural experience, and to a relatively minor degree on wealth. This group has always maintained close relationships with similar groups in Boston, New York, and other coastal cities; it has also maintained a tradition of close relationships with English society, derived from the fact that down to the Confederate War it was common for planters and merchants to send their sons to the English universities and to the Inns of Court. The exclusiveness of this group has meant relatively high prestige in inland communities for all Charlestonians, whether of the Charleston elite or not. The elite of many inland communities stemmed originally from Low-Country planters who removed their families from the coast during the summer malaria season, a group later reinforced by refugees during the Confederate War (Brewster 1947, Petty 1943). In other communities the earliest banks and business houses were organized by Charlestonians. Finally, the fact that the College of Charleston has remained a small institution, offering a free education in a liberal arts curriculum to a selected student body, supports the tradition of social status based on family and culture rather than on wealth.

It is thus evident that speech forms which became established in Charleston would tend to spread inland in South Carolina and adjacent parts of Georgia and North Carolina, regardless of whether they were favored in other parts of the South. Many speech forms current in Charleston not only are dominant in the coastal plain but are found in the South Carolina Piedmont, particularly in the speech of educated informants. Occasionally, as with *batteau* 'rowboat' and the general Southern *carry one home* 'escort, as from a party,' they have even spread into the mountains of western North Carolina.

The analysis of the Charleston dialect in this paper is based upon the field records of the Linguistic Atlas of the United States and Canada, inaugurated in 1930 by the American Council of Learned Societies.

The Atlantic Seaboard collections of the Linguistic Atlas comprise nearly 1600 field records, so that one is able to determine not only what speech forms occur in a given area but how one area compares with the others. The area of Charleston influence has been especially well studied, with 136 field interviews from South Carolina, 75 from eastern Georgia, and 7 from northeastern Florida. From the city of Charleston itself there are 12 interviews (10 white, 2 Negro), a greater number than from any other Atlantic Seaboard community except New York City.[2] Thus there is adequate evidence for determining the complex interrelationships among the various local speech types as well as among the various social levels of speech.

Each field record represents an average of about eight hours of oral interviewing, in a conversational situation, in an effort to get the natural responses of a native informant, well rooted in his community, for about 800 items of everyday speech. These items concern details of pronunciation, such as *horse*, *hoop*, *wheelbarrow*, *greasy*; details of grammar such as *I dove*, or *div*, or *dived*; details of vocabulary, such as the name for the common worm used in fishing.

Each bit of evidence may be plotted on a map of the area for which we have data. When it is found within a sharply defined area, one may draw a line called an *isogloss*, to indicate the boundaries of the area in which this form occurs. Where several isoglosses tend to coincide, we conclude we have a *dialect boundary*. If the speech forms of a given area seem to be spreading into other areas, it is called a *focal area*; an area whose local speech forms are disappearing is a *relic area*; an area with few local peculiarities but subject to influence from several directions is a *transition area* or *graded area*. For more detailed discussion of the history, methods, and aims of linguistic geography, see Pop, *La Dialectologie* (1950).

The key to the speech patterns of the Carolinas and Georgia is the preeminent position of Charleston. The Ulster Scots and Germans of the coastal plain have left scarcely a trace on the patterns of South Carolina speech. The transfer of the state capital to Columbia (about 1800) and the industrialization of the Piedmont since Reconstruction have not yet been reflected in the spread of Columbia or Piedmont speech forms, except in so far as they coincide with the forms of cultivated Charleston speech.

To determine the characteristics of Charleston speech we must return to the three geographical patterns in which Charleston speech forms occur. Here we must be careful to exclude certain classes of forms which occur not only in the area around Charleston but in wider areas as well:

1. Forms characteristic of urban and cultured speech almost everywhere, such as /tʃ/ in *pasture*.
2. Forms characteristic of the Midland and South, such as *bucket* or /ɔ/ in *on*.[3]
3. Forms characteristic of the South Midland and South, as *disremember*, *theirselves*, *hisself*, *corn shucks*, /z/ in *greasy*, or /o/ in *poor*.
4. Forms characteristic of the entire South, such as *all two*, *all both* 'both,' *more prettier*, *Confederate War*, *haunts* /hænts/ 'ghosts,' and *carry one home* 'to escort.'

As previously suggested, Charleston speech forms are distributed in three basic geographic patterns. The first of these is that of Carolina coastal speech forms that are restricted to a narrow strip of the coastal plain in North Carolina (where there was no dominant coastal center) but in South Carolina have spread inland at least to the neighborhood of Columbia and often to the cities of the Piedmont. The northern limit of these

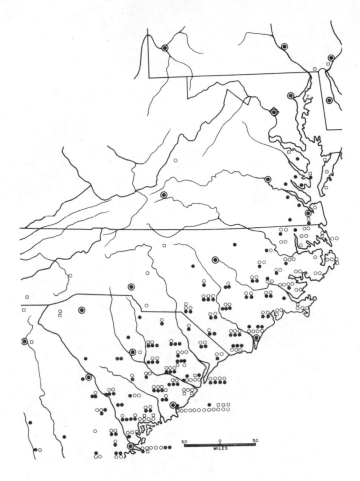

Map 1

Charleston Pronunciation - A

○　/ʌ/ in *bulge*

●　/-b/ in *coop*

□　/æ/ in *tomatoes*

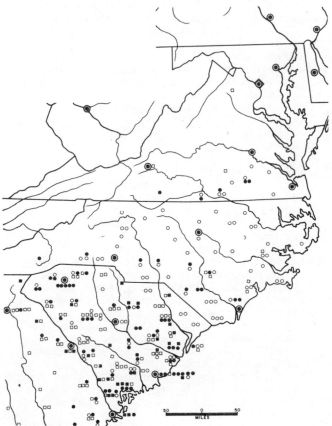

Map 2

Charleston Vocabulary - A

○　*breakfast strip* 'bacon'

●　*clearstone peach* 'freestone peach'

□　*candle fly* 'moth'

■　*candle bug* 'moth'

forms is sometimes the Neuse River, sometimes the Virginia Capes, and occasionally the Delmarva peninsula. In Georgia these forms normally spread throughout the coastal plain. For these items Charleston usage differs from that of the Virginia Piedmont (see Maps 1 and 2).

Pronunciation:

/iu/ occasionally in *puke, music, dues, new*, etc. (Also in New England settlement area, especially in old-fashioned speech.)
/o/ in *wounded* (very old-fashioned).
/ʌ/ in *bulge, bulk*. (Also North and North Midland; Map 1.)
/-b/ in *coop* /kub/ (Map 1).
/war-,wor-/ in *walnut* (also Delmarva and South Midland).

Grammar:

he) *belongs to be* (careful.
church will be over) *time I get there* (also Upstate New York).
I) *ran up with* (him.
I) *ran across* (him.
them boys 'those' (the Virginia Piedmont favors *them there boys*).

Vocabulary:

mosquito hawk 'dragon fly'
press peach 'clingstone peach' (not in the cities of Charleston or Beaufort).
beast 'bull'
troughs, water troughs 'gutters'
hay pile 'hay cock'
take) *a milling of corn* (to be ground
corn dodger 'dumpling'
breakfast strip 'bacon' (Map 2).
clearstone peach 'freestone peach' (Map 2).
earthworm (book word elsewhere).
whicker 'whinny' (also Maine and southeastern New England).
piazza 'porch' (also New England).
spider 'frying pan' (also Northern).

The second pattern is that of forms which have spread inland from coastal ports and plantation areas. Such forms occur near the coast in the Cape Fear Valley of North Carolina, but in South Carolina push inland at least to the Fall Line communities of Cheraw, Camden, Columbia, and Augusta; in Georgia they sometimes spread throughout the coastal plain, more often are confined to the tidewater plantation areas around Savannah, Darien, Brunswick, and St. Mary's. These forms may or may not occur in the communities of northeastern Florida. Forms in this group often occur in the Virginia Piedmont as well; when this happens, as with *crocus sack*, occurrences in the South Carolina Piedmont may have spread from either focus or both (Maps 3 and 4; see also Kurath and R. McDavid 1961).

Pronunciation:

/ɔ/ in *watch, wash* (see Wetmore 1959).
/u/ in *room, broom*, along with /ʊ/. (/ʊ/ is dominant in Northeastern New England, Eastern Virginia, and the Buffalo-Rochester area; see R. McDavid 1949b).
/-rum/ in *mushroom* (also Chesapeake Bay, Eastern New England).
No linking /r/ in *your aunt*.
Centered beginning of /ai,au/ [əi,əu] before voiceless consonants, as in *knife, ice, out, house* (also Eastern Virginia and Canada).
/ɪ/ in unstressed syllables in *funnel, mountain* (also Eastern Virginia and Eastern New England).
[eˑ,eˑə,oˑ,oˑə] in *take, boat*, etc. ([eˑ,oˑ] also in Pennsylvania German area; see Avis 1956, 1961; Map 3.)
/-jə/ in *nephew* (also Eastern Virginia).
/mʌs-/ in *mushmelons* (also Eastern Virginia).
[a,ɑ] in *pasture, hammer, Saturday* (Also Eastern Virginia and Eastern New England; old and receding.)
/-stɪd/ in *instead* (also New England and Upstate New York).
/bɨkʌz/ *because* (also Northern).
[nlɛs] *unless*
Palatalized /k,g/ in *car, garden, girl*, etc. (Also Eastern Virginia.)
/w/ in *whip, wheelbarrow, whetrock* (also Northeastern New England, Hudson Valley, Eastern Pennsylvania).
/-r/ as [ə] or length in *beard, barn, born* (also Eastern Virginia, New York City, Eastern New England).
/ɔ/ as well as /a/ in *pot, crop, borrow, orange*, etc.
/u,ʊ/ in *won't*. (Also Hudson Valley, Chesapeake Bay, Nantucket and Martha's Vineyard; Map 5).
/θ/ in *without* (also Chesapeake Bay, Midland).

Grammar:

/dov/ along with *dived*. (/dov/ is dominant in the North, occurs alongside *dived* in Pennsylvania; Map 7.)
used to didn't (Map 7).
sweat (preterite). (As common as *sweated*.)
swim (preterite). (Old-fashioned; also Virginia Piedmont.)
et (preterite). (Even in cultured speech; also New England and other coastal points, and Southern England.)
he was) *dogbit*. (Not in culture centers; also South Midland.)
he did it) *purpose*. (Rare; also New England, New York State.)
he was) *named for* (his uncle. (Also Eastern New England.)
he fell) *off of* (the horse. (Also South Midland.)
he fell) *out the bed*. (Also Eastern Virginia; Map 7).
he isn't) *home*. (Also New York State and

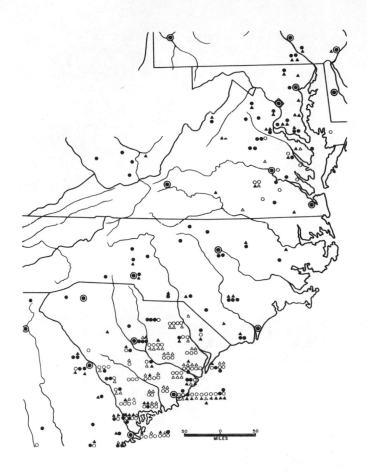

Map 3

Charleston Pronunciation - B

△   /e/ ingliding in *bracelet*

▲   /e/ monophthongal in *bracelet*

○   /o/ ingliding in *coat*

●   /o/ monophthongal in *coat*

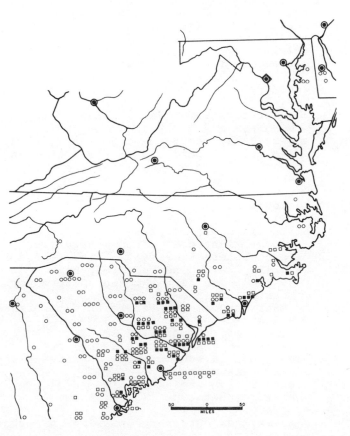

Map 4

Charleston Vocabulary - B

○   *pinders* 'peanuts'

■   *savannah* 'grassland'

□   *sivvy beans, sewee beans* 'lima beans'

Delaware Valley).
two) *yokes* (of oxen. (Also Virginia Piedmont.)
towards (also Virginia Piedmont).
ran acrost (also North Midland).
he do (old-fashioned; also Eastern Virginia).
40) *bushel* (also North Midland).
wait on 'wait for' (also Midland).

Besides these grammatical forms, certain others are far more common in South Carolina than elsewhere:

he's not) *as tall as me.*
I'm not) *as tall as him.*
you can do it) *better than me.*
me and you (can do it.
me and him (are going.
Omission of the nominative relative: *he's the man owns the orchard.*
Omission of the genitive relative: *there's a boy his father is rich.*

Vocabulary:

a little piece (also Midland).
cherry kernel 'cherry seed' (also Delmarva).
armful of wood (also North, North Midland).
coal hod (also New England, Chesapeake Bay).
turnip greens (also North, North Midland).
mutton corn 'green corn' (also northeastern Florida).
cooter 'turtle'
candle fly, candle bug 'moth' (Map 2).
done worked (also Eastern Virginia, spread into South Midland).
sick on the stomach (also Pennsylvania German area, including central North Carolina).
creep 'crawl' (also Northern).
he was) *up in* (Hartford. (Also Southern New England, Upstate New York, New York City, Philadelphia, Virginia, widespread in South Carolina, Georgia.)
savannah 'grassland' (rare in Georgia and not in immediate Charleston area, Map 4).
batteau 'rowboat' (spread into North Carolina, also in Chesapeake Bay and Delaware Bay).
snake fence 'rail fence' (sporadic elsewhere).
cornhouse 'crib' (also Eastern Virginia).
pinder 'peanut' (Map 4).
croker sack (also Eastern Virginia, Martha's Vineyard).
buckra 'white man'
curds 'cottage cheese' (also Chesapeake Bay).
bloody-noun 'bullfrog'
sivvy beans, sewee beans 'lima beans' (Map 4).
mouth organ 'harmonica' (also Northern, North Midland).

These first two groups of forms attest to the importance of Charleston as a focal area from which linguistic forms have spread. For the third group of forms one must consider Charleston and its cultural dependencies as a relic area, in which generally old-fashioned forms are confined to a relatively narrow strip of coast. Some of these forms follow the coastal rice plantation area from Georgetown to the Florida line; others stop at the Savannah River. Inland, they rarely go beyond the area of rice plantations, though a few are found as far up the Santee as the neighborhood of Columbia. Sometimes a form, such as *hall* 'living room,' is not found in the seaport towns but only in the more old-fashioned speech of the surrounding country (Maps 5 and 6).

Pronunciation:

/æ/ in *tomatoes.* (Also Northern; Map 1.)
/u/ alongside /ju/ in *tube, due, new,* etc. (Normal in North Midland, Hudson Valley; dominant in the rest of the North.)
/ɪ/ in *creek* (also North, North Midland).
/vez/ *vase* (sporadic along the coast, common in Canada).
/nɛvjə/ *nephew* (sporadic along the coast, common in Canada).
[a,ɑ] in *glass* (also Eastern New England).
/ʊ/ in *cooter* (Map 5).
/e/ in *again* (also Hudson Valley, Eastern New England).
/o/ in *to.*
Only one front vowel phoneme before /r/: *fair:fear, air:ear,* etc.
/æ/ in *pa, ma* (Map 5).
/æ/ in *palm, calm,* etc. (Even in cultured speech; old-fashioned elsewhere.)

Grammar:

see (preterite). (Rare; also in Eastern Virginia and North.)
a little way (down the road; *a long way* (to go. (Especially in Charleston and Beaufort; in metropolitan areas of other regions.)

Vocabulary:

hall 'living room' (rare).
fatwood 'lightwood' (from Georgetown to northeastern Florida).
cornbarn (rare elsewhere, Map 6).
joggling board 'springboard anchored at both ends' (Map 6).
haycock (uncommon, also North and North Midland).
pinto 'coffin' (chiefly Negro).
worm fence (also North Midland).
wagon pole (also Northern, Chesapeake Bay).
goober 'peanut'
ashbread 'ashcake' (Map 6).
whetseed 'whetstone' (also Albemarle Sound).
yard-ax, table-tapper 'unskilled preacher'
awendaw 'spoonbread'

[278]

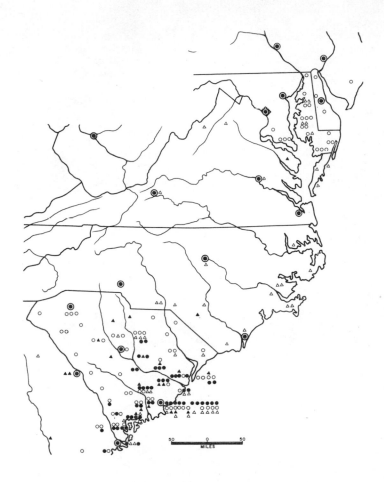

Map 5

Charleston Pronunciation - C

    O   /æ/ in *pa, ma*

    ●   /ʊ/ in *cooter* 'turtle'

    △   /u/ in *won't*

    ▲   /ʊ/ in *won't*

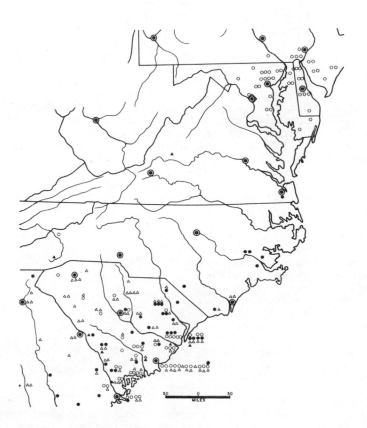

Map 6

Charleston Vocabulary - C

    O   *ground nuts* 'peanuts'

    △   *joggling board*

    ●   *cornbarn*

    ▲   *ashbread* 'ashcake'

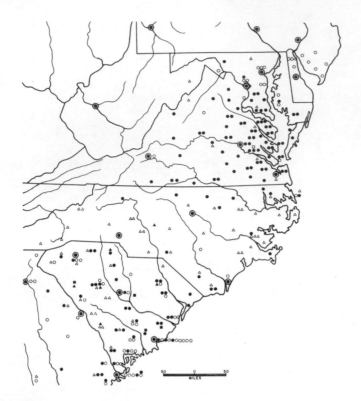

Map 7

Charleston Grammar

○	/dov/ *dived*
●	*out the bed*
△	*used to didn't*
▲	*used to wasn't*
□	*used to warn't*
■	*used to wouldn't*

ground nuts 'peanuts' (receding; to the St. Mary's River; also in the Philadelphia area and British English; Map 6).
bush colt, *bush child* 'bastard'
(*marsh*) *tacky* 'small half-wild horse'
groomsman 'best man' (rare in Virginia).
squinch owl, *skrinch owl* 'screech owl'

Cutting across the three geographical patterns, certain social patterns must be recognized in the speech of this area. The most striking of these patterns is the pronunciation of postvocalic /-r/ in such words as *beard*, *barn*, *four*. Contrary to tradition, a strongly constricted /-r/ is often found in folk speech, not only of the mountains and the cotton-mill villages but also of the sand hills and the Low-Country pine barrens. However, constriction is less strong in younger speakers than in older, in urban speakers than in rural, in cultured speakers than in uneducated; so that the social appraisal of this feature is needed to balance the geographical (cf. Van Riper 1958; O'Cain 1972; R. McDavid 1948, in this volume, pp. 136-42).

In other details, too, urbanization is affecting the speech of the Charleston area just as it affects that of other regions. Two details will illustrate this: 1) *hall* 'living room' is a relic surviving only in rural communities around Charleston and Georgetown; 2) although *press*

peach 'clingstone peach' is the dominant term in the coastal plain from the Virginia Capes south, and is common in both Georgetown and Savannah, it was not recorded from a single informant in either Charleston or Beaufort.

Negro speech, in general, seems to have the same speech forms as white speech. The lexical contributions of the Negro to the Charleston vocabulary are found in Turner's *Africanisms in the Gullah Dialect* (1949) and have been identified by various reviewers (see R. McDavid 1950a, in this volume, pp. 342-48; R. and V. McDavid 1951b, in this volume, pp. 43-51). A list of Gullah vocabulary elements with likely African origins is as follows:

bloody-noun 'bullfrog'
buckra 'white man'
bush child, *bush colt* 'bastard'
cooter 'turtle'
cush 'mush'
da 'colored nurse'
goober 'peanut' (more common in the Virginia Piedmont than in South Carolina).
hu-hu owl 'hoot owl'
joggling board
pinder 'peanut'
pinto 'coffin'
takky 'horse'
titta 'sister'
tote 'carry' (general Southern, also western North Carolina and western Pennsyl-

vania).
yard-ax, *table-tapper* 'unskilled preacher'

Some of these forms, like *cooter*, *pinder*, and *tote*, are used widely by white speakers without any suspicion of their African background; others, like *pinto* and *yard-ax*, are used by whites as conscious Negroisms. But all are known by whites.

Grammatically, the most old-fashioned Negro speech shows a lack of inflection in both noun and verb (*I have drive*, *a pair of shaft*) and /(ʝ)unə/ as the second person plural pronoun, and uses *for* /fə/ rather than *to* or *for to* with the infinitive of purpose, as *he come over for tell me*. Phonologically, old-fashioned Negro speech does not contrast /v/ and /w/, has (along with the speech of the North and North Midland) /s/ rather than /z/ in *grease*, *greasy*, and lacks an /æ/ phoneme. The noticeable differences in intonation patterns await further investigation.

Few of these speech forms of the Charleston area occur only in that area, notably the ingliding [eˑəˑ,oˑə] and such lexical items as *pinder*, *cooter*, *mutton corn*, *sivvy beans*, and *savannah*. The rest are shared with other speech areas of the Atlantic Seaboard; sometimes with the Midland as /-θ-/ in *without*, sometimes with eastern Virginia as *corn house*, *croker sack* and the centered beginning in [əʊt,nəif], sometimes with New York City, as /wʊnt/, sometimes with the Boston area as *piazza*. In the early periods of settlement and expansion from the coast, dialect mixture must have been the norm rather than the exception. It is not surprising, then, that the same speech form (whether in pronunciation, grammar, or vocabulary) may crop up in widely separated areas along the coast, and that the identification of dialect areas is less a matter of individual traits than the combinations in which traits appear. As Primer concluded, "I must again caution all not to understand the above observations on the peculiarities of Charleston pronunciation [or grammar, or vocabulary] as applying to Charleston alone. The peculiar circumstances under which the whole country was settled would exclude any monopoly of sound [or inflection, or word] by any one place." It is not surprising that some of his "Charleston Provincialisms" turn out to be rather widespread, or that investigation has revealed other items which give Charleston speech its individuality, even in the South.

NOTES

[1] Mencken 1948:213, "[Primer] was born in Wisconsin in 1842, but removed to New York as a child. He served in the Civil War as a cavalryman under Sheridan and Custer and was wounded at Antietam. After the war he took to language studies at Harvard, Leipzig, Göttingen and Strassburg, and in 1895 was given a Ph.D. by the last-named. From 1891 until his death in 1913 he was professor of Germanic languages at the University of Texas."

Is it possible that Primer's concern with German made him unable to perceive the most striking feature of Charleston pronunciation, the pure vowels and ingliding diphthongs in *date* and *boat*?

[2] Of the field records from this area [through 1948], 189 were made by R. McDavid, 28 by Guy S. Lowman, Jr., and one by Bernard Bloch. [See O'Cain 1972.]

[3] As in Kurath 1949 and Atwood 1953a, the term 'North' designates New England, the Hudson Valley, and their derivative settlements; 'North Midland,' Pennsylvania and northern West Virginia; 'South Midland,' the Shenandoah Valley and the southern mountains; 'Southern,' the plantation settlements from Chesapeake Bay to northern Florida, plus their immediate derivatives.

This paper offers evidence in support of a position somewhat critical of the theory of over-all patterns of English dialects.[1] Although this position has been repeatedly presented since 1949, when Trager and Smith reached a definitive statement of their analysis of English syllabic nuclei, it has been acknowledged only in Sledd 1955, and has been passed over in such *apologiae* as Hill 1958. The reason for this overpassing is undoubtedly my own failure to present formally, and in detail, the evidence upon which this position is based. To correct the perspective, I have inserted a brief historical footnote in Hill 1962:30-31, 94-95; however, it is well to provide something more extensive for the record.

I am not ashamed to confess my indebtedness to the stimulating ideas of George L. Trager, whom -- to parrot a phrase -- I admire as a scholar as much as any man may this side of idolatry; nor do I disparage the many contributions which Henry Lee Smith, Jr., has made both to the matter of linguistics and to bettering the status of linguists in the academic world and elsewhere. Yet the statement here presented ultimately antedates my acquaintance with either of them. It was first drafted, at the suggestion of Leonard Bloomfield, in 1938, and offered at the New York meeting of the Linguistic Society that year; it was put in the form of a vowel-plus-semivowel analysis at the 1940 Institute. A year later, after I met Trager, an early version was read at the 1941 summer meeting of the Linguistic Society. Publication was delayed, however, by personal difficulties, the pressure of war work, several years of field work for the Linguistic Atlas, the need to acquire a veneer of domestication to the utilitarian ends of departments of literary engineering, and (most significant in recent years) a wish to remain silent rather than confuse scientific discussion by injecting what might be misread as personal feelings. The essence is that, despite a favorable predisposition (which I still hold) toward the Tragerian analysis of English long syllabic nuclei, the evidence gathered in the field convinced me that the over-all pattern, as enunciated in the *Outline of English Structure* (Trager and Smith 1951), could not satisfactorily accomodate all the observable phonemic contrasts in the dialects I knew best, taken *seriatim*, let alone all those dialects taken simultaneously.[2]

The first half of the title, then, suggests the problem of accomodating within a single over-all pattern the phonemic contrasts to be observed in a few groups of dialects spoken south of the Smith and Wesson Line. The principal groups of dialects will be the speech complex in and around my native community, Greenville, South Carolina (an upland industrial center), and that centering on Charleston, South Carolina, the older cultural focus of the Carolina-Georgia coastal plain. Both of these dialect complexes have many subvarieties, reflecting complications of both settlement history and social structure; moreover, recent social mobility (as well as the inland prestige of Charleston) is responsible for the easy borrowing of speech forms, including pronunciations, from one complex to another. [O'Cain 1972 shows that Charleston itself is now even more complicated than when this paper was composed.] In even more drastically mixed communities, such as Columbia (the state capital) or some of the small towns in the Low-Country pine barrens, the complications are so extensive that they cannot be exhaustively treated in a single paper. One must simply assume that any Charleston syllabic nucleus may occur in contrast with any Up-Country syllabic nucleus in some idiolects of these traditional communities.

The second half of the title reflects (as Trager freely concedes) the ultimate indebtedness to Henry Sweet of all phonemic interpretations of English long syllabic nuclei as phonemic sequences of the type vowel plus semivowel. The term 'Sweetening' is employed rather than 'Tragerization' to indicate no prior philosophical commitment to a particular number or vowels or semivowels; 'Tragerization' is restricted to the classical 9V x 3SV analysis, as presented in Trager and Smith 1951.

The problems of an over-all frame of suprasegmental phonemes (accepting the point of view that these phenomena are a part of the phonemic system) is left in abeyance at this time, pending the collection of a body of unrehearsed evidence for independent analysis. That there may be differences in the number, distribution and phonetic qualities of these phenomena would seem a reasonable inference from what we know about the segmental phonemes. This inference is also supported by such informal evidence as:

1. The widespread recognition that

South Midland and Southern dialects --
particularly those of the tidewater region
from Georgetown, South Carolina, to northeastern Florida -- have speech tunes unlike those of North Midland and Northern
dialects.

2. Other structural analyses of suprasegmental phenomena, especially a) Gage's
discovery of the five-pitch dialects in
upstate New York (1958); b) Pike's suggestion that, in some dialects at least,
the two Tragerian terminals /||/ and /#/
may be reduced to one.

3. Interdialectal misinterpretations of
suprasegmental phenomena. For example,
the sequence /'+^/, in such South Midland
dialects as Sledd's and mine, has been in-
terpreted by Joos as /'|'/, because the
phonetic features of Greenville and Atlanta /'+^/ resemble those of Wisconsin
/'|'/.

The consonants, as elsewhere, present
relatively few problems. Intervocalic
/l/, between front vowels, as in *Nelly* and
Billy, is in all these dialects normally
'clear,' rather than 'neutral' or 'dark'
as in dialects farther north. In the
Piedmont (e.g., Greenville), the final
consonant of *fill*, *full* is 'dark,' as in
most other American dialects. In many
dialects of the coastal plain, however, it
is 'clear,' particularly after front vowels, as in *feel* and *fill*, but sometimes
also after central or back vowels, as in
fool, *cull*, and *foal*. The high incidence
of dialect mixture in the South Atlantic
states, plus the fact that the initial
consonant of *log* is 'dark' in certain
other native American dialects, suggests
that a true over-all pattern must set us
clear /l/ and dark /ł/ phonemes, even
though the contrast bears a very low functional load.[3]

The greatest complications, as usual,
occur in the system of syllabic nuclei --
vowels and diphthongs. The procedure of
the Trager and Smith *Outline* will be followed in presenting first the 'simple'
nuclei and then the groups of complex
ones.

Greenville

Simple nuclei:

/i/ lower high-front unrounded, often
   raised, as in *pit*.
/e/ lower mid-front unrounded, often
   raised, as in *pet*.
/æ/ upper low-front unrounded, often
   raised, as in *pat*, *have*, *had*.
/a/ lower low-front unrounded, occasionally raised and retracted. Rare as a simple nucleus, occurring almost exclusively in imitations of Charlestonian pronunciations, as of *man*.[4]
/ʉ/ lower high-central rounded, as in *put*.
   Varies with, occasionally contrasts
   with, lower high-back rounded /u/.

/ɨ/ lower high-central unrounded. Much
   more common under heaviest stress in
   this dialect complex than in Northern or
   North Midland: *wish*, *milk*, *mirror*, *dinner*, *ribbon*, *sister*, *scissors*, *pillow*,
   pencil. As elsewhere, may occur in 're-
   stressed' pronunciations, or with secondary or tertiary stress, in *just*, *such*.
/ə/ upper mid-central raised and retracted, to lower high-back lowered and
   fronted, commonly lightly rounded, as in
   cut.
/a/ lower mid-central to lower low-back
   retracted, unrounded, as in *pot*.
/u/ lower high-back rounded, as in *put*.
   Varies with, sometimes contrasts with,
   lower high-central rounded /ʉ/. Of the
   two, /u/ is more commonly associated
   with urban and plantation, /ʉ/ with rustic or cotton-mill speech. Because of
   social migration, it is possible to have
   contrasts between /bʉł/ 'taurus' and
   /buł/ 'sermo flatulens,' or between
   /pʉł/ 'physical force' and /puł/ 'political influence.' This contrast has
   also been observed in some Kentucky dialects of the Blue Grass region, and in
   Beaumont, Texas.
/o/ mid mid-back, rounded. Rare as a simple nucleus, occasional in *gonna* or in
   the final syllable of *railroad*.
/ɔ/ upper low-back to lower low-back, occasionally advanced, rounded. Rare as a
   simple nucleus; may occur (e.g., *God*)
   as either a) a rustic relic, or b) an
   imitation of prestigious Charleston
   usage, alongside the more common pronunciations with /a/.

All of these simple nuclei may have
lengthening or a weak centering offglide
or both, regardless of what consonant
follows. Both the length and the offglide
become more conspicuous under heavier
stress and in slow, deliberate speech.

Complex nuclei with an unrounded glide
toward a high-front or high-central
position /Vy/.

/iy/ *bee*, *beet*.
/ey/ *bay*, *bait*.
/æy/ *bad*, *halve*.
/ay/ *bite*.
/ʉy/ *push*, *buoy* (occasionally); alter-
   nates with /uy/.
/əy/ *hush*; *third* (occasional among 'r-
   less' speakers).
/ay/ *wash*.
/uy/ *push*, *buoy* (occasionally); alter-
   nates with /ʉy/.
/oy/ *porch*.
/ɔy/ *boy*, *torch*, *George*.

Of nuclei of this type, those above have
been recorded. The upglide is least conspicuous after /i/ (indeed, for some
speakers /iy/ does not occur), most conspicuous after back vowels. In every

[283]

instance the first component of a complex nucleus of this type is characterized by higher tongue position and greater muscular tension than the corresponding simple nucleus, with a resulting sharp difference in vowel quality.

Complex nuclei with a rounded offglide toward a high-central or high-back position /Vw/.

/aw/, /æw/, /ɑw/, /ew/ in *cow*, with the first two by far the most common. Of these /aw/ occurs more frequently in cultivated speech, /æw/ in uncultivated.
/ʉw,uw/ in *do*, with the former more common.
/iw,ɨw/ in occasional (usually pseudo-elegant) pronunciations of *beauty*, etc.
/ow/ in *go*.
/ɔw/ in *law*.

Of diphthongs of this type the above have been recorded. The offglide is least conspicuous after /ʉ/ and /u/ (some speakers do not have either /uw/ or /ʉw/), most conspicuous after front vowels. In every instance the first component of a complex nucleus of this type is characterized by a higher tongue position and greater muscular tension than that of the corresponding simple nucleus, with a resulting sharp difference in vowel quality.

Complex nuclei, with lengthening of the vowel and occasionally a weak centering offglide /Vh/.

/ih/ *bee* (occasionally; varies with /iy/).
/æh/ *baa, sad, salve*.
/ah/ *buy, hide*, in standard speech (i.e., finally or before voiced consonants except /g/ and /nt/; in nonstandard speech, in all positions: *nice, white, tiger, pint*). Some standard speakers have *rifle* 'gun' with /ah/, but *to rifle* with /ay/.
/ʉh/ *do* (occasional; varies with /ʉw/, /uw/, /uh/).
/əh/ *cur, word* (comparatively rare, for 'r-less' speakers).
/ɑh/ *pa, shah*.
/uh/ *do* (occasional; varies with /uw/, /ʉw/, /ʉh/).

Of complex nuclei of this type the above have been recorded. In nuclei of this type, the vowels /i,ʉ,u,ə,æ/ are accompanied by higher tongue position and greater muscular tension than they have when they occur as simple nuclei.

Complex nuclei, with lengthening of the vowel and a strong centering offglide /Vɦ/.

/iɦ/ *weir, weird* (rare).
/eɦ/ *fear*.
/æɦ/ *fair*.
/aɦ/ *fire*.
/ɑɦ/ *far* (occasionally).
/ʉɦ/ *sure, tour* (rare; varies with /uɦ/; disyllabic pronunciations of the type /uwə/ are common).
/oɦ/ *wore, mourning*.
/ɔɦ/ *war, morning*.

Of nuclei of this type the above have been observed. Nuclei of this type are most common among 'r-less' speakers (though very few speakers in the community are completely 'r-less' in the sense in which the term is applied to Southern British Received Pronunciation or standard Boston speech); but most 'r-pronouncing' speakers have minimal contrasts of the type *boa:bore, moa:more, Samoa:some more*. In nuclei of this type the first component is characterized by a more central position than that of the corresponding simple nucleus, with a consequent difference in vowel quality. The difference in quality is most apparent in the sequence /ɑɦ/, where the first component is typically advanced and slightly raised. Thus, in 'r-less' speech such pairs as *hod* and *hard* are normally distinct.

Charleston

Simple nuclei:

The same simple nuclei are recorded as in Greenville: /i/, /e/, /æ/, /a/, /ʉ/, /ɨ/, /ə/, /ɑ/, /u/, /o/, /ɔ/. In addition, speakers normally have another simple nucleus /ʌ/, varying in position from raised upper low-central unrounded to advanced lower mid-back unrounded. A majority of speakers who have /ʌ/ lack the higher /ə/ in stressed syllables, but other speakers have both /ə/ and /ʌ/, contrasting in analogous environments. Other differences in the distribution of the simple nuclei in the two dialect complexes as as follows:
Some Charleston speakers lack a contrast between /i/ and /ɨ/.
Most Charleston speakers have /u/ and lack /ʉ/ as a simple nucleus. Contrasts between /u/ and /ʉ/ are rare.
/a/ is very common in Charleston as a simple nucleus, notably in *takky* 'wild horse,' contrasting with *tacky* 'dowdy,' and as a variant or substitute for /æ/ or /ɑ/.
In words like *pot* and *God*, /ɔ/ is more frequent in Charleston than in Greenville, /ɑ/ less frequent.

A detailed examination of the simple nuclei in many Charleston idiolects would probably reveal that a) some speakers have /æ/, /a/, /ɑ/ and /ɔ/; b) others have /æ/, /a/, /ɔ/ and lack /ɑ/; c) others have /æ/, /ɑ/, and lack /ɔ/; d) others (especially among the Gullah Negroes) have

/a/ and /ɔ/ but lack /æ/ and /ɑ/; e) a
very few (mostly younger-generation,
newly risen whites of humble origins) have
/æ/ and /ɑ/ but lack /a/ and /ɔ/. This
extremely complex situation in the low-
vowel range undoubtedly reflects an early
mingling of speakers representing several
discrete phonemic systems. [See Kurath
1972:118-21.]

Nuclei of the type /Vy/ are relatively uncommon in the Charleston area. The most
frequently recorded nuclei of this type
are:

/əy/ occasionally in *bird*, *hurt*;[5] less
often in *white*.
/ʌy/ especially before voiceless consonants, /g/, and /nt/, as in *bite*, *tiger*,
pint. Some speakers have /ʌy/ in all
positions, /ɑy/ typically in final position and before voiced consonants (except /g/ and the cluster /nt/), as in
buy, *bide*. A few speakers lack /ɑy/.
/ay/ relatively uncommon, as an alternate
of /ɑy/. A few speakers have /ay/ consistently where most Charlestonians have
/ɑy/.
/uy/ (rarely /ʉy/) *buoy*.
/oy/ relatively rare; in old-fashioned
speech, may replace the more common /ɔy/
in *boy*, etc.
/ɔy/ *boy*, *voice*, *void*, *coin*; in old-
fashioned speech /oy/ replaces /ɔy/ in
these words, but /ɔy/ may replace /ay/,
as in *island*.

Nuclei of the type /Vw/ are likewise infrequent. The following are the most
common:

/ɨw/ (less frequently /iw/) in *new*, where
most Charlestonians have /nyʉh/ or
/nyuh/.
/əw/ occasionally in *bout*, etc., alongside
the more common /ʌw/.
/ʌw/ normally before voiceless consonants,
as in *bout*, but occasionally in all positions as in *cow*, *loud*.
/ɑw/ (less commonly /aw/) normally before
voiced consonants and finally, as in
loud, *brown*, *cow*. Some Charlestonians
lack /ɑw/, having /ʌw/ in all positions.

Nuclei of the type /Vh/, with the initial
component characterized by higher tongue
position and greater muscular tension
than that of the corresponding simple
nucleus, are very common in the Charleston area, perhaps more common than anywhere else among native speakers of
American English. In nuclei of this
type a weak centering offglide sometimes
occurs before following consonants,
rarely in final position. The common
nuclei of this type are:

/ih/ *bee*, *beat*.
/eh/ *bay*, *bait*.

/æh/ *bad*, *sad*, *half*, *salve*.
/ah/ often in *ma*, *pa*, *palm*.
/ʉh/ occasionally in *do*. A few speakers
seem to contrast *dew* with /ʉh/ and *do*
with /uh/.
/əh/ occasionally in *bird* (although
Charleston is theoretically an 'r-less'
community, many speakers have /ər/ in
bird, etc.).
/ɑh/ common in *car*; sometimes in *pa*,
shah.
/uh/ *do*.
/oh/ *beau*, *boat*, *bode*.
/ɔh/ *law*, *bought*, *bawd*; sometimes in
shah.

Complex nuclei of the type /Vɦ/, with
lengthening of the vowel and a strong
centering offglide:

In the range /iɦ/, /eɦ/, /æɦ/, many speakers have only one complex /Vɦ/ nucleus,
usually /eɦ/, for *fear* and *fair*. Others
have /iɦ/ in *weird*, *fear*, /eɦ/ in *fair*.
A few have the Greenville pattern of
/iɦ/ in *weird*, /eɦ/ in *fear*, /æɦ/ in
fair.
/aɦ/ occasionally in *fire* (disyllabic
forms of the type /faye/, rarely /faye/,
are more common in Charleston); in *car*,
etc., for speakers who lack /ɑ/.
/uɦ/ (less commonly /ʉɦ/) in *tour*, etc.
/ɑɦ/ in *car*, alternating with /ah/.
/oɦ/ in *board*, *wore*.
/ɔɦ/ in *lord*, *war*.

The replacement of /aɦ/ by /ɑh/ in *car*
is found in standard and nonstandard
speech. In nonstandard speech /oɦ/, /ɔɦ/
are often replaced by /oh/, /ɔh/, so that
woe and *wore*, *Waugh* and *war*, are homonymous.

It is thus apparent that to reconcile
all the phonemic contrasts in these two
South Atlantic dialect complexes in a
Sweet-Trager over-all pattern, we must
have twelve simple vowels and four semivowels, or a total of sixty syllabic nuclei. So far as is currently ascertain-
able, no idiolect in either the Greenville
or the Charleston area -- or anywhere
else -- has the full repertory; but those
lacking in these two areas can be found
elsewhere, as Trager and Smith have previously indicated.
But even this repertory leaves us with
certain leftovers. David Reed has pointed
out, in Hill 1962, that certain Missouri
dialects have contrasting upgliding diphthongs in *lesion* and *vision*, in *vague* and
leg. In some transitional dialects in
South Carolina *vague* has a long tense
upper mid-central vowel (sometimes with a
weak centering offglide), but *leg* has an
upgliding diphthong with a lower mid-front
beginning, in the range of the vowel of
pet. And certain other dialects of the
Southern coast (and no doubt elsewhere)

Table 1:   Nuclei in parentheses ( ) are rare in the dialect, or
                  are to be inferred from their presence in other dialects.

Greenville

Simple Nucleus	V	Vy	Vw	Vh	Vɦ
/i/	pit	bee, beat	(beauty)	bee, beat	weir, weird
/e/	pet	bay, bait	(cow)		fear
/æ/	pat, have	halve	cow	baa, sad, salve	fair
/a/	(man)	mite	cow	buy, hide	fire
/ʉ/	put	push	do	(do)	tour
/ɨ/	ribbon		(beauty)		
/ə/	putt	hush, bird		fur	
/ɑ/	pot	wash	(cow)	shah	far
/u/	put	push	do	(do)	tour
/o/	(gonna)	porch	go		wore
/ɔ/	(God)	boy, torch, George	law		war

Charleston

Simple Nucleus	V	Vy	Vw	Vh	Vɦ
/i/	pit		(new)	bee, beet	(weird)
/e/	pet			bay, bait	beer, bear
/æ/	pat, tacky		(cow)	mad, halve, sad, salve	(bear)
/a/	man, takky		cow	ma, pa	fire, (far)
/ʉ/	(put)	(buoy)		(do), (dew)	(tour)
/ɨ/	ribbon		(new)		
/ə/	(cut)	bird	(bout)	fur	
/ɑ/	pot	buy	cow	shah	far
/u/	put	buoy		do	tour
/o/	(gonna)	(boy)		beau, boat	wore
/ʌ/	cut	bite	bout		
/ɔ/	pot, God	boy		law	war

Composite Pattern

Simple Nucleus	V	Vy	Vw	Vh	Vɦ
/i/	pit	bee	(new)	bee	weird
/e/	pet	bay	(cow), (go)	bay, bait	fear
/æ/	pat	halve	cow	salve	fair
/a/	man, takky	bite	cow	my	fire
/ʉ/	put	buoy, push	do	do	tour
/ɨ/	ribbon	(bee)	(new)	(bird)	(furry)
/ə/	cut	hush, bird, (bite)	(go), bout	bird	(furry)
/ɑ/	pot	wash, bite	cow	shah	far
/u/	put	buoy, push	do	do	tour
/o/	(gonna)	porch	go	go	wore
/ʌ/	cut	bite	bout	(bird)	(furry)
/ɔ/	pot, God	boy, torch	law	law	war

Residual Problems

lesion [liɟʒən]   vs.   vision [vɪɟʒən]
vague [veɟg]   vs.   leg [lɛɟg]
vague [ve·əg]   vs.   leg [lɛɟg]
          room [ry·m] or [ry·yˌm]

[286]

seem to have, in words like *room*, *root*, *rude*, a long tense rounded front vowel, phonetically [y·] or an upgliding rounded high-front diphthong of the type [y·yₐ] -- both nuclei similar to those recorded in Devonshire in similar words. How these phenomena may be properly Sweetened, I leave to future investigators; but it would seem plausible that the over-all pattern might need to be let out a little further. Indeed, though the chance that a given dialect will show hitherto undis-covered contrasts must become progressive-ly less as we learn more about English, the possibility may not be validly ex-cluded from the study of a living lan-guage. An over-all pattern must then in-creasingly approach the finely graded phonic transcription that linguistic geo-graphers have been using for decades. Such is indeed the implication of Stock-well 1959. But true structural dialecto-logy consists in making analyses of sys-tems, and then comparing them, as Moulton does with German-Swiss dialects.

The impossibility of structural dialect comparison through an over-all pattern may in the end be the salvation of the Trager-ian approach for the ends it can best serve. By eliminating the mystique of philosophic comprehensiveness, we make it more useful for what it is: a valuable diagnostic tool, an immensely practical design, a stimulating and provocative ap-proach -- but not the only approach: a caution that may be applied to the new revelation from the banks of the Charles (Chomsky and Halle 1968). Perhaps for presenting the essential picture of phono-logical structure a 'common core' ap-proach -- whether Kurath's or Hockett's (1958) is immaterial here -- may be more useful. In any event, if linguistics is a science -- and if it were not, I'd rather peddle advertising copy on Madison Ave-nue -- we must beware of letting theory harden into dogma, and conversely must be willing to use each approach for what it may contribute to the wider knowledge of man's essential characteristic, the use of language.

NOTES

[1] Originally presented before the Kentucky Foreign Language Conference, 1961.

[2] Another analysis is found in Kurath and R. McDavid 1961. One may convert the current analy-sis, or that in the Trager and Smith *Outline*, into that found in Kurath and R. McDavid 1961, with the residua indicating the essential differ-ences between the approaches.

[3] The theoretical necessity of recognizing /l/ and /ł/ as distinct phonemes has since been sup-ported by the observation that some Scots dialects show minimal contrasts between /l/ and /ł/, and similar contrasts between a clear /n/ and a dark /ꞃ/. Other explanations of these contrasts -- as 'junctural' or 'prosodic' -- seem much less satisfactory.

[4] /a/ also occurs as a short nucleus in *pot*, *God*, etc., in many dialects of the Inland North, ranging from western New England to southern Minnesota, and probably beyond. It is also the initial component in the Eastern New England pro-nunciation of *father*, *park*, *part*.

[5] If we accept a raising of the initial compo-nent as one of the manifestations of /-y/ in *beet* and *bait*, then the upper mid-central beginning of the diphthong in *bird* cannot reasonably be inter-preted as /ɨy/, whether in Charleston, Vicksburg, or New York City.

[When this essay was originally written, Lyndon Johnson was at the height of his power. Field work for the *Dictionary of American Regional English* (Cassidy *et al.* 1981-) had barely begun; editing of the Atlantic Seaboard materials had just resumed; the studies of Pederson and Williamson were dissertations not yet revised for print; and such figures as William Labov and Roger Shuy were hardly known. The amount of updating, apparent by dates or by brackets, testifies to the extent to which the visionary program of the original essay is becoming reality, though much remains to be done.]

With a sub-Potomac accent now enunciating the national policies, the time is fair for examining what we know about Southern speech and what we need to learn. Whatever Southerners felt about Mr. Johnson's policies, no Southerner can deny that his presence made people in other regions less patronizing toward Southern speechways, and removed at least this cause of Southern defensiveness. With another Southerner in the White House, there is now an even more opportune occasion for assessing objectively our speech and its implications. [The presidency of Jimmy Carter, whose speech is strikingly different from that of Lyndon Johnson, is an even more pervasive reminder of the nature of Southern speech and its variety.]

Since Cabell Greet's overview of the subject in Couch's *Culture in the South* (1934), there has been much solid evidence gathered on Southern ways of talking, and a fair amount of scholarly publication. Yet except for the updating of Mencken's *The American Language* (1963), a work whose fundamental structure limited the amount of new material that could be included, almost none of the new evidence has been included in works designed for *l'homme moyen intellectuel*. Even the textbooks, which should have made special efforts to discard timeworn myths for new-won facts, are little improved over those of the 1930's; though the ghost of the mythical 'General American' should have long ago been laid, it still returns to haunt us, sometimes under its old label, sometimes under such new disguises as "consensus English" or "network English," neither of them very palatable in a region where locally identifiable ways of speech are cultural traditions, as soon to be denied as the legitimacy of one's descent.[1]

The distinctive characteristics of Southern speech -- at least, those which outsiders judge as distinctive -- have been attracting attention ever since the Reverend John Witherspoon delivered his castigation of the national idiom in 1781 (cf. Mencken 1963:5-11); but the appraisal of them has generally been casual, impressionistic, unstructured, and uninformed. Among the characteristics most often noted are:[2]

1.   The so-called 'Southern drawl.'
2.   *You-all* as a plural, and allegedly as a singular.
3.   To *tote* groceries from the store.
4.   To *carry* a mule to the barn or a young lady home from a party.
5.   The loss of postvocalic /-r/ in such words as *barn*, *beard*, *board*.
6.   A so-called 'Brooklyn diphthong' [ɜɪ] in *bird* and *turn*.
7.   The positional alternation of 'fast' and 'slow' variants of the diphthongs /ai/ and /au/, giving [əɪ] in *write* but [a·ɛ] in *ride*, [əu] in *house* but [æ·o] in *houses*.
8.   The appearance of a monophthongal [a·] for /ai/ before voiced consonants and finally, but not before voiceless, giving [a·] in *ride* but [ai] in *write*.
9.   The appearance of /ai/ as [a·] in all positions, as in *nice white rice*, a well-known social shibboleth in much of the South.
10.   The alleged falling together of /ai/ and /a/, so that *blind* and *blond* become homonyms.
11.   The alleged falling together of /ai/ and /æ/, so that *right* is indistinguishable from *rat*.

Some of these assumed features, like the two last, seem to be noticed only by outlanders. Some of them, like the last two again, simply do not occur.[3] Some of them contradict others, as with 7, 8, and 9, or with 10 and 11. None of the list is actually universal in the South, however the region may be defined -- whether as the territory of slaveholding states before the Civil War, that of the seceding states, or that in which the plantation system was dominant. To take one feature, the drawl: there is no evidence that Southerners on the average talk any more slowly than Midwesterners, and much evidence that some varieties of Southern speech -- notably that of the Charleston area in South Carolina -- are much more rapid than the varieties of speech in the Middle West. But the myths persist, largely because the evidence is unpublished or confined to scholarly articles and treatises that are seldom noted.

The evidence at hand is of three kinds:
1) detailed phonetic transcription by
trained field investigators, on which is
based the project of a Linguistic Atlas of
the United States and Canada (in this instance, transcriptions are found in three
regional surveys, the *Atlas* of the Middle
and South Atlantic States, that of the
North-Central States, and more recently,
that of the Gulf States); 2) a correspondence survey, involving vocabulary
questionnaires, for the interior South,
conducted primarily by Gordon Wood of
Southern Illinois University; 3) a series
of more localized studies, using field
work or correspondence questionnaires or
sometimes a combination of both methods.

The *Linguistic Atlas of the Middle and
South Atlantic States* (Kurath *et al.*
1979-), launched by Hans Kurath in the
late 1930's, comprises about 1100 field
interviews of over 700 questions each,
with responses elicited by professional
investigators from identifiable local informants and recorded in finely graded
phonetic transcription. The area investigated is roughly that of eighteenth-
century settlement, as far west as the
Altamaha Valley, with four communities as
outposts in northern Florida. [The field
records, after sojourns at Brown and
Michigan, are being edited at Chicago and
South Carolina. The first fascicles are
now appearing.] Although the passage of
time has dated many of its cultural details, this *Atlas* nevertheless constitutes
an indispensable baseline. Out of its archives have come many articles, several
dissertations, and three broad-gauge summary volumes,[4] issued by the University of
Michigan Press: Kurath's *Word Geography
of the Eastern United States* (1949), Atwood's *Survey of Verb Forms in the Eastern
United States* (1953a), and Kurath and Mc-
David's *Pronunciation of English in the
Atlantic States* (1961). Like most scholarly books, these have been printed in
small editions, with limited publicity and
consequent limited distribution; as *par-
ticeps criminis* I note with somewhat wry
amusement that the *Pronunciation* evaded
detection by the survey of scholarly books
issuing from university presses. The *Word
Geography* appeared before there was full
evidence in hand from the South Carolina
Low-Country and eastern Georgia; R. Mc-
David 1955a is brief and cursory, without
accompanying maps [maps have been added
for the reproduction of the article in
this volume, pp. 272-81]. Popular and
pedagogical discussions of the dialects
of the older South usually stem from summaries by Kurath, Atwood, and R. McDavid,
such as that in Francis 1958. The *Linguistic Atlas of the North-Central States*,
with field records available in microfilm
(Marckwardt *et al.* 1976-78), touches the
South only in Kentucky; its evidence also

has been presented largely in scholarly
articles and dissertations (e.g., V. Mc-
David 1956; Marckwardt 1957; R. and V.
McDavid 1960, in this volume, pp. 245-53).
The Handbook and summary volumes, well
underway, should make the evidence accessible to a wider audience (Marckwardt *et
al.* 1980-). The vocabulary of Kentucky
has also been investigated through correspondence questionnaires by Christine
Duncan Forrester; her master's thesis
(1954) is unpublished.

The survey of the interior South by
Gordon Wood has yielded one book (1971)
and a series of articles (1960, 1961,
1963). For Texas there is one first-rate
work, Atwood 1962; it was based on field
investigations of vocabulary only, undertaken by graduate students over a period
of years. Several good local studies by
Atwood's students -- notably by Arthur
Norman in the Beaumont region (1955, 1956)
and by Janet Sawyer in San Antonio
(1957) -- are accessible only in articles
or on microfilm. [The field records for
Oklahoma, by W. R. Van Riper, are in an
early stage of editing, at Louisiana State
University.] LSU also houses some hundred
field records made by students of C. M.
Wise -- uneven in quality but providing a
basis for choosing communities intelligently when more highly trained investigators can be sent into the field. In Alabama there have been two studies of parts
of the plantation area, by James B. Mc-
Millan (1946) and Madie Barrett (1948);
neither has been published. Linguistic
Atlas field work in Missouri began during
the summer of 1966. Frederic G. Cassidy,
of the University of Wisconsin, has several investigators in the South, gathering
material for the *Dictionary of American
Regional English*, a project complementary
to the Atlas as well as significant in its
own right; the investigators have provided the first solid evidence on local
variations in Mississippi. [Beginning in
1968, Lee Pederson has brought to completion the field work for an Atlas of the
Gulf States; editing is well under way.]

The most significant study of Negro
speech is Lorenzo D. Turner's *Africanisms
in the Gullah Dialect* (1949). Juanita
Williamson, of LeMoyne College, Memphis,
has completed a dissertation on the Negro
speech of Memphis (1968); Saunders
Walker, of Tuskegee Institute, has done
one on the folk vocabulary of the eastern
Alabama Negro (1956). There have been
several studies of Louisiana Negro French,
most recently by Raleigh Morgan (1960).
Other French dialects, in Louisiana and
elsewhere, are relatively unstudied. The
same may be said for other colonial languages, though Spanish settlement dates
from 1565 and German settlements, beginning in the early eighteenth century, dot
the historical South from western Maryland
to southern Texas, while Czechs settled in

Texas soon after San Jacinto. The best study of German dialects in the South is Eikel 1966-67. [Gilbert 1971, 1972 enlarge our knowledge considerably.]

The information now at our disposal should give us a far better picture of Southern dialects than we encounter in most popular summaries, but it needs to be made more accessible if we are to have a better understanding of the varieties of English (not to say other languages) now spoken in the South. And in addition to making better use of the data which we now have, we need to fill in many gaps and to undertake other studies -- some of a radically different design -- that will enrich our knowledge and will enable us to cope more effectively with the practical problems confronting the student of Southern speech, the demographer, and the classroom teacher of English, whether in a Southern school or elsewhere.

The highest priority goes to the editing and publication of the data already recorded, classified, and filed. Fairly clear plans were laid down by Kurath at the time the Atlas archives were transferred from Brown to Michigan; they are as applicable now as they were twenty years ago, and developments in typewriter design make it possible to prepare list manuscripts for printing at a fraction of the cost of the hand-lettered maps of the traditional linguistic atlases. [Since 1977 financial support from the National Endowment for the Humanities has yielded remarkable progress in editing the materials from the Middle and South Atlantic and North-Central States. The former should be published within a decade, the latter much earlier, since the microfilming of the field records means that only interpretive volumes are necessary.] For the Middle and South Atlantic *Atlas* the first fascicles are the hardest, the others following easily once the pattern has been established. Next comes Van Riper's evidence on Oklahoma speech. Although Oklahoma is a recently -- and suddenly -- settled part of the United States, it may provide valuable insights for linguistic geographers everywhere on what happens in newly settled territory, and thus may enable us to understand what went on when Englishmen of various origins established themselves in North America, when the Angles and Saxons spilled across the Channel into Britain, or even when the Germanic tribes moved westward in the fifth century; it is an excellent laboratory example, since this time we know in some detail where the settlers came from and we have evidence on the kinds of English they brought with them. Along with these three studies we might put the completion and editing of the Missouri survey.

Priority should go to completing the Atlas survey of the South -- a first-round survey, it should be emphasized, without prejudice to follow-up projects -- from the Altamaha to central Texas, and from Missouri and Kentucky southward to Key West (Atwood's successors at Texas can be counted on to follow up his work on vocabulary with comparable work on pronunciation and grammar). As early as this area was settled, till 1968 it was practically untouched by serious and systematically comparable investigations. Part of the explanation has been the sheer poverty of the region, which has not generated enough wealth to afford the luxury of extensive research; part has been the inability of the genteel tradition of Southern humanistic studies to focus seriously on everyday speech, and the parallel failure of social scientists to concern themselves with language. However, the territory is not excessively large, nor is the population history uncharted. [Pederson's operatives have provided a thousand interviews; and carefully designed editorial plans should see publication in another ten or twelve years. The field records, in microfiche, will appear in 1980.]

The *Dictionary of American Regional English* has been a valuable complement to the regional atlases. Occasionally, as in Missouri, the same investigator has participated in both projects. As the *Dictionary* moves into regions already surveyed for the atlases, it makes possible the assaying of changes in speech patterns the last generation has brought.] Industrialization, urbanization, and mass education -- important social forces in America since 1620 -- have noticeably altered the patterns of Southern dialects since 1930. Even the most informal observations will reveal that /-r/ in words like *barn* and *beard* is being pronounced in communities and among people where it would not have been heard before the Hoover Depression, that /ju/ is giving way here and there to /u/ in *tube*, *due*, *new*, *student*, that *morning* and *mourning* are becoming homonyms.

Even without the incentive of Cassidy's *Dictionary*, it would be necessary to see what changes have taken place. A new survey on the scale of the original Atlas might be hard to defend, since rural ways of life have so often given way to urban, so much of rural life itself has altered, and so many rural customs and the words describing them have become obsolete. But it would be feasible to survey much of the same area with a shorter questionnaire, perhaps focused a bit more on city life, designed to elicit all the phonetic contrasts that could be established in the original investigation (and perhaps a few more)[5] and much of the same information on grammar. We may concede that Northerners set the fashion in the southern half of Florida, and that Virginia diphthongs -- especially the centering beginning of /ai/ before voiceless consonants, as in *ice* --

are no longer prestigious around Washington, but we need to know the limits of this attrition, as well as the possible expansion of Southern speechways in other regions. [Pederson's questionnaire for the Gulf States provides a valuable urban supplement for metropolitan areas. The project for Recordings of Standard English, directed by A. L. Davis, has an inventory of potential phonemic contrasts far more extensive than what is offered in any of the regional questionnaires (see A. L. Davis and L. M. Davis 1969).]

In any future work in Southern dialects, it would be desirable to include detailed investigations of urban and metropolitan areas. At the moment, the only city south of the Ohio that has been adequately studied is Louisville (Howren 1958), though the Atlantic Seaboard and North-Central studies provide evidence for at least first-stage investigations of Charleston, Baltimore, Savannah, Richmond, Atlanta, Macon, and Lexington, Kentucky. [Charleston, Savannah, and Augusta, Georgia, have now been studied in more detail (O'Cain 1972, Hopkins 1975, Miller 1978). Pederson's materials include all major cities in the Gulf States.] As yet, nothing is known about the white speech of Memphis, almost nothing on Washington or New Orleans, nothing on Dallas or Houston or Nashville or Chattanooga or St. Louis or Charlotte or Birmingham or Mobile or Miami, to take a few cities at random. For each city an investigation should cover pronunciation and grammar and vocabulary of various ethnic, age, and educational groups. The research design should indicate the traditional differences between cultivated, common, and folk speech in the community -- in Frances Patton's terms, the difference between "representative" people and those who are not; it must then indicate the traditional differences between the speech of the community and that of the surrounding countryside; finally, it must assess the differences that have been wrought by the passage of time -- whether by mass migration from other areas (particularly important in Washington or Miami), or by the normal centripetal processes of industrialization and urbanization and mass education, which may be most important in the textile centers of the Piedmont. In each of these cities we must determine whether the older type of 'elegant' Southern is losing its prestige, and whether or not speech varieties associated with particular castes or classes are becoming more or less alike. A striking index of the growth of racial tensions in Chicago is the fact that the speech of twenty-year-old Chicago-born Negroes differs sharply from that of contemporary Chicago-born whites, while there are sharper differences among the seventy-year-olds of each race than there are between the two races where that generation

is involved. It would not be surprising if social differences in language had decreased in the South at the same time they were increasing elsewhere, but only systematic investigation can give us the answer.

But not merely the cities deserve intensive studies to show the effects of cultural change and the passage of time. The South has possessed some of the most striking relic areas in the English-speaking world -- areas where the lack of a focal city has prevented the outward spread of local forms, but where geographical or cultural isolation or a combination of these has preserved many older forms that have been lost in other regions. The mountains come first to mind, though they are of more recent settlement and of less sharp isolation than lower Delmarva, Albemarle Sound and the Outer Banks, or the Sea Islands. Are relic forms disappearing, or will some remain? And is it possible that the pronunciation of the mountains will be the Standard Southern of tomorrow? As the children of families of high fertility leave lands of low fertility and move into the cities, they will have economic and educational opportunities their fathers never dreamed of; their children in turn may well be the new elite. The cold facts of Southern demography are that the increase in white population, and in the college population, is coming from the foothill and mountain areas and not from the plantation belts. Even now the Appalachian monophthongal /ai/ in *nice white rice* is heard and accepted where it would have been unthinkable before 1930 -- but this does not yet go for the homonymy of *fire* and *far*, of *tired* and *tarred*. Perhaps other forms, once substandard, are becoming a part of cultivated Southern speech. It would be useful -- not only from the point of view of the pure scientist but from that of the practical teacher -- to sort out the changes that are in progress, so that there will be a minimum lag between the facts of change and the myths that are perpetrated and perpetuated in the classroom. [Wolfram and Christian 1976 is a recent, though controversial, study; see the review by Richard Payne (1978).]

A more intensive study of the speech of the Southern mountains is also desirable from the point of view of the Northern cities to which so many Southern rural whites have migrated in recent years. The rapid growth of Akron following the establishment of the rubber shops was due chiefly to West Virginians; in Cuyahoga County (Cleveland), Ohio, it was estimated that 150,000 West Virginians had arrived in the decade following World War II;[6] in Detroit, Southern rural whites are one of the largest cultural groups on the automobile assembly lines; from eastern Kentucky there is constant migration to the aircraft industries of southern Ohio, and in Chicago there are sizable islands of Southern mountaineer settlement on the North Side. The attempts of well-meaning schoolmarms to bulldoze out the characteristic Southern vowels in the name of correctness and elegance have too often encouraged not only resentment of the condescension implied but apathy toward school work in general -- among a group less than fully habituated to the necessity of long-term schooling. The urbanization of the mountaineer cannot succeed unless his speech is better described than it is now, and unless the school program is directed not toward eradicating a regional accent but toward the replacement of indubitably substandard forms with standard ones. [L. M. Davis 1971 treats mountain speech as found in the Chicago settlements.]

But as important as is the study of the speech of relic areas, and especially of the mountains, the study of Negro speech is far more urgent for teaching programs in all parts of the United States. Not only in Chicago and New York, but in cities as far apart as Boston and Las Vegas, Portland, Oregon, and Miami, Milwaukee and Los Angeles, the Negro population has swollen tremendously during the past two decades. In many Northern cities, Negroes constitute a majority of the school population; in Washington they are more than ninety-five percent. In all of these cities the habitual language patterns of the Negro -- a heritage of his status and education in the South, compounded and reinforced by the residential patterns in the North -- set him off strikingly from the local white middle class and constitute serious obstacles to his economic and educational and social advancement. Such grammatical forms as the uninflected third-person singular present (*it make*, *he do*), or the ommision of auxiliaries (*they done dead*, *she been talking about it*) -- common in southern England and heard widely in the South from uneducated whites as well as from Negroes -- are identifiable in Chicago as 'Negro forms,' by which an unsophisticated teacher can consistently tell the race of the author of a theme. And the same situation is repeated in Oakland and Cleveland and dozens of other cities. Confronted with grammatical problems that will not yield to the conventional middle-class-oriented correction exercises, the Northern teacher either attempts -- and usually unsuccessfully -- to eradicate the home dialect completely or gives up in despair; in either event, the language practices of Northern urban Negroes are one of the principal reasons why Negro unemployment and the consequent relief load remain high, despite a growing number of jobs for skilled labor and service employees. Nothing short of a better-designed teaching program, based upon accurate knowledge of

Southern Negro speech, will suffice; for as fast as a description of Harlem or the South Side is established, new migrants come in to disturb the pattern.

Here is our greatest lack of data. Both Gullah and Louisiana Negro French are rather special cases; and the available description of Gullah is so skewed in the direction of African survivals that much of its structural system has to be inferred (see Kurath 1972:118-24). The Memphis study (Williamson 1968), on the other hand, deals only implicitly with the norms of local cultivated white speech. For the Atlantic Seaboard the Atlas sampling of Negro speech was far coarser than that of white speech -- some fifty records in all. [Pederson has tried to sample Negro speech of all cultural levels throughout the Gulf States.] Even this small sampling would probably show if there is any consistent structural difference between Negro and white speech, since each of these interviews is paired with one for a Southern white of comparable education and social status; few comparisons have been undertaken (Greibeslund 1970, Dorrill 1975). But one should not rest satisfied even with such a study; it would be desirable to make intensive studies of Negro speech in a variety of communities, Northern and Western as well as Southern, with particular attention to unguarded conversation. In such studies many hypotheses could be tested. Some observers have recently asserted that American Negro speech has a different "deep structure" from that of white speech, and they would derive it from an underlying *Gemeinnegrischpidgin*. To a naive social scientist, what is generally known about the operations of the domestic slave trade should be sufficient to refute such an argument; the variety of Negro accents heard in Woodlawn and Englewood (in Chicago) make one wary of simple explanations. Nevertheless, since the arguments have been so plausibly put, by linguists with serious credentials (e.g., Bailey 1965, 1966), it would be well to have enough data, from a wide enough spectrum of communities, to sort out fact from fancy.

One would also like to see a fuller record of language data in those communities where non-English dialects are still spoken, or where speakers of such languages have migrated heavily in recent years. Of rather high priority in the first category are the Spanish-Americans of the Southwest and the Cajuns of southern Louisiana. In 1940, in Lafayette, Louisiana, it was locally estimated that there were three or four hundred thousand native Louisianians for whom French was the native tongue; the inadequacy of the U.S. Census reports -- the 1960 census asked only for the mother tongue of the foreign-born -- gives us barely 1200 speakers of French in Louisiana. Though it is possible that even the Cajun birth-rate cannot compensate for the erosion of their way of life, native speakers of Cajun French are still numerous in Louisiana; furthermore, the conditions under which English is normally acquired in the older French communities of Louisiana are likely to produce dialects little more than *de facto* pidgins. Those who have struggled with Cajun graduates of Louisiana high schools -- many of whom brought to college four years of official exposure to English but an inability to read, write, speak, or understand a standard English paragraph -- would feel that an investigation of Louisiana French, and of the English spoken in areas if French colonization, is still needed. The same is true for border Spanish, and for the English of southwest Texas, in spite of the valuable evidence in Sawyer 1957; in such cities as Miami, where two or more Spanish-speaking groups have settled in recent years, the problem is even more complicated. And though native speakers of German or Czech or Cherokee are not numerous statistically, an examination of Southern dialects of those languages, and of the English spoken by those groups, could teach us much about the problems of language contact. [Pederson's survey and Gilbert's investigations provide at least the beginnings of what is needed.]

Along with the study of Southern speech, English and otherwise, in its multifarious varieties, we should undertake studies of the other aspects of face-to-face communication, even though the exact description of their phenomena is yet to be worked out. We know that language signals alone are not enough; we often comment, "What he said was all right, but I didn't like the way he said it." The way a person says his message involves a number of modalities: *proxemics*, or spatial relationships, including the distance at which communication becomes possible; *haptics*, or matters of physical contact; *kinesics*, or gestures and other bodily movements (Birdwhistell 1952; Pittenger, Hockett, and Danehy 1960); *paralanguage*, or such modulations of the stream of speech as give unusually high or low pitch, unusual loudness or softness, drawl, clipping, nasality, and rasp (Austin 1965). And coming back closer to the essential phenomena of English, no one has yet worked out a systematic comparison of the way dialects differ in stress and pitch and transitions between syllables. Yet these differences are felt so intuitively in the South that by them one can often place an inhabitant of the coastal plain within a few miles of his home -- even if, as with some clergy-men and other public performers, he has taken pains to conceal his origins.

Finally, we need studies of reactions to particular kinds of dialect differences. No region escapes petty ethnocentrism in this respect. A test administered to middle-class white Chicagoans discloses that they consistently interpret the speech of urban-reared white Southern college professors as that of rural uneducated Negroes: the educated Southerner has all the superficial characteristics that Chicagoans associate with Southern Negro speech, notably the loss of postvocalic /-r/ in *barn* and the like (Pederson 1965a). But to redress the balance, there are many Southern professional men who wonder why the educated Northerner sounds so much like the uneducated Southerner: here they are prejudiced because the strong postvocalic /-r/ associated with the Middle West is heard in the South most often from mountaineers, from textile workers, and from marginal farmers in the sand hills and pine barrens. Both reactions are visceral, rather than intellectual; sufficient publicity for both would help to break down the notion that one dialect is inherently better or worse than another, and would strengthen the American tradition of cultural pluralism, by which the best speech for a person to imitate is simply the educated speech of his own community.

It is clear that the amount of work to be done on Southern dialects -- as indeed on the dialects of any American region -- is staggering; but it is also clear that established methods make it possible for us to get very far toward our objectives if we could only have a modest amount of money and a few competent investigators in addition to those already available. The cost of the full set of projects here proposed would perhaps come to a million dollars; an intelligent application of the knowledge to be obtained could probably save that amount in one year in the city of Chicago alone.

NOTES

[1] "Consensus English" has been used by Priscilla Tyler of the University of Missouri, Kansas City; "network English" by William Stewart of Washington, D.C. The diversity of educated accents to be encountered on the streets of Atlanta or New Orleans suggests that we are still far from even a 'consensus Southern.'

[2] This is an *ad hoc* list, based on popular notions. A more accurate -- and more diffident -- summary, first put together by Atwood with the help of other workers on the Atlas project, is to be found in Francis 1958:513-27.

[3] The monophthongal [a·] is identified with the

vowel of *father* when that vowel is somewhat fronted in Northern speech; with the vowel of *rat* when that vowel is lowered. Needless to say, the Southern speaker makes the contrast; the falling together is in the perception of the Northerner. This Southern monophthongal pronunciation in *ice* can create social difficulties in Northern settings.

[4] The method of the Atlas project is summarized in Francis 1958, discussed at length in Kurath *et al.* 1939.

[5] For instance, additional items might show whether there is a two-way or a three-way contrast (or any at all) involving such words as *had*, *sad*, *bad*, or whether there is a contrast between the stressed vowels in such pairs as *scissors:schism*, *sister:system*, *ribbon:ribbing*.

[6] The estimates for Cleveland are informal ones; for Akron there are fairly detailed statistics, and some suggestions why official figures may underestimate the immigration, in Udell 1966.

The times have never been more favorable for analyzing the patterns of Southern speech. First, we now have massive quantities of data, which we never had before; some of it is already accessible to scholars, whatever their residence, and there will be more to come as the *Linguistic Atlas of the Middle and South Atlantic States* (Kurath *et al.* 1979-) finds its way into print [and the records for the Gulf States become accessible]. Second, there is nationwide concern with some of the varieties of Southern speech; as the less-educated Southerners flock to Northern and Eastern cities in search of new opportunities, their pronunciation seems out of place in their new habitat, and their grammar stands in the way of their getting as far in school or in business as their abilities would normally justify. Finally, many of the most important national concerns have been expressed in Southern accents. Despite the bitterness of professional Bostonians, no president has worked harder than Lyndon Johnson for the general welfare, and his efforts have been eloquently supported by those of Martin Luther King and Ralph Abernathy. Nor does the change in administration greatly alter the realities of the situation. Whatever the motives for his "Southern Strategy," Richard Nixon was prepared to accept Southerners as human beings; and Jimmy Carter brought to the White House another variety of Southern speech, with a less flamboyant style but a potentially greater achievement.

So now, in looking at the speech of the South against the background of other varieties of English -- United States, Canadian, British and Commonwealth -- we may begin by deflating a few old myths, some related particularly to Southern speech, but most of them with far wider implications.

The uniformity of Southern speech is grossly exaggerated. Many of our friends from further North speak of "*the* Southern accent" as if it were something monolithic. Actually, within the territory where Southern traditions are important, there is evidence of at least three major speech types: 1) Southern proper, the speech of the old plantation country; 2) South Midland, the speech of the Southern Uplands, ultimately affiliated with that of western Pennsylvania; and 3) North Midland, the speech of Pennsylvania and its immediate dependencies. Within these regional patterns one finds at least nine clearly

marked areas of consequence in the pre-Revolutionary South alone and a number of minor areas (Kurath 1949; for a summary of research see Mencken 1963:Ch. 7, Sec. 4); even a preliminary examination shows more than half a dozen areas in Louisiana and Texas; when the returns are in we can expect to find at least thirty important subvarieties of Southern speech, to say nothing of reflexes of foreign-language settlements of European origin and the semi-creolized dialect of the Gullah Negroes. Truly, as Hans Kurath has repeatedly remarked, the South has the greatest diversity of speech forms to be found in English-speaking North America, with the possible exception of Newfoundland.

The origins of Southern dialects are also generally misunderstood. Many casual observers assert that the warm climate is responsible for a languid drawl. But even if a drawl were a general characteristic of Southern speech -- as it is not -- those who believe in the effects of hot climate would be confounded by the rapid-fire dialogue of the Bengali in eastern India. Similarly, the nasality of Southern Upland speech cannot be explained by either excessive rainfall or excessive dryness -- and both explanations have been offered. More prosaic causes -- social forces -- are responsible.

Nor are there physiological reasons. Though many laymen will assert that there are racial differences in speech, independent of region or education, the solid evidence is all on the other side. In controlled tests, Chicago middle-class whites have consistently identified as the voice of a rural uneducated Negro that of an urban educated Southern-born white -- and Southerners are no more accurate (R. McDavid and Austin 1966). Educated Negroes in Charleston sound much more like the Pinkneys and Rutledges than either group sounds like the uneducated of either race. Concededly, centuries of separate and unequal opportunities have left the average Southern Negro with a larger residue of folk pronunciations and nonstandard grammatical forms; but where investigators have interviewed Negroes and whites in the same community, with equivalent education and income, there is no consistent difference. In a few situations the values are even reversed: before 1954, West Virginia State College had an elite Negro student body -- for the most part the children of highly skilled craftsmen and high-level service employees -- and a distinguished faculty, with degrees from such universities as Northwestern and Chicago. With desegregation, the school began to attract the disadvantaged from the mountains and has had a constant struggle to maintain standards in the face of increasing white enrollment.

It is thus no wonder that popular accounts of the features of Southern dialect should often be wide of the mark. What is referred to as 'the Southern drawl' is probably not a feature of language *per se*; it is rather something else -- a relatively greater length of strong-stressed syllables in comparison with weak-stressed ones. For example, in the American Middle West, the first syllable of *highness* will be perhaps twice as long as the last; in much of the South it will be three or four times as long. But even in the South this 'drawl' is far from universal. It does not appear in Charleston speech, nor in Gullah -- and even where it occurs, the tempo may be far from languid; the effect of drawl may be created by lengthening the strong-stressed syllables and shortening the weak-stressed ones, while the overall tempo remains rapid. The loss of postvocalic /-r/ in *barn*, *beard* and the like -- traditionally associated with 'Southern speech' -- is also far from universal in the South; its distribution is complex, part regional and part social. And the so-called 'broad *a*' [ɑ] in *half*, *past*, *dance* and *tomatoes* is normal for only a small number of Southerners, even among the oldest and best families.

We are thus driven away from our folk beliefs toward the same forces that have created dialect differences elsewhere and at other times.

The most important cause is the pattern of settlement.

Immigrants to a new area bring their speech with them. Students of German dialects still take as their starting point the settlements of Germanic tribes in the fifth and sixth centuries and label certain features of present-day German as Franconian or Alemannic in origin. In the same way it is often possible to identify an American dialect feature with early settlements, say, from East Anglia or Northern Ireland. Since the impact of languages other than English is greatest in the areas where those languages were spoken, one can expect a high incidence of Spanish loans in West Texas, of French loans in southern Louisiana, of German loans in the Shenandoah Valley and on the Yadkin, and of Africanisms in the Sea Islands.

Similarly, speech forms are normally transmitted along major routes of migration and communication. Features of Parisian speech have followed the Rhône to the Mediterranean; features of Pittsburgh speech have moved down the Ohio into the Mississippi Valley. Conversely, a barrier to migration may become a dialect boundary: the Blue Ridge prevented expansion of the Virginia Piedmont in the eighteenth century, and today there is no sharper dialect boundary in the English-speaking world. Not only linguistic traits but other cultural ones are affected by such boundaries. Notice that the Virginia Piedmont prevailingly has the small Southern haystack built around a center pole; the Shenandoah generally has the long Pennsylvania rick or the square stack without a center pole. In vocabulary, in pronunciation, in haystack shapes, in folk songs, in all aspects of traditional life, the influence of the old geographic barrier is still felt.

Ancient political boundaries sometimes become dialect boundaries. In the Rhineland, as Leonard Bloomfield has pointed out, linguistic differences often follow the boundaries of medieval German principalities that were liquidated by Napoleon. In the United States, where political boundaries have rarely constituted a barrier to the movements of people or goods, state lines are much less important; nonetheless, *county site* is common in Georgia as a synonym for *county seat*, but unknown in South Carolina. And if two adjacent states differ in the quality of their educational systems, the political boundary may mark the limits of linguistic features; time and again, Pennsylvania will lack old-fashioned pronunciations or grammatical features that are very common in Maryland and the states further south. The schoolmasters of Pennsylvania simply did a more thorough job.

Where a city or a cluster of cities becomes an important cultural focus, its speech forms will spread into the surrounding area and even beyond. The Fall Line cities of the Virginia Piedmont -- Fredericksburg-Falmouth, Richmond and Petersburg -- have dominated Virginia speech; and the pronunciations of their first families have been emulated in Winchester, in Roanoke, and even in Charleston, West Virginia. In South Carolina, Charleston has played a role similar to that of Richmond and its sister cities in Virginia. In the Gulf States and Mississippi Valley the plantation pronunciation [ɜɪ] in *bird* and the like (a pronunciation strongly resembling what was once common in metropolitan New York, but lacking the stigma of the latter) is found in southeastern Alabama and the Tennessee Valley (but not around Birmingham), in New Orleans and in Vicksburg -- to cite a few instances. Has this radiated from Montgomery or from New Orleans or both?

Finally, the social structure of an area will determine where the sharpest social distinctions in language happen to lie. In the Old South there was a sharp difference between the 'old families' and the rest of the population; in Virginia, when the original surveys for the Atlas were conducted, only in this group did one find the 'broad a' in *dance* or the /æ/ vowel of *patch* in *catch*, instead of the more common /ɛ/ of *fetch*. In inland communities the class markers in language were most likely to be those associated with education, notably the consistent use of the standard preterites and participles of irregular verbs: *I saw*, *did*, *ran* and the like.

If we take the Southern evidence from the first stage of the Linguistic Atlas project, and extrapolate for areas yet uninvestigated, we find a few clear patterns. For our practical purposes we will consider the territorial South as consisting of the fifteen slave states of 1860, plus Oklahoma.[1] Our conclusions are surest for the area from the Mason-Dixon line to the Ocmulgee and northeastern Florida, and almost as sure for Kentucky.

Along the northern boundary we find considerable influence of the North Midland region -- the area settled by the westward expansion of Pennsylvania. West Virginia north of the Kanawha watershed is North Midland, though without a focus to balance against the influence of the Pittsburgh area; its most characteristic feature to outlanders is the intrusive /r/ in *wash*, *push*, *bushel*, *judge*, *mush*. Further east, the Pennsylvania German area and the Delaware Valley with the cultural focus at Philadelphia have long influenced parts of Maryland and Virginia. There are offshoots of the Pennsylvania German settlements in both central Maryland and the Shenandoah Valley. In Delaware there is a major speech boundary between Wilmington and the more rural southern part of the state; the strength of this boundary suggests that Wilmington has been a cultural satellite of Philadelphia since before the Revolution. Baltimore, a latecomer as Atlantic Seaboard communities go, had a well-defined core of old Southern families, but soon came under the influence of Philadelphia. Today, with industrialization, its ties to the North Midland are growing stronger, those to the South growing weaker. This tendency was evident even as early as the 1930's, when for practical purposes the regional boundary ran through the city, but younger and better educated speakers favored North Midland forms. Postvocalic /-r/ was pronounced; *horse* and *hoarse* were homonyms; *whip* and the like began with /w-/, not with /hw-/.

The South Midland region also derives from Pennsylvania, but less directly. In the middle of the eighteenth century, when the Ulster Scots in Pennsylvania reached the Alleghenies and found further progress westward blocked by the French and their Indian allies, they turned southwest into the Shenandoah. Some of them recrossed the Blue Ridge and followed the eastern slopes into the Piedmont of the Carolinas and Georgia; others descended the Clinch and Holston to the neighborhood of Knoxville and beyond; still others followed the Kanawha into the Ohio Valley. In the beginning, these Ulstermen were strongly opposed to the institutions and mores of the Plantation South; they were independent subsistence farmers, with little use for money crops or chattel slavery; their traditions are reflected by the migration of the Lincolns into the free land north of the Ohio, by the fission of West Virginia from the parent state and by the continuing political cleavage between planter and mountaineer in nearly every part of the South. The picture is obscured, however, by other facts of cultural and political history: in all of the South, as cotton became profitable and the decay of chattel slavery was arrested, money crop agriculture spread into the upper Piedmont and the rich bottom lands of the inland rivers; local government fell into the hands of those who accomodated themselves to the interests of the plantation economy; local autonomy was suppressed behind a facade of "states rights" and "the Solid South." Despite the extent of the South Midland settlements -- from Harper's Ferry to San Antonio -- it was not until after the Confederate War that the region developed cultural foci comparable to Philadelphia and Pittsburgh in the North Midland. Louisville, Lexington, Nashville, Memphis were outposts of the cultural values enunciated in Richmond, Charleston, Savannah, Montgomery, and New Orleans. Linguistically, the South Midland has been passive until recent years, receptive to speech forms from outside foci -- occasionally the North Midland but more generally the planting and mercantile coastal South. The prevalent loss of postvocalic /-r/ in the uplands among younger and more sophisticated speakers -- as in *park your car* -- is a case in point: in my boyhood in Greenville, South Carolina, this loss was characteristic of young people of better families in the city; outside the city, the small farmers, mountaineers and textile workers retained the /-r/ essentially unimpaired. The receptivity of the South Midland to plantation speech forms has led to debate among scholars as to whether it belongs dialectally with the Midland or the South.[2] In either event, its transitional quality is undeniable.

Passive though the South Midland is in comparison with the South, it has its own subdivisions. At least three of these have been identified along the Atlantic Seaboard: 1) the Shenandoah Valley; 2) Southern West Virginia, with southwestern Virginia and eastern Kentucky; 3) the Carolina and Georgia mountains. Each has a few characteristic features, though -- as with the South Midland in general --

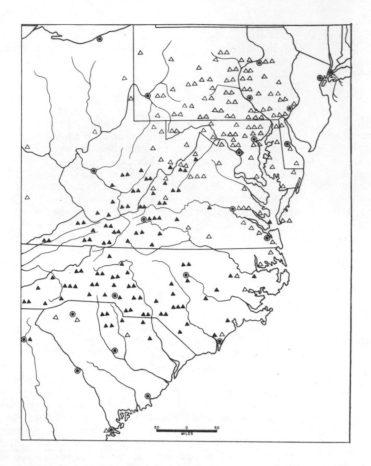

Map 1

Migration from Pennsylvania

△ *flannel cake* 'pancake'

▲ *family pie* 'cobbler'

features not shared with other areas are
fewer than one might expect.

The Shenandoah Valley was historically a
route of diffusion of Midland settlers
from Pennsylvania into the Southern uplands. Few words mark this route: *flannel cake* 'pancake,' focusing in Philadelphia and extending to the head of the Valley; *family pie* 'cobbler,' beginning in
the Shenandoah and spreading into the
Carolina Piedmont (Map 1).

West Virginia from the Kanawha south,
along with southwestern Virginia and the
easternmost counties of Kentucky, has a
few peculiar words of its own. Perhaps
the most characteristic is *hobby* or *hobby
bread*, to designate a small hand-shaped
loaf of cornbread, smaller than the traditional *pone*, and generally baked three to
an oven or skillet. Less widespread in
West Virginia, but extending through the
Carolina mountains, is *redworm*, a regional
term for *earthworm* (Map 2). A few mountain terms extend toward the seacoast,
along the valleys of the Yadkin-Pee Dee
and the Cape Fear, with the speech of
mountain Ulstermen and Cape Fear Highland-
ers for once reinforcing each other.
Among these words are *big house* for the
living room and *fireboard* for the mantelpiece (Map 3). Yet none of these South
Midland areas is well defined; all are
under pressure from both the older plantation centers and the newer cities.

The areas of the South proper have been
much more distinctive than those of the
South Midland, because (as noted) every
focal community lay in the plantation
area; plantation families that prospered
with the plantations set the prestige
patterns.

Throughout the South there are a few
words of general currency. One of the
most typical -- if somewhat less frequently heard today, in a generation of technological change -- is *lightwood* /laitəd/
(homonymous with the plantation pronunciation of *lightered*) for fatty pine kindling. Equally characteristic is *blate*
'bawl' (the sound made by a calf), as illustrated on Map 4. But even within the
South there are a few well-defined belts.
Along the coast below the Fall Line, the
dragon fly is a *mosquito hawk*, a clingstone peach is a *press peach*, and *budget*,
bulge, *bulk* have the vowel of *cut*; above
the Fall Line, we find, respectively,
snake doctor, *plum peach*, and the vowel of
put (Map 5).

The two strongest focal areas in the Old
South, the Virginia Piedmont and the
Charleston area, have several things in
common. In pronunciation, the two areas
share with Canadian speech striking alternations of the diphthongs /ai/ and /au/
according to the phonetic environment,
with a strongly centralized variety occurring before voiceless consonants, as in

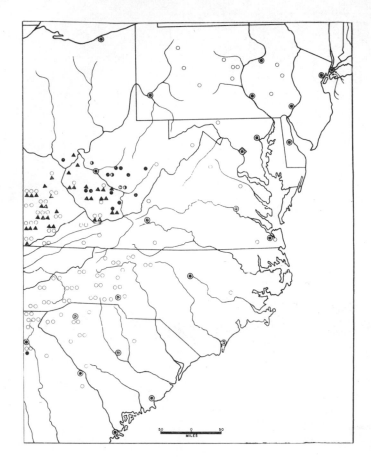

Map 2

Southern Mountains

○   *redworm* 'earthworm'

▲   *hobby* 'small corn cake'

●   *check* 'lunch'

◑   *jackbite* 'lunch'

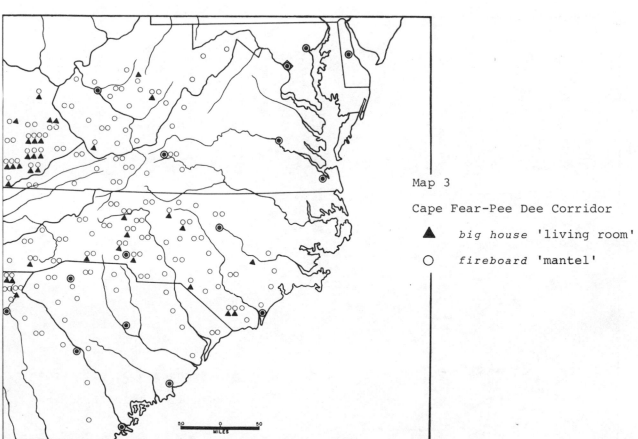

Map 3

Cape Fear-Pee Dee Corridor

▲   *big house* 'living room'

○   *fireboard* 'mantel'

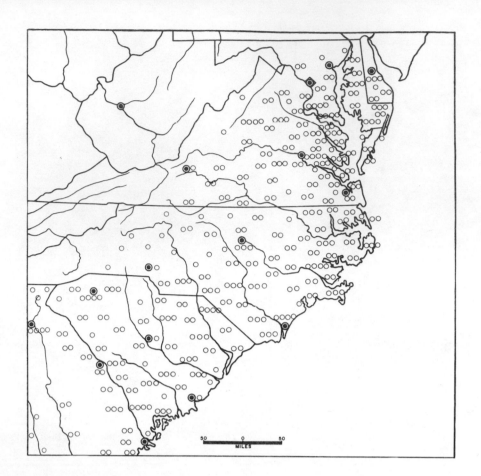

Map 4

The South

○   *blate* 'bawl'

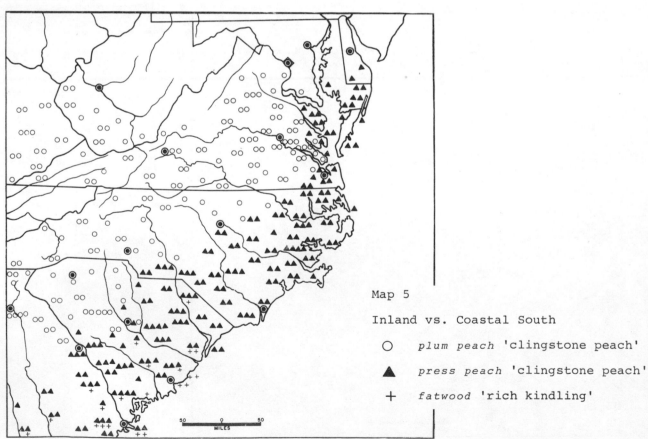

Map 5

Inland vs. Coastal South

○   *plum peach* 'clingstone peach'

▲   *press peach* 'clingstone peach'

+   *fatwood* 'rich kindling'

[300]

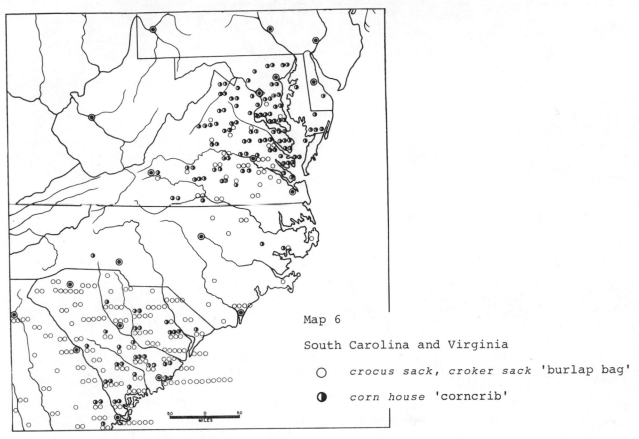

Map 6

South Carolina and Virginia

○　*crocus sack, croker sack* 'burlap bag'

◐　*corn house* 'corncrib'

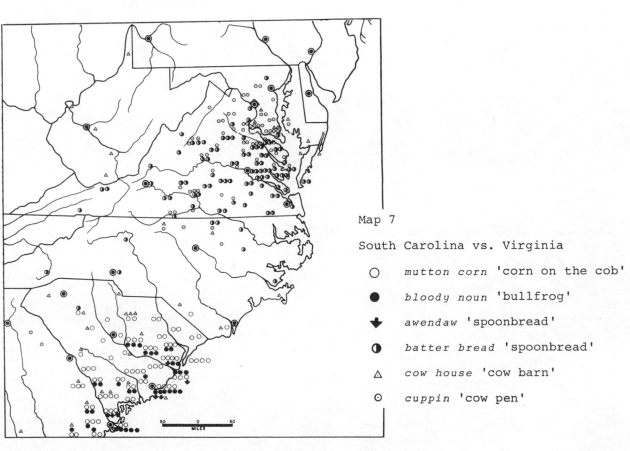

Map 7

South Carolina vs. Virginia

○　*mutton corn* 'corn on the cob'

●　*bloody noun* 'bullfrog'

▼　*awendaw* 'spoonbread'

◐　*batter bread* 'spoonbread'

△　*cow house* 'cow barn'

⊙　*cuppin* 'cow pen'

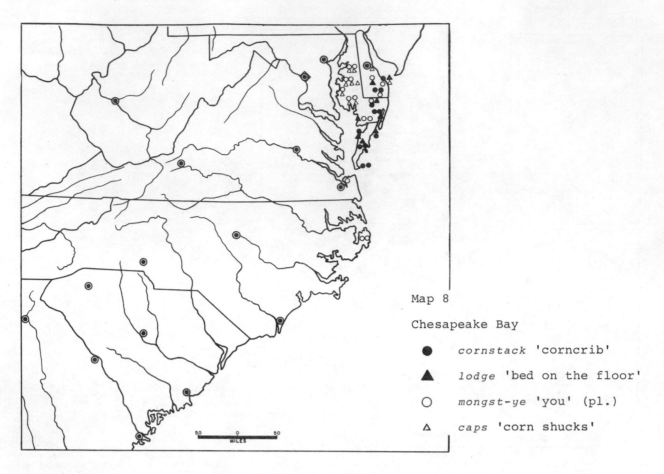

Map 8

Chesapeake Bay

●   *cornstack* 'corncrib'

▲   *lodge* 'bed on the floor'

○   *mongst-ye* 'you' (pl.)

△   *caps* 'corn shucks'

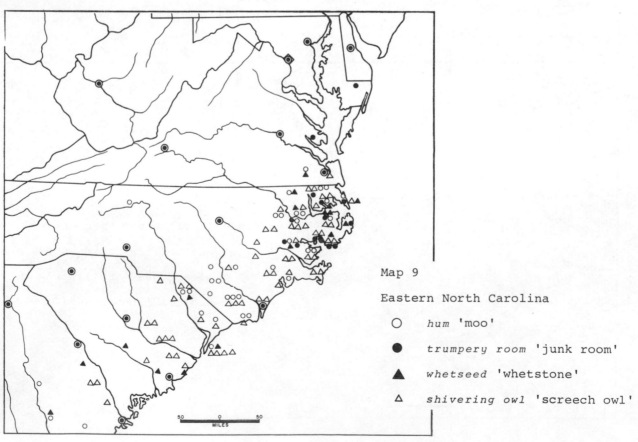

Map 9

Eastern North Carolina

○   *hum* 'moo'

●   *trumpery room* 'junk room'

▲   *whetseed* 'whetstone'

△   *shivering owl* 'screech owl'

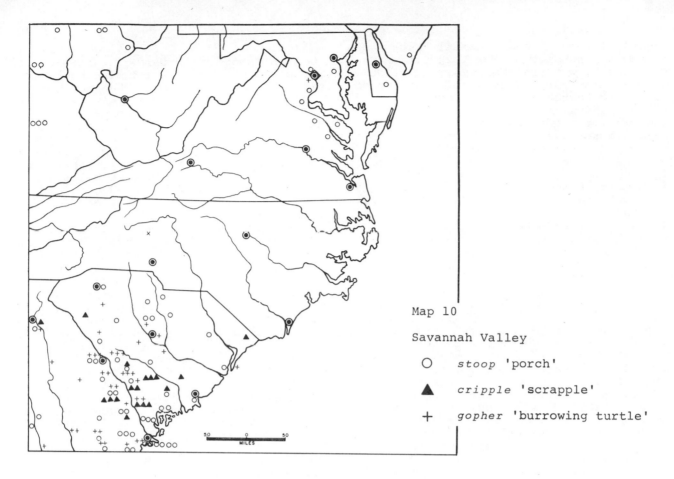

Map 10

Savannah Valley

○   *stoop* 'porch'

▲   *cripple* 'scrapple'

+   *gopher* 'burrowing turtle'

ice and *house*. A few vocabulary items are also shared, such as *corn house* for *corn-crib* and *croker sack* for burlap bag (Map 6). In other respects, however, the two areas are sharply different. Virginia has the Africanism *goober* for peanut; South Carolina has *pinder*. Virginians call spoonbread *batter bread* -- a term unknown in South Carolina. Conversely, *mutton corn* for the more common *roasting ears* is a South Carolina term unfamiliar to Virginians. Such traditional Virginia pronunciations as /əfrɛd/ for *afraid* and /hʌm/ for *home* are not found in Charleston, whose peculiar ingliding /e/ and /o/, as in *date* and *boat*, sound as exotic in Richmond as in Dubuque (Map 7).

In contrast to focal areas like the Virginia Piedmont and the South Carolina Low-Country, the Old South has its relic areas, lacking influential centers to make their words and pronunciations fashionable; as a result their characteristic speech forms are chiefly retained by the older and less sophisticated, with others taking on the usage of the Virginia Piedmont, the South in general, or the nation as a whole.

One of the most striking relic areas has been Chesapeake Bay, heavily indented with bays and tidal rivers that have inhibited communication until the last two decades. Here we find *cow pound* for the more common *cow lot*, *caps* for *corn shucks*, *cornstack*

for *corncrib*, *baseborn* (*child*) for *bas-tard*, *mongst-ye* instead of *you-all* as the polite plural, and the archaic *housen* for *houses* (Map 8). Eastern North Carolina, caught between the two adjacent mountains of conceit, tenuously preserves *shivering owl* for *screech owl* and *hum* as a synonym for *moo*; *trumpery room* (instead of the Virginia *lumber room* or the more common *junk room*) and *whetseed* for *whetstone*, are practically confined to the shores of Albemarle Sound (Map 9). Further south, there are relics of German settlement around Salisbury, North Carolina, and Newberry, South Carolina -- with survivals of *rainworm* for *earthworm* and *smearcase* for *cottage cheese*. The Ulster Scots settlement around Kingstree, South Carolina, has kept the Northern Irish *chay!* as a call to cows. The descendants of the Saltzburgers in the Savannah Valley still use *cripple* to designate the delicacy known in Philadelphia as *scrapple* -- the term apparently coming from a South German word meaning drippings. The Savannah Valley also uses *stoop* for *porch*, especially an unroofed one; since *stoop* is tradi-tionally derived from Dutch and associated with the Hudson Valley, its occurrence along the Savannah -- where there was no Holland Dutch settlement -- so far is in-explicable. Perhaps the term was brought south by the architects who designed the mansions of the Savannah well-to-do --

houses with more than a casual resemblance to the brownstones of New York City. Further south, with the territory undefined, we encounter *gopher* designating a kind of burrowing turtle and *prairie* designating a damp meadowland -- their oldest meanings in North American English, if somewhat overshadowed by what they refer to in the upper Mississippi Valley (Map 10).

Although there is little evidence to distinguish the speech of Southern Negroes from that of Southern whites with comparable social advantages, there is one striking exception: the Gullah country of the South Carolina-Georgia coast. In this area, large numbers of slaves were imported in a relatively short time to work such money crops as indigo, rice and Sea Island cotton; endemic malaria discouraged white settlers, and encouraged long summer absences on the part of the few who lived there. Slavery, peonage, swamps and tidal rivers discouraged movement. For these reasons many speech forms of probable African origin are still established in these communities, though hardly known inland; in the same area the forces of geographical and cultural isolation also preserved old and humble speech forms that the slaves acquired from the whites among whom they worked.[3]

To this point we speak on the basis of systematic evidence elicited in personal interviews by trained investigators. Once we cross the Appalachians, however, we are without this kind of evidence so far, save for Kentucky and Oklahoma and a few local studies. Nevertheless, the evidence we have is sufficient for an observer to make certain general observations on the patterns of Southern dialects before the age of mass-production industry and the subsequent age of automation.

In the New South, as in the Old, social differences in language were more sharply marked than in the regions to the North. Status was determined by family background, education and wealth, with family at least ostensibly the most important -- since the older families dominated the economy and had most of the opportunities for education and other indices of cultural prestige. Many schools designed for the less affluent soon became oriented to the dominant system of values; typical was Sweet Briar, originally founded to educate Virginia mountain girls, but by the 1920's popularly regarded as an advanced finishing school. The outsiders who built up new fortunes by skill or luck or a convenient lack of scruples adjusted so skillfully to the prevailing patterns of prestige that the community often forgot their humble beginnings -- even in the first generation of prominence.[4] And the common economic ruin following the Confederate War only emphasized the inalienable advantages of family and culture, as contrasted with the ephemeral status of wealth.

As the South expanded westward, Southern society continued to be dominated by the planters and merchants. When cotton culture expanded in the early nineteenth century, the plantation system -- and with it, a relatively large slave population -- spread into rich upland areas. Some of the original South Midland small farmers rose into the planter class; others were pushed into the unproductive hills and pine barrens, crossed the Ohio into territory where slavery was forbidden (the Lincolns are the most notable representatives), or pushed further west. The social distinction between the planter and the redneck was fundamental in Southern society; the planters, a small minority, manipulated the political attitudes of the region for at least a generation after Reconstruction, and by such political contrivances as the creation of new counties with disproportionate representation kept at least a veto on significant legislative change until the recent decisions of the Federal courts.

But the planter group of the inland South was far more diverse than its coastal counterpart. A few of the older families, like the Hamptons and Hugers, either added new plantations in the Mississippi Valley to their older holdings along the coast or transferred the bulk of their operations from exhausted soil to new. They found, however, a local planter group -- mostly French -- already established and were soon augmented by the successful entrepreneurs who had made wealth on the frontier -- as gory and violent as any of the later manifestations of the American tradition of the Wild West. As a consequence of this mobility, many features originally associated with the South Midland found their way into plantation speech, even in those areas most heavily settled from the plantation belt of the Old South.

The westward dialectal expansion of the Old South is a crazy quilt if compared to the orderly and well-marked belts of coastal plain, Piedmont and mountains that we find along the Atlantic. Even in eastern Georgia the pattern begins to be confused, with the plantation areas expanding inland largely between the Savannah and the Ogeechee, and then sweeping west across the Piedmont; however, barely thirty miles west of Brunswick and St. Marys we encounter swamps, wiregrass and piney woods, settled by marginal farmers. Cherokees and Creeks long blocked expansion into the lower valleys of the Chattahoochee and Flint, which were first settled by land-hungry uplanders rather than by the westward extension of plantation holdings. The fertile bottom lands of the Mississippi and its tributaries produced an intricate interlacing of plantation and small farming areas, with the respective domination by Southern and South Midland features. To take one characteristic example, the Black Belt of Alabama, the lower Mississippi Valley, and the Tennessee Valley towns as far upriver as Athens and Decatur show the loss of /r/ coloring in *barn*, *beard* and *bird* -- and often in the last the diphthong associated with older New York City speech; but the hill country around Birmingham and the pinelands of eastern Mississippi exhibit an /r/ as strong as anything to be found in the Middle West. A similar crazy-quilt pattern would not be unlikely in Arkansas and Missouri.

The territorial expansion of the South was not conducted solely by Southerners and South Midlanders. Pennsylvanians, Yankees and York Staters pushed into Missouri; in combination with the German exiles and the mountaineers who had always opposed slavery, they were able to keep the *Show Me State* in the Union -- though at the price of local feuds that started Jesse James on his short career as an outlaw and on his longer one as the first juvenile delinquent to become a folk hero. And though the American Indians -- except in Oklahoma -- were largely brushed aside, two other groups maintained their identity, and indeed modified the invading Anglo-American culture: the Spanish-Americans of Texas and the French of Louisiana. Loans from these two groups, in fact, mark respectively the two principal focal areas of the Gulf States: the hacienda country of the Southwest and the plantation area of southern Louisiana, with its metropolitan focus at New Orleans. Since these patterns persist in the vocabulary despite the cultural changes of the last fifty years, it is likely that they will also be found in pronunciation and even in grammar. Other probable focal areas in the New South -- though the extent of their influence has not yet been determined -- are the Kentucky Blue Grass, Metropolitan St. Louis, Memphis, the Nashville Basin and the Montgomery-Mobile axis in southern Alabama.

Since dialect patterns are rarely static, particularly in times when the population is rapidly growing, we should have expected this outline of Southern dialect patterns to have been modified over the past generation by the simple passage of time. But modification has been accelerated by a number of fundamental economic and social changes whose impact is likely to be even greater in the future.

The three principal forces operating in American society to create a different dialect situation from that to be found in Europe have been industrialization, urbanization, and general education. For a long time these forces were less active in the South than in other regions. In comparison with other parts of the United States, the Southern regions have been the most predominantly agricultural (with a large proportion of small, marginal farms), the most predominantly rural, the least literate and sophisticated. Although in all of these respects the South as a whole is still behind the rest of the nation, the discrepancy is far less than it used to be. In industry and education the best Southern achievements rank with the best in other regions, though they are much less numerous.

Industrialization began in the 1830's, when such leaders as William Gregg developed cotton mills to provide employment for poor whites crowded off the land by the competition of slave labor and the low fertility of subsistence farms; to Gregg is due the unhappy tradition of Southern textiles as the most segregated and least unionized American industry. But it was not till after Reconstruction that the era of textile expansion began. Throughout the Piedmont of the South Atlantic states, almost every county seat and many smaller places became ringed with cotton mills, whose operatives -- in company villages, with company stores, company schools and company churches -- became a *de facto* third race in the pattern of segregation. Drawn from the pine barrens, the sandhills, the mountains and other areas of marginal farming, the textile workers swelled the population of urban areas; though their speech had little prestige, they altered the structure of urban society in such a way that through the educational opportunities of their children and grandchildren they would inevitably affect the patterns of local cultivated speech.

Though textiles was the first industry to become established in the South, it was not alone. Tobacco manufacturing and coal mining soon followed -- both, like textiles, employing relatively low-skilled labor at the outset and suffering disproportionately from economic cycles. But more sophisticated industries ultimately developed -- steel, paper, shipbuilding, aircraft manufacturing among them. Especially on the Gulf coast, large fields of oil and gas brought rapid industrialization, centering first on refining and then on petrochemicals. And the tendency of giant corporations to decentralize only hastened the industrialization of the South.

Industrialization requires the easy movement of raw materials to the factory and of finished products to the consumer. The industrializing South eagerly improved its means of transportation -- railroads, roads, waterways. Moreover, since the distribution of industrial products is most efficiently handled through larger centers, industrialization inevitably led to the growth of cities. The urbanization of the South was also furthered by the general mechanization of agriculture and by the specific decline in cotton growing and the rise of timber cropping and cattle raising, which required fewer hands and sent large numbers to the towns. The stores and services -- from groceries to gin mills -- that sprang up to supply the mill workers and handle industrial products absorbed much of the labor surplus; some of the new arrivals quickly moved into the growing middle class, which was also swelled by newcomers from other regions. The expansion of Southern cities has been uneven; but this has been true in other regions as well. Some, despite their size, have remained little more than overgrown mill villages; some -- like the Texas metropolises -- have ostentatiously displayed great wealth and a reactionary social philosophy; a few, notably Atlanta, have walked open-eyed into the twentieth century and developed a character of their own. But throughout the South the typical cultural leader everywhere is now not the planter but the urban businessman, often not a Southerner except by adoption.

For the industrialization and urbanization of the South could not have been accomplished on Southern resources alone. With plentiful natural resources and a large labor supply, the region had a shortage of capital and management talent. Although a few giant corporations were developed by Southern capital and leadership to the point where they could compete successfully on the national scene, most Southern industries soon passed into the control of Eastern capital; the vast majority of Southern factories are now owned by national corporations, and managed by representatives from the central organization.

This side of the change in Southern population is often overlooked. Everyone knows that hundreds of thousands of Southern Negroes have moved North -- so that there are now more Negroes in the Chicago metropolitan area than in all of South Carolina. In Cleveland, Detroit, Philadelphia, New York, Negroes from the South and their children are a large part of the population; in such cities they are also one of the major economic problems, since the demand for unskilled labor is declining and many of them lack the training for the new clerical and technical jobs that automation is creating. We are all aware that many poor whites have also gone North -- to the assembly lines of Detroit, the rubber shops of Akron and the airplane factories of Dayton -- and have created their share of social problems. We are also aware that within the South there has been a flow of both races from the country to the city -- to Louisville and Little Rock, to Memphis and Birmingham and Atlanta. If we think of Northern migration southward, we are likely to think of the resort traffic and retirement colonies

that have made the southern half of Florida an enclave of the Middle Atlantic states and the Middle West. We forget the more diffuse -- and for that reason, probably the more influential -- migration of plant superintendents, bank cashiers, store managers, industrial chemists, tool and die makers, and now of college professors, as the needs of the South outran local supplies and new opportunities made positions competitive with those available in other regions.[5]

This has been most noticeable as the quality of Southern education has improved. Not unfittingly, some of the first steps were taken by the Reconstruction governments; the constitution of 1868 was the first one that committed South Carolina to general education. The ensuing century has seen the South, by and large, contributing to education a much larger proportion of its wealth than other regions -- though the discrepancy in resources to tax meant that expenditures per pupil in Mississippi were nowhere near what they have been in Ohio or California. Progress has not been easy, as nostalgia, fundamentalism and petty politics have often hamstrung the best-designed programs. But no one can deny that the general quality of Southern education has improved, at all levels. If the Johns Hopkins, the first real graduate university in the United States, failed to keep its preeminence (and in any event it is situated in a city whose Southern affiliations are rather weak), Duke is now unquestionably in the first rank today, and from Charlottesville to Austin, from Miami to Louisville, the better institutions have as high standards and as cosmopolitan an atmosphere as anyone could desire. As with industrialization and urbanization, education has advanced unevenly in the South, as indeed in other regions. But this development, too, will have a profound effect on Southern speechways.

The combined force of these developments promises to affect Southern speech in several ways.

First of all, the balance of population and wealth has shifted irreversibly from the plantation. The textile and tobacco centers of the Piedmont -- increasingly diversified -- centers of heavy industry like Birmingham, petrochemical foci like Baton Rouge, and the variegated industrial complexes like Atlanta and Louisville and Houston have reduced many of the old Southern towns to backwaters, surviving on the custom of Florida-bound tourists. Where seaports flourish -- as Norfolk and Savannah and New Orleans -- it is because they have exploited their geographical advantages to facilitate industrialization.

With industrialization and urbanization, wealth can be expected to replace family as a force for social prestige; since most of the new managerial class --

whether Southerners or not -- come from outside the plantation area, the influence of plantation speech will be diluted. Industrialization and urbanization will speed the disappearance of the more local terms in the vocabulary, especially those associated with the mule-powered farm. Not all readers of this article can tell a *froe* from a *hamestring*, and I suspect all are less likely to make *curds* at home than to buy *cottage cheese* at the supermarket.

As higher education becomes more general, for the near future a smaller proportion of those attending college will be the children and grandchildren of college graduates. In this way the influence of the old elite will be further attenuated, and the characteristics of educated Southern speech will become somewhat different. Since the majority of the white population of the South is found in areas where the South Midland influence is strong, the enlargement of the ranks of the educated is bound to increase the importance of the South Midland component of Southern speech, at the expense of coastal Southern. Education will also tend to eliminate such folk grammatical forms as *div* or *seed*, and such pronunciations as /dɪf/ for *deaf* or /waʊndɪd/ for *wounded*. It is probable, given the prevailing attitude in American schools, that many Southerners will adopt the fashion of full rather than reduced vowels in final syllables, so that *Tuesday* and *borrow* will come to have final /-e/ and /-o/ respectively. And even educated Charlestonians may come to avoid *ain't* in polite conversation with their equals.

Some of this change is already under way. As early as 1946 I noticed that upland vowels were common among native Savannians; in 1949, I found that Knoxvillians were losing the distinction between *horse* and *hoarse*, between *merry* and *marry* and *Mary*. Seven years ago, I discovered that the younger speakers in the Kanawha Valley were pronouncing *tube* and *due* and *new* as /tub/, /du/ and /nu/ in the fashion of northern West Virginia. In 1965, in a sample of recordings from high-school students in Charleston I found little of the traditional pronunciation of *date* and *boat*; and the daughter of a couple from Gloucester County, but grown up in Arlington, spoke to me without a trace of the Piedmont *out* and *night*.

Let us not be nostalgic, however; change in language is inevitable -- and always moved by social forces. Besides, the South is still so linguistically diverse that many of our local speech forms will survive in spite of outside pressures. And our traditions of speech are so powerful that some distinctive Southern varieties of speech are likely to endure for the foreseeable future. This, in fact, may be a source of strength toward solving our educational problems; unlike Chicago or Detroit, where uneducated arrivals from the South -- of whatever race -- are sharply set off from the natives by both grammar and pronunciation, each Southern community finds its basic pronunciation patterns shared by all races and social classes, and the grammatical problems the same where educational and cultural backgrounds are similar. We do not need separate programs for separate groups -- only one program intelligently designed and effectively taught. Our knowledge of Southern dialects may help Southern communities to show how the rest of the nation can solve the language problems of the classroom.[6]

NOTES

[1] Most of the field work in the pre-Revolutionary South, as far west as the Ocmulgee in Georgia, was done in the two periods 1933-39 and 1945-48; that in Kentucky, mostly 1952-55; in Oklahoma 1958-62. Louisiana has been investigated, less professionally, by the students of C. M. Wise, mostly 1933-48. Texas vocabulary was fairly well investigated by the students of E. Bagby Atwood; its pronunciation less systematically, though there have been several first-rate studies. Field work in Missouri began in 1966. Elsewhere, we have largely vocabulary evidence collected by correspondence, but very reliable so far as it goes, thanks to the high standards of the investigator, Gordon Wood, of Southern Illinois University. [The Linguistic Atlas of the Gulf States, under Lee Pederson, will cover all truly 'Southern' areas; field work was completed in 1978.]

[2] On the basis of vocabulary, Kurath (1949) considered it a part of the Midland, conceded that pronunciation features might group it with the South. In discussing the affiliations of Texas dialects, E. Bagby Atwood (1962) grouped Southern Coastal and South Midland together as 'General Southern.'

[3] See Turner 1949. Analogous phenomena in Louisiana Negro French have been discussed by many observers, notably Raleigh Morgan (1960).

[4] A not atypical example is given in Cash 1941.

[5] The development of Washington has been atypical, reflecting two disparate trends. Originally it was a small Southern town, and the lower echelons of government service held a disproportionate number of Southerners. Beginning with the 1930's, however, the expansion of government activities has drawn into the metropolitan area large numbers of Middle Westerners and Easterners to fill professional, technical, administrative and policy-

making positions; in the same period, the extension of equal opportunities to Negroes and the desegregation of the public schools have attracted many Negroes from the South. As middle-class whites -- especially families with children -- have fled to the suburbs, a peculiar situation has developed. In the suburbs the speech patterns are mixed, but with something other than the local Southern cultivated standard beginning to predominate; in the city proper, Negroes constitute about 55% of the population, over 90% of the school enrollment, and the cultivated speech of local middle-class Negroes (itself strongly akin to local cultivated white speech) has been largely swamped by the new immigrants. [The proportion of Negroes has continued to rise in the 1970's.]

[6] [As of 1978, it is generally conceded that the desegregation of schools has been more successful in the South than in other regions.]

More than a century after Appomattox emotional issues aroused by the conflict of the Union and the Confederacy are still alive, even affecting presidential campaigns. In his abortive efforts to stop the 1968 candidacy of Richard Nixon for the Republican nomination the putatively liberal Nelson Rockefeller waved the bloody shirt and disparaged his opponent for seeking reconciliation with the South, while the Alabama maverick George Wallace launched his third-party candidacy on the ground (among others) that the interests and feelings of the South had been ignored by Democrats and Republicans alike. [As late as 1978, the elected president, Jimmy Carter, of Georgia, had not been fully accepted in New England.] In view of these still passionate regional feelings it is in order to appraise the names by which the regional conflict of 1861-65 has been known by twentieth-century Americans.

The primary data for this paper were derived from the archives of the Linguistic Atlas of the United States and Canada, a group of autonomous projects sponsored by the American Council of Learned Societies.[1]

It is possible that the backgrounds of field workers and their interest in the subject are reflected in the variety of responses they were able to elicit. Let us consider the two authors of this paper, both of whom served as field workers: V. McDavid, a native of Minnesota, had rarely heard any name but *Civil War* -- at home, in school, or during field work in her state; R. McDavid, a native South Carolinian and (as he puts it) a grandson of one of the few authentic privates in the Confederate Army, was not only interested in local oral traditions but, in Southern schools, had been educated to the proprieties of designations -- notably one, that *Civil War* was an inaccurate and unfair term. However, since none of the principal field workers was limited to his own region, the personal biases have fairly well canceled each other out except as indicated below.

Differences in names for the conflict appeared before the last Confederate stragglers laid down their arms. Historians have noted that the earliest names reflected the personal attitudes of writers toward the causes of the war, but that later the names came to be applied more objectively and dispassionately.[2] The names seemed to reflect three principal explanations: 1) a conspiracy by evil men -- abolitionists in the North or slavocrats in the South; 2) the question of states' rights -- whether a state had the right to secede, or the federal government the right to suppress secession by force of arms; 3) slavery. Of the three the second has been responsible for most of the varying names both in the historical literature and in folk speech.

In the first generation after Appomattox several writers offered assorted versions of the conspiracy. However, serious historians did not accept these or the names they generated. J. T. Headley and Horace Greeley, Northerners, wrote about *The Great Rebellion*; and Alexander H. Stephens, Vice-President of the Confederacy, wrote about *The War Between the States*. Among the historians of that time the constitutional question of states' rights was reflected in the alternatives to *Civil War*.

The Linguistic Atlas materials offer a greater variety of terms than the histories do. Many of the informants take the terms rather seriously, as one might expect on realizing that some of the oldest served in uniform, that others recalled the war and Reconstruction, and that many others learned the names shortly afterward from veterans or their widows.

Some thirty folk names for the war appear in the field records. However, six of them are of so much greater frequency than the rest that we shall pay most attention to them: *Civil War*, *Rebellion*, *Confederate War*, *War Between the States*, *War Between North and South*, and simply *The War*.

There is interesting evidence of another sort in the major historical dictionaries: the *Oxford English Dictionary* (1884-1928), the *Dictionary of American English*, by Craigie and Hulbert (1936-44), and the *Dictionary of Americanisms*, by Mathews (1951). These dictionaries, with dated citations from written and printed materials, provide evidence on how the term *Civil War* developed. It was first used in a generic sense with reference to the war of 1861-65. From this habit developed the use of *Civil War* as a proper noun.

The dictionaries do not give us any very early citations for this specific use. However, one comes to light from the New York *Tribune* for December 25, 1861, in the column of its London correspondent, who wrote that "The Great Republic . . . may not prove able to cope with England, though backed by the *civil war*." That correspondent is better known for other reasons than providing the earliest citation for the specific American sense of *Civil War*. He was Karl Marx.

Confederate War is not in the historical dictionaries at all, though it is perhaps the second commonest term in folk usage. It is not in the dictionaries because it is not the term of historians or politicians; it is merely a term used among the people.

The Rebellion (*Great Rebellion*, *War of the Rebellion*) was used by Northern politicians from the beginning. It was the term consistently used by the federal government, as in Andrew Johnson's presidential proclamation of amnesty in 1865. An early example is found in the title of Headley's *The Great Rebellion: A History of the Civil War in the United States* (1863-66).

For the fourth and fifth commonest terms -- *The War Between the States* and *The War Between the North and the South* -- the dictionaries are nearly as disappointing as with *Confederate War*. The earliest citation for each is from 1900.

In the field records, as one might expect, the commonest term is *Civil War*. It is overwhelmingly the most prevalent in all states, North and South, and among all age groups. In only a few communities do we find *Civil War* not used by at least one informant: two in Virginia, three in North Carolina, five in South Carolina, and one in Georgia. Even in South Carolina *Civil War* is used by more informants than is any other term -- 76 to 67 for *Confederate War*.[3]

What is surprising, at least to an outsider, is the natural use of *Civil War* in the South. Professional Southerners have long inveighed against it, especially in election years; and in the North (as V. McDavid has observed) one often comes across the comment that Southerners reject the term. Here, as often happens, folklore is refuted by the Atlas evidence.[4]

Rebellion and *Confederate War* show patterns of distribution both by regions and by age of the informant. Moreover, *Rebellion*, in particular, reflects the informant's interpretation, however acquired, of the cause of the war -- the question of states' rights and the legitimacy of secession.

In New England *Rebellion* is nearly as common as *Civil War*, especially in Maine, New Hampshire, and Vermont. It is not limited to the oldest New England informants; many of the younger ones also use the term. Most informants also say *Civil War*.

In the Atlantic states the area in which *Rebellion* is widespread includes New England, New York State, and roughly the northern third of New Jersey and Pennsylvania. From New England westward, even in the area of Yankee settlement, its incidence falls off; even within its territory of predominance it is very rare in metropolitan New York and the lower Hudson Valley.[5]

Outside the area of New England settlement *Rebellion* is much less common and is normally confined to the oldest informants. There are nine examples in southern Pennsylvania (five in the Philadelphia area and three among the Pennsylvania Germans), one in southern New Jersey, six in West Virginia, two in Delaware, and one in the District of Columbia. Even farther south the term is not unknown: there are two examples in South Carolina, one on the Eastern Shore of Virginia, and one each from the mountain areas of North Carolina and Georgia. Most of these were from poor-white backgrounds or from communities where there was little sympathy for slavery or secession.[6]

As we go farther west, *Rebellion* becomes less common. There are perhaps fifteen examples in each of the North-Central states alongside fifty to sixty for *Civil War*. There are five examples from Kentucky, one from an Ohio River community, and the rest from the eastern part of the state, where the mountaineers were fiercely hostile to slavery and usually vote Republican today. Since everywhere in the North-Central region *Rebellion* is commonest in the speech of the oldest informants, it is plainly a dying term. Quite possibly field work done today in New England would reveal a similar trend, though the fact that New England was the ideological center of abolitionism and radical Reconstruction may still give *Rebellion* greater local vitality there, just as it had wider currency in the 1930's.

Confederate War (*War of the Confederacy*) is an extremely interesting item to the linguistic geographer. Ignored by lexicographers, it shows a striking regional pattern and, in fact, is the commonest folk term in the South Atlantic states. It is lacking in the Shenandoah Valley and in the Northern Neck of Virginia, reflecting partly ideological dissent between planter and upland farmer, partly the federal neutralization -- full occupation -- of the Northern Neck throughout most of the conflict. However, within the area where it is found it is used by informants of all types, though it is commonest among the oldest generation. As with *Rebellion*, age is more important than education for an informant's choice of the term *Confederate War*.[7] At the time when the field work was done it had not ceased to be a natural term, and in South Carolina it is nearly as common as *Civil War*.

Outside the area of concentration, however, there are few occurrences of *Confederate War*: three in West Virginia and one in Ohio. It is lacking in the border states of Delaware, Maryland and Kentucky, and in the data from Alabama and Louisiana it is far less common than in the Old South.

The term *War Between the States* has a somewhat artificial status. After the fighting ceased, Southern apologists continued to justify secession on constitutional grounds. This attitude is expressed in the memoirs of Confederate President Jefferson Davis and more explicitly in those of his Vice-President -- Alexander H. Stephens -- entitled *A Constitutional View of the Late War Between the States* (1868-70).

The War Between the States occurs only three times in New England, always in the speech of cultivated informants. It is very rare in the Middle Atlantic states (New York, Pennsylvania, West Virginia, New Jersey) and in the border states of Delaware and Maryland. In the South, as an alternate to *Civil War*, it is second only to *Confederate War*. It is used somewhat more frequently by the younger and better-educated informants than by the oldest. This apparently supports an investigator's intuition (and R. McDavid's sense of indoctrination in school) that it is a term deliberately taught as representing Southern attitudes. In contrast with *Confederate War*, which did not occur, there are several examples of *War Between the States* in the North-Central region. However, it is much less common than *Rebellion* except in Kentucky.

The War Between the North and the South has a peculiar distribution. Far less common than *War Between the States*, it occurs almost always in the speech of older and less-educated informants. It thus contrasts with *War Between the States*, which is used primarily by younger speakers. Geographically its principal concentration is in the lower Potomac Valley and upper Chesapeake Bay, where, as a territorial rather than an ideological designation, it expresses the neutrality that region sought in vain.

There are three minor terms with distributions on which one may speculate. *War of Secession* (*Secession War*) occurs once in New Brunswick, once in New Hampshire, once in New York, twice in Pennsylvania, once in Virginia, twice in Georgia, and twelve times in South Carolina. This may possibly reflect R. McDavid's interviewing techniques; more likely, since he also did the greater part of the field work in Georgia, it points to South Carolinians' consciousness of history and to pride in their state's role as *The Cradle of Secession*. *Southern War* appears three times in New Hampshire, three in New York State, twice in Virginia, and twice in South Carolina. *Rebel War* is found once in New York, twice in North Carolina, once in South Carolina, and once in Georgia. Apparently to Southerners being a *rebel* is ideologically less offensive than participating in a *Rebellion*.[8]

The euphemism *Late Unpleasantness*, a favorite jocular term among younger Southerners today, occurs only once, as does the sentimental *War Between the Blue and the Gray*.

One other term is very common -- simply *The War*. As one might expect, it occurs chiefly in the South. Its pattern is rather hard to interpret, because its occurrence in a given field record depends on the practices of the field worker. It is usually a casual form, appearing in free conversation, and most likely occurred when the field worker encouraged conversation as a source of unguarded response.[9] It is seldom a direct response. But it is interesting that more than two generations after Appomattox, with two world wars and several minor ones intervening, many Southern informants felt that the *Civil War* was sufficiently identified as *The War*. Of course, it makes a difference when the fighting is on one's own farm -- and most of it took place in Southern territory.[10]

It is interesting to examine the evidence on synonyms for *Civil War* against the patterns of dialect regions which were presented in Kurath 1949 and confirmed by Atwood 1953a and Kurath and R. McDavid 1961 as well as by various articles. According to this analysis there are three major dialect regions of the Atlantic Seaboard: 1) Northern -- New England, the Hudson Valley, and derivative settlements westward; 2) Midland -- Pennsylvania and its derivative settlements to the west and southwest; 3) Southern -- the older plantation area of the coastal plain and lower Piedmont and its derivatives in the West. *Rebellion* here shows up in a characteristic Northern pattern. Its focus is in New England, the center of abolition sentiment; it is relatively uncommon in New York City and the lower Hudson Valley; its limits in the northern parts of New Jersey and Pennsylvania coincide with those for such words as *pail*, such grammatical forms as *see* as a past tense, and such pronunciations as the unrounded vowel /a/ in *on*, *fog*, *hog*. *Confederate War* has a characteristic Southern distribution, though it is lacking in the Northern Neck of Virginia and in Delaware and Maryland. From the Rappahannock River south its limit follows the crest of the Blue Ridge, the principal boundary of the Southern region. Since few Southern forms have crossed into the Ohio Valley, *Confederate War* would be unlikely in the North-Central states. Contrariwise, the presence in the North-Central states of *Rebellion*, a New England term, is not surprising from what is known about settlement history. That *Rebellion* occurs south of the usual limits of Northern terms is not surprising, partly because of the political alignments of the nineteenth century, partly because the process of dialect mixture has often resulted in a southward spread of Northern terms such as the negative verb phrase *hadn't ought* (Map 1).[11]

Many of the other terms in the list appear only once or twice. One interesting group is found in New England. As we mentioned earlier, historians have discovered three main theories of the origins of the war: conspiracy, constitutional issues, and slavery. Most of the widespread terms reflect the question of states' rights. None of these recorded for the Atlas suggest conspiracy. Only in abolitionist New England do we find names that reflect the slavery issue: *The Abolition War*, *The Nigger War*, *The Abe Lincoln War*, *The War for the Blacks*. That some of these show less than complete enthusiasm merely confirms the well-attested fact that American thinking, especially about wars, has never been monolithic, not even in New England in the 1860's.

There are some forty field records from Afro-American informants, most of them in the South. The terms they use are predominantly those of their white neighbors: *Civil War*, *Confederate War*, *War Between the States*. One, however, went beyond local tradition to call it *Freedom War*.

Several Canadians have been interviewed in border communities as well as in regional surveys of Canada. In some records the term *Civil War* was not elicited, as presumably of no interest to Canadians; in others they were not recorded. Of the twenty-six who responded in New Brunswick[12] and southern Ontario twenty gave *Civil War*, three (all in New Brunswick) gave *Rebellion* or *War of the Rebellion*, and three (all in Ontario) gave *War Between North and South*. In Ontario, furthermore, there are three designations not known in the States or, if known, have a different background: *American Civil War*, *American War*, and *Yankee War* [13]

Informants sometimes offered comments about the terms they used. These are valuable because they reveal trends or attitudes.

Several older New England informants repeat what must have been a current joke about the name of the war. After they gave the term *Civil War* the field worker reported them as going on to say, "It wasn't very civil." This pun is not confined to New England; it occurs in records from the South, including some made for the recent studies in South Carolina and Georgia.

Many informants in the North said that *Rebellion* was old-fashioned or going out of use. The evidence bears them out. Similarly, many Southern informants said that *Confederate War* was old-fashioned and that *War Between the States* was the modern term. Other Southerners made such comments as that *Civil War* is now in very bad taste. Another, however, said that *War Between the States* is only a joke.

Several Southerners further observed that *Civil War* had been proscribed by the United Daughters of the Confederacy, founded in 1894. Since the Daughters also insisted on *War Between the States*, which, except for Stephens' book, was not widely known before the turn of the century, it is clear that the prevailing attitudes of the South toward the two terms are closely related and have been fostered by professional Southerners, especially the U.D.C. The Daughters have always been zealous in protecting Southerners against the ravages of Northern propaganda, and in no detail of this campaign have they been more zealous than in promoting the use of *War Between the States*. For a long time they were successful in keeping *Civil War* out of textbooks used in Southern schools; and when a Southern newspaper inadvertently used the offending term, the editor would receive a stinging reprimand. So successful was the campaign of *Schrecklichkeit* that, for self-protection, style sheets in the city room often carried instructions that in stories from wire services *Civil War* must be replaced by *War Between the States*. The substitution became so mechanical that the New Orleans *Times-Picayune* finally carried a story describing an aviator who had flown against Franco as having participated in the *Spanish War Between the States*.[14] Even to the grandson of a Confederate combat veteran this is carrying linguistic delicacy a bit too far.

NOTES

[1] This article appeared originally in an issue of *The Southern Speech Journal* dedicated to the memory of a distinguished Southern professor, C. M. Wise, one of the pioneers in the study of Southern dialects. It is based on a paper presented by V. McDavid at a meeting of the Faculty Research Club of Chicago State University, April 1965. The authors acknowledge the support of the American Council of Learned Societies for the Atlas project and their permission and that of the regional editors for using the data.

The collections investigated, totaling some 2200 records, are: 1) the *Linguistic Atlas of New England*, edited at Brown University by Hans Kurath and Bernard Bloch, published 1939-43; 2) the *Linguistic Atlas of the Middle and South Atlantic States*, now being edited at the University of South Carolina (Kurath *et al.* 1979-); 3) the *Linguistic Atlas of the North-Central States*, now being edited at the University of Chicago (Marck-

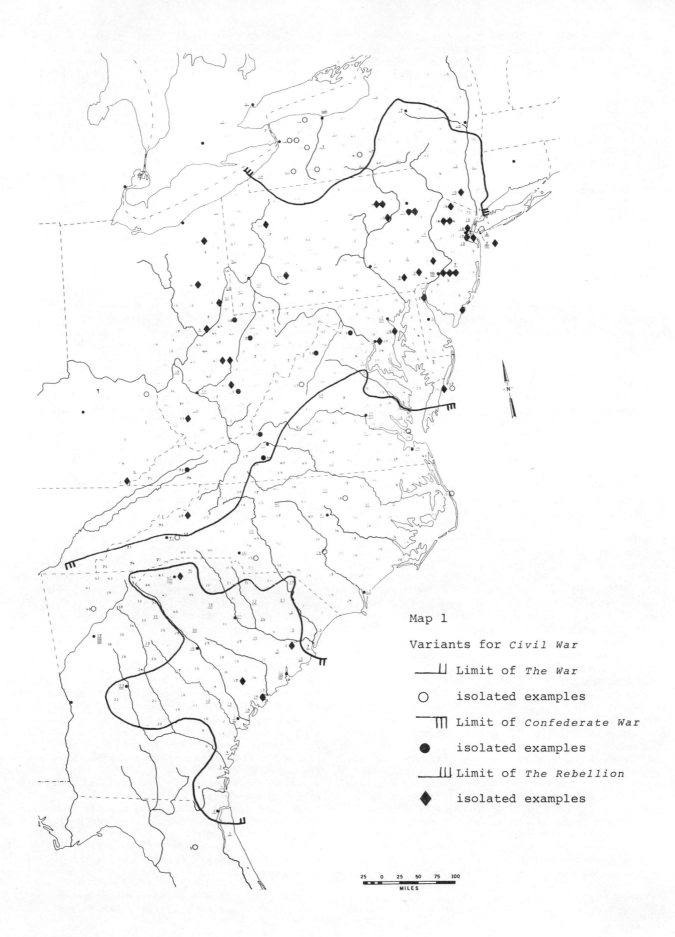

Map 1

Variants for *Civil War*

⌐⌐ Limit of *The War*

◯ isolated examples

⊤⊤ Limit of *Confederate War*

● isolated examples

⊥⊥⊥ Limit of *The Rebellion*

◆ isolated examples

25 0   25 50 75 100
MILES

wardt *et al.* 1980-); 4) the *Linguistic Atlas of the Upper Midwest* (Allen 1973-76); 5) the Linguistic Atlas of Louisiana, some hundred field records made since 1933 by students of Claude M. Wise and Claude L. Shaver, of Louisiana State University; 6) two special collections made for local projects, a) 38 records made in 1962 for Pederson 1965a, and b) some twenty field records made in the late 1940's for Barrett 1948. Other regional archives were not used because the item was not included in the regional questionnaires.

[2] For a summary of the attitudes of historians and of the names they employed the authors are indebted to Arvarh Strickland, of Chicago State.

[3] Most South Carolinians, even those with little formal education, were very conscious of history and of the rhetoric of nomenclature. Moreover, R. McDavid, who did most of the interviews in South Carolina, was a native, had many personal introductions to his informants through his father's political contacts, and deliberately sought conversational responses.

[4] T. Harry Williams, Professor of History at LSU, pointed out orally that many of the military figures of the Confederacy used *Civil War* from the beginning. [*Civil War* was used on both sides of the Atlantic to designate the secession of the American colonies. An examination of contemporary documents would be interesting.]

[5] As Kurath 1949 pointed out, the Hudson Valley and New York City often do not follow general Northern usage. Moreover, there are special reasons why such a folk term as *Rebellion* might not be common in the metropolitan area. That area has become heavily urbanized and in recent years has drawn hundreds of thousands of immigrants from Southern and Eastern Europe. New Yorkers are much more interested in historical justification for Israel, Italy, or Poland (to name a few at random) than in that of regions of the United States. It is also possible that the draft riots of 1863 made them less self-righteous than New Englanders in their attitudes toward the South. [New York City voted against Lincoln in both 1860 and 1864; before the outbreak of hostilities the mayor of New York, Fernando Wood, proposed that the city secede from the state and establish itself as a free port.]

[6] Political slogans such as "the Solid South" have concealed the strong regional divisions within the South. However, even in 1861-63 there was notable dissent, manifested most strikingly in the secession of West Virginia from the parent state and in the strong Union sympathies of eastern Tennessee and western North Carolina. Many small farmers in all parts of the South referred to the war as "a rich man's war and a poor man's fight." For sectional divisions in the South see Key 1949.

One may note that one elderly South Carolinian said he used *The Rebellion* "'cause that's when the Yankees rebelled against the Constitution."

[7] It is still used by educated Charlestonians. One of them, at a meeting of Southern historians, remarked, "I am sick of you Virginians blaming us for dragging you into the *Confederate War;* you dragged us into the Revolution." As a term without invidious overtones it has been adopted by many younger Southern intellectuals.

[8] *The War for Southern Independence*, favored by some Southern historians, never caught on. [It has, however, been adopted by the historian Eugene Genovese.] This term contrasts with another minor variant, *The War of Northern Aggression.* *The War of the Sections* occurs once in a Virginia history.

[9] *The War* is commonest in the records made by R. McDavid, who encouraged his informants to talk freely and recorded proportionately more unguarded responses. It would be the natural usage in telling about earlier times, though one of the other terms would be offered as a direct response.

[10] This is often overlooked by Americans from other regions, who express amazement at the regional sensitiveness of Southerners and their willingness to support an aggressive foreign policy by military means. With a white population of 5,500,000 the Confederacy had 258,000 military dead, approaching the losses of the United States in World War II. Economic losses included the loss of nearly all invested capital and the destruction of most railroads and factories, to say nothing of the loss of crops and livestock. The military occupation -- twelve years in some states -- was the longest in Western history, far longer than that imposed on Germany or Japan; and there were no congressional billions for rebuilding.

[11] Even in South Carolina and Georgia there is less resentment toward the Middle Westerners who made up Sherman's army of devastation than toward the New Englanders who contributed the propaganda.

[12] Actually there was considerable interest in New Brunswick. Many New Englanders (skedaddlers) crossed the border to avoid the draft. One of their settlements is still known as *Skedaddler's Ridge*. And many from New Brunswick served as substitutes. Some Canadians observe that New Brunswick has never been so prosperous since.

[13] One informant on the Niagara peninsula rejected *Rebellion*, which he said should be applied only to the Canadian revolts against British rule in 1837-38. H. Rex Wilson, of the University of Western Ontario and a leading Canadian dialectologist, observes that many Canadians use *Rebellion* for the American Revolution. In W. S. Avis's *Dictionary of Canadianisms* (1967) *Rebellion* appears in the sense of the revolts of 1837-38 and in the later Northwest Rebellion; *American War* designates either the American Revolution or the War of 1812; *Yankee War*, the latter. To a Canadian, *Civil War* would be most likely to describe the English civil strife of the 1640's.

Two similar forms, *The Great American War of 1861* and *The American War 1861-65*, appear in two Virginia county histories.

[14] For this story we are indebted to "Pie" Dufour, of the New Orleans *Times-Picayune*.

Part III
Critical Dialectology

DIALECTS IN CULTURE

With the publication of the essential part of the *Sprach- und Sachatlas Italiens und der Südschweiz* (Jaberg and Jud 1928-40), the first two volumes of the *Linguistic Atlas of New England* (Kurath et al. 1939-43), and the handbooks for both these works, one would expect students of dialect to study the principles upon which these works were compiled. And since the editors of these works, and their students, have discussed those principles at length in print, it is difficult to believe that any serious scholar could remain in ignorance.[1] It is therefore disappointing to see how many of these principles are violated in J. S. Hall's monograph on the phonetics of Smoky Mountain speech. Although the author spent much time in research, his methodology throughout is so faulty that the work is difficult to assess and almost impossible to use unless one knows the dialect already.

Hall had much in his favor. His study covers a limited area, so that he could make a far more intensive survey than could field workers in New England or the South Atlantic States. He seems to have handled informants easily; and through his connection with the CCC he could observe mountain life at close range, make tests of local dialects at the CCC camps, and obtain introductions to representative older informants under conditions which would give him the informants' confidence. To cover the Smokies he had nearly as much time for field work as Lowman had in all Pennsylvania. And often, as in his analysis of the /oɟ/ diphthong, he reveals that he has the gifts of clear observation and intelligent analysis.

Unfortunately, Hall does not make use of his advantages. How far he fails may be seen by examining (A) his methodology, (B) his analysis, (C) his data. His methodology we may contrast with that of the New England *Atlas*, as described in the *Handbook of the Linguistic Geography of New England* (Kurath et al. 1939); his analysis, with Bloch's and Trager's investigation of the syllabic phonemes of their dialects; his data with what I find in my own dialect (that of Greenville, South Carolina, on the margin of the Blue Ridge)[2] and have observed through field work in Up-Country South Carolina and other parts of the South.

A. Hall's announced purpose is "to describe the sounds of one of America's most interesting vernaculars"(1). For "interesting" one should probably read 'quaint,' for to the linguist all dialects are equally interesting as examples of living speech. Throughout the monograph Hall underlines what to him is the exotic in Smokies speech: "their picturesque life and surroundings"(2), "an air of serene pastoral beauty"(7), "quaintly used"(38), "the old pronunciation of *boil* v. is picturesquely exemplified"(47), "a colorful example"(57), "the curious pronunciation . . . colorfully illustrated" (60), "naively reflected"(68), "pleasing rusticity"(80), "the curiously inverted phrase [ˈhænt ˈnobʌdɪ ˈsɪd ɪt]"(88).

The area of Hall's study embraces Haywood and Swain Counties in North Carolina, and Blount, Cocke, and Sevier Counties in Tennessee -- those counties within whose limits is located the Great Smoky Mountains National Park. It is regrettable that he did not also study informants from surrounding territory -- the reader cannot tell from Hall's statements even whether informants were studied from these five counties beyond the limits of the Park -- so that he might determine whether the Smokies are a dialect area to themselves.[3] Of course, it was impossible and unnecessary to survey the surrounding area as closely as the Smokies proper, but he should have studied informants beyond the Park boundaries, both from the five counties of his study and from the adjacent Monroe County in Tennessee and Graham, Madison, and Jackson Counties in North Carolina. The field records for the Atlas of the South Atlantic States, by Lowman, might indicate whether there is a dialect boundary on the east and south between the Smokies and the Blue Ridge area, but Hall does not refer to them.

The motivation for Hall's study seems ill-founded: that the Smokies constitute a relic area, long removed from the main currents of American culture, in which he could find vestiges of earlier stages in the growth of the language; and that the speech of the area "does not show the deep impress of the schoolmaster's influence." For unschooled speech, it is unnecessary to go into the Smokies: it can be found almost anywhere in the South outside the metropolitan centers and the plantation caste. Besides, the Smokies are not a relic area: initial settlement was too recent;[4] population has tended to become denser; contact with the outside world -- especially the focal areas of the Carolina Piedmont and the Upper Tennessee Valley -- has grown easier. In North Carolina one can more easily find relic areas along the coast (especially the Banks islands from Hatteras to Manteo), first settled a century before the Smokies and far less accessible to the outside world.

Hall does not attempt to define dialect areas within the Smokies (there are not even topographical and political maps, much less maps setting off speech areas or indicating the distribution of particular forms), but assumes a uniform speech throughout the area. Yet his own evidence refutes this assumption and suggests that the Smokies are a transition area of dialect mixture: a) the area was settled from three directions -- the Tennessee Valley, western North Carolina, and Up-Country South Carolina (11-12); b) there are two types of front vowel neutralization before nasals (15, 19). Just how many and how diverse these dialects are cannot be told from Hall's monograph, but a uniform speech throughout the Smokies seems improbable.

Hall does not state how many informants he used, or indicate their types by age groups or culture groups, or tell how many forms he secured from each. This sharply contrasts with Atlas practice, and weakens a reader's confidence in Hall's conclusions.

There is no indication that Hall used work sheets, and much that he did not: several times he mentions forms inadequately represented in his transcriptions, though such forms could easily have been obtained by some modification of the Atlas work sheets. For example, he suspects that his transcriptions do not represent accurately the usual pronunciation of *rock* (27); he mentions a "few instances" of *hospital* (28) (cf. item 84.7 in the New England work sheets); his records have few examples of "'long *i*' before *p* and *b*" (43); the prefix *pro-* "is not well represented"(58); *genuine* was noted in "few instances"(68) (but cf. 51.3 in the New England work sheets); weak-stressed /i/ is not recorded before /-tʃ/ (75) (but *spinach* is familiar enough); he cites few examples of the initial cluster in *shrink*, *shrub*, *shrivel* (99), one of the shibboleths of Southern speech (but *shrank*, *shrunk* appear in the New England work sheets: 27.7, 27.8). Although Hall makes much of the necessity for a technique to put informants at their ease (2) -- an indirect apology for not using work sheets -- the Atlas field workers have found that work sheets both speed up interviews and provide a natural framework for questions about local culture. Random notations only waste time.

In contrast with the Atlas, Hall spent the greater part of his time in the field on phonographic recordings -- seven of his ten months in the Smokies. Such procedure is questionable: phonographic recordings are useful only if one is already expert in a language or dialect (Bloomfield 1942: 10); they waste time, for they must be transcribed impressionistically before they can be used; they leave out important forms and include much irrelevant and repetitious material. Attempts to fill in the gaps by dialect test recordings, such as the fable of Arthur the Rat, are worthless. Such test records are artificial, designed primarily for sophisticated informants, and far less natural than questions based on work sheets. If Hall had used Atlas work sheets during his ten months in the field, he could have made between fifty and eighty complete field records, far more representative, descriptive, and manageable than 138 double-faced phonograph records, including 65 of ballads and other music and twenty of Arthur the Rat.

Hall spent much time studying naive spellings in local manuscripts, and dialect spellings in novels and sketches. This type of study should be made: where no living speakers remain, or where the object of study is an earlier stage of the language, it is the only possible type of study. But so long as living informants are available -- especially if the local culture is changing rapidly -- they should be consulted and the books ignored. Besides, so-called dialect spellings cannot be trusted: the writer -- often from another speech area -- will interpret the dialect in terms of his own phonemic system; and apparently there is a standardized literary 'dialect spelling,' largely respellings more nearly phonemic than conventional English orthography. As Orbeck discovered some time ago (1927:7-10, 74-75, 141-43), and Penzl and I have recently confirmed (Penzl 1941, R. McDavid 1942b), orthographic evidence at best can indicate only phonemic differences, and not always those.[5] In the time he spent reading and annotating literary items, Hall could have made at least a dozen field records from work sheets.

Hall could have stated historical information more compactly than he does: in his introduction is a short sketch of the settlement history, but Chapters II and III also contain some historical data (49-50, 106). Much of these last two sections is purely speculative and could safely be omitted.

Nowhere does Hall give a phonetic chart or indicate the values of the symbols he employs. Frequently he remarks, meaninglessly, that a symbol (he makes the error of identifying a *phoneme* with a *phonetic symbol*) has its usual American quality.[6] Presumably he follows the modification of IPA used in *American Speech*; but he nowhere states this practice, nor does the use of this alphabet by others justify his not giving a phonetic chart or otherwise indicating the values of his symbols. Anyhow, the alphabet is inadequate, or he has inadequately mastered it: he declares that *remember* "sounds very much like [ṛˈmɛmbɚ]"(53); treats voiceless /d/ as equivalent to /t/ (75); indicates only two degrees of retroflexion -- full and zero; nowhere indicates aspiration; fumbles over transcribing the diphthong in *law* (31); indicates free nasality only three times (23, 24, 34) and ignores nasality as a morpheme alternate in sandhi (McMillan 1939); overlooks the glottal stop as an allophone of the /t/ phoneme, and uses the symbol only once (91), to indicate a prosodic feature of the colloquial affirmative response.

B. Hall divides his analysis into three parts: Chapter I, "The Vowel Sounds of Stressed Syllables;" Chapter II, "The Vowel Sounds of Unstressed and Partially Stressed Syllables;" Chapter III, "The Consonants." This plan is defective: he ignores the difference, phonemic in English, between close juncture, internal open juncture, and external open juncture (compare *syntax* and *tin-tax*; Trager and Bloch 1941:225-26, Bloch and Trager 1942: 35-36, 47); pitch, not phonemic in English as regards single words, but possibly a phonetic criterion by which dialects may be set off from one another, he mentions only in passing (13, 14, 19); stress he mentions several times (13, 14, 19, 34, 43-44, 48, 51, 53, 61, 71, 74) but gives no unified treatment. The vowels of "partially stressed syllables" (medial stress) are best treated in English along with those of "stressed syllables" (loud and reduced-loud stress), rather than with those of "unstressed syllables" (weak stress). And since the consonant analysis of English is easier than the vowel analysis, and differs less from dialect to dialect, it would appear sound methodology to discuss the consonants before the vowels.

For the stressed-vowel phonemes Hall uses a system of twelve "simple vowels" and three "diphthongs," employing two symbols for one simple-vowel phoneme, and for the first element of two of his diphthongs a symbol [a] which he does not use for any of the simple vowels. Time-honored though this analysis may be, it seems incomplete and bulky. Bloomfield described Chicago English in terms of nine discrete vowel symbols (1935); Bloch and Trager required only six vowel symbols for Eastern and Western varieties of Central American (1942:50-52; Trager and Bloch 1941:223-46);[7] only six, moreover, are needed to analyze the vowel system of my own dialect (that of Greenville, South Carolina), not greatly different from that of the Smokies. It would seem likely that the dialect Hall describes has fewer than twelve vowel *phonemes*, though undoubtedly

he needs more *phonetic symbols* than he employs to describe the *allophones*.

More serious is the mistaken viewpoint at the basis of Hall's analysis. Instead of recording the phonetic facts and conducting the phonemic analysis according to the forms occurring in Smokies speech, he appears to have made a partial analysis of his own speech, or of some Northern or Central dialect (possibly this is what he means by "normal American"), and classified forms according to the vowels with which they are pronounced in that dialect.[8] Perhaps he adopts this device to facilitate the comparison of Smokies speech with English of earlier periods; it is inadvisable, however, to attempt comparisons before the dialect under examination has been thoroughly described; and this device of Hall's makes systematic description of Smokies speech impossible. The fact that *bulge* and *bulk* always occur in the Smokies with the /u/ phoneme (Hall's [ʊ]) is indicated under his discussion of [ʌ] rather than under [ʊ]. Where phonemic neutralization occurs before nasals -- as sometimes of /i/ and /e/ (Hall's [ɪ] and [ɛ]), sometimes of /e/ and /a/ (Hall's [ɛ] and [æ]) -- the analysis is confused: he reports that "all degrees between [ɪ] and [ɛ] are represented" before nasals (15); that "[ɛ] is often raised to or toward [ɪ]"(19); and that "the opposite tendency to lower [ɛ] to or toward [æ] is also frequent before nasals"(19). What these statements may imply is that there are two dialects in the Smokies, differentiated by the treatment of front vowels before nasals; in one of them, as in the South Carolina Piedmont, /i/ and /e/ are neutralized in these positions, in the other /e/ and /a/. These phenomena could all be treated in one section. Similarly, Hall seems needlessly disturbed to find that only two front short vowel phonemes, one higher and one lower, occur before /-r/, and that each has a rather wide range of freely alternating allophones (16) [in the Charleston area, many speakers have only one front vowel before /-r/ or its /ə/ reflex, so that *ear* and *air* are homonyms]. Hall's treatment of [æ], like many conventional treatments, ignores the *phonemic* difference between simple /a/, as in *pat, hand* (v.), and diphthongal /aj/ (phonetically [æẹ]), as in *bad, cash, hand* (n.); thus /hízhajnz ɚblak/ *his hands are black*, but /ʃihanzim ðᵊtrajʃ-bajsket/ *she hands him the trash-basket*.[9] In handling the low-back vowels, Hall is particularly inept. He worries about a "choice" between the symbols [ɑ] and [ɒ] instead of attempting to describe the phoneme and its allophones. Here as elsewhere he is phonemically bound by his own system. In the Smokies, as in most of the Upland South, the vowel of *law* is a diphthong -- roughly [ɒọ], phonemically /ow/; the vowel of *father* is a simple vowel, low-back and often extremely retracted [ɑ], phonemically /o/. The extreme backness of the latter is likely to confuse a student working with inadequate phonetic apparatus.[10] In his analysis of the syllabic of *law*, Hall properly notes that it is often diphthongal, but naively asserts that it "suggests the diphthong [au]," further evidence of being bound by his own phonemic pattern. In much of the Upland South the syllabics of both *cow* and *law* are diphthongal; the former is generally upper low-front to mid-back (phonetically [æọ]), the latter low-back partially rounded to mid-back (phonetically [ɒọ]), so that there is no confusion; any resemblance of the latter to the diphthong in Hall's pronunciation of *cow* is irrelevant to a description of Smokies speech. The "striking . . . complete unrounding" of the stressed syllabics in *Florida*, *forehead*, *laurel*, *orange*, etc. (33) is typical of the Upland South (R. McDavid 1940) [this observation is also supported by the studies of C. K. Thomas]. Likewise the list of words in which "[o] rather than [ɔ] occurs before r" reflects usual Southern practice (Kurath 1940). The analysis of the preterites of *ride*, *drive*, *rise* /rid;driv,drɒv;riz/ is a part of Smokies morphology, not of phonology. The instability of the [ɔɪ] diphthong is typical of the South Carolina Piedmont.[11]

The vowels with weak stress are handled even less systematically than those with loud stress. Weak stress vowels in English are very difficult to analyze; the only satisfactory attempt is that of Trager and Bloch (1941:229-31, Bloch and Trager 1942:50). Yet it seems obvious that Hall should not include medial and weak stress in the same division of his vowel analysis; and the analysis of weak stress syllabics in initial and medial syllables on the basis of orthography is not only poor methodology but a confession of defeat. Hall's treatment of weak stress syllabics in final syllables is better; some attempt is made to list forms according to the vowel phonemes of Smokies speech, or at least according to allophones; but again there is too much emphasis on orthography. The analysis of the suffix morphemes -*ville*, -*land*, -*ment* (71-72) largely ignores the relative positions of the suffix and loud stress, which determine whether the morpheme appears in the alternant with medial stress or in that with weak stress; in the weak stress alternant of -*ville* the very dark /l/ is typical, not "extreme"(104). The analysis of weak stress /i/ before nasals in final syllables (74) should include *organ* and the proper name *Morgan*, both of which often have /i/ in the South Carolina Blue Ridge and in middle Tennessee. *Captain* is usually /kapəm/, phonetically [kæ'pm], rather than /kaptən/ (82) in rural Piedmont and mountain speech. Morpheme alter-

nation, rather than simple phonetic substitution, seems to be the explanation of forms of the types /fejvərojt/ *favorite*, /kəvərlid,-led/ *coverlet* (75).

Hall's methodology is poorest in his chapter on consonants. Nowhere does he attempt to describe the consonant system, but confines himself to differences between the Smokies and his undescribed "General American." As elsewhere, many of the forms cited are poorly analysed. That the comparative particle *than* has more than one form in morpheme alternation (/ðan/:/ðən/:/ən/:/-n/) is well known, although the rules of this alternation have not yet been worked out. The standard local form of *yeast* in Up-Country South Carolina is /ijst/ (86); /jijst/ is a learned form. In most of the South, *Campbell* and *McCampbell* are /kaməl,məkaməl/. The transcriptions [kunt,dɪnt,wʌnt] (88) *couldn't*, *didn't*, *wasn't*, are ambiguous: from them one would infer monosyllabic forms, which seem improbable in the South; more likely -- and frequently heard -- are two-syllable forms with a weak glottal stop or glottal or velar spirant before a phonetically syllabic [ŋ] (phonemically /ən/). Interpretation of the front glide in [θɪu] *threw*, as "perhaps the remnant of an old [r]" is fanciful and unnecessary. Simplification of final consonant clusters could be best treated by stating what clusters occur after what vowels, stressed and unstressed (90) (cf. Bloomfield 1933: 131-34). Such forms as *a aunt*, where literary usage would have *an*, are common in rural Southern speech.[12] Instead of listing "excrescent" homorganic stops following /m,n,ŋ/ Hall should state the combinations in which non-nasal consonants follow nasals; if such forms as /fents/ *fence*, /wormpθ/ *warmth*, are normal in Smokies speech, there is nothing excrescent about the clusters /-nts,-mpθ/. If diphthongs are analyzed phonemically as short vowel plus semivowel, it is easy to explain such forms as Hall's ['sæwɚ,'pæwəl,'tæwəl] (93); one- and two-syllable variants of forms containing /-w/ diphthongs before final /-r,-l/ occur in free alternation in most Southern dialects. Following the diphthongs /ij,ej/, /l/ is often syllabic in the Upland South: forms of the types /fijəl/ *feel*, /jejəl/ *Yale* (lock) (94) are common. Hall does not cite the typical Southern cluster /sr-/ in forms like *shrink*, *shrub*, *shred*, though the cluster /sw-/ in such forms is twice cited (99). Allophones of the /t/ phoneme before weak-stressed /əl,ən/ (phonetically syllabic [l,ŋ]) are incompletely treated: Hall does not mention the apicalized glottal stop noted by Trager (1942) as an allophone of his /t/ phoneme and probably more common in the Upland South than in the East. The alternation between such forms as *éverwhàt* and *whàtéver* (or *whatéver*) is part of the morphology, not of the phonology. Concern whether *éverwhère* "represents" *everywhere* or *wherever* (105) is unnecessary; that a form *éverwhère* is used in the Smokies in well-defined syntactic situations is the only relevant statement (and properly part of the syntax); what occurs in other dialects is unimportant. Postvocalic /-r/ deserves a single treatment, among the consonant phonemes, rather than a treatment in several parts, some with the vowels and others with the consonants. Hall speculates about the future of postvocalic /-r/, but without maps or charts to support his speculations; contrast Bloch's treatment of postvocalic /-r/ in New England (1938).

C. Many of Hall's other analyses are weak. The undefined learned terms "apheresis," "aphesis," "syncope," and "metanalysis" confuse rather than clarify his statements. It is unnecessary to suggest reasons for shortened forms like /katəluwt∫/ beside the longer /katəluwt∫ij/ *Cataloochee* (74); it suffices to state that both forms occur. The forms /bə́k-âgər,bə́k-êjkər/ *buck-ague* may indicate folk analysis and analogical creation of agentive forms rather than phonetic development (79). The proper name *Odus* is not merely a folk spelling, but occurs in well-to-do urban families. Hall cites many forms which suggest likely spelling pronunciation or folk analysis of book words probably of limited occurrence: *civilian* (55), *Italian*, *violin* (56), *microphone* (61), *incinerator* (66), *Zephyr* (70), *massacre*, *sabre* (79), *quadruple* (88), *cuckold* (91). It is of doubtful relevance to cite pronunciations of place names which could be learned only from chance encounter or from books: *Arizona* (25), *Utah* (31), *Norfolk* (32), *Colorado* (59), *Idaho*, *Omaha* (60), *Alamogordo* (New Mexico) (81). Hall concerns himself too much with abnormalities, such as the exclamatory form /wij won/ (phonetically ['wi: 'wɑ:·n]), uttered by a girl of high-school age (40). Forms from sermons —— /dorknes/ *darkness* (72), /ənatəmejtəd/ "anathemated" [?] (100) —— or from songs —— as /-ijn/ instead of /-iŋ,-in/ in the present participle (16) —— are suspect; preachers and singers often use forms different from those of ordinary speech.[13] Hyperforms or attempted corrections may occur on phonograph records when the informant tries to dress up his speech for outsiders: /ont/ for *aunt* (24); /stamp/ *stamp* (v.) instead of /stomp/ or /stowmp/ (26);[14] /karektər/ *character* (61); /intərestiŋ/ *interesting* (64); the rarity on the disks of /aks/ instead of the more formal *ask* (99); the pronunciation of orthographic *l* in *calm*, etc. (104). Work sheets properly used would give field records against which any such abnormalities might be checked.

It is unnecessary to list all forms cited by Hall which occur outside the Smokies: he himself recognizes that Smokies speech does not differ greatly from many other Southern dialects,[15] though his preoccupation with the phonemic system of his "General American" makes him emphasize apparently strange or quaint forms. But of the forms which he cites as rare, illiterate, only reported, or not appearing in his records, I use in my normal speech: /hjer/ *here*, *hear*; /der/ *dear*, *deer*; /jer/ *year*; /wu∫/ *wish* [the high-central [ɨ] is probably more common, but in 1943 the possibility that this vowel contrasted with that of *pit* and *put* was yet to be raised]; /ker/ *care*; /l∫er/ *chair*, *cheer*; /sker/ *scare*; /pəwr/ *poor*; /jəwr/ *your*; /nəw-kâwnt/ *no-account* (adj.); /tinəsij/ *Tennessee*; /dəreklij/ *directly*; /vojgrəs/ (never associated etymologically with either *vigorous* or *vicious*) 'mean-tempered;' /korpəmtər/ *carpenter*; /tərpəmtojn/ *turpentine* (both of these, as in all normal Southern pronunciation, with the medial syllable phonetically a syllabic [m̩]); /ruwkəs/ *ruckus*; /ijbəm/ *even*; /sebəm/ *seven*; /ələbəm/ *eleven*; /hebəm/ *heaven*; /smidʒin/ *smidgen*; /kəndʒər/ *conjure*; /əmbəl/ *humble*; /juwmər/ *humor*; /frejəl/ *frail* (v.) 'to thrash (a person) thoroughly' (never associated with *flail*); /həwlt/ *hold* (n.). I use jocularly or proverbially, as part of the folk dialect: /wijpənz/ *weapons*; /howrspitəl/ *hospital*; /fərən,fərənər/ *foreign*, *foreigner*; /∫əwr/ *sure*; /nogin/ *noggin* 'head;' /kərlojnij/ *Carolina*; /howŋgrij/ *hungry*. Many other supposedly rare forms occur outside the Smokies: /rejəl,rejlij/ *real*, *really*, are common among middle-aged educated speakers in middle Tennessee. *Bleat* is always /blejt/ among rural speakers in middle Tennessee and the South Carolina Piedmont. In most of South Carolina, rural informants recall the 'Dutch oven,' and /əbəm/ is a common form. Despite Hall's failure to hear it, /bor/ *bear* probably occurs in the Smokies; in middle Tennessee /bor-grâjs/ *bear-grass* is the common name for the yucca. In the rural South, /kəmints/ *commence* is normal. The surname *Jordan* is often /dʒərdən/. The form /owl/ *oil* is very common [for other speakers, *all* may have an upgliding diphthong [ɔoɬ,ɒɬ], while *oil* has a centering one [ɔəlɬ]. The three surnames *Robison*, *Robertson*, *Robinson* are homonymous in Up-Country South Carolina and Louisiana upper-class speech: /robərsən/ or /robəsən/. Final weak-stress /-ij/ where other dialects would have /-ə/ is by no means confined to the Smokies area: *Saluda* (the river, town, or county in South Carolina, or the town in North Carolina) is often /səluwdij/; a native of White County, Tennessee, said that the proper pronunciation of *Sparta*, the county seat, was /sportij/; a native of *Golconda*,

Illinois, called it /gəwlkondiჳ/. In the South, the morpheme -boro in place names is nearly always /-bərə/. Mountain as /mawntiŋ/ is frequent; Fountain Inn (Greenville County, South Carolina) is often /fawntiŋ-in/ in local speech. Throughout the South the suffix morpheme -ville in place names is frequently preceded by the possessive: St. Martinville, Louisiana, is often St. Martinsville, in writing as well as speech; I have heard my own city called /grijnzvəl/. Among my schoolmates /njuwnojted/ for United was common.

In addition, there are many clear errors of statement. In Heywood County, North Carolina, I heard forty (as usual in the South) with the syllabic of law, never with that of low. A shoat is not "a young pig," but a half-grown animal, older than a pig but not yet a full-grown hog. A staple is not "a kind of nail," but is used for quite different purposes. A /vormənt/ varmint (vermin is only a book word) is not any "wild animal or bird" but only a small predatory animal, especially one addicted to chicken stealing, such as the fox, weasel, or skunk; sometimes the word is used metaphorically, of a treacherous or unpleasant person, but I have never used or heard the form as descriptive of a bird. Okra has probably as wide social distribution as pneumonia. Hendersonville is in Henderson County, North Carolina, not in Transylvania County. To lowrate means 'to censure,' not merely "to criticize." The forms /skruwtʃ/ and /skrawdʒən/ are best simply listed as forms, rather than explained by involved etymologies. It is the business of the descriptive linguist to state the forms that occur, not to invent ingenious explanations.

In the four pages of Hall's bibliography there are strange omissions. He does not list the records for the Linguistic Atlas of the South Atlantic States, though Lowman's work in western North Carolina might have improved his methodology. He does not cite any of the works on phoneme analysis, in Language and its Supplements, by Bloomfield, Sapir, Swadesh, Twaddell,

Bloch and Trager, and others. He overlooks the discussion of dialect geography in Bloomfield's Language (1933), and Kurath's recent delineation of American dialect areas (1940). He has apparently not consulted the bibliography of linguistic geography in the New England Handbook, though the works of Bloch, Caffee, Daddow, Orbeck, and Penzl might have been helpful. It is not necessary to append a ponderous bibliography to a descriptive linguistic study, but it is important that the author show familiarity with proved methodology. Among the list of "Dialect Novels, Stories, and Works Descriptive of Southern Appalachian Life and Culture," one does not find Mildred Haun's The Hawk's Done Gone (1940), the truest representation of Smokies life in fiction and probably the only novel by a native of the area; nor does one find any reference to the romances, short stories, and sketches of William Gilmore Simms, who was better than most authors at representing local dialect in literature. For "Diaries, Journals, MSS" and for "History and Geography," Hall does not seem to have consulted the extensive Flowers collection of Caroliniana at Duke University, or to have made use of the work of Odum and other rural sociologists at the University of North Carolina.

Possibly Hall's induction into military service caused hasty publication, which led to errors that might otherwise have been avoided. But no haste to publish can account for bad methodology, both in field work and in analysis. In Hall's work these errors are particularly regrettable: the scattering of the younger natives and the dying of the older ones will soon make it impossible for a linguist to study the Smokies afresh. Consequently a reviewer, though applauding Hall's energy and welcoming the information he collected, cannot approve his use of his informants or his analysis of his data. Perhaps, if the war ends early enough, Hall may make a more systematic study of Smokies speech before the last native informants are gone.

NOTES

[1] See, for example, R. McDavid 1942a (in this volume, pp. 5-9); Bloch and Trager 1942; Bloomfield 1933:Ch. 5, Ch. 19.

Fieldwork in Up-Country South Carolina, which supplied much of the evidence on which this review is based, was made possible by a fellowship from the Julius Rosenwald Fund.

[The review attempts to analyze the dialect in question, as well as the speech of Greenville, South Carolina, in terms of the Trager and Bloch six-vowel analysis of 1941. That creakings appear in the statement is not surprising; one should

examine Chapter 45 in this volume, which used the nine-vowel Trager and Smith analysis, and Chapter 59, which reverted to the unitary analysis adopted by Kurath and R. McDavid, in The Pronunciation of English in the Atlantic States (1961). Relevant also is "Confederate Overalls," in this volume, pp. 282-87.]

[2] The phonemic structure of the Greenville dialect was discussed before meetings of the Linguistic Society of America at New York (1938) and Chapel Hill (1941); see also "Confederate

Overalls," in this volume, pp. 282-87.

Following the practice of Trager and Bloch 1941, phonetic transcriptions are enclosed between square brackets, phonemic transcriptions between slant lines. Since the dialects of the Smokies and of Up-Country South Carolina differ principally in the assignment of forms to a given phoneme rather than in the phonemicization, the following symbols are used for the stressed syllabics of both dialect groups: /i,e,a,o,ə,u/ for the six short vowels of *pit*, *pet*, *pat*, *pot*, *putt*, *put*; /ij,ej,aj,oj/ for the diphthongs in *beat*, *bait*, *pass*, *bite*; /aw,ow,əw,uw/ for the diphthongs in *bout*, *bought*, *boat*, *boot*.

Numbers in parentheses refer to pages of Hall's monograph.

[3] "The relation of Smokies speech to that of the Southern Appalachians in general is an interesting question but one which surpasses the limits of the present purpose and the knowledge of the writer" (5). "Many of the phenomena here discussed are widespread. . . . It is no doubt impossible to single out any feature in the pronunciation of the Great Smokies as peculiar to that area"(85). Yet six weeks of field work -- less if the short Atlas work sheets were used -- would determine whether isoglosses coincide with the boundaries of the Smokies. On the North Carolina side, Hall could have checked what the records of the South Atlantic Atlas suggest. (Bernard Bloch adds editorially: "Hall did in fact spend a day several years ago at the office of the Linguistic Atlas, consulting the manuscript field records on file there.")

[4] Settlement was not legalized till the treaty of 1791 (9). Swain County was not organized till 1871 (8). "One of the older present residents of the area [western Swain County] states that his family came . . . in 1882 when he was a boy, and that his parents had previously settled in Cashiers Valley, having come there from South Carolina. . . . Other first settlers of that area came from Burke County, North Carolina [about fifty miles east of Asheville] about 1883"(11). In such a community one would expect dialect mixture, rather than any strongly local type of speech. Yet Hall characterizes an informant from this recently settled area as "a picturesque character of the remote and isolated Hazel Creek [Swain County, North Carolina], who in the author's belief is one of the last of the old mountain men of the Smokies" (29).

[5] Thus in the English of southwestern Louisiana, /θ/ and /ð/ do not occur. Such spellings as *tink*, *team* for *think*, *theme*, and *Mermentheau* for *Mermenteau* (a river) indicate the absence of a phoneme /θ/. But such words as *then*, *those*, always spoken with initial /d-/, I have never observed written with *d-*.

[6] See 13, 14, 18, 22, 26, etc. The findings of Marckwardt and his colleagues demonstrate that the Middle West, long supposed to be the center of "General American," is clearly divisible into at least two subareas; Kurath, on the evidence of Atlas records from the Middle and South Atlantic states, replaces the old terminology with a division of American dialects into Northern, Central, and Southern. In any event, however, the only relevant norms for Hall's study were those of Smokies speech; and the only scientifically valid procedure would be to describe the range of sounds within each phoneme of that speech.

[7] (Bernard Bloch adds editorially: "We have since come to the conclusion, however, that the dialects in question, and perhaps most other dialects of English, can be more conveniently described in terms of *seven* vowel phonemes. We should now transcribe the words in our table 2 [Trager and Bloch 1941:243] as follows: *pit* /pít/, *pet* /pét/, *pat* /pǽt/, *pot* /pát/, *cut* /két/, *put* /pút/; *beat* /bíjt/, *bait* /béjt/, *bite* /bájt/, *Hoyt* /hójt/; *bout* /báwt/, *boat* /bówt/, *boot* /búwt/; *idea* /àjdíh/, *yeah* /yéh/, *balm* /báhm/, *law* /lóh/, *huh* /héh/; . . . *beer* /bíhr/, *bear* /béhr/, *bar* /báhr/, *bore* /bóhr/, *burr* /béhr/, *boor* /búhr/. To the syllabics consisting of vowels + /h/ is to be added /æh/, as in *ashen* (contrast *passion* with /æ/); to the series *mirror* /mírər/, *merry* /mérij/, *marry* /mǽrij/, *sorry* /sárij/, *hurry* /hérij/, *jury* /džúrij/, is to be added *story* /stórij/ (contrast *glory* /glóhrij/ with the syllabic of *law*.) [For those who consider the nine-vowel analysis a revealed dogma, this footnote should be helpful; for several years many of Trager's students had held just as passionately to the six-vowel analysis, and Bloch's acceptance of a seventh in 1943 made me willing to accept a tenth in 1951 if the data called for it.]

[8] "*Hotel* is always [ˈhoˌtɛl] in the Smokies; it is included in this list [of forms with weak-stressed initial syllables whose syllabic is orthographically represented by *o*] because General American is taken as the norm"(57).

[9] See Trager 1940, Trager and Bloch 1941. Trager's contrast, based on the phonetics of his own dialect, is between /a/ as in *bade* and /eh/ as in *bad*; the difference in our analyses reflects a different phonemic structure as well as different phonetic features. The significant linguistic fact is that such a phonemic difference -- regardless of which analysis the phonetic features of the dialect demand -- exists in many dialects of American English and should be noted when it occurs.

[10] In the phonetic alphabet for the New England *Atlas*, one symbol was used for the low-back position, indicating (when unaccompanied by diacritics) a vowel with slight rounding. For other sections, two symbols are used, for rounded and unrounded low-back vowels. The differences between the Atlas field workers in transcribing low-back vowels (see the *Handbook*, 126-27) suggests that each field worker should know intimately the phonemic patterns of his own speech, and should prepare a descriptive phonemic analysis of the speech of each informant.

[11] In my dialect, forms of the types *boy*, *quoit* are often dissyllabic, patterning like *doughy*, *poet*; forms of the type *oil* may be dissyllabic /owil,owəl/, or monosyllabic rhyming with the type

call /owl,kowl/; the forms *coin* and *cawin'* are homonymous and dissyllabic: /kowin/.

[Here a unitary phonemic analysis seems to require less elaborate explanations.]

[12] Such forms are easily elicited from informants, and have been found in the compositions of college students in southwestern Louisiana. [They are almost universal in British folk speech.]

[13] Thus in the Litany a New Haven Anglican priest uttered *cowardice* with medial-stressed final syllable: /kâwərdòɹs/.

[14] In Up-Country South Carolina, /stamp/ and /sto(w)mp/ are never confused. One /stamps/ a letter but /sto(w)mps/ his foot. The latter is locally often written *stomp*; the spelling *stamp*, as in Arthur the Rat ("stamping her feet on the ground"), would encourage an artificial pronunciation.

[15] See note 3 above. If Hall's methodology were sounder in the field and in analysis, it would be unnecessary to cite these forms with wider distribution than that indicated in the monograph. But relying largely on chance data collected without systematic work sheets, and basing the analysis on a mythical "General American" rather than on the usage of the Smokies area, Hall is suspect in his statements of distribution and social standing. The comparison with forms in the Greenville dialect may be instructive. Since Greenville is on the fringe of the mountain area, and was originally settled by much the same cultural groups as first settled the Smokies, any relic forms current in Greenville should be carefully looked for in the Smokies. Moreover, since urban speech is ordinarily more susceptible than rural to external cultural influences, one should take with caution Hall's labels of "illiterate," "uneducated," and the like if the form so labeled is still currently respectable in Greenville.

A difficulty that linguistics faces in obtaining recognition as a science is that few competent linguists have attempted to present the principles and the results of their science to the public. In this respect linguistics is far behind other sciences. Huxley publicized the discoveries of nineteenth-century biology and geology; Jeans and Russell have popularized post-Einsteinian physics; and the Oak Ridge scientists have been convincingly articulate about nuclear fission and its economic and social implications. Even other branches of anthropology have been better publicized by their practitioners than linguistics -- as in the works of Boas, Malinowski, Hooton, and Ruth Benedict. But linguists, who know most about language, seem of all scientists to use it least well in presenting their science to the uninitiated. In the last century, Max Müller and William Dwight Whitney could popularize without abandoning scientific principles; but today, with the exception of one journalistic report ("Science Comes to Languages" 1944) and one radio program,[1] the scientific linguist generally writes in technical language for other linguists, while the popularizer ignores the principles of linguistic science and becomes a purveyor of get-culture-quick nostrums.

To this pattern the work of Mencken is a refreshing exception. Though not an academically trained linguist, he is a careful observer and bases his work, like all descriptive linguists, on the assumption that a language is what its speakers actually use. Furthermore, he presents his case in a style that any literate person can follow.[2]

The thesis of *The American Language*, in all its editions (1919, 1921, 1923, 1936), has been that the language of the United States has developed into something quite different from the standard English of Great Britain, until it is now not just a divergent dialect, or group of dialects, but a language in its own right, not only established in this country but displacing British English in international use and bringing about changes -- especially in vocabulary -- even in the language of England itself, and is to be criticized by its own standards and not by some arbitrary norm. Though most linguists would hardly go so far as to accept 'American' as a separate language -- even Mencken, though proving divergence, does not demonstrate the mutual unintelligibility which linguists insist upon as a criterion for setting up separate languages -- they can find no quarrel with Mencken's insistence on appraising American usage on its own merits. That, after all, is what Fries has done in his *American English Grammar* (1940), and what underlies the work of the *Linguistic Atlas of New England* (Kurath *et al.* 1939-43).

Supplement I, while capable of being understood and enjoyed on its own merits, is basically an attempt to bring up to date a part of the material covered in the fourth edition of *The American Language* (1936); a second supplement is expected to appear some time next year.

As in the earlier editions, one notices from the outset that Mencken, like any good linguist, possesses a broad knowledge of his subject and a scientific attitude towards his data. He has made every effort to obtain pertinent information. He has read widely, both in the language and about it; he has kept up with current scholarship; he has utilized clipping bureaus to gather information not generally assembled, and has encouraged the criticism and cooperation of other scholars, generously acknowledging the information given to him. In drawing his conclusions, however he may phrase them, he is a scientist: he proceeds on the principle that one man's dialect is as good as another; and he ridicules Anglomania, regional or social snobbery, prudery, and other influences preventing the effective use or the rational appraisal of the resources of the language.

Supplement I covers the ground of the first six chapters of the 1936 edition: I. "The Two Streams of English;" II. "The Materials of Inquiry;" III. "The Beginnings of American;" IV. "The Period of Growth;" V. "The Language Today;" VI. "American and English." The method is to take up points in the 1936 edition for which new evidence has been found or new summaries or interpretations have been made, and to state the new conclusions. Since the *Dictionary of American English* (Craigie and Hulbert 1936-44), completed since 1936, is the best record in dictionary form of usage in this country, Mencken naturally introduces the evidence of the *DAE* on almost every point, elaborating or emending it in the light of his own findings and those of other scholars. By its nature and scope, this supplement is more concerned with lexicography than with other phases of linguistics. The mass of details is so great that a reviewer is almost obliged to speak in general terms; it would be futile to draw up long lists of particular forms and attempt to point out every instance where more is known of usage or etyma than Mencken has presented.

Throughout the opening chapter especially, Mencken makes clear how actual usage asserts itself, regardless of the pronouncements of self-appointed guardians of the language on both sides of the Atlantic. From John Witherspoon of Princeton, in 1781, down to contemporary newspaper quacks, there have been repeated efforts to purge the 'ungrammatical' and 'improper,' to rule out coinages and neologisms; but Americans have gone on using words as the situation demanded and freely coining new ones, with the result that the American vocabulary has grown increasingly rich and colorful even though in some respects a little bizarre. The richness and color and grotesqueness alike Mencken points out with relish.

In the beginning most learned men, both British and American, looked down on the colloquial language of the United States. There were efforts -- as in England a century earlier, and as unsuccessful -- to set up some sort of Academy to 'ascertain' and purify the language, but the commonsense views of such men as Jefferson prevailed (20).[3] That Noah Webster was a close observer and found it not only patriotic but good business to defend American usage against attempts to make it conform to the patterns favored in England -- this fact not only counterbalanced Webster's personal and sectional authoritarian tendencies, but made his writings one of the strongest forces in behalf of a separate standard for this country (21-27). Writers as well as educators attempted to direct the course of the language: James Fenimore Cooper, for instance, held out for the diphthong /ay/ in *either*, *neither*, on the analogy of the relationship between German spelling and pronunciation, and insisted on /iw/ or /yuw/ rather than /uw/ in *new*, though elsewhere deploring the "common fault of narrow associations to suppose that words are to be pronounced as they are spelled" (119).[4] Whitman, in keeping with his traditional role as a prophet of grass-roots American literature, insisted on American standards and on the right of a language to grow in accordance with the spirit of the people speaking it, but his own practice showed an addiction to the very type of finishing-school English that he inveighed against (124). In contrast with the literary Brahmins and prophets, Mencken reemphasizes the part that the humorists -- especially Mark Twain -- played in developing American standards, by freely using class and regional dialect

to heighten their caricatures and by spreading the more colorful words among the American reading public (126-33).

The second chapter, the shortest, attempts to determine the nature of characteristically American words, and to classify the types of Americanisms. In general, an "American" word is considered to have something "rude and busteous" about it -- to typify the forcefulness and vigor and creative energy with which this nation is conventionally associated. A parallel is drawn -- not to be pressed too far -- between the prodigal creative vigor of the expanding United States in the nineteenth century, and that of England during the Elizabethan era (153-56).

The third and fourth chapters, on the beginnings of American and the period of growth, deal chiefly with the sources of new words in the American vocabulary during the colonial period and the nineteenth century: with borrowings from the languages of the American Indians and of non-English-speaking immigrants, with new compounds formed from English morphemes, with altered meanings to describe new physical phenomena and social institutions, and with outright coinages -- the vocabulary of drinking and of politics being here treated in particular detail. With his usual interest in social satire, Mencken often emphasizes the amusing side of the vocabulary, but where there is new evidence on a disputed point -- as on the long-disputed origin of *O.K.* -- he has carefully introduced this evidence and supplied documentation (269-78). [It was further updated in Mencken 1963.]

Chapter 5, "The Language Today," discusses the sources of new words -- especially headlines, columnists, the argot of such magazines as *Variety* and *Time*, and trade names -- and illustrates the development of such new productive affixes as *-teria*, *-burger*, and *-eroo* (350-72). Mencken's copious citations of verbs derived without change from nouns (382-92) bear out the contention of many linguists that the chief distinction between verbs and nouns in modern English is not in form but in syntactic function.

The final chapter in the *Supplement*, "English and American," not only cites divergences in the vocabularies of the two countries, but also (especially in the section on euphemisms) pokes fun at the occupational and racial sensibilities of many Americans, and at their attempts to designate themselves and their work by names either indicating a superior social status -- like the pseudo-engineers (581-84) and the undertakers (567-72)[5] -- or avoiding the social stigma traditionally associated with the conventional names (611-37).

It is apparent from this summary that *Supplement I* is not, strictly speaking, concerned with linguistics in the narrowest sense. Its matter, save for occasional references to phonological or morphological details, is essentially lexical, and frequently digressive in discussing the sociological context in which new forms have originated. But no linguist denies that the lexicon is a part of the language, and that one of the significant features of any language is the way in which its lexicon is enriched. It is natural and commendable that Mencken, writing for a lay audience, repeatedly emphasizes the nature of the American society in which the American vocabulary has developed.

Some linguists may dislike the rather unfavorable picture of their profession which Mencken has drawn. The charge that the Linguistic Society has no interest in American usage, the fun poked at the "mysterious entities called phonemes"(102), the excessive praise showered upon the American Dialect Society as now constituted (105) [a generation later, the praise is more justly bestowed] -- these details indicate either a bias or a lack of familiarity with the facts. The discussion of the Linguistic Atlas would indicate that in Mencken's estimation, Kurath and his associates have failed to make clear the divergences in pronunciation which are the most reliable criteria for setting off dialect areas (113-14). Perhaps Mencken's criticisms are at least partly justified. No linguist will deny that there has been warm, even acrimonious (as well as highly technical) controversy among linguists as to the most accurate scientific analysis of English phonemes (to say nothing of the phonemes of other languages), that our stimulating symposia on English phonemics have yielded relatively few papers and almost none written for a lay audience, and that systems of transcription devised by expanding the IPA need overhauling in the light of what has been learned of non-Indo-European sound systems (cf. Bloch and Trager 1942). If our faces are red when Mencken twits us with our shortcomings, the remedy is to take note of them and to adjust our practice so to reach the potential audience who are interested in language but have not had our special type of training.

That Mencken's orientation justifies him in criticizing the practices of professional linguists and lexicographers is shown by the consistency with which he presents usage as the only reliable criterion. I have found only one minor divergence from this point of view: "The other objection to *Negro* has to do with the fact that the word is frequently mispronounced and tends to slide into the hated *nigger*. In the South it is more commonly heard as *nigrah*, and not only from white lips"(125-26). A more accurate linguistic statement would be that /nigrǝ/ and /nigǝr/ are not mispronunciations but

forms which, though historically explainable, have come to stigmatize the group which they designate, and that this group has consequently fostered the use of the spelling pronunciation /niygrow/ as more dignified and less derogatory. The stigma, not the "mispronunciation," is what Negroes object to (see R. McDavid 1960b, in this volume, pp. 146-49). With this minor exception, Mencken's point of view is completely descriptive -- as in his appraisal of Farmer's *Americanisms -- Old and New* (1889) (97), in his awareness of the limitations of the *DAE* (9, 108-09),[6] in his condemnation of normative grammar (163, 321), and in his discussion of *shall* and *will* (402-04).

It is not surprising that *Supplement I*, like preceding editions of *The American Language*, should testify to the author's prejudices. Anglomania in its varied forms is the object of perhaps the sharpest attack (the Protestant Episcopal Church, for instance, is characterized as "the crown colony of the Church of England"[500]), but there are also repeated sallies against Puritanism (113, 186, 234, 649, 671),[7] prohibitionists (305, 431, 522, 644), censorship (641-49), the New Deal (102, 299, 300, 303-06, 308, 411-18),[8] and professors of pedagogy (236, 528).[9] While not in the strictest traditions of academic scholarship, these asides do not lessen the soundness of Mencken's conclusions and serve to keep up the reader's interest. Less justifiable, perhaps, are the long digressions on formulae for alcoholic drinks (252-62), on the origin of the verb *to goose* (390-92), and on the author's coinage of the term *ecdysiast* as a more dignified professional title for a strip-tease artist (585-87).

Since this supplement follows the outline of the 1936 edition, it is inevitable that there should be some repetitiousness, with the same form sometimes being discussed two or three times. There are also a number of minor errata and omissions. Thus, by 1944 all three volumes of Kurath *et al.* 1939-43 had appeared, not merely the first (105). Among the writers who skilfully used dialect, Mencken does not mention the Southern novelist William Gilmore Simms. In the South, during Reconstruction and since, *scalawag* (293) has been chiefly applied to those white Southerners who collaborated with the occupation governments; the adventurers from other sections who often headed those governments were, and are, usually known as *carpet-baggers*. The common folk meaning of *smooch* 'to kiss,' is not given (238). The former sportswriter for the *New York Times* is not James M. Kieran but John (304). *Trojan horse* (306) has been applied more often to infiltration by Nazis than to that by Communists. *Sanitate*, as a verb (396), was used by Kipling in *Departmental Ditties*.[10] And *son-of-a-*

bitch, the American epithet-of-all-work, not only has the endorsement of Shakespeare (*King Lear* 2.2.22), but is traceable to the fourteenth century.[11] A person with a ready memory and the habit of reading in odd corners of literature could annotate many more details.

But these shortcomings are very small. Mencken deserves no blame for not being omniscient. *Supplement I*, like the four preceding editions of *The American Language*, is primarily intended to summarize the most important facts about the language we speak, and about the attitudes that people have held and now hold toward it. Mencken has added many details to our knowledge, has rendered many others accessible to that large body of the reading public which does not dig into academic journals and monographs, and has presented them in such a way that almost any reader -- in spite of the digressions, or perhaps baited by them -- is likely to want to continue to the end of the volume. In so entertainingly presenting the basic argument of descriptive linguistics, that a language is what it is and not what professors or critics would seek to make it, Mencken has done other linguists a valuable service. It is hoped that some of our professional scholars will be able to present the results of general linguistics to the public with some of the facility with which Mencken has presented the case for what he calls the American language.

NOTES

[1] "Where Are You From?," with H. L. Smith, Jr., was presented over the Mutual network from 1939 to 1942.

[2] [Although somewhat scornful of the highly technical terminology of American linguistics, Mencken was a member of the Linguistic Society, and actively supported the work of the Linguistic Atlas. This review and the one which follows are the only notice of *The American Language*; they pleased Mencken very much.]

[3] Authoritarianism, to be sure, is not dead, nor are its exponents found only among schoolteachers and speech correctors. An editorial in the *Saturday Evening Post*, "Is There a Lexicographer in the House?" (1946), deplores the "ungoverned tendency here in America" to admit to the dictionary "every novelty with which frontier wits and modern saloon columnists have sought to dazzle their giddy readers," remarking that "our English cousins try, in a scholarly way, to encourage a reasonably disciplined approach to it [the English language]," and calling for a lexicographer who "could cut away some of the spurious branches without injuring the tree." Even some linguists seem inclined to marshal authorities rather than to evaluate usage for what it is worth. Several of the textbooks prepared under the recent Intensive Language Program were condemned by reviewers because the foreign linguistic forms described, though admittedly possible, were not the forms approved by academies or orthoepists.

[4] The records of the Linguistic Atlas show that /uw/ prevails in Eastern New England, Pennsylvania, Maryland, New York City, and the lower Hudson Valley, and competes with /iw/ elsewhere on the Atlantic Seaboard north of the Potomac; /uw,iw/ has also been found in the Charleston-Beaufort-Savannah area.

[5] A cemetery outside Columbia, South Carolina, is advertised as "the new and modern burial estate."

[6] "It must be remembered that the *DAE*'s examples do not always show the first actual use; all they indicate is the first *printed* use encountered by its searchers"(9).

[7] "The pioneers who trekked westward . . . were not, perhaps, as vicious as the Puritans of early New England, but by the same token they lacked almost altogether the cultural aptitudes and propensities that, in the Puritans, even **Calvinism** could not kill"(234).

[8] "Of late the professors of semantics have divided into two factions. The first, led by metaphysicians, lifts the elemental business of communicating ideas to the level of a baffling and somewhat sinister arcanum standing midway between the geometry of the fourth dimension and the Freudian rumble-bumble; the other, led by popularizers, converts it into a club for use upon the enemies of the current New Deals"(102).

[9] "Of all the evangelists of Better Things who had flourished since 1800 only Noah Webster left any permanent mark upon the American people. He taught them how to spell -- a faculty that they were not to lose until the emergence of pedagogy as a learned profession, cradled at Teacher's College, Columbia"(236).

[10] "A Legend of the Foreign Office," line 2 (1886).

[11] *Of Arthour and of Merlin*, Auchinleck MS, lines 8475-78 (Macrae-Gibson 1973):

He [Wawain] grad aloude to king Taurus
'Abide þou þef malicious!
Biche-sone þou drawest amis
Þou schalt abigge it ywis!'

In this passage, as in others where *biche* appears in the same poem, the epithet is used to stigmatize the Saracens, traditional medieval villains, of whom Taurus was one of the leaders. Since the Koran labels the dog as especially unclean, the epithet is a pointed insult.

In his preface to *Supplement II*, Mencken
announces that it will probably be his
last book-length treatment of American
English. It is hoped that time, health,
and inclination will enable him to recon-
sider, and to produce at least a third
supplement covering topics treated in the
fourth edition of his book *The American
Language* (1936) but not in the present
supplement or in its predecessor of 1945.[1]
Whether a third supplement appears or not,
it is likely that *The American Language* --
begun as a task for his left hand during
the First World War, when a conflict between his opinions and the policies of the
federal government led to the suspension
of his editorial work for the *Baltimore
Sun* -- will be the work by which Mencken
is longest remembered. And in any history
of the study of American English it will
bulk large.

At some future date -- probably when
Mencken is dead and cannot object -- the
doctoral dissertation of an ambitious student will trace Mencken's development as a
linguist through the four editions and the
two supplements of *The American Language*
and through his various miscellaneous
articles on the subject. At the moment it
may serve to point out a few of the reasons why *The American Language* is one of
those works, all too rare in any of the
sciences, which combine basic soundness
with popular appeal.

No one denies that Mencken writes entertainingly. His willingness to include humorous examples and amusing digressions,
his barbed -- often ribald -- epithets for
various phenomena of American society, can
be counted on to attract and hold the layman's interest. But this is no mere
shallow cleverness; Mencken states his
arguments in clear English and supports
them with frequent examples -- a practice
that many academic linguists might profitably follow. In addition, he almost always indicates his sources in detail, so
that a critical reader may verify the evidence for himself.

But cleverness, clarity of style, and
amplitude of examples and footnotes do not
of themselves make a scientific work valuable. When the science is linguistics,
what one particularly wants to know is the
author's attitude toward language and
toward the study of language, and his
method of procedure. And here, too,
Mencken's work stands the test.

One of the most fruitful developments in
modern linguistics is the realization that
linguistics is a social science -- that a
language is a social instrument, reflecting the relationships between people in a
given cultural framework, and that linguistic phenomena must be studied in their
relationship to other cultural phenomena,
on their own merits and not in terms of
arbitrary norms. It is here that Mencken's
experience as a practicing journalist for
some forty years has somewhat compensated
for his lack of formal linguistic training. He is aware that American English is
what people actually say in their dealings
with one another, not what one would have
them say. He understands as clearly as
any other linguist that many of the traditional 'grammatical errors' against which
textbooks of composition are directed are
part of standard colloquial usage. And he
repeatedly insists that more linguists
ought to concern themselves with the way
in which Americans actually speak.[2] His
unfamiliarity with some of the technical
tools of linguistics, particularly practical phonetics and phonemic theory, occasionally leads him to an awkward statement
or an erroneous observation, more often a
failure to press an observation to its
logical conclusion or to a feeling of diffidence toward those who do. But such
lapses are comparatively rare.

Supplement II, like its predecessor, is
organized by chapters according to the
plan of the fourth edition. It includes
Chapters VII, "The Pronunciation of American;" VIII, "American Spelling;" IX,
"The Common Speech;" X, "Proper Names in
America;" XI, "American Slang." Of
these, Chapters VII and IX are of greatest
interest to the linguist, as dealing most
directly with linguistic problems; but
throughout the book the emphasis is on the
social influences operating on the language. A comprehensive list of words and
phrases cited and a full index make the
book easy to use.

Chapter VII starts with the sound observation that differences in pronunciation
(that is, not only in phonemic structure
but in the number and distribution of allophones) are more enduring than differences in vocabulary, that though the folk
words of a given area may disappear, the
local pronunciation pattern is likely to
remain. Mencken properly dismisses as ab-
surd the notion that the American climate
is responsible for dialect differences,
but seems to give too much credit to Noah

Webster as a linguistic influence -- for instance in preserving the secondary stress of such words as *secretary*. He contrasts the position of British Received Standard as a prestigious class dialect with the failure of any counterpart to arise in this country, and emphasizes the extent to which what he calls "General American" has gained favor as a model of usage. He discusses some of the systems used for indicating pronunciations differences, and suggests that intonation patterns may be the easiest means of identifying dialects. In his discussion of the vowels and consonants he works in terms of the conventional alphabet instead of using the simpler approach in terms of phonemics;[3] he seems to magnify unnecessarily the difficulties in using a phonetic or phonemic alphabet.[4] After indicating roughly the distribution of the three principal dialects which he distinguishes -- Eastern, Southern, and "General American"[5] -- he discusses briefly some of the more important national and regional studies, and follows with a state-by-state inventory of recorded local speech peculiarities and research that has been done on them, concluding with some mention of the English used in foreign-language settlement areas and a fairly long discussion of Negro speech. In no part of this inventory does he confine himself to phonological items, but brings in vocabulary and grammar wherever information is available. The contrast between, say, the long treatment given to Virginia and the brief paragraph about Michigan indicates how uneven has been the investigation of local dialects so far, and how much more work needs to be done. The studies discussed are not all of the same value -- Mencken seems to give more weight to Brooks 1935 than it deserves[6] -- but with few exceptions he mentions everything of significance.[7]

The chapter on spelling is of only marginal interest to linguists, but throughout it Mencken has stressed the operation of social and cultural forces. It contains a good brief sketch of the development of the Merriam-Webster dictionaries,[8] discusses a few of the differences between British and American orthographic practices, and gives a fairly detailed summary of the various schemes that have been devised during the past thirty years for reforming English spelling, with a few asides on similar attempts for other languages. Most of these attempts failed; the notable exceptions are the romanization of Turkish under Ataturk and the simplification of the Russian alphabet under the Soviet government -- two administrations that had no need to worry about public opinion in general, or in particular about a large literate population accustomed to an older system. In contrast, none of the schemes proposed for reforming English spelling has made any great head-way; for literacy is normal in our culture, and readers and printers accustomed to the conventions of English orthography, with all their absurdities, shun any drastic change. An interesting small-scale example of the pressure of a cultural pattern is cited from Faroese, where an early alphabet, theoretically phonetic, was replaced by one similar to that of Icelandic (312).

Chapter IX, "The Common Speech," like the corresponding chapter in the 1936 edition, assumes in general that folk grammar is relatively uniform throughout the United States -- an assumption contradicted by Atwood's recent investigation of verb forms in the folk speech of the Eastern United States [finally published as Atwood 1953a; cf. also V. McDavid 1956]. Mencken summarizes the recent efforts of linguists -- S. A. Leonard, Pooley, Barnes, Fries, Marckwardt, Curme, and Sturtevant among them -- to bring the study and teaching of grammar into closer relation to the actual facts of cultivated usage than was the practice during the vogue of the normative tradition typified by Richard Grant White. He skilfully draws upon the arguments of linguists that such forms as the double negative, *ain't*, and *I seen him* are undesirable in standard colloquial English, not because they are "incorrect grammar" but because they connote an inferior social status. He brings in evidence to refute the old charge that European peasant dialects or languages in nonliterate cultures have vocabularies of only a few hundred words.[9] Besides discussing the controversial Southern use of *you-all* -- inconclusively, as is inevitable in any discussion not based upon a mass of controlled data -- he points out that such forms as *it's me* and *who did you see?* have won acceptance on all except the most formal or finicky levels of usage.[10]

Chapter X, on proper names, provides some of the most entertaining reading for the layman, but little of direct interest to the linguist. The emphasis is again on the operation of cultural processes: immigrants from non-English-speaking countries replace their names with English ones, shorten them, or make minor changes to fit them into the phonemic and orthographic patterns of American English. Conversely, since Italian names have become familiar to native Americans, recent immigrants from Italy are less likely than earlier ones to change their names; and European and American Jews migrating to Palestine, where modern Hebrew is the official language, often adopt Hebrew names. The popularity of saints' names and later of Old Testament names attests the part that religion has played in our culture; both types have become relatively less popular with the increasing secularization of the last century. The popularity of nicknames as given names, especially for boys, and the seemingly contrary tendency to give exotic and fanciful names to girls -- both practices most common in the Southwest -- arise from the cultural situation: with a short, informal name a man, especially a politician, can avoid the charge of standoffishness; on the other hand, the unusual name is favored for a woman as a symbol of the elegance and refinement to which, by the advertising standards of a mass-production era, all women are presumed to be entitled. The section on place names gives a fair appraisal of the virtues and shortcomings of the U.S. Board on Geographical Names and indicates, by states, what local research has been done. Practices in naming telephone exchanges, apartment houses and hotels, restaurants, bungalows, trains and Pullman cars, merchant and naval vessels, churches, racehorses, and newspapers are also discussed, and the chapter ends with a few pages on the nicknames for states and their inhabitants.

The final chapter, on American slang, indicates two origins: the effort to achieve novelty of expression (manifest in the language of newspaper columnists and radio comedians), and the occupational jargon of various activities, legitimate or criminal (*slang*, it must be remembered, was originally a designation of criminal jargon). As these activities, for instance those related to the automobile and the airplane, become a part of everyday experience, some of the slang comes into general and even standard use. Increasing specialization, as our culture has grown increasingly complex, has led to the multiplication of such jargons, some of them growing naturally, others (as that of baseball) fostered by those who write about the activity. A number of short specimen glossaries are given as examples of occupational slang; and the origin of many terms, particularly such World War II items as *GI* and *jeep*, is discussed in some detail.

Not only Mencken's awareness of language as a social instrument, his clarity and facility of expression, and his liberal acknowledgement of sources, but also many observations on details indicate his appreciation of the principles and some of the problems of linguistics, especially in relation to American English. Thus, he emphasizes the relative social homogeneity of the English-speaking population of the American colonies (7-11, 20).[11] He notes the absurdities in the standards of 'correct diction' proposed by many departments of speech, especially that of Columbia University (17, 26, 33); the fact that British pronunciations are most affected among people suffering from social insecurity (20-24); the persistence of the tendency in English to shift the primary stress to the initial syllable of a word (47-48, 250); and the importance of

studying intonation, stress, pitch, and vowel length as well as the quality of vowels and sonsonants (54-60). He points out the greater frequency in the South than elsewhere of /-in/ rather than /-iŋ/ as the ending of the present participle (91) [cf. Atwood 1953a, V. McDavid 1956]; the difference in vowel quality, in most Southern dialects, between the stressed syllabic in *eye* and that in *father* (125); and for the Philadelphia area -- the chief Atlantic Seaboard focus for this change -- the loss of initial /h-/ in such words as *wheelbarrow* (203, 209) [cf. R. and V. McDavid 1952b, in this volume, pp. 185-98]. He recognizes that stress and vowel quality are criteria determining whether compounds should be written as one word (324); that multidialectalism, shifting from standard to folk forms according to the audience, is very common (347);[12] and that snobbery toward folk speech, especially toward its grammatical forms, is strongest among the group just removed from the folk (346). His own prejudices are frankly expressed, and are responsible for the pungent epithets with which he salts his allusions to such varied topics as Columbia Teachers College,[13] Richard Grant White,[14] Franklin D. Roosevelt and the New Deal,[15] the use of the syllabic of *father* in such words as *dance* and *ask*,[16] the aping of British pronunciation,[17] English departments,[18] textbooks of composition,[19] the Modern Language Association,[20] military bureaucracy,[21] and the cultural backwardness of the Middle West and the Inland South.[22] Though a sophisticated reader may become surfeited, these Menckenisms generally serve to hold his attention.

There are points to which a linguist should raise objections. In particular, Mencken seems not to understand fully one of the principles of dialect lexicography: that the dialect of an individual or of a locality includes not only the words peculiar to that person or place, but words which that person or place shares with other persons or places -- that before a word can be identified with any region or class, its occurrence must be recorded wherever it is found.[23] Moreover, it is doubtful if Americans have been as "conscious" of pronunciation as Mencken suggests (5-6). Tidewater Southern is far from uniform, but like Tidewater New England is extremely complex: Norfolk, Wilmington, and Charleston, to mention only a few, are distinctive types (14, 122). The discussion of the Army Language Program (if it warrants a place in this book at all) is entirely too brief: Mencken does not mention the summary in *Fortune*, "Science Comes to Languages" (1944); pays too much attention to Cross's embittered attack (67); mentions none of the articles written by linguists participating in the program; and -- what is particularly to the point -- says nothing about the Army manuals devised for teaching English to foreigners.

Many objections can be made from a linguistic viewpoint to particular statements. *Mall*, *Albany*, and *Raleigh* are poor examples of the so-called 'broad *a*,' since all three are very commonly pronounced with a rounded vowel or diphthong (75). The syllabic of *hearth* is often of the phonemic types /ər,əh,əy/, in standard as well as folk speech (79). *Forehead* is usually /farid,fɔrid/ in the South (95), and *Wednesday* is everywhere /wɛnzdiy,-dey/ except in extremely affected speech or in the natural speech of a few individuals (96). The initial cluster /sr-/ in *shrink* and *shrimp* is not only almost universal in the South but common elsewhere too (98). The arrangement of linguistic entries on the maps of the *Linguistic Atlas of New England* (Kurath *et al*. 1939-43), in spite of Mencken's misunderstanding, does indicate the social status of the informants, and detailed information is available in Kurath *et al*. 1939 (111). The so-called "illiterate" forms /ketʃ/ *catch*, /sæysiy/ *saucy* (of a child's manners), and /nekid/ *naked* are forms that I regularly use; I have recorded /rentʃ/ *rinse* from cultivated Southern speakers, and /guwmz/ *gums* from fairly well-educated speakers in Michigan (120) [President Ruthven of the University of Michigan regularly said /guwmz/, to the distress of the high-school graduate who assisted his dentist]. The form /griyziy/ *greasy* not only is normal for all classes of Southerners, but is used by many speakers in the New York and Philadelphia areas and generally in the sections of Pennsylvania, Ohio, Indiana, and Illinois south of a line roughly following Parallel 40 (122-23). To label the 'Egypt' section the "most interesting" dialect area in Illinois seems to betray a preference for the strange over the normal (139). Such locutions as *I live over to Wayne Avenue* are by no means confined to Chicago (141); they are found in Atlas field records from both New England and the South Atlantic states. Pronunciations of the type /tʃæs,dʃæs/ not only are not "incredible" but are not confined to New York State (184). *Tote* 'carry,' though most frequent in the South, appears often in the *Linguistic Atlas of New England*; *tote road* still occurs in northern lumbering areas; the verb *pack* 'carry' seems to be more common than *tote* in the Southern Appalachians and in Middle Tennessee (194). Philadelphia is a source, rather than an importer of Southern Piedmont expressions (204); among Philadelphia words, Mencken does not list the most typical item *pavement* 'sidewalk.' *Dry-land frog* 'toad,' *green beans* 'string beans,' and *homemade cheese* 'cottage cheese' are not exclusively Virginian (231), nor did Mrs. Nixon (1946) imply that they are. That Tagalog "has made little more actual progress [in the Philippines] than Gaelic in Ireland"(243) seems doubtful, in view of the several million persons who speak it as their native language. Systematic simplified spelling would not "vastly multiply homophones"(292), but would merely indicate them: a common confusion of writing with language. Mencken's observation that the sounds indicated by *ch* in German *licht* and *loch* are different is good phonetics but probably bad phonemics: in German the distinction is automatic, just like the Piedmont Virginian's distinction between the diphthongs of *house* and *houses* or of *rice* and *rise*. A lack of distinction between the pronunciations of *bawd* and *bored*, *whore* and *haw*, *source* and *sauce* (356) would seem as strange to Bostonians and Charlestonians as to Middle Westerners, even though the former have no postvocalic /r/ (Kurath 1940). *Zdenka*, listed among the weird names bestowed on girls (492), is a good Serbo-Croatian name. *Cuffy* and *Cuff* (513) still survive as racial labels and salutations among the Negroes of the Charleston area. There is a reasonable doubt whether the surviving American Indian languages have changed as much in the last three centuries and a half as English or Spanish (527) (Nida 1947:121). Finally, the rather loose organization of the book almost inevitably leads to a certain amount of repetition and padding.

Yet, summing up all these objections, what do we find they amount to? Simply that Mencken's knowledge does not equal the knowledge of all specialists in American English combined, and that -- approaching the subject originally as a layman -- he has not completely mastered all the principles of linguistic science, particularly of phonemic analysis and linguistic geography, two aspects of linguistics where there is still controversy among linguists.[24] It is not necessary to apologize for these defects. No professional linguist has ever attempted a study of American English on as large a scale or dealing with as many ramifications as Mencken's; every linguist who has taken the trouble to communicate with Mencken has found him ready to accept information, suggestions, and criticism, to examine new findings and methods, and to encourage the investigation of special topics. Throughout, Mencken has consistently argued for the descriptive rather than the normative approach to language study; he has consistently treated the language spoken in this country as a record of the manifold and varied activities of the American people. If today it is a little easier than it was thirty years ago to persuade teachers of English that grammar should be taught according to the way the English language actually works, if today linguists and laymen alike are becoming increasingly aware that linguistics is a social science and that the study of linguistic phenomena must be correlated with that of other social and cultural activities, a considerable part of the credit must be given to the labor which Mencken has put into his study of the American language.

NOTES

[1] Chapter XII of the 1936 edition deals with the future of American English; an Appendix treats non-English languages. "I had hoped to take up in a second Appendix certain themes not discussed at all in the fourth edition -- for example, the language of gesture, that of children, the names of political parties, cattle brands, animal calls, and so on"(v).

[2] "Not until the Linguistic Society followed in 1924 was there any organized attack upon language as it is, not as it might be or ought to be, and even the Linguistic Society has given a great deal more attention to Hittite and other such fossil tongues than to the American spoken by 140,000,000-odd free, idealistic and more or less human Americans, including all the philologians themselves, at least when they are in their cups or otherwise off guard"(336). It is interesting to note that this criticism of the Linguistic Society, though still unfair, is far milder than that in *Supplement I* and in earlier editions -- to say nothing of Mencken's criticisms of other learned societies.

[3] The quotations from Robert Bridges and Leroy T. Laase (71) are essentially in phonemic terms. Among suggestions for revising the alphabet of the IPA, Mencken does not include Bloch and Trager 1940, 1942.

[4] Trager and Smith 1951 argues that all dialects of English can be adequately represented by an alphabet of thirty-three characters (nine vowels, three semivowels, twenty-one consonants), plus marks for stress, pitch, and juncture. For a slight demurrer, see "Confederate Overalls," in this volume, pp. 282-87.

[5] Kurath has shown that the Northern type, spreading from western New England, and the Midland types, spreading from Pennsylvania, divide the Great Lakes Basin, and that the Midland types include much of the territory traditionally regarded as Southern. The lexical evidence for these conclusions is to be found in Kurath 1949.

[6] Brooks compares forms found in the Uncle Remus stories of Joel Chandler Harris and forms recorded by Payne (1908) with forms listed in the *English Dialect Grammar* of Joseph Wright (1905). Even if the dialect imitated by Harris were the same as that recorded by Payne -- and Harris was brought up in eastern, not western Georgia -- the fact would remain that eastern Alabama is a recently populated tertiary settlement area with a population of mixed origins, so that an examination of its dialect for possible sources in the British Isles would seem to be of little value.

[7] Among the omissions are Bloch and Trager 1942; Trager and Bloch 1941; Hawkins 1935, 1942; and Henry Lee Smith, Jr.'s popular radio presentation, "Where Are You From?" (Mutual network, 1939-42).

[8] Mencken's list of rivals of the Webster dictionaries does not include the *American College Dictionary* (1947), which probably appeared after *Supplement II* went to press.

[9] Early in 1948, a professor of speech at a midwestern university told a convention of dairymen that the vocabulary of many rural Americans was only about a thousand words.

[10] However, Mencken does not formally state the conclusion that in modern colloquial English the form of the pronoun is determined by its position in the sentence: *I* and *who* occur before a verb, *me* and *whom* after a verb or preposition.

[11] Most of the settlers who came from the British Isles were of the rising middle class, with both aristocracy and peasantry scantily represented. See Bridenbaugh 1938.

[12] An earlier reference (107) partially contradicts this observation. It is a commonplace, however, that many educated Southerners -- especially political figures like Huey Long and Eugene Talmadge -- automatically revert to folk dialect when addressing a folk audience.

[13] "The wizards of Teachers College, Columbia, began supplanting it [Webster's *Spelling Book*] with spellers of their own"(5); "[the apostrophe] has been dropped from the title of *Teacher's* College, Columbia, the Lhasa of American pedagogy" (325); "the more intelligent inquirers -- most of them *not* pedagogues, but philologians"(336).

[14] "He had no training in philology, but was a very cocksure fellow, and did not hesitate to pit his opinions against those of such authorities as William D. Whitney. During the Civil War he served gallantly as a Federal jobholder in New York"(23).

[15] "Roosevelt II, whose native speech was a somewhat marked form of the Harvard-Hudson Valley dialect, toned it down with similar discretion when he spoke to his lieges, and his caressing rayon voice did the rest"(45).

[16] "The broad Southern *a* is now losing ground even in Tidewater Virginia, but is holding out better among the women than among the men"(74). Field experience seems to indicate that in every social class women preserve relatively fewer folk forms, lexical or grammatical, than their husbands

and brothers.

[17] "It is a strange fact that a man born and bred to this dialect [New York City] later became one of the most adept practitioners of Oxford English known to linguistic pathology. He was William Joyce, who alarmed the British during World War II in the character of Lord Haw Haw" (193).

[18] Quoting from I. E. Clark's study of Ring Lardner: "The language of the English teachers, enforced by the psychology of the Department of Education, only confused him" (333).

[19] "The enormous proliferation of public-schools produced a heavy demand for textbooks of grammar, and nearly all of them were written by incompetents who simply followed the worst English models" (334).

[20] "When the Modern Language Association was launched at the new Johns Hopkins in 1883 it met a fate even more grisly [than that of the American Philological Association], for the young college professors who flocked into it passed over the living language with a few sniffs and threw all their energies into flatulent studies of the influence of Lamb on Hazlitt, the dates of forgotten plays of the Seventeenth Century, the changes made by Donne, Skelton and Cowper in the texts of forgotten poems, and such-like pseudo-intellectual gymnastics" (335-36).

[21] "The papers published by soldiers during World War II -- not the official papers edited by Army press-agents, but those produced by soldiers on their own" (596). "During the war a naval officer of rank and fancy suggested that *leather-teat* be substituted [as a designation for a woman Marine], but this stroke of genius was frowned on by the High Command" (779).

[22] The Inland South is called "the Get-Right-with-God-Country" (328) and "the Bible and Bilbo country" (639). In answering A. W. Read's explanation of the pronunciation of *Missouri* as *Missoura* as due to "the disinclination of the carnivora of a proud and once bloodthirsty state to let it pass under a name which suggests a diminutive," Mencken observes that Read "overlooks the unchallenged presence of the same diminuitive in *Mississippi*, one of the least infantile names on the American map, and in the names or pet-names of such testosteronic towns as *Boise*, Idaho; *Tulsy*, Okla.; *Hickory*, N.C.; and *Corpus Christi*, Texas" (544). "Kentucky has also been called the *Hemp State*, . . . not because of the activity of its busy and accomplished hangmen, but because it produced large crops of hemp" (628). ". . . since the Scopes trial at Dayton in 1925 it [Tennessee] has been called the *Monkey State* with painful frequency, and will probably be a long time living down that derisive designation. The effort to repeal natural selection by law made the State ridiculous throughout the world, and its civilized minority has suffered severely from its ensuing ill fame" (639).

[23] See Kurath's preface to Nixon 1946.

[24] The 'neolinguistic' school, building on the theories of Matteo Bartoli, consider dialect geography from an entirely different point of view from that of American dialect geographers. See R. A. Hall 1946, Bonfante 1947.

It is regrettable that there has been so
little cooperation between American linguists and teachers of speech. As linguists have rightly complained, some
speech departments, ignoring the facts of
the language, have set up arbitrary norms
of so-called correct pronunciation without
reference to any living dialect on land or
sea. Yet linguists, in turn -- though recognizing language as a social instrument
and themselves as social scientists --
have too often overlooked the social
drives, for prestige or at least for satisfactory group identification, on which
the notion of corrective speech courses is
founded. Though any dialect is correct in
all its aspects -- phonological, grammatical, and lexical -- for the cultural context in which it flourishes, yet one of
the traditional American rights is that of
changing from one's native cultural context to another, and -- like it or not --
certain linguistic features, even on the
phonological level, are frequently associated with an inferior economic or educational status.[1] Lacking detailed information about the facts of usage in various
dialect areas -- information which it is
the business of the linguist to supply --
the most conscientious speech teacher can
easily misjudge what a student must do to
achieve that satisfactory group identification. It is not surprising that some
teachers attempt to reshape according to
their own model any dialect remarkably
different from their own -- not simply to
rectify stammering, lisping, foreign accents, or slum speech. This same lack of
information undoubtedly plays into the
hands of that small minority (unfortunately a well-remembered minority) of speech
teachers who insist upon some fanciful
model of elegance which they have either
concocted themselves or inherited from
their preceptors.[2] Merely to ridicule all
teachers of speech on the basis of this
minority, as some linguists do, accom-
plishes nothing but only evades the linguist's responsibility as a social scientist: the social drives on which the appeal of speech courses is built are too
powerful, and must be met somehow. It is
incumbent on those linguists who know the
facts concerning the relative prestige of
various speech forms in various dialects
of American English to put this data at
the disposal of others,[3] recognizing the
drive for group identification and indicating what features are most likely to
prevent such identification;[4] on his
part, the teacher of speech should concentrate on those features in order to gain
the greatest returns for a given expendi-
ture of energy.[5] At present, however,
such liaison is an ideal rather than a
fact, and the linguist or speech teacher
who has explored the other man's problem
is comparatively rare.

One of those exceptions, fortunately, is
C. K. Thomas. A successful teacher, he is
well aware of the diversity of American
English -- he has recorded samples of the
speech of some 7000 informants[6] -- and in
particular has added a great deal to our
knowledge of New York speech, both Metropolitan and Upstate (Thomas 1935-37,
1942). His present book incorporates his
experience both in pedagogy and in research, and as such must be given serious
consideration by those in search of an introductory textbook in phonetics.

One is impressed from the beginning with
the clarity and conciseness of Thomas's
presentation. Using a 'broad' form of IPA
transcription (beginning students are
likely to be confused by a multiplicity of
shift signs and other diacritics) and recognizing that the layman generally thinks
of pronunciation in terms of the conventional alphabet,[7] he follows his three introductory chapters -- a general introduction, a description of the vocal mechan-
ism, and a classification of speech
sounds -- by twelve chapters on the sounds
of American English, beginning with those
symbols which in conventional English orthography most often represent the sounds
to which the IPA symbols are assigned.
Though the order of presentation is somewhat unorthodox, it seems good pedagogy to
proceed from the familiar to the unfamiliar.[8] A long chapter on regional types
explains the basis on which he divides the
United States into seven dialect areas and
includes transcriptions of specimens from
each of them, with two from what he calls
the 'General American' area. The final
chapter, on standards of pronunciation,
offers no get-prestige-quick shortcuts but
the sound advice that cultivated usage is
the only authority and that observation is
the only means of discovering that usage.
The pedagogical value of the book is en-
hanced by the exercises; footnotes and
chapter bibliographies (unfortunately
there is no general bibliography) direct
the student to more complete treatments of
some of the topics briefly discussed.

[335]

As befits a work produced by one who is both linguist and speech teacher, Thomas's book is not only generally good but has many particular virtues to which the reader should be directed. Fundamental is the observation with which the preface opens and the last chapter closes, that a language -- like any other part of a culture -- inevitably has local variations throughout its area. The conventional nature of linguistic symbols is emphasized (v), as is the fact that pronunciation and spelling may have little to do with each other -- though one must recognize the social forces that occasionally lead to spelling pronunciations (7-8). The defects of dictionaries and their keys are admitted. The evidence is given for treating the vowel of *cut* and the unstressed vowel of *sofa* as stress-conditioned members of the same phoneme -- though Thomas does not make that formal statement and continues to use the symbols [ʌ] and [ə] respectively (95). The 'elocutionary tradition' centering in New England explains the prestige among many many speech teachers of certain New England pronunciations, especially the 'broad *a*' [a,ɑ], and students are warned that tinkering with one's speech in the effort to acquire an alien dialect with greater cultural or social prestige often leads to a way of speaking that is not only artificial but ridiculous (86-88, 102). The unstressed vowels are recognized as more difficult to analyze than the stressed ones (77-78), and phrasal stress -- with the smaller number of vowel distinctions and the weakening or loss of initial /h-/ in unstressed syllables -- is recognized as a normal phenomenon of English which neither student nor teacher ought to tamper with (102, 110). The popular notion of dialect is cleverly presented: "In his own judgment, the linguistically naive person speaks English; the other person speaks a dialect"(171). Probably the most important detail is Thomas's recognition of the phonemic principle -- that speech sounds do not occur just as so many noises, but as patterns of noises, that the patterns may differ from dialect to dialect, and that the speech teacher as well as the linguist must recognize the structure of each dialect as made up of a number of significantly contrasting units, some with a perceptually wide phonetic range.

In a book of this type, there are many statements and attitudes to which a reviewer with some field experience may take exception, as possibly weakening a very useful work. The most important of these concern Thomas's division of American English into dialect types, his phonemic analysis, and his definition of what constitutes substandard speech.

Thomas has done a useful service in helping to break down the long-fostered notion that American English is divided into three types: Eastern, Southern, and 'General American.' He has subtracted New York City from the 'Eastern' area (some scholars put it in 'General American'), and Middle Atlantic and Western Pennsylvania from 'General American,' and has set off the Southern Mountain area from 'Southern,'[9] but he still leaves the very clearly distinguished and sharply defined Richmond and Charleston-Savannah major focal areas unidentified within the Southern area.[10] Moreover the Great Lakes States are by no means as homogeneous an area as Thomas would make them: to mention only one of the more important items, the line between Northern /grɪysɪy/ and Southern and South Midland /grɪyzɪy/ -- a feature which Thomas describes as "more personal than regional"(154) -- divides Ohio, Indiana, and Illinois roughly along Parallel 40.

In his presentation of the phonemes of American English, Thomas works in terms of IPA broad transcription rather than of a structural analysis. Thus he treats the initial and final consonants of *church*, *judge* /č,ǰ/ not as unit phonemes but as consonant clusters, and the syllabics of *see, say, so, Soo* /iy,ey,ow,uw/ as unit phonemes. Yet the pattern of the language suggests no initial cluster parallel to /*ťš-/, and the fact that the syllabics of *pit, pet, pat, pot, putt, put* occur only before consonants -- plus the usual upgliding diphthongization of the syllabics of *see, say, so, Soo* -- is a powerful argument in favor of analyzing the latter as short vowel plus semivowel.[11] The analysis as short vowel plus semivowel makes it easier to symbolize structurally the characteristics of the Charleston-Savannah area, where the syllabics of *say* and *so* are ingliding diphthongs, as having /eh, oh/ where other American dialects have /ey,ow/. Thomas also multiplies his unit phonemes by using unit symbols ([ɜ] and [ɚ] respectively) for the stressed and unstressed syllabics of *girder*: a phonemic transcription for a so-called 'r-retaining' dialect would probably be /gərdər/ or /gəhrdər/, for a so-called 'r-less' dialect (where Thomas would use the transcription ['gɜdə]) /gəhdər/ or /gəydər/, with a statement that the final /-r/ is lost unless followed by an initial vowel in close juncture.[12] There is no mention that in many dialects a phonemic contrast exists between the syllabic of *bad* and that of *bade* -- in my speech between the types /æy/ and /æ/, in other dialects between /æh/ and /æ/ or /eh/ and /æ/. Nor is there any mention of the high-central short vowel phoneme /ɨ/, in many dialects distinct from both /i/ and /u/ (the syllabics of *pit* and *put*), occurring in my speech as the stressed syllabic in such words as *wish, milk, dinner, sister,* and *ribbon*.[13] Thomas is not alone in neglect-

ing any of these points; and in particular on the question of analyzing the syllabics of *see, say, so, Soo,* and *girder* it
seems that he considers the analysis as
unit phonemes easier to handle pedagogically. One can only wish that a teacher
of Thomas's ability would try to see if
the analysis of these syllabics as short
vowel plus semivowel was not at least as
easy to teach.

Defining substandard usage is difficult
at best, and in an area as large as the
United States there are likely to be sharp
differences of opinion. But among the
details which Thomas indicates as substandard are the following:

1. Syllabics of the type /æw/ in *now,
house* (107).
2. Loss or weakening of postvocalic
/-l/ in *million, film, milk, will you* (42).
3. The form /bæbdɫs/, *Baptist* (37).
4. Simplification of postvocalic consonant clusters in *land, old, candidate,
facts, kept, asked,* etc. (40, 119, 138).
5. The form /kyuwpan/, *coupon* (55, 100).
6. The form /nekɫd/, *naked* (57).
7. Phonetically syllabic [ŋ] as in
[beɫʔkŋ] *bacon* (81, 117).
8. The form /wuwnɫ/, *won't* in New York
City (95).
9. The form /pə(r)ɫikyə(r)liy/, *particularly* (136).
10. Linking /-r/ in such phrases as *the
idea of, saw him* in New England (147).
11. Forms of the type /məymə(r/, *murmur*
in New York City and parts of the South
(75, 147).
12. Simplification of the initial clusters /hy-,hw-/ to /y-,w-/, as in *humor,
whip* (104).
13. Homonymy of *for, far* in the South
(90).

Of these, numbers 1, 2, 4, 5, 6, 7, and 9
occur regularly in my own speech.[14] I
have often encountered number 3 in the
speech of educated Southerners, and usually number 10 in the speech of educated
Eastern New Englanders. Lowman recorded
forms of the types /wuwnɫ,wunɫ/ for two-
thirds of the cultivated speakers of the
New York metropolitan area, and in
Charleston they are prestigious forms.
Such forms as /məymə(r),səytənliy/ are
upper-class speech in New York City
(though possibly a little old-fashioned),
and in the Deep South are prestigious as
associated with the plantation class.
Homonymy of *far, for* is rare in the South
Atlantic states on any level, and in
western Louisiana and East Texas seems to
be without social connotation. The simplification of initial /hy-,hw-/ is a more
complex problem. However, according to
the records of the Linguistic Atlas, *humor*
is prevailingly /yuwmər/ south of the New
York-Pennsylvania line; and such words as
whip and *wheelbarrow* prevailingly have

initial /w-/ east of the Alleghenies from
Albany to Baltimore (with /w-/ forms
spreading among younger and more sophisticated speakers), and often along the New
England coast from Boston north and the
South Atlantic coast from Georgetown
south (R. and V. McDavid 1952b, in this
volume, pp. 185-98). To toss such forms
in the same barrel with /diyz,dowz/ *these,
those,* /aytælyən/ *Italian,*[15] and /siŋiŋ/
singing, seems to involve a question of
perspective. For most of the forms listed
in this paragraph it is a case of pay your
money and take your choice.

A few other details might be differently
presented. Whisper is not the same thing
as voicelessness (28-29). *Nephew* often
occurs with /v/ in the coastal South (38).
Clapboard is far from an unfamiliar word
in the Northern area (118). Intervocalic
voiced /-ɫ-/ is distinguishable from /-d-/
on a fortis-lenis basis (116). Simplification of consonant clusters is less
likely to be noticed (especially unfavora-
bly) than intrusive consonants because it
is a more normal phenomenon of American
English (139). Such a form as /haləwiyn/
Halloween may be a survival of earlier /a/
rather than an innovation (151); such
relic forms with /a/ occur sporadically
along the Atlantic Seaboard in the speech
of old-fashioned Atlas informants. A
rounded vowel is frequently recorded for
pot, rock, crop in the South Carolina and
Georgia coastal plain (152). Such forms
as [nəɫs,həus] *nice, house,* with a centering beginning -- very common in Michigan
and the Adirondacks (where they seem to
occur as often before voiced as before
voiceless consonants) as well as in the
Virginia Piedmont and the South Carolina
and Georgia Tidewater (where they generally occur as variants of /ay,aw/ before
voiceless consonants) -- probably represent more a survival of an earlier stage
in the development of English diphthongs
than "an extension of Canadian usage"(153-
54). And the weakening or loss of intervocalic /-r-/ in *barrel* is not confined to
the South (145). The bibliographies omit
both Pike's *Phonetics* (1943) and his *Phonemics* (1947); Bloch and Trager 1942;
Trager and Bloch 1941; and Trager's analyses of the phonemic bifurcation of 'short
a'(1940).

One cannot overlook these details. Some
of them -- in particular the hesitance to
make phonemic statements -- come close to
being fundamental; one must hope that
they will be corrected in subsequent editions. Nevertheless, one should not reject the book on their account: most if
not all of them are not errors that spring
from taking a wrong direction, but those
that develop when one does not go far
enough in the right direction. Where
Thomas's dialect divisions differ from
those of the Atlas, the explanation may
lie in the different type of questionnaire

and the different circumstances under which the interviews were conducted.[16] Where one objects to his phonemic analyses, one must admit that Thomas is not the only one who does not accept the analysis of English phonemes that has been worked out by Bloomfield and his students, but that the same type of analysis that Thomas uses is sometimes found even in what purport to be treatises on phonemic analysis.[17] And in disagreeing with Thomas over what constitutes substandard usage,

one must remember that Thomas himself admits that the problem is complicated, and that no hard and fast rule can be applied. Within its limits and for its purposes, the book is good. It should be a successful and teachable introductory textbook; it should help dispel normative notions; and it should point the way toward the cooperation of linguists and teachers of speech, who are both -- though in different ways -- concerned with the effectiveness of language as a social instrument.

NOTES

[1] A part of the work of the applied anthropologist is to educate people out of the notion that other people may be inferior by belonging to economically or educationally unprivileged groups, and out of considering the dialects of such groups as inferior. Until that end is attained, however, the practical problem will remain.

An example of the extent to which dialectal prejudice is found is the recent experience of a Cornell student, a native of Oklahoma, who -- inquiring by phone if an apartment was available -- was almost rejected unseen because the owner of the building identified the student's standard Oklahoma speech with the speech of Negroes.

[2] Such unrealistic attitudes are not confined to teachers of speech, but are probably at least as common among teachers of English and of modern languages. One has only to remember that several of the textbooks prepared by linguists under the Intensive Language Program were pounced upon because they contained forms which, though admittedly current in cultivated speech, were not the forms recommended by academies or orthoepists.

[3] Kurath and R. McDavid 1961 summarizes data from Linguistic Atlas records along the Atlantic Seaboard. For treatments of New York City speech see Frank 1949, Hubbell 1950.

[4] The type of evaluation will vary from individual to individual, even within the same family, depending on each person's sense of cultural security and on how he judges his success in achieving group identification. Linguistics is therefore one of the branches of anthropology that must cooperate with psychology in the study of personality. For a suggestion of the type of cooperation needed (though linguistics is not directly mentioned), see Linton 1945.

[5] The best teachers of speech -- probably a majority of the profession -- recognize that the artificial standards of elegance which some teachers try to perpetrate actually prevent satisfactory group identification (except with small culturally marginal groups) because those who have acquired artificial speech patterns are often regarded as freaks.

[6] Unfortunately, Thomas nowhere indicates the type of interview or questionnaire. From the

selections in Chapter 21, it may be inferred that the reading of a selected prose text constitutes at least a part.

[7] Even such an astute observer as H. L. Mencken discussed American pronunciation in terms of the conventional alphabet as late as 1948.

[8] Although tables of vowels and consonants are given, they are buried in the middle of the book (96, 103); they might be more useful if they were printed at the beginning (or end), for ready reference. Thomas explains that the tables were printed in the middle of the book for deliberate pedagogical reasons, so that the students would not be confronted with the full array of symbols until they had been introduced to them individually. When he used Kenyon 1924, his students found the tables of symbols at the beginning both bewildering and discouraging.

[9] In Kurath 1949 Thomas's Middle Atlantic, Western Pennsylvania, and Southern Mountain are included as subdivisions of the Midland, identified respectively as Philadelphia, Pittsburgh, and South Midland.

[10] The bundles of isoglosses setting off the Richmond and Charleston areas are at least as sharp as those for Philadelphia and Pittsburgh. To take but one example, very sharp lines set off both Richmond and Charleston areas as having forms of the type /rum,brum/ room, broom, as opposed to the inland forms /ruwm,bruwm/. See R. McDavid 1949b.

[11] The analysis of these syllabics as short vowel plus semivowel helps explain the occurrence of the 'intrusive [w],' which Thomas has observed following the stressed syllabic in going, do it, etc. The explanation would be that the phoneme /w/, occurring postvocalically, sometimes becomes ambisyllabic or is doubled.

[12] Or, if the structure of the phoneme system in the dialect permits, simply as /gərdər/, with the statement that the allophone of /-r/ following /ə/ in stressed syllables is the length and tenseness that distinguish the stressed syllabic of murder from that of mudder.

[13] Thomas mentions the high-central vowel, but

only as a nondistinctive careless allophone of /i/ (49).

[14] In my native cultural area, my group would consider a pronunciation of the type /neykɨd/ as substandard -- as a spelling pronunciation affected by those trying to climb socially but unsure of their status, a linguistic analogue to flashy clothes.

[15] Kurath *et al*. 1939-43:map 453 shows that in New England /aytælyən/ is not restricted to the uneducated. [It is also in the natural speech of President Carter.]

[16] Thomas could not be expected to know all the details of what is in the Atlas, since only the New England section has been published (Kurath *et al*. 1939-43) and very little of the other data has been systematically analyzed.

[17] Pike 1947 has the same analysis of English diphthongs that one finds in Thomas's book; the only difference is that Pike goes to greater length to defend his position. R. A. Hall 1950a likewise treats the syllabics of *see*, *say*, *so*, *Soo* as unit phonemes. [So does Kurath and R. McDavid 1961; see also "Confederate Overalls," in this volume, pp. 282-87. However elegant the trageremic solution, the evidence is too refractory.]

Kurath's *Word Geography* is the first attempt to bring to a general audience some of the findings for the Linguistic Atlas of the United States and Canada, of which he has been director since its inception in 1930. Although field work for the Atlas has been under way almost continuously for the past two decades, and the New England section has appeared in print (Kurath *et al.* 1939-43), few scholars have attempted to correlate its findings with those of the other social sciences (R. McDavid 1946, in this volume, pp. 131-35). The *Word Geography* should stimulate similar investigations on the part of historians and sociologists.

Kurath's thesis is that the basic patterns of American dialects along the Atlantic Seaboard (the only area for which field work has been completed) are determined by the settlement history, modified by the trading areas of the major cities. As an introduction he shows that there are three levels of usage in America -- folk speech, common speech, and cultivated speech -- none of them sharply set off from the others. All three types have clear regional varieties, with folk speech exhibiting the greatest amount of difference and cultivated speech the least. He goes on to discuss the characteristic vocabulary of the eighteen dialect areas he has found along the Atlantic Seaboard, and the distribution of regional and social variants for particular items, illustrating the limits of speech areas and the distribution of individual words by well-prepared maps. A complete word index makes it easy for the reader to find the information about items in which he may be particularly interested.

The *Word Geography* compels a sharp revision of the traditional regional analysis of American dialects. No longer can one speak glibly of a 'General American' type of speech including everything west of the Hudson and north of the Mason-Dixon Line. Instead Kurath shows that it is necessary to set up Northern, Midland, and Southern regional groupings. The Northern region includes New England, the Hudson Valley, and their derivative settlements in northern Pennsylvania, upstate New York, and Ohio. The Midland includes the Pennsylvania settlements of the Philadelphia Quakers, the Susquehannah Valley Germans, and the Ohio Valley Ulster Scots, and their derivative settlements both to the west and at least as far south as the

Carolina and Georgia Piedmont and mountains. The Southern region includes the original plantation area -- coastal settlements from Chesapeake Bay south, and their hinterland. Within each of these regions there are clearly defined local areas. Thus New York State is divided among Greater New York, the Hudson Valley, and Upstate -- the last a continuation of northwestern New England, from which most of the early upstate settlers came. Maps indicate the characteristics of each of these areas. Greater New York, like metropolitan areas everywhere, has few distinctly local expressions, the only identifiable one being *school gets out* (33, 79; Map 156). The Hudson Valley shows many isolated relics of Dutch settlement (Maps 100, 101, 102, 120), and others which have spread elsewhere, such as *stoop* (18, 25, 52; Map 7), *pot cheese* (18, 24, 71; Maps 8, 14, 125), *cruller* (18, 21, 24, 25, 69; Maps 14, 120), and *sawbuck* (25, 35, 37, 59; Map 81). Upstate shows such Western New England words as *Dutch cheese* (18, 21, 24, 71; Maps 8, 125) and *horning* for the serenade to newly married couples (18, 23, 24, 78; Map 154). The predominance of New England settlers upstate has prevented the spread of Midland forms from Pennsylvania.

The demonstration of Midland elements in the speech of the South Atlantic states has hitherto been obscured by excessive attention to political oratory about the 'Solid South.' Kurath's observations, however, are supported by historical facts. Both tradition and records indicate the settlement of the Southern mountains and the Carolina and Georgia Piedmont by the migration southward from Pennsylvania. The record of economic and political diversity within the South -- especially evident in the strong anti-secession sentiment in all areas where Kurath has found Midland speech forms -- suggests how the Atlas can help a reinterpretation of historical data.

Kurath's meticulous scholarship is open to few objections. He perhaps does not make as much as he might of the influence on the Southern and South Midland speech of the dominant plantation caste, so that secondary cultural centers fairly far inland have taken over features of plantation speech not shared by inland rural speakers (R. McDavid 1948, in this volume, pp. 136-42). Although he suggests this influence (39, 45, 80), he nowhere summarizes it. But even for this detail he provides the evidence from which others may draw the conclusions.

The soundness of Kurath's analysis is corroborated by the results of dialect research undertaken after the *Word Geography* went to press. Recent field work in South Carolina and Georgia shows that most of Kurath's dialect boundaries for the South Atlantic states can simply be extended. The completed upstate New York field work reveals extraordinary uniformity outside the Hudson Valley (R. McDavid 1951a, in this volume, pp. 219-31). Work in the Great Lakes Basin shows that Northern, North Midland, and South Midland belts extend westward to the Mississippi, throughout the areas previously lumped together as 'General American' (A. L. Davis 1949). One can only hope that historians as well as linguists will use and amplify the new interpretation of American dialects as evidence of American social history, which Kurath has provided in his *Word Geography*.

Turner's book, the product of seventeen years of research, should inaugurate a new approach to the study of American Negro speech. It has long been known that Gullah, the dialect spoken by Negroes along the South Carolina and Georgia coast, is sharply different not only from all varieties of standard English but also from the folk dialects of the United States and Canada. The peculiarities of Gullah have been exploited by writers and raconteurs (R. Smith 1926), but little of its structure was known prior to Turner's investigations.

For the linguist and the cultural anthropologist, Gullah occupies a peculiar position as probably the unique example of a creolized language developing in the United States. The situation in which Gullah developed is a familiar type to those who have studied contact and creolized languages elsewhere (e.g., R. A. Hall 1943): Negroes from various parts of Africa were brought to the South Carolina and Georgia rice plantations, where white inhabitants were in a decided minority,[1] and opportunities to become familiar with the standard language were limited.[2] Furthermore, the development and preservation of Gullah as a creolized language has been helped by both geographical and cultural isolation (G. G. Johnson 1930:9-10): the coastal plantations were normally separated from the mainland by tidal streams or swamps;[3] the institution of slavery till 1865, and the rigid Southern caste system since then -- often reinforced by peonage[4] -- have kept a large proportion of the Gullah Negroes from any appreciable contact with the outside.

Unfortunately, until recently linguists have neglected to make a serious investigation of Gullah. Several students have published accounts of the language -- notably Bennett 1908-09, R. Smith 1926, Gonzales 1922, G. G. Johnson 1930, Stoney and Shelby 1930, and Crum 1940. Only Smith is a linguist;[5] none has had much acquaintance with African languages or with other creolized languages spoken by Negroes in the New World;[6] and most of them are white Southerners who under the Southern caste system would find difficulty in approaching Negro informants on terms of intimacy.[7] Under these circumstances, it is not surprising that, despite individual exceptions in some details, the prevailing interpretation of Gullah has been one which minimizes the features derived from African languages[8] and attributes most of the characteristic features of Gullah either to seventeenth-century British dialects[9] or to some form of baby talk used by plantation overseers to the simple-minded representatives of undeveloped primitive cultures, who in turn distorted this simplified form of the language through their ignorance, laziness, or physical inability to reproduce the sounds of English.[10]

Turner has had several advantages over every previous investigator of Gullah. In addition to the obvious fact that as a Negro he could approach the Gullah people on terms of intimacy denied to any white investigator, he has been trained in dialect geography and field methods by Kurath and Bloch; he has studied African languages and has checked his materials with native speakers of many languages in the areas from which the Gullah Negroes were probably transported;[11] and he has also investigated the creolized Portugese spoken by Brazilian Negroes. On the basis of the data at his disposal he has identified several thousand items in Gullah with possible African sources -- a mass of evidence which should go far towards correcting the tendencies of previous investigators to dismiss the African element in Gullah as inconsequential. The presentation in the present book is soberly factual, the conclusions are conservative, even the details are rarely questionable.[12]

However, though recognizing what Turner has accomplished, one must point out that his new book is not the work which linguists have looked for. A descriptive grammar of Gullah has long been needed; it is not provided here.[13] It is true that Turner's aim is not to give a descriptive grammar of Gullah but to identify elements of African origin; yet one may suggest that this purpose would have been better served had he provided a structural description before proceeding to comparison. After all, it is one thing to suggest the carry-over of a number of details; it is another to indicate basic structural similarities.[14] [It should not be overlooked that Turner's data in this book -- notably the texts -- are so clearly presented that it is possible for another scholar to make at least a broad structural sketch of his own. For instance, in developing his *Areal Linguistics* (1972), Kurath made such an analysis and concluded 1) that the lexicon of

Gullah is primarily English; 2) that the phonology seems to be different from that of any present-day English dialect; 3) that the grammar contains both English and non-English elements.]

The arrangement of the book suggests that its purpose is not primarily linguistic: Chapters 1 "Backgrounds;" 2 "Phonetic Alphabet and Diacritics;" 3 "West African Words in Gullah" (personal names; other words used in conversations; some expressions heard only in stories, songs, and prayers); 4 "Syntactical Features;" 5 "Morphological Features;" 6 "Some Word-Formations;" 7 "Sounds;" 8 "Intonation;" 9 "Gullah Texts." A more orthodox linguistic approach would have been to proceed from phonology (Chapters 2, 7, 8) through morphology (Chapters 5, 6) and syntax (Chapter 4) to a presentation of the texts from which the analysis and any glossary would be derived; each stage of the description could be accompanied by a treatment of African and Brazilian analogues and possible sources; vocabulary items not found in the texts -- particularly the list of personal names -- could be included in an appendix. Such a presentation would not only provide the description of Gullah that linguists have desired but would so emphasize the African contribution as to convince even the most skeptical reader.

The chapter on backgrounds points up the conditions favorable to the preservation of Africanisms in Gullah: the geographical and cultural isolation of the Sea Island rice and cotton country, the lack of contact with the standard language, the preference -- encouraged by discriminatory tariffs against the importation of slaves from the British West Indies -- for slaves shipped direct from Africa.[15] The account of other attempts to analyze Gullah shows the extent to which such writers have accepted the judgments of their predecessors,[16] and the unfamiliarity of those writers with African languages or with Negro speech in other parts of the Western Hemisphere.

The chapter on West African words in Gullah is by far the longest; in fact, the list of Gullah personal names constitutes nearly half the book. It is pointed out that many of these names -- nicknames or so-called 'basket names' -- the Gullah freely use among themselves but seldom reveal to the white man.[17] As an introduction to this list of names, there is an account of name-giving practices in various parts of West Africa, reflecting religious, economic, political, and military aspects of African culture. The considerable number of names derived from Arabic and from the history of Mohammedanism, and the smaller number traceable to Portugese, suggest types of culture contacts between West Africa and the Mediterranean world before the slave trade with North America

began. Of the names which Turner lists, a very large proportion are shown to be names actually in use today in Africa; every name included has at least been recognized by native speakers of some African language as possible in their own community. Because the Gullah, like other Americans, very frequently do not know the meaning of their names, Turner often supplies several possible etyma for a single name; some of the most frequently cited languages are Efik, Fon, Twi, Wolof, and Yoruba. Each name is listed opposite its possible etyma, without any attempt to draw extreme conclusions.[18] The phonetic resemblances of individual names, the overall similarity in the patterns of name giving, are most impressive.

To the dialect geographer the list of "other words used in conversation" is interesting for what it shows of cultural borrowing of African vocabulary items into Southern American English.[19] The distribution of such of these words as have been recorded for the Linguistic Atlas of the South Atlantic States reinforces Turner's suggestion that many words in everyday use in that area are of African origin and have taken over by the whites from their contacts with Negroes: the foci from which these words have apparently spread had large Negro populations early in their history (Petty 1943). *Pinto* 'coffin' has been recorded sporadically from the Pee Dee River to Savannah -- chiefly from Negroes, sometimes offered by white informants as a characteristic 'Negro word.'[20] *Buckra* 'white man' has spread into the South Carolina Piedmont, especially in the contemptuous designation of poor whites as *poor buckra*. *Joggling board* (cf. Gullah [ʤʊgɑl-bod, ʤʊglʊ-bod]) -- less often applied to a seesaw than to a long limber plank anchored at both ends and used, as a swing might be used, by nurses dandling infants, by children at play, and by courting couples -- is known throughout the plantation country from Georgetown to the Altamaha River, and in inland communities frequented by plantation families in the malaria season. *Jinky board, janky board* (cf. Gullah [tʃika-bod]) is a Berkeley County, South Carolina, name for the seesaw. *Pinder* 'peanut' is found from Chesapeake Bay and the Potomac River southwest through the Piedmont and mountain areas of Virginia and North Carolina, through the Piedmont of South Carolina and Georgia, and along the coastal plain from Georgetown south. *Cooter* 'turtle' is found throughout the coastal plain and the lower Piedmont from the Cape Fear River to Florida. *Cush* 'a kind of mush' is frequently recorded in the coastal plain.[21] Of words not recorded in the Atlas, *hoodoo* 'curse' (noun and verb) has spread far beyond the South; *okra* is a staple Southern vegetable; *gumbo* 'a thick soup with an okra base' (cf. Gullah [gʌmbo] 'okra') is nationally known; *benne* 'sesame' is a common ingredient of cookies and candy in the Charleston and Savannah areas; *da* is the usual Charleston name for a child's Negro nurse; *Geechee* is commonly used, with mildly insulting connotations, by Up-Country South Carolinians as a nickname for any Low-Countryman, especially one from the Charleston area; *jigger* (or *chigger*) is the common Southern name for a minute insect with a proclivity for burrowing in human flesh; *war mouth* (also known as *more-mouth*; cf. Gullah [wɔmɛʊ̈], Mende [wɔ] 'large') is a common coastal-plain name for a kind of catfish; *pojo* 'heron' is widely known in the Charleston area; *tabby* 'a type of structural material made of cement and oyster shells, often with pieces of brick intermixed' is frequently used for foundations or house walls in South Carolina and Georgia coastal communities; *shout* 'religious dance' is a typical practice of the less formally organized Protestant groups in the South, white as well as Negro.[22]

As with patterns of nomenclature, evidence of Africanisms in Gullah grammar is less a matter of individual details than of carrying over of structural resemblances,[23] though such resemblances are less clear in Turner's treatment than they would have been if Gullah had been described systematically on the basis of its own phenomena. Actually, the Indo-European bias shown in long paradigms and an over-detailed treatment of the absence of inflection in Gullah obscures the case for African survivals. The term 'verbal adjective' for a type of predicate nucleus found in certain types of clauses, such as [i tɔl] 'he is tall,' is likely to be confusing; whether [tɔl] here functions as a verb or as an adjective could be determined by a structural analysis.

So far as Gullah word formation is concerned, dialect geography supports Turner's suggestion that many Gullah compounds and onomatopoetic expressions may reflect African practice: *yard ax* 'poorly trained irregular preacher' and its synonym *table tapper* have been recorded chiefly in the Georgetown and Charleston areas and in the Santee Valley; *huhu owl* 'hoot owl, large owl' is found occasionally in the South Carolina coastal plain; *bloody noun* 'large bullfrog' (cf. Gullah [blʌdɪnɛʊn]) has been recorded in the Santee and Savannah Valleys, and along the coast from Georgetown to the Florida line.[24] Not recorded in the Atlas but commonly considered to be of Negro origin are such metaphors as *sweet-mouth* 'to flatter' and *bad-mouth* 'to curse.'[25]

Perhaps the greatest advantage of a more systematic treatment of the Gullah data would appear in the phonology, which is diffused through Chapters 2, 7, and 8. A simple statement of the phonemic system of Gullah, followed by a description of the allophones of individual phonemes -- both those allophones that are in free variation and those that are in complementary distribution, like the syllabics of *house* and *owl* -- might show striking evidence of African background by comparison with similar statements of the structure of some of the West African languages.[26] From the data as presented it is clear 1) that Gullah has fewer vowel and consonant phonemes than any dialect of standard American English; 2) that some English consonant clusters do not occur, but some non-English clusters found in African languages, such as initial clusters of nasal followed by homorganic stop, do occur. It is probably significant that recorded West African languages have relatively few vowel phonemes (Westermann and Ward 1933). It is even more significant, though the point is not made in this book, that the phonemic system of Gullah and the phonetic values of individual allophones show striking uniformity in all the communities where the dialect is spoken, although these communities occur discontinuously along three hundred miles of coast in the region in which dialects of American English show the greatest local diversity.[27]

A few minor exceptions may be taken to some details of the phonological treatment. A linguist who has investigated dialects spoken in various parts of the United States will be somewhat bewildered by a statement that a particular phonetic symbol represents "the sound of the English vowel" in such and such a word. Is the "considerably retracted variety of [ɪ]"(15) phonemically distinct or not?[28] If in Twi [o] and [ɔ] are separate phonemes (19), the difference should be indicated where Twi forms are cited. In Gullah, as probably in all dialects of American English, [ʌ] and [ə] seem to be members of the same phoneme: in Gullah [ə] does not occur in stressed position, but both [ə] and [ʌ] occur in free variation in certain unstressed syllables, with the former allophone favored "in the newer type of Gullah . . . by persons who try to distinguish stress"(19-20). The diphthongs of *white*, *mine* and *house*, *cow* are probably to be interpreted as /ay,aw/ respectively; it is not necessary to indicate positional variants in complementary distribution, such as are found in many varieties of American English, including white speech of the South Carolina and Georgia tidewater area (21). One cannot interpret [c,ɟ] both as separate phonemes and as subsidiary members of the /k,g/ phonemes; examination of the texts shows that /k/ and /c/, /g/ and /ɟ/ contrast phonically in Gullah, as do the corresponding sound types in all dialects of standard English, though frequently Gullah has /c,ɟ/ where the corresponding standard English words have /k,g/. Does the statement that [ŋ] "appears to be a subsidiary member of the [n] phoneme"(27) refer to its use in Yoruba or in Gullah? In the texts, there seems to be a phonemic contrast. Is [ɲ] to be interpreted as a unit phoneme or as a cluster /ny/? Its occurrence in syllable final position in /boɲ/ 'tooth' suggests the former. Unless nasalized vowels are phonemic in Gullah, there is no need to mark them as such; the phenomenon can be handled by a statement that in some words (the commonest could be listed) the phonemic sequence vowel plus nasal consonant appears phonetically as a nasalized vowel. If Gullah has a phonemic accent system, whether of stress or pitch (30), the accent should be indicated not only in individual words but particularly in texts (Trager 1941). The chapter on intonation starts with the familiar observation that Gullah intonation is different from that of standard English (cf. Bennett 1908-09:337, G. G. Johnson 1930:17) and describes several intonation features in some detail. However, as in other details of the phonology, there is no attempt to set up a phonemic system of intonation, such as was constructed by Wells 1945 or Pike 1945. There is no mention of juncture, though juncture phenomena have been analyzed for English (Trager and Bloch 1941) and for at least two African languages, Fanti (Welmers 1946) and Hausa (Hodge 1947).

The Gullah texts suggest to anthropologists several directions in which the culture of the Gullah people might be investigated. Of particular interest to the student of myth diffusion is the fragment from the story of the tortoise and the deer, which I recorded in 1940 from the last native speaker of Catawba.[29] As previously suggested, these texts would be more useful if the transcription were phonemic, including marks for accent and intonation. Furthermore, as Turner admits, most of the texts -- taken down at an early stage in his investigations -- contain relatively few of the Africanisms recorded in his vocabulary lists; it would be interesting to see if more African lexical items would appear in connected texts taken after he had achieved terms of intimacy with his informants.

The bibliography is fairly long but lacks Welmers and Harris 1942, Greenberg 1941, Hodge and Hause 1944, Bloch and Trager 1942, the studies of English intonation by Pike and Wells, Nida's *Morphology* (1946), and Pike's *Phonemics* (1947) and *Tone Languages* (1948). Indicating the volume would make it easier for scholars to consult articles which Turner has cited from journals.

Yet these specific objections must not blind the reader to Turner's contribution. They are merely raised, in some detail, because linguists want to know what Gullah is like as a language, both for its own sake and for the light it throws on creol-ized and contact languages in other parts of the world. Turner himself is aware of this; his future publications will undoubtedly provide this knowledge. He has certainly achieved the limited objective set for this book -- of showing that the language of the Gullah Negroes contains many features that can be explained only in terms of the African background. Certainly no one can now safely say that Gullah is merely a combination of seventeenth-century British dialects and baby talk, somehow mangled by the inept articulation of ignorant and lazy savages. Once more anthropological training and linguistic method have dissipated a myth.[30]

Possibly one of Turner's most significant contributions lies in the intriguing problems which his book poses for the student of Southern American English phonology. Leaving out such obvious results of culture contact as the occasional occurrence of the Gullah bilabial /f,v/ in white speech of the South Carolina and Georgia coastal plain, there are several structural features that must be explained. Gullah /l/ is usually very clear in all positions; clear /l/ has frequently been recorded, even in postvocalic position, from coastal-plain white informants. Despite the fact that Pike minimizes the dialectal differences in intonation patterns (1945:105-06), differences do occur: even naive observers have noticed that Southerners often end a sentence with a rising intonation, such as is found in Gullah and in some West African languages (250). From an impressionistic point of view there is something in the intonation patterns of the Georgetown-Charleston-Beaufort area that is not found elsewhere in American English. This does not imply that all of these features or any of them can be certainly ascribed to African influence. If British dialects are ever adequately investigated, patterns of geographical distribution in England may prove to be an adequate explanation. But the fact that these phenomena occur in white speech in and near the Gullah country, in a region marked by large early slaveholdings, suggests borrowing; linguists cannot afford to be cocksure that all borrowing of phonological features was in one direction, however strong the probabilities.

Perhaps the greatest value of any scholarly work is not in the questions that it answers but in those which it enables other scholars to ask. In this respect, Turner's book is one which no student of American English can afford to ignore.

[The suggestion that a wide range of evidence be drawn on before sweeping conclusions are reached is still pertinent. However, in the last two decades, what with the profit in poverty for educational entrepreneurs, the most sweeping generalizations have been drawn by those who would assert African and creole substrata and deny that features of British or Irish dialects of the seventeenth century might be better preserved among American Negroes than among their white counterparts, or indeed among Southern Americans of all races than among speakers of other regional varieties of American English.

Part of the difficulty has risen from the practical nature of most recent research -- the attempt to provide better teaching materials in the expanding Black Belts of Northern and Western cities. Investigators have assumed 'Standard English' to be the prestigious local varieties in such metropolitan areas -- a more accurate designation for this hypothetical 'standard' is 'Suburban White Inland Northern English' -- and have largely ignored the existence of Southern varieties of standard speech, some of them, as in Richmond, Charleston, and New Orleans, antedating even the founding of Chicago. The delay in obtaining funds for editing the Linguistic Atlas materials, where a certain amount of comparable evidence is available, makes it difficult to evaluate the more extreme statements; and indeed, the situation in which the Linguistic Atlas records were made in the 1930's, before the days of lightweight high-fidelity recording apparatus, curtailed the amount of syntactic evidence that could be recorded. And it appears, in many discussions of varieties of nonstandard English spoken by Negroes, that the grammatical details -- especially the syntactic -- provide the most striking contrasts to the standard English spoken by educated whites in Northern metropolitan areas.

The suggestion of Labov (1966) that one must investigate a range of personal styles, for each informant, could be profitably followed. In his biographical study of George Wallace (1968) and in his more recent portrait of Congressman Mendel Rivers for *Life* (1970), Marshall Frady presents his subjects as using in their informal speech (and for Wallace, even from the platform) a wide range of grammatical features putatively associated with 'Black English,' such as the lack of inflections for noun plural and genitive,

for verb preterite and participle and third-singular present indicative, and the absence of the present of the copula *to be* where standard English would expect it with participles, predicate nouns, and predicate adjectives. I have myself observed these features in radio broadcasts of interviews with Wallace. In fact, my wife and her professional colleagues have observed that the absence of the copula is very common in my own speech, when I am talking informally to my peers; and I have observed the same phenomena among my contemporaries in South Carolina.

In informal conversation at a conference at Tuskegee Institute (1968) James Sledd remarked on the difficulty of reaching a definitive solution on the extent of creole language influence on the dialects of American Negroes; a person would need a detailed knowledge, not only of African languages and creoles and pidgins, but of synchronic and diachronic variations of English and several Romance languages. And in the meanwhile one cannot overlook the definitive evidence from Early Modern English, from more recent Irish English, and from other dialects -- such as New-Foundland (Paddock 1966) and that of the upland American South -- where creole influence is improbable. Some of this comparative evidence has been made available in L. M. Davis 1970, Greibesland 1970, Dorrill 1975, and in O'Cain 1972, a sociolinguistic study of Charleston, South Carolina.

Whatever the final scholarly conclusions, one is faced with the fact that in many American communities -- including most of the metropolitan areas of the North and West -- there are large bodies of Negroes, poor and uneducated, whose speech patterns differ strikingly from those of local upper-class whites, and that the problem of providing better education, including better programs in reading and writing, faces the school systems at the practical level, regardless of the ultimate origin of these dialectal differences. Indeed, teachers and administrators and local molders of opinion could almost always profit from greater respect for speechways different from their own, whether the speaker is a Harlem junkie or a Texas president.]

NOTES

[1] On St. Helena Island there were 2000 slaves to 200 whites (G. G. Johnson 1930:127). "On St. Helena Island today there are approximately twenty-five Negroes to one white person"(Crum 1940:54). On Johasee Island the plantation overseer was the only white man resident the year round (Crum 1940:42). Plantation owners and their families normally tried to spend the malaria season, November to May, at inland or Northern resorts; see Brewster 1947.

[2] "It is not likely that the African characteristics of the negroes have stood in the way of their acquiring a better English, but rather that they have learned as much from the white man as he gave them opportunity to learn"(Krapp 1925:1.253).

Even religious instruction for the slaves proceeded slowly, in the face of objections to giving them any education at all and legal prohibitions against teaching them to write. See Crum 1940: 173-231, *passim*.

³ Edisto Island was not connected with the mainland by a bridge and causeway till 1918 (Crum 1940:29); an all-weather road has been available for little more than a decade. On one field trip Turner was trapped on the causeway by a spring tide and had to abandon his car.

⁴ Peonage was not officially abolished till 1907. Extralegal forms of peonage have been tolerated since that time.

⁵ Bennett, Gonzales, Stoney, and Shelby are professional writers; Smith is a folklorist with traditional philological training; Johnson is a sociologist; Crum is a religious educator. Only Johnson has undertaken any serious study of the American Negro. Accounts by Krapp and other students of the English language are largely derivative from Bennett.

⁶ Stoney has had some acquaintance with West Indian Negro English. Significantly, he is less inclined than most to reject the possibility of African influence.

⁷ Slavery, peonage, dispossession from lands acquired by purchase after the Civil War (Crum 1940: 322-43), the disabilities of the Southern caste system, and the fanning of anti-Negro prejudice by Southern politicians have led to secretiveness and suspicion in Negro responses to white investigators; see R. Smith 1926:11, Crum 1940:27, 80. For a literary interpretation of this secretiveness, see Heyward 1925:174-83.
Turner reports (11-12) that Guy S. Lowman, Jr., principal field worker for the Linguistic Atlas of the United States and Canada, found considerable difficulty in interviewing Gullah informants, even though Turner was accompanying him. Despite the myth that Southerners understand the Negro and know how to deal with him, I encountered the same difficulty in interviewing South Carolina and Georgia Negro informants for the Atlas.

⁸ Possibly Southern writers on Gullah have been led to discount the possibility of African influence by their own appreciation of the psychology of the plantation owner, who would naturally not wish a large proportion of new slaves to come from any single tribe or language area, lest they be able to conspire against him in a language that he and the privileged and trusted slaves of the plantation could not understand.

⁹ It is not surprising that many English relic forms seldom heard elsewhere in North America should be found in Gullah; geographical and cultural isolation would favor the retention of any forms that had once attained currency, whatever their origin.

¹⁰ "To express other than the simplest ideas, plain actualities, is, however, difficult"(Bennett 1908-09:338); "intellectual indolence, or laziness, mental and physical, which shows itself in the shortening of words, the elision of syllables, and modification of every difficult enunciation" (Bennett 1908-09:40); "it is the indolence, mental and physical, of the Gullah dialect that is

its most characteristic feature"(Bennett 1908-09: 49); "Gullah, that quaint linguistic mongrel"(E. Stanhope Sams, "Preface" to R. Smith 1926:5); "Slovenly and careless of speech, these Gullahs seized upon the peasant English used by some of the early settlers and by the white servants of the wealthier colonists, wrapped their clumsy tongues about it as well as they could, and, enriched with certain expressive African words, it issued through their flat noses and thick lips as so workable a form of speech that it was gradually adopted by the other slaves"(Gonzales 1922:10); "Simple language concepts of the unseasoned slaves . . . with their simple dialects"(Crum 1940:113).
This traditional interpretation appears to stem from Bennett's article; examination of later interpretations of Gullah shows that even much of Bennett's phraseology has been taken over practically unchanged. See for instance Krapp 1924.
It should not be necessary to refute the myth that phonemic systems and allophones are racially determined; yet as late as 1949 an allegedly scientific newspaper columnist (Wiggam 1949) announced that the Negro is unable to pronounce postvocalic /-r/ because his lips are too thick.
Attribution of features of Gullah phonology to English peasant speech is probably fanciful, since peasantry made up a relatively small proportion of pre-Revolutionary settlers; see Bridenbaugh 1938. The rapid tempo of Gullah speech is evidence enough that the alleged indolence is a purely mythical explanation.

¹¹ "To a person who is not familiar with West African culture, it might seem possible to explain Gullah culture entirely in terms of western influence"(Bascom 1941).

¹² One may suggest that, despite possible African etyma, it is unlikely that the personal names [pidi] and [kusʊ] are of African origin, to say nothing of the place names *Coosaw*, *Pee Dee*, *Tybee*, *Wahoo*, *Wando*, and *Wassaw* (307). The Pee Dee were one of the Siouan tribes in South Carolina; *Coosaw*, especially in the longer place name *Coosawhatchie*, is probably Muskoghean. The possibility that any of the coastal place names in Georgia are of African origin is remote, since that colony prohibited slavery in its original organization under Oglethorpe.

¹³ I have recently learned that Turner some time ago completed the manuscript of such a sketch; its publication, however, is not likely in the near future.

¹⁴ Emphasis on vocabulary borrowings can lead to such basic misinterpretations of linguistic method as the statement sometimes heard that, because of its many lexical items derived from Romance, English is no longer a Germanic but a 'mixed language.'

¹⁵ Nathaniel Heyward, greatest of the rice planters, always bought "fresh Africans as long as that cheap supply remained available"(Phillips 1918:249-250, quoted by Crum 1940:44-45).

¹⁶ All these writers, most of them white South-

erners, reason from common linguistic misconceptions, which may be summarized as follows:

1. Any form different from what I call standard is therefore inferior.

2. Any form associated with a less privileged social class is therefore inferior.

3. Any form associated with a caste to which the stigma of inferiority is attached is therefore inferior.

The fallaciousness of such assumptions, and of others on which the traditional attitudes toward American Negro culture have been based, is pointed out in Herskovits 1941.

[17] The instability of Gullah personal names and the discrepancy between Gullah name-giving practices and those of white Americans was noted particularly by Northern white teachers brought South by the Freedmen's Bureau after the Civil War to staff the new schools for Negroes. See Crum 1940: 313.

[18] Mathews (1948) attempts to derive the folk term *doney* 'sweetheart' through a Gullah personal name from the latter's African etymon, Bambara [doni] 'a burden.' However, the Linguistic Atlas records *doney* most frequently in areas where there is least reason to suspect Negro influence: the Shenandoah Valley and central and western North Carolina.

[19] Preliminary field work in the South, and all records from Delaware, Maryland, Virginia, and North Carolina were made by Lowman prior to 1941. Field work in South Carolina, eastern Georgia, and northeastern Florida was completed by RIM in the summer of 1941 and 1946-48, under grants from the Julius Rosenwald Fund and the American Council of Learned Societies.

[20] *Pinto* is used chiefly for the old-fashioned hexagonal coffin (occasionally pentagonal, with the omission of the footboard); informants often explain the name by commenting that the narrowness of the coffin pins the corpse's toes together -- a spurious etymology which was seldom questioned prior to Turner's investigations.

[21] Despite possible Kongo (Angola) and Kikongo (Belgian Congo) etyma, and suggested related words from other African languages, it is problematical whether Southern *tote* 'to carry' is really of African origin. True, *tote* in this sense is characteristic of the Southeastern states; but *tote road*, *tote team*, *tote wagon*, and *tote sled*, as well as *tote* itself (more often meaning 'to haul' than 'to carry') have been recorded in northern New England, upstate New York, northern Michigan, and northern Minnesota, where African influence is unlikely. Despite the fact that no satisfactory English etymon for *tote* has been proposed, its occurrence in these Northern states suggests that such an etymon is nevertheless probable, and that the prevalence of *tote* in the South Atlantic states may be due to reinforcement by a homonymous synonym of African origin rather than to African sources alone.

Turner does not list *takky* 'horse,' generally recorded along the South Carolina coast in the form *marsh takky*, and often supposed to be of African origin. Presumably the proposed African etyma are dubious.

[22] It would have been very useful if Turner had indicated the geographical distribution within the Gullah country of each lexical item, including personal names. In 1941 he suggested that groups of words and names traceable to particular African languages were found clustered in particular Gullah communities, and that this geographical distribution can be correlated with the pattern of slave settlement. See Turner 1941:73.

[23] It is interesting, and hardly coincidental, that the morphemes {də} 'a verb of incomplete predication' and {pas}, used to introduce a term of comparison, correspond to similarly used morphemes in Taki-Taki and Haitian Creole respectively. See R. A. Hall 1948:100-01, 109; Comhaire-Sylvain 1936:43-44, 50.

[24] An onomatopoetic variant /budɨdəŋk,bə-,-duŋk/ seems to be confined to the Georgetown area.

[25] Such phrases as *put the mouth on* 'hex' are also frequently heard, and are considered to be of Negro origin.

[26] The significance of similarities in phonemic structure rather than in phonetic details was pointed out in Sapir 1925.

[27] This uniformity is shown in Turner's field records, now in the files of the Linguistic Atlas. It was confirmed by Lowman in a report to Kurath after Lowman had made sample recordings from all of Turner's principal informants.

[28] Such a phonemic distinction occurs, for instance, in my own speech between the stressed syllabics of *ribbing* /ribɨn/ and *ribbon* /rɨbən/. See Trager and Smith 1951.

[29] The occurrence of this story (in telling it the informant used the African-derived *cooter* 'turtle') is interesting because the Catawba not only lived very far inland but traditionally avoided contact with Negroes and were in turn avoided by them.

[30] The implications are not confined to the linguistic interpretation of Gullah. The demonstration of a persisting African linguistic heritage suggests the persistence of other African cultural traits, and controverts the Southern myth of Negro inferiority and cultural poverty. An awareness of these implications of Turner's book is probably responsible for some Charlestonians labeling favorable press notices elsewhere as "nigger propaganda."

For no varieties of English is accurate information more necessary or desirable than for those varieties spoken in Australia. An area of three million square miles with a population less than eight million means a population density of less than three to the square mile. Nearly a third of the population is found in the metropolitan areas of Sydney and Melbourne, and over forty percent in the five largest cities -- a situation of cities in the wilderness unmatched in the English-speaking world. For various reasons, metropolitan London probably contributed a larger proportion of the early settlers of Australia than it did of any other British colony or dominion. Although the influence of polite British society -- and of Received Standard, the caste dialect of that society -- has inevitably been felt, the distance from London to Sydney and the well-publicized origins of the first families of Australia have probably reduced the impact of that influence. Even the environment in which Australian English developed -- flora, fauna, physical geography, and native customs -- is remarkably different from that in any other area of white settlement. Consequently, one has a right to expect several kinds of linguistic developments in the century and a half since the earliest settlements: the acquisition of new lexical items, the development of new meanings for familiar terms, the rise of new local dialects, and the establishment of one or more dialects with social prestige. It is possible that a good study of Australian speech could help answer a number of questions of linguistic theory that have been raised by students of dialect geography.

Unfortunately, no existing treatise on Australian speech provides the data from which these answers may be derived. Even more unfortunately, Baker's book -- the result of years of work on a subject in which he is intensely interested -- does not provide that data either. This does not mean that Baker's book is without merit: I personally found it both entertaining and informative, and after reading it I feel I possess a much better understanding of Australian culture than I did before. But it does mean that he has failed to come to grips with the fundamental problems, so that the important work in Australian English is still to be done.

The linguistic features of greatest significance and of most permanent interest to linguists are those that are most intimate and habitual and least spectacular, least subject to overt influence. Thus a feature of phonology is likely to persist longer than one of grammar or vocabulary: features of vocabulary may be displaced by cultural borrowing or made obsolete by a technological change within the speaker's own culture;[1] a feature of grammar may be eliminated by the spread of literacy and public education; a feature of phonology is much more difficult for an outsider even to identify accurately, much less meddle with. Even in vocabulary items, the most significant ones are those dealing with simple matters of everyday life; the colorful vocabulary of gold miners, moonshiners, or shrimp fishermen may be most interesting in itself and accurately portrayed by poets or novelists, yet be used by a comparatively small part of the population.[2]

Baker's emphasis, however, is of a different type. He has a wide interest in the complex of geographical, historical, and social forces that contributed to the development of Australian society; he has presented a wealth of entertaining anecdotes and what seems to be accurate information about the words associated with each of these influences. In contrast, he has only one chapter on pronunciation -- in which he deplores the "Australian accent" on esthetic grounds but resents efforts to set up Received Standard in its stead -- and two bare mentions of grammar, in which a normative attitude is manifest.[3] And nowhere does he go into specific details as to the social or geographic distribution of speech forms within Australia.

When it comes to cases, Baker is only partially a linguist. The "Australian language," so far as he is concerned, seems to be the vocabulary. Although he is very eloquent in wanting Australian writers to write in an Australian idiom, his comments on Australian pronunciation indicate that he wishes to modify and "improve" that pronunciation[4] -- though he properly deplores the tendency of Australian radio announcers to ape the pronunciation of British Received Standard.[5] Although he is anxious to have a scientific study of the speech of Norfolk and Pitcairn Islands -- the dialects developed among the descendants of unions between *Bounty* mutineers and Polynesian women -- he is less interested in recording and analyzing Melanesian Pidgin than in having it replaced by "Basic English."[6]

The publisher's blurb on the dust jacket of *The Australian Language* features a laudatory comment by H. L. Mencken. It is easy to see why Mencken would enjoy what Baker has written: the style is that of straightforward reporting, with a minimum of professional gobbledygook, and the colorful anecdotes of Australian mores would naturally delight the founder of *The American Mercury* and the reporter of the monkey trial in Dayton, Tennessee. Furthermore, Baker offers clues that may some day be utilized by the linguists who make a systematic study of Australian dialects. But Baker shows small appreciation of the methods of scientific linguistics, and his book no more belongs in a class with Mencken's *The American Language* (1936) than Frances Trollope's *Domestic Manners of the Americans* (1832) -- another entertaining and accurate anecdotal treatment -- with Kluckhohn's *Mirror for Man* (1949).

NOTES

[1] Thus changes in merchandising practices have meant that many articles formerly produced at home or on the farm or by local craftsmen are now more easily available through chain stores and mail-order houses. Thus many items of the folk vocabulary in the United States have been replaced by neutral or euphemistic commercial terms, such as *spider* by *frying pan*. The introduction of tractor-drawn farm machinery has rendered obsolete for many people, even on the farm, much of the vocabulary dealing with horses and mules.

[2] The questionnaires for dialect atlases have emphasized those concepts that are part of the experience of most people and that are easy to bring into a conversation.

[3] "The Australian is an adept in the many forms of pleonasm, repeated negatives, misrelated participles and possessives, and general misuse of even the simplest rules of 'pure' grammar. There unfortunately exists such little appreciation for correct modes of speech that his own lack of interest in improvement is confirming his errors into national habits"(262).

"This question of mutilated grammar is something distinct from the use of slang, and the issues should not be confused. It matters not one whit that Australia should hear and absorb American slang: but it is a matter of fundamental importance that children should come to believe it not only permissible but meritorious to befoul every precept of grammar with slovenly distortions"(287).

[4] Baker seriously discusses -- not once but several times -- the theories that climatic conditions or native laziness may be responsible for the noticeable characteristics -- what Baker calls "objectionable features" -- of Australian pronunciation (e.g., 324, 342, 352-53).

Such attitudes are not confined to Australia. Frequently one encounters assertions that the pronunciation habits of American Negroes are due to the thickness of their lips and the shape of their tongues, or that the South Midland drawl springs from laziness inspired by the warm climate. In one Western university the member of the school of pedagogy charged with training high-school English teachers recently explained Minnesota pronunciation patterns on the theory that the climate causes all Minnesotans to suffer from sinus trouble!

[5] Even the Australian Broadcasting Corporation, which Baker suggests unduly favors Received Standard as the official dialect of radio announcers, is more sympathetically disposed toward using natural educated speech of their country than the Politburo of American radio announcers and their fellow travelers in speech departments, who seem determined to foist on the public a type of dialect natural to no one.

[6] "The noxious form of speech known as pidgin English"(219); "If pidgin will help us understand the aboriginal, then let our authors not fear to use it. It is another matter altogether, of course, whether some determined attempt should not be made to educate the aborigines to speak purer English -- say, through the medium of Basic English"(228); "Here is yet another pidgin 'dialect' -- another of those semi-phonetic monstrosities which must make New Guinea natives shake their heads in despair at the idiocies and inconsistencies of white men"(238-39); "The jargon of pidgin English, which the riff-raff and scum of the seven seas had spread across the Pacific from whaling and sealing ships!"(240).

Of Baker's ten recommendations to the Federal Government summarizing the argument of his book, two are concerned with pidgin:

"6. That a Government effort be made to discourage the education of aborigines at mission stations in the use of pidgin English, Basic English being an ideal means for educating natives (Chapter XIII, section 3).

7. That if denominational missions in New Guinea are to be permitted to reduce pidgin English to written form, standardization be insisted upon; that, in any case, such activities be discouraged (Chapter XIII, section 5)"(359).

Students of dialect geography, especially those concerned with English, should welcome the appearance of Dieth and Orton's questionnaire as evidence that a linguistic atlas of England is at last under way. Such an atlas, incorporating the procedures that have been successfully utilized by linguistic geographers in other countries, is long overdue.[1] What we know of the distribution of linguistic forms in the British Isles is found principally in the fifth volume of Ellis's *Early English Pronunciation* (1869-89) and in Wright's *English Dialect Dictionary* (1898-1905) and *English Dialect Grammar* (1905). These are monumental works, without which we would be helpless. But they were based on methods which we now know to be inadequate: a multiplicity of investigators, many with less training than enthusiasm; uneven coverage of the country; recording whatever seemed to the observer to be 'dialect' in his locality, without reference to the overall distribution of the same item of flora, fauna, human activity, or material culture. Consequently the record is spotty, both in lexicon and in grammar.

No scholars regret this situation more than those who have been conducting investigations in the dialects of the United States. Too often they do not find in Ellis or Wright any evidence from which to adduce the relationships between American and British regional speech. To take a single example: the geographical distribution of American designations for the earthworm (Kurath 1949:74-75; Maps 139, 140) suggests that most of these terms must have come to the colonies from the British Isles. Yet of these terms only two, *eaceworm* and *angledog* (plus a few terms as yet unrecorded in the United States), are found in Wright. As American scholars amass systematic evidence about the distribution of linguistic forms in the New World (see R. McDavid 1951c; R. and V. McDavid 1956a, in this volume, pp. 86-106), they have increasingly lamented the lack of evidence from the Old World. This questionnaire suggests that much of that evidence will soon be available.[2]

This questionnaire -- like those of the French, Italian, and American atlases -- is designed for use in the field by trained investigators making impressionistic transcriptions in a finely graded phonetic alphabet. In its present version, the fifth, it represents the results of five years' work, including field checks in six English counties and parts of Scotland. The authors acknowledge their indebtedness to the published questionnaires for other European atlases, as well as to Wright's *Dialect Dictionary*. They do not state that they disregarded the American atlases, but one may infer that they did not use them (see Viereck 1973). Thus the English and American questionnaires show a number of differences -- some arising from the difference in the status of the dialects in the two countries; some from differences in regional and national culture; some from differences in the interests of those directing the projects, differences dependent in turn on differences in the conception of what a dialect is (cf. Martinet 1952).

As American scholars use the term, a dialect is any regional or social variety of a language, set off from other such varieties by differences in vocabulary, grammar, or pronunciation. At the present state of our investigations, vocabulary is the chief criterion for setting off the Hudson Valley from Western New England and Upstate New York; pronunciation is the easiest way to set off Greater New York from the Hudson Valley. American dialect areas have arisen in various ways: all of them derive from the history of settlement; relic areas have persisted because of their geographical or cultural isolation; focal areas have arisen from the economic or cultural prestige of a community, such as Boston or Philadelphia, or of a social group, such as the planter class of the Virginia Piedmont or the planter and merchant class of the South Carolina and Gerogia coast. If relic areas attest survivals of early usage, focal areas attest innovations. To the American student, both relics and innovations are important; local names for a pile of hay in the field are no more -- and no less -- a part of dialect than local names for a baby carriage.

Furthermore, in the United States and Canada social varieties of a dialect exist within dialect areas. Beside clear-cut differences between the folk speech of two dialect areas, we have equally clear differences in cultivated usage. Moreover, the intermediate variety of speech -- what Kurath and Atwood call "common speech," as distinct from folk speech and cultivated speech -- not only differs from region to region but has a differing relationship to the regional standard and the regional folk speech. In some Atlantic Seaboard areas, such as eastern Virginia, cultivated speech is often sharply distinguished from the other two varieties; in the Midwestern small town, differences in the cultural level may be barely perceptible in local speech, with the cultured speaker adopting standard grammatical forms, giving up many items of the folk vocabulary, but retaining local pronunciation. Consequently the American atlases include urban informants as well as rural, and several levels of age and sophistication.

The demography of England is remarkably different from that of the United States. In our sense of the word there has been no immigration since 1066; and even the Norman Conquest is less like our immigration than like the familiar process by which a New York corporation buys control of a Middle Western factory and replaces the old managerial personnel with new people trained in one of the Eastern branches. Dialect differences have had a long time to develop, though both historical trade routes and new industrialization have affected the patterns in which speech forms occur.

It is probably awareness of this longer historical perspective that has led the directors of the English survey to work from a more restricted definition of dialect than that which Americans use.[3] They do not plan to include either cultivated or common speech,[4] but concentrate on the folk speech of the oldest living generation. In their search for data they are frankly oriented towards the past; they are not concerned with the spread of innovations but with the survival of relics. They direct their investigation largely to the rural areas, where relics might be expected to survive in greatest number.[5] Their questionnaire therefore disregards the accretions to the vocabulary during the past century of industrialization, urbanization, and widespread education.[6]

The questionnaire is divided into nine "books," or major topical divisions: I. The Farm; II. Farming; III. Animals; IV. Nature; V. The House and Housekeeping; VI. The Human Body; VII. Numbers, Time, and Weather; VIII. Social Activities; IX. States, Actions, Relations. Each book is divided into "chapters" or sub-topics, 8 to 14 to the book. The number of questions in each chapter varies from 3 to 26. The total number of questions is about 1125; in the United States the "long" questionnaires (used along the Atlantic Seaboard) contain 750-800 questions, the "short" questionnaires (used in other regional surveys) 550-625. Those familiar with the American questionnaires will notice several differences between the arrangement adopted by Dieth and Orton and that adopted by Kurath.[7] Most of these are inconsequential, since any

topical arrangement of a questionnaire is bound to be somewhat arbitrary. The only significant difference is that Dieth and Orton put nearly all morphological and syntactic items in their ninth book, while Kurath distributes them in smaller blocks scattered through the questionnaire. The English arrangement would probably be impractical for direct interviewing in the American cultural scene; by focusing the informant's attention on questions of grammar, it would tend to draw from even an illiterate not his natural forms but those he thinks are "correct." In England, however, with old-fashioned informants and a clear distinction assumed between dialects and the standard language, the field workers should not encounter such inhibitions.[8]

A little over a fourth of the items in the English questionnaire will provide evidence for comparison with the American materials. Most differences in the contents reflect differences we have mentioned in the basic philosophy of the investigations.

The English questionnaire includes far more details from the minutiae of old-fashioned rural life: weeds, small parts of farm implements, details of animal anatomy, subdivisions of farm chores, small sections of farm buildings. It includes more taboo items -- those dealing with the sexual and excretory functions of man and beast -- though it does not seek the folk terms for either *pregnant* or *bastard*. It has a section dealing with coins -- the American questionnaire has none -- and more questions dealing with holidays and measures.

On the other hand, the English questionnaire has no section designed to elicit the pronunciation of place names. It has none of the political or cultural terms that the American atlases included for pronunciation (though sometimes these items also reveal lexical variants): *general, colonel, judge, actress, secretary, library, post office, hotel, theater, railroad station, hospital, nurse, student, education, college*. The few items dealing with school do not include one of the most profitable entries in the American atlases -- *played hookey* and its synonyms (cf. Kurath 1949:79; Maps 157, 158. Are English schoolchildren more dutiful in their attendance? Or are English truant officers more efficient?). These differences are motivated by a desire to concentrate on the local and the relic, to omit the general and the innovation -- even if the latter might show regional differences in pronunciation.

The reasons for other differences are not clear, especially for the smaller number of greetings and food terms in the English questionnaire. Moreover, our available evidence shows that many items which Dieth and Orton do not include set off dialect areas in both England and the United States. Take, for example, the verb *grease* and the adjective *greasy*. In the eastern United States, forms with /z/ predominate south of the latitude of Philadelphia, Columbus, Fort Wayne, and Peoria; in England they have been recorded east of a line running from the Wash south to London, roughly the same area in which English folk dialects seem to lack constriction of postvocalic /-r/ (see Kurath and Lowman 1970). I wish Dieth and Orton had included these terms. I should also like to have the data on such pronunciation items as *God*, *crop*, *tube*, *due*, *scarce*, *frost*, *spoon*, *coop*, *cooper* (or the surname), *hoops*; such lexical items as *clabbered milk*, *cherry stone*, *frying pan*, *stone* and *rock*, *pot*, *wagon tongue*, *toadstool*, *earthworm* (*worms* is included for pronunciation), *moth*, *dragon fly*, *midwife*. To the plurals of *foot* and *year*, I should like to see added other plurals of nouns of measure -- such as *pound*, *rod*, *mile*, *yoke of oxen*, *head of lettuce*, and *bushel* (or whatever equivalent measure is used; one might wonder why the *bushel* is universal in the United States, but not generally known in England).[9] I should like to see to what extent *you* has developed new plurals in English dialects -- or are such forms as *youse*, *you-uns*, *mongst-ye*, *you-all*, and *yoona* completely American developments? I should like to see a little more evidence on the syntax of prepositions: *all at once*; to *run across* an old friend, or *run into*, *up on*, *onto*, or *afoul of*; to name a child *for*, *after*, *from*, or *at* someone; to be sick *to*, *at*, *in*, or *on one's stomach* (are all speakers of British English merely *sick*?). I should like to see more evidence on verb forms;[10] I should particularly like to know the Eng-

lish dialectal forms for the preterite of *dive*. Though *dove* /dov/ is apparently very rare in British speech, in the United States it is almost universal in the North; in several other areas it seems to be spreading as the socially preferred form.[11] In fact, I wish Dieth and Orton could include nearly all the items that have been profitable throughout the eastern United States. But this I know is impossible. No questionnaire can be exhaustive; and the director of every survey has the right to decide which items are most profitable for the purposes of his investigation.

I like the format of the questionnaire. Most praiseworthy is the fact that it has appeared in print before the investigation is too far advanced; other students of English can comment on the contents as I have done, so that Dieth and Orton will have the benefit of experience and criticism from many parts of the English-speaking world. The index (I note the omission of *half past*) should help both the casual reader and the field worker find their way around; it is disturbing to have to look through the entire questionnaire to find where to insert a conversational response.[12] The provision of index notations to the purpose of particular questions (phonological, morphological, or syntactical) and the rather full contents for eliciting responses should make for efficient use of the questionnaire, as will the device of showing pictures of objects difficult to describe.[13]

In all, Dieth and Orton have prepared an excellent questionnaire. One can only wish them the best of success in using it, and the early completion of the long-needed linguistic atlas of England.

NOTES

[1] Our only systematic information is found in fifty field interviews (using a short version of the American questionnaire and a wide-meshed network) made in southern England in 1937-38 by Guy S. Lowman, Jr., principal field investigator for Linguistic Atlas of the United States and Canada. See Kurath and Lowman 1970, Viereck 1975.

[2] An independent but related survey of Scotland is now under way, using not only field investigation but printed questionnaires distributed by mail (see McIntosh 1952, reviewed in this volume, pp. 356-61; McIntosh *et al.* 1951, reviewed in this volume, p. 355). This combination of methods -- field work supplemented by check lists to be filled in by the informants -- has been utilized effectively in the Upper Midwest (Allen 1973-76).

[3] For the theory of dialect upon which Dieth and Orton base their survey see Dieth 1948, Orton and

Dieth 1951.

[4] The position of Southern British Received Standard as a prestigious class dialect possibly justifies the omission of cultured speech, though many Scots and Northern Englishmen stick to their own standards and resent attempts to impose Received Standard upon them. Less desirable is the failure to study the intermediate types of speech. By whatever designation we may choose to call them -- "common speech" or "local standard" -- these types have not received adequate study in any European investigation.

[5] The American atlases have investigated rural areas more intensively than urban, because of both the higher survival of linguistic relics and the greater stability of the population. However, it has included 25 informants from Greater New York City, 12 from Charleston, 8 from Philadelphia, 7 from Savannah, 6 each from Baltimore and Rochester,

5 each from Boston and Richmond.

[6] Dieth and Orton plan a shorter questionnaire for the investigation of the town dialects; this "will omit the books relating to husbandry, but on the other hand will include more notions relating to the life of the artisan and the syntactical aspects of his speech"(611).

[7] The new England questionnaire appears in Kurath *et al.* 1939:147-58. For a comparison of the various American questionnaires used through 1951, see R. and V. McDavid 1951a. [For later versions, see Davis, McDavid, and McDavid 1969.]

[8] In actual practice, nearly all the American field workers have sought to record grammatical responses from unguarded conversation, as a supplement to direct questioning if not as a substitute for it. A. L. Davis and RIM particularly have tried to record as much as possible of all interviews from free conversation.

[9] Although the uninflected plurals are generally commonest in old-fashioned speech and rare in cultivated American usage, the geographical distribution of the uninflected forms in the United States varies from word to word. See R. and V. McDavid 1964, in this volume, pp. 199-218.

[10] The variety of verb forms from the Atlantic Seaboard is admirably treated in Atwood 1953a [see also V. McDavid 1956]. Atwood includes charts showing the regional distribution of 28 forms; of these, the English questionnaire provides data on only 11.

[11] See Atwood 1953a:9, Fig. 6. *Dove* is not found in the Lowman records from southern England. The difference in its status -- rarity in England, regional standard in the United States -- suggests that *dove* should perhaps be considered an Americanism, though it is not listed in Mathews 1951.

[12] An index of the New England questionnaire was prepared to facilitate editing the materials; an index of forms recorded in the New England *Atlas* (Kurath *et al.* 1939-43) was compiled by Atwood and his graduate seminar at the University of Texas.

A map inventory and word list, prepared by Audrey Duckert, is incorporated in the second edition (1973) of Kurath *et al.* 1939.

[13] No directions in a questionnaire, no matter how elaborately they are framed, can eliminate the need for alertness and discrimination on the part of the field worker. Some contexts may prove more productive than those provided in the questionnaire; some items included for pronunciation may turn out to have lexical variants. But the directions will cut down the possibility of false starts.

For example, in the New England *Atlas goal* was included as a pronunciation item (/gol/ or /gul/), and was sought in the context of the place to which children run in their tag games. In New England, *goal* is the usual word in this context; in other areas one gets *bye*, *home*, *base*, *den*, or *hunk*. Lowman consistently recorded the lexical variant for this context; some of the investigators in the Middle West sought only for the pronunciation of *goal*, regardless of the context in which it was obtained. A few have sought the form in the New England context, and then looked for *goal* in some other context. More explicit directions would have prevented this uncertainty.

The questionnaire for the Scottish dialect survey represents a new attempt to obtain by correspondence the materials for a linguistic atlas. Although Wenker used the correspondence method for the German *Atlas* (Wrede *et al.* 1927-56), in recent surveys -- such as the French, Italian, and American atlases -- it has generally been disregarded in favor of investigations on the spot by trained field workers. The reasons the correspondence method has lost favor have been that laymen -- even schoolteachers -- are normally 1) not adequately trained to make accurate records of dialect forms; 2) unwilling to admit that they, or their habitual associates, use forms stigmatized as 'incorrect,' 'vulgar,' or otherwise lacking in social prestige. The skilful field worker can elicit many forms that the average citizen could not -- or would not -- write down on paper.

But though no one questions the desirability of field investigations, recent experiments have indicated that correspondence materials can provide valuable data if the investigator exercises care in framing his questionnaire. The German survey attempted to use the correspondence technique where it is least likely to succeed -- for recording phonetic differences. A. L. Davis has shown that a carefully selected multiple-choice questionnaire of lexical items will provide a picture of dialect distributions differing little from that obtained by a preliminary survey in the field (1949). In the Upper Midwest Harold B. Allen has used a modification of Davis's questionnaire to supplement the data obtained by field work (Allen 1973-76). In Wisconsin Cassidy has used an extensive questionnaire to obtain by correspondence the data for a survey of the folk lexicon (1948). Other investigations (e.g., R. McDavid 1940) have indicated that lay observers are competent to record the distribution of the phonemes if not their phonetic quality. In devising the Scottish questionnaire, McIntosh has kept in touch with Davis and Cassidy and has drawn on their experience.

The Scottish questionnaire, like that for the German *Atlas*, has been distributed through the public school system. The local schoolmaster puts it in the hands of someone competent to fill it out. It is not designed to supplant investigation in the field, but to enable the field investigation to be conducted more efficiently. The authors hope to use it 1) to set up their network at less expense than a preliminary field investigation would entail; 2) to obtain the bulk of the lexical material, leaving to the field workers the task of eliciting most of the phonetic and grammatical materials and the more difficult parts of the lexicon; 3) to obtain a wider coverage than a normal field survey would permit. Since this first questionnaire is experimental, the questions are not confined to any one topic but represent many aspects of the folk vocabulary; several items were included at the request of American dialectologists, since McIntosh is anxious to facilitate the comparison of Scottish and American materials. Most items are designed to elicit lexical variants, but a few deal with grammatical or phonemic differences; the directors of the survey shrewdly estimate that Scotsmen's pride in their own speech is stronger than any reverence they may have for British Received Standard.

The questionnaire is used to obtain information on both Scots (Scottish English) and Gaelic. In communities where the directors suspect that Gaelic is still spoken, two questionnaires are to be filled out -- one by a speaker of Scots, the other by a speaker of Gaelic. In addition to the 210 questions which are answered in every questionnaire, 10 are provided for Gaelic speakers alone. The questionnaire has been sent to some 3000 communities, including Northern Ireland and the northern counties of England.

The questionnaire is sturdily put together, attractively bound, and accompanied by clear and specific instructions about the purposes of the survey and the questionnaire. Preliminary reports indicate that it has already gathered much valuable data. With several such questionnaires supporting competent field investigation, McIntosh and his associates should be able to give us what we have long needed -- accurate information about the distribution of linguistic forms in Scotland.

Scholars have many reasons to welcome
McIntosh's book, the first in a series of
monographs based on the current investigation of Scottish dialects. The significance of the book, be it said at the outset, is not in the raw data it contains;
actually it discusses only a few speech
forms and their distribution. But it
augurs well for our future understanding
of the regional and social varieties of
Scottish speech. We can be sure that the
survey is in good hands; it will be vig-
orously pursued; it will provide the
study of Scots speech with valuable material to complement the work of Craigie's
Dictionary of the Older Scottish Tongue
(1931-) and Grant and Murison's *Scottish
National Dictionary* (1931-76); and the
friendly relations between McIntosh and
American dialect geographers should lead
to the gathering of data that will help us
to interpret the Scottish contribution to
American speech. In broader terms, McIntosh's *Introduction* offers a sound critical appraisal of the aims and methods of
dialect geography in the light of recent
developments in linguistics. What is perhaps most important, McIntosh writes well,
presenting undiluted linguistic truth so
effectively and so clearly that the specialist need not feel insulted or the layman overwhelmed.

The need for a new survey of British
dialects, making use of modern techniques,
has been recognized for some time. No one
should underestimate the work of the English Dialect Society, or the invaluable
data in Ellis's *Early English Pronunciation* (1869-89) and in Wright's *English
Dialect Dictionary* (1898-1905) and *English
Dialect Grammar* (1905). But as with many
pioneer works, the techniques by which
these studies were prepared have been
greatly improved in the past two generations. The volunteer work of the enthusiastic but untrained amateur needs the direction of a specialist; for the haphazard collection of anything that strikes
the investigator's fancy, it has been necessary to substitute systematic investigation of selected items, to provide comparable data on grammar, pronunciation,
and vocabulary;[1] and the assembling of
data from whatever communities amateurs
could be persuaded to work in, has been
replaced by surveys over a network of communities reflecting the economic, social,
and cultural history of the area. It is
no reflection on Ellis and Wright that the

Edinburgh group should have begun a new
investigation of Scotland, or that in England a similar investigation (though differing somewhat in method) is being inaugurated under Harold Orton of Leeds and
Eugen Dieth of Zurich (Dieth 1948; Orton
and Dieth 1951; Dieth and Orton 1952, reviewed in this volume, pp. 351-54).

Perhaps even more important than the new
techniques of dialect investigation is the
changing estimate of what constitutes dialect. Rarely nowadays do investigators
limit their inquiries to the old-fashioned
informant and the speech of the uneducated; rarely do they assume a polar opposition between a uniform standard language (Kurath's "cultivated speech") and
diverse local dialects (Kurath's "folk
speech"). Instead, they generally recognize that cultivated speech as well as
folk speech may have regional varieties,
and that between cultivated speech and
folk speech is a vast body (largely uninvestigated) of "common speech" -- the habitual vehicle of communication for the
yeoman or independent small farmer, the
small storekeeper, the skilled craftsman --
with distinct geographical varieties centering around regional or local commercial
centers. Not only do all three varieties -- folk speech, common speech, and
cultivated speech -- vary from place to
place, but the relationship of the three
is not everywhere the same. In many
places the common speech, in some the cultivated speech, clings to characteristically local pronunciations, words, and
grammatical forms; in other places, only
the oldest and least sophisticated folk
speakers retain the old forms. Moreover,
dialect forms are not just relics of older
usage that persist in relic areas; equally important are the innovations that have
arisen or spread in focal areas. A true
picture of dialect usage must take account
of both the preservation of relics and the
spread of innovations.

The Scottish survey is important for an
understanding of the relationship between
British and American dialects. Speakers
of Scots constituted an important part of
the American colonial population. High-
landers settled the Cape Fear Valley in
North Carolina, and in Georgia formed the
military colony of Darien at the mouth of
the Altamaha, established to protect Savannah against the Spaniards. Ulster
Scots set up independent frontier communities in New Hampshire and in northeastern

South Carolina; the main body of their migration settled the Pittsburgh area in western Pennsylvania, from which they spread south through the Shenandoah Valley into the Piedmont and mountain areas of the Carolinas and Georgia. The important role of the Scots in Canadian history is apparent even to a casual student; it is possible there are more speakers of Scots Gaelic in Nova Scotia than in Scotland. In view of these facts, the student who would see American dialects in their true perspective will find the distribution of dialect features in Scotland and Northern Ireland only slightly less important than that in England itself.

The Scottish survey, a joint project of the Departments of English and Celtic at the University of Edinburgh, will record both Scots (Scottish English) and Gaelic usage. It is concerned not only with the dialects of Scotland proper, but also with those of Northern Ireland, the Isle of Man, and the northernmost counties of England -- regions long affiliated with Scotland, both culturally and linguistically. So far, the evidence has been assembled only through two correspondence questionnaires, distributed to some 4100 communities; at the time the *Introduction* went to press, not all of the first questionnaires had as yet been returned, much less analyzed. The second questionnaire was distributed only last year; field investigations, as well as further questionnaires, lie in the future. As anyone familiar with dialect work can appreciate, it will be some time before the survey is completed and the results are published. In the meantime, since the success of the project depends on continued public interest and public cooperation, McIntosh and his colleagues are bringing out a series of monographs on related topics, the first one naturally being the explanation of the project. The ultimate publication of the Scottish *Atlas* itself (Mather and Speitel 1975-) will modify the conclusions of some of the volumes, but will not supersede them.[2]

The *Introduction* explains to the scholar and the educated layman the purposes of the survey, the problems that such investigations meet, and the solutions here proposed. It appeals to national pride by properly identifying Scottish speech as an aspect of Scottish culture. It avoids all pretense to omniscience or finality by pointing out that the study of regional and local speech is never completed as long as the language endures, but must be undertaken many times and with many techniques.

At the outset McIntosh delimits the scope of the Scottish survey by showing how the investigation of the living language at a particular time requires a different procedure from that of a historical dictionary (such as Craigie's or Grant and Murison's), a study of place names, or the compilation of local glossaries. He is careful to explain that a collection of local glossaries would not be equivalent to a linguistic survey, since the compiler of such a glossary seldom attempts to provide a complete local vocabulary but concentrates upon the oddities -- the things that he feels are 'dialect' -- and so usually misses many distinctive items. McIntosh shows how dialect studies may be either descriptive[3] or comparative; comparative studies in turn may be either diachronic, comparing different historical stages of the same dialect, or diatopic, comparing different dialects at the same time. Diatopic studies are therefore the immediate business of the linguistic geographer, regardless of the descriptive or historical uses to which his data may subsequently be put.

McIntosh wisely indicates that the investigator of dialects cannot work in a vacuum, but must cooperate with other social scientists: historians, social anthropologists, geographers, and students of material culture. Population history is always important in interpreting the distribution of linguistic forms; in Scotland the significant movements of population largely took place before there were documents to record them, but they can be traced and must be reckoned with. As a force altering the number and nature of local dialects -- operating on all, though differently on each one -- the linguistic geographer must take account of the standard language. For McIntosh this is not equivalent to British Received Standard, but something like the working definition which Fries uses: that variety of the language (itself with many local variations) used by those in positions of respect who conduct the important affairs of the English-speaking world. He rejects the notion of a 'pure dialect' as something that has never existed. Moreover, he points out, dialect boundaries -- even in Scotland -- are rarely very sharp, so that it is often difficult to determine where one local variety leaves off and another begins. On these questions, though he has said nothing really new or startling, he has said it more deftly and more intelligently than it is often said.

On questions of method, the book is more controversial. McIntosh takes sharp issue with some of the traditional methods in linguistic geography, especially some of the theories of Gilliéron (or rather, their rigid application by Gilliéron's disciples): the use of a single uniform questionnaire throughout the area, and of a single field worker whose job it is to record automatically -- and to submit without editing -- a minute impressionistic transcription of the responses of each informant. McIntosh suggests that for the Scottish survey it might be profitable to reexamine the techniques of investigation, to determine whether all types of evidence need to be collected by the field worker. Utilizing not only recent experimental dialect studies but lessons from statistics, demography, and phonemic theory, he concludes that the field worker ought to be used only for those purposes for which he has no substitute -- in the main, phonetic recording[4] -- and that the bulk of the lexical evidence might well be gathered by correspondence questionnaires, such as those which the Scottish survey is already using.

The arguments of McIntosh against the traditional procedures are plausible, though I do not find them completely convincing in principle, and though I doubt whether the Scottish methods would be applicable to North America: 1. Good field workers are hard to find, hard to train, and hard to keep enthusiastic about field work for more than a few years. 2. The typical European 'portmanteau questionnaire' of 2000 items or more is bound to yield many blanks if there are marked differences in local culture.[5] 3. Field work is an expensive means of collecting data, which should be used only when no other satisfactory means is available. 4. For most of the lexical items fine impressionistic transcriptions (or even phonemic transcriptions) are superfluous, since -- to take a specific example -- the comparison between the cow calls *co-boss* and *sookie* does not involve a single potential phonemic contrast in analogous environments.[6] Allowing a week for interviewing each informant with the long questionnaire (a reasonable estimate in the light of American experience with somewhat shorter ones), McIntosh shows that in five years a good field worker would be able to complete little more than 250 interviews, a far from adequate sample for Scotland. Therefore the field worker should collect data on fewer items -- most of them dealing with matters of pronunciation -- and visit more communities.

Since the field worker will be recording chiefly pronunciation, his questionnaire should be designed to record as many known or suspected phonetic differences as possible. McIntosh recognizes three types of pronunciation differences, as Kurath and I do in Kurath and R. McDavid 1961: 1) differences in the incidence of the phoneme -- is the syllabic of *stone* /o/ or /e/ or /i/? 2) differences in the pronunciation of the phoneme or one of its allophones -- what is the phonetic quality of /r/ or of intervocalic /t/? 3) differences in the phonemic system -- have OE /hw-/ and /f-/ fallen together? In discussing attempts to answer these questions, McIntosh is not afraid to use technical concepts, but explains how linguists operate in terms of the phonemic principle, which assumes there are fixed structure points in the

sound system of every informant. Since no list of words can anticipate all contrasts, it may be necessary to add items to the questionnaire in order to handle local problems.[7] Furthermore, the field worker should be allowed to comment on his practice and to point out where he may have failed to adjust adequately to the differences between two closely related neighboring dialects.[8] The field worker thus assumes a more important role than that which Gilliéron assigned him.

As the phonetic investigation depends on fixed points in the sound system of the informant, the investigation of vocabulary depends on the choice of fixed points in the informant's experience of the external world. Although no informant will know everything that one might care to ask about, the lexical items chosen should be common to the experience of most. (Sometimes, it is true, a cultural item of limited distribution, such as the Charleston *joggling board*, may be critical for determining the extent of a dialect area.) Assuming a skilful field worker, the lack of a response may have one of two causes: the item may not occur, as coasting is unknown in the flat and snowless South Carolina coastal plain; or the item, though it occurs, may lack a name, as the familiar strip of grass between the sidewalk and the street -- a *tree lawn* in Cleveland, a *boulevard* in Minneapolis, a *parking* in northern Illinois -- has no name in the South Carolina Piedmont. A useful lexical item should have a number of regional or social variants; *caboose* would be unprofitable in the United States, since all railroads -- and all people familiar with railroads -- use only that term. On the other hand, a term may have such an overwhelming number of variants, with very slight connotative differences, that they reflect no pattern of regional or social distribution. Early in the New England field investigation, the questions calling for synonyms of *prostitute* and *intoxicated* were dropped; and in the Rocky Mountain area, contrary to local expectations, *gun* and *silver dollar* proved unprofitable.

Besides making sure that the lexical items in his questionnaire provide useful information on the distribution of linguistic forms in Scotland (the correspondence questionnaires were first tried on a group of Edinburgh undergraduates), McIntosh is concerned with the problem of making his data comparable with findings in other parts of the English-speaking world. Many Scots terms will not appear in the United States; conversely, neither the peanut nor the poor white is a normal part of Scottish culture. But there are so many valid comparisons in such activities as housekeeping, cooking, animal husbandry, and children's games, that since his last visit to the United States in 1949, McIntosh has often sought the advice of American linguistic geographers on the makeup of his questionnaires. One of these questionnaires consists largely of lexical items; but it includes a few items of morphology and some dealing with problems of phoneme incidence and phonemic contrast.[9]

Since McIntosh is writing for the layman as well as for the specialist in linguistic geography, he is careful to answer the questions which an amateur might raise. Though he is particularly concerned with getting records from the relatively old-fashioned informants, since their type of speech is disappearing, he is well aware that 'old-fashioned' and 'modern' are relative terms -- that resistance to innovations varies not only from place to place (being much stronger, say, in the Outer Hebrides than in a suburb of Edinburgh) but from speaker to speaker, and even from occasion to occasion in the same speaker. One need not be distressed by this variability: it is a part of the normal linguistic situation in any period, though it is accentuated in times of rapid linguistic change. The question whether men or women make better informants -- a question that seems to worry a number of linguists (cf. "Le Langage des femmes" 1952, R. McDavid 1953c) -- McIntosh dismisses as irrelevant. Toothlessness, too, he feels need not disqualify an otherwise satisfactory informant; it may be a normal characteristic of elderly uneducated informants in isolated rural communities, just as continual tobacco chewing is a normal part of the conversational situation for some American social groups. McIntosh recognizes, furthermore, that an interview is not a mechanical process. Though an experienced field worker tries to control the contexts in which questions are asked and answered, and though he knows the cues that are most likely to set up satisfactory responses, he does not hold the interview to rigid patterns, but manipulates the sequence of questions according to the informant; the less formality the better, especially if the investigator wants to get trustworthy grammatical data. As American students have found out, the field worker (or the person through whom the questionnaires are distributed) is likely to obtain the highest degree of cooperation if he appeals to local or regional pride; McIntosh, by stressing the importance of the data as an aspect of Scottish history and Scottish culture, has had excellent press relations and full cooperation from the Scottish Office of Education. As for publication, McIntosh rejects as too expensive the older method of hand-lettered maps, like those that appeared in the French, the Italian, and the New England atlases. Instead, he favors publication in the form of tables.

Lest some of his readers be disappointed at obvious omissions in the final survey, McIntosh is careful to explain that he does not expect to say the last word or get anything approaching all the data. This observation is particularly applicable to the study of grammatical variations. With care, one may assemble comparative morphological evidence as easily as lexical, but linguists have not yet devised satisfactory procedures for a thorough and systematic investigation of differences in syntax. Before undertaking such an investigation on a national scale, McIntosh advocates local pilot studies to experiment with different techniques. As methods develop, many kinds of future dialect studies may be undertaken: comparative studies of intonation and voice quality, detailed analyses of the sources and levels of usage in the speech of a region, and systematic descriptions of local dialects. (Phonological descriptions are few enough, and in their descriptions of English dialects linguists have rarely gone further.)

The most important question to raise at this point is the validity of the evidence gathered by correspondence, since so much of the Scottish material will be of this sort. Any method can fail if handled clumsily; the correspondence method, also, is less effective for some kinds of vocabulary items than others, and would probably be less effective in the United States than in Scotland. But even American experience has shown that a carefully prepared questionnaire, with careful indoctrination of those through whom it is distributed, enables the investigator to derive useful data through correspondence. In the Great Lakes area, A. L. Davis found that a selected multiple-choice questionnaire distributed to a limited number of communities gave essentially the same picture of dialect patterns that the preliminary field work had revealed (1949). In the Upper Midwest, Harold B. Allen has supported his two hundred field interviews with a thousand multiple-choice check lists; they have made the evidence from field records much more meaningful than it would otherwise have been (1973-76). D. W. Reed has had equal success with check lists in California; he has found them particularly useful in setting up the network of communities for field work. In Wisconsin, F. G. Cassidy has relied almost exclusively on correspondence for his study of the folk vocabulary.[10] Of course, one must not lump together correspondence data with field material, but present each type separately. In this way the reader can see for himself if the two techniques yield different results.

Perhaps because McIntosh wished to simplify his statements for the benefit of the layman, a few of his observations need qualification. No matter how carefully devised, a correspondence questionnaire cannot probe for lexical variants in the way that a field worker can; if the first response (as often in the Middle West) is a general term, the field worker can modify the form of his question. Even in Scotland, I suspect that the correspondence method will prove only partially successful in probing for grammatical variants; though their tradition of 'correctness' is less vigorous than the American (and meets a stronger resistance from pride in local usage), notions of propriety and the prestige of the standard language may still inhibit informants from writing down what they actually say.[11] No matter how hard one tries to focus a questionnaire on pronunciation alone, some items will turn out to have lexical variants in some localities. Thus the word *goal* 'place to which children run in certain games' was included in the New England *Atlas* for its pronunciation; but in other parts of the Atlantic Seaboard the same question usually called forth *base*, *bye*, *hunk*, *line*, or *den* (cf. Kurath *et al.* 1939-43, Kurath 1949). A minor point: McIntosh's use of *informer* (74) where

Americans would use *informant* is an unpleasant reminder of the public honors recently rendered those who have made profitable careers out of testifying against their neighbors; but since the Scottish law term for professional informing is *delation*, perhaps *informer* does not have the associations for McIntosh that it has for Americans and Irishmen. Finally, the repeated use of Scottish place names makes me wish that McIntosh had included a map showing the location of every place mentioned in his book; though such names may be no problem for Scotsmen, Peebles and Black Isle are as strange to most Americans as Orangeburg and the Juniata would be to the average Scot.

But these are small objections. The book as a whole is intelligent and lucid. Readers interested in Scottish dialects, scholars and amateurs alike, will look forward to the appearance of the Scottish atlas and the other monographs in this series. And American linguists writing for a popular audience could profit by McIntosh's example.

NOTES

[1] To take one small example, the Atlantic Seaboard states have a variety of terms for the earthworm, distributed in regional patterns that reflect settlement history and suggest that most of them must have come from the British Isles. Yet of these terms the *English Dialect Dictionary* includes only the Narragansett Bay *eaceworm* and the Windsor (Connecticut) *angledog*. See Kurath 1949:74-75; Maps 139, 140.

[2] The second monograph in the series, University of Edinburgh Linguistic Survey of Scotland Monographs, is Jackson 1955.

As McIntosh points out (96), the monumental appearance of such supposedly definitive works as Wright 1898-1905 may lead some scholars to assume that it is unnecessary either to preserve the original research materials or to supplement, corroborate, or correct it by later studies. Many British scholars have reported difficulty in enlisting support for a linguistic atlas, since a widespread opinion holds that Ellis and Wright have recorded everything.

[3] McIntosh reminds us that good pedagogical prescriptive treatments are essentially descriptive, since they limit themselves to the features of the single dialect (upper-class Parisian French, British Recieved Standard, or middle-class Chicago English) which the instructor feels will best serve his students' needs. What linguists criticize in many prescriptive treatments is not their prescriptiveness, but the choice of an inappropriate model (such as British pronunciation as a standard for Americans), an erroneous description (as when the preterite *dove* is deplored as 'colloquial' or 'substandard,' though in American com-

munities where both *dived* and *dove* occur, the latter is generally favored by younger and more sophisticated speakers), or the implication that the choice between linguistic forms is an ethical choice between good and evil rather than a social choice between appropriate and inappropriate.

[4] Even for phonetic studies, portable tape recorders can supplement the field worker's notes. Though recorders can be used only where electric current is available, and must be carefully tended during the interview, the recording can be played repeatedly, will catch many more conversational responses than even the best field worker can jot down, and provide better evidence than impressionistic transcriptions for such problems as stress, intonation, and juncture. On the other hand, the interviewer who relies solely on the tape will spend much more time transcribing the data than he would spend in a field interview, and may find important material obscured by noise or not on the tape at all. The best solution is to conduct the interview in the way that one has found most effective, transcribe impressionistically during the interview, and use the tape as a check.

[5] The questionnaire published by Orton and Dieth contains about 1125 items, heavily weighted in favor of relics to be found only in relatively isolated communities. See Dieth and Orton 1952, reviewed in this volume, pp. 351-54.
One can spend too much time attempting to devise a foolproof questionnaire for field investigations. Orton and Dieth spent five years on their questionnaire before they published it; within five years after the American atlas was first proposed, the field workers had completed the survey

of New England and Lowman had undertaken his preliminary survey of the South Atlantic States. The most carefully prepared questionnaire must allow for modification in the light of field experience; as Gilliéron himself recognized, a perfect questionnaire can be made only after the dialects have been exhaustively investigated.

[6] A lexical variant sometimes yields valuable information on the phonemic structure of the dialect. In American English there is lexical variation between *toadstool*, *frogstool*, and other terms. In New England, many informants preserve the old-fashioned monophthongal or ingliding 'New England short o' [oə] only in the initial syllable of *toadstool*, while (for these informants) the upgliding diphthong [ou] occurs in the simplex *toad*. Thus the complete picture of the phonemic system of such dialects depends on the pronunciation of *toadstool*, which had been included in the questionnaire primarily as a lexical item. See Avis 1956, 1961.

[7] *Cot* 'small bed' is not a part of the questionnaire for any of the American regional atlases. But in areas where the field worker suspects that some informants lack the contrast between unrounded and rounded low-back vowels (western Pennsylvania, northern Michigan, Minnesota, western Canada) the field worker may use *cot* for comparison with *caught* or *tot* with *taught*. Other potential contrasts may elude even the most alert field worker and require independent investigation. See Ives 1952, Gleason 1955.

[8] The field worker can avoid some of these problems by zig-zagging across suspected dialect boundaries rather than working parallel to them.

[9] Lest this seem a retrogression to the discarded techniques of the German *Atlas* (Wrede *et al.* 1927-56), we should remember that Wenker asked for *phonetic* data from what amounted to 40,000 miscellaneous field workers at a time when the phonemic principle was not yet an axiom of linguistics. If the test words are carefully chosen, most informants can furnish *phonemic* data -- as whether *creek* has the syllabic of *leek* or *lick* or *lake* -- without having to use any phonetic symbols.

[10] [However, for the *Dictionary of American Regional English* (Cassidy *et al.* 1981-), Cassidy relied primarily on field work.]

[11] Informants are reluctant to write a linguistic form which they have been taught is incorrect, no matter how often they use it in conversation. A striking example is the complete absence of *ain't* in the Vulgar English materials examined for Fries 1940. In field interviews I have often heard informants deny using, and stigmatize as illiterate, forms which I had recorded several times in their conversation.

Atwood's *Survey* -- the second full-length survey based on the collections of the Linguistic Atlas project --is an important contribution to the study of present-day American English. Like its predecessor, Kurath's *Word Geography of the Eastern United States* (1949), it substitutes for prejudice a scientific judgment based on observation of the living language, and should help in the reestablishment of the descriptive rather than the prescriptive approach as the determining principle where one is dealing with the status of competing linguistic forms.

The particular importance of Atwood's study lies in the fact that this is the first large-scale study of English grammatical forms derived from comparable data obtained by systematic sampling of the spoken language of locally and socially identified informants over a wide geographical area.[1] As such, it is probably an even more significant contribution to the study of present-day English than either Kurath's *Word Geography* or Kurath and R. McDavid 1961. The average speaker, or teacher, is far readier to grant regional variations in cultivated usage for vocabulary and pronunciation than he is for grammar. Travel, the radio, and previous studies have made us all aware that pronunciation and vocabulary vary from region to region, that educated New Yorkers, Philadelphians, and Charlestonians of the same social level may use different words in the same biosocial context or pronounce the same words differently. But we are less willing to concede the existence in grammar of the same variety of equally acceptable regional standards. However much we differ in actual practice, in our attitude toward language most Americans at least pay lip service to the ideal of one uniform standard of grammar, from which all deviations are wrong. Yet the history of English -- or of any other language, for that matter -- reveals that there have always been regional differences in standard grammatical usage, and that by dialect borrowing grammatical forms (like words or pronunciations) have spread from one region to another, even into the dialect of the cultural focus of the area in which the language is spoken. One of the most striking examples in English is the personal pronoun of the third person plural: *they*, *their*, *them*. By the thirteenth century all these case forms were well established in Northern English, but

still unknown in the London area. Toward the end of the fourteenth century, Chaucer used the nominative *they* regularly, the genitive *their* and the dative-accusative *them* very infrequently. By 1500 *they*, *their*, *them* were all established in standard London English. Atwood's study happily reminds us that competition between grammatical forms still exists in standard American English, with some forms spreading and others disappearing.

The method Atwood employs is a simple one, but one requiring intelligent judgment and painstaking examination of the evidence. His first step is to list all items in the Atlas questionnaires that might reveal differences in verb forms,[2] grouping them in the following categories: 1) Tense Forms; 2) Personal Forms; 3) Number and Concord; 4) Negative Forms; 5) Infinitive and Present Participle; 6) Phrases (sometimes several items in the questionnaires may deal with the tense forms of a single verb, or with a particular negative or personal form). The second step is to examine all of the Atlas field records and record on separate charts or tables the data for each of these items. The third step is to determine the distribution of competing forms, both regionally and socially. Where there seem to be significant regional patterns in the distribution of particular forms, Atwood has provided maps, 28 in all (Figs. 2-29). Fig. 1 indicates the geographical scope of the survey; Figs. 30-31 show two bundles of isoglosses indicating the significance of verb forms for setting off dialect areas -- the South from the Midland, the South and South Midland from the North Midland. Atwood's statements are consistently clear and easy to follow.

Before making his regional and social interpretations, Atwood wisely observes certain precautions in evaluating the data he intends to interpret. He recognizes that no two field workers operate in exactly the same fashion, regardless of their skill or training, and that such personal differences may bulk large in transitional areas covered by two field workers -- as Vermont by Lowman and Bloch, the South Carolina Up-Country and Upstate New York by Lowman and me. The field workers may prefer certain types of informants, may manipulate the questionnaire differently, may stick closely to direct responses or freely record incidental forms from the informant's unguarded conversation. It is true that these personal biases often correct one another; nevertheless, it is important that the interpreter of the data should recognize such problems and state them frankly, so that the reader will not be misled.[3]

Besides calling attention to differences in the field workers' practices, Atwood is properly conservative in accepting the forms which the field workers have recorded. For this study he counts only direct responses (forms given in response to the questionnaire) and conversational responses (forms picked up on the fly, from the informant's unguarded remarks); he has disregarded suggested responses (forms prompted by the field worker) and reported responses (forms which the informant says he has heard from others, but doesn't admit using himself). Atwood's comment on this practice is well taken:

> As a result of this procedure, I believe it legitimate to conclude that the non-standard verb forms are at least as frequent in popular speech as my tabulations show them to be. In some areas, particularly, they are probably more frequent, since, no matter how skillful a fieldworker may be, there are many informants who hesitate to use a form that is perfectly natural to them because they feel that it might be disapproved as "incorrect." (3)[4]

With such a conservative approach to data recorded by trained field workers from definitely localized and socially identified informants, it is to be expected that Atwood's conclusions would be sober rather than spectacular, but all the more convincing for their sobriety. They deserve careful scrutiny from the dialect geographer, the social historian, and the much-abused teacher of high-school or college English. Among the most important conclusions are the following.

1. The evidence supports the scheme of dialect areas which Kurath's *Word Geography* set up on the basis of vocabulary. It shows convincingly that, despite Mencken's eloquence (1936:416-73, 1948:332-94), there is no such thing as a uniform American Vulgate, spoken and written by the uneducated in all regions. Instead, there are verb forms characteristic of the North (New England, the Hudson Valley, and their derivative settlements), the Midland (Pennsylvania and its derivative settlements, including the Southern uplands), and the South (the old areas of plantation culture). Within these large regional divisions, one finds verb forms characteristic of well-defined smaller areas, both focal areas (the Hudson Valley, the Pennsylvania German area, Eastern Virginia, and the South Carolina Low-Country) and relic areas (Northeastern New England, the Delmarva peninsula, Eastern North Carolina, and the Southern Mountains). Many of these regional and local forms are con-

fined to old-fashioned speech and are lacking in the metropolitan centers; but some are well established in cultured speech and are even spreading to other areas. Typical regional distributions are shown by the following forms:

The North: *see* (pret.).

The North without the Hudson Valley: /wʌnt/ *won't*.

The Hudson Valley: /wunt/ *won't* (also South Carolina Low-Country).

Northeastern New England: /gwain/ *going* (also South).

The Midland: *boilt* (past participle).

The South Midland: *dogbit* 'bitten by a dog.'

The Pennsylvania German area: *got awake* 'woke up.'

Western North Carolina: /ækst/ 'asked.'

The South: *heern* 'heard' (also Northeastern New England).

Eastern Virginia: *clome* 'climbed.'

The South Carolina Low-Country: *dove* 'dived' (also North).

Delmarva: *wurdn't* /wɜdnt/ 'wasn't.'

Eastern North Carolina: *hadn't ought* (also North).

2. The evidence on the social status of verb forms should be very helpful to the teacher of English and the writer of textbooks. As Atwood's book gains circulation and is supplemented by other works based on the grammatical evidence from the Atlas (e.g., V. McDavid 1956, R. and V. McDavid 1960, Allen 1973-76), one can organize the preparation of teaching materials and one's classroom practices around the actual facts of cultivated usage rather than around what someone has said cultivated usage ought to be. At such a time, teachers of English will be able to devote their attention to the effective use of the standard English which nearly every college freshman has already mastered; they can eschew the time-honored drillwork in the detection and correction of 'grammatical errors.' Many of these proscribed forms are not errors at all, but standard English; others, though nonstandard, are confined to relatively small areas of the English-speaking world. Conversely, many so-called 'correct' forms are actually used by a minority of cultivated speakers.

To illustrate: most handbooks of composition denounce *hadn't ought*, *laid* as the preterite of *lie*, and *dove* /dov/ as the preterite of *dive*, in terms that suggest that these three forms are equally characteristic of uneducated speech in all regions. Atwood shows that, in reality, these three forms have three very different patterns of distribution. *Hadn't ought* (32-33, Fig. 26) is essentially a regional form; except for a small area in northeastern North Carolina, it occurs only in the North; in New England it is used by a third of the cultured informants. *Lay*, the so-called 'standard' preterite of *lie*, is universal in cultured usage only in southwestern New England; it is predominant on Chesapeake Bay and in Eastern North Carolina -- parts of the South where one expects to find old-fashioned forms still in use; in general, a minority of cultured speakers use *lay* as the preterite, while a majority use *laid* (18). *Dove* is predominant throughout all the North, plus all of New Jersey; it occurs alongside *dived* in eastern Pennsylvania, the Pittsburgh area, and the plantation area of the South Carolina-Georgia coast; in communities of divided usage, *dove* is usually favored by younger, urban, and educated informants (9, Fig. 6). Thus *hadn't ought* is a regional form which constitutes no problem for most speakers of American English; *laid* is one of two competing standard forms in a complex interrelationship of linguistic and social forces; *dove* is, in general, actually a prestige form, spreading because it is indicative of a superior social status.

3. Finally, this survey should remind scholars again of the contributions which linguistic geography can make toward an understanding of the relationships between linguistic forces and other social and cultural forces. As a summary, it will be useful in interpreting the data now being gathered in the North-Central States, the Upper Midwest, the Rocky Mountains, and the Pacific Coast. It should whet the appetite of scholars to find out what has happened to the English language in what is largely unknown territory -- the Gulf States, the lower Mississippi Valley, Texas and the Southern Plains, and Canada. It should direct the attention of scholars and teachers -- and one hopes, of foundations as well -- to the importance of publishing the Middle and South Atlantic materials as soon as possible. Interpretative studies, like this and Kurath's *Word Geography*, are invaluable; but they are no substitute for an edited Linguistic Atlas of the Middle and South Atlantic States.

In Atwood's study I find a few omissions, either of verb forms or of additional contexts in which some of his cited forms might be found. I suspect most of

these were omitted either because field workers were inconsistent in their practice or because the data presented no clear picture. Nevertheless, most teachers will regret that he did not consider the data on *shall* and *will* -- even though this data is available for New England alone. The distribution of *hadn't ought* is very interesting; the interesting, and somewhat different, distribution of *had ought* does not appear. I miss discussion of the perfective *done* (as in *I've done worked all day*), a construction which I use myself and which I recorded frequently in South Carolina. The distribution of *lay out* and *laid out* 'played hookey' (see Kurath 1949:79, Map 158) might illuminate the status of *lay* and *laid* in the South. An exhaustive study of the Atlas questionnaires might disclose a few other omissions, a total trivial in comparison with Atwood's exhaustive treatment of 88 entries representing over a hundred items from the questionnaires.

I also find a few minuscule omissions from the maps. The area of the Atlas survey omits the three Ontario communities (Welland, Kingston, Brockville) investigated as part of the survey of New York (data from Welland is included on Figs. 9 and 15), five or six communities in upstate New York, one in Ohio (Lawrence County), and a couple in South Carolina. But here, too, the errors are so slight that only exhaustive familiarity with the survey can disclose them. They do not affect the presentation of evidence, either in the text or on the maps.[5]

For several years I have waited for the publication of Atwood's study; now that I have it in my hands, I am not disappointed. I have already made frequent use of it in the few months since it appeared; in the future, I shall require all my advanced students to examine it. It is the kind of study that needs to be multiplied, and that surely will be multiplied when funds are obtained to publish the Atlas materials from the Middle and South Atlantic States and put the data in the hands of a wider community of scholars.[6]

NOTES

[1] Fries 1940 also judges the status of grammatical forms according to the social status of the informants who actually use them. Fries' study differs from Atwood's, however, in three important ways: 1) it is based on letters written to a government bureau, so that the investigator is limited to the grammatical forms that the writers happened to use; 2) the informants are classified only by social status and not geographically, so that one cannot draw any conclusions about regional usage; 3) for various reasons -- either an educationally-imposed taboo on writing some forms

that freely occur in speech, or the formality of the relationship between a petitioner and a government office -- some very common linguistic forms rarely or never appear in these letters, even those written by speakers of what Fries calls "Vulgar English." The most notable example of this kind is *ain't*, which does not appear at all.

Wright 1905 assumes a rather unified Standard English; furthermore, it is not based on strictly comparable materials like those of the Atlas.

[2] The New England questionnaire is found in

Kurath *et al.* 1939:147-58. For a comparison of all questionnaires used in the Atlas project through 1951, see R. and V. McDavid 1951a, through 1967, Davis, McDavid, and McDavid 1969.

[3] These problems are likely to be most numerous in areas investigated by several field workers over a period of years, and more critical for a study of grammatical forms than for either pronunciation or vocabulary.

[4] Even direct and conversational forms may present somewhat different pictures. Some of my informants in the South -- chiefly the moderately educated, but occasionally cultured informants as well -- would use *ain't*, multiple negatives, and nonstandard verb forms freely in conversation but never offer them in response to direct questioning; in fact, they would be indignant at my even suggesting that they might use forms which they associated with the speech of Negroes and poor whites. After several such experiences, I adopted the practice of recording grammatical forms from free conversation wherever possible, and reduced direct probing for them to a minimum.

[5] Four of the maps omit some of the evidence from southwest Virginia and western North Carolina. Atwood indicates the omissions in a note immediately preceding the maps.

[6] [With the assistance of the National Endowment for the Humanities, the publication of the Middle and South Atlantic materials has begun (Kurath *et al.* 1979-) and the editing of those from the North-Central States is well along.]

Down in the Holler is another of the publications which have given Vance Randolph a deserved reputation as our leading authority on Ozarks folk culture -- on language and living, on manners and morals and music. In this volume he has enjoyed the assistance of George P. Wilson, an enthusiastic partisan of the amateur's interest in dialect study, and for eight years secretary of the American Dialect Society.

The materials in this book are derived from Randolph's own observations of his Ozark neighbors over several decades. What he has published before, he has reworked, amplified, and annotated.

Randolph's method of dialect investigation is one which many scholars would like to emulate: to pick one's community, settle down there, win the confidence of one's neighbors, and spend the rest of one's life recording what one hears. When combined with training in phonetics and general linguistics, this method can produce exceptionally full and accurate records of the usage of a community; many of the best dialect monographs by European scholars have been produced by a variant on this method, with the investigator returning summer after summer to the same village until the record is essentially complete. Even without accurate phonetics (and Randolph freely admits his lack of phonetic training), in the hands of a sensitive investigator it yields valuable information about vocabulary, grammar, and many aspects of pronunciation. As any experienced field worker recognizes, there is no substitute for evidence recorded from an informant's unguarded conversation.

Randolph's purpose, as he defines it, "is to write down what I have heard the Ozark hillman say, how he said it, and what he meant by it" -- the presentation of linguistic evidence in its social context. This leads to an anecdotal treatment, with linguistic forms the occasion for a series of entertaining stories which Randolph enjoys telling. Some of these stories I recognize from my field experience as a part of the American store of folk anecdote; others are localized in the Ozarks scene. The anecdotal treatment leads to an emphasis of some aspects of the vocabulary to the neglect of others: taboo and euphemy get an entire chapter, while animals, furniture, implements, cooking, and sports get only incidental treatment. But an author as an artist has the right to emphasize what he wishes; if the omissions leave us a little uncertain, we can be dead sure of the inclusions.

Randolph likes living in the Ozarks and recording the speech and culture of his neighbors. He has established excellent rapport with his informants that makes possible accurate observation of the linguistic phenomena associated with intimate aspects of life. This appears particularly in his searching criticism of fictional representations of Ozark speech -- a section of interest to everyone who has ever grappled with a 'literary dialect.' The interesting presentation should make this a popular book for students of American culture. What is more, it provides a great deal of evidence which the scholar can utilize for at least a preliminary interpretation of the position of Ozarks speech in relation to other varieties of present and earlier English.

What the scholar misses is the framework to facilitate this interpretation. This omission is not Randolph's fault, for he does not pretend to be what he is not. But the book would be more effective if the statements about the position of the dialect had drawn on what has been learned in the last two decades about the regional and social varieties of American English. To disparage the work of "professors" (a curious attitude, with one of the authors holding professorial rank), does not dispose of the serious scholarship with which a writer on American dialect ought to be familiar.

Charles C. Fries's *American English Grammar* (1940) is but one of several studies attempting to define standard English on the basis of actual cultivated usage rather than the prejudices of normative grammarians. Those familiar with such studies will find nothing unusual, or even worthy of mention, in *it sure was me*; that is standard English, as are *in back of*, *named after* someone, and *over and above* one's expenses. To *knock up* 'make (a woman) pregnant' is somewhat crude but heard throughout the United States. The compound preposition *for to*, introducing an infinitive of purpose, is common everywhere in nonstandard English.

An even more surprising oversight is the lack of any reference to the Linguistic Atlas project. The New England volumes and the accompanying handbook appeared in 1939-43. Field work for the Middle and

South Atlantic States was completed in 1949, when Kurath's *Word Geography of the Eastern United States* also appeared. In the North-Central States, the Upper Midwest, the Rocky Mountains, and the Pacific Coast field work has progressed under the direction of A. H. Marckwardt, Harold Allen, Marjorie Kimmerle, and David Reed. These scholars and their associates have published much about methods of investigation, the study of population history, the interpretation of data, and the position of particular American dialects (e.g., Atwood 1951, 1953a) -- to say nothing of specific data about individual items Randolph has recorded.

A scholar familiar with the Atlas materials can see from Randolph's evidence that Ozarks speech must be classified with the speech of the American Midland, deriving ultimately from the Pennsylvania settlements. Like the speech of the Southern mountains, it is probably a relic variety of South Midland, gradually yielding to the pressure of Southern Lowland speech of the river valleys, and to the Northern and North Midland speech of the Northern plains. But one would like to know more of the status of competing forms. Is Ozarks speech a dwindling relic of a type that was once spoken throughout the area from the South Carolina Piedmont to central Texas? Or has it always been sharply differentiated from the speech of the surrounding lowlands? Who settled the Ozarks, and when, and why? (It would have been very helpful if the authors had included a map, giving the boundaries of what they consider the Ozarks area, and indicating the location of the many geographical features which are mentioned in the book.) How should one explain the presence in Ozarks speech of such South Carolina Low-Country forms as *pinder* 'peanut' and *cooter* 'turtle;' or *dove* as the preterite of *dive* -- a form predominant in the area of New England settlement, common in the Charleston area, but rare in the Midland; or of *run* 'small creek,' predominant in Pennsylvania but rare in the Appalachians south of the Kanawha? To answer these questions we need another type of study from that which Randolph has made. It nowise lessens the value of his work that he has not provided such a study: his materials have a unique value that nothing else could have. But other studies will be necessary; and since Randolph announces that this is to be his last publication dealing with Ozarks speech, one hopes he will help future investigators to obtain the cooperation of his neighbors without which no field work can succeed.

When the survey of the Gulf States and lower Mississippi Valley is completed [Lee A. Pederson, of Emory University, has begun it], we will have a much better idea of the significance of the Ozarks as a relic area. This is not to be shown by listing individual speech forms and offering parallel quotations from earlier literature. If such examples are evidence that the Ozark hillmen speak 'Elizabethan' English, one could make as good a case for the older-generation folk speech of any area in rural America. Relic forms may be found anywhere; it is the pattern of recurring relics, with large numbers of speakers in the same area using the same relic forms, that makes a relic area -- such as Cape Cod, Chesapeake Bay, Albemarle Sound, Western North Carolina, or the Ozarks.

Delineating these patterns will take time. Meanwhile, we can be very thankful that we have *Down in the Holler*. It is valuable linguistic evidence as well as good reading.

This is a posthumous work of the late Robert L. Ramsay, whose interest, energy, and inspiration have provided for Missouri possibly a more thorough study of place names, past and present, than is available for any other state. From 1928 to 1948, eighteen of Ramsay's M.A. candidates investigated Missouri place names section by section; the results of their research are incorporated in a master file now approaching forty thousand names. The present publication is a popular presentation, in topical rather than alphabetical form, of part of the data in one of these theses, showing the cultural influences that are reflected in nearly six hundred names of one county.

The cultural influences producing American place names are indicated by the subdivisions of this study: "Franklin and Washington: the County's Reverence for Great Americans;" "New Haven and Pacific: Borrowed Names from Other Sections of the U.S.;" "Krakow and Japan: Loans from All Over the World;" "Missouri, Meramec, and Other Indian Survivals;" "Boeuf, Bourbeuse, and Tavern Rock: the French Imprint on Franklin County;" "Fort San Juan and the Spanish Bequest;" "Daniel Boone and Other American Pioneers;" "Kiel, Dissen, and Etlah: the German Heritage;" "Franklin County Mines and Methods of Naming Them;" "Millers, Innkeepers, and Postmasters;" "Landowners and Local Families;" "Franklin's Landscapes, and Its Flora and Fauna;" "Union and Enterprise: the County's Ideals;" "Jacob's Well and Jordan Creek: Bible Names of Franklin County;" "Buzzard's Roost and Reed's Defeat: a Touch of Humor." Each of these sections is compact, incorporating both pleasant anecdote and solid information. As usual in place-name studies, some surprising origins appear; for example, *Japan* (locally /ˈdʒepən/) derives its name from the local Catholic parish, the Church of the Holy Martyrs of Japan, "named for the twenty-six priests and lay brothers of Spanish, Portugese, and Japanese blood who were crucified for their faith on February 5, 1597, in the great persecution that almost wiped out Japanese Christianity for three hundred years"(20). A map, a list of field workers and informants, and an index will prove useful to the reader.

Since Ramsay completed the manuscript only four days before his death, one can pardon such occasional slips as the apparent statement that the Rock Island connects with the Southern Pacific at Omaha, Denver, and Kansas City (19) -- though a proofreader could easily have corrected this. The work epitomizes what Ramsay's career demonstrated -- that place-name research provides not only valuable information on linguistic and cultural history, but a great deal of pleasure for the investigator.

Haugen's book is one of the most interesting studies yet published of the development of Old World languages on New World soil. Broader in scope than its title implies, it throws light not only on bilingualism but on the entire theme of making new Americans from Old World stock, on culture contact, on the transition of the United States from a predominantly agricultural society with many self-sufficient local communities to a complex, highly interdependent industrial economy. What has happened to compact Norwegian settlements in Wisconsin has happened also -- though less dramatically because not involving a change of languages -- to New England villages and to Kentucky county seats.

An American-Norwegian himself, Haugen not only could develop tentative hypotheses from observing acculturation in his own family and community but could easily establish rapport with informants. A distinguished linguist, especially accomplished in Scandinavian dialects and in linguistic geography, he has rigorously applied proved methods, modified where necessary. His examination of secondary materials -- e.g., emigration and immigration records, church histories, newspaper circulation lists -- provides accurate and almost exhaustive information about the background against which the drama of the American-Norwegian community was acted out. Finally, his style is consistently lucid and easy, so that the most casual reader may profit.

The first volume treats the sociocultural forces operating on the dialects of American Norwegian. Beginning with an analysis of the problem of the bilingual and a working definition of bilingualism, Haugen discusses the patterns of settlement and the forces which operated first to shift American Norwegian toward American English and then to displace it entirely. Many of the forces were basic to the American scene and may be summarized as the tendency of a dominant language to displace the languages of minority groups, especially through business and the schools. Other forces were the result of far-off political events, such as the anti-German sentiments fomented by patrioteers in World War I (which created suspicion of all foreign language groups but especially of those speaking Germanic languages) or the restrictive legislation of the 1920's that shut off the flow of Norwegian immigration. But other forces were

present in the American-Norwegian community itself. Like all immigrant groups, it included speakers of many old-country dialects, some sharply divergent from the rest. The literary language of the early migration, Dano-Norwegian, differed greatly from the everyday dialects of the immigrants; the Nynorsk or Landsmål, a new literary language developed from Norwegian dialects toward the end of the nineteenth century, was never established in the American Norwegian. The gradual disappearance of Norwegian in the United States may be traced by such processes as the change of the language of preaching and by the circulation losses of Norwegian-language newspapers. By 1949, in only scattered communities was the youngest adult generation using Norwegian freely.

The direction of the change was apparent even while the number of Norwegian-speaking monolinguals was at its height. Perhaps most noticeable to a casual observer was the shift from the historical Scandinavian system of patronymics (still the legal system in Iceland) to the American system of surnames. But in other parts of the vocabulary, too, the shift was in the direction of English. Many loanwords were taken into American Norwegian to describe physical or cultural phenomena unfamiliar in the homeland, or Norwegian words underwent a semantic shift to the meaning of their American English cognates; when an American-Norwegian community might have adopted any one of several Norwegian words (or meanings of the same Norwegian word), it generally chose the one closest to the pattern of American English. More subtle but no less real was the indebtedness to American English through loan translation, a device by which the American name of a cultural loan was analyzed by the speakers of Norwegian, and one or more of the components translated. Although loan translation is a familiar process -- as when *hydrogen* becomes *Wasserstoff* in German, or German *Zeitgeist* is adopted into English as *the spirit of the age* -- Haugen's discussion is very illuminating.

Where the first volume discusses the cultural history of the American-Norwegian community, the second describes Haugen's methods and analyzes the results. Basically the method is that of the Linguistic Atlas of the United States and Canada, with modifications to take care of the bilingual situation. A systematic questionnaire (II.645-53) was devised to elicit comparable data; a modification of the International Phonetic Alphabet was used to indicate both Norwegian and American English speech sounds with a minimum of diacritics; the interviewing was conducted by trained field workers in selected communities, under conditions approximating natural conversation; mechanical recordings supplemented the impressionistic notations. In keeping with the practice of American linguistic geography (but differing from many older dialect studies which record mostly relic forms from very old-fashioned informants), Haugen's informants represented various age groups and from one to three generations of American residence; in each community Haugen tried to sample the speech of the youngest Norwegian-speaking generation. There is a valuable table of informants (II.618-35), a selection of thirty-one texts (II.482-555), a selected vocabulary of English loans, and a comprehensive list of abbreviations.

To single out particular merits of so excellent a book may seem gratuitous; three, however, impressed me: 1) the interpretation of the role of bilingualism in linguistic borrowing; 2) the classification of bilingual situations, since the problems of English loans into an early colonial language like Pennsylvania German are unlike those of English loans into the standard Norwegian of Norway; 3) the careful choice and definition of terms. Linguists will also be interested in observing 1) that in older loans non-Norwegian sounds were replaced, while in later ones the phonetic shape is often unaltered; 2) that many older loans reflect pronunciations now nonstandard or obsolete in Wisconsin English; 3) that loans are adapted morphologically to certain favored classes -- nouns to the masculine gender, verbs to the first weak conjugation (compare the long-established pattern for verbs borrowed into English).

I find very few errors. More troublesome is the small scale of the maps, which are difficult to read. There will probably be objections to Haugen's system of transcription, which often uses compound symbols where I would prefer unit symbols.

The University of Pennsylvania Press and the American Institute of the University of Oslo are to be congratulated on publishing so important a work in so attractive a format at a relatively modest price. It is a book which I am sure to reexamine many times.

Pop has performed a heroic service in com-
piling his survey of the work in linguistic geography up to the middle of the
twentieth century. Even the linguist who
is little concerned with dialect problems
in his own research must often discuss
such problems for the benefit of students.
Up to now, if any such linguist wished to
go much beyond the comparatively brief
statements in Bloomfield 1933 or other
general works, he has faced a painful task
in even assembling a working bibliography.
Now, he can find at least the basic information in Pop's monumental two volumes --
the work of a dialectologist who could not
find a handy survey of his branch of linguistics and decided to supply the need.

Following an introductory chronology of
the development of dialect studies, Pop
surveys in turn the Romance languages
(French, Franco-Provençal, Provençal, Ca-
talan, Spanish, Portugese, Italian, Rheto-
Romansch, Dalmatian, Sardinian, and Ruma-
nian); then, in less detail, because his
primary interest is in Romance, and his
first intention was to deal only with Romance dialectology, Germanic, Celtic,
Slavic, Finno-Ugrian, modern Greek, Albanian, Berber, Bantu, Arabic, Chinese, the
languages of India, and Korean. For each
language or dialect area he indicates the
principal investigations -- completed, in
progress, or proposed -- with information
concerning the area, the method of investigation, the kind of questionnaire (if
any), the kind of investigator, the kind
of notation, and (where criticism is
available) the significance of the project. A concluding chapter summarizes the
lessons in method that one can derive from
the esperience of previous investigators,
indicates a few of the contributions of
dialectology to general linguistics, and
pleads for the establishment (since realized, at the University of Louvain) of an
international center for dialectology.
Since *La Dialectologie* will probably be
used most often as a reference book, it is
gratifying to have not only a detailed
topical index ("Table analytique") and indices of relevant geographical and personal names, but also four chronological
tables (by types) of published works on
linguistic geography, three tables of
works in progress or proposed, and a table
of illustrations. For many of the sections there are detailed critical bibliographies.

The amount of factual information is

almost stupefying. Whenever Pop could
get precise details, he published them.
A typical example: most of us have been
content to know that the German *Atlas*
(Wrede et al. 1927-56) is based on information from about forty thousand communities; Pop informs us that there were
44,251 responses from 40,736 communities,
and gives the specific bibliographical
reference for this information.

On questions of theory and method, Pop
is not so fruitful. A disciple of Gilliéron, he is largely satisfied with the
methods of the French *Atlas* (Gilliéron
and Edmont 1902-10) and does not concern
himself much with the newer techniques
that have been devised to take care of
situations which had not been anticipated
when Edmont mounted his bicycle and rode
out into the French countryside. But who
could perform a like labor of compilation
and interpretation (and under serious difficulties) and still find energy for simultaneously providing a fresh critical
perspective? The theoretical interpretation can wait, and will be all the better
for the facts which Pop has provided.

Understandably, there are some gaps.
Even in the Romance section, he omits the
1946 proposal for an exhaustive investigation of Italian place names. He has no
mention of the considerable work in Japanese dialects, perhaps because most of it
has been published in Japanese (see Brower
1950). And -- as an American -- I wish
there had been more space devoted to both
North American English and North American
French. Each specialist will dredge up a
few errors where Pop has touched on his
specialty: e.g., the number of communities investigated in New England is given
as 431, when it was actually about half
that number -- 431 being the number assigned to the northernmost community in
New Brunswick. And since the maps of most
linguistic atlases contain a wealth of
phonetic detail, some of the illustrations
are too crowded to be useful.

Judging the work as a whole, it is almost incredible that one man could have
compiled and organized so much useful information in so short a time with so relatively few errors. Pop has performed a
unique service to linguistics by publishing *La Dialectologie*, by establishing the
International Center, and by founding the
journal *Orbis* as an organ through which
dialectologists in various countries may
keep each other informed. Thanks to Pop's

indefatigable energy, future linguistic surveys should be spared many of the mistakes that have been made in the past.

An examination of regional speech as revealed in documents from the eighteenth and nineteenth centuries, *Tarheel Talk* is an interesting book, not only for the student of American English but for students of all aspects of American culture. Furthermore, both in its accomplishments and its limitations it offers valuable lessons in method to those students of language who must work with documentary evidence from an earlier period.

The evidence upon which *Tarheel Talk* is based is derived from the manuscripts in the Southern Historical Collection at the University of North Carolina. Drawn from all parts of the South, but naturally representing North Carolina better than any other state, the Collection includes legal papers, personal and business letters, account books, diaries, church records, and the like -- unedited, normally with known date and locality of composition, and many times with specific and detailed information about the author. As with manuscripts used for the *Middle English Dictionary* (Kurath, Kuhn *et al*. 1952-), such evidence throws light on various linguistic and cultural problems: pronunciation, grammar, vocabulary, word meanings, linguistic attitudes, the growth of public education, and the status of families, communities, and institutions. A work of this kind demands an unusual combination of abilities in the investigator. Before the evidence can be used at all, there must be patience, dogged industry, and meticulous care in seeing that forms in a variety of hands are transcribed faithfully, with sufficient context to offer a fair chance for reasonable interpretation. And the interpretation demands a delicate balance of imagination and caution: imagination in seeing the possible implications of the evidence, caution in not pressing the conclusions farther than the evidence will support them. By these standards, Eliason has done well.

The plan of *Tarheel Talk* is straightforward: a preface is followed by three introductory chapters (1. "The Background;" 2. "The Writings;" 3. "Language Attitudes and Differences"), three analytical chapters (4. "Vocabulary;" 5. "Pronunciation;" 6. "Grammar"), appendices listing word usages and significant spellings, and a word index.

The opening chapter begins with a fundamental caution which Eliason often repeats: one must always remember that the similarities between varieties of American English are more numerous (and in the long run, far more important) than the differences; furthermore, few linguistic features are limited to North Carolina or originated there. It also points out -- as linguists have long known, but too few of the general public are aware -- that every variety of American English draws on the resources of many British dialects, that each of the original colonies was an area of dialect mixture, with present-day regional and local speech types developing out of generations of give and take.[1] It accepts as generally valid the scheme of dialect areas in North Carolina which Kurath sets up in *A Word Geography of the Eastern United States* (1949): a major division between Southern speech of the coastal plain and the Pennsylvania-derived South Midland speech of the Piedmont and mountains, with two coastal subareas centering on Albemarle Sound and the Cape Fear Valley, and the prestigious Southern usage of the Virginia Piedmont thrusting into the northern tier of counties between the Roanoke and the Neuse. Social distinctions, too, are recognized: Eliason accepts the familiar observation that the sharpest differences between folk and cultivated usage in the New World are to be found in the southeastern United States. Finally, migration and education (and implicitly, industrialization -- though the industrial development of North Carolina comes later than the period covered in Eliason's book) are noted as forces effecting changes in the language in the direction of homogeneity, even while regional and local varieties were developing out of an earlier general heterogeneity.

From manuscript source materials Eliason has arrived at a number of conclusions about language attitudes that contradict the traditional picture of nineteenth-century American English. True, it was considered good that a man should strive to improve his use of the language; however, such improvement was largely evaluated in terms of style, vocabulary, and spelling, with grammar a matter of little concern and pronunciation essentially of none -- probably reflecting an aristocratic tolerance of diversity that is still more prevalent in the South and South Midland than anywhere else in the United States.[2] In the materials Eliason examined, there was practically no attention to dialect differences, within or without

North Carolina. Writers from western North Carolina apparently had a more casual style than those from the eastern counties; on the other hand, perhaps because education was harder to obtain at home, Western Carolinians tended to make better use of their opportunities.[3] In the earlier letters, women wrote more colloquially than their husbands did; by 1850, however, the situation had been reversed. Folklore, proverbs, and slang appear rarely, whether spontaneously or as citations. There are few comments about foreigners' speech, and little evidence as to the usage of Germans, Scots, or Irish. Especially surprising are Eliason's comments about Negro speech:

> Most [slave letters] are semiliterate, of course, some displaying an almost total ignorance of conventional English. In this respect they are just like overseers' reports, reflecting as accurately as any writing can the actual folk speech of the lowest level. Otherwise, their only peculiarity is that the language used indicates something of the attitude slaves had, or were expected to have, toward their master and mistress. There are no letters written by slaves to one another, which might reveal this attitude in a somewhat different light. (112-13)[4]

The chapter on vocabulary concerns itself chiefly with Americanisms, with particular attention to terms of North Carolina origin (like *buncombe* and *scuppernong*) and items for which the Southern Historical Collection supplies earlier citations or fuller data than the historical dictionaries. However, it also treats obsolete, slang, and local terms; neologisms; pet names, kinship terms, and titles; proper names (lacking, regrettably, *Matrimony Church*, whose records are one of Eliason's best sources); taboo and euphemy. The chapter on pronunciation is organized by phonological types; that on grammar by parts of speech. These chapters are a mine of entertaining and useful data; on the other hand, since they deal with specific linguistic forms, they do provide a number of opportunities for a reviewer to indicate where individual statements might be rephrased -- especially when the reviewer is a sixth-generation speaker of an Up-Country South Carolina dialect, a field worker for the Linguistic Atlas (in South Carolina, Georgia, and Kentucky), and co-author with Kurath of *The Pronunciation of English in the Atlantic States* (1961). The following observations should not be considered as picayune objections, unappreciative of the difference between manuscript evidence and field transcriptions from local informants, or of the difficulties in interpreting manuscript evidence; in fact, I must share responsibility for statements I would modify, in that I have not yet been able to bring to completion some of the pro-

jects on which I have been working during the last decade.

Vocabulary: *Put in* 'ante up,' as 'to put in at shooting matches'(143) is still a part of the gambler's vocabulary, especially in poker. *Open sow* (143) 'sow not with young' may not be explained in dictionaries but in the South is a normal part of the vocabulary of hog raising. Among apparently obsolete terms, *osnaburg* 'a kind of coarse cloth, similar to burlap'(155) is still extant; not only was it offered by many Atlas informants, but it has been used by the U.S. Army as a foundation for camouflage. *Funeral* 'formal obsequies'(157), as contrasted with *burying* 'interment,' is still in use in upper South Carolina, as is *rising* as a designation for a boil. *Bealing* 'boil' is still occasionally heard in old-fashioned South Midland speech. At least in South Carolina, there seems to be a regional difference -- Up-Country vs. Low-Country -- in the distribution of *pail* and *piggin* (162) as terms for the old-fashioned stave-handled bucket. Older South Carolina informants usually distinguish between *comfort* 'tacked quilt' and *coverlid* 'quilted bedspread'(162); likewise between *infare* 'formal reception after a wedding' and *serenade* 'shivaree'(163) -- though folk speech could easily confuse two such ceremonial functions, and apparently some North Carolinians did. Field work also throws light on the absence of *dad* and near absence of *daddy* (169) in Eliason's materials: many Atlas informants indignantly rejected these terms on the ground they were 'properly' used only of elderly Negroes.

Pronunciation: Spellings like *evey* for *every* and *funal* for *funeral* (209) would likely represent not loss of postvocalic /r/ but of prevocalic, deriving from such common dissyllabic pronunciations as /ɛvrɪ/ and /fjunrəl/. The pronunciation of *afraid* as /əfrɛd/ (216) is still fairly widespread in cultivated speech of the South Atlantic states, with the prestige of its American focus in the Virginia Piedmont (Atwood 1951); in *great* (which Eliason does not cite) the /ɛ/ pronunciation is even more widely disseminated. In *keg*, the /æ/ pronunciation (222) is far from superseded: in folk speech and common speech it is the most widespread pronunciation east of the Mississippi, and it is not unknown in cultivated speech. For some spellings indicating phonemic alternants of /ɪ/ and /ʊ/, as *wosh* for *wish* (225) and *hindred*, *jist* for *hundred*, *just* (230) the explanation may be found in a high-central short unrounded vowel, phonemically distinct from /ʌ/ and /ɛ/ and /ɪ/ and /ʊ/, such as the vowel I use in *wish*, *milk*, *mirror*, *sister*, *scissors*, *ribbon* (see Trager and Smith 1951).

Grammar: Omission of the relative pronoun is still fairly common in colloquial cultivated speech of the South Atlantic states, though even in this region it is probably not as common as seventeenth-century drama suggests it was in colloquial cultivated usage of the Early Modern period. And not only does the indefinite article still appear as *a* /ə/ before vowel initial in folk and common speech throughout the South and South Midland (242), but it occurs rather frequently in the speech and writing of urban-reared native Ohio college students (R. and V. McDavid 1956b).

For these details, and for some more general matters, Eliason could have made sharper statements if he had been able to spend more time with the Atlas archives. For instance, although the vowels in *tune*, *new*, and *suit* (206-07) have the same Middle English and Early Modern English ancestry, their development in the United States has not been identical: /tjun,nju/ are practically universal throughout the South and South Midland, but in these areas /sjut/ is rare and is often considered an affectation by those to whom /tjun,nju/ are normal. The pronunciation of *creek* with /ɪ/, rare south of the Kanawha, nevertheless occurs in central North Carolina, in the area of German settlement; and its occurrence today in the older settlements along Chesapeake Bay and the South Carolina coast lessens one's surprise at finding it in nineteenth-century records from the conservative areas of eastern North Carolina.[5] The expanded preposition *in* (*the*) *room of* 'instead of' is shown by Atlas evidence to be a characteristic North Carolina form (R. and V. McDavid 1954). Slightly annoying to an Atlas field worker is the statement: "The *Atlas* informants are aged, and their speech old-fashioned"(194). Actually, one of the significant innovations of the American linguistic atlases was the insistence on including, in every community, at least two age or educational levels. My informants have ranged from 19 to 104, from illiterates to Pulitzer Prize journalists and internationally known artists, though all have had deep local roots. But such points of dispute turn out to be few indeed; and the conclusion one reaches from comparisons between Eliason's statements and those based on the Atlas materials is that the two approaches complement each other, and that where they deal with the same phenomena each study reinforces the conclusions the other has reached.

In short, this is a good book, to which I will frequently return -- and so will other students of American English. Furthermore, from remarks in *Tarheel Talk* and elsewhere, I am happy to learn that this will not be Eliason's last contribution to the study of Southern regional speech, for he and his students plan to continue exploiting the Southern Historical Collection. Nor, I suspect, will he stop there; he is too good a social anthropologist to ignore the changes which growing population, expanding industry, and increased education are bringing to even the remote coves of the Appalachians and the isolated hamlets scattered along the Outer Banks Islands from Manteo to Hatteras. Only sampled by the Atlas survey (155 records for North Carolina, never more than four in a county, and no pretensions at being exhaustive) and apparently even more skimpily represented in the Southern Historical Collection, the richly diverse dialects of such relic communities threaten to disappear before they can be adequately recorded for future study. But one can expect that -- given competent field workers -- the author of *Tarheel Talk* will bring to the study of living linguistic relics in present-day North Carolina the same perceptiveness and energy he has brought to the study of the past.

NOTES

[1] For example, in the focal areas along the Atlantic Seaboard, the cultural centers have long maintained economic and social ties with the London area. Yet no single variety of standard American English has all five of the following characteristics of present-day British Received Pronunciation: 1) loss of constriction or postvocalic /-r/ in *bird*, *barn*, *beard*; 2) /w-/ in *whip*, etc.; 3) two low-back rounded vowels as phonemic entities, with /ɔ/ in *cot* and /ɔ:/ in *caught*; 4) the so-called 'broad *a*' ([a,ɑ]) in *grass*, *France*, *command*, etc.; 5) homonymy of *hoarse* and *horse*, *mourning* and *morning*, etc.

[2] Even today the educated Southerner is likely to look askance at someone who 'talks too correctly' (i.e., who is excessively meticulous in adhering to the rules of the traditional grammars), and to ridicule or distrust someone who attempts to adopt pronunciations noticeably different from those of the area where he was brought up.

[3] In the South Atlantic states, almost without exception, the major institutions of higher education have grown up in the Piedmont and mountains rather than in the coastal plain. Presumably, the yeomanry of the uplands had a larger stake in seeing that there were local opportunities for going to college, since the wealthier Low-Country planters could afford to send their sons North, or even to England.

[4] As Eliason points out, there was no North Carolina area in which Negro slaves (especially newly arrived Negroes) were concentrated as heavily as they were in the rice and Sea Island cotton

areas of the South Carolina and Georgia coast. Consequently, North Carolina Negroes never developed such a highly creolized dialect as Gullah. It is also true that in the early nineteenth century, Negroes whose speech was heavily permeated with Africanisms would normally not be able to write at all.

On the other hand, it must be conceded that since the failure of Reconstruction, the Southern pattern of segregation has resulted in an educational differential between poor whites and Negroes, so that the latter would be more likely to preserve nonstandard forms which both groups used before the Confederate War. Such characteristic 'Negro' forms as the lack of plural inflections in nouns and of preterite and participial inflections in verbs are also preserved in the black ghettoes of Middle Western industrial cities, and are often found in the speech and writing of Negro college students who have graduated from Ohio urban high schools. On the other hand, where the Negro population is relatively small, as in Minnesota, there are no grammatical features which one might label as 'Negroisms.'

[5] Automatically, the more data recorded from a community or an individual, the more likelihood that the investigator will discover variants in usage. For instance, in the Upper Midwest, especially in the areas of most recent settlement (where one might reasonably expect variety in usage) the use of supplementary check lists has uncovered many vocabulary variants that did not show up in the field records made by Allen and his colleagues; likewise, investigators who have tried to record grammatical forms from free conversation sometimes find as many as four variants for a single item (e.g., *saw*, *see*, *seed*, *seen* as preterites of *see*). The documents in the Southern Historical Collection often provide a similar variety in responses; an intensive field investigation of Albemarle Sound, the Outer Banks, or the Cape Fear Valley would provide many examples of such variety.

The death of E. Bagby Atwood, on October 6, 1963, not only has impeded the study of Texas dialects but has delayed the development of new research techniques and new theoretical interpretations of the data.

Coming to American dialectology from medieval literature, Atwood had previously produced one major work, Atwood 1953a.[1] He had also assembled a table of characteristic features of the major dialect areas of the Atlantic Seaboard (1950b); expanded or adapted by others, as in my chapter in Francis 1958, it is a basic reference. *The Regional Vocabulary of Texas* was to have been the first stage in his study of the speechways of his native state.

Atwood's book is divided into eight chapters: I. "The Area;" II. "The Method;" III. "Topical Survey of the Vocabulary;" IV. "Geographical Aspects of Usage;" V. "Dialect Mixture and Meaning;" VI. "Obsolescence and Replacement;" VII. "Lexicographical Pilón" (etymologies and meanings of "Border Spanish"); VIII. "Word Atlas" (125 maps, with a brief introductory essay). An appendix explains the procedures for encoding and sorting the materials by IBM machines; a word index lists all forms mentioned.

The opening chapter sketches the geographic regions and settlement history of Texas -- the latter largely an extrapolation from what is known about relatively small groups. Of English-speaking settlers, few were born north of the Potomac and Ohio Rivers; particular communities varied as to whether coastal or inland Southerners predominated. Of foreign groups, Germans and Czechs settled in central Texas; ,Latin-Americans, most numerous after 1850, chiefly in the south and southwest. In 1860, thirty percent of the population were slaves, concentrated, like their free descendants, in East Texas. West Texas was long dominated by cattle ranching and East Texas by cotton farming; today the reverse is true. Sheep herding remains concentrated in the southwest; corn is grown principally in East Texas; oil is found in various large fields. The picture is one of variable topography, diverse but not heterogeneous settlement patterns, growing population, and a changing economy.

The methods of dialectology derive from Gilliéron and Edmont 1902-10: 1) one informant per community; 2) a standardized questionnaire; 3) a trained field worker, conducting interviews on the spot in a conversational situation and recording responses immediately in finely graded phonetic notation; 4) publication in large maps, giving the full phonetic responses. These principles were followed by Jaberg and Jud 1928-40 and by Kurath *et al.* 1939-43, but with modifications: several field workers, to facilitate gathering the data; several informants per community, to test social differences and the dimension of time. For the Middle and South Atlantic States the New England questionnaire was modified for the local culture. In later American surveys, lightweight apparatus and rural electrification have made possible recordings on tape; multiple-choice correspondence questionnaires have supplemented lexical data gathered in the field. In his survey of the Gulf States and Interior South, Gordon Wood relied exclusively on correspondence materials (1971).

Atwood's methods derive from the conviction that personal field work is necessary, a belief that vocabulary might (as in Scotland) be investigated independently of pronunciation, and the discovery that student field work with an experimental questionnaire was yielding reliable data. An incidental course assignment thus became a method of systematic inquiry, not only by Atwood but by colleagues in other Southwestern institutions.

Atwood's questionnaire is an adaptation of those used on the Atlantic Seaboard. The investigators were given general instructions, but were not compelled to follow a specified routine. These investigators were students, whose chief qualification was interest in the project. Their informants were, normally, relatives and friends, almost always lifelong residents of their communities and old enough to remember farming and ranching before mechanization; only fifteen percent were under 50.

This method has obvious advantages: besides saving money and time, the student interviewers were at least informally acquainted with local demography and social history; moreover, they did not have an outsider's problem of winning acceptance. The disadvantages are also obvious. In addition to "the youth and inexperience of the fieldworkers"(32), reliance on relatives and close friends may hinder efforts to record taboo information. Furthermore, such students would choose disproportionately many respectable informants, disproportionately few poor whites -- let alone

Negroes, Indians, and Latin Americans.[2]

For analysis, Atwood divided Texas into six segments: Northwest, West, Southwest, North, Central, and East -- labels reflecting history and local tradition but implying no preconceived notions of dialect distribution. The responses were encoded on IBM cards for mechanical sorting and listing. Atwood is cautious about drawing conclusions, and reminds his readers that his work, like all good dialect investigations, is based on selective sampling.

The third chapter is organized by topics: weather, landscape, the house, goods and chattels, time and distance, the premises, various fauna, something to eat, family matters, social and daily life, verb forms and syntax. The glosses are clear and accurate; the only one I would expand is *varmint* (77), which in my Southern and South Midland experience is not "any small wild animal," but a predator, especially one addicted to raiding hen houses -- weasel, mink, fox, coon, possum, skunk, bobcat, and the like. The older difference between *clapboards* (split) and *weatherboards* (sawn) is specified. In Texas, as in many areas to the east, /dov/ is the prevailing preterite of *to dive*, favored by the younger and better educated. Many Texans, like South Carolinians, observe that the greeting *Christmas gift!* (68) was exploited by Negro servants to gain extra contributions from their patrons. The *cornbread* family (63) is well glossed; e.g., *egg bread* is primarily "a better variety of cornbread, made with meal and eggs," only "occasionally a synonym for *spoon bread*," the only meaning given in Kurath 1949 and in *Webster's Third New International Dictionary* (1961). Texans use many Eastern terms for the burlap bag: the Chesapeake Bay *grass sack*, the Eastern Virginia-South Carolina *croker sack*, the North Carolina *tow sack*, but not the West Virginia *coffee sack*.

Of South Midland terms familiar in Texas, I recognize *poke* 'paper sack,' *French harp* 'harmonica,' *to pack* 'carry' from West Virginia and Middle Tennessee, *back stick* from the Southern Appalachians, and *wardrobe* 'built in closet,' common in the Nashville Basin. Of my boyhood terms I miss *ash cake* (and its synonyms *ash bread* and *ash pone*), the characteristic South Carolina *pinders* 'peanuts,' the Low-Country *po' buckra* 'poor white,' and *corn dodger* 'dumpling,' the Southern Coastal *piazza* 'porch,' the Up-Country *turn of corn* 'load to be taken to the mill,' and *hoosier* 'a rustic, especially an uncouth one.' But *gully washer* predominates for torrential rain, alongside such familiar congeners as *toad strangler* and *stump mover* (38). I too recorded the pronunciation *ceasting* (39), chiefly from Negroes. In the South and South Midland, as in Texas, a *branch* is properly smaller than a creek; a *hydrant* (46) is properly outdoors, for the garden hose, a *spicket* (or *faucet*) on the kitchen sink; the outdoor toilet is occasionally a *Federal Building*, without party connotations.[3] *Sourbelly* (62) I knew for *sowbelly*. *Gumbo* had a higher viscosity rating than *vegetable soup*. *Cush* (64), a kind of cornmeal mush, also appears in Charleston. Humble homes in South Carolina often had *puncheon floors* (77); a *chamber* was not a bedroom, but a vessel with a handle, kept under the bed for nocturnal emergencies; *hog-killing weather* was crisp and cold; *cold enough to freeze the horns off a billy goat* was severe indeed; a praying mantis was often a *devil's horse*. And though the territoriality of *chigger* and *redbug* was not investigated in the South Atlantic states, the insect has plagued me under both labels since 1921.

Chapter IV treats Eastern sources of the Texas vocabulary and new dialect patterns discovered in the Southwest. The greatest number of Texas words are those which Atwood labels "General Southern," that is, found alike in Kurath's Southern (the old plantation country) and South Midland (the Southern Appalachians and Upper Piedmont). In fact, Atwood (79) contends that the South Midland is a part of the South rather than of the Midland -- the region settled from Pennsylvania and deriving its speech patterns from that source. Characteristic General Southern words are *pallet* 'improvised bed on the floor,' (corn) *shucks*, *you-all*, *pully bone* 'wishbone,' *light bread* 'white bread in loaves,' and *clabber cheese* 'cottage cheese.' Of Coastal Southern words the most widely distributed in Texas are *chittlins* 'edible hog intestines' (now familiar on the Chicago South Side), *snap beans* 'string beans,' *to tote* 'carry,' *to carry* 'escort,' and *to low* 'moo.' The Midland as a whole contributes a large number: *sook!* 'call to cows,' (quarter) *till*, *to wait on* 'wait for,' *piece* 'distance,' *want off*, *green beans* 'string beans,' and *blinds* 'roller shades.' The North Midland offers only *string beans* and *whinny*, both found in other regions; the North, only *pail* and *cherry pit*, perhaps as commercial terms, and *hadn't ought*.

Atwood next investigates western and northern limits of Southern influence. Both General Southern and Coastal Southern words become less frequent as one moves from East Texas into the Trans-Pecos and New Mexico, or from Texas northward across Oklahoma, but no clear boundary appears. Since Southern words are rare in California, the Trans-Pecos and New Mexico may be considered a transition area; another transition area may appear in western Oklahoma and southeastern Colorado. In general, Southern usages are more widely distributed than the older interpretations of Texas speech suggested -- probably through the early prestige of plantation culture and the recent westward spread of cotton farming.

Atwood also finds specifically Southwestern speech areas, notably Southern Louisiana and the old cattle country of Southwest Texas. Louisiana offers *banquette* 'sidewalk,' *pirogue* 'boat used for river fishing,' *armoire* 'wardrobe,' *lagniappe* 'small gift to a customer,' *bayou*, *gallery* 'porch,' and restricts the *shivaree* to weddings when at least one of the participants has been married before. Southern Louisiana also lacks such General Southern words as *Christmas gift!*, *whetrock*, *branch*, and *pully bone*.

Southwest Texas, the heart of the old cattle-range country, is a focal area from which have spread terms -- mostly of Spanish origin -- dealing with cattle raising, ranch life, and topography. A few of these terms are largely confined to Southwest Texas, e.g., *resaca* 'small body of standing water,' *vaquero* 'cowboy,' and *llano* 'a plain.' Some are heavily concentrated in the Southwest, e.g., *chaparral*, *hacienda*, *reata* 'rope,' and *mott* 'grove of trees in open country.' Others have spread to West Texas, e.g., *olla* 'water jug,' *arroyo* 'dry creek bed,' and *pilón* 'small gift to a purchaser.' Still others are widely distributed, e.g., *mesa*, *corral*, *bronc*, *lariat*, *canyon*, *burro*, *norther*, *tank* 'artificial pond,' *dogie* 'calf,' *cinch* 'saddle girth,' *pinto* 'spotted horse or pony,' and *chaps* 'leather devices for protecting the legs when riding in brush country.'

Minor areas also appear. In West Texas, especially the South Plains area, one finds *sugan* 'bed roll,' *surly* 'bull,' *draw* 'stream bed, usually dry,' and *shinnery* 'scrub oak.' In central Texas are concentrations of *roping rope*, *grass sack*, and *Tarv(i)ated road* 'blacktop.' Among the Texas Germans occur *plunder room* 'store room,' *clook* 'setting hen,' *smearcase* and *kockcase* (two varieties of homemade cheese), and such rarer terms as *Opa* 'grandfather,' *Oma* 'grandmother,' *krebbel* 'doughnut,' and *silze* 'pork loaf.' Arkansas immigrants fostered such Appalachian terms as *back stick* and *redworm* 'earthworm.' *Cup towel* 'dish towel,' for some reason, extends but little beyond the borders of Texas; its distribution in other regions is yet uncharted.

With Southwestern and Southern Louisiana focal areas, one finds prominent bundles of isoglosses separating Texas from Louisiana, Louisiana from Texas and Arkansas, and the Acadian French area of southern Louisiana from the northern and western parts of the state. Nevertheless, Atwood -- remarking that "far too many lines have been drawn already" -- refuses to draw boundaries in the absence of grammatical and phonological evidence.

Since Texas is a region of dialect mixture, terms from various Eastern areas often exist side by side. Sometimes competing forms yield blends, e.g., *freeseed* (*freestone* + *clearseed*), *fire mantel* (*fireboard* + *mantel*), *head souse* (*head cheese* + *souse*). At other times, specialization of meaning occurs: a *rock wall* is held together by cement, a *rock fence* not; a *mouth organ* is smaller than a *harmonica*; a metal container is a *bucket* for water, a *pail* for milk; *banquette* is applied only to the older style of sidewalk, of brick or boards.

Atwood finds that among university students (sampled for recent usage) many terms are disappearing and others coming in, in response to mechanization of agriculture, mass distribution, and general education -- including greater familiarity with dictionaries. Radio, television, and movies have little effect, because (as Kurath suggests) their audience is passive. The vocabulary of horse-drawn vehicles and of the farm is familiar to few of the younger generation; folk terms like *snake doctor* are yielding to book words like *dragon fly*. The vocabulary of ranching, however, is still widely known, since it carries prestige. Mail-order catalogs apparently are dropping older folk terms; whether this causes or reflects obsolescence is an open question. Sometimes a homemade product cannot be adapted to commercial distribution; e.g., the lamented *teacake*, a kind of cookie, has yielded to a miscellaneous array of store-bought confections. Cultural prestige probably favors New Orleans *praline* over Texas *pecan patty*. Education hastens the disappearance of rustic terms like *Pappy*, *antigodlin*, *rench*, *widow woman*, and *racket store*.[4] Atwood always gives the percentages of usages by age groups, so that the reader may draw his own conclusions.

"Lexicographical Pilón" shows that in Border Spanish, as in Texas English, many terms have strikingly different referents from their Castilian ones. The 125 maps are carefully designed, and present the evidence effectively. The appendix is illuminating to scholars who expect mechanical morons to clarify their own muddled thinking: a machine will impartially reflect any errors in the plan and force laborious manual corrections; the depth of sorting can impose or save extensive manual labor. The index, with contrasting type faces and generous type sizes, is unusually legible. Finally, in an academic world where transformational grammarians hound adherents of older structuralism as grimly as Castro's bearded ones pursue suspected Yanqui sympathizers, Atwood's wry humor is refreshing: "Some [informants] know no difference between a *hydrant* and a *faucet*, . . . or, for that matter, between a *burro* and a *burrow*"(36); a bull is glossed as "male bovine (with original equipment)"(57); "if anything is likely to lead to another Civil War [Atwood omits such Southern synonyms as *Confederate War*] it is the Northerner's accusation that Southerners use *you-all* to refer to only one person."

All in all, *The Regional Vocabulary of Texas* is an attractive and interesting book, a monument to a distinguished colleague, cut off in his prime.

NOTES

[1] The first systematic large-scale study of grammatical variation in spoken American English, it constituted the most solid body of evidence in Bryant 1962, though incredible blunders attribute not only Atwood's findings but even his exact words to someone else.

[2] See Labov 1963. Labov also notes the hiatus just east of Dallas and Austin -- an area of relatively low population, but a transition area in which one might expect isoglosses.

[3] South Carolina, Michigan, and New York informants also know this designation of a place for plenary sessions; in Canada the analogous *Parliament Building* is common.

[4] Atwood suggests confusion with the *racket* used in tennis; as a naturalized Chicagoan I suspect our local economic enterprises. In South Carolina *racket store* was uncommon; however, Greenville had a *Red Hot Racket*.

These works -- frankly pedagogical in their outlook -- provide clear evidence that a department of speech can now be as good an academic address for a linguist as such traditional homes as English, Romance, Germanics or classics, or the currently fashionable domains of mathematics and philosophy.[1] It is through the efforts of such men as Thomas and Bronstein, linguists and teachers of speech, that this change has taken place.

Thomas's book, a second edition of a work first published in 1947 (see Atwood 1948; R. McDavid 1949d, in this volume, pp. 335-39), is half again as long as its predecessor. The explanations are more detailed but less technical; the exercises are more numerous; the attitude is more descriptive, with fewer *ex cathedra* judgments. These changes reflect the new evidence on American pronunciation and on dialect distributions: not only in the various linguistic atlases but in Thomas's own growing file of recordings (principally of the speech of undergraduates), totaling, at the time the second edition went to press, some 14,000 speakers "from over 2,500 of the 3,000-odd counties in the United States"(vii).

The most obvious effects of the new evidence are seen in Chapter 22, "Speech Areas," notably in the accompanying map (232). Older discussions of American dialects -- following J. S. Kenyon and George Philip Krapp and Kurath 1928a -- had set up three principal areas: 1) 'Eastern' -- eastern New England, sometimes with New York City added; 2) 'Southern' -- everything south of the Mason-Dixon Line (or the Potomac) and the Ohio, plus Arkansas, Louisiana, southern Missouri, eastern Oklahoma and eastern Texas; 3) 'General American' -- everything else. In the 1947 edition Thomas increased the number of dialect areas and sharply contracted the territory of 'General American,' but kept that term. In the current edition it no longer appears. The roster of "major speech areas" includes:

A. Eastern New England.

B. New York City.

C. Middle Atlantic: eastern Pennsylvania, New Jersey, Delaware, Maryland.

D. (1)[2] The South: Virginia to the Big Bend country of Texas, including most of Arkansas and the southern fringe of Oklahoma.

E. Western Pennsylvania.

F. Southern Mountains: Tennessee, most of Kentucky and West Virginia, and the inland fringes of Virginia, the Carolinas, Georgia, Alabama and Mississippi.

D. (2) North Central: western New England, the Hudson Valley, and the New England settlement area as far west as the Dakotas and the northeast corner of Nebraska.

G. Central Midland: the Ohio Valley, Missouri, Kansas, New Mexico, Colorado, Utah; most of Wyoming, Nebraska, and Oklahoma; west Texas, northern Arkansas, southwestern South Dakota and the southern fringe of Iowa.

H. Northwest: Washington, Oregon, Idaho, Montana, western North Dakota, northwestern South Dakota, and the northern fringe of California and Nevada.

I. Southwest: Arizona, most of Nevada and California.

Students of American dialects will note certain differences between Thomas's scheme and others:[3] 1) lumping together of the Hudson Valley and the Inland Northern area derived from western New England; 2) rather generous assignment of territory to 'the South,' and the failure to differentiate such distinctive subareas as Eastern Virginia and the South Carolina Low-Country;[4] 3) extension of the Southern Mountain area to include the plantation country of the Tennessee and Cumberland Valleys (in Tennessee, Mississippi, Alabama and Georgia), but not the red-hill country of central Alabama, where Mountain pronunciation is usual; and 4) the very large and undifferentiated Central Midland area, within which one finds not only bundles of isoglosses representing incidental features but significant isoglosses for structural features as well. In sections of the Ohio Valley, in the St. Louis area, and in sections of the Rocky Mountains (but not in intervening areas) *barn* and *born* are homonymous, with /ɒ/, normally distinct from *borne*, with /o/. In these areas, and some adjacent territory, *cot* and *caught* are homonyms. Thomas's Central Midland needs subdividing, and so do his Northwest and Southwest.[5]

Thomas quite properly points to the mass of evidence, particularly the number of informants, on which he bases his conclusions. Yet one might note that in addition to numbers one must consider the selection of speakers, the kinds of data, and the interpretation. Thomas's informants were, by and large, young adults, with some exposure to higher education; the Linguistic Atlas chooses speakers of three generations and three degrees of sophistication.[6] The Atlas evidence includes grammar and vocabulary as well as pronunciation, and is elicited in a conversational situation of several hours for each informant. Thomas's evidence is for pronunciation alone, and is elicited by the reading of a standard text, a matter of a few minutes. Even the pronunciation evidence is of different kinds: Thomas relies heavily on his favorite group of words -- those containing the low-back vowels before intervocalic /-r-/ -- a class not so heavily represented in the Atlas materials, which however offer much more evidence than Thomas's text on other features. There are differences in the phonetic symbolization: Thomas uses few diacritics and does not differentiate rounded and unrounded vowels in the low-back range. With such immense opportunities for divergence, it is remarkable -- and a tribute to the objectivity of all investigators -- not that differences occur but that the same general pattern emerges from all investigations.

Three other features of Thomas's work need discussion.

I. Order of presentation. As in the first edition, he presents vowels and consonants unsystematically and piecemeal: [p,b,m,f,v,t,d,n,l] in Chapter 4; [s,z,k, g,i,ɪ,ə] in Chapter 5; [w,ɟ,e,ɛ] in Chapter 6. Thomas insists that this order works for him; other teachers will have to decide whether it fits their needs.

II. Analysis and symbolization. Thomas uses brackets for both phonetic and phonemic transcriptions, as a "practical step," to avoid confusing the student. Yet this practice may breed confusion of its own, especially in the treatment of the low-back vowels, where [ɒ] may represent 1) the phoneme /ɔ/ of *caught*, in contrast with *cot*, in some Inland Northern communities; 2) the phoneme /ɒ/ of *cot*, in contrast with *caught*, in eastern Virginia; 3) a phoneme /ɒ/ found in both *cot* and *caught*, in such areas as Eastern New England and Western Pennsylvania.[7]

III. Attitude. My experience, both as native speaker and observer, leads me to dissent from some of Thomas's value judgments.

1. High-central [ɨ] in *spirit*, *river*, *such*, *just*, is hardly "careless." It is a part of the phonemic system for many cultivated speakers, as a phoneme contrasting with both /ɪ/ and /ʊ/; I have it, *inter alia*, in *dinner*, *Elizabeth*, *milk*, *mirror*, *pretty*, *pillow*, *till* (prep. and conj.), *ribbon*, *sister*.[8]

2. Like many cultivated Southerners I have a retracted /ɛ/ in many words, and in *yellow*, *trestle*, the replacement of /ɛ/ by /ʌ/ -- in even the most careful styles of speech.

3. In *won't*, /ʌ/ is not "old-fashioned," nor is /u/ "substandard . . . of the New York City area." The former is pretty well restricted to the New England settlement area but occurs on all social levels; /u,ʊ/ are found in Canada and in the Charleston area on all levels, like /u/ in New York City.

4. In *humor*, /ɟ-/ seems far more common than /hɟ-/, in all regions and all classes of speakers. For other words /ɟ-/ is less widely distributed, but is not substandard, since its distribution is regional rather than social. In *wheel* and the like, /w-/ is usual in all types of speech in several parts of the Atlantic Seaboard (R. and V. McDavid 1952b); in such inland urban communities as Chicago, /w-/ and /hw-/ occur side by side, often as alternative pronunciations for the same speaker, but with no implication that either one is "substandard."

5. Neutralization of the contrast between intervocalic /-t-/ and /-d-/, as in *latter* and *ladder*, which Thomas labels "careless," is an innovation that seems to be spreading, especially among the younger and better educated speakers (157).

6. The assimilated /-lz/, as in *worlds*, *fields*, is normal for many cultivated speakers; the pronunciation /-ldz/ is likely to attract unfavorable attention as an affectation (186).

7. In *catch*, /ɛ/ is not "likely to be dismissed as substandard wherever it occurs"(210).[9] In some areas, in fact, /æ/ may be considered an affectation assumed by the socially insecure.

8. Far from having "little currency today," the centered beginning of the diphthong /aɪ/ before voiceless consonants is standard Canadian, favored by eastern Virginians (Atwood 1951), and current in the Charleston area. Before voiced consonants or in final position it is somewhat old-fashioned; nevertheless, it is still heard in the rural Inland Northern territory and in parts of the South.

9. In the South, despite Thomas's diffidence (227), the social status of /ɛ/ in *naked*, *great*, *afraid*, is significantly different from that of /e/ in *head*. The former is always acceptable; the latter, associated with mountain speech, is usually regarded as rustic.

10. As Mencken pointed out years ago (1936:429, 430), the informal *bust* and *cuss* are as standard in their spheres as *burst* and *curse* in theirs; the latter might well be labeled not "standard" but "formal" (88). The quaint *passel* would be rejected by millions of speakers who would use *bust* and *cuss* without blinking.

11. For *captain*, the informal [kæpm̩] is as correct in "good speech" as the more formal [kæptən] (104),[10] which is likely to be restricted to official situations. And [bekŋ] for *baking* or *bacon* is not sub-

standard (105, 159) but a normal assimilation.

12. *Annual* (134) is normally /ænjəl/.

13. The simplification of clusters, as in /fæks,kɛp,kænədɪt/ for *facts*, *kept*, *candidate*, undoubtedly varies in status from region to region (161); my own reaction, unlike Thomas's, is that among cultivated speakers the unassimilated forms would be rejected as pedantic.

14. In *peer*, etc., the syllabic nucleus has many variants: not only /i,ɪ/ but /e, ɛ/ as well.[11] Likewise, /æ/ is often found in *where*, *there*, etc.

15. The neutralization of the contrast between /ɔ/ and /o/ before /-r/, as in *war*, *wore*, is very widespread, with its focus in the Hudson Valley and eastern Pennsylvania (111). In Thomas's "Central Midland" this neutralization is usual, except where /ɑ/ and /ɔ/ are neutralized before /-r/, as in *barn*, *born* -- a neutralization also widespread in western Louisiana and East Texas.

16. *Used to*, as a quasi-auxiliary, rarely has /-tt-/ (175), but is normally /just ə/.

Bronstein's work, like Thomas's, is written with the varying needs of the speech major in mind; but there are many differences in both organization and detail. The first part, "Our Language Today," begins by discussing American English as a cultural phenomenon, changing in response to the interactions of a complex polyhedron of forces, with the full range of standard usage never fully represented in even the best general reference works.[12] This is followed by a discussion of the phonetic concept, the rationale of the phonetic alphabet, and the phonemic principle; the linguistic attitude is sound, but not tailored to the specifications of any party line. Finally there is an account of the diversity within the English speech community, and a summary of typical pronunciation differences from one region to another.

The second part is a straightforward discussion of the segmental speech sounds of American English -- stops, fricatives, frictionless consonants; front, back, and central vowels; diphthongs and triphthongs. There are mouth diagrams and vowel charts,[13] descriptions of the articulation of speech sounds, notes on allophonic and diaphonic variations, and comments on the regional and social differences in the incidence and the phonetic quality of particular phonemes.

The last part deals with connected speech: sound changes, loss and addition of sounds, the pronunciation of foreign words, pitch and melody, terminal contours. Here Bronstein's treatment is again more systematic than Thomas's, showing familiarity with the research of the past two decades and guarded sympathy with the Trager-Smith analysis of the suprasegmentals.

There are two appendices. The first sketches the history of the English language, including attitudes toward variant pronunciations. The second contains the full IPA, the McDavid and Francis map of dialect areas and migration routes (Francis 1958:580),[14] three charts and a table from Kurath *et al.* 1939, and five samples of phonetic transcriptions from live speech.[15] Perhaps more important, there is a long discussion of the Trager and Smith binary analysis of English syllabic nuclei. Since this analysis has been so influential in the last fifteen years,[16] Bronstein presents its theoretical basis, arguments for and against, and the actual transcription practices of various scholars.[17] Bibliographies following each chapter are full, accurate, and up to date. In short, *The Pronunciation of American English* could be used either for a first course in English phonetics or as a supplementary text in the structure of English or an introduction to linguistics if the principal text, like Gleason's (1955) or Hill's (1958), is skimpy in its phonetic discussions.

Bronstein's work has many commendable features, such as a sensible definition of dialect (9), some skepticism about overall patterns (51, 144-45, 314-15), and a recognition that dialects may differ in the number of phonemic entities. On the other hand, he does not seem to recognize the falling together, in certain areas, of such pairs as *cot* and *caught*. And occasionally I disagree with his usage judgments, though less frequently than with those of Thomas:

1. I cannot complain about /wɔnə/, as a reduced informal variant of *want to*, though I might boggle at /dʒit/ *Did you eat?*

2. For *posts*, /pos/ is a normal form (76).

3. The bilabial allophone [ɸ] of /f/ in *cupful* is not careless, but predictable in normal transition (83).

4. In the ordinals *fifth* and *sixth* I normally have /fiθ/ and /sɪks/, with the latter undifferentiated in the plural (85).

5. There is no evidence that "substandard speakers are generally consistent in avoiding the use of /ju/" in *tune*, *duty*, and the like. In the South and South Midland, /ju/ is shared by all classes.

6. Viscerally, I normally judge a final /o/ in *tomato*, *fellow*, etc., as an affectation (169).

7. Such forms as /frɔs/ *frosts* and /æst/ *asked* are not -- in my experience -- "commonly associated with less educated speech." I use them freely, and in the most formal situations. Perhaps it is good that in a country as large as ours, with all kinds of personality types and

all kinds of reactions to the pressures toward homogeneity, variant pronunciations not only exist on the standard level but have their defenders.

In short, neither book is perfect, but both have their merits not only as practical texts but as repositories of information not readily accessible elsewhere. And both are tokens of that interdisciplinary cooperation which we hope will characterize our science in the remaining third of this century.

NOTES

[1] Cordial and profitable cooperation among linguists, speech therapists, speech teachers, neurologists, surgeons, and psychologists marked the workshop on the Nomenclature of Communicative Disorders, held at Carmel, California, in January 1964, under the auspices of the Rehabilitation Codes.

[2] On Thomas's map, both "the South" and "North Central" are labeled D. The differentiation here is my own. In Bronstein and possibly in later printings of Thomas, the North Central area appears as J.

[3] E.g., Kurath 1949:Map 3. For inland North America see Marckwardt 1957 and Allen 1964. Dialect areas in the Southwest are diffidently proposed in Atwood 1962.

[4] Thomas dismisses these, while including Metropolitan New York, solely on the number of speakers. One might argue that distinctiveness is still a relevant criterion.

[5] Preliminary field work in Montana (O'Hare 1964) discloses an apparent dialect boundary along the Continental Divide, reflecting settlement history.

[6] Since teachers' colleges, until recently, were widely regarded as second-class institutions, drawing their populations from the socially insecure lower-middle class, the high proportion of Thomas's informants taken from such institutions may distort his interpretation of what constitutes standard English. This is particularly true in the South.

[7] Kurath and R. McDavid 1961:7, and synopses 3-21, 80-85. This review generally follows their phonemic transcription.

[8] Thomas nowhere discusses the occurrence of the high-central vowel in the weak-stressed syllables of *careless*, *haunted*, *mountain*, *towel*, etc. In such words Kurath considers this vowel an allophone of /ɪ/. See Kurath and R. McDavid 1961:168, Map 149.

[9] R. McDavid 1953a. See also Kurath and R. McDavid 1961:139-40, Map 74. Many Southerners, incidentally, have a three-way contrast between such words as *had*, *have* [æ], *sad*, *salve* [æˆ·], *bad*, *halve* [æˆ·ɨ]. Thomas ignores the structural status of the last two variants, dismissing them, wherever they occur, as "unpleasant"(91).

[10] In the South the informal variant is heavily predominant, especially as a courtesy title to a work-boss or patron.

[11] Kurath and R. McDavid 1961:115-23. Many speakers in the Charleston area have only one front vowel before /-ə/ (the reflex of earlier postvocalic /-r/), so that *fear* and *fair* are homonyms.

[12] This is true even of *Webster's Third New International Dictionary* (1961), although individual entries sometimes show a plethora of variants.

[13] In view of Bronstein's interest in the Linguistic Atlas project, it is regrettable that he omitted the Atlas modification of IPA, as found in Kurath *et al.* 1939:Chapter IV, especially 123, 133.

[14] Earlier, Bronstein includes maps showing the traditional analysis before 1940 (44), the division according to Thomas 1958 (46), and the principal divisions for the Atlantic Seaboard according to Kurath 1949 (47).

[15] Thomas presents transcriptions of regional types, based on his collectanea. They appear to be consensus transcriptions, statistical abstractions rather than the usage of identifiable informants.

[16] This analysis first appeared in an article by Trager and Bloch (1941). It was modified and elaborated by Trager and Smith in *An Outline of English Structure* (1951). It has been widely adopted in introductory textbooks and in manuals for the teaching of English as a second language -- sometimes, one suspects, mechanically, without an understanding of its theoretical basis or an inquiry into its fitness for a particular task.

[17] Four of these generally follow Trager and Smith: W. Nelson Francis, H. A. Gleason, Jr., Charles F. Hockett, Sumner Ives. Five work from other analyses: Thomas, J. S. Kenyon, Allan F. Hubbell, Kenneth Pike, Clifford Prator.

The Linguistic Atlas of the United States and Canada, begun in 1931 with field work in New England (Kurath *et al.* 1939-43 and the autonomous Allen 1973-76 are the only parts published as yet), was designed as a first-stage survey of American English, a framework within which later and more detailed investigations might be developed. Labov's study is the most intensive investigation of this kind and has been a model for many kinds of special dialect studies.

Naturally, there are reasons why an intensive study of an urban community -- and particularly of New York -- should require different techniques from those employed in the broad-gauge Atlas study. The Atlas used three broad groups of informants: 1) the old-fashioned, of limited education; 2) the common or middle group, with some high-school experience; 3) the cultivated, with a college education or equivalent and identification with the local traditions of cultural prestige. It insisted on natives of the community, and if possible on several generations of local residence; in most communities it rejected recent foreign-language immigrant groups, and everywhere rejected those self-consciously concerned with 'speech improvement.' For its purposes the Atlas did well to impose these limits; otherwise it could not have sorted out the basic regional types in American English, gauged the direction of change, and provided a working base for those scholars of future generations who will sort out the contributions to American English from the various dialects of the British Isles and from the other colonial languages.

But any community has more than three social levels, which may or may not be distinguished by language features, and New York is immeasurably more complex. The native New Yorker is a rarity; the population has grown in recent years largely by overseas immigration of speakers of other languages and by internal migration by speakers of lower-class dialects of other regions. Finally, the public schools of the city have had an almost sadistic commitment to 'speech improvement,' and to denigration of the native idiom; one of Labov's happiest achievements is the recognition and measurement of an Index of Linguistic Insecurity -- of discrepancy between what an informant thinks he should say and what he actually says.

In comparison with the Atlas investigations (the interviews were conducted in 1940), Labov chose a random sampling of a selected area, the Lower East Side, utilizing the network of relationships established by the Mobilization for Youth Program. He restricted himself to a limited number of pronunciation variables -- notably the postvocalic /r/ of *beard* and the like, the initial consonants of *thin* and *then*, the syllabic nuclei of *bad* and *off*. He shortened the interview time considerably (to about twenty percent of the average time required for the 800-question Atlas interview). He deliberately elicited data for a variety of styles, ranging from the reading of formal word lists to an account of an incident in which the informant thought he would be killed. He elicited not only pronunciations, but judgments on the status of pronunciations, including the informants' own usage, and he applied rigorous statistical method to the examination of the data.

The principal conclusions one may derive are 1) that the prestige standards of New York City speech have changed in the last generation; 2) that a strongly constricted /r/ in *beard* is spreading among the younger and better educated; 3) that lower vowels have more prestige than higher ones in *bad* and *off*, but that there are slightly different reactions among various ethnic groups. In general, one agrees with Labov's thesis that pronunciation variations in New York City are not haphazard, but pattern with age, social status, and style of utterance.

There is no point in overloading a brief review with an inventory of the relatively few places where Labov seems to misunderstand or misinterpret the method or findings of the Linguistic Atlas. More important, it would seem, is the fact that certain groups are not represented -- notably the old stock white Protestants, who still make up a very large proportion of the New York upper class, and whose speech patterns seem -- admittedly from familiar rather than scientific observation -- to suggest other values than those found in Labov's informants (is this a sharper stratification than he has observed?). But one should not expect a single investigation to accomplish everything, and Labov has certainly succeeded in making us aware of the complex polyhedron of forces operating in New York City, or indeed in any community, though elsewhere the Index of Insecurity may be less significant.

BIBLIOGRAPHICAL INDEX

List of Abbreviations:

AS   *American Speech*
CE   *College English*
CJL *Canadian Journal of Linguistics* (formerly *Journal of the Canadian Linguistic Association*; entries for both titles are listed as *CJL*)
DN   *Dialect Notes*
IJAL *International Journal of American Linguistics*
Lg   *Language*
LSA Linguistic Society of America
NCTE National Council of Teachers of English
PADS *Publication of the American Dialect Society*
SIL *Studies in Linguistics*

Indexed page numbers are listed in Roman type, chapter numbers in italics.

Aitken, A. J.   See Craigie and Aitken 1931-.
Allen, Harold B.   1952   The Linguistic Atlas of the Upper Midwest of the United States. *Orbis* 1.89-94.   (99)
----- 1957   On Accepting Participial *drank*. *CE* 18.283-85.   (122, 251)
----- 1958   *Readings in Applied English Linguistics.* New York: Appleton-Century-Crofts. [2nd ed., rev., 1964]   (42n2)
----- 1959   Canadian-American Speech Differences along the Middle Border. *CJL* 5.17-24.   (103)
----- 1964   Aspects of the Linguistic Geography of the Upper Midwest. Marckwardt 1964:303-14.   (100, 384n3)
----- 1973-76   *Linguistic Atlas of the Upper Midwest.* 3 vols. Minneapolis: Univ. of Minnesota Press.   (8, 72, 84n4, 99, 104, 129n2, 184n6, 193n1, 201, 217n2, 231n1, 237n6, 237n13, 258, 314n1, 353n2, 355, 359, 363, 385)
        1947   *The American College Dictionary.* Ed. by Clarence Barnhardt. New York: Random House. [*ACD*]   (185, 333n8)
        1969   *The American Heritage Dictionary of the English Language.* Ed. by William Morris. Boston: Houghton, Mifflin.   (22n2, 125n3)
Andreyev, N. D.   1962   Models as a Tool in the Development of Linguistic Theory. *Word* 18.186-97.   (17)
Atwood, E. Bagby   1948   Review of Thomas 1947. *Lg* 24.326-30.   (381)
----- 1950a   *Grease* and *greasy*: A Study of Geographical Variation. *University of Texas Studies in English* 29.249-60.   (64, 266n17)
----- 1950b   *Outline of the Principal Speech Areas of the Eastern United States.* [mimeograph]   (66n1, 106n12, 377)
----- 1951   Some Eastern Virginia Pronunciation Features. *University of Virginia Studies* 4.111-24.   (252n13, 367, 374, 382)

Atwood, E. Bagby   1953a   *A Survey of Verb Forms in the Eastern United States.* Ann Arbor: Univ. of Michigan Press. [Review: R. McDavid 1954c]   (xxi, 32, 42n1, 84n1, 88, 106n12, 108, 111, 114, 122, 129n3, 156, 174, 203, 238, 243, 245, 252n8, 266n17, 281n3, 289, 311, 330, 331, 354n10, 354n11, *52*, 367, 377)
----- 1953b   A Preliminary Report on Texas Word Geography. *Orbis* 2.61-66.   (101)
----- 1962   *The Regional Vocabulary of Texas.* Austin: Univ. of Texas Press. [Reviews: Labov 1963, R. McDavid 1964d]   (xxi-xxii, 72, 101, 105, 184n6, 289, 307n2, *58*, 384n3)
Atwood, E. Bagby *et al.*   1948   *Word Index to The Linguistic Atlas of New England.* Austin: Chauntecleer Press. [mimeograph]   (85)
Austin, William M.   1965   Some Social Aspects of Paralanguage. *CJL* 11.31-39.   (28, 42n5, 293)
----- See also R. McDavid and Austin 1966.
Avis, Walter S.   1953   The Past Participle *drank*: Standard American English? *AS* 28.106-11.   (122, 251)
----- 1954-56   Speech Differences along the Ontario-United States Border. Vocabulary: *CJL* 1[Preliminary Number].13-18; Grammar and Syntax: *CJL* 1.14-19; Pronunciation: *CJL* 2.41-59.   (103)
----- 1956   The Mid-Back Vowels in the English of the Eastern United States. Diss., Univ. of Michigan.   (105n6, 276, 361n6)
----- 1961   The 'New England Short *o*': A Recessive Phoneme. *Lg* 37.544-58.   (276, 361n6)
Avis, Walter S. *et al.*   1967   *A Dictionary of Canadianisms on Historical Principles.* Toronto: W. J. Gage.   (5, 31, 124, 314n13)
Ayres, Harry M.   1933   Bermudian English. *AS* 8.1. 3-10.   (195n27)
Baehr, Rufus F.   1964   Need Achievement and Dialect in Lower Class Adolescent Negroes. Diss., Univ. of Chicago.   (73, 152, 161)
Bailey, Beryl Loftman   1965   Toward a New Perspective in Negro English Dialectology. *AS* 40.171-77.   (292)
----- 1966   *Jamaican Creole Syntax: A Transformational Approach.* Cambridge: Cambridge Univ. Press.   (292)
Baker, Sidney J.   1945   *The Australian Language.* Sydney: Angus and Robertson. [Review: R. McDavid 1951e]   (xx, *48*)
Barnhardt, Clarence   See *The American College Dictionary* (1947).
Barrett, Madie W.   1948   A Phonology of Southeast Alabama Speech. Diss., Univ. of North Carolina.   (106n17, 184n6, 289, 314n1)
Bascom, W. R.   1941   Acculturation among the Gullah Negroes. *American Anthropologist* 43.43-50.   (347n11)
Baugh, Albert C.   1935   *A History of the English Language.* New York: Appleton-Century. [2nd ed., 1958, Appleton-Century-Crofts]   (136)

Benét, Stephen Vincent 1943 *Western Star*. New York: Farrar and Rinehart. (259)

Bennett, John 1908-09 Gullah: A Negro Patois. *South Atlantic Quarterly* 7.332-44, 8.39-42. (44, 342, 345, 347n10)

Birdwhistell, Ray L. 1952 *Introduction to Kinesics: An Annotation System for Analysis of Body Motion and Gesture*. Louisville: Univ. of Louisville. (28, 293)

----- 1956 *Kinesics*. Louisville: Univ. of Louisville. (28, 42n5)

----- 1970 *Kinesics and Context: Essays on Body Motion and Communication*. Philadelphia: Univ. of Pennsylvania Press. (28)

Bloch, Bernard 1935 The Treatment of Middle English Final and Preconsonantal *r* in the Present-Day Speech of New England. Diss., Brown Univ. (105n6)

----- 1938 Post-vocalic *r* in New England Speech. *Actes du IVème Congrès International du Linguistes* (Copenhagen: Munksgaard), 195-99. (321)

Bloch, Bernard and George L. Trager 1940 *Tables for a System of Phonetic Description*. New Haven: Preliminary ed. (7, 333n3)

----- 1942 *Outline of Linguistic Analysis*. Baltimore: LSA. (7, 9n2, 319, 320, 322n1, 327, 333n3, 333n7, 337, 345)

Bloch, Bernard See also Trager and Bloch 1941.

Bloomfield, Leonard 1933 *Language*. New York: Holt. (20, 42n8, 129n2, 258, 320, 322, 322n1, 371)

----- 1935 The Stressed Vowels of American English. *Lg* 11.97-116. (319)

----- 1942 *Outline Guide for the Practical Study of Foreign Languages*. Baltimore: LSA. (8, 318)

Bloomfield, Morton See Sledd 1964.

Bonfante, Giuliano 1947 The Neolinguistic Position. *Lg* 23.344-75. (334n24)

Botkin, B. A. 1953 The Spiels of New York. *New York Folklore Quarterly* 9.165-75. (174)

Bowman, Elizabeth 1966 The Minor and Fragmentary Sentences of a Corpus of Spoken English. *IJAL* 32.3.2. [Indiana Univ. Research Center in Anthropology, Folklore, and Linguistics Publication 42] (124)

Brengelman, Frederick H. 1957 The Native American English Spoken in the Puget Sound Area. Diss., Univ. of Washington. (104)

Brewster, Lawrence F. 1947 *Summer Migrations and Resorts of South Carolina Low-Country Planters*. Durham: Duke Univ. Press. [Historical Papers of the Trinity College Historical Society, Series 26] (139, 274, 346n1)

Bridenbaugh, Carl 1938 *Cities in the Wilderness: The First Century of Urban Life in America, 1625-1742*. New York: Ronald. (259, 333n11, 347n10)

Bright, Elizabeth S. 1971 *A Word Geography of California and Nevada*. Berkeley: Univ. of California Press. [Univ. of California Publications in Linguistics, 69] (72, 101, 105)

Bright, William See R. McDavid 1966a.

Bronstein, Arthur J. 1960 *The Pronunciation of American English: An Introduction to Phonetics*. New York: Appleton-Century-Crofts. [Review: R. McDavid 1966b] (xxii, 59)

----- See also R. McDavid 1970.

Brooks, Cleanth 1935 *The Relation of the Alabama-Georgia Dialect to the Provincial Dialects of Great Britain*. Baton Rouge: Louisiana State Univ. Press. (44, 195n28, 330, 333n6)

Brower, Robert H. 1950 *A Bibliography of Japanese Dialects*. Ann Arbor: Univ. of Michigan Press. [Univ. of Michigan Center for Japanese Studies Bibliographical Series, 2] (371)

Bryant, Margaret 1962 *Current American English*. New York: Funk and Wagnalls. (106n17, 380n1)

Buck, Carl Darling 1949 *A Dictionary of Selected Synonyms in the Principal Indo-European Languages*. Chicago: Univ. of Chicago Press. (107)

Caffee, Nathaniel See Kurath 1940.

Carrière, Joseph M. 1939 Creole Dialect of Missouri. *AS* 14.109-19. (104)

Cash, Wilbur J. 1941 *The Mind of the South*. New York: Knopf. (139, 307n4)

Cassidy, Frederic G. 1941 Some New England Words in Wisconsin. *Lg* 17.324-39. (97)

----- 1948 On Collecting American Dialect. *AS* 23.185-93. (103, 264n1, 265n7, 266n18, 355)

----- 1961 *Jamaica Talk: Three Hundred Years of the English Language in Jamaica*. London: Macmillan; New York: St. Martin's Press. (103)

Cassidy, Frederic G. et al. 1981- *Dictionary of American Regional English*. Cambridge, MA: Belknap Press. [*DARE*. In preparation: projected publication date] (xix, 5, 23n10, 31, 59n1, 87, 105, 125n5, 172, 237n16, 288, 289, 290, 361n10)

Cassidy, Frederic G. and Audrey R. Duckert 1953 A Method for Collecting Dialect. *PADS* 20. (103)

Cassidy, Frederic G. and Robert LePage 1967 *A Dictionary of Jamaican English*. Cambridge: Cambridge Univ. Press. (23n10, 31, 103, 124)

Cassidy, Frederic G. See also S. Robertson 1934.

Catford, J. C. 1957a The Linguistic Survey of Scotland. *Orbis* 6.105-21. (14)

----- 1957b Vowel-Systems of Scots Dialects. *Transactions of the Philological Society*, 67-117. (14)

Chase, Stuart 1948 *The Proper Study of Mankind: An Inquiry into the Science of Human Relations*. New York: Harper. (184n4)

Chomsky, Noam 1957 *Syntactic Structures*. The Hague: Mouton. [Review: Lees 1957] (10, 27)

Chomsky, Noam and Morris Halle 1968 *The Sound Pattern of English*. New York: Harper and Row. (287)

Christian, Donna See Wolfram and Christian 1976.

Clarke, Nona See Wolfram and Clarke 1971.

Comhaire-Sylvain, Suzanne 1936 *Le Créole haïtien: morphologie et syntaxe*. Wetteren: De Meester. (45, 348n23)

Corbin, Richard and Muriel Crosby 1965 *Language Programs for the Disadvantaged: The Report of the NCTE Task Force on Teaching English to the Disadvantaged*. Urbana: NCTE. (68)

Couch, W. T. See Greet 1934.

Craigie, Sir William and A. J. Aitken 1931- *A Dictionary of the Older Scottish Tongue, from the Twelfth Century to the End of the Seventeenth*. Chicago: Univ. of Chicago Press. (356, 357)

Craigie, Sir William and James R. Hulbert 1936-44 *A Dictionary of American English on Historical Principles*. 4 vols. Chicago: Univ. of Chicago Press. [*DAE*] (5, 9, 103, 124, 309, 325, 327, 328n6)

Crinklaw, Donald 1976 Ladue Lockjaw, or How I Learned to Love the St. Louis Language. *St. Louisian* 8.10.59-61. (257)

Crockett, Henry J., Jr. See Levine and Crockett 1967.

Crosby, Muriel See Corbin and Crosby 1965.

Crum, Mason 1940 *Gullah: Negro Life in the Carolina Sea Islands*. Durham: Duke Univ. Press. (50n9, 342, 346n1, 346n2, 347n3, 347n7, 347n10, 347n15, 348n17)

Curme, George O. 1931 *Syntax*. Boston: Heath. [A Grammar of the English Language, vol. 3] (23n13)

----- 1935 *Parts of Speech and Accidence*. Boston: Heath. [A Grammar of the English Language, vol. 2] (23n13, 217n1)

Danehy, John J. See Pittenger, Hockett and Danehy 1960.

Darwin, Charles 1859 *On the Origin of Species by means of Natural Selection, or the Preservation of Favoured Races in the Struggle for Life*. London: Murray. (18)

Davis, A. L. 1949 A Word Atlas of the Great Lakes Region. Diss., Univ. of Michigan. (97, 106n12, 144, 184n6, 238, 249, 252n4, 264n1, 266n17, 341, 355, 359)

Davis, A. L. and Lawrence M. Davis 1969 Recordings of Standard English Questionnaire. *Orbis* 18.385-404. (291)

Davis, A. L. and Raven I. McDavid, Jr. 1949 *Shivaree*: An Example of Cultural Diffusion. *AS* 24.249-55. (vii, xii, xvi-xvii, 84n11, *26*, 237n14)

----- 1950 Northwestern Ohio: A Transition Area. *Lg* 26.264-73. (viii, xi, xvii, 97, 192, 233, 235, *31*, 266n17)

Davis, A. L., Raven I. McDavid, Jr. and Virginia McDavid 1969 *A Compilation of the Worksheets of the Linguistic Atlas of the United States and Canada and Associated Projects*. 2nd ed. Chicago: Univ. of Chicago Press. (84n8, 354n7, 365n3)

Davis, Lawrence M. 1970 Some Social Aspects of the Speech of Blue-Grass Kentucky. *Orbis* 19. 337-41. (49, 346)

----- 1971 *A Study of Appalachian Speech in a Northern Urban Setting*. Chicago: US Office of Education, Department of Health, Education, and Welfare. [Project O-E-142] (49, 63, 156, 292)

----- See also A. L. Davis and L. M. Davis 1969.

Dearden, E. Jeannette 1943 Dialect Areas of the South Atlantic States as Determined by Variations in Vocabulary. Diss., Brown Univ. (105n6)

DeCamp, David 1954 The Speech of San Francisco. Diss., Univ. of California, Berkeley. (101, 110)

----- 1958-59 The Pronunciation of English in San Francisco. *Orbis* 7.372-91, 8.54-77. (101, 110, 129n4, 156, 174)

Dickens, Charles 1850 *The Personal History of David Copperfield*. London: Bradbury and Evans. [Issued in 20 monthly parts, May 1849-November 1850] (193n4)

Dieth, Eugen 1848 Linguistic Geography in New England. *English Studies* 29.65-79. (70, 84n2, 353n3, 356)

Dieth, Eugen and Harold Orton 1952 Questionnaire for a Linguistic Atlas of England. *Proceedings of the Leeds Philosophical and Literary Society, Literary and Historical Section* 6.9.605-760. [Review: R. McDavid 1953d] (xx, 104, *49*, 356,

360n5)

Dieth, Eugen See also Orton and Dieth 1951.

Dil, Anwar S. See R. McDavid 1979.

Dollard, John 1937 *Caste and Class in a Southern Town*. New Haven: Yale Univ. Press. (144)

Dorrill, George T. 1975 A Comparison of Negro and White Speech in Central South Carolina. M.A. Thesis, Univ. of South Carolina. (46, 292, 346)

Dorson, Richard M. 1956 *Negro Folktales in Michigan*. Cambridge: Harvard Univ. Press. (173)

Dowd, Jerome 1926 *The Negro in American Life*. New York: Century. (49n1)

Downer, James W. 1958 Features of New England Rustic Pronunciation in James Russell Lowell's *Biglow Papers*. Diss., Univ. of Michigan. (50n15, 105n6, 109, 157)

Drake, James A. 1961 The Effect of Urbanization on Regional Vocabulary. *AS* 36.17-33. (66n2)

Duckert, Audrey See Cassidy and Duckert 1953, Kurath *et al.* 1939.

Dulong, Gaston 1954 L'Atlas linguistique de la Gaspésie. *CJL* 1[Preliminary Number].23-25. (104)

Dunlap, Howard G. 1974 Social Aspects of a Verb Form: Native Atlanta Fifth-Grade Speech -- the Present Tense of *be*. *PADS* 61-62. (161)

Dwight, Timothy 1821-22 *Travels in New England and New York*. New Haven: Dwight. (195n18)

Edmont, Edmond See Gilliéron and Edmont 1902-10.

Eikel, Fred, Jr. 1966-67 New Braunfels German. *AS* 41.5-16, 254-60; 42.83-104. (290)

Ekwall, Eilert 1912 On the Origin and History of the Unchanged Plural in English. *Lunds University Årskrift* Afd. 1, Bd. 8.3. (217n1)

----- 1946 *British and American Pronunciation*. Upsala: Lundequistska. [American Institute in the University of Upsala, Essays and Studies on American Language and Literature, 2] (136)

Eliason, Norman 1956 *Tarheel Talk: An Historical Study of the English Language in North Carolina to 1860*. Chapel Hill: Univ. of North Carolina Press. [Review: R. McDavid 1958c] (xxi, 253n16, 57)

Ellis, A. J. 1869-89 *On Early English Pronunciation*. 5 vols. London: Trübner. [Early English Text Society, Extra Series, 2, 7, 14, 23, 56] (26, 80, 192, 193n8, 195n18, 351, 356)

Elphinston, James 1787 *Propriety Ascertained in her Picture: or, Inglish Speech and Spelling Rendered Mutual Guides*. London: J. Walter. (192)

Emerson, O. F. 1891 The Ithaca Dialect: A Study of Present English. *DN* 1.85-173. (195n23, 231n1)

Farmer, John S. 1889 *Americanisms -- Old and New*. London: T. Poulter. (183, 327)

Fasold, Ralph and Walter A. Wolfram 1970 Some Linguistic Features of Negro Dialect. *Teaching Standard English in the Inner City*, ed. by Roger Shuy and Ralph Fasold (Arlington: Center for Applied Linguistics), 41-86. (51n31)

Fishman, Joshua *et al.* 1966 *Language Loyalty in the United States*. The Hague: Mouton. [Janua Linguarum, Series Maior, 21] (66n9)

Flanagan, John T. 1940 A Note on *shivaree*. *AS* 15.109-10. (181)

Flaten, Nils 1900 Notes on American-Norwegian with a Vocabulary. *DN* 2.115-26. (183)

Flexner, Stuart See Wentworth and Flexner 1960.

Flom, George T. 1926 English Loanwords in American Norwegian. *AS* 1.541-58. (183)

Forgue, Guy Jean and Raven I. McDavid, Jr. 1972 *La Langue des Américains.* Paris: Aubier Montaigne. (105)

Forrester, Christine D. 1954 A Word Atlas of Kentucky. M.A. Thesis, Univ. of Kentucky. (249, 252n4, 289)

Foster, Charles W. 1971 The Phonology of the Conjure Tales of Charles W. Chesnutt. *PADS* 55. (50n15)

Fowler, H. W. 1926 *A Dictionary of Modern English Usage.* Oxford: Clarendon. (193n15)

Frady, Marshall 1968 *Wallace.* New York: World. (48, 346)

----- 1970 Sweetest Finger this side of Midas. *Life* 68[Feb. 27].7, 52-60. (48, 346)

Francis, W. Nelson 1958 *The Structure of American English.* New York: Ronald. (2, 66n1, 111, 129n3, 158n4, 266n17, 289, 293n2, 294n4, 377, 383)

Frank, Yakira H. 1949 The Speech of New York City. Diss., Univ. of Michigan. (105n6, 106n12, 110, 111, 129n4, 145n9, 156, 174, 196n33, 231n1, 338n3)

Frazier, Alexander See R. McDavid 1967b.

Frey, J. William 1942a The German Dialect of Eastern York County, Pennsylvania. Diss., Univ. of Illinois. (104)

----- 1942b *A Simple Grammar of Pennsylvania Dutch.* Clinton, SC: privately printed. (104)

----- 1945 Amish "Triple-Talk". *AS* 20.85-98. (104)

Friedan, Betty 1963 *The Feminine Mystique.* New York: Norton. (32n2)

Fries, Charles C. 1940 *American English Grammar.* New York: Appleton-Century. (17, 30, 38, 117, 122, 123, 126, 151, 199, 218n9, 252n2, 253n16, 325, 361n11, 364n1, 366)

----- 1952 *The Structure of English.* New York: Harcourt Brace. [Review: Sledd 1955] (12, 123, 124)

Gage, William W. 1958 Grammatical Structures in American Intonation. Diss., Cornell Univ. (283)

Gilbert, Glenn 1971 *The German Language in America: A Symposium.* Austin: Univ. of Texas Press. (290)

----- 1972 *Linguistic Atlas of Texas German.* Austin: Univ. of Texas Press. (290)

Gilliéron, Jules and Edmond Edmont 1902-10 *Atlas linguistique de la France.* Paris: Champion. (13, 71, 79, 158n6, 187, 258, 371, 377)

Gleason, H. A. 1955 *Introduction to Descriptive Linguistics.* New York: Holt, Rinehart, and Winston. (361n7, 383)

Gonzales, Ambrose 1922 *The Black Border: Gullah Stories of the Carolina Coast.* Columbia, SC: State. (50n9, 342, 347n10)

Gove, Philip See *Webster's Third New International Dictionary* (1961).

Grandgent, C. H. 1893 American Pronunciation Again. *Modern Language Notes* 8.277-78. (185)

Grant, Madison 1916 *The Passing of the Great Race: or, The Racial Basis of European History.* New York: Scribner's. (49n4)

Grant, William and David Murison 1931-76 *Scottish National Dictionary.* Edinburgh: Scottish National Dictionary Association. (356, 357)

Greenberg, Joseph H. 1941 Some Problems in Hausa Phonology. *Lg* 17.316-23. (50n14, 345)

----- 1955 *Studies in African Linguistic Classification.* New Haven: Compass. [Reprinted from the *Southwestern Journal of Anthropology* for the Language and Communication Research Center, Columbia University, and the Program of African Studies, Northwestern University] (50n14)

Greet, W. Cabell 1931a A Phonographic Expedition to Williamsburg, Virginia. *AS* 6.161-72. (195n26)

----- 1931b A Record from Lubeck, Maine, and Remarks on the Coastal Type. *AS* 6.397-403. (195n26)

----- 1933 Delmarva Speech. *AS* 8.4.56-63. (195n26)

----- 1934 Southern Speech. *Culture in the South,* ed. by W. T. Couch (Chapel Hill: Univ. of North Carolina Press), 594-615. (288)

Greibeslund, Solveig C. 1970 A Comparison of Uncultivated Black and White Speech in the Upper South. M.A. Thesis, Univ. of Chicago. (46, 49, 292, 346)

Haden, Ernest F. 1942 The French-Speaking Areas of Canada: Acadians and Canadians. *ACLS Bulletin* 34.82-89. (104)

Haden, Ernest F. and Eugène Joliat 1940 Le Genre grammatical des substantifs en Franco-Canadien empruntées à l'anglais. *PMLA* 55.839-54. (104)

Haislund, Niels See Jespersen 1909-49.

Hall, Edward T. 1959 *The Silent Language.* Garden City, NJ: Doubleday. (28, 42n5)

----- 1966 *The Hidden Dimension.* Garden City, NJ: Doubleday. (42n5)

----- See also Trager and Hall 1953.

Hall, Joseph S. 1942 *The Phonetics of Great Smoky Mountain Speech.* New York: King's Crown. [*American Speech* Reprints and Monographs, 4. Review: R. McDavid 1943] (xii, xix, 243n3, 42)

Hall, Robert A., Jr. 1943 *Melanesian Pidgin English: Grammar, Texts, Vocabulary.* Baltimore: LSA. (45, 342)

----- 1944 Chinese Pidgin Grammar and Texts. *Journal of the American Oriental Society* 64.95-113. (45)

----- 1946 Bartoli's 'Neolinguistica'. *Lg* 22. 273-83. (334n24)

----- 1948 The Linguistic Structure of Taki-Taki. *Lg* 24.92-116. (45, 348n23)

----- 1950a *Leave Your Language Alone!* Ithaca: Linguistica. [2nd ed., 1950 (Garden City, NJ: Doubleday), entitled *Linguistics and Your Language*] (339n17)

----- 1950b Review of Turner 1949. *AS* 25.51-54. (45, 265n12)

Halle, Morris See Chomsky and Halle 1968.

Hallowell, A. Irving See Spier, Hallowell and Newman 1941.

Hankey, Clyde 1960 A Colorado Word Geography. *PADS* 34. (100, 105, 266)

Hanley, Miles L. 1933 *Serenade* in New England. *AS* 8.2.24-26. (181)

Hardy, Thomas 1886 *The Mayor of Casterbridge.* London: Smith, Elder. (184n5)

Harris, Charles C. 1952 Papiamentu Phonology. Diss., Cornell Univ. (45)

Harris, Rachel S. 1937 The Speech of Rhode Island. Diss., Brown Univ. (105n6)

Harris, Zellig 1951 *Methods in Structural*

Linguistics. Chicago: Univ. of Chicago Press. (17, 22n3)

Harris, Zellig See also Welmers and Harris 1942.

Haugen, Einar 1950a The Analysis of Linguistic Borrowing. *Lg* 26.210-31. (43, 97, 197n50, 265n12)

----- 1950b Problems of Bilingualism. *Lingua* 2. 221-90. (197n50)

----- 1953 *The Norwegian Language in America: A Study of Bilingual Behavior*. 2 vols. Philadelphia: Univ. of Pennsylvania Press. [Review: R. McDavid 1955c] (xxi, 8, 72, 104, 110, 183, 197n50, 252n10, 55)

----- 1956 Bilingualism in the Americas: A Bibliography and Research Guide. *PADS* 26. (157)

Haun, Mildred 1940 *The Hawk's Done Gone*. Indianapolis: Bobbs Merrill. (322)

Hause, Helen E. See Hodge and Hause 1944.

Hawkins, Jane D. 1935 The Speech of Chepachet, Rhode Island. M.A. Thesis, Brown Univ. (333n7)

----- 1942 The Speech of the Hudson River Valley. Diss., Brown Univ. (105n6, 333n7)

Headley, Joel Tyler 1863-66 *The Great Rebellion: A History of the Civil War in the United States*. Hartford: Hurlbut, Williams. (310)

Hempl, George 1891 Unstressed *wh*. *Modern Language Notes* 6.310-11. (185)

----- 1894 American Speech-Maps. *DN* 1.315-18. (80)

----- 1896 *Grease* and *greasy*. *DN* 1.438-44. (64, 239, 266n17)

Herndobler, Robin 1977 White Working-Class Speech: The East Side of Chicago. Diss., Univ. of Chicago. (129n4, 156)

Herskovits, Melville J. 1941 *The Myth of the Negro Past*. New York: Harper. (44, 45, 47, 50n13, 348n16)

----- 1948 *Man and his Works: The Science of Cultural Anthropology*. New York: Knopf. (18, 143)

Herzog, George 1941 Cultural Change and Language: Shifts in the Pima Vocabulary. Spier, Hallowell and Newman 1941:66-74. (106n19)

Heyward, DuBose 1925 *Porgy*. New York: Doran. (347n7)

Hill, Archibald A. 1958 *Introduction to Linguistic Structures*. New York: Harcourt, Brace. (15n4, 282, 383)

----- 1962 *First Texas Conference on Problems of Linguistic Analysis in English*. Austin: Univ. of Texas. (178, 282, 285)

Hockett, Charles F. 1958 *A Course in Modern Linguistics*. New York: Macmillan. (15n5, 42n8, 287)

----- See also Pittenger, Hockett and Danehy 1960.

Hodge, Carlton T. 1947 An Outline of Hausa Grammar. *Lg* 23.4, Suppl. [*Lg* Diss. 41] (50n14, 345)

Hodge, Carlton T. and Helen E. Hause 1944 Hausa Tone. *Journal of the American Oriental Society* 64.51-52. (50n14, 345)

Hopkins, John R. 1975 The White Middle-Class Speech of Savannah, Georgia: A Phonological Analysis. Diss., Univ. of South Carolina. (129n4, 157, 291)

Howren, Robert R. 1958 The Speech of Louisville, Kentucky. Diss., Indiana Univ. (129n4, 156, 291)

Hubbell, Allan F. 1950 *The Pronunciation of English in New York City: Consonants and Vowels*. New York: King's Crown. (105n6, 129n4, 145n9, 156, 174, 196n33, 231n1, 338n3)

Hulbert, James R. See Craigie and Hulbert 1936-44.

----- 1946 Is There a Lexicographer in the House? *Saturday Evening Post* 219.14 [Oct. 6]. 164. (328n3)

Ives, Sumner 1950a The Dialect of the Uncle Remus Stories. Diss., Univ. of Texas. (50n15, 88, 109, 157)

----- 1950b A Theory of Literary Dialect. *Tulane Studies in English* 2.137-82. (88, 157, 193n4)

----- 1952 American Pronunciation in the Linguistic Atlas. *Tulane Studies in English* 3.179-91. (88, 361n7)

----- 1954 The Phonology of the Uncle Remus Stories. *PADS* 22. (88)

Jaberg, Karl and Jakob Jud 1928-40 *Sprach- und Sachatlas Italiens und der Südschweiz*. 8 vols. Zofingen: Ringier. (71, 126, 159, 177, 258, 317, 377)

Jackson, Kenneth H. 1955 *Contributions to the Study of Manx Phonology*. Edinburgh: Nelson. [Univ. of Edinburgh Linguistic Survey of Scotland Monographs, 2] (360n2)

Jagendorf, Moritz 1953 The Rich Lore of a Rich Hotel, The Plaza. *New York Folklore Quarterly* 9.176-82. (174)

Jespersen, Otto 1909-49 *A Modern English Grammar on Historical Principles*. 7 vols. Copenhagen: Munksgaard. [Phototyped ed., rev. and pub. by Niels Haislund] (185, 191, 192, 194n13, 194n16, 197n51)

Johnson, Glenn H., Jr. 1950 A Dialect Study of Colorado Freshman at the University of Colorado. M.A. Thesis, Univ. of Colorado. (264n1)

Johnson, Guion G. 1930 *A Social History of the Sea Islands, with Special Reference to St. Helena Island, South Carolina*. Chapel Hill: Univ. of North Carolina Press. (342, 345, 346n1)

Johnston, Wm. 1764 *A Pronouncing and Spelling Dictionary*. London: Johnston. (191, 192)

Joliat, Eugène See Haden and Joliat 1940.

Jones, Daniel 1917 *An English Pronouncing Dictionary*. New York: Dutton; London: Dent. (185)

----- See also Michaelis and Jones 1913.

Jones, John 1701 *Practical Phonography*. London: R. Smith. (192)

Joos, Martin 1962 *The Five Clocks*. *IJAL* 28.2.5. [Indiana Univ. Research Center in Anthropology, Folklore, and Linguistics Publication 22] (30, 33, 42n2, 125n2)

Jud, Jakob See Jaberg and Jud 1928-40.

Kennedy, Arthur G. 1927 *Bibliography of Writings on the English Language from the Beginning of Printing to the End of 1922*. Cambridge and New Haven: Harvard Univ. Press, Yale Univ. Press. (19)

----- 1935 *Current English*. Boston: Ginn. (194n9)

----- See also Mencken, Pound, Malone and Kennedy 1945.

Kenrick, William 1773 *New Dictionary of the English Language*. London: Rivington. (192)

Kenyon, John S. 1924 *American Pronunciation*. Ann Arbor: Wahr. (20, 105n7, 195n19, 338n8)

Kenyon, John S. 1948 Cultural Levels and Functional Varieties of English. *CE* 10.31-36. (42n2)

Kenyon, John S. and Thomas A. Knott 1944 *Pronouncing Dictionary of American English*. Springfield, MA: Merriam. [Review: Kurath 1944] (185)

Key, V. O., Jr. 1949 *Southern Politics in State and Nation*. New York: Knopf. (314n6)

Kimmerle, Marjorie M. 1952 *Bum, poddy*, or *penco*. *Colorado Quarterly* 1.87-97. (100)

Kimmerle, Marjorie M., Raven I. McDavid, Jr. and Virginia G. McDavid 1951 Problems of Linguistic Geography in the Rocky Mountain Area. *Western Humanities Review* 5.244-64. (viii, xviii, 100, *34*)

Kipling, Rudyard 1886 *Departmental Ditties and Other Verses*. Lahore: Civil and Military Gazette Press. (327, 328n10)

Kirby, Thomas A. See Kurath 1940.

Kluckhohn, Clyde 1949 *Mirror for Man: The Relation of Anthropology to Modern Life*. New York: Whittlesey House. (184n4, 350)

Knott, Thomas A. See Kenyon and Knott 1944, and *Webster's New International Dictionary of the English Language, Second Edition* (1934).

Kökeritz, Helge 1932 *The Phonology of the Suffolk Dialect: Descriptive and Historical*. Upsala: Appelberg. (192, 193n3, 197n49, 197n52)

Krapp, George P. 1924 The English of the Negro. *American Mercury* 2.190-95. (43, 347n10)

----- 1925 *The English Language in America*. 2 vols. New York: Century. [Review: Kurath 1927] (20, 44, 105n7, 124, 136, 192, 194n18, 346n2)

Kroeber, A. L. 1950 Anthropology. *Scientific American* 183.3.87-94. (45)

Kruisinga, Etska 1905 *A Grammar of the Dialect of West Somerset: Descriptive and Historical*. Bonn: Hanstein. (197n49)

Kuhn, Sherman M. See Kurath, Kuhn *et al.* 1952-.

Kurath, Hans 1927 Review of Krapp 1925. *Lg* 3. 131-39. (105n7)

----- 1928a American Pronunciation. *Society for Pure English Tract* 30.279-97. (107, 195n20, 381)

----- 1928b The Origin of the Dialectal Differences in Spoken American English. *Modern Philology* 25.385-95. (195n20)

----- 1940 *Mourning* and *morning*. *Studies for William A. Read*, ed. by Nathaniel Caffee and Thomas A. Kirby (University, LA: Louisiana State Univ. Press), 166-73. (242, 320, 322, 332)

----- 1941 Star-Gazing. Paper presented at the Linguistic Institute, Chapel Hill, North Carolina. (9n1)

----- 1944 Review of Kenyon and Knott 1944. *Lg* 20.150-55. (239)

----- 1949 *A Word Geography of the Eastern United States*. Ann Arbor: Univ. of Michigan Press. [Review: R. McDavid 1950b] (xiv, xx, xxi, 23n11, 42n1, 49n5, 50n8, 84n1, 88, 90, 105n5, 106n12, 108, 110, 111, 113, 114, 119n1, 129n3, 145n3, 145n7, 149n1, 175n2, 176, 183n1, 186, 187, 189, 190, 192, 200, 201, 216, 223, 231n1, 232, 233, 234, 235, 237n5, 237n9, 237n16, 238, 239, 245, 252n3, 252n10, 258, 266n13, 281n3, 289, 295, 307n2, 311, 314n5, 333n5, 338n9, *46*, 351, 352, 360, 360n1, 362, 364, 367, 373, 378, 384n3, 384n14)

Kurath, Hans 1968 The Investigation of Urban Speech. *PADS* 49.1-7. (113)

----- 1972 *Studies in Area Linguistics*. Bloomington: Indiana Univ. Press. (46, 51n19, 285, 292, 342)

Kurath, Hans *et al.* 1939 *Handbook of the Linguistic Geography of New England*. Providence: Brown Univ., for American Council of Learned Societies. [2nd ed., rev. by Audrey Duckert (New York: AMS), 1973] (7, 79, 84n3, 85n10, 104, 105n1, 108, 129n2, 158n4, 185, 193n1, 196n34, 197n44, 197n45, 217n2, 230n1, 294n4, 317, 323n10, 332, 354n12, 365n2, 366, 383, 384n13)

----- 1939-43 *Linguistic Atlas of New England*. 3 vols. in 6. Providence: Brown Univ., for American Council of Learned Societies. [Repr., 3 vols. (New York: AMS), 1972. Reviews: Marckwardt 1940b, Menner 1942, Dieth 1948, R. and V. McDavid 1952a, O'Cain 1979] (xiv, 26, 70, 71, 72, *10*, 104, 105n1, 108, 115, 126, 135n3, 159, 170, 184n6, 193n1, 217n2, 223, 230n1, 233, 234, 244n8, 258, 262, 312n1, 317, 323n10, 325, 327, 332, 339n15, 339n16, 340, 354n7, 354n12, 360, 366, 377, 385)

----- 1979- *Linguistic Atlas of the Middle and South Atlantic States*. Chicago: Univ. of Chicago Press. (v, 26, 51n33, 72, 104, 168, 184n6, 193n1, 217n2, 223, 230, 236n1, 258, 289, 290, 295, 312n1, 365n6)

Kurath, Hans, Sherman M. Kuhn *et al.* 1952- *Middle English Dictionary*. Ann Arbor: Univ. of Michigan Press. (8, 31, 84n4, 86, 105n4, 107, 111, 113, 199, 373)

Kurath, Hans and Guy S. Lowman, Jr. 1970 The Dialectal Structure of Southern England: Phonological Evidence. *PADS* 54. (198n57, 216, 353, 353n1)

Kurath, Hans and Raven I. McDavid, Jr. 1961 *The Pronunciation of English in the Atlantic States*. Ann Arbor: Univ. of Michigan Press. (2, 14, 23n11, 42n1, 66n1, 66n2, 68, 84n1, 88, 108, 112, 113, 119n1, 119n3, 129n3, 146, 156, 245, 276, 287n2, 289, 311, 322n1, 338n3, 339n17, 358, 362, 374, 384n7, 384n8, 384n9, 384n11)

Labov, William 1963 Review of Atwood 1962. *Word* 19.266-72. (380n2)

----- 1966 *The Social Stratification of English in New York City*. Arlington: Center for Applied Linguistics. [Review: R. McDavid 1968] (xii, xxii, 38, 72, 105, 120n4, 129n4, 130n8, 145n9, 151, 156, 160, 174, 231n1, 346, *60*)

----- 1972 *Language in the Inner City: Studies in the Black English Vernacular*. Philadelphia: Univ. of Pennsylvania Press. (31)

Lane, George S. 1934-35 Notes on Louisiana-French. *Lg* 10.323-33, 11.5-16. (45)

----- 1952 Le Langage des femmes: Enquête linguistique à l'échelle mondiale. *Orbis* 1.10-86. (359)

Larsen, Vernon S. and Carolyn H. Larsen 1966 Reactions to Pronunciations. R. McDavid and Austin 1966:49pp. (66n11)

Lea, Homer 1912 *The Day of the Saxon*. New York: Harper. (49n4)

Learned, M. D. 1888-89 The Pennsylvania German Dialect. *American Journal of Philology* 9.64-83, 178-97, 326-39, 425-56; 10.288-315. (104)

Lees, Robert B. 1957 Review of Chomsky 1957.

Lg 33.375-408. (v)

Leonard, Sterling A. 1932 *Current English Usage.* Chicago: Inland, for NCTE. (122)

LePage, Robert See Cassidy and LePage 1967.

      1853 Letters about '*umble* in *David Copperfield. Notes and Queries,* 1st Series.8.54, 229, 298, 393-95, 551. (193n4)

Levine, Lewis and Henry J. Crockett, Jr. 1967 Speech Variation in a Piedmont Community: Postvocalic /-r/. *Explorations in Sociolinguistics,* ed. by Stanley Lieberson. *IJAL* 33.4.2.76-98. [Indiana Univ. Research Center in Anthropology, Folklore, and Linguistics Publication 44] (142n21)

Lewis, C. S. and E. M. W. Tillyard 1939 *The Personal Heresy, a Controversy.* London: Oxford Univ. Press. (10)

Lieberson, Stanley See Levine and Crockett 1967.

Linton, Ralph 1945 *The Cultural Background of Personality.* New York: Appleton-Century. (338n4)

Littré, Émile 1863-69 *Dictionnaire de la langue française.* 4 vols. Paris: Hachette. [7 vols. (Paris: Gallimard Hachette), 1956-58] (181)

Lloyd, Donald J. 1954 Let's Get Rid of Miss Driscoll. *The Educational Forum* 18.341-48. (125n2)

Loban, Walter D. 1963 *The Language of Elementary School Children.* Urbana: NCTE. [NCTE Research Report 1] (161)

Lounsbury, Thomas R. 1904 *The Standard of Pronunciation in English.* New York: Harper. (193n8)

Lowes, John Livingston 1919 *Convention and Revolt in Poetry.* Boston: Houghton Mifflin. (27)

Lowman, Guy S., Jr. See Kurath and Lowman 1970.

Luick, Karl 1921-40 *Historische Grammatik der englischen Sprache.* Leipzig: Tauchnitz. (192)

McDavid, Raven I., Jr. 1940 Low-Back Vowels in the South Carolina Piedmont. *AS* 15.144-48. (320, 355)

      1942a Some Principles for American Dialect Study. *SIL* 1.12.1-11. (vi, xiii, *1*, 322n1)

      1942b Phonological Evidence from Naive Spellings in Southwestern Louisiana. Paper presented at LSA Annual Meeting, Indianapolis. (318)

      1943 Review of J. S. Hall 1942. *Lg* 19.184-95. (viii, xii, **xix**, 269n2, *42*)

      1944 The Unstressed Syllabic Phonemes of a Southern Dialect: A Problem of Analysis. *SIL* 2.51-55. (viii, xi, xviii, *35*)

      1946 Dialect Geography and Social Science Problems. *Social Forces* 25.168-72. (vii, xv, *16*, 135, 143, 181, 264, 340)

      1947 Review of Mencken 1945. *Lg* 23.68-73. (viii, **xix**, 22, *43*)

      1948 Postvocalic /-r/ in South Carolina: A Social Analysis. *AS* 23.194-203. (vii, xi, xv, *17*, 181, 197n56, 280, 340)

      1949a American Dialect Studies since 1939. *Philologica* [Prague] 4.43-48. (105n2)

      1949b Derivatives of Middle English [o:] in the South Atlantic States. *Quarterly Journal of Speech* 35.496-504. (266n16, 276, 338n10)

      1949c /r/ and /y/ in the South. *SIL* 7.18-20. (viii, xviii, *36*)

      1949d Review of Thomas 1947. *SIL* 7.89-99. (viii, xx, 322n1, *45*, 381)

      1949e Review of Mencken 1948. *Lg* 25.69-77. (viii, xix-xx, 22, *44*)

McDavid, Raven I., Jr. 1950a Review of Turner 1949. *Lg* 26.323-33. (viii, xx, 49n5, 51n19, 197n50, 265n12, 280, *47*)

      1950b Review of Kurath 1949. *New York History* 31.442-44. (viii, xx, 49n5, *46*)

      1950c The Linguistic Atlases: An Instrument of Research in the Social Sciences. Report prepared for the ACLS. [mimeograph] (109-11)

      1951a The Folk Vocabulary of New York State. *New York Folklore Quarterly* 7.173-92. (viii, xi, xvii, 105n5, 203, *29*, 236n1, 252n3, 341)

      1951b Midland and Canadian Words in Upstate New York. *AS* 26.248-56. (viii, xii, xvii, 105n5, 130n7, 203, *30*)

      1951c Two Decades of the Linguistic Atlas. *Journal of English and Germanic Philology* 50.101-10. (105n2, 351)

      1951d Dialect Differences and Inter-Group Tensions. *SIL* 9.27-33. (vii, xv-xvi, *18*, 247, 264)

      1951e Review of Baker 1945. *SIL* 9.13-17. (viii, xx, *48*)

      1953a Notes on the Pronunciation of *catch. CE* 14.290-91. (117, 384n9)

      1953b Regional and Social Patterns in Southern Pronunciation. Paper presented at the Sixth Kentucky Foreign Language Conference. (106n11)

      1953c Review of *Orbis* 1. *IJAL* 19.246-50. (359)

      1953d Some Social Differences in Pronunciation. *Language Learning* 4.102-16. (vii, xv, *13*)

      1953e Review of Dieth and Orton 1952. *Journal of English and Germanic Philology* 52.563-68. (viii, xx, *49*, 356, 360n5)

      1953f Review of McIntosh et al. 1951. *Journal of English and Germanic Philology* 52.568-70. (viii, xx, 353n2, *50*)

      1954a Linguistic Geography in Canada: An Introduction. *CJL* 1[Preliminary Number].3-8. (103)

      1954b Review of McIntosh 1952. *Lg* 30.414-23. (viii, xx-xxi, 353n2, *51*)

      1954c Review of Atwood 1953a. *IJAL* 20.74-78. (viii, xxi, *52*)

      1954d Review of Randolph and Wilson 1953. *Journal of American Folklore* 67.327-30. (viii, xxi, *53*)

      1955a The Position of the Charleston Dialect. *PADS* 23.35-49. (viii, xi, xviii, 105n5, 106n11, 252n3, *37*, 289)

      1955b Review of Ramsay 1953. *Modern Language Notes* 70.222-23. (ix, xxi, *54*)

      1955c Review of Haugen 1953. *American Anthropologist* 57.1339-41. (ix, xxi, *55*)

      1955d Review of Pop 1950. *IJAL* 21.81-83. (ix, xxi, *56*)

      1958a The Dialects of American English. Francis 1958:480-543. (106n12, 145n1, 245)

      1958b Linguistic Geography and Toponymic Research. *Names* 6.65-73. (vii, xvi, *25*)

      1958c Review of Eliason 1956. *Journal of English and Germanic Philology* 57.160-65. (ix, xxi, *57*)

      1960a The Dialectology of an Urban Society. *Communication et rapports du premier congrès international de dialectologie générale*, ed. by A. J. Van Windekens (Louvain: Centre International de Dialectologie Générale, 1964), 68-80. [Congrès held 1960, published 1964] (vi, xi, xiv, 7)

McDavid, Raven I., Jr. 1960b A Study in Ethnolinguistics. *Southern Speech Journal* 25.247-54. (vii, xii, xvi, 110, *19*, 327)

----- 1960c Hans Kurath: A Portrait. *Orbis* 9. 587-610. (vii, xi, xv, *12*)

----- 1961a Structural Linguistics and Linguistic Geography. *Orbis* 10.35-46. (vi, xi, xiii, *2*)

----- 1961b Confederate Overalls: or, A Little Southern Sweetening. Paper presented at the Fourteenth Kentucky Foreign Language Conference. (xviii-xix, 15n4, *38*, 322n1, 322n2, 333n4, 339n17)

----- 1962 Dialectology and the Classroom Teacher. *CE* 24.111-16. (vii, xvi, *21*)

----- 1964a Mencken Revisited. *Harvard Educational Review* 34.211-25. (vi, xiii, *3*)

----- 1964b American English. *CE* 25.331-37. (vii, xv, *14*)

----- 1964c Dialectology and the Teaching of Reading. *The Reading Teacher* 18.206-13. (vii, xvi, *22*)

----- 1964d Review of Atwood 1962. *Journal of English and Germanic Philology* 63.841-46. (ix, xxi-xxii, *58*)

----- 1965a American Social Dialects. *CE* 26. 254-60. (vii, xv, *15*)

----- 1965b Dialectology and the Integration of the Schools. *Zeitschrift für Mundartforschung*, NF 4.2[*Verhandlung des zweiten internationalen Dialektologenkongresses*, ed. by L. E. Schmitt]. 543-50. [Dialektologenkongress held 1965, published 1968] (vii, xvi, *20*)

----- 1965c Can Linguistics Solve the Composition Problem? *Chicago Schools Journal* 46.193-200. (vii, xvi, *23*)

----- 1966a Dialect Differences and Social Differences in an Urban Society. *Sociolinguistics*, ed. by William Bright (The Hague: Mouton), 72-83. (vii, xiv, *8*)

----- 1966b Sense and Nonsense about American Dialects. *PMLA* 81.2.7-17. (vii, xiv, *9*)

----- 1966c Review of Thomas 1958 and Bronstein 1960. *Lg* 42.149-55. (ix, xxii, 322n1, *59*)

----- 1967a Historical, Regional, and Social Variation. *Journal of English Linguistics* 1. 25-40. (vi, xi, xiii, *5*)

----- 1967b System and Variety in American English. *New Directions in American English*, ed. by Alexander Frazier (Urbana: NCTE), 125-39. (vi, xiii, *4*)

----- 1967c Word Magic: or, Would You Want Your Daughter to Marry a Hoosier? *Indiana English Journal* 2.1.1-7. (viii, xii, xviii, *33*)

----- 1967d Needed Research in Southern Dialects. *Perspectives on the South*, ed. by Edgar T. Thompson (Durham: Duke Univ. Press), 113-24. (viii, xix, *39*)

----- 1968 Review of Labov 1966. *American Anthropologist* 70.425-26. (ix, xii, xxii, *60*)

----- 1970 Changing Patterns of Southern Dialects. *Essays in Honor of C. M. Wise*, ed. by Arthur Bronstein et al. (Hannibal, MO: Standard, for the Speech Association of America), 206-28.

(viii, xix, *40*)

McDavid, Raven I., Jr. 1979 New Directions in American Dialectology. *Varieties of American English: Essays by Raven I. McDavid, Jr.*, ed. by Anwar S. Dil (Stanford: Stanford Univ. **Press**), 257-95. (105)

McDavid, Raven I., Jr. and William M. Austin 1966 *Communication Barriers to the Culturally Deprived*. Chicago: US Office of Education, Department of Health, Education, and Welfare. [Cooperative Research Project 2107] (42n5, 66n3, 153n1, 295)

McDavid, Raven I., Jr. and Virginia G. McDavid 1951a *A Compilation of the Worksheets of the Linguistic Atlas of the United States and Canada and Associated Projects*. Ann Arbor: Linguistic Atlas of the United States and Canada. [See also A. L. Davis, McDavid and McDavid 1969] (354n7, 365n3)

----- 1951b The Relationship of the Speech of American Negroes to the Speech of Whites. *AS* 26.3-17. (vi, xi, xiv, *6*, 63, 197n50, 265n12, 280)

----- 1952a The *Linguistic Atlas of New England*. *Orbis* 1.95-103. (vii, xi, xiv, *10*)

----- 1952b *h* Before Semivowels in the Eastern United States. *Lg* 28.41-62. (vii, xvii, 84, 116, *27*, 272, 331, 337, 382)

----- 1954 The Habitat of Prepositions. Paper presented at the American Dialect Society Annual Meeting, New York. (375)

----- 1956a Regional Linguistic Atlases in the United States. *Orbis* 5.349-86. (vii, xiv-xv, *11*, 351)

----- 1956b Elimination of the Alternation between *a* and *an*. Paper presented at the LSA Annual Meeting, Philadelphia. (375)

----- 1958 Linguistic Geography and the Study of Folklore. *New York Folklore Quarterly* 14.3.242-62. (vii, xvi, *24*)

----- 1960 Grammatical Differences in the North-Central States. *AS* 35.5-19. (viii, xvii-xviii, 97, *32*, 289, 363)

----- 1964 Plurals of Nouns of Measure in the United States. Marckwardt 1964:271-301. (vii, xvii, *28*, 252n9, 354n9)

----- 1969 The *Late Unpleasantness*: Folk Names for the Civil War. *Southern Speech Journal* 34. 194-204. (viii, xix, *41*)

----- 1973 *Cracker* and *hoosier*. *Names* 21.161-67. (256)

McDavid, Raven I., Jr. and Sara Witham 1974 Poor Whites and Rustics. *Names* 22.93-103. (256)

McDavid, Raven I., Jr. See also Mencken 1963; Kurath and R. McDavid 1961; Kimmerle, R. and V. McDavid 1951; A. L. Davis, McDavid and McDavid 1969; Forgue and R. McDavid 1972; A. L. Davis and R. McDavid 1949, 1950.

McDavid, Virginia G. 1956 A Survey of Verb Forms in the North-Central States and Upper Midwest. Diss., Univ. of Minnesota. (84n1, 97, 99, 108, 111, 122, 129n3, 156, 174, 218n7, 252n1, 289, 330, 331, 354n10, 363)

----- See also Kimmerle, R. and V. McDavid 1951; A. L. Davis, McDavid and McDavid 1969; R. and V. McDavid 1951a,b, 1952a,b, 1954, 1956a,b, 1958, 1960, 1964, 1969, 1973.

McGlothlin, William J. 1926 *Baptist Beginnings in Education: A History of Furman University.*

Nashville: Sunday School Board of the Southern Baptist Convention. (141n15)

McIntosh, Angus 1952 *An Introduction to a Survey of Scottish Dialects.* Edinburgh: Nelson. [Univ. of Edinburgh Linguistic Survey of Scotland Monographs, 1. Review: R. McDavid 1954b] (xx-xxi, 14, 58, 104, 353n2, *51*)

McIntosh, Angus *et al.* 1951 *Linguistic Survey of Scotland, First Questionnaire.* Edinburgh: Linguistic Survey of Scotland. [Review: R. McDavid 1953e] (xx, 353n2, *50*)

McMillan, James B. 1939 Vowel Nasality as a Sandhi-Form of the Morphemes *-nt* and *-ing* in Southern American. *AS* 14.120-23. (319)

----- 1946 Phonology of the Standard English of East-Central Alabama. Diss., Univ. of Chicago. (106n17, 184n6, 289)

McQuown, Norman 1971 *The Natural History of an Interview.* Chicago: Joseph Regenstein Library of the University of Chicago. [Manuscripts on Cultural Anthropology 15.97] (28, 156)

Macrae-Gibson, O. D. 1973 *Of Arthour and Merlin.* London: Oxford Univ. Press. [Early English Text Society, Original Series 268] (328n11)

Macris, James 1955 An Analysis of English Loanwords in New York City Greek. Diss., Columbia Univ. (72)

Malmstrom, Jean 1958 A Study of the Validity of Textbook Statements about Certain Controversial Grammatical Items in the Light of Evidence from the Linguistic Atlas. Diss., Univ. of Minnesota. (111, 252n4)

Malone, Kemp See Mencken, Pound, Malone and Kennedy 1945.

Marckwardt, Albert H. 1940a Folk Speech in Indiana and Adjacent States. *Indiana Historical Bulletin* 17.120-40. (97, 217n6, 250)

----- 1940b Review of Kurath *et al.* 1939, Kurath *et al.* 1939-43:Vol. 1. *Lg* 16.257-61. (84n2)

----- 1941 Middle English ŏ in the American English of the Great Lakes Area. *Papers of the Michigan Academy of Sciences, Arts and Letters* 26.561-71. (97, 238, 242)

----- 1942a *Introduction to the English Language.* New York: Oxford Univ. Press. (195n21)

----- 1942b Middle English *wa* in the Speech of the Great Lakes Region. *AS* 17.226-34. (97, 238)

----- 1957 Principal and Subsidiary Dialect Areas in the North-Central States. *PADS* 27.3-15. (100, 252n10, 289, 384n3)

----- 1964 *Studies in Language and Linguistics in Honor of Charles C. Fries.* Ann Arbor: The English Language Institute, University of Michigan.

Marckwardt, Albert H. *et al.* 1976-78 *Linguistic Atlas of the North-Central States: Basic Materials.* Chicago: Joseph Regenstein Library of the University of Chicago. [Manuscripts on Cultural Anthropology, 200-208] (72, 104, 252n4, 258, 289)

----- 1980- *Linguistic Atlas of the North-Central States.* [In preparation; projected publication date] (v, 51n33, 72, 104, 175n2, 184n6, 193n1, 201, 217n2, 237n13, 237n16, 245, 252n1, 258, 289, 313n1)

Marshall, Howard W. and John M. Vlach 1973 Toward a Folklife Approach to American Dialects. *AS* 48. 163-91. (145n1)

Martinet, André 1952 Review of Pop 1950. *Word*

8.260-62. (351)

Martinet, André 1962 *A Functional View of Language.* Oxford: Clarendon. (129n3)

Mather, J. Y. and H. H. Speitel 1975- *Linguistic Atlas of Scotland.* London: Croom Helm; New Haven: Archon. (58, 104, 124, 198n57, 216, 357)

Mathews, Mitford M. 1948 *Some Sources of Southernisms.* University, AL: Univ. of Alabama Press. (51n27, 348n18)

----- 1951 *A Dictionary of Americanisms on Historical Principles.* Chicago: Univ. of Chicago Press. (5, 31, 124, 309, 354n11)

Maurer, David W. 1950 The Argot of the Professional Dice Gambler. *Annals of the American Academy of Political and Social Sciences* 269. (173)

----- 1951 The Argot of the Racetrack. *PADS* 16. (173)

----- 1955 Whiz Mob: A Correlation of the Technical Argot of Pickpockets with their Behavioral Pattern. *PADS* 24. (173)

----- 1963 *The Big Con.* New York: New American Library. [Rev. ed.] (173)

----- 1974 *The American Confidence Man.* Springfield, IL: Thomas. (173)

Maurer, David W. and Victor Vogel 1954 *Narcotics and Narcotic Addiction.* Springfield, IL: Thomas. [3rd ed., 1967] (173)

Maurer, David W. See also Mencken 1963.

Mencken, H. L. 1919 *The American Language.* New York: Knopf. [1st ed.] (xiii, 16, 20, 22, 121, 325, 329)

----- 1921 *The American Language.* New York: Knopf. [2nd ed., rev. and enl.] (xiii, 20, 22, 325, 329)

----- 1923 *The American Language.* New York: Knopf. [3rd ed., rev. and enl.] (xiii, 20, 22, 121, 325, 329)

----- 1936 *The American Language.* New York: Knopf. [4th ed., cor., rev., and enl.] (xiii, 20, 21, 22, 51n28, 106n18, 122, 123, 158n7, 194n10, 199, 254, 325, 327, 329, 330, 333n1, 350, 363, 382)

----- 1945 *The American Language: Supplement I.* New York: Knopf. [Review: R. McDavid 1947] (xix, 21, 22, 122, 146, 254, *43*, 329, 333n2)

----- 1948 *The American Language: Supplement II.* New York: Knopf. [Review: R. McDavid 1949e] (xix-xx, 21, 22, 121, 122, 160, 185, 196n32, 281n1, *44*, 338n7, 363)

----- 1963 *The American Language: The Fourth Edition and the Two Supplements, Abridged with Annotations and New Material.* Ed. by Raven I. McDavid, Jr. with the assistance of David W. Maurer. New York: Knopf. (xiii, 2, 21, 22, 23n14, 24n16, 121, 124n1, 129n3, 254, 288, 295, 326)

Mencken, H. L., Louise Pound, Kemp Malone and Arthur G. Kennedy 1945. *American Speech 1925-1945: The Founders Look Back.* *AS* 20.241-46. (20, 125n9)

Menner, B. J. 1942 Review of Kurath *et al.* 1939-43:Vol. 2. *Lg* 18.45-51. (84n2)

Meredith, M. J. 1933 "Belling the Bridal Couple" in Pioneer Days. *AS* 8.2.22-24. (181)

Meriwether, Robert Lee 1940 *The Expansion of South Carolina, 1729-1765.* Kingsport, TN: Southern. (139, 141n10, 191, 273)

Meyerstein, Goldie P. 1959 Selected Problems of

Bilingualism among Immigrant Slovaks. Diss., Univ. of Michigan. (72)

Michaelis, Hermann and Daniel Jones 1913 *A Phonetic Dictionary of the English Language*. New York: Stechert. (185)

Miller, Michael 1978 Inflectional Morphology in the Speech of Augusta, Georgia: A Sociolinguistic Description. Diss., Univ. of Chicago. (129n4, 157, 291)

Mitchell, Margaret 1936 *Gone with the Wind*. New York: Macmillan. (26, 55, 176, 259)

Mitzka, Walther and L. E. Schmitt 1951-73 *Deutscher Wortatlas*. 20 vols. Giessen: Schmitz. (71)

Morgan, Raleigh 1960 The Lexicon of Saint Martin Creole. *Anthropological Linguistics* 2.7-29. (289, 307n3)

Morris, William and Mary Morris 1975 *Harper Dictionary of Contemporary Usage*. New York: Harper and Row. (125n3, 193)

Morris, William See also *The American Heritage Dictionary* (1969).

Murison, David See Grant and Murison 1931-76.

Myrdal, Gunnar 1944 *An American Dilemna: The Negro Problem and Modern Democracy*. New York: Harper. (43, 45, 49n2, 50n13)

Needleman, Morriss H. 1949 *A Manual of Pronunciation*. New York: Barnes and Noble. (185)

Neilson, William D. See *Webster's New International Dictionary of the English Language, Second Edition* (1934).

Newman, Stanley S. See Spier, Hallowell and Newman 1941.

Newmark, Leonard See Sledd 1964.

Nida, Eugene A. 1946 *Morphology*. Ann Arbor: Univ. of Michigan Press. (345)

----- 1947 *Linguistic Interludes*. Glendale, CA: Summer Institute of Linguistics. (332)

Nixon, Phyllis J. 1946 A Glossary of Virginia Words. *PADS* 5. (332, 334n23)

Norman, Arthur M. Z. 1955 A Southeast Texas Dialect Study. Diss., Univ. of Texas. (101, 110, 289)

----- 1956 A Southeast Texas Dialect Study. *Orbis* 5.61-79. (289)

O'Cain, Raymond K. 1972 A Social Dialect Survey of Charleston, South Carolina. Diss., Univ. of Chicago. (46, 49, 129n4, 142n21, 174, 280, 282, 291, 346)

----- 1979 The *Linguistic Atlas of New England* Reprinted: A Review Article. *AS* 54[December]. (84n2, 129n2)

Odum, Howard W. 1910 *Social and Mental Traits of the Negro*. New York: Columbia Univ. (49n1)

O'Hare, Thomas 1964 The Linguistic Geography of Eastern Montana. Diss., Univ. of Texas. (104, 384n5)

O'Hern, Edna M. See Putnam and O'Hern 1955.

Orbeck, Anders 1927 *Early New England Pronunciation as Reflected in Some 17th-Century Town Records of Eastern Massachusetts*. Ann Arbor: Wahr. (192, 259, 318)

Orton, Harold et al. 1962-71 *Survey of English Dialects: Basic Materials*. 4 vols., each in 3 pts. Leeds: Arnold. [Review: Viereck 1973] (8, 26, 70, 104, 124, 126, 198n57, 216)

Orton, Harold and Eugen Dieth 1951 The New Survey of Dialectal English. *English Studies Today* 1.63-73. (353n3, 356)

Orton, Harold See also Dieth and Orton 1952.

Paddock, Harold 1966 A Dialect Survey of Carbonear, Newfoundland. M.A. Thesis, Memorial Univ. of Newfoundland. (42n9, 51n31, 346)

Pap, Leo 1949 Portugese-American Speech. New York: King's Crown. (72, 104)

Pater, Walter 1876 Romanticism. *Macmillan's Magazine* 35[Nov.].64-70. (27)

Payne, L. W., Jr. 1908 A Word List from East Alabama. *DN* 3.279-328, 343-391. (44, 333n6)

Payne, Richard C. Review of Wolfram and Christian 1976. *Journal of English Linguistics* 12.83-92. (291)

Pederson, Lee A. 1965a The Pronunciation of English in Metropolitan Chicago. *PADS* 44. (61, 62, 64, 66n2, 72, 105, 129n4, 151, 156, 160, 174, 293, 314n1)

----- 1965b Some Structural Differences in the Speech of Chicago Negroes. Shuy 1965:28-51. (64, 66n2, 105)

Penzl, Herbert 1934 The Development of Middle English â in New England Speech. Diss., Univ. of Vienna. (105n6)

----- 1941 The Phonetic Interpretation of Naive Spelling. Paper presented at LSA Summer Meeting, Chapel Hill and Durham. (318)

Perry, William 1775 *The Royal Standard English Dictionary*. Edinburgh. (192, 195n18)

Petty, Julian J. 1943 *The Growth and Distribution of Population in South Carolina*. Columbia, SC: State Council for Defense, Industrial Development Committee. (46, 139, 141n12, 274, 343)

Phillips, George 1856-60 Ueber den Ursprung der Katzenmusiker. *Vermischte Schriften* (Vienna: Braumüller), 3.26-92. (184n8)

Phillips, Ulrich B. 1918 *American Negro Slavery*. New York: Appleton. (347n15)

Pike, Kenneth L. 1943 *Phonetics*. Ann Arbor: Univ. of Michigan Press. (337)

----- 1945 *The Intonation of American English*. Ann Arbor: Univ. of Michigan Press. (161, 345)

----- 1947 *Phonemics*. Ann Arbor: Univ. of Michigan Press. (337, 339n17, 345)

----- 1948 *Tone Languages*. Ann Arbor: Univ. of Michigan Press. (345)

----- 1967 *Language in Relation to a Unified Theory of the Structure of Human Behavior*. The Hague: Mouton. [2nd ed., rev.] (22n1)

Pittenger, Robert E., Charles F. Hockett and John J. Danehy 1960 *The First Five Minutes: A Sample of Microscopic Interview Analysis*. Ithaca: P. Martineau. (42n5, 156, 293)

Pittenger, Robert E. See also Smith and Pittenger 1957.

Pop, Sever 1950 *La Dialectologie*. 2 vols. Louvain: Univ. de Louvain. [Recueil de travaux d'histoire et de philologie, 3rd series, fasc. 38-39. Reviews: R. McDavid 1955d, Martinet 1952] (xxi, 12, 84n2, 129n2, 158n4, 274, 56)

Pope, Liston 1942 *Millhands and Preachers: A Study of Gastonia*. New York: Oxford Univ. Press. (141n8)

Potter, Edward 1955 The Dialect of Northwestern Ohio: A Study of a Transition Area. Diss., Univ. of Michigan. (97)

Pound, Louise See Mencken, Pound, Malone and Kennedy 1945.

Primer, Sylvester 1888 Charleston Provincialisms. *PMLA* 3.84-99. [Also: *American Journal* of Philology 9.198-213; Phonetische Studien 1. 227-43] (195n22, 272)

Primer, Sylvester 1889 The Huguenot Element in Charleston's Pronunciation. PMLA 4.214-44. (197n50)

----- 1890 The Pronunciation of Fredericksburg, Virginia. PMLA 5.185-99. (195n22)

Proctor, Richard A. 1885 The Misused h of England. Atlantic Monthly 55.593-601. (193n2)

Putnam, George N. and Edna M. O'Hern 1955 The Status Significance of an Isolated Urban Dialect. Lg 31.4.2. [Lg Diss. 53] (58)

Pyles, Thomas 1949 Linguistics and Pedagogy: The Need for Conciliation. CE 10.389-95. (185)

----- 1952 Words and Ways of American English. New York: Random House. (106n16, 148)

----- 1964 The Origins and Development of the English Language. New York: Harcourt, Brace and World. (42n8)

Ramsay, Robert L. 1953 The Place Names of Franklin County, Missouri. Columbia, MO: Univ. of Missouri Studies. [Review: R. McDavid 1955b] (xxi, 54)

Randolph, Vance and George P. Wilson 1953 Down in the Holler: A Gallery of Ozark Folk Speech. Norman: Univ. of Oklahoma Press. [Review: R. McDavid 1954d] (xxi, 53)

Raup, H. F. 1957 The Names of Ohio's Streams. Names 5.162-68. (177)

Read, Allan Walker 1939 The Speech of Negroes in Colonial America. Journal of Negro History 24. 247-58. (49n3)

Read, William A. 1911 Some Variant Pronunciations in the New South. DN 3.497-536. (195n24)

Reed, Carroll E. 1949 The Pennsylvania German Dialect Spoken in the Counties of Lehigh and Berkes: Phonology and Morphology. Seattle: Univ. of Washington Press. (104)

----- 1952 The Pronunciation of English in the State of Washington. AS 27.186-89. (101)

Reed, Carroll E. and Lester W. Seifert 1954 A Linguistic Atlas of Pennsylvania German. Marburg/Lahn: Becker. (8, 104, 110)

Reed, David W. 1954 Eastern Dialect Words in California. PADS 21.3-15. (101)

Reed, David W. and J. Spicer 1952 Correlation Methods of Comparing Idiolects in a Transition Area. Lg 28.348-59. (97)

Riley, William See Shuy, Wolfram and Riley 1968.

Robertson, Ben 1942 Red Hills and Cotton: An Up-Country Memory. New York: Knopf. (141n13, 142n16)

Robertson, Stuart 1934 The Development of Modern English. New York: Prentice-Hall. [2nd ed., rev. by Frederic Cassidy, 1954] (195n20, 197n51)

Rudnyćkyj, J. B. 1952 Slavic Linguistic Atlas of Canada and USA. Orbis 1.109-12. (104)

Sapir, Edward 1921 Language: An Introduction to the Study of Speech. New York: Harcourt, Brace. (20)

----- 1925 Sound Patterns in Language. Lg 1.37-51. (348n26)

----- See also Spier, Hallowell and Newman 1941.

Sawyer, Janet B. 1957 A Dialect Study of San Antonio, Texas: A Bilingual Community. Diss., Univ. of Texas. (72, 74, 110, 129n4, 156, 289, 293)

Schmitt, L. E. See Mitzka and Schmitt 1951-73, R. McDavid 1965b, Strang 1968.

1944 Science Comes to Languages. Fortune 30.2.133-35, 236-40. (105n3, 325, 331)

Scott, Fred Newton 1917 The Standard of American Speech. English Journal 6.1-11. (121)

Sebeok, Thomas et al. 1952-68 Studies in Cheremis. 10 vols. Publications of the Indiana University Research Center in Anthropology, Folklore, and Linguistics; and elsewhere. (168)

Seifert, Lester W. See C. Reed and Seifert 1954.

Shelby, Gertrude See Stoney and Shelby 1930.

Sheldon, E. S. 1890 A New Englander's English and the English of London. DN 1.33-42. (194n8)

Shewmake, Edwin F. 1920 English Pronunciation in Virginia. Diss., Univ. of Virginia. (195n25)

Shuy, Roger W. 1965 Social Dialects and Language Learning. Urbana: NCTE. (130n9, 167)

Shuy, Roger W., Walter A. Wolfram and William K. Riley 1968 Field Techniques in an Urban Language Study. Arlington: Center for Applied Linguistics. (105, 145n10)

Shuy, Roger W. See also Fasold and Wolfram 1970.

Simms, William Gilmore 1850-51 Katharine Walton. Godey's Lady's Book 40-41[Feb.-Dec. 1950]. [1st ed., Philadelphia: Hart, 1851] (51n18)

Skeat, W. W. 1901 The Influence of Anglo-French Pronunciation upon Modern English. Transactions of the Philological Society 31.439-68. (197n55)

Sledd, James H. 1955 Review of Trager and Smith 1951 and Fries 1952. Lg 31.312-45. (282)

----- 1959 A Short Introduction to English Grammar. Chicago: Scott, Foresman. (15n4)

----- 1964 Review of Morton Bloomfield and Leonard Newmark, Linguistic Introduction to the History of English (New York: Knopf, 1963). Lg 40.465-83. (39)

Smith, Henry Lee, Jr. and Robert E. Pittenger 1957 A Basis for Some Contribution of Linguistics and Psychiatry. Psychiatry 20.61-78. (42n5)

Smith, Henry Lee, Jr. See also Trager and Smith 1951.

Smith, Reed 1926 Gullah. Bulletin of the University of South Carolina 190.14-21. (342, 347n7, 347n10)

Spears, Mabel Y. 1949 W'ere, w'en, w'y, w'ich, w'at. CE 11.38-39. (193n7)

Speitel, H. H. See Mather and Speitel 1975-.

Spicer, Edward A. 1943 Linguistic Aspects of Yaqui Acculturation. American Anthropologist 45.410-26. (106n19)

Spicer, J. See D. Reed and Spicer 1952.

Spier, Leslie, A. Irving Hallowell and Stanley S. Newman 1941 Language, Culture, and Personality: Essays in Memory of Edward Sapir. Menasha, WI: Sapir Memorial Publication Fund.

Stanley, Oma 1937 The Speech of East Texas. New York: Columbia Univ. Press. [American Speech Reprints, 2] (195n29)

Stefánsson, V. 1903 English Loan-Nouns Used in the Icelandic Colony of North Dakota. DN 2.354-62. (183)

Stephens, Alexander H. 1868-70 A Constitutional View of the Late War Between the States. Philadelphia: National; Chicago: Zeigler, McCurdy. (311)

Stockwell, Robert P. 1959 Structural Dialectology: A Proposal. AS 34.258-68. (287)

Stoney, Samuel and Gertrude Shelby 1930 Black

Genesis: A Chronicle. New York: Macmillan. (342)

Strang, Barbara 1968 The Tyneside Linguistic Study. *Zeitschrift für Mundartforschung*, Beihefte, NF 4.2[*Verhandlung des zweiten internationalen Dialektologenkongresses*, ed. by L. E. Schmitt].788-94. (151)

Strickland, Ruth G. 1962 The Language of Elementary School Children: Its Relationship to the Language of Reading Textbooks and the quality of Reading of Selected Children. *Bulletin of the School of Education, Indiana University* 38.4. (161)

Sturtevant, Edgar H. 1947 *Introduction to Linguistic Science*. New Haven: Yale Univ. Press. (143)

Sumner, William G. 1940 *Folkways*. Boston: Ginn. [Originally published 1907] (184n4)

Sweet, Henry 1874 The History of English Sounds. *Transactions of the Philological Society* 22.461-623. (192)

----- 1888 *The History of English Sounds from the Earliest Period*. Oxford: Clarendon. [new and rev. ed. of Sweet 1874] (197n54)

Thomas, C. K. 1935-37 Pronunciation in Upstate New York. *AS* 10.107-12, 208-12, 292-97; 11.68-77, 142-44, 307-13; 12.122-27. (195n30, 196n38, 231n1, 335)

----- 1942 Pronunciation in Downstate New York. *AS* 17.30-41, 149-57. (195n30, 196n38, 231n1, 335)

----- 1947 *An Introduction to the Phonetics of American English*. New York: Ronald. [Reviews: Atwood 1948, R. McDavid 1949d] (xx, 105n7, 158n8, 194n9, *45*, 381, 382)

----- 1958 *An Introduction to the Phonetics of American English*. New York: Ronald. [2nd ed. Review: R. McDavid 1966b] (xxii, 105n7, *59*)

Thompson, Edgar T. See R. McDavid 1967d.

Thompson, Harold W. 1939 *Body, Boots, and Britches*. Philadelphia: Lippincott. (168, 237n4, 237n10)

Tidwell, James N. 1948 The Literary Representation of the Phonology of the Southern Dialect. Diss., Ohio State Univ. (50n15)

Tillinghast, Joseph A. 1902 *The Negro in Africa and America*. New York: Macmillan. (49n1)

Tillyard, E. M. W. See Lewis and Tillyard 1939.

Trager, George L. 1940 One Phonemic Entity Becomes Two: The Case of 'short a'. *AS* 15.255-58. (132, 323n9, 337)

----- 1941 The Theory of Accentual Systems. Spier, Hallowell and Newman 1941:131-45. (345)

----- 1942 The Phoneme /t/: A Study in Theory and Method. *AS* 17.144-48. (7, 320)

----- 1949 *The Field of Linguistics*. Norman, OK: Battenburg. [*Studies in Linguistics* Occasional Papers, 1] (12)

----- 1958 Paralanguage: A First Approximation. *SIL* 13.1-12. (42n5)

Trager, George L. and Bernard Bloch 1941 The Syllabic Phonemes of English. *Lg* 17.223-46. (7, 268, 269n1, 319, 320, 322n1, 323n2, 323n7, 323n9, 333n7, 337, 345, 384n16)

Trager, George L. and Edward T. Hall 1953 *The Analysis of Culture*. Washington: ACLS. (22n4)

Trager, George L. and Henry Lee Smith, Jr. 1951 *An Outline of English Structure*. Norman, OK: Battenburg. [*Studies in Linguistics* Occasional

Papers, 3. Review: Sledd 1955] (10, 14, 27, 120n4, 145n1, 162, 176, 282, 283, 287n2, 333n4, 348n28, 374, 384n16)

Trager, George L. See also Bloch and Trager 1940, 1942.

Tressider, Argus 1943 The Sounds of Virginia Speech. *AS* 18.261-72. (196n31)

Tressler, J. L. 1934 Should the National Council Act as an American Academy? *English Journal* 23. 293-98. (122)

Trollope, Frances 1832 *Domestic Manners of the Americans*. London: Whittaker, Treacher. (350)

Tucker, Lael 1949 The Kiss, the Tree, and the Bullet. *Harper's Magazine* 198.1187.40-51. (184n4)

Turner, Lorenzo D. 1941 Linguistic Research and African Survivals. *ACLS Bulletin* 32.68-89. (44, 51n22, 348n22)

----- 1949 *Africanisms in the Gullah Dialect*. Chicago: Univ. of Chicago Press. [Reviews: R. A. Hall 1950b, R. McDavid 1950a] (xiv, xx, 41, 42n10, 44, 45, 47, 50n11, 72, 104, 110, 149n2, 157, 173, 184n6, 191, 265n12, 280, 289, 307n3, *47*)

Udell, Gerald R. 1966 The Speech of Akron, Ohio: A Study in Urbanization. Diss., Univ. of Chicago. (66n2, 72, 129n4, 151, 156, 294n6)

Uskup, Francis 1974 Social Markers of Urban Speech: A Study of Elites in Chicago. Diss., Illinois Institute of Technology. (130n8)

Van Riper, W. R. 1958 The Loss of Postvocalic *r* in the Eastern United States. Diss., Univ. of Michigan. (105n6, 106n13, 280)

Van Windekens, A. J. See R. McDavid 1960a.

Viereck, Wolfgang 1973 A Critical Appraisal of the *Survey of English Dialects*. *Orbis* 22.72-84. (351)

----- 1975 *Lexikalische und grammatische Ergebnisse des Lowman-Survey von Mittel- und Südengland*. Munich: Fink. (26, 141n9, 181, 193n3, 197n48, 198n57, 216, 237n14, 353n1)

Vlach, John M. See Marshall and Vlach 1973.

Vogel, Victor See Maurer and Vogel 1953.

Walker, John 1791 *A Critical Pronouncing Dictionary and Exposition of the English Language*. London: Robinson. (192)

Walker, Saunders 1956 A Dictionary of the Folk Speech of the East Alabama Negro. Diss., Western Reserve Univ. (103, 111, 289)

Wanamaker, Murray G. 1965 The Language of Kings County, Nova Scotia. Diss., Univ. of Michigan. (101)

Ward, Ida C. See Westermann and Ward 1933.

Warner, W. Lloyd 1941-59 Yankee City Series. 5 vols. New Haven: Yale Univ. Press. (144)

Watson, John F. 1843 Notitia of Incidents at New Orleans in 1804 and 1805. *American Pioneer* 2. 227-37. (181-82)

Weber, Robert H. 1965 A Comparative Study of Regional Terms Common to the Twin Cities and the Eastern United States. Diss., Univ. of Minnesota. (100, 110)

Webster, Noah 1789 *Dissertations on the English Language*. Worcester, MA: Thomas. (195n18)

----- 1934 *Webster's New International Dictionary of the English Language, Second Edition*. Ed. by William A. Neilson and Thomas A. Knott. Springfield, MA: Merriam. [*WNID-2*] (114, 185, 194n11, 194n12)

1961 *Webster's Third New International Dictionary of the English Language*. Ed. by Philip Gove. Springfield, MA: Merriam. [*WNID-3*] (xiv, 17, 25, 33, 73, 114, 121, 124, 125n3, 193, 255, 378, 384n12)

Weinreich, Uriel 1953 *Languages in Contact*. New York: Linguistic Circle of New York. [Publications of the Linguistic Circle of New York, 1] (104)

Wells, Rulon 1945 The Pitch Phonemes of English. *Lg* 21.27-39. (345)

Welmers, William E. 1946 A Descriptive Grammar of Fanti. *Lg* 22.3, Supplement. [*Lg* Diss. 39] (50n14, 345)

----- 1949a Secret Medicines, Magic, and Rites of the Kpella Tribe of Liberia. *Southwestern Journal of Anthropology* 5.208-43. (50n14)

----- 1949b Tonemes and Tone Writing in Maninka. *SIL* 7.1-17. (50n14)

----- 1950a New Light on Consonant Change in Kpella. *Zeitschrift für Phonetik und Allgemeine Wissenschaft* 4.105-17. (50n14)

----- 1950b Notes on Two Languages of the Senufo Group. I. Senade: *Lg* 26.126-46; II. Sup'ide: *Lg* 26.494-531. (50n14)

Welmers, William E. and Zellig S. Harris 1942 The Phonemes of Fanti. *Journal of the American Oriental Society* 62.318-33. (50n14, 345)

Wentworth, Harold 1944 *American Dialect Dictionary*. New York: Crowell. (5, 184n6)

Wentworth, Harold and Stuart Flexner 1960 *Dictionary of American Slang*. New York: Crowell. (124)

Westermann, Diedrich and Ida C. Ward 1933 *Practical Phonetics for Students of African Languages*. London: Oxford Univ. Press. (344)

Wetmore, Thomas H. 1959 The Low-Central and Low-Back Vowels in the English of the Eastern United States. *PADS* 32. (105n6, 276)

Whatmough, Joshua 1960 Note in *Language*. *Lg* 36.187-88. (52)

White, Newman I. *et al.* 1952-64 *Frank C. Brown Collection of North Carolina Folklore*. 7 vols. Durham: Duke Univ. Press. (169)

Whitehall, Harold 1935 Some Fifteenth-Century Spellings from the Nottingham Records. *University of Michigan Publications in Comparative Literature* 13.61-71. (197n52)

Whitney, William Dwight 1874 The Elements of English Pronunciation. *Oriental and Linguistic Studies, Second Series* (New York: Scribner's), 202-76. (193n8)

Whorf, Benjamin L. 1941a Languages and Logic. *Technology Review* 43.6.2-6. (131)

----- 1941b The Relationship of Habitual Thought and Behavior to Language. Spier, Hallowell and Newman 1941:25-93. (131, 136)

----- 1943 Phonemic Analysis of the English of Eastern Massachusetts. *SIL* 2.21-40. (267)

Widén, Bertil 1949 *Studies on the Dorset Dialect*. Lund: Gleerup. [Lund Studies in English, 16] (193n3)

Wiggam, Albert E. 1949 Let's Explore Your Mind. *Cleveland Plain Dealer*, July 3. (43, 145n2, 347n10)

Williamson, Juanita V. 1968 A Phonological and Morphological Study of the Speech of the Negro of Memphis, Tennessee. *PADS* 50. (49, 72, 105n6, 129n4, 157, 289, 292)

Wilson, George P. See Randolph and Wilson 1953.

Wilson, H. Rex 1959 The Dialect of Lunenburg County, Nova Scotia. Diss., Univ. of Michigan. (101)

Winter, Nevin O. 1917 *A History of Northwest Ohio*. Chicago: Lewis. (238)

Wise, C. M. 1933 Southern American Dialect. *AS* 8.2.37-43. (195n24)

Witham, Sara See R. McDavid and Witham 1974.

Wolfram, Walter A. 1969 *A Sociolinguistic Description of Detroit Negro Speech*. Arlington: Center for Applied Linguistics. (145n10, 156)

Wolfram, Walter A. and Donna Christian 1976 *Appalachian Speech*. Arlington: Center for Applied Linguistics. [Review: R. Payne 1978] (291)

Wolfram, Walter A. and Nona Clarke 1971 *Black-White Speech Relationships*. Arlington: Center for Applied Linguistics. (51n29)

Wolfram, Walter A. See also Shuy, Wolfram and Riley 1968; Fasold and Wolfram 1970.

Wolle, Muriel 1941 *Ghost Cities of Colorado*. Denver: Smith-Brooks. (264n2)

----- 1949 *Stampede to Timberline*. Boulder: Univ. of Colorado. (264n2)

Wood, Gordon R. 1960 An Atlas Survey of the Interior South. *Orbis* 9.7-12. (289)

----- 1961 Word Distribution in the Interior South. *PADS* 35. (289)

----- Dialect Contours in the Southern States. *AS* 38.243-56. (289)

----- 1971 *Vocabulary Change*. Carbondale: Southern Illinois Univ. Press. (105, 289, 377)

Workman, William D. 1960 *The Case for the South*. New York: Devin-Adair. (146)

WPA Writer's Program 1940a *The Ohio Guide*. New York: Oxford Univ. Press. (238)

----- 1940b *New York: A Guide to the Empire State*. New York: Oxford Univ. Press. (237n4)

Wrede, Ferdinand *et al.* 1927-56 *Deutscher Sprachatlas*. Marburg/Lahn: Elwert. (71, 258, 355, 361n9, 371)

Wright, Joseph 1892 *A Grammar of the Dialect of Windhill in the West Riding in Yorkshire*. London: Paul, Trench, Trübner. [English Dialect Society, 67] (191)

----- 1898-1905 *The English Dialect Dictionary*. 6 vols. London: Frowde. (9, 19, 26, 44, 71, 181, 191, 197n49, 198n57, 255, 256, 351, 356, 360n1, 360n2)

----- 1905 *The English Dialect Grammar*. Oxford: Frowde. (19, 26, 44, 185, 191, 197n49, 333n6, 351, 356, 364n1)

Wright, Joseph and Elizabeth M. Wright 1924 *An Elementary Historical New English Grammar*. London: Oxford Univ. Press. (197n49)

Wyld, Henry C. 1920 *A History of Modern Colloquial English*. London: Unwin. (192, 197n52, 265n13)

----- 1927 *A Short History of English*. New York: E. P. Dutton. [3rd ed., rev. and enl.] (192)

Zachrisson, Robert E. 1927 *The English Pronunciation at Shakespeare's Time as Taught by William Bullokar, with Word-Lists from All his Works*. Upsala: Almqvist and Wiksells. [Skrifter utgivna av Kungl. humanistika vetenskaps-samfundit i Uppsala, 22.6] (191)